HUNGER STRIKE

For Sian

HUNGER STRIKE

Margaret Thatcher's Battle with the IRA

1980–81

THOMAS HENNESSEY

IRISH ACADEMIC PRESS

First published in 2014 by

Irish Academic Press
8 Chapel Lane
Sallins
Co. Kildare, Ireland

© 2014 Thomas Hennessey

British Library Cataloguing in Publication Data
An entry can be found on request

ISBN: 978 0 7165 3176 0 (paper)
ISBN: 978 0 7165 3223 1 (ebook)

Library of Congress Cataloging-in-Publication Data
An entry can be found on request

Printed in Ireland by SPRINT-print Ltd.

Contents

List of Abbreviations

CLF	Commander Land Forces
FCO	Foreign and Commonwealth Office
DFA	Department of Foreign Affairs
DUP	Democratic Unionist Party
GOC	General Officer Commanding
ICJP	Irish Commission for Justice and Peace
ICRC	International Committee of the Red Cross
INLA	Irish National Liberation Army
IRSP	Irish Republican Socialist Party
MEP	Member of the European Parliament
MI5	Security Service
NHAC	National H-Block Armagh Committee
NIO	Northern Ireland Office
PAB	Political Affairs Branch
PIRA	Provisional Irish Republican Army
RUC	Royal Ulster Constabulary
SDLP	Social Democratic and Labour Party
SIS	Secret Intelligence Service
TD	Teachta Dála (Dáil Deputy)
UDA	Ulster Defence Association
UDR	Ulster Defence Regiment
UVF	Ulster Volunteer Force
UUP	Ulster Unionist Party

Dramatis Personae

Gerry Adams	Vice-President of Sinn Féin
Michael Alexander	Diplomat and foreign policy secretary to Mrs Thatcher
Michael Alison	Minister of State, NIO
Sir Robert Armstrong	Cabinet Secretary (UK)
Humphrey Atkins	Secretary of State for Northern Ireland, 1979–81
John Blelloch	Deputy Under-Secretary NIO
Lord Carrington	Secretary of State for Foreign and Commonwealth Affairs, 1979–82
Owen Carron	Bobby Sands' election agent; MP for Fermanagh–South Tyrone, 1981–83
Jimmy Carter	President of the United States 1977–81
Don Concannon	Minister of State, NIO, 1976–79
General Sir Timothy Creasey	General Officer Commanding Northern Ireland, 1977–79
Father Oliver Crilly	ICJP member
Bishop Edward Daly	Roman Catholic Lord Bishop of Derry
Michael Devine	Hunger-striker
Kieran Doherty	Hunger-striker
Sean Donlon	Irish Ambassador to the United States
Professor James Dooge	Irish Foreign Minister-Designate
Father Denis Faul	Roman Catholic chaplain, Maze Prison
Sir Leonard Figg	British Ambassador to Ireland
Dr Garret FitzGerald	Taoiseach, 1981–82
Sir Ian Gilmour	Lord Privy Seal (Deputy Foreign Secretary)
Charles Haughey	Taoiseach, 1979–81
Roy Harrington	Private Secretary to Humphrey Atkins
Sir Nicholas Henderson	British Ambassador to the United States
John Hermon	Chief Constable of the RUC
Stanley Hilditch	Governor of Maze Prison
Liam Hourican	Press Secretary to Garret FitzGerald
Brendan Hughes	PIRA O/C Maze Prison, hunger-striker
Francis Hughes	PIRA prisoner, hunger-striker

John Hume	Leader of the SDLP
Martin Hurson	Hunger-striker
Walter Kirwan	Assistant Secretary, Department of the Taoiseach
General Sir Richard Lawson	General Officer Commanding Northern Ireland, 1979–1982
Brian Lenihan	Irish Minister for Foreign Affairs, 1979–81
Hugh Logue	ICJP member
Jack Lynch	Taoiseach, 1977–79
Kevin Lynch	Hunger-striker
Roy Mason	Secretary of State for Northern Ireland, 1976–79
Raymond McCreesh	Hunger-striker
Joe McDonnell	Hunger-striker
Thomas McElwee	Hunger-striker
Brendan McFarlane	PIRA OC Maze Prison
Martin McGuinness	Senior member of the Republican Movement
Danny Morrison	Irish Republican; editor of *An Phoblacht/Republican News*
Dermot Nally	Cabinet Secretary-General (Ireland)
Sir Kenneth Newman	Chief Constable of the RUC, 1976–80
Rory O'Bradaigh	President of Sinn Féin; PIRA Army Council member
David O'Connell	Sinn Féin politician; PIRA Army Council member
Patsy O'Hara	Hunger-striker
Bishop O'Mahoney	ICJP member
Cardinal Tomás Ó Fiaich	Roman Catholic Primate of All Ireland
James Molyneaux	Leader of the UUP
David Neligan	Head of the Anglo–Irish, Information and Cultural Division of the DFA
Reverend Dr Ian Paisley	Leader of DUP
James Prior	Secretary of State for Northern Ireland, 1981–84
Francis Pym	Secretary of State for Defence
Ronald Reagan	President of the United States, 1981–89
Bobby Sands	PIRA OC Maze Prison; hunger-striker; MP for Fermanagh– SouthTyrone
Sir Kenneth Stowe	Permanent Under-Secretary NIO, 1979–81
Margaret Thatcher	Prime Minister 1979–90
William Whitelaw	Home Secretary
Philip Woodfield	Permanent Under-Secretary NIO, 1981–83
D. J. Wyatt	Deputy Under-Secretary NIO

Introduction

With the announcement, in April 2013, that Baroness Thatcher had died, the President of Sinn Féin, Gerry Adams, offered a withering assessment of the former premier:

> Margaret Thatcher did great hurt to the Irish and British people during her time as British Prime Minister ... Here in Ireland her espousal of old draconian militaristic policies prolonged the war and caused great suffering ... Her failed efforts to criminalise the republican struggle and the political prisoners is part of her legacy ... she ... will be especially remembered for her shameful role during the epic hunger strikes of 1980 and 81. Her Irish policy failed miserably.[1]

Adams' comments reflected the dynamic impact that Mrs Thatcher, as Prime Minister, had on Anglo-Irish relations in general, and the politics of Northern Ireland in particular. Under her premiership the Anglo-Irish Agreement was signed in 1985, laying down the foundations for the British-Irish governmental management of the Northern Irish 'Troubles' that, arguably, led to the Good Friday Agreement in 1998.

Before the defining moment of the Falklands War, and the seminal clash with militant trade unionism during the 1984–85 Miners' Strike that changed British industrial relations forever, the first test of Mrs Thatcher's resolve was the confrontation with the Provisional IRA (PIRA) in the hunger strikes of 1980–81. Here was the clash of the iron will of Irish Republican prisoners, who were prepared to die, and who regarded themselves as prisoners of war (POWs), with the 'Iron Lady' who, in one of most famous speeches, declared that she was 'not for turning.' To the Prime Minister, the PIRA hunger-strikers (and their Irish National Liberation Army (INLA) colleagues) were terrorists, criminals who killed and maimed soldiers, police and civilians to drive the British out of Northern Ireland against the will of the majority of the people in that 'Province'. Mrs Thatcher also experienced personal losses at the hands of Republicans, which confirmed this impression, with the loss of close friends such as Airey Neave (assassinated by the INLA) and Ian Gow (assassinated by the PIRA), both killed by car bombs. In 1984, the Provisionals came within a whisker of killing Mrs

Thatcher herself during a bomb attack at the Conservative Party conference in Brighton.

When Margaret Thatcher became Prime Minister of the United Kingdom of Great Britain and Northern Ireland in May 1979, she inherited a conflict that made her own country – not some faraway land – the most dangerous place in the world to be a British soldier: it was in places such as the small village of Crossmaglen, and the surrounding country roads and fields of South Armagh, that young servicemen lost their lives to improvised explosive devices (IEDs), and where, since 1970, the Provisional IRA had waged its own war to end British rule in Northern Ireland. By 1979, however, the British Army was taking a secondary role in the fight against the PIRA, mainly supporting the overwhelmingly Protestant police, the Royal Ulster Constabulary (RUC), with backup from the (again, overwhelmingly Protestant) Ulster Defence Regiment (UDR), which served exclusively in Northern Ireland.

Mrs Thatcher's first Secretary of State for Northern Ireland was Humphrey Atkins, who directly governed the 'Province', as successive Secretaries of State had done, since 1972, when the Northern Ireland Parliament had been swept away – and along with it majority Unionist (Protestant) rule over the minority Nationalist (Catholic) population there. For many in Great Britain, including those in the Government, Northern Ireland appeared to be an intractable problem. So, when taking over as Secretary of State, Atkins prepared a series of memoranda for his colleagues setting out the parameters of Her Majesty's Government's (HMG's) policy in Northern Ireland. They also provide a snapshot of Northern Ireland as it appeared to London in 1979. Atkins wrote:

> Our policy in Northern Ireland can best be considered under three headings: politics, law and order, and social and economic affairs. Each is inseparably connected with the other two, like the three stands of a rope. Each interacts on the other. If all three pull together the rope is strong; if one strand is weaker than the others or subjected to greater strain, the rope could part.

Atkins painted a picture of the background, for unfamiliar colleagues, of the situation in Northern Ireland. Nearly two thirds of the one and a half million people of Northern Ireland lived within thirty miles of Belfast, the capital. Outside Belfast (population 360,000) and Derry/Londonderry (50,000), there were 'few villages on the English pattern: people live in small towns and a pepper-pot scattering of rural homesteads.' Agriculture was the most important single industry (10% of the overall working population of half a million). Farms (average size seventy-five acres) were less than half the average size in the UK, and almost wholly owner-occupied. There was 'nothing else going' for Northern Ireland in terms of natural resources: no indigenous energy (oil, coal or natural gas); no ready access to markets; and many disincentives to industrial investment. Some 20% (140,000) of the workforce was in manufacturing, uncomfortably concentrated in such declining industries as textiles and shipbuilding. Since 1974, 30,000 manufacturing jobs had been lost. Unemployment, at over 11%, was double the national rate, and the highest of any UK region. Male unemployment ranged from over 10% in Belfast to over 31% in Strabane. As a result of low income and a high birth rate (Protestant as well as Catholic), many more households in Northern Ireland had a lower standard of living than in Great Britain. Weekly household income averaged £79 compared with £93 in the UK as a whole. The rate of infant mortality was higher. Housing conditions were worse. Of the dwellings in use, 20% were statutorily unfit, compared with 7.3% in England and Wales. Hospital services and roads, however, were probably better, and education and recreation was as good as in Great Britain. The crime rate, both overall and for juveniles, was significantly lower than in England and Wales, notwithstanding terrorism. Belfast was a 'particular headache', with concentrations of deprivation and social need greater than anywhere else in the UK. In a group of predominantly Catholic wards in the Belfast urban area, 60% of adult males were unemployed, and over two-thirds of the households lacked basic amenities.

Into this depressing socio-economic mix, Atkins threw in the 'most pervasive political fact about the people of Northern Ireland': that one million were Protestants and half a million were Catholics.

> Not one of these voted in 1979 either for us or for the British Labour Party. The two distinct communities are divided by religion, race, allegiance and politics. Work, friendship and some recreational activities may span the divide. But housing, education, ways of life, culture, and attitudes to history do not. People know to which community they belong and they live, and vote, accordingly.

The proportion of votes cast for the Protestant 'orange' and Catholic 'green sides hardly fluctuated from election to election.' The Catholic minority 'feels threatened by the Protestant majority in Northern Ireland and in the rest of the UK; the Protestant majority feels threatened by the Catholic majority in Ireland as a whole. Violence is a time-honoured reaction by either side immediately the threat from the other looms large.'[2] This 'double minority' problem 'makes genuine negotiation very difficult.' Atkins believed that the results of the recent European election, in 1979, had almost certainly made it more difficult to get some political movement. Reverend Ian Paisley, the hard-line leader of the Democratic Unionist Party (DUP), had scored an emphatic personal victory among Protestants; even if his organization remained second in other elections, when competing against the more moderate Ulster Unionist Party (UUP), it was the first election in which the whole of Northern Ireland could vote for him as a candidate, with Northern Ireland treated as one constituency. The European election also confirmed the position of the Social Democratic and Labour Party (SDLP) as the dominant representatives of the Catholic minority.[3]

Meanwhile, the 'Direct Rule' of Northern Ireland from London was 'nobody's first choice' of government. It lacked the 'red blood of politics'; under it political life had few outlets, and politicians lacked responsibility. It was not seen to be democratic, and gave both sides – and their friends in the United States, for example – a licence to criticize the British Government. It did, however, give guarantees to both communities: 'to the Protestants that they are part of the United Kingdom and to the Catholics that they are being freed from discrimination. It is impartial, sensitive and, to an extent, positive government. It brings together into an indivisible whole the inter-acting strains of economic and social affairs, politics and security.'[4] On law and order, Atkins pointed out that 'Terrorism does not blanket the Province. Most of the Province is almost permanently free of it.' The pattern of deaths and injuries from terrorism had changed since 1973, following the worst year (1972) of the 'Troubles':

Deaths (Injuries in brackets)	1st half of 1973	1st half of 1976	1st half of 1979
RUC and RUC reserve	7(61)	15(172)	10(81)
Army and UDR	48(334)	13(99)	16(56)
Civilians	105(1029)	147(1253)	18(225)
	160(1424)	175(1524)	44(362)
Shooting attacks	3321	890	360
Bombing attacks	778	634	332

'Note the big drop in civilian deaths and injuries since 1973 and reduction in shooting and bombing attacks', Atkins pointed out to his colleagues. Over the same period, the size of the police force – the full-time Royal Ulster Constabulary and the part-time RUC Reserve – had grown from 6,900 to 11,000, while the peak strength of the regular British Army had fallen from over 17,000 to just under 13,000. There were some 7,500 in the Ulster Defence Regiment.

The Provisional IRA aimed in the longer term, noted Atkins, to force the British out of Ireland and create a thirty-two-county Socialist Republic; 'and more immediately to force us' into a declaration of intent to withdraw and an amnesty for terrorist prisoners. He also noted how, in the early 1970s, the Provisionals were welcomed into the Catholic ghettos to help protect the community against the Protestants, 'But now the Catholics have become sickened by their brutal methods and apparently pointless and unattainable aims. So they do not now operate from a broad and secure base with large bodies of men.' The major responsibility for action against terrorists now rested with the police and not the Army (as it did during the early years of the Troubles). Thoroughly demoralized and inadequate in the early 1970s, the Royal Ulster Constabulary had been steadily built up in terms of strength, experience, confidence and acceptance. They now policed the greater part of Northern Ireland, including most of Belfast, with the support, if they needed it, of the UDR. The regular Army still played a major part in supporting the RUC in about a third of Belfast, as well as in other sensitive areas, notably along the border. Meanwhile, 876 people were convicted of terrorist offences in the first half of 1979. Given all of this background, Atkins noted how Northern Ireland was viewed from across the Irish Sea:

> Not surprisingly in view of the scale of its problems, Northern Ireland strikes the newcomer as turned in on itself. Though the people are well used to visiting experts and pundits, they show a relative indifference to how they are regarded elsewhere, except for a resentment of the apparent indifference in Great Britain as tragedy is piled on tragedy.[5]

This was the Northern Ireland setting faced by Mrs Thatcher, who began her premiership as the hunger strikes of 1980–1981 were played out. Their consequences continue to reverberate to this day. As a result of the refusal of Mrs Thatcher's Government to concede 'special category status' to the Republican prisoners in Her Majesty's Prison The Maze – which the prisoners believed would also give them 'political status' – Sinn Féin, the political wing of the PIRA, entered into electoral politics when Bobby Sands, on hunger strike, was elected MP for the constituency of Fermanagh-South Tyrone. Eventually, a few years after the Good Friday Agreement, Sinn Féin became the dominant Nationalist party in Northern Ireland, finally supplanting the SDLP, which had also supported the goal of a united Ireland but opposed the pursuit of it via violence. Many today would agree with the words of Padraig O'Malley, writing in 1991, about the aftermath of the hunger strikes: 'In the broader political arena there was no question as to who had won and who had lost. Sinn Féin and the IRA were seen as indisputable winners, for although they had lost in the narrow sense that they had to call off the hunger strikes and accept what was on offer ... they won in the larger sense'[6] due to their electoral advance. The conclusion of this book reassesses such claims regarding the legacy of the hunger strikes in the context of the bedding in of the institutions of the Good Friday Agreement.

The book also deals with some of the other controversies surrounding the hunger strike. In Ireland – a land where commemorations are legion – the thirtieth anniversary of the first hunger strike, of 1980, led one of those who participated in it, Leo Green, to declare from a public platform:

> On the day the second Hunger Strike ended we knew we hadn't lost. We had secured the key demand on the right to wear our own clothes. That opened up a space within the prisons to make further progress. And, within a short space of time, the rest of the ... demands followed. The price was enormous. But we hadn't just not lost – we had won.[7]

The hunger-strikers occupy an exalted position in the Republican pantheon, so when it has been suggested that some of the ten men who died agonizing deaths on hunger strike need not have done so, there was bound to be controversy. This controversy originated from within the Republican family. The version of events that has dominated within Sinn Féin circles has been that it was the intransigence of Mrs Thatcher that led to the deaths of ten Republicans on hunger strike. In 2005, however, the former public relations officer (PRO) of the prisoners, Richard O'Rawe – himself incarcerated within the Maze – broke ranks, and in his book *Blanketmen* made a number of allegations against the then PIRA leadership outside the prison. O'Rawe's claims struck at the heart of the Sinn Féin leadership's version of events.

O'Rawe claimed, contrary to the Sinn Féin 'official' version of events that the prisoners controlled the hunger strike, that it had, in fact, been the IRA Army Council – the seven-man ruling body that ran the war against the British – that had had unrestricted control, 'and that, for us prisoners, the Army Council was the umbrella under which all the other contentious issues sheltered.' He also alleged that the British Government had made a substantial offer to settle the hunger strike following the release of a conciliatory statement O'Rawe had written on behalf of the prisoners on 4 July 1981. This offer, sometimes known as the 'Mountain Climber' offer, was presented, it was claimed, on at least two different occasions to senior Republicans Gerry Adams and Danny Morrison by mediators from Derry, who had been in contact with British Government representatives. The first occasion had been shortly before the fifth hunger-striker, Joe McDonnell, died on 8 July 1981, and the second was after the sixth hunger-striker, Martin Hurson, died on 13 July.

O'Rawe also alleged that the then Sinn Féin national director of publicity, Danny Morrison, told Bik McFarlane, Officer Commanding (O/C) of PIRA prisoners in the Maze, the details of the offer when they met in the prison hospital on 5 July. O'Rawe claimed that McFarlane wrote him a message outlining what was on offer. They both accepted it, believing that there was enough in it 'to end the hunger strike with honour.' Shortly after McFarlane had communicated the acceptance of the offer to the outside leadership, though, a secret communication was smuggled into the prison from Gerry Adams, 'informing us that there was not enough in the offer to settle the hunger strike,' and that 'more was needed'. McFarlane and O'Rawe accepted what 'we believed to have been the position of the IRA Army Council.' In O'Rawe's view: 'Adams's comm [communication] rejecting the offer ensured the prolongation of the hunger strike, with six more hunger strikers dying in its wake.' Later there were claims that the full Army Council was unaware of any of this, and that events were being run by a small number of Republicans grouped around Adams.

As controversial was O'Rawe's suggestion that there were only two possible explanations as to why the IRA Army Council would reject the prisoners' acceptance of the offer. The first was that it believed that the British Government would make a better offer before Joe McDonnell died, 'a perfectly understandable, if dangerous, approach, given that the British had not closed down the communication channel.' The second explanation was that the Army Council wanted to 'accelerate an electoral strategy' by getting a Republican candidate, Owen Carron, returned for Bobby Sands' seat in Fermanagh-South Tyrone: 'Since this could not, in all likelihood, be achieved without the hunger strike, I suggested that the Army Council would have had to be prepared to sacrifice hunger strikers in order to achieve that aim', recalled O'Rawe.[8]

Brendan McFarlane, however, has disputed O'Rawe's claims: 'There was no concrete proposals whatsoever in relation to a deal.' As to whether the two agreed that there was a basis for a deal to end the hunger strike, McFarlane was clear: 'That is totally fictitious. That conversation did not happen. I did not write to the army council and tell them that we were accepting [a deal]. I couldn't have. I couldn't have accepted something that didn't exist.' He insisted that the 'prisoners took the decisions' on the continuation of the hunger strike, not the outside leadership of the Republican Movement.[9] Also among those critical of O'Rawe's claims was Danny Morrison, who believed that as:

> ... a result of his attacks Richard has been ... lauded by revisionists, anti-republican journalists and the usual suspects ... Richard's book has helped no one but the enemies of the struggle. Not the hunger strikers' families, not the blanket men, not the republican cause, not his friends and comrades, and, certainly, not himself. What Richard O'Rawe has written is repugnant but it has exposed him as a minor figure against the inviolable memory of the hunger strikers, their sacrifices and their greatness.[10]

Now, with the release of British Government archives covering the hunger strike – together with the diary of Brendan Duddy, the secret backchannel (known as 'Mountain Climber') between the British and the PIRA during this period – it is possible to resolve some, although not all, of the controversies surrounding O'Rawe's claims. It is surprising to find that Mrs Thatcher's hand was literally all over the 'deal' sent to the Provisionals – revealing the key involvement of a Prime Minister who claimed that she refused to negotiate with terrorists. As Prime Minister, Mrs Thatcher did not manage the day-to-day handling of the hunger strikes, but she had the last word on the policy options offered to her. In this respect the Government's strategy rested with the Prime Minister – she was thus, in a memorable phrase used by one of her Northern Ireland ministers, 'the lady behind the veil'. The question as to who remained in control of the hunger strike – whether it was the prisoners themselves or whether Gerry Adams (who has always denied he was in the IRA) was a 'man behind the balaclava' type figure – remains contentious given O'Rawe's claims.

There have been many memoirs, oral histories, polemics, hagiographies and interviews regarding the hunger strike – including outstanding books, such as David Beresford's *Ten Men Dead* and Padraig O'Malley's *Biting From the Grave* – but what follows is a history of the hunger strike, and the background to the dispute that led to it, based on unpublished archival material; when combined with Republican sources published elsewhere it offers an insight into the minds of the main decision-makers and participants in one of the defining episodes of modern British-Irish history. The book also tries to address some of the wider questions such as whether Mrs Thatcher's Government adopted the correct stance in confronting the Republican prisoners in the Maze in the manner in which it did. It also considers the legacy of the hunger strike in the context of the Provisional IRA's campaign more generally, including what was achieved in the shorter and longer terms. While some of these conclusions may be contentious, one thing is not: after the hunger strike, the political landscape in Northern Ireland, and the path of British-Irish history, was changed utterly.

NOTES

1   Sinn Féin http://www.sinnfein.ie/contents/26085
2   TNA CAB 148/183 OD(79) 12, 5 July 1979 Northern Ireland: The Overall Situation Memorandum by the Secretary of State for Northern Ireland.
3   TNA CAB 148/183 OD(79)13, 5 July 1979 Northern Ireland: Politics. Memorandum by the Secretary of State for Northern Ireland.
4   TNA CAB 148/183 OD(79) 12, 5 July 1979 Northern Ireland: The Overall Situation Memorandum by the Secretary of State for Northern Ireland.
5   TNA CAB 148/183 OD(79) 12 5 July 1979 Northern Ireland: The Overall Situation Memorandum by the Secretary of State for Northern Ireland.

6   Padraig O'Malley, *Biting at the Grave. The Irish Hunger Strikes and the Politics of Despair* (Boston, 1991) p.211.
7   *An Phoblacht*, 27 October 1980.
8   Richard O'Rawe, *Afterlives. The Irish Hunger Strike and the Secret Offer that Changed Irish History* (Dublin 2010) pp.16–18.
9   *Irish News*, 12 March 2005.
10 *Daily Ireland*, 9 March 2005.

Chapter 1

Contours of Conflict:
The Prisons, 1972–79

Following the suspension of the Unionist-dominated Northern Ireland Parliament at Stormont, the first Secretary of State appointed to run Northern Ireland, from London, was William Whitelaw. It was he, in 1972, who introduced 'special category' status for prisoners convicted of terrorist offences, which would form the backdrop to the hunger strikes to follow.

The background to this decision was a spiralling cycle of violence that had, seemingly, brought Northern Ireland to the point of civil war: British troops had been deployed, in 1969, by the then Labour Government to keep the warring Protestants and Catholics apart; in 1970, the Provisional IRA had begun a bombing campaign on commercial targets; in 1971, the 'Provos' killed their first British solider as part of their crusade to drive the British State out of the 'Occupied Six Counties' of Northern Ireland; in the same year, the Conservative Government agreed to introduce, under pressure from the Unionist Government at Stormont, internment without trial against the IRA; and, in early 1972, the discipline of British paratroopers broke down as they ran amok at an anti-internment march in Derry/Londonderry, killing thirteen civilians.

The Northern Irish Government and Parliament were swept away soon afterwards in the disastrous wake of the 'Bloody Sunday' killings. The Provisionals proved to be a match for any outrage by the security forces – not least on 'Bloody Friday', when they detonated twenty-two bombs around Belfast, killing eleven people and injuring over 100. By this stage, elements of the Protestant community were taking matters into their own hands, following the apparent inability of the authorities to maintain law and order, with the formation of their own Loyalist paramilitary groups such as the Ulster Defence Association (UDA), alongside the pre-existing Ulster Volunteer Force (UVF). All of this was taking place, not far away in some distant continent at the end of the Empire, but within the United Kingdom of Great Britain and Northern Ireland itself.

When Whitelaw took over the Northern Ireland Office (NIO) and introduced special category status – applicable to both Republican and Loyalist prisoners

– he did so under pressure to secure an PIRA ceasefire in 1972, and to end a hunger strike by a senior Republican commander, Billy McKee. Even then, in a meeting with senior Provisionals, Gerry Adams and David O'Connell, the Northern Ireland Office official Philip Woodfield, who delivered Whitelaw's terms for a ceasefire, made the situation clear: 'the Secretary of State could not concede political status for convicted prisoners; he was, however, ready to consider representations about specific matters, and had already made certain arrangements which had led to the calling off of the hunger strike'.[1] As this was the first encounter between Her Majesty's Government and the Provisional IRA, Woodfield offered his impressions of the two Republican representatives in a minute that was later read by the Prime Minister, Edward Heath:

> Mr O'Connell is about forty and Mr Adams is twenty-three. There is no doubt whatever that these two at least genuinely want a cease fire and a permanent end to violence. Whatever pressures in Northern Ireland have brought them to this frame of mind there is little doubt that now the prospect of peace is there they have a strong personal incentive to try and get it. They let drop several remarks showing that the life of the Provisional IRA man on the run is not a pleasant one.
>
> Their appearance and manner was respectable and respectful – they easily referred to Mr Whitelaw as 'the Secretary of State' and they addressed me from time to time as 'Sir'. They made no bombastic defence of their past and made no attacks on the British Government, the British Army or any other communities or bodies in Northern Ireland. Their response to every argument put to them was reasonable and moderate. Their behaviour and attitude appeared to bear no relation to the indiscriminate campaigns of bombing and shooting in which they have both been prominent leaders.[2]

In June 1972, therefore, Whitelaw authorized the introduction of special category status. This meant that Republican and Loyalist convicted prisoners now enjoyed certain privileges not granted to non-paramilitary inmates. Special category prisoners were:

i)   not to be required to work;
ii) allowed to wear their own clothes;
iii) allowed to receive one parcel weekly, which could include food and tobacco;
iv) allowed to send out one letter weekly at public expense; and
v)   allowed one visit of thirty minutes' duration weekly.

Despite the fact that Whitelaw had considered special category status as not conceding 'political' status to prisoners, it did allow Republican and Loyalist prisoners to view it as classifying them as prisoners of war.

As a result of the rapid increase in the number of prisoners, as well as the number of persons detained at the time under emergency legislation, it was necessary to house large numbers of inmates in 'compounds' rather than in cells. They were held at a disused RAF base near Lisburn, several miles outside Belfast, known as 'the Maze' or 'Long Kesh'. This, with imagery reminiscent of Second World War POW camps surrounded by barbed wire, watchtowers and Nissen huts, all reinforced the Republican prisoners' perception of themselves as political prisoners fighting against a foreign occupation.

A compound at the Maze, Long Kesh, consisted of four Nissen huts. Two of the huts, and half of another, were divided into cubicles and used for sleeping accommodation; half of one hut was used for recreation, and the fourth hut was used as a dining room. Ablutions, a study hut and exercise yard completed the unit. Each compound could house up to eighty to ninety inmates. Republican and Loyalist prisoners virtually ran their own compounds, leading to a significant loss of control over the prisoners by the authorities.

The rapidity of the increase in the prison population is noteworthy. On 1 January 1969, the total prison population in Northern Ireland, tried and untried, of men and women, including those in borstal, was only 712. By the end of 1973, there were 688 special category prisoners including twenty-five women. By 31 December 1974, the number had increased to 1,116, including fifty-one women. At the end of 1974, there were 545 male special category prisoners in compounds at the Maze, 502 in compounds at Magilligan and eighteen in Belfast. The women were in Armagh Prison, the only women's prison in Northern Ireland. The whole question of special category status for certain convicted prisoners, and the use of compound accommodation, was closely examined by a committee under the chairmanship of Lord Gardiner, a former Lord Chancellor, to consider, in the context of civil liberties and human rights, measures to deal with terrorism in Northern Ireland. Delivered in January 1975, the committee's report stated:

> Prisoners of the compound type, each compound holding up to 90 prisoners, are thoroughly unsatisfactory from every point of view; their major disadvantage is that there is virtually a total loss of disciplinary control by the prison authorities inside the compounds, and rehabilitation work is impossible.

The report recommended that the earliest opportunity should be taken to end special category status, and that the first priority should be to stop admitting new prisoners to it.[3] Gardiner was clear that 'The introduction of special category status for convicted prisoners was a serious mistake.' It was recommended that it should be 'made absolutely clear that special category prisoners can expect no amnesty and will have to serve their sentences'.[4] To the British Government, and the majority of people in Northern Ireland, the prisoners and internees in these compounds were not freedom fighters but terrorists, with no justification for engaging in political violence. As the Gardiner Report put it:

> Political dissent is as old as political society; its roots may be resistance to oppression or simply idealism. The new factor in the long history of dissent is the effectiveness of the weapons its more extreme proponents can command. Terrorism is probably more widespread in both the industrial and developing world than at any other time in recent history. There are a number of reasons for this, which include the relative ease with which arms, money and terrorist skills can cross frontiers, the effect of mass communications in both facilitating and glamourising violence, and above all the vulnerability of complex industrial societies. *But the greater ease with which terrorism can be organised does not legitimise it.*
>
> This is particularly evident in the case of Northern Ireland. To work through the process of political persuasion for a united Ireland, a Northern Ireland integrated with the United Kingdom or even a sovereign Northern Ireland is quite legitimate. But the terrorist organisations reject the democratic process, and they can only embitter relations between Britain and Ireland. They cannot bludgeon the British out of Ireland ... They can offer no gifts to the people of Northern Ireland by way of greater freedom, security, or prosperity which the people cannot now attain by legal and democratic means. Moreover, they command the support of only a small fraction of either the minority or the majority community in Northern Ireland. Because they are attempting to destroy Northern Ireland as a political society, terrorists who break the law – which in Northern Ireland gives greater protection to the accused than in most disturbed communities – are not heroes but criminals; not the pioneers of political change but its direst enemies.[5]

As the NIO recognized, one of the problems with special category status was that community attitudes to crime and to prison were sometimes 'blurred when offenders can be represented as Loyalist and Republican prisoners of war.' Special category status was 'erroneously regarded as a badge of respectability', particularly amongst young prisoners. No matter what efforts were made to persuade a young prisoner, or his parents, that it was very much in his own interests to accept work or training as an ordinary prisoner 'rather than spend his time in idleness under the evil influence of adult prisoners in a special category compound, the family attitude is almost invariably that they can hold up their heads in the local community if their son is with his paramilitary colleagues; but they would be ashamed to regard him as an ordinary criminal.' It was considered that special category status encouraged prisoners, their organizations and their families to hold firmly to the 'mistaken belief that one day they will be the subject of an amnesty.'[6]

In November 1975, the Secretary of State, Merlyn Rees, announced the Labour Government's intention to start to phase out special category status. This phasing-out process began with effect from 1 March 1976; no prisoner convicted of an offence committed on or after that date would be granted special category treatment, regardless of the nature of his offence.[7] Rees had already announced the phasing out of internment. By this point, many paramilitary prisoners were being convicted under the Diplock Courts system and emergency legislation, which saw suspected terrorists tried by one judge with no jury sitting. Rees made it clear that those prisoners who had already been granted special category status would not be deprived of it. This did not, however, mean that prisoners convicted *after* 1 March 1976 for offences committed *before* that date would be deprived of special category status. As an NIO official admitted: 'It would be a nonsense if a prisoner convicted in 1980 of a murder committed in 1970 were to be allowed to start a life sentence as a special category prisoner when our declared object is to phase out that status.' Despite this, the reality remained largely unchanged: prisoners continued to be convicted and granted special category status after 1 March 1976 for offences committed before that date. Thus, during the period from 1 March 1976 to the end of that year, there were 230 new admissions to special category. By 13 September 1977, there were another fifty-eight.[8]

It remained a key governmental aim to attempt to break paramilitary control over prisoners in the compounds. The Permanent Search Team (established in 1976) descended on the compounds without warning to conduct searches on its own terms, and almost succeeded in eliminating the prisoners' stocks of mock weapons, training manuals, uniforms and escape equipment, all of which had become commonplace. A Thames TV programme for example focused on a 12 July colour parade in 1976. Although embarrassing events like this were becoming uncommon – their rarity was admitted by the most senior NIO civil servant, the Permanent Under-Secretary (PUS), Sir Brian Cubbon – there was still paramilitary control in the compounds. This paramilitary oversight was designed to minimize the influence of prison staff on the lives of the inmates, maximize that of the paramilitaries themselves and generally further the aims of their respective organizations. In the long term, the Government had no announced plans for dealing with the problem beyond waiting for the numbers to reduce, but as Cubbon observed: 'Our ultimate objective must be to get them into cells.

This is consistent with the commitments made by Mr Whitelaw when special category was introduced, which did not include any entitlement to be housed in compounds rather than cells.[9] Eventually, all prisoners who would formerly have been placed in special category were placed in cells, most of them in HM Maze Prison, where eight new cell blocks of 100 cells each were constructed. These blocks were known as 'H-Blocks' because of their design in the shape of a letter 'H'.[10]

The struggle with Republican prisoners over the loss of special category status began on 14 September 1976, when PIRA Volunteer Kieran Nugent was convicted of hijacking a vehicle, and was sentenced to three years' imprisonment. When he was taken to the Maze, Nugent refused to wear the prison uniform issued to him on the grounds that he was not a criminal but a political prisoner. This began the 'blanket protest', in which the prisoner, by refusing to wear prison uniform, was naked except for a blanket. The demand from the 'Blanketmen' was for restoration of special category status, or in their view, political status, as prisoners of war. However, what exactly constituted political status was not always obvious. As the protest evolved, later, into the 'dirty protest', the prisoners had no clear demands other than to be awarded special category status. As the NIO noted, in 1978, it seemed that the prisoners were protesting for the right to:

i) wear their own clothes at all times;
ii) not to work;
iii) enforce their own discipline.[11]

At an anti-H-Block campaign conference in Dublin held on 16 December 1979 to elect a Southern sub-Committee, four broad demands were put forward:

i) prisoners' rights not to wear uniform;
ii) not to do prison work;
iii) to have freedom of association;
iv) to organise recreational and educational facilities and have weekly visits, letters and food parcels.[12]

An NIO note, of March 1980, of a meeting held the previous day at the Maze between Cardinal Tomás Ó Fiaich, Bishop Edward Daly and officials, recorded the Cardinal as saying that in his opinion the protesters' demands were specific, and amounted to demands for:

i) own clothes;
ii) no obligation to work;

iii) full [restoration of lost] remission of prison sentences;
iv) no deprivation of visits and letters, etc.[13]

This was the point at which, according to NIO files, full remission seemed to have crept in to the demands. The *Socialist Worker* of 1 June 1980, meanwhile, announced Charter 80's 'Charter for Political Status' as being:

i) the right of prisoners to wear their own clothes;
ii) the right to refrain from prison work;
iii) the right to free association amongst political prisoners;
iv) the right to organise their own educational and recreational facilities, and receive one visit, one letter and one parcel a week;
v) the right to full remission of sentences.

This became the final statement of the demands for special category status. As was noted by an NIO official: 'only two and a half of the protesters' present demands' dated from HMG's original five commitments on special category status in 1972.[14]

One of the protesting prisoners was Bobby Sands, a Provisional IRA Volunteer in his twenties from Belfast. He had previously been interned without trial, released and arrested again, having been caught in the act of firebombing a property. From his own account, one can see the evolution of a Republican paramilitary:

> From my earliest days I recall my mother speaking of the troubled times that occurred during her childhood. Often she spoke of internment on prison ships, of gun attacks and death, and of early morning raids when one lay listening with pounding heart to the heavy clattering of boots on the cobble-stone streets and as a new day broke, peeked carefully out of the window to see a neighbour being taken away by the Specials [auxiliary police].
>
> Although I never really understood what internment was, or who the Specials were, I grew to regard them as symbols of evil. Nor could I understand when my mother spoke of [James] Connolly and the 1916 Rising and of how he and his comrades fought and were subsequently executed – a fate suffered by so many Irish rebels in my mother's stories.
>
> When the television arrived, my mother's stories were replaced by what it had to offer. I became more confused as 'the baddies' in my other mother's tales were always my heroes on the TV. The British army always fought for 'the right side' and the police were always 'the good guys'. Both were to be heroised and imitated in childhood play.

The history that Sands learnt at school was always English history, often focused on English historical triumphs in Ireland and elsewhere. He often wondered 'why I was never taught the history of my own country', and when his sister, a year younger than him, began to learn the Gaelic language at school, he 'envied her. Occasionally, nearing the end of my school days, I received a few scant lessons in Irish history. For this, from the republican-minded teacher who taught me, I was indeed grateful.' He started work, which, 'although frightening at first, became alright,' especially with the reward at the end of the week. Dances, clothes, girls and a few shillings to spend 'opened up a whole new world to me. I suppose at that time I would have worked all week, as money seemed to matter more than anything else.' Then came the violence of 1968, 'and my life began to change. Gradually, the news changed. Regularly I noticed the Specials, whom I now knew to be the "B" Specials, attacking and baton-charging the crowds of people who all of a sudden began marching on the streets.' From the talk in the house, 'and my mother shaking her fist at the TV set, I knew that they were our people who were on the receiving end.' Sands' sympathy and feelings 'really became aroused' after watching the scenes at Burntollet, where some off-duty B Specials joined other Protestants attacking students marching under a Civil Rights banner. 'That imprinted itself in my mind like a scar, and for the first time I took a real interest in what was going on. I became angry.'

In 1969, 'events moved faster as August hit our area like a hurricane. The whole world exploded, and my own little world just crumbled around me.' The TV did not have to tell the story now, for it was on Sands' own doorstep. Belfast was in flames, 'but it was our districts, our humble homes, which were burnt. The Specials came at the head of the RUC and Orange hordes, right into the heart of our streets, burning, looting, shooting and murdering.' There was 'no one to save us,' except 'the boys', as Sands' father called the men who defended the district with a handful of old guns: the IRA. As the 'unfamiliar sound of gunfire was still echoing, there soon appeared alien figures, voices, and faces, in the form of armed British soldiers on our streets. But no longer did I think of them as my childhood "good guys", for their presence alone [provided] food for thought.' Before he could determine the solution, though, 'it was answered for me in the form of early morning raids, and I remembered my mother's stories of previous troubled times. For now my heart pounded at the heavy clatter of the soldiers' boots in the early morning stillness, and I carefully peeked from behind the drawn curtains to watch the neighbours' doors being kicked in, and the fathers and sons being dragged out by the hair and being flung into the backs of sinister-looking armoured cars.' This was followed by murder, Sands witnessing: 'the shooting dead of our people on the streets in cold blood.' The TV now:

> ... showed endless gun battles and bombings. The people had risen
> and were fighting back, and my mother, in her newly found spirit of

resistance, hurled encouragement at the TV, shouting 'give it to them boys!'

Easter 1971 came, and the name on everyone's lips was 'the Provos', the people's army, the backbone of nationalist resistance.

I was now past my eighteenth year, and I was fed up with rioting. No matter how much I tried or how many stones I threw I could never beat them – the Brits always came back....

I had seen too many homes wrecked, fathers and sons arrested, neighbours hurt, friends murdered, and too much gas, shootings, and blood, most of it my own people's.

At eighteen-and-a-half I joined the Provos. My mother wept with pride and fear as I went out to meet and confront the imperial might of an empire with an M1 carbine and enough hate to topple the world.

In the autumn of 1972, Sands was charged, and for the first time faced jail. He was nineteen-and-a-half. Sands was imprisoned in the Maze internment camp, and surrounded by barbed wire, where he spent three-and-a-half years as a 'prisoner-of-war' with special category status. 'I did not waste my time. I did not allow the rigours of prison life to change my revolutionary determination an inch. I educated and trained myself both in political and military matters, as did my comrades.'

Upon his release in 1976, Sands was 'more determined in the fight for liberation'. He reported back to his local IRA unit, and threw himself straight back in to the struggle. 'Quite a lot of things had changed. Belfast had changed. Some parts of the ghettos had completely disappeared, and others were in the process of being removed. The war was still forging ahead, although tactics and strategy had changed.'

At first, Sands found it somewhat hard to adjust, but he settled into the run of things and, 'at the grand old age of twenty-three', he got married. The 'liberation struggle', meanwhile, had to be continued. Thus, six months after his release, 'disaster fell a second time as I bombed my way back into jail!' With his wife being four months pregnant, the shock of capture, the 'seven days of hell' in Castlereagh interrogation centre, a quick court appearance and remand, 'the return to a cold, damp cell, nearly destroyed me. It took every ounce of the revolutionary spirit left in me to stand up to it.' Jail, 'although not new to me, was really bad, worse than the first time.' Things had changed enormously since the 'withdrawal of political status.'

Both Republicans and Loyalist prisoners were mixed in the same wing, where the greater part of each day was spent locked up in a cell. The 'screws' (prison officers), 'many of whom I knew to be cowering cowards, now went in gangs into the cells of Republican prisoners to dish out unmerciful beatings. This was to be the pattern all the way along the road to criminalisation: torture, and more torture, to break our spirit of resistance.' Sands 'was meant to change from being a revolutionary freedom fighter to a criminal at the stroke of a political pen, reinforced by inhumanities of the most brutal nature.' As he was led from the courthouse, his mother, 'defiant as ever, stood up in the gallery and shook the air with a cry of "they'll never break you, boys", and my wife, from somewhere behind her, with tear-filled eyes, braved a smile of encouragement towards me.'

Sands became a blanketman on the following day, 'and there I was, sitting on the cold floor, naked, with only a blanket around me, in an empty cell.' The days were 'long and lonely.' The sudden and total deprivation of such basic human necessities as exercise and fresh air, association with other people, his own clothes, and things like newspapers, radio, cigarettes, books and a host of other things, 'made life very hard. At first, as always, I adapted. But, as time wore on, I came face to face with an old friend, depression, which on many an occasion consumed me and swallowed me into its darkest depths.' Only the occasional letter from home got past the prison censor. Gradually, his appearance and physical health began to change drastically: 'My eyes, glassy, piercing, sunken, and surrounded by pale, yellowish skin, were frightening.' He had grown a beard, 'and, like my comrades, I resembled a living corpse. The blinding migraine headaches, which started off slowly, became a daily occurrence, and owing to no exercise I became seized with muscular pains.'[15]

From the perspective of prison management, the protest was 'an important facet of the special category battle, and not only could the numbers of new committals swell the ranks of existing protestors, but there is always the danger of some of the present conformers joining the protestors, either by choice or as a result of pressure from within the [paramilitary] command structure.' As E. N. Barry, an NIO official responsible for prisoners, concluded: 'There is no room for compromise.'[16] In 1978, the prisoners escalated their protest. A statement from the prisoners' public relations officer announced:

> On March 20, we, the Republican prisoners-of-war 'on the blanket' in H-Blocks 5 and 3 intensified our protest to highlight the inhumane and degrading way we are being treated. We are being beaten, daily, because we refuse to wear the British criminal uniform ... The first stage of our protest involved all the blanket-men, almost 300. We refused to wash, shower or brush and mop out our cells. The system immediately retaliated by arbitrarily picking out 12 men and placing them in the punishment calls.
>
> On March 27, we felt it necessary to escalate the protest. Since last week, our cells have become dirty and smelling, but undeterred, we entered the second stage by refusing to slop-out (a privilege of leaving

the cell to empty one's chamber pot down a lavatory). This privilege, which didn't apply to all our comrades, was regularly withdrawn by the screws as a form of punishment/harassment.

We also refused to leave our cells to get fresh water in our water containers, but we told the screws we would accept a bucket in which to slop our filled chamber pots. And we said we would hand our water containers out for the orderlies to refill and leave back in our cells.

Two of our comrades were then taken from their cells and put in punishment.

After Tuesday's breakfast, we set our dirty dishes and water containers outside the cell. The screws hurled them back in and some men received minor injuries. Some burst water containers soaked bedding.

For that day's toiletry, we were handed half a sheet of toilet paper, and our chamber pots were not emptied.

We received our dinner cold – it was served half-an-hour late. Dishes which we left out were used as missiles against us, before being removed. Another comrade was taken hostage and shipped off to punishment block.

At 8.30 p.m. lock-up, there was no point in putting out our water containers. The chamber-pots were overflowing. We urinated into the boots – part of the criminal uniform – then threw the urine out of the window. On top of this, men had to leave excrement lying in a corner of the cell.

My own cell is stinking, and my body has a sickening smell about it. We expect great harassment and more beatings because of this stage of the protest.[17]

This marked the commencement of the 'dirty protest', in which the prisoners smeared their own excreta onto the walls of their cells. A prison situation report of 10 April gives a flavour of the new protest. In Block H3, it was the day for the routine change of linen (sheets and pillowcases). The inmates threw out the dirty items and would not accept the clean replacements. These were put in the cells anyway. The protestors emptied chamber pots, but from such a height as to cause splashing, and refused to use disinfectant. Inmates refused to leave cells, except for statutory visits and to see the doctor when being examined for fitness for cellular confinement. Two inmates attended welfare visits with the welfare officer. All H3 inmates refused to clean cells, or to wash and shower. On the same morning in H5, inmates on cellular confinement refused to put their bedding out, which was removed by orderlies. Slopping out was into buckets, so as to cause splashing. Disinfectant was refused. Some inmates refused to put on trousers to go and see the doctor, so the doctor saw them in their cells. Miles (the Deputy

Governor) visited all prisoners in H3 and H5 Blocks, entered all the cells and stood close to each prisoner and spoke to each man. He examined the pots in each cell – a little urine was in some, but no solid waste. The cells were untidy, but with only surface dirt.[18]

In response, the prison authorities introduced special measures to deal with the situation. External walls, walkways and inner perimeter wire fences contaminated by excreta and rubbish thrown out by the inmates were cleaned daily by scraping, brushing and hosing. Polythene sheeting was used to collect excreta thrown through the inner-facing windows and was then burnt. Excrement thrown out through windows was removed by suction cleaning. Disinfectant powder (hypochlorite) was liberally used after cleaning. Internal corridors in the cell blocks were cleaned daily, again by washing and suction cleaning. In the cells, a rotational system was in force whereby prisoners were removed from dirty cells, which were then cleaned. Industrial cleaning apparatus was used – steam hoses with added disinfectant fluids. After cleaning, the cells were dried out, and if necessary repainted, before prisoners were returned to them.[19]

The prisoners hoped that the dirty protest would draw support, outside the H-Blocks, for their demand for special category status. All Republican propaganda, concerned with the prisoners, was directed towards this end. The prisoners disputed that they were treated humanely. In a statement, one of them declared that the 'Republican prisoners-of-war' in H-Blocks 3 and 5, Long Kesh, and B-Wing, Crumlin Road Gaol, wished to highlight the 'torture and inhuman' treatment that has been practised on them in the form of 'institutionalised violence … We are kept in total solitary confinement, never being allowed to leave our cells. We do not receive any form of fresh air or exercise whatsoever. Most of us have had no form of exercise for over a year.' After several months of this, 'we are physically shattered. Every man suffers from some sort of medical complaint. We become exhausted at the slightest physical exertion. The food we receive here is inadequate and usually inedible, because it is cold, ill-prepared or simply disgusting. We do not receive any food parcels, therefore we are dependent upon what the prison authorities serve us. When the food is bad (it usually is) we go without! In our circumstances this is a very serious loss.'[20]

Only very limited support, however, was forthcoming from the wider population. One who did take an interest was the independent Nationalist MP for Fermanagh–South Tyrone, Frank Maguire, who, on one occasion, took up the complaint that prisoners were denied warm food. Assistant Governor Murphy disputed this. He recorded how, on 27 February (evening meal) and on 28 February 1979 (breakfast, lunch and evening meal), 44 prisoners in C-Wing H-Block 3 refused to take their meals from the prison staff who were handing them out. Accordingly, the meals were placed on the floor of each prisoner's cell. On 28 February, when carrying out adjudications in the cells of prisoners

Kelly and Whelan, Murphy noted that there was not the normal protest of banging of chamber pots and shouting. On completion of the adjudications, he made the usual gesture of asking each prisoner whether he had anything that he wanted to say to him. Both Kelly and Whelan, who were accommodated in separate cells, complained of cold food. Murphy discussed the matter there and then with the prisoners and the Prison Class Officer, while Whelan informed the Assistant Governor that he did not wish to pick up his plate of food when it was in the doorway and not completely in his cell. He added that this was a further protest, although the food had always been distributed in this manner. Murphy noted:

> At no time has any prisoner forfeited any meal, the food was delivered to the cell in a warm condition and the prisoners admitted being awkward. I informed both Whelan and Kelly individually, that I thought that they were being rather stupid in depriving themselves of warm food. It should be noted that all meals were fully eaten in the main, apart from the normal plastering of potatoes on the cell walls with the human excreta. All prisoners have now stopped their protest of refusing to take their hot meals when placed on the cell floor and there have been no further complaints. On one of the days in question 28 February 1979 (lunch) I sampled the meal which consisted of: Roast Beef, Boiled potatoes, Cabbage and Gravy, followed by Creamed Rice Pudding. I am satisfied that there are no grounds for complaint.[21]

In the face of general apathy from the public, it was from segments of the Roman Catholic Church that the cause of the prisoners was taken up. Father Alex Reid, of Clonnard Monastery in Belfast, suggested to Don Concannon, the Minister of State at the NIO, that the necessary facilities be provided for the prisoners 'because I believe it will be very difficult to resolve the situation in the prison if the prisoners cannot consult properly among themselves. I appreciate that the authorities are not prepared to recognize any prisoner as a spokesman for any group, but I think the results of such consultations could be communicated to the authorities in some way that would not violate any rule or compromise any principle.' Reid suggested that these facilities should be given to one or two people 'from outside who are concerned about prisoners' welfare and the anxieties of relatives.' This could be arranged by giving permission for a special welfare visit to one or two people who would speak on behalf of relatives to two or three prisoners. The 'good faith of such people can be guaranteed in any way that the authorities might think necessary. I believe that such a visit could have a helpful and moderating influence on the situation.'

Reid also gave his own impression of the situation in the prison 'in the hope that it will throw some extra light on the problem': about 300 prisoners were refusing to accept the present prison discipline because they believed it was designed to categorize them as common criminals. They absolutely refused to think of themselves as common criminals and, therefore, rejected the policy that, as they saw it, sought to treat them as such. To them, a common criminal was 'a person who was motivated by considerations that were private and personal to himself when he committed the offence for which he was sentenced.' The offences for which they themselves were sentenced were, to their way of thinking, motivated not by private but by political considerations. Their offences, they would maintain, arose directly from the political situation in Northern Ireland, and should not, therefore, be classified as common crimes. In support of this contention, they quoted the nature and the circumstances of their offences, and also the legislation under which they were arrested, interrogated, tried, convicted and sentenced. This legislation was special to Northern Ireland, and was enacted because of its political situation:

> The conviction that they are not common criminals runs very deep, and gives rise to a determination that they will not submit to being treated as such, no matter what happens. The evidence of this determination is their willingness to endure and to go on enduring the appalling conditions which they have created for themselves by refusing to co-operate in such elementary matters as wearing clothes, washing themselves, slopping out their cells, etc. The danger in this determination is that it will lead to further extremes in which many of the prisoners may refuse even to eat. If this happens the consequent escalation of tensions inside and outside the prison will lead inevitably to further violence, suffering and tragedy.
>
> The position of the prisoners then, as I see it, is not that they refuse to accept their sentences or are unwilling to submit to prison discipline but that they refuse to submit to a discipline which, as they see and experience it, categorises and treats them as common criminals.

Reid agreed that the issue of freedom of association might also present difficulties, but if the problems of the prison uniform and prison work were solved, 'this and other issues would tend to solve themselves'. Like the other priests who attended at the Maze Prison, he was 'deeply concerned about the situation there because of the suffering it involves, especially for relatives, and also because of the tensions it engenders in the community. As you know, these kinds of tensions tend to bring about violence and bloodshed, and it is this danger that gives the main cause for concern.' Reid was not suggesting that the authorities should in any way bow to the threat of violence, 'but when one thinks of what violence means in personal terms to those who are the victims of it, one feels impelled to do everything possible to defuse any situation that has the potential of violence.'

Looking at the situation in the Maze Prison, recognizing its potential for violence and remembering what violence meant in personal terms, Reid was convinced that what was called for now was the kind of expertise that enabled those in authority to combine firmness about principles with flexibility about their application. He pointed to the example of the Government of the Republic of Ireland, which:

> ... may be helpful here. As you know, they do not, in principle, recognize political status for prisoners, or give any special status to any prisoner, but they so manage the affairs of their prisons that they are able to avoid the kind of confrontation we are experiencing here. Portlaoise Prison [in the Republic] is an example of this. The approach of the authorities in the Republic and the way they have managed to handle their prison problems are worthy, I believe, of serious and detailed examination because they may give helpful guidelines.[22]

Concannon, however, dismissed Father Reid's first point that a way should be found to enable the prisoners to consult among themselves and that the authorities should agree to admit some persons from outside who were concerned about the welfare of the protesters and the anxieties of their relatives:

> ... I do not believe that in fact the prisoners have any great difficulty in consulting among themselves; they gather together to attend Mass on Sundays and are able to shout to one another from their cell windows, which they have broken. As to visits from outside, the protesting prisoners have their monthly statutory visits, and I would suppose that some of the visitors who come in to see them fall in the categories mentioned.

Nor were the authorities prepared to give facilities to so-called 'welfare' organizations, whose real objective would be to facilitate communications between the protesting prisoners and those outside who supported them. Any individual prisoner who wished to see the Governor or one of his staff, or a member of the Board of Visitors, could do so on application in the normal way.

Reid's discussion as to the reasons why the prisoners concerned were unwilling to accept that they should be treated in accordance with the rules that applied to all convicted prisoners was in 'essence the argument ... that a murder for political reasons is not the same as a murder in other circumstances.' This was wholly unacceptable to the Government. Concannon noted that most of the prisoners' offences were not offences under emergency legislation – for example murder, attempted murder and firearms and explosives offences. All of them had been convicted in open courts. Although it had been necessary, with the approval of Parliament, to suspend jury trials for terrorist cases, other safeguards of the normal criminal procedures applied, including the requirement on the prosecution to prove its case beyond reasonable doubt. Where convictions were based on confessions, the courts had the power – which they used on occasion – to exclude or disregard any statement made by the accused if the interests of justice so required. To Concannon, Father Reid's proposal, reduced to its essentials, was that the Government should respond to the PIRA campaign by allowing sentenced prisoners to wear their own clothes and to perform work of their choosing rather than that provided by the authorities: 'We are not prepared to take either of these steps; surely this would be "bowing to the threat of violence"' – which Reid said he was not advocating – concluded the Minister of State. Reid's letter repeatedly mentioned 'flexibility': 'But what he is really asking is that we recognise the claim of these prisoners to be treated in a special way because of the nature of their offences – and that we then extend the same treatment to all other sentenced prisoners.' All the evidence was that there was very little public support for the special category campaign; the great majority of people agreed with the Government's view that those who killed, maimed and destroyed property and jobs should, if convicted by the courts, be treated in the same way as other prisoners.[23]

One of the problems for the protesters was that there was still little public support for the prisoners' campaign, and the authorities could remain confident that they could resist the demand for special category status. The prisoners, however, were given a major morale boost when, following his visit to the H-Blocks in July 1978, the Roman Catholic Archbishop of Armagh, Dr Tomás Ó Fiaich, issued a statement:

> There are nearly 3000 prisoners in Northern Ireland today. This must be a cause of grave anxiety to any spiritual leader. Nearly 200 from the Archdiocese of Armagh are among a total of almost 1800 prisoners in the Maze Prison at Long Kesh. This is equivalent of all the young men of similar age groups in a typical parish of this Diocese.
>
> Last Sunday I met as many as possible of these Armagh prisoners as the Bishop appointed to minister to themselves and their families conscious of Christ's exhortation about visiting those in prison. I am grateful for the facilities afforded me by the authorities.
>
> On this, my second visit as Archbishop of Long Kesh, I was also aware of the grave concern of the Holy See at the situation which has arisen in the prison, and I wanted to be able to provide the Holy See with a factual account of the present position of all prisoners there, something which I shall do without delay.

Having spent the whole Sunday in the prison I was shocked by the inhuman conditions prevailing in H-Blocks 3, 4 and 5, where over 300 prisoners are incarcerated. One would hardly allow an animal to remain in such conditions, let alone a human being. The nearest approach to it that I have seen was the spectacle of hundreds of homeless people living in sewer-pipes in the slums of Calcutta. The stench and filth in some of the cells, with the remains of rotten food and human excreta scattered around the walls, was almost unbearable. In two of them I was unable to speak for fear of vomiting.

The prisoners' cells are without beds, chairs and tables. They sleep on mattresses on the floor and in some cases I noticed that these were quite wet. They have no covering except a towel or blanket, no books, newspapers or reading material except the Bible (even religious magazines have been banned since my last visit), no pens or writing material, no TV or radio, no hobbies or handicrafts, no exercise or recreation. They are locked in their cells for almost the whole of every day and some of them have been in this condition for more than a year and a half.

The fact that a man refuses to wear prison uniform or to do prison work should not entail the loss of physical exercise, association with his fellow prisoners or contact with the outside world. These are basic human needs for physical, mental health, not privileges to be granted or withheld as rewards or punishments. To deprive anyone of them over a long period – irrespective of what had led to the deprivation in the first place – is surely a grave injustice and cannot be justified in any circumstances. The human dignity of every prisoner must be respected regardless of his creed, colour or political viewpoint, and regardless of what crimes he has been charged with. I would make the same plea on behalf of Loyalist prisoners, but since I was not permitted to speak to any of them, despite a request to do so, I cannot say for certain what their present condition is.

Several prisoners complained to me of beatings, of verbal abuse, of additional punishments (in cold cells without even a mattress) for making complaints, and of degrading searches carried out on the most intimate parts of their naked bodies. Of course, I have no way of verifying these allegations, but they were numerous.

In the circumstances I was surprised that the morale of the prisoners was high. From talking to them it is evident that they intend to continue their protest indefinitely and it seems they prefer to face death rather than submit to being classed as criminals. Anyone with the least knowledge of Irish history knows how deeply rooted this attitude is in our country's past. In isolation and perpetual boredom they maintain their sanity by studying Irish. It was an indication of the triumph of the human spirit over adverse material surroundings to notice Irish words, phrases and songs being shouted from cell to cell and then written on each cell wall with the remnants of toothpaste tubes.[24]

An NIO spokesman commented that the Government was 'most surprised' that Archbishop Ó Fiaich's lengthy statement about his visit to HM Maze Prison 'makes no reference to the essential fact that it is the prisoners themselves who have made conditions what they are.' He added: 'These criminals are totally responsible for the situation in which they find themselves. It is they who have been smearing excreta on the walls and pouring urine through cell doors. It is they who by their actions are denying themselves the excellent modern facilities of the prison. It is they, and they alone, who are creating bad conditions out of very good conditions.' Each and every prisoner had been tried under the judicial system established in Northern Ireland by Parliament. Those found guilty after the due process of law, if they were sent to prison by the courts, 'serve their sentences for what they are – convicted criminals. They are not political prisoners; more than 80 have been convicted of murder or attempted murder, and more than 80 of explosives offences.' They were members of organizations that were responsible for the deaths of hundreds of innocent people, the maiming of thousands more, and the torture by kneecapping of over 600 of their own people:

> This protest action is the basis of a propaganda campaign which has been mounted by the IRA. It has been roundly condemned north and south of the Border. Not surprisingly there have been allegations made to the Archbishop about ill-treatment of prisoners by prison staff. There is no truth in these allegations, and prison officers know that any such complaints by prisoners are thoroughly and promptly investigated and, if substantiated, lead to disciplinary action.[25]

Within the prison, there was a constant battle between the prisoners and the authorities. On 2 October 1978, Governor's Order No. 85 was issued to rationalize the search routine of those prisoners located in H-Blocks 3, 4 and 5 who refused to conform to prison rules, with the following procedures to be strictly observed:

(1) When prisoners are moved from Wing to Wing, either individually or as a joint exercise, each prisoner will be strip-searched. During the search he will be required to spread his legs in a wide position, thus any article he may attempt to conceal between his hips should fall to the ground. A metal detector will also be used to detect any foreign body concealed

on the prisoner's person. Should prisoners refuse to co-operate in the search staff are authorised to use force in order to open the prisoner's legs. Any force used should be consistent with the amount of resistance shown by the prisoner. Where force has to be used in order to successfully complete a search, a record of the incident should be carefully recorded. The Principal Officer/Senior Officer [in charge] of the search operation will be responsible for recording and signing the record.

(2) When prisoners leave the Wing prior to a visit taking place, they will also be required to undergo a strip search similar to Para (1) above. Should any prisoner refuse to be searched their visit will be terminated and the prisoner returned to his cell. This will include all visits except those to a legal advisor. When a prisoner refuses to be searched prior to a legal visit the Governor will be immediately informed.

(3) On return from a visit, if it is suspected that a prisoner is concealing prohibited articles and he refuses to co-operate in the search procedure he will be located in the Cell Block and the Governor informed.[26]

Roy Mason, the Secretary of State, raised a query: why was it necessary to conduct these close body searches of protesting prisoners in the H-Blocks? It occurred to him that if these men were naked in their cells for twenty-four hours a day, then they had very little scope to hide anything. If this were the case, then why subject them to this further, apparently unnecessary, indignity? As Mason's Private Secretary observed, 'the Secretary of State is not in general disposed to be over-sympathetic to these men who have created the problems in the H-Blocks for themselves, but he does rather wonder about the question of searching.'[27]

W. R. Truesdale, Director of Prison (Ops), replied that to achieve their objectives, the protesting prisoners, and their supporters outside, 'know that they must defeat the prison system. Everything the protesters do is intended to prevent the prison from operating efficiently or to bring the prison system into disrepute.' In the case of H-Block protesters, 'we are dealing with dedicated men who give no quarter and who will stop at nothing to "beat the screws".' In the circumstances in which the protestors had placed themselves, great importance was attached to every point scored against the prison system, and successful smuggling must rank high in terms of boosts to morale. There were two main reasons for attempting to ensure that H-Block protestors did not achieve success in smuggling unauthorized articles:

(a) As in any contest, the participants aim to destroy their opponents' morale. To defeat the 'H' Block protest, prison Governors must ensure that the prisoners concerned are not allowed to think they can flout authority with impunity. (The continuing steam cleaning cycle is also a successful move in this direction).

(b) As mentioned above, the smuggling of letters is prevalent, and in the circumstances of the protest, the content of such letters is not always as innocent as might first appear. Good prison security is based not only on reliable physical obstacles and procedures but also on the ability of the prison Governor and his staff to anticipate problems. To this end, the gathering of prison intelligence, from whatever source, is important. Clandestine correspondence, carefully assessed, is a valuable pointer to prisoners' morale, proposed escape attempts, serious smuggling, the naming of prison officers as potential targets and even trafficking by prison officers.

If the inmates of H-Blocks 3, 4 and 5 showed by their behaviour that they accepted the prison regime, then there would be no justification for close body searches except in special cases, acknowledged Truesdale. However, 'these men have totally rejected the fact that they are sentenced criminals and are subject to prison authority.' It followed that, as the man responsible for the continued safe custody of the prisoners placed in his charge, the Governor 'must be allowed to exercise his professional judgement of what is required to maintain the security of his prison.' Given that a complete relaxation of body searching would be interpreted as a victory by both the prisoners and their supporters, whilst a reduction to random searches would undoubtedly encourage continued smuggling, 'the sensible action would seem to be that which the Governor had already taken in issuing his Governor's Order No. 85 of 2 October 1978.'[28]

Ed Maloney, a journalist who had been given access to the H-Blocks, reported on one of the prisoners he met, a 24-year-old from the New Lodge Road district of Belfast, who was serving a recommended life sentence for murder. The prisoner had not washed, and his teeth were completely yellow, his skin a 'cadaverous shade of white, and stretched tightly across his cheekbones. His eyes were sunk deep into dark-rimmed sockets, and throughout the visit never ceased to wander.' The prisoner explained how breakfast consisted of cornflakes or porridge, a pint of tea and two unbuttered slices of bread. If the prisoners suspected that their food had been tampered with, it joined the excreta pasting their cell wall: 'One day my cellmate found a dead mouse at the bottom of his mug of tea, and we think that sometimes the screws piss into the tea as well' claimed the prisoner. He added that the idea of warders searching a cell that contained only two foam rubber mattresses and six thin blankets was especially galling: 'We're first of all given an anal search, and then made to stand outside the cell in puddles of urine while the screws poke through our mattresses. If we make a move, other screws jump on top of us.' Maloney reported how anal searches, which followed and preceded every excursion from cells, were often the cause of violence, and were regarded by the prisoners as petty harassment designed to break their wills: 'I was made to stretch my legs open and was searched twice before this visit. They'll do it twice more before I get back into my cell. How could I get the time and opportunity to hide anything? It's done for badness.'[29]

There was, however, a security issue to take into account. As Bobby Sands explained in a communication, or 'comm', smuggled out to 'Liam Og' (a senior Sinn Féin official): 'The boys have to swallow, then vomit the comms back up. It doesn't always work, plus some of our comms are just going out as we get yours, and often our opinion changes upon your advice or information and leads to contradictions at times.'[30] The comms were also hidden anally.

Allegations of abuse of the prisoners by the staff were frequent. Often, the prisoners were championed by Father Faul of Dungannon, who was one of the Prison Chaplains, and a vociferous critic of security force abuses. On one occasion he alleged that prisoners were compelled to run in pairs naked down one wing while being struck on the head, body and privates: 'They were then searched intimately in a circular area which was the most public part of the prison. They were made to kneel down and then beaten into the other wing.' As there were 45 prisoners under the age of 21 in H-Block 3, Faul felt that the continuing use of intimate body searching accompanied by episodes of brutality was 'a very serious matter.' This intimate body searching was not carried out in H1, H2, H8 or H9, and he asked why they were being used once or twice a week on naked prisoners in H3, 4 and 5. The answer seemed to be, he believed, that orders were being given that were contrary to Article 3 of the European Convention on Human Rights, which forbade cruel, inhuman and degrading treatment.[31]

On another occasion, in October 1978, the NIO was forced to deny a claim that prisoners in the H-Blocks were in urgent need of medical attention after being doused with boiling water by warders. A spokesman said that there was no truth in the allegations that the prisoners had suffered serious burns and were in need of medical care after their cells had been hosed down. But a statement from Republican prisoners claimed that: 'Following the hosing down of prisoners and cells, 16 Republican prisoners are now in urgent need of medical attention. Immediately after the hosing, the cells of some Republican prisoners were invaded by prison orderlies and "screws", who threw boiling water, injuring a number of prisoners. Of these, four have serious burns. These are as follows: Gerry Dowdell, Gerard Jackson, Martin Kavanagh and John Boyle.' Father Faul said that he himself saw scald areas on prisoners' backs, in one case measuring 12 by 5 inches, which could not have been caused by contact with hot-water pipes as the Northern Ireland Office was alleging.[32] From the other side of the fence, at a meeting of the Protesting Prisoners' Review Group, Governor Miles was asked if there was any basis for these reports. Miles replied that there were two cases that had been highlighted. In one of these, the doctor had found no evidence whatsoever of scalding. In the second case, there was evidence of blistering, but it seemed likely that this damage was caused by contact with hot piping. In neither case did the prisoner make a complaint, and no Prison Officer was named in any of the press reports. Miles did say, however, that although unfounded, reports of this nature could have a damaging effect.[33]

In 1978, four protesting prisoners, including Kieran Nugent, made representations to the European Commission of Human Rights (ECHR) that were admitted for consideration. As an NIO official noted, if HMG failed to win this case, then the prisoners:

> … would thus become prisoners of war – or political prisoners – and eligible for release on the conclusion of hostilities. The Courts would be seen as political courts and not courts of law. The RUC would become political police, not the impartial guardians of the law. Terrorism would become respectable. Obviously, therefore, the granting of any of these claims as rights is out of the question. But should the regime be modified without in any way making a concession on these claims?[34]

While not all protesting prisoners fought the authorities with the same intensity, some resisted as hard as they could. The authorities fought back equally hard. For example, Kieran Nugent was the subject of disciplinary charge on 22 September 1976 for refusing to wear prison clothing or work; since 5 November 1976, the charges had been repeated at regular 14-day intervals; since 6 October 1978, these had occurred at 28-day intervals. He had been regularly awarded 14 days' loss of remission; 14 days' loss of privileges; 14 days' loss of earnings and 3 days' cellular confinement. By 1978, Nugent had now lost all his available remission.

Thomas McFeely was another protesting prisoner. He was convicted on 4 February 1977 of attempted wounding; of possession of a firearm with intent to endanger life; of use of a firearm with intent to prevent arrest; of possession of a firearm in suspicious circumstances and of two offences of robbery. He was sentenced on the first four offences to concurrent terms of imprisonment of 14 years, 12 years, 12 years and 10 years; for the two offences of robbery he was sentenced to two concurrent terms of 12 years' imprisonment, to run consecutively to the sentences for the other offences. On 10 March 1977, the Governor ordered McFeely to be removed from association with other prisoners because he had been trying to set himself up as their leader, and had been giving them orders. The chairman of the Board of Visitors approved his removal from association under Rule 24 as he was considered to be becoming a menace to good order and discipline. The only suitable accommodation for a prisoner subject to

Rule 24 was the punishment cells; this was because the punishment cells provided the only accommodation in HM Maze prison where a prisoner might be held away from other prisoners. However, removal from association was not a punishment, and resulted in no loss of privileges whatever.

On 18 April 1977, McFeely was transferred to H-Block 5, after having agreed to behave like other prisoners, only to be removed again to the punishment cells under Rule 24 on 9 January 1978 for being a disruptive influence and again giving orders to other prisoners. McFeely declared himself to be on hunger and thirst strike. On 11 January he was transferred to H3 after coming off his strike and undertaking not to set himself up as a spokesman. He was again moved to the cell block on 13 March after being a disruptive influence and giving orders to other prisoners, renewing his hunger strike. On 14 March he refused a medical examination. On 19 March the Medical Officer examined him and found no cause for concern.[35] Under the headline 'Concentration Camp Horrors', *An Phoblacht* informed Republican supporters about McFeely's struggle against the authorities:

> A hunger strike traditionally excites Irish pity. A hunger and thirst strike causes dread. The reason is very simple. A protester can last months on hunger strike, always with the hope of reprieve, although too often the damage caused is irreparable. But hunger and thirst strikes usually end very quickly in death.
>
> Two men went on hunger and thirst strike in H-Block 3, Long Kesh Concentration Camp, on March 13. Thomas McFeely, Claudy, Co. Derry, married, the father of three beautiful children, sentenced to 26 years; and Sean Campbell, New Lodge Road, Belfast.
>
> Bluntly, the reason why they took this terrible course was that the horrors of H-Block had been increased to such an extent that human beings could not take any more. Death, even under the great suffering of hunger and thirst strike, would be preferable to the H-Block tortures.
>
> Consequently, Republican POWs have been forced to survive under a prison regime as ruthless and as fascist that the only occasions on which our naked comrades are permitted to leave their cells are on Sundays to attend Mass or during the week if, for some medical reason, it is absolutely necessary to pay the prison doctor a visit.[36]

On 21 March, McFeely stopped his hunger strike. On 30 March he was transferred to H5 after assuring a deputy governor that he would not give orders to other prisoners.[37] The view of Governor Stanley Hilditch (in overall control of the Maze) was uncompromising. He saw no possibility of, or need for, compromise on the application of the whole range of punishments, which was necessary to maintain prison discipline. Many prisoners had lost all their remission and control had, therefore, to be exercised through the loss of other privileges. Any change in policy would, he felt, be taken as a sign of weakening on the Government's part. Hilditch gave no credence to the 'humanitarian' viewpoint, which, in his opinion, had been successfully countered by the Government's 'self-infliction' publicity.[38]

Despite the failure for the special category campaign to generate sufficient support outside the Maze, there remained an underlying concern at the potential trouble the protest could generate. This point was raised when the Taoiseach, Jack Lynch, met with his British counterpart, Prime Minister James Callaghan. Lynch thought that it was of great importance that the British Government should find some way of removing the grounds for the grievances of the IRA prisoners in Long Kesh. He expressed the view that this issue constituted one of the IRA's few remaining political assets, which they would continue to exploit for so long as the situation remained frozen. Left to themselves, the Taoiseach said, many of the relatives and friends of the prisoners involved in the protest would seek to persuade the prisoners to call off their action; the IRA took great care, however, to ensure that the prisoners received no visitors who were of this mind. Instead, those who visited the prisoners encouraged them in their stand and, more importantly, led them to believe that their protest action was a focus of world sympathy and attention and that they were playing a leading role in the political struggle of the IRA. Lynch further urged Callaghan to consider whether it might not be to the advantage of the British Government to allow the prisoners access to newspapers and the radio, so that they could find out for themselves how little sympathy or attention they commanded in fact. This would have an immediate effect on their morale, and would weaken the hold that the IRA sympathizers visiting them from outside exerted over them. This could lead to the removal of one of the IRA's most potent political weapons. On this occasion, the Prime Minister confined himself to saying that he would give careful consideration to what Lynch had said. Given the sensitivity of the issue, Callaghan and Lynch agreed that there would be no public reference to the fact that the Long Kesh issue had been discussed during their meeting. Lynch, in fact, asked whether he should tell Irish journalists that the subject had not been mentioned.[39]

When the Taoiseach's concerns were passed on, Roy Mason stressed to Downing Street that the dirty protest had attracted scant sympathy and much condemnation in Northern Ireland. Yet PIRA sustained the protest, both for their own internal reasons and as a political weapon on the wider scene. Anything that could properly be done to bring home to the prisoners themselves and to others that their propaganda campaign was a 'hollow sham' would be welcome. Mason appreciated the constructive character of Lynch's remarks, but the regime in the H-Blocks was kept under review. There were obvious risks in making changes that could be construed by Provisionals as significant concessions, so strengthening the prisoners' resolve and casting doubts on the Government's determination. There was also the risk that equipment and material supplied to prisoners would be vandalized and used in the protest, as had happened in the past. But Mason was concerned that the prison regime should be as humane as possible, within the rules, so he undertook to consider the suggestions that had been put to him, both for their own sake and as a further means of demonstrating the futility of the protesters' campaign. It would then be for the prisoners, and those who supported them, to make up their minds as to whether there was any point in continuing the protest. The Secretary of State felt 'bound to remain sceptical about any immediate and direct effect of detaching many prisoners from the main body of protesters.'[40]

It was not long after the Callaghan–Lynch meeting that, in March 1979, the minority Labour Government fell, and the Prime Minister called a general election. Republicans looked forward to the departure of Roy Mason, 'who came here with so much confidence and so many boasts departs very soon as a defeated man, and we will grind the next British War Lord into the ground as we have done with Mason! It matters little who rules at Westminster; they'll still send their gunmen and tanks and SAS murderers to repress the Irish people.' But by a combination of political work, street resistance and uncompromising revolutionary guerrilla warfare, 'we will inflict a political defeat on the British government's will to stay in Ireland.' The Provisionals were defiant:

> We shall make their occupation of Ireland so costly in terms of moral corruption and political bankruptcy that it will be domestically and internationally unacceptable. And to highlight the question of British occupation in Ireland, we are now quite capable of striking at British targets wherever they can be found.
>
> In the philosophy of Loyalism is an enemy of Irish freedom. We are opposed to Loyalism and we are opposed to the setting up of an independent Six Counties. Loyalists had an independent Six Counties for over 50 years and practised sectarianism and discrimination.
>
> Peace will only come about when Britain stops interfering in our country and when our people can determine their own future. Those that resist the development of a democratic and peaceful Ireland are out to maintain privilege, division and sectarianism, and are tools of Imperialism.
>
> We are out to break the back of British Rule in Ireland, a process which inevitably involves the disintegration of Loyalism as a racialist, sectarian philosophy.
>
> Another enemy of freedom which we clearly recognise as our enemy is the Free State [Irish] Fianna Fail government. They are opposed to the

development of a united Ireland based on the 1916 proclamation because it would spell an end to their corrupt collaborationist party. Traditionally they have exploited the working class in the 26 counties by offering, but only paying lip-service to, Irish Unity. Their repression of Republicans, in common with their opposition to the legitimate demands of workers, will intensify in the months ahead as we increasingly expose their hypocrisy and offer the underprivileged and oppressed sections of the community an independent banner around which to rally. As we break British Rule we break Fianna Fail, and all other reactionary interests in Ireland.

We demand a British Declaration of Intent to withdraw, an Amnesty for all political prisoners and recognition of the Irish people's right to self-determination. Backing up those demands will be the muscle of the Republican Movement drawing its support and personnel from the courageous ranks of the oppressed. There will be no capitulation, no respite. In the immortal words of Padraig Pearse:

'WE HAVE THE STRENGTH AND THE PEACE OF MIND OF THOSE WHO NEVER COMPROMISE'.[41]

NOTES

1   TNA CJ4/1456 The IRA Truce 26 June–10 July 1972.
2   TNA PREM 15/1009 Note of a Meeting with Representatives of the Provisional IRA.
3   TNA CJ4/2730 The Current Protest Campaign in the Northern Ireland Prisons Against the Refusal of the Authorities to Grant 'Special Category' Status to Convicted Prisoners.
4   Summary of Conclusions and Recommendations *Report of a Committee to consider, in the context of civil liberties and human rights, measures to deal with terrorism in Northern Ireland, etc.* (1975) (Parliamentary papers. Cmnd. 5847).
5   *Report of a Committee to consider, in the context of civil liberties and human rights, measures to deal with terrorism in Northern Ireland* Cmnd.5847 paras.7–8.
6   TNA CJ4/2729 Special Category Status.
7   TNA CJ4/2730 The Current Protest Campaign in the Northern Ireland Prisons Against the Refusal of the Authorities to Grant 'Special Category' Status to Convicted Prisoners.
8   TNA CJ4/2729 Grant of Special Category Status to Prisoners Convicted of Offence Committed after 1 March 1976.
9   TNA CJ4/2729 Special Category Prisoners, 31 October 1977.
10 TNA CJ4/2730 The Current Protest Campaign in the Northern Ireland Prisons Against the Refusal of the Authorities to Grant 'Special Category' Status to Convicted Prisoners.
11 TNA CJ4/3639 Marson to Buxton Prisoners' Demands, 23 October 1980.
12 *Loc.cit.*
13 *Loc.cit.*
14 *Loc.cit.*
15 *Republican News*, December 16 1978.
16 TNA CJ4/2729 Prisoners Protesting Because They Have Not Been Granted Special Category Status.

17   The *Irish News*, 31 March 1978.
18   TNA CJ4/2730 H3/H5 Situation Report, 10 April 1978.
19   PRONI NIO/12/68 Appendix I, Special Measures to Combat Health Risks Arising from the Conditions Imposed by Inmates of H3, 4 and 5, Maze Prison.
20   *An Phoblacht*, 8 Marta 1978.
21   PRONI NIO/12/15 Murphy to George, 12 March 1979.
22   PRONI NIO/12/128A Reid to Concannon, 25 July 1978.
23   PRONI NIO/12/128A Concannon to Fitt, 13 December 1978.
24   TNA CJ4/2730 NIO Belfast to Dublin Telegram No. 060, 1 August 1978.
25   PRONI NIO/12/68 Northern Ireland Office Comment by Northern Ireland Office Spokesman on Archbishop Ó Fiaich's Statement, 1 August 1978.
26   TNA CJ4/2728 Governor's Order No. 85, Searching of Non-Conforming Prisoners, 2 October 1978.
27   TNA CJ4/2730 Searching of Prisoners, 30 October 1978.
28   TNA CJ4/2728 Truesdale to PS/Secretary of State, 15 November 1978.
29   Magill, December 1978.
30   Denis O'Hearn, *Nothing But an Unfinished Song: The Life and Times of Bobby Sands* (Nation Books, 2006) p. 279.
31   The *Irish News*, 9 October 1978.
32   *Ibid.*
33   PRONI NIO/12/68 Note of the Second Meeting of the Protesting Prisoners' Review Group held at Maze at 10.15 a.m. on Wednesday, 11 October 1978.
34   TNA CJ4/2730 Protesters in the H-Blocks, 20 October 1978.
35   TNA CJ4/2728 Observations of the Government of the United Kingdom on the Admissibility of Application No.8317/78, Lodged by Thomas McFeely, Kieran Nugent, John Hunter and William Campbell.
36   *An Phoblacht*, 29 Marta 1978.
37   TNA CJ4/2728 Observations of the Government of the United Kingdom on the Admissibility of Application No.8317/78, Lodged by Thomas McFeely, Kieran Nugent, John Hunter and William Campbell.
38   PRONI NIO/12/68 Note for the Record A.E. Huckle, Division 3(B), 31 October 1978.
39   TNA CJ4/2728 Prime Minister's Private Secretary to J. G. Pilling, 27 November 1978.
40   TNA CJ4/2728 Hopkins to Cartledge, 4 December 1978.
41   *An Phoblacht / Republican News*, 21 April 1979.

Chapter 2

Mrs Thatcher's Northern Ireland Policy

In May 1979, Britain went to the polls to elect a new Government. The general election was won by the Conservative Party, led by Margaret Thatcher. Even before she became Prime Minister, Mrs Thatcher had personal experience of Republican violence – although it was not at the hands of the Provisionals. The INLA had assassinated Airey Neave, the Conservative Party spokesman on Northern Ireland, who was killed by a bomb placed under his car in the House of Commons car park on 30 March 1979. Neave, who had escaped from Colditz during the Second World War, was the man who ran Mrs Thatcher's successful campaign to oust Edward Heath as Tory leader in 1975. He was a mentor to Thatcher, and she felt a deep personal loss when he was killed. The moment when the future Prime Minister was told that an MP had been killed by a car bomb – at that stage, she had no idea it was her friend – was captured by a television crew as Mrs Thatcher campaigned in the general election.

On 16 May, at St Martin's in the Field, Trafalgar Square, the new Prime Minister delivered the memorial speech for Neave. In it she revealed not only her thoughts and feelings about her friend, but also how she perceived those who had committed what she considered to be a cowardly terrorist attack:

> Airey Neave was my very dear and deeply trusted friend. When we were in Opposition, he was head of my Private Office, a Member of the Shadow Cabinet and our Spokesman on Northern Ireland.
>
> Had he lived, he would have been a Member of the Cabinet.
>
> But just after 3 o'clock in the afternoon following the day the General Election was announced, Airey, who had come through all manner of personal trials in the war; who held the Distinguished Service Order, the Military Cross and the French *Croix de Guerre*; whose escape from Colditz, the prison which the Germans claimed was escape-proof, had become a legend in his lifetime; who played a prominent part at the

Nuremberg trials, Airey the quiet, Airey the soft-spoken, was murdered by a terrorist's bomb.

So, on an afternoon in early Spring, the gentlest of men, who utterly abhorred and was sickened by violence, became its victim ... In the Autumn of last year, Airey's study of the Nuremberg trials was published. In her foreword, Rebecca West wrote of Airey: 'It is, I think, against his principles to care much about danger, but he would do all he could to spare the rest of us unnecessary risk'.

[Following phrase in speaking text: "Words written with astonishing insight".]

In the final chapter, Airey reflected on the meaning of the Nuremberg experience which had a lasting influence on his life, and the great struggle of good against evil, freedom against tyranny, that the war embodied.

'Before our eyes', he wrote, 'the problems of race and terrorism are a frightening reminder of Hitler's example. Those who use terror to gain their political ends are the heirs of his Revolution of Destruction however much they may claim to represent opposing doctrines'.

It is deeply poignant to recall those words today. But I want to recall something else Airey wrote at the time that his book was published. He gave me a copy, with this inscription: 'Remembering that tyranny has many sides and freedom but one.' ... And the best of all memorials to Airey Neave, man of peace, taken by violence, is for us who remain, and those who come after us, never to weaken, never to weary of the struggle, but to hold fast, as he held fast, to the end, until that work is done.[1]

The day on which Mrs Thatcher became Prime Minister, her most senior civil servant, the Cabinet Secretary Sir John Hunt, wrote to her: 'Northern Ireland is likely to become a more urgent political problem following the election than it has been for many months past.' Though the previous Administration had tried to make progress, explained Hunt, in practice everybody was marking time in the months before the election. Both the Unionists and the SDLP believed that they stood to gain more after the election than before, and so neither was prepared to move from its entrenched positions. The Unionists wanted to return to fully devolved Government of the pre-1972 Stormont kind. They were 'firmly opposed to any kind of power-sharing in Government with the minority.' The SDLP sought to participate in the government of Northern Ireland, and 'they will resist any moves which, in their view, will make it more difficult for them to achieve their long-term aim of a united Ireland.' The impression had built up in Northern Ireland that the period of political inactivity before the election was a prelude to some new initiative by an incoming Government with the authority of a fresh mandate. Expectations were also high in Dublin and the United States. The

Irish Government had 'in general been reasonably helpful to us over Northern Ireland in the recent past, but they are under constant pressure to take a tougher, more nationalist line.'

One source of that pressure was from the Irish lobby in the United States. The United States Government came under similar pressure from the same direction. The approach of a presidential election year in the United States would add to this pressure. There was, therefore, 'clear need for the Government to move into a higher gear. But however high the expectations of a new approach by the Government may be, the reality is that the room for manoeuvre is very tightly constrained', Hunt warned the Prime Minister.[2] Indeed, during a follow-up conversation on 4 July after a summit with other Western leaders, the need to keep the White House onside with regard to Northern Ireland was emphasized to Mrs Thatcher by President Jimmy Carter:

> Prime Minister: Hello, how are you?
>
> President Carter: Just great. I hope you got home safely.
>
> Prime Minister: Yes, very safely, to a lot to do …
>
> President Carter: One other point that I'd like to talk to you briefly about. I've been asked by Senator Kennedy and Chip [sic] O'Neill to talk to you briefly about the Northern Ireland question, so that we don't have another …
>
> Prime Minister: … problem, yes.
>
> President Carter: … altercation as we did with Speaker O'Neill and [Secretary of State] Vance. Do you have, I know in the campaign both you and Jim [Callaghan] avoided that issue [in the general election].
>
> Prime Minister: We wouldn't have it as a Party issue at all. We'd have been wrong to have had it as a Party issue.
>
> President Carter: Do you have any analysis that's been done within your own Party or Government that you might send to me that I could read over just to describe both the present situation and any prospects for the future.
>
> Prime Minister: I will get one prepared and have it sent over. As a matter of fact my next appointment is with Humphrey Atkins, our Secretary of State for Northern Ireland, so that can be done.
>
> President Carter: I don't have any background knowledge about it and just hearing directly from you about the present situation and prospects for the future would help to guide me … any restraints on it otherwise I would like to share it confidentially with Senator Kennedy and O'Neill.
>
> Prime Minister: Yes, I'll l remember that when drafting it. Anything that's confidential to you I will put separately.

President Carter: Good. Well, right, thank you very much. I hope you have time to get some rest.

Prime Minister: It's not allowed to politicians. But it was very interesting I thought. Well, thank you very much for phoning. Best wishes. Goodbye.

President Carter: Goodbye.[3]

A series of papers outlining the Northern Ireland situation from the British point of view (on which the Prime Minister made a number of alterations herself), were dispatched to Carter. She wrote to him on 20 July:

Dear Mr President,

You asked me on the telephone if I could let you have a note of our position on Northern Ireland. I have set this out as briefly as possible in the four enclosed papers, one on the background, one on present Government policy, one on terrorism, and one on security policy and its impact on human rights. I am happy that you should show these papers to anybody to whom you think that they might be useful.

The essence of our position today is that as a Government we have a good majority in the House of Commons and five years in which to make progress over this problem, and all those directly concerned know this. Our present view is that we can best make progress by patient and persistent negotiation with the parties rather than by more precipitate action. We have already taken an initiative, in the sense of starting discussions with all those with a concern in the matter; but this does not mean that we expect an early solution. There is a wide gap between the outlook and aspirations of the two communities in Northern Ireland, and it will not easily be bridged.

I know that you are in close touch with Jack Lynch, and I am sure that he understands our position. I myself met him shortly after taking office, and both Humphrey Atkins and [Lord] Peter Carrington [Foreign and Commonwealth Secretary] have had useful talks in Dublin with Irish Ministers during the past few weeks. We recognise that they have a legitimate interest in the matter, and in the outcome; but they recognise that the responsibility is ours alone. Of course Irish unity remains their long term aspiration, but they are at one with us that any settlement must have the broad consent of both sides of the community in Northern Ireland, a principle which you endorsed in your statement of August 1977. To seek to impose a settlement in the face of opposition from either community would only aggravate and prolong the troubles.

I have included the paper on our security policy and its impact on Human Rights in Northern Ireland because the subject is often a live one in the United States. We are as concerned, as I know you are, to safeguard civil liberties to the fullest possible extent: we have a fundamental duty to protect all the law abiding citizens of Northern Ireland from murder and maiming by terrorists, which is the most important human right of all. I know that Tip O'Neill and others have been quite concerned about human rights. We have done all we can to encourage understanding of our problems. We have been extremely appreciative of the efforts which he and several of his colleagues have made to reduce the flow of funds from Irish-American sources in the United States to terrorist organisations over here, and more generally to put the record straight on the 'Irish question' in those circles. It is an unhappy fact that perspectives on Ireland – and not only in the United States – are still apt to owe more to the 19th Century than to the facts of the present day world.

I have tried to keep these papers as short as possible; but Sir Nicholas Henderson [HM Ambassador] had a very full briefing on all aspects of the Irish question before taking up his post in Washington, including a visit to Northern Ireland. You may be sure that we shall keep him fully informed as our thinking develops.

Warm personal regards.
Yours sincerely
Margaret Thatcher[4]

The President thanked Mrs Thatcher for the information, and assured her: 'I will be giving this important material the closest possible study, and have already found it most useful in understanding the basis of present British policy. I am sure we will be in further touch regarding developments in Northern Ireland, but in the meantime I wanted you to know how much I appreciate your thoughtfulness in preparing this information for my use.'[5]

This, then, was the broad canvas upon which HMG operated with regard to Northern Ireland. But there were also, as Sir John Hunt explained to Mrs Thatcher, more practical concerns. He warned the Prime Minister that 'there is at the present time an underlying and rather worrying difference of view between the Northern Ireland Office and the Ministry of Defence (MOD) about the handling of the security situation', and 'I think you ought to be aware of it.' This was going to be discussed in the Overseas and Defence Cabinet Committee (OD), which was composed of most of the senior Ministers in the Government. The MOD was concerned that, while the situation on the streets had improved, the hard core of the PIRA had become more professional. They wanted to see tougher security measures, but accepted that these largely depended upon cross-border co-operation from the Dublin Government. Accordingly, they sought a political 'initiative' that would secure this support. As a first step, they wanted an interdepartmental study, chaired by the Cabinet Office, of the 'cross-Border problem.' Some people in the MOD also wanted to see the appointment of a Resident Minister in Belfast and a Director of Operations overseeing the Army and RUC. The NIO, on the other hand, tended to see these suggestions as 'undeserved criticism from soldiers who would like to be let off the leash. More substantively, while they are anxious to make progress,' they doubted whether the grounds existed at the time for a major political initiative. The NIO also doubted whether, even if such grounds existed, there was very much more that the Dublin Government could do, unless the Irish police, the Gardai, was much improved on the Irish side of the Border.

Having discussed the matter fully with both Departments (Hunt chaired the Official Committee on Northern Ireland), the Cabinet Secretary did not think that there was as much between them as some senior officials and generals believed. It was, however, most undesirable for there to be misunderstandings over the cross-border problem between the NIO and the MOD, and if the way to defuse this was a small working party chaired by the Cabinet Office, 'I think we could take this on, provided this is what OD wants.' Hunt did not, however, think that the Prime Minister needed to float the idea at the OD Committee unless Francis Pym, the Defence Secretary, himself pressed for it. If, however, he went further and suggested the appointment of a Resident Minister in Belfast or a Director of Operations, and he had already canvassed both with Atkins,

> I think you ought either to kill both ideas or say that you will reflect on them yourself (they are certainly not suitable for remission to a normal interdepartmental committee). Over the years many of us have felt that the case for a Resident Minister in Belfast is a strong one, but it has always come up against the stumbling block that the Secretary of State of the day feels that his support must lie at Westminster and that he has perforce to commute: I doubt whether Mr Atkins will feel any differently.

The appointment of a Director of Operations would raise great difficulties vis-à-vis the RUC, and would be a major reversal of the policy of giving 'primacy to the police' over security in Northern Ireland, added Hunt. The essential questions then were:

> Do Mr. Atkins's general impressions of the present situation in Northern Ireland accord with those of his colleagues? This will almost certainly prompt Mr. Pym to say that he was profoundly depressed by his recent

visit to Belfast, and could lead straight in to a general discussion of the politico/security situation ... Is Northern Ireland likely to become a major factor in the United States [Presidential] elections? How much time will the Dublin Government give Mr Atkins before they start stirring up trouble? Will there be a problem over Army morale unless we are seen to be doing something? On this same question of whether time is working for or against us, how much significance should be attached to Paisley's sweeping victory in the recent Euro-elections? ... Despite the big drop in civilian casualties since 1973 has the PIRA threat really diminished? Mr. Atkins may say yes: but Mr. Pym is likely to take the view that, although the casualties have diminished in scale, the PIRA threat, particularly in the Border area, has actually grown in terms of sophistication and our ability to cope with it, even though its popular base has shrunk. Is there more we can do on our own account to improve cross-Border security? Or does it depend on help from the Dublin Government? What are the prospects of getting more from them?[6]

Pym did indeed raise his concerns with the OD: the terrorists were becoming more professional, and a 'duel' was developing between them and the security forces. The soldiers' morale remained good, but they 'could not see an end to the situation', and their repeated postings to Northern Ireland were bad for the morale of their families. Better intelligence was desirable, but this presented difficulties in the border area, and many known terrorists could not be arrested for lack of legally admissible evidence. Pym stressed that while the primacy of the police in security was not in question, the Chiefs of Staff were not satisfied with the existing arrangements for command and control in anti-terrorist operations, and they had asked him to convey this to the Committee. Mrs Thatcher, summing up the discussion, concluded that the meeting endorsed the general approach to Northern Ireland as set out by Atkins: 'But time was not necessarily on our side ... The emergency had now lasted for 10 years, and public opinion would not accept its continuance, or the present casualty rate in the security forces, indefinitely.' There would also be increasing international pressure. Meanwhile, concluded the Prime Minister, Atkins, in consultation with Pym, should consider the points that had been raised about the direction, under his overall authority, of anti-terrorist operations, and report his conclusions to the Committee.[7] Before Atkins could report back, however, a dark day for the British in Ireland proved to be a turning point and, arguably, laid the foundations for long-term success in the campaign against the Provisional IRA.

The Provisionals' most spectacular success in the entire Troubles came on 27 August, when they assassinated the Queen's cousin, 79-year-old Lord Mountbatten of Burma – also killed were his 14-year-old grandson, a 17-year-old boatman, and Dowager Lady Brabourne – in a bomb attack in County Sligo in the Irish Republic, where the elderly aristocrat was holidaying. On the same day, PIRA bomb attacks back in Northern Ireland, at Warrenpoint, County Down, killed eighteen British soldiers. The Provisionals described the killing of Mountbatten as 'a discriminate operation to bring to the attention of the English people the continuing occupation of our country'. They went on:

> The British army acknowledge that after ten years of war it cannot defeat us, but yet the British government continue with the oppression of our people and the torture of our comrades in the H-Blocks. Well, for this we will tear out their sentimental imperialist heart. The death of Mountbatten and the tributes paid to him will be seen in sharp contrast to the apathy of the British government and the English People to the deaths of over three hundred British soldiers, and the deaths of Irish men, women and children at the hands of their forces.

The Provisionals continued:

> The Mountbatten Assassination
> We used a 50lb bomb, all gelignite, detonated by remote control …
> It caused the political effects we wanted it to cause and which were expected before hand. That is, the British government and a fair sized majority of English people – they are living in a monarchy, after all – would react to the death of Mountbatten in a way they wouldn't react to the death of a 70-year old Irishman killed by the Brits or at the hands of the RUC.
> English people had an affinity with the likes of Mountbatten which they don't have for Irish people. Some 2,000 dead Irish and it means nothing to them, and there's been dead Irish people down the centuries. English people just don't care – well, they're going to have to care.
> Mountbatten has been described as a father figure of the Royal Family, a pillar of post-imperialist Britain; but Britain is still an imperialist power while it remains in occupation of the six counties.
> When they've finished cursing, of course, and damning us, they'll have to question the value of continuing with their occupation of Ireland. Because that's why he died.

> Warrenpoint Ambush
> The first bomb was 1,100lb, the second 80lb. It was the second one which caused most of the deaths. Both were remote detonated. The

British army has been very, very fortunate in escaping major losses since the sophisticated remote was developed – very, very lucky.

The importance of Warrenpoint was that after ten years, a full platoon was wiped out, the biggest Brit loss in the country for 58 years. Before that, there was the 18 auxiliaries wiped out by the IRA in November 1920.

Overall effects

The connection between Mountbatten and Warrenpoint is that both have helped sap the will of the English people to stay in Ireland.

It's OK saying 'you're only stiffening their upper lip. Hitler couldn't do it, how can you?' They had no choice when Hitler was bombing London.

They have a choice now. They have to go and they will go.

Loyalists

An IRA army council statement recently pointed out that loyalists would face psychological problems in accepting the implications of a British declaration on withdrawal. They are going to have to come to terms with that. We are not going to grant them – or the people of Cork or anywhere else – privileges.

If the Brits went in the morning, the result depends on the scenario for withdrawal. Loyalists must have that 'steel wall' against which they put their back taken away from them. The British guarantees must be removed.[8]

In contrast, in her condemnation of the attacks, the Prime Minister felt that by their actions the terrorists had added yet another infamous page to their 'catalogue of atrocity and cowardice.' By their involvement in the death of Lord Mountbatten, they would 'earn the condemnation and contempt of people of goodwill everywhere.' By the same token, the 'senseless murder' of members of the security forces had reinforced the repugnance felt for those who sought to 'advance their political ends by these evil means.' The Government would spare no effort to ensure that those responsible for these and for all other acts of terrorism were brought to justice: 'The people of the United Kingdom will wage the war against terrorism with relentless determination until it is won', declared the Prime Minister.[9]

The day after the attacks, the Prime Minister called a meeting at Number 10 Downing Street, which was attended by the Home Secretary, Willie Whitelaw; the Defence Secretary, Francis Pym; Atkins; the Lord Privy Seal, Sir Ian Gilmour (and number 2 at the Foreign and Commonwealth Office); the Chief of the General Staff, Field Marshal Sir Edwin Bramall; and Kenneth Stowe, the Permanent Under-

Secretary at the NIO, to discuss the implications and the Government's next moves. Atkins gave his colleagues an account of his visit to Warrenpoint earlier that day, and of his discussions with the security authorities. He said that although there were very strong indications that the bombs that ambushed the British convoy at Warrenpoint had been detonated from across the border, there was as yet no firm evidence of this; and that, similarly, it had not yet been established that any small arms fire had come from across the border. The, Irish police, the Garda, had already detained two suspects in connection with the Warrenpoint explosions, and two more in connection with the murder of Lord Mountbatten and his companions.

There was general agreement that the key to the situation in Northern Ireland lay in Dublin, and also to some extent with the Pope, who would be visiting the Republic in October. The Prime Minister said that the Government had to take decisions on the future approach to the Irish Government, as well as on what the UK required of the Republic. It was agreed that the British Government could, if necessary, take steps to make the rest of the world more aware of the shortcomings of the Irish Government's policies towards the terrorists, and of the implications of those shortcomings. This could help to change the Irish Government's attitude on the extradition issue – Irish courts refused to extradite Republican suspects on the grounds that their offences were 'political'. The UK might be able to exert some leverage against the Republic in the context of the new British Nationality Act, although any moves in this direction would be complicated by the fact that both countries were members of the EEC. It might also be possible to step up administrative action against Irish immigrants to the UK, along the lines of the steps already being taken at UK channel ports against Algerians and Turks. It was, however, agreed that before a more confrontational policy with regard to the Irish Republic was considered, a further attempt should be made, at a meeting between the Prime Minister and Jack Lynch, to enlist the Irish Government's effective co-operation, particularly in the intelligence field. If no progress resulted, other measures would have to be considered.

Atkins then informed his colleagues of possible new measures that could be adopted within Northern Ireland, all of which carried both advantages and disadvantages. These included the reintroduction of executive detention (internment); increased use of the UDR; more vigorous use of special forces such as the Special Air Service (SAS); changes in the law, for instance making it possible to accept as evidence in court the testimony of police officers of the rank of superintendent or above concerning membership of proscribed organizations; the proscription of the PIRA's political wing, Sinn Féin; the closing of border roads; the withdrawal of police from border areas, thus relieving the Army from the duty of protecting the police; and the dispatch of more troops to Northern Ireland, although there was general agreement that this last option should not be pursued further. There was also some discussion of how co-operation between the RUC and the Army, particularly in the intelligence field, could be improved, possibly by the appointment of a Director of Operations who could exercise overall day-to-day control of operations, both by the police and by the Army. Possible ways of improving intelligence concerning terrorist activities south of the border were also discussed. It was agreed that an arrangement with the Irish Government whereby British helicopters could cross the border freely and conduct surveillance within an area of, for example, five kilometres south into Irish territory, would be of very considerable assistance to border security operations.

The final decisions agreed at the meeting were that Pym and Atkins would prepare a joint paper for Cabinet on 30 August, which was not to be circulated in advance, covering both the objectives that the Government should pursue in any future discussions with the Irish Government, in order to improve cross-border security and to 'stiffen the Irish Government's policies towards the terrorists'; and also covering possible ways of improving the British Government's own security effort in Northern Ireland, including the improvement of co-operation between the Army and the RUC in intelligence and operational matters. It was also agreed that the Foreign and Commonwealth Office (FCO) would pursue urgently the question of ensuring that Jack Lynch was invited to attend the ceremonial funeral of Lord Mountbatten in Westminster Abbey the following week, and that the invitation, when extended, would be accompanied by a message from the Prime Minister inviting Lynch to meet her during his visit to London for talks 'on the Irish problem.'[10] In the meantime, Mrs Thatcher prepared to go on a sudden visit to Northern Ireland – Operation LIMITATION – on 29 August, to see and hear for herself what soldiers, police officers, prison officers and ordinary civilian workers thought of the problems they faced. An itinerary was rapidly drawn up:

10.00 Arrive Aldergrove [Airport outside Belfast]
10.15 Arrive Musgrove Park Hospital by helicopter, Visit civil and military sides
11.10 Depart Hospital
11.20 Arrive Belfast City Hall to visit Lord Mayor and (hopefully) a cross-section of councillors
12.15 Walkabout City Centre
12.45 Depart Girdwood Barracks by helicopter
13.00 Arrive 3 Brigade, Portadown
Buffet lunch, all ranks
14.10 Briefing by GOC, Brigadier Thorne, Major Ridley ... and Colonel Thomson ...

Followed by helicopter visit to Crossmaglen
15.45 Arrive Gough Barracks
17.20 Depart Gough
18.00 Depart Aldergrove[11]

A series of briefings was provided for the Prime Minister by Atkins that set out the issues she had to consider, both in the short term and the long term. The first question posed to Mrs Thatcher was: 'What is the Government's security policy?' It was then explained to her that the policy 'is and remains the elimination of terrorism by the establishment of the rule of law, and the extension of the pattern of normal policing throughout the whole of Northern Ireland.' But was this an adequate policy? The Prime Minister was told: 'You must look at it in a political framework, not merely in isolation.' Success must be measured by the 'degree to which the terrorists have progressively become isolated from the community to which they belong.' The activities in which they engaged reflected this: attacks on the security forces, assassinations and the like, as did the secretive, cellular organization that they had had to adopt. 'Will the policy continue then?' The answer was that the broad policy would continue, but there was plenty of room for the development of operations within it. The activities of the security forces were being changed and refined all the time to match and thwart the terrorists' activities. The development of methods of surveillance to cope with the terrorists' own more security-conscious methods was a case in point ('obviously I cannot go into detail about that', observed Atkins), but intelligence remained a key area. Those concerned were working to maintain the impetus and to make the most effective use of resources.

Were there no new measures then, asked Atkins. Selective detention was one of them; the power remained there under the Emergency Provisions Act, though it had not been used for the last four years: 'I must continue to reserve the possibility of using detention if the situation could not be controlled by other means', Atkins explained. Should the security forces not be freed of present restrictions? The only restrictions under which the police and Army operated:

> ... are those of the rule of law. But these are not restrictions: these are our ultimate protection. We could only undo this by imposing martial law, and I cannot imagine anything which would give the terrorists greater encouragement. We should utterly lose the sympathy and confidence of a large part of the people of Northern Ireland. Meanwhile it is false to suggest that the hands of the security forces are tied. The circumstances in which they may use their arms are clearly laid down, and follow the principle of law that no more force should be used than is reasonable in the circumstances. The British Government will not put the security forces above the law in any part of the United Kingdom.

As to what more could be done about security co-operation with the Irish authorities, the 'horrible' incidents of 27 August demonstrated, if any proof were required, that the Provisional IRA paid no heed to the border. Although co-operation with the Republic was already 'great', the key principle that any measures should satisfy was that the terrorists should not be permitted to draw any benefit from the fact of an international boundary: 'It would be wrong for me to be specific', Atkins told the Prime Minister, 'but the first requirement is mutual confidence, and on that level the position is very good.' There was a problem with resources that faced the Irish authorities as much as the British. On the question of whether the border should not 'be some sort of "warzone"', Atkins declared: 'I am prepared to look at any practical option.' At first sight, though, the main objection to that sort of concept was the enormous size of force that would be required. There was little point in making 300 miles of border prohibited territory 'if you cannot enforce it.' Atkins left aside the effect on the innocent inhabitants of the territory, although that would be counter-productive also:

> This illustrates two fundamental points of our policy: first that whatever we do against the terrorists we must not alienate the community at large, since that will vastly compound our problem and block off any route to political progress; and secondly that we have to treat the terrorists for what they are – not a hostile army, but a small and isolated band of thugs and killers with no popular support behind them. Both these facts point clearly to the primary need for careful and dedicated police work, backed up of course by military power.

On the general question of 'Why are British troops in Northern Ireland?' Atkins outlined how the troops were there because Northern Ireland was a part of the United Kingdom, 'where ordinary decent men and women are facing criminal violence which the police cannot deal with on their own.' So long as that was the situation, the troops would have to remain. It was:

> A fundamental human right that the individual should look to the State to protect him against murderers and criminals. The IRA has shown total contempt for human life and happiness. It has killed and tortured Catholics and Protestants. It is dedicated to the overthrow of all democratically established institutions in both the North and South of Ireland. It is evil and it cannot be allowed to win.

Atkins emphasized that here was 'no military or security solution' to the problem of providing the people of Northern Ireland with an acceptable form of government. Security measures were required to deal with a security threat.

At present 'it is the IRA who are seeking violent "solutions", not the British Government. And after nearly ten years, these tactics have left them as far away from "victory" as ever.' They operated with less public support than ever before. Indeed, by their actions they 'positively harm the cause of Irish unity.' Atkins was confident that terrorism 'can and will be beaten; and the Army will play a vital role in this.' It was misleading, however, to talk of a fight between the Army and the terrorists. The RUC was the lead for security operations throughout Northern Ireland. The police called on the Army or the UDR for support as required. Both the police and the Army acted on behalf of the people of Northern Ireland, 'who are playing their own part by showing that they reject violence, and that they want it to stop. With the full support and co-operation of decent people, both here and in Northern Ireland, the police and the Army will certainly defeat the terrorists', declared Atkins.

As to why Britain did not simply withdraw the troops or give notice of its intention to withdraw, Atkins told the Prime Minister: 'Withdrawing the troops whilst violence continues would make neither moral nor practical sense.' An abandonment of British responsibility for Northern Ireland would, in the present and foreseeable circumstances, mean the expulsion of the majority of that community from the United Kingdom in conditions of great chaos and uncertainty. There would be a real risk of civil war in Ireland. Britain could not be free either of the responsibility for or the effects of that increased violence. Nor was there any reason to believe that a British ultimatum to withdraw would lead to the creation of agreed and stable forms of government in an independent Northern Ireland: 'Quite the opposite.' Such a move would greatly increase fear and tension. The constitutional future of Northern Ireland was a matter for the people there to decide. As far as independence was concerned, all the major parties, and the overwhelming bulk of the population, dismissed it. It was not at this time even a possible option. As to why the British Government did not meet the requirement that successive Irish Governments had requested – that HMG recognize that Ireland would ultimately have to be united and declare now its interest in achieving unity in due course – Atkins explained to Mrs Thatcher that it was 'dangerous to speculate about the long-term future of Northern Ireland, and I will not do so.' The Government's position was clear:

> We will not stand in the way of Irish unity if it appeared that unity had the willing consent of the people of Northern Ireland. But there is absolutely no sign that a majority of people in the North do want this. In the Border Poll of 1973, 58% of the total electorate (not of those voting) were opposed to unity with the South; and in the recent general and European elections 70% of votes were cast on both occasions for candidates in favour of continued Union with Great Britain. The Government will respect those democratically expressed views.[12]

The briefings given to Mrs Thatcher in Northern Ireland by the Army and the RUC illustrated the differences between them. The military held a strong belief in the value and necessity of a major independent UK intelligence operation in the Republic. It also favoured the closure of a certain number (35) of border crossings, together with the necessary change in the law to allow them to be policed; improved integration of their own and the RUC's operational control; and the establishment of more joint operations rooms. The Army again raised the subject of a Director of Operations, to exercise overall day-to-day operational control, responsible only to the Secretary of State. Overall the Army took a 'gloomy view' of the PIRA's increasing operational and technical competence. They pointed out to the Prime Minister that in, for example, the Crossmaglen area, 80 soldiers had been killed since the Troubles began, as against only 9 terrorists. The Army also had great respect for the PIRA's competence in, e.g., radio and electronics.

The RUC, however, took a more optimistic view of the general course of the campaign against the PIRA. They pointed out to Mrs Thatcher that the Garda would co-operate only with them, and never with the Army. The RUC went on to argue that the Garda's level of professional competence was nevertheless very low: they therefore attached importance to persuading the Irish to instruct the Garda to set up special crime and surveillance units. The police claimed that whereas they had adapted successfully to the new type of enemy they now faced, for example by switching the emphasis from interrogation to surveillance, the Garda had not changed their tactics, and were still using the 'old techniques'. Less enthusiasm was shown regarding the usefulness of joint operations rooms with the Army. Although the RUC agreed with the Army that the PIRA's new cellular structure was impossible to penetrate, they pointed out that PIRA members did talk loosely once an operation had been concluded, and that this could provide useful intelligence. Unlike the Army, who in the border areas could move only by helicopter or on foot, the police were able to maintain regular road patrols by using hired, unmarked vehicles. The RUC claimed that, if their strength were increased by 1,000, they should after 2½ years be able to relieve the Army of all but a reserve role. Reflecting on these different briefings, Mrs Thatcher's Private Secretary, Bryan Cartledge, told her:

> The fact remains that in 3 Brigade's area about 200 identified terrorists are holding down 3,800 troops and 3,700 UDR personnel. In the Province as a whole, not more than 500 terrorists are holding down 12,666 troops and 7,522 UDR personnel – together with 6,374 regular and 4,560 part-time RUC …
>
> The RUC, who will be responsible for Ulster's law and order when the Army have left, inevitably take a rather different and longer-term view of the problem from that of the Army …

You have seen the physical conditions in Crossmaglen, which are probably typical of the Army operational outposts: they are pretty dreadful. They, together with the constant tension, are perhaps not calculated to produce a very objective view of the overall problem ...

The fact remains that there is clearly a very deep difference of approach between the Army and the RUC, and it must be open to question whether significant improved cooperation between them can be achieved without some structural change (joint operations rooms, Director of Operations, or whatever) on the lines suggested by the Army [and] there has to be some way of adjudicating quickly between conflicting views in any given operational emergency.[13]

On a personal note, the effect of the Prime Minister's visit, particularly to Crossmaglen, was to provide a major morale boost to the soldiers she saw. Major Nicolas Ridley, who had briefed Mrs Thatcher in South Armagh, wrote her a personal thank you note: 'To lose one's Commanding Officer is always a blow: to lose one of the stature of Colonel David Blair is doubly hard, as one has rarely to privilege to serve under a man of such charm and ability. In our close knit family regiment the loss was felt deeply by all ranks.' Although Ridley believed that Blair's death had in no way affected the efficiency of the Battalion, he told the Prime Minister: 'the personal concern you showed for your soldiers by visiting Crossmaglen displayed the sort of leadership this country has so long been needing' and it had done much to fortify the Battalion for the remainder of its tour in Northern Ireland. Ridley also thought that the Prime Minister might like to know that 'many of the villagers of Crossmaglen who normally refuse to talk to us except to express hostility to the British have been coming up to my soldiers expressing great respect and admiration for you and sadness that they could not have met you personally when you visited.'[14]

As well as the soldiers and policemen she met, the Prime Minister took an interest in the families who were bereaved. For example, Mrs Thatcher was kept abreast of how the wife of Major P. J. Fursman, also killed at Warrenpoint, was coping with her husband's death. The Prime Minister was informed:

The news is much better. Mrs Fursman ... visited Warrenpoint with her brother and now fully accepts why there is no body. She has returned to England, and although obviously deeply distressed, is stable and in as normal a condition as could be expected.[15]

The most significant outcome from the Mountbatten and Warrenpoint killings was the creation of a more integrated intelligence apparatus. In the aftermath of the attacks, the divisions between the NIO and the MOD – and consequently the divisions between the RUC and the Army – were resolved. Atkins and Pym, tasked with coming up with an improved system, presented their conclusions to the Cabinet on 30 August. Atkins explained to the Cabinet how the events of 27 August had led Pym and him to bring forward proposals for immediate action on two questions that had been concerning them since taking office. These were how to improve the direction and co-ordination of security operations in Northern Ireland, and how to obtain more co-operation in security matters from the Irish Republic. On the first question, their agreed proposal was for a new high-level Security Directorate in Northern Ireland. This would be responsible to Atkins, would operate on a 24-hour basis and would be designed to reconcile the differences that inevitably arose between the viewpoints and methods of the RUC and the Army – particularly as RUC morale, manpower and effectiveness had been transformed since they had regained primary responsibility for the prevention and detection of all crime. This was an important development that could not be jeopardized, since greater RUC strength offered the best hope of achieving the desired reduction of Army involvement in the security field.

Pym added that their proposals were based on agreement about the need to improve co-ordination between the RUC and the Army, and about the key role of the head of the new Directorate. The latter should be a man of seniority and stature, who was not a serving soldier or a civil servant from the Northern Ireland Office. The Foreign Secretary, Lord Carrington, then explained to the Cabinet that there was a mood of shame in the Republic following the Mountbatten murders. It was, therefore, a good moment for the Prime Minister to make a determined effort in talks with Jack Lynch, 'who was much less unsympathetic to us than his likely successor', to bring home the importance of co-operation in security matters. A full list of British requirements in this area was to be prepared and put to the Taoiseach. As the Foreign Secretary pointed out, however, the resources available to Lynch were limited, and 'we should not be too optimistic about his likely response. If it was inadequate we should not hesitate to reveal publicly what we had asked for.'

In discussion there was general agreement within the Cabinet that 'our most important need was to seek greater co-operation from the Irish Government and to publicise the fact that we were doing so. The two main difficulties facing our security forces were the existence of safe havens in the Republic and the lack of intelligence from south of the border.' If the Irish Government proved unwilling to co-operate, 'we would need to consider such means as we had of bringing pressure to bear on them'. While British public opinion might not be averse to using pressure, it would be right first to try to persuade Lynch of 'our common interest in defeating terrorism.' As regarded the proposed Security Directorate, some doubt was felt within the Cabinet about the danger of appointing too eminent a man to head it, giving the matter too much publicity. The Secretary of State for Northern Ireland's position might appear to be undermined; public opinion might regard organizational changes as an inadequate response to the present crisis; and credit might be lost if the new system failed to produce measurable results. The basic trouble seemed to be a 'difference in diagnosis' between the Chief Constable, Sir Kenneth Newman, and the RUC, who felt the situation to be slowly improving, and the GOC and the Army, who were less sanguine. It would be difficult for the head of the Directorate to bridge this gap. Against that, it was urged that the new Directorate, if properly presented with stress on its around-the clock role, could serve to show that the Government was actively seeking to improve the security effort rather than passively awaiting the next tragedy.

In further discussion it was noted that the quality of the Army's leadership might be somewhat better than the RUC's, that extensive further recruiting for the RUC might be no easier than police recruiting had proved in Great Britain, but that in the Chief Constable's view an adequately enlarged RUC could in time relieve the Army of almost all its security duties. If, however, it proved impossible to bring terrorism under control within the framework of the existing legal system, it might in the end be necessary to modify the system and perhaps even move towards the introduction of martial law in areas of particular terrorist activity. The growing professionalism of the IRA and the high level of casualties in the security forces were new factors, against which radical counter-action might well be required.

Mrs Thatcher, summing up the discussion, said that the Cabinet were agreed that she should invite Lynch for talks in London at the time of Lord Mountbatten's funeral. She would arrange for the invitation to be issued and announced forthwith. The Foreign Secretary, in consultation with the Secretary of State for Northern Ireland and the Secretary of State for Defence, would prepare a list of requirements to be put to him, which would be made public if he failed to respond. Lord Carrington, in consultation with other Ministers as appropriate, would take all possible steps to ensure that through the media 'we maintained psychological pressure on the Irish Government.' Atkins would arrange for an immediate announcement to be made about extra recruitment for the RUC, while the establishment of the new Security Directorate was agreed. But a decision on how far to publicise it would 'not be taken until we knew who its head would be.' This would be decided by Atkins and Pym, in consultation with Mrs Thatcher. Meanwhile, Atkins would bring forward early proposals for a political initiative to increase democratic participation in the processes of government in Northern Ireland, and he and Pym would, in consultation with the Law Officers, arrange for a review of the restrictions on the use of firearms by members of the security forces.[16]

When the Prime Minister discussed, in greater detail, the arrangements for heading up the Security Directorate, with Carrington, Pym and Atkins, the last two were agreed that they were not instituting a 'Director of Security Operations' with authority to command and control security operations in Northern Ireland. As Atkins told Mrs Thatcher, that would be 'wrong in principle, contrary to our policy', and indeed it could only be brought about by recalling Parliament to pass legislation to strip the police of their independent status and make them subordinate to Atkins as Secretary of State. As it was, the Directorate as proposed would need very careful presentation to the RUC, who would greatly resent it if it appeared that they – 'as an independent and Ulster force' – were in any way to be taken over. The maintenance of their morale and status was fundamental to the effectiveness of HMG's security policy. Atkins wrote to Mrs Thatcher: 'As I have emphasised to you, it is only by holding fast to this policy and extending normal policing throughout the Province that we shall get the Army out of Northern Ireland.' The leader of the Directorate and his team would be subordinate to, and accountable to the Security Policy Group, which Atkins led, and it was the essence of their task that their work should result in a more effective use of security forces while operating through existing command structures. As Atkins explained: 'It is I hope clear from this why he should be of a senior rank in the public service, but not outranking the heads of the existing commands, over whom he will have no authority. This leads me to conclude that it is the quality of the man, not his eminence in another field, which we should be concentrating on – and I would certainly question the wisdom of putting someone into this as a post-retirement occupation.' Nevertheless, Atkins recognized the concern that Mrs Thatcher had expressed to him that the leader of this team should be a person of standing whose appointment would add to public confidence, in Northern Ireland and in Great Britain:

> I have to say that in my judgment an officer seconded from or retiring from the Diplomatic Service would signally fail to meet this requirement: a Foreign Office figure could and almost certainly would be spitefully attacked by Unionists as yet another indication of the GB mentality which treats Northern Ireland as a colony. If you conclude that a public figure is necessary then I would suggest that we should look in the direction of a distinguished policeman with experience in the deployment of large forces and in dealing with threats to security both by way of urban violence and terrorism. Such a person would be better qualified in my view to get the best out of the Security Directorate than someone new to this game.[17]

As for the proposed meeting with the Taoiseach, the effects of 27 August were not only felt in Britain. The shock of Mountbatten's killing in the Republic led to Jack Lynch writing personally to Mrs Thatcher and describing how the PIRA's admission of responsibility brought 'shame to all true Irishmen and women.' When the Prime Minister suggested that she might soon meet the Taoiseach for talks on security matters, she was pushing at an open door, as Lynch replied to say how 'accompanied by my wife, I propose to represent my Government at the funeral and Memorial Service for Earl Mountbatten in London'. He offered to hold talks while there: 'I would hope that our discussions will pave the way for worthwhile progress in the various closely related areas relevant to ending the violence which has brought grief to so many homes throughout Ireland and in Britain over the last ten years.'[18]

When the Prime Minister met with the Taoiseach, on 5 September, she thanked him for being ready to have talks with her in the wake of the previous week's double tragedy. Since the events of 27 August, she had been making it clear in public that she was sure that he was as anxious as she was to stamp out terrorism: a threat not just immediately to Northern Ireland, but to democracy as a whole. The events of the previous week had aroused public expectations in the United Kingdom that concrete action would be taken to combat terrorism. The co-operative efforts that their two Governments had made in the past were not enough; the opportunity had to be seized to improve their joint efforts against the PIRA, and she saw the purpose of their meeting as being to discuss what measures their two Governments could take together.

In reply, Lynch stressed that the horror and revulsion that had been felt in the UK towards the events of 27 August was matched by the public reaction in the Republic; but to those feelings, in the Irish case, was the added shame that the deaths of Lord Mountbatten and those with him had occurred on Irish territory. He had been concerned that the reaction in the UK might have repercussions for Irish people living there, particularly since some British newspapers had given the impression that the deaths had been caused in some way by Irish negligence. He fully agreed with what the Prime Minister had said about the need to stamp out terrorism. Terrorism in the Irish Republic posed not only a security threat, but was also damaging economically: in his view there was a real risk that terrorism might in the long term retard economic growth in the Republic, particularly because of its effect on foreign investment and tourism. Successive Irish Governments had taken a number of substantial steps to combat the activities of the PIRA. They had increased the strength of the Garda and of the Irish Army; they had committed as many resources as they could afford to the policing of the border; they had encouraged close and successful co-operation between the Garda and the RUC; and they had a range of anti-terrorist laws that was perhaps stronger than that of any other European country. The question now was what more could be done. Various ideas had been aired in the press, such as direct co-operation between the British and Irish armies, RUC participation in the Garda's interrogation of suspected terrorists and joint British and Irish patrols on the border, but, warned Lynch, all these ideas would raise difficulties for the Irish Government.

The Prime Minister, however, reiterated that existing co-operation between the two Governments in the security field was not working well enough and had to be improved. The feeling in the UK that members of the IRA were safe once they were south of the border was stronger than ever, 'and there would be severe public reaction in this country if today's meeting did not point the way towards substantial improvement in security co-operation between the authorities of their two countries.' Mrs Thatcher had a number of specific measures to suggest – and she had been meticulous about not revealing in public, before their meeting, what she wished to put to the Taoiseach. Before they discussed the details of them, she wished to make it plain that all the steps that she was asking the Irish Government to take, the British Government was ready to introduce itself, on a reciprocal basis. She was seeking nothing that she was not prepared to offer in return.

The two premiers then discussed a series of measures, beginning with extradition and extra-territorial jurisdiction – the main problem being that the Republic's courts declined to extradite suspected terrorists to Northern Ireland if their offences were deemed 'political'. The Prime Minister pointed out that the British Government already extradited people in the UK to the Republic of Ireland. In the years 1976–78, the numbers had been 27, 31 and 26 respectively. Moreover:

> ... these figures included some of our own nationals who had been extradited to the Republic to face charges there. We had extradited the Littlejohn brothers to the Republic on charges of robbery, and when one of them had been recaptured in the UK following their escape from custody while in the Republic, he had been returned again to the Irish authorities. Similarly we had in recent years extradited a number of British nationals to other foreign countries. We were prepared to do this in the interests of the rule of law, and we would like to see other countries, including the Republic, acting similarly.

The British Government knew that the Irish Government had constitutional difficulties over extradition. Mrs Thatcher understood, for example, that the EEC Agreement relating to the European Convention on the Suppression of Terrorism contained a special accommodation for the Republic, by which it would have no obligation to extradite, but which would impose an obligation to consider the prosecution of those whom it did not extradite. This made it all the more important that, when the Irish Government did undertake such prosecutions, it did so with the best possible chance of securing convictions. The key to getting evidence on which convictions would be obtained turned, very often in terrorist cases, on translating intelligence into evidence that would stand up in court. The Prime Minister explained that the RUC felt very strongly that this process would be helped enormously if they were allowed to participate in the Garda's interrogation of suspected terrorists who were questioned in the Republic about incidents in Northern Ireland. However much information the RUC gave the Garda about a particular suspect, interrogation was more likely to have a successful outcome if those conducting it included police officers with first-hand knowledge of the case. The British Government would, therefore, like to see RUC officers allowed to interview, in Garda stations and in the presence of Garda officers, persons suspected of terrorist offences in the North: 'We were ready to provide the same facilities for the Garda in Northern Ireland', added the Prime Minister.

Lynch's comment was that extradition raised difficult constitutional problems for the Irish Government. Extradition was a judicial process that had never been intended to apply to people who were simply suspected of offences and who were wanted for interrogation. Moreover, a number of other European countries, including France, Denmark and Belgium, never extradited their own nationals. With regard to the proposal that the RUC should participate directly in the Garda's interrogation of suspected terrorists held in the Republic, he was advised that this could be counter-productive. The Garda felt that such a practice might very well alienate the local population and jeopardize their readiness to supply intelligence to them: this was particularly true in the rather special circumstances that affected the area a few miles south of the border with Northern Ireland. Moreover, the station in which interrogation took place might well be a target for terrorist action, and there would, therefore, be a physical risk to the Garda and RUC officers involved. A further problem about this proposal was that there was a very real risk, in the view of his Attorney General, that the courts in the Republic would exclude as inadmissible a confession that was obtained by interrogation during which an RUC officer had been present. This might seem extraordinary, but the attitude of the Irish courts on matters of this kind could only be described as officious. Nonetheless, Lynch recognized that something like 80% of all convictions obtained against terrorists depended on confessions resulting from interrogation, and he was, therefore, prepared to look further at the Prime Minister's proposal.

The next issue to be discussed was a Garda anti-terrorist squad. The Prime Minister observed that earlier in the year the Garda had deployed to the border a special anti-terrorist squad, which the RUC thought had been highly successful. Unfortunately, it seemed that the unit had been disbanded after a short time. Lynch, however, said that he was not aware of any major change in the deployment of the Garda along the border, though it was true that, in order to combat the rise in crime generally, and in particular IRA bank raids elsewhere in the Republic, some police had been withdrawn from the border, where it was thought that this would not be detrimental to security. He was ready to consider whether a squad of the kind the Prime Minister had described should be used along the border. Lynch's most senior civil servant, the Irish Cabinet Secretary General, Dermot Nally, who was accompanying the Taoiseach, here interjected that he understood that the special unit had been disbanded because the Garda had concluded that it was less effective than local forces using local knowledge. In response, the Prime Minister insisted that co-operation between the RUC and the Garda would be much improved if a Garda liaison officer were attached to the RUC's headquarters in the North, and similarly if there were an RUC officer at Garda headquarters. Lynch, however, pointed out that a joint RUC/Garda Committee had been set up at Deputy Chief Constable level in 1974, and these liaison arrangements were still working. It might, though, be that there was a need for some strengthening of these links.

The premiers next discussed helicopter overflights. Mrs Thatcher pointed out that suggestions had appeared in the press that British security forces should have the right of hot pursuit into the Republic. There was a misunderstanding about this. What HMG wanted to propose was that British helicopters should have standing authority to overfly the Republic to a depth of 10–15 kilometres in order to look for terrorists: 'We were not proposing that British troops or police should cross the border on the ground,' but a measure of the kind she had described would do much to stop the PIRA thinking that they had a safe haven across the border. It might have been possible for information from the helicopters to be transmitted directly to the Garda and the Irish Army, instead of relaying it to them via the RUC, which might save a good deal of time. Lynch commented that it very rarely happened that British security forces pursued suspected terrorists to the border and then saw them escape. As regarded the overflight of helicopters, the Irish authorities already gave automatic approval to advance requests for British helicopters to overfly Irish territory, even though this was a politically sensitive matter, but he agreed to consider the Prime Minister's proposal to see whether it would be effective in its operation.

The Prime Minister next argued that there would be much to be gained if there were co-operation between the armies of the two countries on the border to match the co-operation between the RUC and the Garda. Lynch, though, thought that there might be difficulties about this proposal. The Irish Army operated in the Republic in aid of the civil power, and they worked through the Garda. In any case, he understood that the RUC were sensitive about direct co-operation between the two armies, and they preferred to be the sole channel between the security forces on either side of the border. Mrs Thatcher concluded by stressing that it was important that there should be a very early follow-up to the proposals that she had put to Lynch and he had agreed to consider. She therefore suggested that Atkins should meet the Irish Minister for Justice, Gerry Collins, together with the RUC Chief Constable, Sir Kenneth Newman, and the Garda Commissioner, in the next two to three weeks to monitor progress.[19]

Before the Irish formally responded to the British proposals, the major event that grabbed most peoples' attention in Ireland was when, in late September, His Holiness Pope John Paul II visited the Republic – the first time a Pontiff had set foot on the Emerald Isle. At Drogheda he appealed to the 'men of violence' to end their campaign. This led Atkins to warn the Prime Minister that 'we may be faced suddenly with a situation which we have not discussed, namely a PIRA announcement of a ceasefire, or of the offer of a ceasefire conditional upon certain responses by the Government.' Atkins set out the options if there were a ceasefire, 'so that we are not exposed to the criticism that we are losing the opportunity which the Pope has, almost magically, created.' Provisional Sinn Féin had announced their intention to hold a press conference on 2 October, at which the PIRA's response was likely to be revealed: 'I doubt if the Pope's appeal for an end to violence is likely to be heeded by PIRA or [the] INLA: they have settled for a long haul and will not give up without something substantial to show for it', Atkins told Mrs Thatcher. Indeed, there had already been 'one attack today' on the Army in Belfast, probably conducted by the PIRA, which 'fortunately (and fortuitously)' resulted only in two soldiers being slightly injured. Nevertheless, the Government needed to be ready with an appropriate response to any move the PIRA might make. Atkins suggested that the Government's response should be as follows:

> a. If PIRA were to declare a ceasefire (which would certainly be only for short-term tactical reasons) our response should be that we welcome any reduction of violence and that if terrorism dies then nothing could do more to encourage the restoration of political and economic progress in Northern Ireland. We should re-affirm, however, that our policy will continue to be to enforce the rule of law and that those who commit no crimes have nothing to fear.
>
> b. The more likely PIRA move is to declare that they will continue violence unless the British Government meets certain conditions. Our general response to such an approach must be that, as the Pope himself has said, political progress cannot be brought about by violence. If their conditions demand immediate political proposals, we must reaffirm that we shall bring our proposals to the Westminster Parliament when our consultations have been completed. If they demand moves towards 'justice' (the word which the Pope himself used) such as the concession

of special category status for 'prisoners of war', we should emphasise that we shall discriminate neither against nor in favour of those convicted of terrorist offences. As the Pope said – 'Nobody may ever call murder by any other name than murder the spiral of violence may never be given the distinction of unavoidable logic or necessary retaliation.' If they demand civil rights for the Catholic minority, we shall be able to stand firm on the record of successive British Governments in tackling discrimination.

    c. Another possibility is that PIRA may seek covertly to negotiate a ceasefire, and there are already straws in the wind to suggest this possibility. I am re-inforcing my existing instructions to Ministerial colleagues and senior officials in my Department that such approaches are to be reported to me and that it is to be made clear in response to them that the Government is not prepared to enter into negotiations with terrorists.

If any of these situations arose, Atkins, of course, would 'consult you and colleagues most closely concerned very urgently so that we may avoid the Government being spuriously thrown on to the defensive. If, in the event, nothing emerges from PIRA … we can consider then how to respond to any subsequent PIRA moves of this kind.'[20]

There was, though, no PIRA ceasefire. The senior Republican, Danny Morrison, commented on how: 'What disappointed me was that the Pope having made, in fact, having overstated, his position by concentrating for half an hour on "the men of violence", "terrorism" and "subversion", did not balance it with a reference to the British partition of Ireland or the inhumanity being carried out by the British on hundreds of defenceless political prisoners.'[21] When it came, the official response of the Provisionals to the Pope's plea to them to end their armed struggle was, therefore, in the negative:

> To understand this conflict it is necessary to analyse the root causes of the problem. The Pope himself stressed this point and acknowledged that it is not a religious war. This is something that we have always maintained.
>
> The struggle is not merely for civil rights within the six county state. Rather it is a war of national liberation against English occupation and colonialism which has lasted, not just 10 years, but 810 years, having its roots in the Norman invasion of 1169 … colonialism in Ireland is an anachronism and must be brought to an end.
>
> To understand this conflict it is necessary to analyse the root causes of the problem. The Pope himself stressed this point and acknowledged that it is not a religious war. This is something that we have always maintained.[22]

By the beginning of October, as Sir John Hunt explained to Mrs Thatcher, the 'severely limiting factor' remained the 'unwillingness' (a word underlined by the Prime Minister) of the Irish to contemplate some measures, and their 'inability' to implement others. Thus the Army in Northern Ireland wanted to be able to pursue terrorists across the border and into the territory of the Republic. They also wanted to be free to deal directly with the Irish Army on counter-terrorist matters, and for the latter to have the same special emergency powers as they enjoyed themselves. The MOD, including the Chief of the General Staff (the senior British officer in the Army) – although not Army HQ Northern Ireland – was persuaded that these proposals were not worth putting forward to the Irish at the present time. In the meantime, Hunt asked the Prime Minister to think, once again, about what HMG's public attitude should be: 'If the Irish Government are prepared to do less than we hope'. The questions put in Dublin to British officials suggested that the Irish were certainly preparing to offer some overflight concessions for British helicopters. This helicopter concession would be welcome, as the Army attached particular importance to improving the existing level of surveillance south of the border.[23]

Atkins met with the Irish on 5 October. The atmosphere in the meeting was friendly throughout, though the Irish Minister for Justice, Gerry Collins, 'who did most of the talking, went out of his way to score points related to the effectiveness of the RUC and the British Army whenever he could.' Atkins referred to the need to ensure effective policing on both sides of the border, and asked for the reactions of the Irish Ministers to the proposals made at the Downing Street meeting. In reply, Collins said that the Republic was not convinced that the effectiveness of the current measures in the North was all it could be, and there might be improvements that could be adopted by the RUC. Nevertheless, on their side, they had decided:

(i)   to increase the strength of the special Garda task force enabling it to give a quicker response especially in difficult areas of the border;
(ii) to increase the strength of the special investigation section of the Garda technical bureau so as to increase the teams available; and
(iii) to increase the strength of the Garda generally in the border areas.

Collins believed that these measures would improve the effectiveness of the Garda, though their procedures would be kept under continuous review. He thought that there was an implied note of criticism of the Garda in the suggestions that the British Government had put forward, and he emphasized that the Garda were always willing to co-operate: he did not know of any incidents where they had declined to do so. Atkins, however, welcomed the decisions that the Irish had taken, 'which went a long way to meeting the points which we had raised, with the exception of surveillance.'[24]

In his report of the meeting to Mrs Thatcher, Atkins explained how an extra 1,000 recruits for the RUC was going to be matched on the Irish side by more Gardai in selected border areas. It was agreed that certain border areas, notably South Armagh, needed reinforcing on both sides. The Irish and the Garda Commissioner 'clearly appreciated' the arguments of the RUC Chief Constable that long-term surveillance and in-depth investigations were a crucial element in bringing terrorists successfully before the courts. They agreed that the exchange of information across the border in both directions was a key to this. Co-ordinated operations for pre-determined tasks were acknowledged as the best way of deploying manpower on either side of the border, and special efforts were needed in problem areas, especially co-ordinated patrolling in the more dangerous ones. The Garda Commissioner and the Chief Constable also agreed to review their procedures together, and to make the changes that were necessary.

On the key issue, the Irish came with a 'most carefully prepared and constructive concession': they were now ready to permit helicopters to cross the border as a direct follow-up of serious incidents, subject to a number of detailed operational conditions that 'we were able to accept. The only shortcoming is their insistence that the maximum depth of penetration should be 5 kilometres at 1,500 feet, while we regard 10 kilometres as the useful minimum.' There was no immediate prospect of getting more than this. Atkins had the GOC's Chief of Staff at hand, and with his concurrence he accepted the offer, on the understanding that they should have to review the arrangement month by month. The Irish were equally insistent on this, since 'they are highly suspicious of the dangers of abuse, and frightened of the political side effects of regular appearances of British helicopters in their border areas.' It was part of the agreement on helicopters that British Army pilots should be able to communicate with the Garda on the ground. On ground-to-ground communication more generally, the Irish also conceded that there would be occasions when the British Army would need to get in touch without delay with the forces on the other side. To meet this point, the Irish were putting a Garda officer into every Irish Army unit operating on the border so that direct communication would be available in emergencies.

With regard to RUC interviews of suspects in the South, the Irish argued strongly, and with much supporting evidence, that the courts in the Republic would never admit statements that had been obtained with the participation of the RUC in questioning. They claimed that, in any event, given the rules currently applied by their courts, police questioning unsupported by other evidence never yielded any results, and that to allow it would have the effect of drying up their current sources of information, as well as putting the policemen concerned on both sides at personal risk. They made it plain that they would not be able to give way over this, and suggested instead that the British ought to tackle the problem by means of closer consultation between the RUC and Garda, which should bring improvements in the Garda performance over questioning. While Atkins 'expressed our real disappointment that they could not help us on this point', he was guided by the Chief Constable, who had a separate and constructive meeting with the Garda Commissioner, at which it was agreed that there were other routes to the same end. 'I did not make this an issue publicly. It was quite clear that the valuable breakthrough on helicopter overflights would have been at risk had I pressed the issue that far.' The Irish, noted Atkins, 'dislike the idea of formal liaison officers.' After Atkins had pointed to the political effect of the proposal in demonstrating their joint dedication to the cause, they agreed that each force should nominate an officer who would be available around the clock as contact with the other headquarters.[25]

The Prime Minister, while noting that progress had been made, expressed some disappointment with the outcome. She did 'not think that enough has been achieved', and asked, in particular, whether it was not the case that 'we wanted regular helicopter controls in order to get advance information of terrorist activity as well as follow-up after incidents.'[26] So, in an effort to convince his boss, Atkins had his Private Secretary, Roy Harrington, send her a report in which the Prime Minister was assured that, on incidents relating to British helicopter flights into the Irish Republic, 'the Irish produced everything we wanted.' Mrs Thatcher scribbled 'No' next to this sentence. Atkins' view, however, was that the Army 'are entirely happy' with the limitation to five kilometres, and with monthly reviews. 'If we can justify it, we can press for an extension.' Present arrangements for overflight after giving prior notice would continue, and the Irish would be stationing a helicopter of their own at Dundalk to patrol the difficult border area: 'We shall, therefore, have joint patrolling by helicopters.' The proposed arrangements for communication between helicopters and the Garda, and between the British Army and Garda officers specially attached to their Army, were 'entirely satisfactory.' The arrangements for nominated senior liaison officers were 'probably better' than the original idea of an exchange of liaison officers, who would not have been available on a 24-hour-a-day basis. When, reported Harrington, Atkins had reviewed the conclusions of the meeting with the GOC, the Chief Constable and the new Security Co-ordinator, it was agreed that the meetings had produced a quite new and substantially higher level of co-operation, 'on which we can build at the further meetings which are to take place.'[27]

At this stage, the new Security Co-ordinator had been appointed. He was a Whitehall man of substance: Sir Maurice Oldfield, the former 'C' or Chief of the Secret Intelligence Service (SIS) – more commonly known as MI6. In early October, Mrs Thatcher read his initial report on the situation he found in Northern Ireland. It was entitled 'But ie Buts'. This might be regarded as light-hearted title for a paper on a serious subject – 'and it might also be considered presumptuous for one who has been in Northern Ireland for exactly one week to make such a comment' wrote Oldfield. 'I have however found the same refrain going through my talks at all levels and in all departments. They went something like this: "Our personal relations are very good, but ..."; "We have no difficulty in agreeing at the operational level, but there are questions of higher policy"; and "Of course the task is clear, but ..." This suggested, to Oldfield, that while recognizing the valid reasons for these reservations, 'our aim should be to convert the conjunction "but" into and".' He observed, with regard to the differences between the Army and the RUC: 'I always knew Northern Ireland had many religions, but I never realised that it could give rise to so much theology – and a good deal of it pretty dogmatic.' Oldfield believed measures were needed that would produce visible results in the following six months. A Joint Operations Staff would, he feared, duplicate, or triplicate, the existing chain of command in the Army and RUC. He suggested looking critically at the arrangements for the conduct of operational liaisons between the police and military at local level, and then following the channels from these arrangements upwards. Such an examination would enable a determination of what new organization (if any) might be needed at the top. The Security Co-ordinator's staff would have a mixture of functions. It would have an investigate function, and be prepared to 'serve as a court of appeal.' It should produce independent advice on the planning, management and command problems relevant to security operations. It should act as a think-tank, and also as a 'ginger group'. It would not have executive powers, and would discharge its responsibilities though the departments within whose constitutional responsibilities action lay. It should also keep a 24-hour watch. Finally, as an envoi to the end of his report, the former SIS Chief recalled a story about his old CIA counterpart Allen Foster Dulles, 'who kept a card on his office desk. This card faced the visitor and read: "Do you come with a solution to your problem or are you yourself part of it?" Let us hope we can together find our solutions.'[28]

By December, Oldfield and Kenneth Stowe had produced a joint paper on security, reviewing Northern Ireland strategy for the coming year. In it they stated that the core policy (of enforcing the rule of law by the police with Army support) 'stands: progress was being made, but slowly; there will be setbacks'. The Planning Staff – i.e. the Security Co-ordinator's Staff – was now virtually complete and ready to operate; the aim was to achieve some visible improvements in the short term, while developing more effective measures for the long term. The weakness was that 'terrorist incidents tend to be spectacular and positive, whereas the security forces' operations risk appearing negative (PIRA were deterred, so nothing happened); were too slow (an arrest was made for a crime two years ago); and do not equate with terrorist acts (one terrorist arrested may have a dozen coups behind him).' To many people, especially in Northern Ireland, the law and the courts appeared too soft on terrorism. 'Our successes are not exploited positively and sensitively', concluded Oldfield and Stowe. They argued that:

Our policy should:

a. promote the intelligence effort which is the ultimate matchwinner: the review … has to be implemented;

b. strengthen the law against the terrorist, maintain and develop the police machinery for interrogation, and speed up the law's application: (a review is in hand on the first point);

c. prepare options which can be used in quick reactions to and therefore exploitation of terrorists' acts;

d. make the most of the help the Republic can give; in the process demonstrating to them our commitment;

e. concentrate security forces' effort on the 'black' areas and also re-assess the effort in the grey areas to coordinate better the police, army and civil administration;

f. consider plans on common assumptions about police development and army manpower for the period under review bearing in mind their implications in the longer term, (say three years).

Any outcomes would be assessed by the Security Policy Meeting: chaired by the Secretary of State, its other members were the Chief Constable, GOC, the Security Co-ordinator and the PUS.[29] Atkins approved the Oldfield–Stowe plan, and the Prime Minister was informed that, under the aegis of the Security Co-ordinator, 'much has been done, and more is planned, to improve the effectiveness of the security effort.' Measures had been taken to improve the security of prison officers, and the profile of the security forces in West Belfast had been raised. A scheme had been agreed for the selective closure of cross-border roads when the opportunity arose, and the various measures agreed with the Irish Government for the improvement of cross-border security were being implemented. Action had been taken to improve the use of intelligence resources.[30] Out of the Mountbatten and Warrenpoint deaths, a slow intelligence revolution, under Oldfield, the supreme Spook, was under way.

Notes

1   Thatcher Foundation Speech at Airey Neave's Memorial Service, 16 May 1979.
2   TNA PREM 19/80 Hunt to Prime Minister, 2 May 1979.
3   TNA PREM 19/79 Transcript of a Telephone Conversation Between the Prime Minister and the President of the United States on Tuesday, 4 July 1979.
4   TF Prime Minister letter to President Carter (Northern Ireland).

5   TNA PREM 80 President Carter to Prime Minister, 6 August 1979.
6   TNA PREM 19/83 Hunt to Prime Minister, 9 July 1979.
7   TNA CAB 148/183 OD (79) 4th Meeting. Cabinet Defence and Overseas Committee, 10 July 1979.
8   *An Phoblacht*, 1 September 1979.
9   TF Written Statement on Warrenpoint and Mountbatten murders, 27 August 1979.
10   TNA PREM 19/79 Pattison to Pilling, 28 August 1979.
11   TNA PREM 19/385 Prime Minister's Engagements, Wednesday, 29 August 1979.
12   TNA PREM 19/385 Notes on Northern Ireland for the Prime Minister.
13   TNA PREM 19/385 Cartledge to Prime Minister, 29 August 1979.
14   TNA PREM 19/385 Ridley to Prime Minister, 1 September 1979.
15   TNA PREM 19/385 Note to Prime Minister, 31 August 1979.
16   TNA CAB 129/66 Cabinet Limited Circulation Annex, 30 August 1979
17   TNA PREM 19/79 Atkins to Prime Minister, 31 August 1979.
18   TNA PREM 19/83 Lynch to Thatcher.
19   TNA PREM 19/79 Note of a Meeting Between the Prime Minister and the Taoiseach held at 10 Downing Street at 14.45 on Wednesday, 5 September 1979.
20   TNA PREM 19/82 Atkins to Prime Minister, 1 October 1979.
21   *An Phoblacht/Republican News*, Saturday, 6 October 1979.
22   *An Phoblacht/Republican News*, Saturday, 6 October 1979.
23   TNA PREM 19/82 Hunt to Prime Minister, 2 October 1979.
24   TNA PREM 19/82 Meeting Between the Secretary of State for Northern Ireland, the Irish Minister for Foreign Affairs and the Irish Minister for Justice on 5 October 1979.
25   TNA PREM 19/82 Atkins to Prime Minister, 5 October 1979.
26   TNA PREM 19/82 Whitmore to Harrington, 10 October 1979.
27   TNA PREM 19/82 Harrington to Prime Minister.
28   TNA PREM 19/83 Oldfield note, 16 October 1979.
29   TNA PREM 19/385 Northern Ireland Strategy 1980 – Security.
30   TNA PREM 19/385 Memo to Prime Minister.

Chapter 3

The First Hunger Strike Begins

Meanwhile, the dispute in the H-Blocks rumbled on. In November 1979, the NIO picked up intelligence of a possible hunger strike in the Maze. Humphrey Atkins immediately informed Mrs Thatcher:

> A hunger strike would be a deliberate and ruthlessly determined act to achieve political status for terrorist prisoners. This is the objective of the dirty protest itself, and it is an indication of its failure that a hunger strike is being considered. I am sure that we must not give in, or do anything that can be used as a sign that we are not resolute.

He pointed out how, after taking medical and legal advice in 1974, the then Government decided that there would no medical intervention in any future hunger strikes, and, following a 1974 Government statement, after medical and legal advice, not to initiate medical intervention during a hunger strike: 'The effect is that prison authorities and the prison doctors will allow the inevitable deterioration – and consequent death – of a hunger-striker to take place unless the prisoner specifically asks for medical intervention.' While the 1974 statement did not rule out forced feeding, the decision was left to the clinical judgement of the doctor concerned, 'but I think it unlikely that any prison medical officer in Northern Ireland would resort to forced feeding. In my view we must stand firm on the 1974 statement.'

To make sure that any prisoners intending to embark on a fast were fully aware of the Government's position, Atkins intended to announce, by way of an arranged written answer in the House of Commons, 'our policy on the medical management of protesting prisoners. This will not, of course, refer to a hunger strike, but it will make clear that it is not the practice, or the intention, to force medical care upon any prisoner for his own individual benefit. This will get our general policy about the medical role in prisons on record before a hunger strike takes place.' If there were a hunger strike of a co-ordinated kind by dirty protesters, 'it will be, as I have said, an act of desperation: there will be international interest in it and, perhaps, concurrent fears among the general public about a terrorist campaign. We shall need to say firmly and quickly what our policy is and be prepared to combat the aggressive propaganda which would accompany the strike.' Atkins sought Mrs Thatcher's agreement, and that of colleagues, that:

i.   we should sustain our determination not to yield on the issue of political status for terrorist criminals;
ii. we should be prepared to face up to a hunger strike with the 1974 procedures, and say so as soon as a hunger strike is called.[1]

The Prime Minister's support was forthcoming – as was that of Atkins' Cabinet colleagues. This was the view widely shared by those in Government; as Atkins explained to a fellow MP:

> The IRA are a small and isolated group of terrorists, representing no-one but themselves and engaged in a brutal attempt to coerce a law-abiding people and a democratic government into their way of thinking. They do not themselves observe the laws of war; indeed, they have brutally murdered members of the security forces who have fallen into their hands. They cannot themselves expect to be treated by the authorities as if they were prisoners of war.
>
> I believe that any concession to the IRA on this point would encourage the terrorists to hope that an amnesty may one day be granted; a hope which would only, by encouraging terrorists and potential terrorists in the belief that they can escape punishment for their crimes, feed the fires of violence. It is my firm resolve that terrorists duly convicted by the courts shall suffer the full penalties prescribed by the law. I have no sympathy whatever with the claim that the perpetrators of serious and violent crimes should escape the rigours of the law merely because they claim to be motivated by 'political' considerations; and I see no reason why gangsterism should escape the punishment of the law.[2]

There was, however, no hunger strike, perhaps because the European Court of Human Rights option – initiated in 1978 – was still in play. But in June 1980, the ECHR published its findings on the PIRA prisoners' application. The applicants' main complaint was that their right to freedom of conscience and belief (under Article 9) had been denied them because the prison authorities sought to apply to them the normal prison regime. The British Government argued that the right to freedom of belief did not extend to opinions or attitudes about whether some prisoners should enjoy a more favourable regime than others, and, furthermore, that the requirements to do prison work and wear prison clothing were necessary and lawful adjuncts to any prison regime. The Commission found 'that the right to such preferential status for a certain category of prisoners is not amongst the rights guaranteed by the [European] Convention [on Human Rights] or by Article 9 in particular', and observed that the applicants were not entitled to the status of political prisoner under national law, under the Convention or under 'the existing norms of International law'. The Commission concluded that 'the protest cannot derive any legitimacy or justification from the Convention and cannot be attributed to any positive action on behalf of the respondent Government'. The Commission added that 'it [did] not consider there to be anything inherently degrading or objectionable about the requirement to wear a prison uniform or to work', and found the applicants' complaints under Article 9 inadmissible.

The PIRA applicants (Nugent, McFeely and two others) also argued that the regime under which they lived amounted to inhuman and degrading treatment in breach of Article 3 of the Convention. The Government pointed out that some of these complaints (for example, the alleged denial of exercise, library facilities and toilet facilities) were completely unfounded, in that basic rights such as these had never been removed, and remained available to all prisoners. Other allegations (for example, that the protesters were denied educational facilities, remission, extra visits, extra letters and periods of free association), it was argued, were misleading in that privileges of this kind might, under Prison Rules, be removed by the prison governor as part of a disciplinary award in the interests of maintaining good order within the prison. Finally, other complaints (for example, that the protesters were 'forced' to go naked, to stay in their cells 24 hours a day, to live in cells bare of furniture and in disgusting and unhygienic conditions) were misleading in that the circumstances about which the applicants were complaining were self-imposed. In fact, the Commission declared all the applicants' complaints under Article 3 inadmissible. It recognized 'the fact that they choose not to avail of the above opportunities to leave their cells is plainly their own responsibility'; that in relation to the applicants' refusal to take exercise or use the library facilities, 'they alone must bear responsibility for the choice they have made'; and 'that any inadequacy in the medical attention they received or are receiving as a result of such behaviour is attributable to their own actions in furtherance of the protest'. The Commission was 'satisfied with the general provision of medical care at the Maze', including that given to the protesters. In relation to their unhygienic living conditions, the Commission said that it had no doubt that the conditions were 'inhuman and degrading' within the meaning ascribed to them under the Convention, but observed that 'these conditions are self-imposed by the applicants as part of their protest for "special category status" and, were they motivated to improve them, could be eliminated almost immediately'. The Commission also found that a range of other measures about which the applicants complained were either not breaches of the Convention or were justified as necessary in a democratic society in the interests of public safety and for the prevention of crime or disorder.

The Commission, however, did not reach a decision on the admissibility of two particular aspects. These were prisoners' rights to correspondence and the effectiveness of national remedies for prisoners' complaints. Restrictions that the Prison Rules of England and Wales imposed on prisoners' correspondence were already being considered by the Commission in connection with alleged breaches of the Convention, and so the Commission decided to adjourn consideration of this case until that in Great Britain had been settled. In relation to the effectiveness of national remedies for prisoners' complaints, the Commission found that 'this issue gives rise to difficult questions of law and fact which require further observation in the light of the parties' observations', and accordingly adjourned its consideration of the admissibility of this aspect of the applicants' complaints. As the NIO noted, these two aspects were peripheral to the applicants' main complaints, and were relevant to *any* convicted prisoner in Northern Ireland, not just to protesting prisoners.

Although the Commission's ruling did 'vindicate the Government's refusal to grant special category and rejects the claims of ill-treatment', it did also, in paragraph 64 of its judgment, contain a note of criticism. The Commission was concerned about what it saw as a lack of flexibility in the approach of the State authorities towards exploring ways of resolving the protest. The Commission believed that efforts should have been made to ensure that the prisoners took 'regular exercise in the open air with some form of clothing (other than prison clothing) and [make] greater use of the prison amenities under similar conditions'. It also said that 'arrangements should have been made to enable the applicants to consult outside medical specialists even though they were not prepared to wear prison uniform or underwear'.[3] Despite these minor concerns, the ECHR was clear: the blanketmen had no justification for their demand for political status according to domestic or international law. There was now little option for the prisoners but to either carry on the protest with little hope of victory, or to resort to the ultimate weapon: a hunger strike to force the Government to cave in to their demands.

It therefore fell to the senior PIRA Officers Commanding within the H-Blocks to prepare for a hunger strike. In effect, this meant the senior O/C, Brendan 'The Dark' Hughes and Bobby Sands. Hughes was the 'operational commander'[4] for the PIRA's 'Bloody Friday' bombing onslaught in Belfast in 1972. Twenty-two bombs were detonated in the space of about 80 minutes – 11 people were killed, including two teenage boys and a mother of seven; 130 people were injured. Hughes was arrested in 1974, and sentenced to 15 years in prison as a special category prisoner; he was subsequently convicted for another offence, after 1 March 1976, and thereby surrendered his special category status. It was under

Hughes' command that prisoners began the dirty protest. Now, when Hughes and Sands asked for volunteers, looking for six, they had 148 prisoners put their names forward. Hughes found 'it was very, very hard ... very, *very* hard to pick people.' Sands wrote a personal letter to each volunteer, warning them that embarking on a hunger strike would entail tremendous suffering and probably death. It was then up to the other OCs in each H-Block to make a physical and psychological profile of the candidates. On this basis, Hughes and Sands drew up a shortlist, also taking into account the convictions of volunteers in terms of their possible impact on public relations. Six men were chosen to represent the Six Counties in the North, with a seventh added to match the number of signatories of the 1916 Proclamation of the Irish Republic in 1916. There was, however, some disagreement between Hughes and Sands when the former told the latter that he would not be going on hunger strike; it would be Hughes who would represent County Antrim, from which both men came. Instead, Sands would be the new overall OC in the Maze. The final part of the plan was to establish two additional stand-by emergency squads of six or seven men who would join the fast at a key point, possibly as the first hunger-strikers approached death.[5]

As rumours surfaced of a hunger strike, a British official visited the Department of Justice in Dublin on 6 and 7 October, to investigate how the Irish authorities dealt with their paramilitary prisoners in Portlaoise Prison. The official was informed that there were currently about 170 'subversive' prisoners, or about 15% of the sentenced population: 'This of course is totally different from our own situation: we have something like three-quarters with affiliations with paramilitary organisations of one sort or another. They were also not serving such long sentences compared with the majority of ours', noted the official. The 'subversives' had been concentrated at Portlaoise for some years, prior to which they had caused extensive problems in other prisons, culminating in a riot at Mountjoy Gaol. The British official also confirmed that all prisoners in the Republic were allowed to wear their own clothes – there was no restriction laid down centrally about the range of 'own clothes' that prisoners might wear. This was left to Governors, and difficulties rarely arose. Work was a different matter. The subversives were not required to do ordinary prison work, and never had been (prior to 1974 or thereabouts they also had virtually free association). They were required to keep their cells clean, and in return for this they got the standard daily gratuity – at present 30p a day – which was paid to all prisoners regardless of the nature of their prison employment. They also got the standard one-quarter remission. This position was peculiar to Portlaoise. In all other establishments the authorities decided on the tasks on which the prisoners were to be employed, and, so far as the official could ascertain, the prisoners had no more choice in the matter than under the UK system.

The subversives were divided into three groups for the purposes of the organization of their day. They were unlocked at about 8 a.m. They slopped out and washed, and collected their breakfast from the hotplate. During the period until 9.15–9.30, the cells were left unlocked. There were three forms of activity: outdoor exercise, indoor recreation and craft work: 'As I understood it, roughly a third of the prisoners are engaged on each of these activities at any one time (assuming that the weather is such as to permit outdoor exercise). The prisoners are merely observed from outside whilst in the craft workshop(s).' At lunchtime, the prisoners collected their meal, took it to their cells and were locked in while they ate. Communal dining was not a feature of the South's prison system. The afternoon session lasted from about 2.15–4.30, and the same procedure then took place for the tea meal. From 5.30 to about 7.15, there was the third and final session of the day. At 8 p.m., the prisoners were locked up for the night. There was no free association period as such, but the way in which the regime operated seemed to permit a great deal of free association during the day. Saturdays, the official was told, were no different from other days, and Sundays were also much the same apart from attendance at Mass. The 'official line' was that the prisoners' command structures were not recognized. In reality, however, the authorities found it convenient to deal with spokesmen in order to sort out matters affecting the prisoners generally (spokesmen did not attempt to speak on behalf of others about individual matters, such as marital or private affairs, but did so in regard to general matters such as food, organization of craft work etc.) Portlaoise was a single cell block on four levels. The top two floors were occupied by Provisional IRA prisoners, the next by some PIRA and the INLA men, and the ground floor by Official IRA and others. There was no access from one floor to another at any time. The different groupings did not exercise, have indoor recreation or do craft work together, but were kept separate at all times.[6]

On October 10, the H-Block Information Centre in Belfast announced that a hunger strike would begin on October 27.[7] In the wake of this, Father Alex Reid wrote to NIO Minister Michael Alison making, 'in his usual courteous way', further suggestions to end the prison protests. His recommendation that the Government should consider the abolition of prison uniform as an advanced humanitarian and penological move was 'a distinctly shrewd observation.' This very possibility was raised in a preliminary way during the NIO's review of the ECHR decision. It was also the subject of further consideration as part of the remit of a second working party, which was reviewing in depth the questions of work and clothing. As for the remaining questions – or demands by the prisoners – S. C. Jackson, of the NIO, commented: 'Father Reid seems rather over-optimistic in assuming that these could be so easily dealt with. The nature of the IRA as a terrorist organisation and the brutal intransigence it has displayed over the "prison struggle" would not lead one to suppose that the remaining demands could so simply be accommodated – apart of course from our giving in.' Father Reid's assertion that 'for almost a year now the demand for political status has been officially dropped' needed to be challenged. This simply was 'not true, as a study of any Republican utterances will show.' Presumably, thought Jackson, he referred to the entirely spurious distinction between 'political status' and the 'five humanitarian demands' that were the PIRA's latest presentational gambit. Father Reid seemed to 'look forward to consolidating his position as an intermediary', but Alison was asked whether 'he wishes to continue according Father Reid "Ministerial" status; this would rather tend to encourage him in his self-appointed role and could lead to others of similar outlook expecting similar treatment.'[8]

Some movement on clothing seemed the most obvious option for HMG. A decision was made to introduce 'civilian-style' clothing. The conduit for laying the foundation for revealing this change in policy was through Cardinal Ó Fiaich: on 23 October, accompanied by Bishop Edward Daly, of Derry, he called on the Secretary of State, in London, to discuss the impending hunger strike. Atkins revealed to the Cardinal the background to the Cabinet's consideration of the matter that day. There was no doubt that the hunger-strikers included determined people who were intent upon killing themselves if allowed to do so. The Government would not force-feed them, and if they persisted there was a considerable risk that some at least of the hunger-strikers would die. The demand that they were making was for political status, which would never be granted. The Government had the support of the Pope in their insistence that murder did not become excusable because of the motives for which it was committed. In that, the Government also had the support of the ECHR. Atkins then revealed that the Government had, however, decided to make a change in the rules relating to clothing. Prisoners, he explained, were permitted to wear their own clothes for visits, for association between the hours of 5.00 p.m. and 8.00 p.m. in the evening, and at weekends. They were also permitted to wear their own clothes for exercise periods, although many of them chose not to do so. Such clothing had to be approved by the prison authorities. At work, the prisoners wore prison uniform. The Government had decided to make available a range of 'civilian clothing' for working hours.

Ó Fiaich was not impressed, and criticized the fact that the clothing would be provided by the prison authorities; he would strongly have preferred the prisoners to be able to provide their own clothes for use throughout the day. Atkins countered that for security reasons, for the maintenance of good order within the prison and also to some extent because of the need to carry the prison staff with him, he felt it necessary to retain the degree of control involved in what was proposed. He would have liked to have had the range of civilian clothing available immediately, but unfortunately it would take a little time to provide. The change would be formally announced that afternoon, and would apply to all prisoners in Northern Ireland. Bishop Daly, however, pressed strongly for prisoners to have the freedom to wear their own clothes at all times, subject to approval of the type of clothing. The Government had gone five-sixths of the way to giving what was needed on this matter, and it was a great disappointment that, contrary to what they had expected from news reports, the Government was limiting the concession in the way in which the Secretary of State had described. He urged Atkins to reconsider. There was a considerable risk that the prisoners would reject the proposition, whereas, if they had been given freedom of choice, Daly would have felt able to go into the prison and recommend that the prisoners accept what was on offer. He could not be sure what the result would have been – and would have liked there to have been some movement on the question of work as well – but there would have been some hope of ending the hunger strike at least. He could hardly argue for the present, more limited, concession.

Atkins, for his part, emphasized the extent to which the Government had moved, and reminded the Cardinal and the Bishop of the severe criticism to which he was already being subjected, which he had expected, and which he had had to take into account. Daly continued to insist that a more generous gesture was needed. To give so much of what had been asked for, but to hold back the final element within it, would harden attitudes rather than soften them. He had been visiting the Parish of Omagh, talking to the families of prison officers, among others, and he believed that they would support such a change. (He commented that Omagh had not a single man in prison: 'it is the most apolitical parish in the diocese'). The more limited concession being offered would be seen by the prisoners as merely a different form of uniform. The positive elements of the Government's proposals continued to be emphasized by Atkins to the Cardinal and the Bishop: prison uniform would be abolished, relatives could be encouraged to send in clothes for use outside working hours, and the clothes to be provided for work would be of a 'civilian pattern'. Bishop Daly again urged the Government to alter its position. The Secretary of State insisted that he would not do so, and pressed Daly to say, since he regarded the Government as having gone five-sixths of the way towards a satisfactory change in respect of clothing, whether this change was to be welcomed or not. Daly declined to answer, saying that the prisoners would have preferred a free choice. He was concerned that this limited concession would be wholly unsuccessful, and that the result would be a disastrous situation within weeks when striking prisoners became ill or died. In that event, he would be out on the streets himself leading protests. He had been invited to head a committee of protest in Derry. Had there been a full-hearted concession on clothing, he would have declined the invitation, but now he considered that he would probably have to accept it. The Cardinal then asked how many different types of clothing would be made available. Atkins replied that this could not yet be predicted because there was at present no civilian-type clothing immediately available. The Cardinal felt that, because of the limited nature of the concession and the time before it was in effect, it would be regarded as niggardly rather than magnanimous, and could be dismissed by the prisoners. This was in his view the central issue, and if the Government had gone the whole way it would have ended the hunger strike, and might indeed have achieved what all concerned wanted: a real, progressive step towards the ending of the entire protest. In so doing, the position and influence of the IRA would have been considerably weakened.[9]

The meeting did not go as well as Atkins might have hoped. When he publicly announced the 'concession' to allow all male prisoners to wear prison-issue civilian-style clothes, the news provoked considerable criticism – from virtually everyone. While the Alliance Party refrained from significant public comment, John Hume for the SDLP made clear his support for the efforts of Cardinal Ó Fiaich and Bishop Daly, 'and he seems to share the views of the Catholic churchmen who have expressed "disappointment" that the measure "stops short of what is demanded by the situation".' Hume was clearly worried that the hunger strike may overshadow the SDLP's new political strategy, which was due to be unveiled at the Party Conference on 7 November. In the Republic, the hunger strike brought problems for the Taoiseach, Charles Haughey, during the run-up to a crucial Donegal by-election, when he felt it necessary to disassociate himself and his party from the remarks of Miss Síle de Valera MEP, who criticized Mrs Thatcher's attitude towards the hunger-strikers as 'callous, unfeeling and self-righteous'. International attention was 'beginning to stir' – in the Soviet Union, *Pravda* had given their support to the hunger-strikers, who they viewed as 'fighters for the freedom of Northern Ireland', and the French Communist Party delivered a strongly worded statement to the British Ambassador in Paris. However, support for the Government's line had come from an editorial in the *Washington Post* (5 November), which said that the Prime Minister was 'entirely right' when she said that the authority of the State was at risk.[10]

But the two key audiences that the NIO had to address were the minority Catholic community and the majority Protestant community. The latter required assurance that there would be no 'sell out'. On 28 October, the leaders of the Ulster Unionist Party, the Democratic Unionist Party, the Ulster Progressive Unionist Party, the United Ulster Unionist Party and the Unionist Party of Northern Ireland came out with a unanimous statement condemning HMG for its attempt 'to do a shabby deal with the IRA', adding:

> The Government must learn that the Unionist family, whatever their internal differences, are one in their determination to defend and maintain the Union and see the IRA defeated ... They cannot and will not tolerate any deals with Ulster's enemies ... [they condemn HMG] for capitulating [on clothing] to the demands of convicted criminals who have been engaged in a campaign of self-inflicted degradation at

the Maze and Armagh prisons. This further treachery reveals the abject refusal of the Government to acknowledge the real character of militant Republicans. It is hardly credible, given the lessons of past experience, that Mr Atkins could have underestimated the IRA's ability to exploit every concession in furtherance of their evil and murderous ends. The dishonesty of the Government and its attempt to deceive the House of Commons as well as the people of Northern Ireland stand exposed.

Other Unionist politicians joined in the clamour of protest at what HMG had done. But, noted the NIO, the unanimity of 28 October 'is a fragile thing.' It was not easy for the likes of Mrs Ann Dickson (Leader of the liberal UPNI) to put their name to the same piece of paper as Dr Paisley (DUP): 'extreme passion on a very narrow common cause brought the five momentarily together.' The alliance was 'unlikely to be a continuing phenomenon.' The Protestant community was 'even more difficult than the Catholic to consider as a whole, and its attitudes (except as given expression by the articulate and usually extreme few) hard to fathom.' It was difficult to generalize about the Protestant community: 'Superficially, it is warm and extrovert and it has articulate spokesmen, but its real feelings it keeps to itself.' Opinion polls over the years had given cause to hope that the silent majority were moderate, tolerant and ready to move forward: 'But perhaps they are just silent'. It was impossible to go over the heads of the leaders to the community at large: 'Their silence is only to be broken by the few who may or may not give a fair picture.'

There were some signs, however, of a new mood. Despite continuing anxieties in Northern Ireland, there was, in contrast to the early seventies, no evidence of a great wave of Protestant opinion wanting to impose itself. March's Orange Order security demonstration, planned over three months, and boycotted by the paramilitary Ulster Defence Association and DUP, brought out only 15,000 (many of whom disappeared quickly into the pubs *en route*) instead of the 40–50,000 hoped for. The Unionist parties were more interested in competing amongst themselves than fighting what might be thought to be the enemy. The UDA, under the leadership of 'Supreme Commander' Andy Tyrie, had been waging what they themselves saw as an uphill propaganda battle, not only for the ear of the world, but also for the consciousness of Ulster's Protestant people – above all the working class, which they largely represented. It was to little avail, as Tyrie admitted privately during the previous week: 'Our biggest problem at the moment is moral rearmament, the morale of the people has dropped so low'. Although there had been some reports of a recent spate of applications to join the UDA, these had been discounted, 'and the impression one gets is of an apathetic UDA membership, far from anxious to take again to the streets.'

Tension had undoubtedly increased, however, in the Protestant as well as the Catholic community, particularly where the cause for fear was most patent, in for example County Fermanagh, where isolated Protestants (forming the minority there) were under threat from PIRA gunmen, or in the towns and cities where the communities living cheek by jowl had memories of past confrontation. Again and again, moderate Protestant opinion – Bishop Eames, of the Church of Ireland, for one – had pressed their worry that, if the situation was not well handled, the gains of the last ten years would be lost. But that same moderate opinion, and Protestant opinion generally, was concerned not with the narrow issue of the hunger strike or the H-Blocks campaign, but with the whole matter of government in Northern Ireland. They feared that they were now seeing another Republican attack on the fabric of government and on the structure of the community in Northern Ireland. They, like the Catholic community, were looking to HMG for evidence that such attacks were going to be firmly and wholeheartedly resisted: 'and they howl in fury at any sign – such as a concession to the prisoners or too blatant a gesture to the South – that the Government is weakening. The principal message … to the Protestant as to the Catholic Community is one of reassurance.'

Despite the one moment of unified action, the parties, particularly the UUP and DUP, were locked in conflict. The Protestant Churches were not a homogenous body, and were divided on doctrine and practice. With one important exception, they did not, however, compete much among one another for allegiance. The Loyalist paramilitary organizations, noted the NIO, had difficulty in handling both the H-Block campaign and the hunger strike. Some Loyalist prisoners had been on the blanket protest since it began in 1976. None had ever joined the dirty protest. Over the years, the UDA had shown concern lest some sort of special status or privileges be accorded to Republican prisoners, and that the Loyalist prisoners would be overlooked. Whenever there had been rumours that HMG was about to make a move, the number of Loyalist prisoners on the blanket had gone up, and Andy Tyrie had 'gone into action, without much success, to try to get the world to realize that there are Loyalists in gaol.' The UVF, who did not by and large get on well with the UDA, had been conspicuous in this context, principally for their prisoners feuding with UDA prisoners. Their principal demand had been for segregation, both from Republican prisoners and from other Loyalist prisoners.

Once the hunger strike became a certainty, and following the 23 October announcement of the clothing concession, the UDA, sometimes alone, sometimes jointly with its political affiliate, the New Ulster Political Research Group (NUPRG), had come out with a series of statements, 'muddled and superficially contradictory. Tyrie's problem is to say and do simultaneously a number of things which are scarcely compatible.' He wanted to 'be in on the act' if any concessions were made, and yet not align himself with Republican demands. He wanted to persuade his following that the situation now in the Republican camp was akin to the Easter Rising, and that massive sectarian violence was about to break out. To appear responsible he urged restraint, but at the same time had been 'fully behind' that year's Loyalist assassinations, and 'strongly endorsed the policy of picking off' what he described as 'known Republicans'. A UDA statement of 29 October of its intent to eliminate such people had 'of course' provoked calls for its proscription, but there had been subsequent statements somewhat backtracking, because Tyrie, 'while pretending not to mind the prospect', wanted to avoid the proscription of the UDA. The situation was thus confused and confusing,

> ...but it is probably fair to say that ... the UDA do not care what HMG does provided the Loyalist prisoners get whatever may be on offer to the Republicans: that they will pursue their long-established but (at least until recently) increasingly effective terrorist campaign: and that they are ambivalent as to whether they want to raise or lower the temperature on the streets. They certainly want to be ready for sectarian violence should it come.

There was less information on which to base an assessment of UVF attitudes. Essentially, they too wanted to dissociate themselves from the Republican prisoners, while enjoying any changes in regime the latter may get. The UVF following was 'tiny' compared to that of the UDA, and they did not have the same potential for mass influence. Thus, as far as the Government was concerned, 'The Message' it needed to send out was as follows:

> Our predominant concern must be to reassure the Protestant community that:
>
> a) the security situation is under control;
> b) HMG plans no precipitate action in the political field.

> We must convince them that on H Blocks and the hunger strike we intend to stand firm on our present public position – ie that while we will continue in our endeavours to operate a humanitarian prison regime there is no question of our making any concessions which would be tantamount to conceding political status (and we must bear in mind that for most of the vocal Protestant community any move at all will be evidence that HMG is on the way down the slippery slope).
> We must also show clean hands in respect of 'deals with the enemy' – a favourite Unionist charge. This means careful and honest presentation of any talks we may have with Catholic churchmen including in particular Cardinal Ó Fiaich and Bishop Daly. It also means we must be more careful

than ever not to give cause for allegations that we are improperly in touch with intermediaries such as Fathers Reid, Faul ... or with other potential PIRA representatives such as Councillor Canning [in Dungannon].[11]

One of the key factors restricting any Government concession to the hunger-strikers was the feared reaction in the Protestant community; the counterbalance was trying to appease the Catholic community as well. Cardinal Ó Fiaich and Bishop Daly had pronounced themselves as 'deeply disappointed' that the announcement 'stops short of what is demanded in the situation.' In H3, Sands and Hughes had studied Atkins statement. After an all-night conference, the prisoners rejected the Government's offer, seeing it as an attempt to undermine the hunger strike. Sands accused the Government of engaging in 'a cruel piece of teasing and political brinkmanship in an attempt to defuse the momentum and growing support for the blanketmen'. The wearing of 'our own clothes we regard as a basic human right and as only one of our five demands ... We are not criminals and we are ready and willing to meet an agonizing death on hunger strike to establish we are political prisoners.'

Sands, as he told to a Sinn Fein official – in a smuggled comm – believed that the British offer was a sign of weakness, and that all the prisoners demands could be secured. He urged the official to get a message to the 'people in the districts' that 'with more active support and pressure we can badger them totally.' Sands also noted: 'Screws morale [is] at [an] all-time low following concessions bid yesterday. They'll be sickened before it's all over.' That night, Hughes, after lights out, made a speech to the other prisoners describing the approach of the 'final battle': some men on the wing would probably die before the battle was won, but, he added, there were casualties in any war. 'Whenever you went on any Army job outside you ran the risk of dying ... The same applies in here.' There was no alternative to the hunger strike given 'the Brit enemy's callousness toward us.' Hughes concluded by urging his comrades to: 'Be true to your people and be faithful to the Republic.'

Tommy McKearney, one of the men who would be going on hunger strike, then spoke a few words, ending his speech with the phrase that Spartan mothers told their sons before going to battle: 'Come home with your shield – or on it.' When somebody light-heartedly shouted: 'Sure, we'll be carrying you shoulder-high round The Moy!' (in County Tyrone, where McKearney hailed from), he answered: 'In a coffin'.[12] Seven hunger-strikers were named to begin their strike by refusing breakfast on Monday 27 October. They were:

> Brendan Hughes (PIRA);
> John Nixon (INLA);
> Thomas McFeely (PIRA);

Raymond McCartney (PIRA);
Leo Green (PIRA);
Sean McKenna (PIRA); and
Thomas McKearney (PIRA).

The scene was now set for the beginning of the trial of strength between the Thatcher Government and the prisoners. The Government was aware that intelligence in the days leading up to the hunger strike demonstrated considerable confusion in the minds of the PIRA leadership with regard to how best to use terrorism in support of the hunger-strikers. Their dilemma was 'obvious: can they cajole and bludgeon at the same time?' Most reports suggested that cajolery was at least temporarily the order of the day. There was, for example, intelligence that attacks on off-duty UDR, RUC and prison officers were to be suspended; Gerry Adams was reported to have insisted on a disclaimer of the shooting of a UDR woman in Strabane on 13 October. How firm this policy was, or how rigorously it could be held to, remained to be seen, and it seemed unlikely that it would be sustained indefinitely, if only because it was in such conflict with the leadership's earlier determination to intensify the campaign that winter. As a member of the Relatives Action Committee (concerned about the bad publicity of the Strabane murder) put it: 'How can we give up the war when that's what they are in gaol for?' What did seem likely was that 'Adams is giving the most careful thought to how and when best to use terrorism in support of the prisoners. And it is highly probable that even if terrorism in the Province is kept at a low pitch, efforts will be made to mount attacks on the mainland and against British targets abroad.' There had been good intelligence in the past that this would be the PIRA's policy in the event of a hunger strike. Recent reports had suggested that IRA Active Service Units (ASUs) had been prepared for the British mainland (possibly originally as part of the 'winter campaign'), and an important recent Irish police find of explosives and explosive devices was also certainly bound for either the UK mainland or the Continent. However, the PIRA's capacity for such activity was 'currently limited.'[13]

As the hunger strike began, Atkins asked his officials for urgent consideration to be given to the likely developments surrounding the Maze protest, which might require of Ministers decisions or statements of a 'political rather than an operational kind'. The assessment of some of the elements of the way in which the protest might develop were based on discussion at two meetings, on 29 October, between the NIO (including Prisons Branch and Liaison Staff), the Army's Chief of Staff and the RUC Deputy Chief Constable. The operational contingency planning was considered by two Co-ordinating Committees – one of which was chaired by the NIO's John Blelloch, a Deputy Secretary who would emerge as one of the key British figures in the ensuing events. This review concluded that the aim of the

Provisionals was to sustain a campaign of peaceful demonstrations attracting mass support from the Catholic community. To this end, they were prepared to consider limiting their violence so as not to alienate the 'humanitarian lobby', though such limitation would not affect attacks on uniformed security forces, or exclude attacks on the British 'mainland', and might not be obeyed by all PIRA and INLA groups. These tactics presented the security forces with a dilemma that had been familiar throughout the campaign: 'Too firm a hand in dealing with initially peaceful demonstrations may provoke the Catholic community and set back the progress made in establishing the acceptability of the RUC. Too loose a rein may outrage the Loyalists and cause some of them to take the law into their own hands.'

It was concluded that this phase of the campaign surrounding the Maze protest was likely to come to an end at a point that was as yet unpredictable. Clearly, a death or deaths among the hunger-strikers would be a highly emotive event with incalculable consequences. But even before this, the Provisionals were likely to be faced with the failure of the campaign because HMG was not going to give way on their demands. Their resulting frustration would tempt them to try to re-run the events of 1968–1970, deliberately seeking to provoke reaction from the Protestants and the police so that once again they could pose as the sole, and necessary, defenders of the Catholic community. It was not yet entirely clear what the UDA/UVF plan was, and they were probably not yet clear themselves, but a continuing campaign of assassination against leading Republicans was to be expected, and might in itself force a change of strategy upon extreme Republicans. As in the early stages of the Troubles, Dr Paisley's 'brutal oratory', particularly if other Unionist politicians felt they had no choice but to climb on this 'bandwagon', had the capacity to inflame passions in both communities.

None of these elements should be seen in isolation; they were all interconnected. A variety of disconnected events (an incident involving the security forces; the assassination of a Loyalist politician) could produce a quite sudden change of community temper. The operational requirement to act sensitively was fully recognized by the security forces. But there was also a political requirement for steps to break up the cohesion on the Maze protest issue that was building in each of the Protestant and Catholic communities, and to seduce moderates away from extremists. HMG 'should not be left as a lone voice pleading for cool heads. We must get others to speak.' The key figures were the Protestant church leaders, the cross-community Alliance Party, John Hume, the leader of the SDLP, 'the Cardinal' and Bishop Daly. The Cardinal and Bishop Daly were 'at the moment not under control. They feel that they have been slighted by HMG and are sulking.' For this reason, and because 'any formal meeting initiated from our side would be taken as a sign that we are contemplating moves which we are not contemplating, it is difficult for the Secretary of State to meet them now in order to urge them to raise their voices against violence or actions which could lead to violence. But we need to maintain contact.'

There was a possible further category of development in which essentially political, rather than violent, influences inside or outside Northern Ireland sought to play a role of their own. The possible permutations were too numerous to delineate in summary. The left wing of the Labour Party (Charter 80), the US President, Charles Haughey, various humanitarian bodies (such as Amnesty), Churchmen; any of these and many more could erupt onto the scene with ready-made solutions or offers of mediation. In the same context within Northern Ireland, the 'respectable' political parties on either side of the divide might seek to wrest the initiative away from paramilitary leaders by some initiative of their own: 'Our response will need to be tested against the two legs of our own policy; no go on political status but flexibility on genuinely humanitarian issues.'[14]

The battle would be for public opinion, which meant getting the public tone right. As Julie Ireland, of the NIO's Political Affairs Branch (PAB), commented on a submission by the Secretary of State: 'we need to seduce moderates away from the extremists in both communities. But are we going to achieve this, at least as far as the Catholic community is concerned, through a line as tough as that taken in the outline speech …? We must be firm, but we must also be seen to be reasonable.' She had two points to make on the speech:

(a) It is surely counterproductive to say that PIRA are, or are about to be, defeated. In any case, nobody is going to believe that if the hunger strike fails, the PIRA will disappear. They will have lost a major battle, but not the war.

(b) What do we mean when we talk about the 'failure' of the hunger strike? It will be perceived to mean the hunger strikers will die without winning political status. This is not an event we should appear to be eagerly awaiting – as the outline speech might be taken to imply. The Government does not want the hunger strikers to die, and it should say so.

If HMG was to avoid falling into the PIRA's 'delicate trap, we must stand firm on political status, but we must be seen to be concerned, both about the hunger-strikers and the situation PIRA are trying to create.' HMG could emphasize – as did the outline speech – that the PIRA was trying to exacerbate inter-community tensions. HMG could encourage the two communities to see each other's point of view. ('Would you like the Shankill Butchers to get political status?' was one message that might have been employed, referring to the notorious Protestant gang of serial torturers and murderers). Perhaps HMG could also have suggested that the hunger-strikers were merely pawns in the PIRA's game: 'In brief, I am arguing for a more visibly compassionate response to the hunger strike.'[15]

S. J. Leach, also of the NIO's PAB, shared 'Miss Ireland's view that a speech by the Secretary of State which was as hard-nosed as the draft outline … might prove counterproductive.' The key section was paragraph two of the outline: 'The Provisional IRA have staked everything on a last throw. If they fail, they are defeated. If they win, all that has been achieved in the past 2 or 3 years is lost.' To Leach, this seemed 'potentially provocative: it almost amounts to "seeing the prisons as an extension of the battleground", which is precisely the sectarian failing which the speech goes on to castigate.' It was also, of course, somewhat risky to make a firm prediction that one single event – the 'failure' of the hunger strike – would lead to the defeat of the PIRA. An outcome in which all the hunger-strikers abandoned their strike without winning any concessions would be a severe blow for the PIRA, but it was far more likely that some, at least, would die, 'and even if the strike still "fails" in the sense that HMG stands firm, it could well be argued that the ramifications of such a "failure" would severely affect "all that has been achieved in the past 2 or 3 years" just as much as it would affect PIRA's credibility.' To sum up, 'although I do not quite see how HMG could actively make "a more visibly compassionate response" to the strike (as Miss Ireland suggests) without edging towards some compromise on points of principle, I do believe that we should avoid adopting an unnecessarily tough (and somewhat simplistic) public posture.'[16]

As for events in the prison, at the beginning of the strike the seven remained in their dirty cells, with three of them sharing their cells with protesters who were still taking food. On 6 November, however, all seven were moved to individual furnished cells in a wing of H-3 Block to facilitate medical supervision. The hunger-strikers did not foul or damage their cells, and prison staff commented on their co-operative attitude as the strike got properly under way. During this first fortnight, the strikers were visited by their families, the prison chaplains and prison staff. On 3 November, Brendan Hughes was visited by Tim Pat Coogan, editor of the Irish Press, and by Danny Morrison of Provisional Sinn Féin. On 3 November, the Maze was filmed by a crew from Channel 5, New York. The dirty protest at the Maze, meanwhile, continued, with some 150 further prisoners joining the protest during the period. By 7 November, at HMP Maze there were 510 dirty protestors and fifty-three prisoners refusing to work. There remained twenty-eight women on a dirty form of protest at HMP Armagh.

The hunger-strikers' and the protestors' morale was reported to be high, based on optimistic reports of the development of the H-Block campaign at home and abroad. An intercepted note provided evidence of this, and referred also to twelve further candidates for the hunger strike if any of the seven should die or give up the strike.[17] Also on 7 November, the seven hunger-strikers were moved to the observation wing, where it would be easier to monitor them. Their condition was still not giving rise to concern.[18] Bobby Sands, however, was concerned: by 9 November, two weeks into the fast, he saw all the hunger-strikers during Mass except McKearney, who had a cold. He 'noticed when we shook hands that all of the boys' hands were fairly cold.' Sands noted that the hunger-strikers were 'slightly lazy, that is, they're neglecting to mention important wee points.' Hughes had recovered from an earlier kidney complaint, but was now suffering from a pain in his testicles from shouting out the prison hospital window to Sands every night, in Irish, so the prison officers could not understand him. Tom McFeely was by far the strongest-looking. The one Sands was worried about was Sean McKenna, who was 'looking by far the worst'. Most of the warders were behaving well towards the hunger-strikers, so Sands urged them to exploit the situation: 'In general, the screws are overly nice. Some are even crawling rather pathetically. I told the boys to request letters and pens', he reported in a smuggled comm.[19]

To gauge the mood in the Catholic-Nationalist community, the NIO's S. J. Leach attended the SDLP Conference at Newcastle, on 7–9 November, to monitor the party's views on the hunger strike. The H-Blocks debate took place on the evening of Friday, 7 November, on the basis of the following emergency motion from the Executive Committee:

> Conference deplores the ineptitude of the British Government's handling of the 'H' Block issue; urges that prisoners be allowed to wear their own clothing in line with progressive practice in other countries; condemns the inhuman conditions which exist in 'H' Block; calls for immediate action to implement a new regime based on respect for individual dignity; appeals to the hunger strikers to allow the matter to be settled through further discussion; reminds all who publicly comment on the issue of its potential for deepening community divisions and calls on them to direct their efforts towards a peaceful resolution of the issue.

Seamus Mallon proposed the resolution in a 'measured and sober speech', which stressed the 'potentially enormous repercussions of the hunger strike' and the corresponding determination of the SDLP to 'demonstrate responsibility and leadership in facing up to the issue and helping to resolve it by peaceful means'. He criticized HMG's handling of the clothing question, reiterated John Hume's argument that 'the only punishment to which a prisoner should be subjected is the deprivation of liberty', and urged the hunger-strikers to give up their protest in the interests of saving life, both inside and outside the prison. Finally, he asked all the speakers who followed him to watch their words with care and say nothing that might exacerbate the problem. On the whole, this injunction was followed. The recurring themes in the debate were:

— HMG's ineptitude in allowing itself to become 'a prisoner of the prisoners' demands' (in the words of Sean Farren, Chairman-elect of the Party) by failing to defuse the issue in the early stages;
— The SDLP's overriding desire to play what role it could in solving the problem and ameliorating tension and suffering; [and]
— However notwithstanding this, the fact that HMG was in the driving seat and alone had the power, through re-examining its position, to resolve the crisis through humanitarian measures.

A number of speakers, most notably Paddy Duffy, argued that while the SDLP would always be opposed to political status, the five demands contained nothing exceptionable on humanitarian grounds, and should be supported. (On the specific issue of clothing, he commented that he thought there was a great deal of mileage in 'the tracksuit proposal', under which prisoners could continue to wear in their cells the sportswear used for exercise.) Michael Canavan's speech included a condemnation of those 'on the extreme wing of the Irish tradition' who were trying to present the dispute as a fight for Irish unity. After an unsuccessful attempt from the floor to amend the motion to record party support for all five demands (not just the clothing one), the motion was passed unanimously.

This concluded the formal consideration of the issue, although the presence of about 100 'Smash H-Block' demonstrators outside the conference hotel was a feature of the following day's proceedings. The pickets, who had produced a carefully drafted handout for the occasion, failed to gain entry to the hotel, although at one stage, when an attempt to do so seemed imminent, John Hume and Seamus Mallon went out to talk to them. (Challenged to say whether he would meet the National Smash H-Block Committee, Hume replied that the SDLP was a democratic party, he would certainly be willing to consider this and that the Committee should get in touch with party headquarters. Much to his annoyance, noted Leach, this was written up in at least one newspaper the following day as if he had *requested* a meeting with the Smash H-Block Committee.) The pickets made a serious attempt to disrupt Hume's keynote address to the Conference on Saturday afternoon – a demonstrator with a loudhailer succeeded in positioning himself just outside the Conference Hall, and chanted slogans throughout the speech. This, though, was entirely counterproductive: Hume determinedly succeeded in making himself heard, and delegates supported and applauded him with a vigour that was, if anything, strengthened by the presence of the hecklers.

In conversation with delegates, Leach found no significant evidence that the 'basic instincts of the Party on this question were anything but sound.' Dr Joe

Hendron (chairman of the Constituency Representatives) was typical of many in saying that his gut reaction to the strike – enhanced, if anything, by the 'blatant blackmail' attempts of the Smash H-Block Committee – was that the Government should not concede an inch. He was also typical, however, in continuing by saying that, as a politician concerned for the survival of his party, he had to go beyond gut reaction: it was undeniable that the issue was a very emotive one for people who voted SDLP, and the party would suffer increasingly if it was not resolved. Sean Farren also stressed the hunger strike's potential to damage the party: if hunger-strikers actually died, the electoral consequences in 1981 could be severe. The SDLP would never compromise in its opposition to political status, but criticism of the Government would become even more intense if no move were made on 'humanitarian' grounds to solve the issue. Leach heard many complaints about the handling of HMG's decision not to allow the prisoners to wear their own clothing: the general view was that although this would not have stopped the strike, it would have scuppered the chances of attracting much popular support, putting the SDLP in a much easier position. Paddy Duffy stressed to Leach that one factor in the current reaction was the clear impression among the minority population that the Cardinal and Bishop Daly had been 'conned'. Like many others, Duffy believed – 'and I found it difficult to shake him', lamented Leach – that HMG had in fact intended to permit prisoners to wear their own clothes, and had resiled from this as a result of Loyalist pressure.

To sum up, Leach found that delegates very much wanted the strike to be resolved through movement by HMG to accommodate some or all of the five demands, but principally clothing, on humanitarian grounds. On the other hand, they were totally opposed to any concessions on the 'political status' question, which would strengthen the credibility of the Provisionals. When pressed on this contradiction, most argued that the hunger strike was the result of HMG's ineptitude, and it was therefore up to HMG to sort it out. Seamus Mallon commented that although the resolution set out the party's willingness to play its part in settling the issue, in practice the ball was in HMG's court, and the SDLP had no intention of sticking its neck out unless it felt reasonably sure that this would contribute to a positive settlement. For the same reasons, the party would not be going out of its way in public to stress those aspects of the issue that were helpful to HMG. Finally, Leach had a brief discussion with John Hume at lunch on Sunday, 9 November. He made two important points:

(i) At his meeting with the Secretary of State and PUS on 5 November he had taken pains to clarify the areas which HMG regarded as points of principle. Arising out of this he had had some ideas – which he was still working on – which he thought might provide a way out.

(ii)   However he had no intention of falling into the same trap as the Cardinal and Bishop Daly, who had incurred all the disadvantages of appearing to be negotiating on behalf of the H-Block protesters, although they did not in fact know what the protesters would accept as the price of calling off this action. If and when he came forward with a proposal, the Secretary of State could be sure that it was guaranteed to achieve the desired result. (He also mentioned that Bishop Daly, whom he had seen last week, remained sore.)[20]

Mike Bohill, also of the Political Affairs Branch, had attended the Conference and forwarded a few supplementary comments on Leach's minute. His central comments were:

(a)   H-Blocks hung like a cloud over the whole weekend. The urgency of the issue forced other aspects – constitutional progress, the economy etc – into the shade.

(b)   I doubt if there were more than a handful out of the 500 who attended the conference who did not perceive the H-Blocks issue in any terms other than humanitarian. No-one urged political status; the Secretary of State can rest assured that he has complete support on that point. Only Paddy Duffy (and his Cookstown Branch) sought special category status, but did not make any headway. On the other hand, there was a widespread and honestly-held conviction amongst rank and file members that HMG was directly responsible for the appalling conditions of H-block, for the present impasse, and for the hunger strike.

(c)   There was widespread sympathy for the 5 demands (excepting anything explicitly inferring political status), but especially the clothing issue. Few if any saw, or at least would admit, any contradiction in terms with their rejection of political status. Their argument was presented in simple and stark terms: deprivation of freedom was punishment enough. What HMG was doing in H-Blocks was imposing additional punishments which could not be justified on humanitarian grounds. (Even the most vile murderers have their dignity, and this human dignity must be respected.) This, and only this, was the issue with which the SDLP was concerned.

(d)   This sense of injustice ran so deep that I am personally aware of at least two leading SDLP figures who signed the book of support which Saturday's protesters produced – but only after deleting the words with other political prisoners from demand no 3.
So long as the H-Blocks issue is regarded as primarily a matter of humanitarian concern, it is inevitable that SDLP support for the protesting prisoners demands will grow; at the same time, however, it will be mirrored

by a growing – if forlorn – call to the protesters to call off the hunger strike.

(e) Unlike Mr Leach, I found no evidence to support the view that allowing the prisoners to wear their own clothes would not have prevented the hunger strike. On the contrary, Paddy O'Hanlon was emphatic that it would have and that, even now, it would stop the strike if introduced. As you are aware, he usually has his ear fairly close to the ground in S[outh] Armagh. Rory McShane, a leading Newry solicitor and rising young SDLP star, was similarly sure.[21]

On 14 November, Mike Bohill took a call from Arthur Keenan, HMG's Civilian Representative (CIVREP), who passed on the information that Jim Canning, the Nationalist councillor identified as a possible backchannel, had made contact with him earlier that morning. Canning reported that another person, Byrne, had seen both Tommy McKearney and McKearney's father. Byrne claimed that 'McKearney Jnr' had indicated that the hunger strike revolved around only two issues: the clothes and work issues. The other three issues 'can be dismissed.' McKearney had made it clear to Byrne that, on the clothes issue, they were not ruling out completely the wearing of prison uniform, but that it should be up to them to decide/have a say in when and under what circumstances. On the work question, they similarly sought greater flexibility on what should constitute work. McKearney Jnr had again confirmed to Byrne that he was prepared to die if these two issues were not resolved. McKearney Snr confirmed that he would stand by his son's decision.[22]

Despite the widespread concern in the Nationalist community, one of the main problems for those supporting the hunger-strikers was drumming up public support for them. On 16 November, a protest march, organized by the National H-Block/Armagh Committee (NHAC) was held in Downpatrick. Mike Bohill took an interest in it: 'Together with two temporary P[olitical] A[ffairs] B[ranch] conscripts (one aged 9 years, the other 3 years), I attended the smallest of yesterday's three H-Blocks protest marches', he reported to his superiors. Since he had no desire to be seen as a sympathizer, he limited his presence to observing the preliminaries, viewing the march, and listening to the speeches at the march's ultimate destination. The points he considered noteworthy were:

(a) The march was poorly attended. About 300 marched – the vast majority being male teenagers, together with a handful of men, women and children...

(b) The organisation was good. There were plentiful supplies of banners and placards, and stewards to keep the march orderly...

(a) The band which led the march had to be bussed in from Annalong (over 20 miles away), despite the fact the East Down area has a plentiful supply of its own brass/silver/pipe bands.

(b) There were no major local figures present. All the speakers, stewards and organizers – together with a sizeable number of marchers – were from outside the area. There were no clergy involved.

(a) Few turned out to watch the march during its two-mile journey, despite the band and the fairly mild weather.

(b) The speeches at the end of the march were predictable and unremarkable.

All in all, the organizers 'cannot have been encouraged by the response', he concluded.[23]

Meanwhile, David Gilliland and D. J. Wyatt, from the NIO, spent an hour with Bishop Edward Daly in Derry on 19 November. Wyatt recalled:

We had a friendly and relaxed conversation. He was manifestly glad to have this opportunity to re-establish contact about the Maze Prison protest on a confidential basis. I think we were entirely successful in re-establishing friendly relations. We agreed that the events of 23 October were water over the dam, and the Bishop professed himself content that there had been no intention to deceive him or the Cardinal. We would, he said, have noted that no such suggestion had ever emanated from him or the Cardinal.

The Bishop was much more honest than Wyatt had expected in admitting that no moves that were possible for the Government to make would satisfy the strikers, who would take any concessions and ask for more. He did not believe that if HMG had given prisoners the right to wear their own clothing that this would have headed off the hunger strike. His concern was rather that the Government should do everything in its power to show itself to be so reasonable and humane that even though the hunger strike might continue, the community would refuse to support it. Daly was very worried that all the hard work that had been put in by many people, not least the police, in turning the community away from support for the Provisionals was now being undone. He had made his resolute opposition to the hunger strike and its supporters as clear as he could, and had instructed the clergy in his Diocese not to offer the demonstrators any kind of support. The Bishop thought that at some time the Government would have to make some further move to demonstrate its concern over the protest. Choosing the correct time, which was probably not yet, would be important. It would be equally important that the response of community leaders should be orchestrated in advance; people should not be taken by surprise. Apart from a 'rather unconvinced' reference to some ideas floated by one of the Maze chaplains, Father Toner, at his meeting with Michael Alison earlier in the week, Bishop Daly 'did not appear to have any ideas about where we go from here.'[24]

On 20 November, it was decided to administer the prison wing containing the hunger-strikers with staff from the prison hospital. In response to this, the seven hunger-strikers, continuing their co-operation with prison staff, decided to take baths and asked for pyjamas. They also said that in future they would slop out, which prison officers had been doing for them prior to that time. Hughes asked for association with the other hungers-strikers, and Nixon requested a haircut. These responses by the hunger-strikers amounted to conforming with the prison regime. The seven were treated from this point as sick, conforming prisoners. By 21 November, the hunger-strikers had lost between 9 and 14lbs, but their health still gave no cause for concern. At this time there were 482 dirty protestors and 30 prisoners on a no-work protest.

The number of women protesters at Armagh remained at 28, but there were increasing rumours that a number of women prisoners were about to begin a hunger strike in support of the demand for political status. These rumours were supported by requests by the women prisoners to take their additional privilege visits for November in order to inform relatives of their intentions. It was rumoured that among the female hungers-strikers would be Mairead Farrell (their spokeswoman), Mary Doyle and Christine Beattie. The Republican Press Centre in Belfast confirmed that three or four women prisoners at HMP Armagh were expected to go on hunger strike in the near future. Their statement said that this action 'would remove the simple concession of civilian clothes from being a central issue' and would 'clarify (the women's) demands and those of the H-Block protesters as a package of five demands amounting to political status.' The morale of protesters, hunger-strikers and the prison staff was assessed by the NIO as remaining high, although the initial momentum of increasing numbers joining the dirty protest in support of the hunger strike had dropped away and was continuing to decline gradually.[25]

As the confrontation slowly built towards its conclusion, an internal NIO paper, 'The Hunger Strike – Looking Ahead', considered ways in which the hunger strike and special category status campaign might develop, the options open to HMG against the overall background of the Provisional campaign and the Government's political and security aims. By this stage the seven hunger-strikers had been refusing food for 28 days. By about Christmas their condition was likely to be critical. The Government's established aims were:

(a) To end the hunger strike without increasing the polarisation of the two communities.

(b) To break the campaign for political status; success in this will remove a potentially divisive element from the NI political scene and destroy a propaganda weapon abroad: even more important, it will deny the Provisionals what they regard as a central objective.

These aims were wholly consistent with, and were part of, the Government's wider policy for political development and the full establishment of law and order. As part of that policy, 'we have sought to retain the confidence and co-operation of the majority of the Catholic community (who have over the last few years identified themselves with our policy) without at the same time alienating the Protestants.'

The hunger strike, meanwhile, 'finds PIRA at a crossroads. It follows a period of some 18 months during which PIRA have suffered severe attrition. They are in military difficulties, and there are signs that the PIRA leadership are becoming disenchanted with the prospects of success in the military campaign and are concerned by Security Force effectiveness on both sides of the border and their own inadequate response to it.' NIO Liaison Staff had work in hand to try to establish what was going on within the IRA leadership and how it might decide to handle the terrorist campaign. But there had been enough signals, when looked at as a whole over the previous twelve months, to suggest that the leadership might be looking for a way out. Possibilities included a *de facto* ceasefire and a split in the organization. At the same time, there had been firm intelligence from a variety of sources that the PIRA was also trying to mount major terrorist activity. This could, in the PIRA's eyes, be a last fling to try to put themselves into a good negotiating position, or the start of a new period of effectiveness, or, more loosely, represented an alternative policy option to be run in tandem with bringing the campaign to an end, 'it being in the lap of the gods and the Security Forces which option wins.'

'The Hunger Strike – Looking Ahead' argued that the hunger strike could not have come at a worse moment for the leadership, since it threw into further confusion the already complicated policy problems with which they had been confronted over the last year or so. It was clear that the strike was not of their choice or to their liking, but it had also been evident that the leadership saw the plight of the prisoners as a chance for the PIRA to regain popular support, particularly if the campaign in support of them and reactions to HMG's handling of the issue triggered off sectarian violence and revalidated the PIRA's claim to be defenders of the Catholic community. This aspect of the problem was not an easy one for them to handle: 'they can coax or bludgeon but not both at once.'

Many of the points touched on were explored in greater detail in the paper: 'But one important factor to bear in mind throughout this ensuing discussion is the inter-relationship between the Provisional military campaign, the Political Status Campaign and the hunger strike.' Political status was an essential part of what the PIRA was fighting for: recognition of their legitimacy as a prelude to 'Brits out' and an amnesty for their prisoners. To come to any accommodation that ruled out the achievement of that objective would be such a fundamental blow to all the movement stood for in that it 'would almost certainly be its death warrant.' The hunger strike, although part of Republican tradition, was not a weapon they would at this moment have chosen to use to try to secure political status, partly because they did not believe that HMG was prepared to cave in, or even subscribe to a face-saving (for the PIRA) compromise. Equally, because of the huge number of their men who were now in gaol, the PIRA was deeply constrained in a way that their predecessors in the 1935–42 and 1956–62 campaigns were not. They could not accept terms or bow silently out with thousands of their men liable to serve a large part of their lives in gaol: 'The prisons issue cannot be disentangled from the campaign as a whole.' In terms of what was to follow, none of the hunger-strikers at this point gave any real cause for medical concern. Some reports said that their morale was good and their resolution firm. At least some of them were probably willing to fast until death. Several things, however, had been going against the Provisionals:

(a) There are reports that some of the strikers are wavering and want to deal a deal on less than the five demands;

(b) there have also been signs that some of the PIRA/PSF leadership are inclined to such a deal;

(c) the Provisionals' campaign of support has not really got going;

(d) indeed the campaign has actually lost a good deal of the moderate support with which it started; [and]

(e) the Provisionals believe that the Government will not give in, and are bound to have been reinforced in this belief by ministerial statements.

It was a matter of judgement whether these indications meant that if HMG did nothing then the hunger strike would collapse – and if so, whether it would collapse before or after a death. The Provisional IRA was showing signs of panic, but they were also showing signs of preparing themselves for a renewed military effort. On balance it did not seem likely that the hunger strike, or the campaign in support of it, would collapse in the immediate future. Indeed it seemed quite probable that, as the existing tactics appeared to be producing too little progress for the Provisionals, they would seek to raise the stakes. Reports of the PIRA's intentions were conflicting, reflecting the views of different elements in their leadership. One report spoke of an Intention to mount a thirty-two county campaign, while others spoke of action in the six counties only. There were also contrary reports of co-ordinated action and of licence for individual groups to 'do their own thing'. 'We cannot at present predict the precise pattern which will emerge' admitted the paper. [26]

By 28 November, the seven hunger-strikers were receiving daily medical examinations, and although their condition gave no immediate cause for concern, their blood analysis showed signs of deterioration. On 27 November, the Prison Medical Officer had decided that the hunger-strikers were no longer strong enough to receive visitors in the prison visiting area. Arrangements were therefore made for visits to take place in two empty cells in the hunger-strikers' wing. The hunger-strikers again received visits from relatives and parish priests. Eilish Kelly continued to visit several of the strikers, as well as Pat Finucane (another solicitor and member of the National Smash H-Blocks Committee), both ostensibly visiting on legal matters. Finucane's brother was a dirty protester at the same time. On 25 November, McFeely was visited by a Fergus Black, who was described as a friend or relative. Black turned out to be a reporter from the *Irish Press*. The *Irish Press* of 26 November published a report of the interview with McFeely, in which he claimed that morale was high, although McKearney's condition was giving cause for concern. McFeely was quoted as saying: 'We are all going downhill fast, but there will be no compromise. We are going all the way … if there are repercussions it won't be our fault. It will be the British Government's.'[27] By this point, the number of dirty protestors had reduced to 470, and the number of prisoners on a no-work protest had dropped to 17. There were now 29 female prisoners at Armagh on their own form of dirty protest. Rumours still abounded that some of the women would begin a hunger strike on Monday 1 December. Token three-day fasts by seven Republican remand prisoners at a time had begun at Belfast Prison.

On 2 December, the seven hunger-strikers were transferred to the Prison Hospital. This move was to facilitate closer medical surveillance rather than the result of any significant deterioration in the strikers' health. They continued to receive daily medical examinations, and although there was no undue cause for concern, three had complained of minor ailments, nausea, headaches and vomiting. As expected, three female prisoners had begun a hunger strike on 1 December. The three strikers were Mairead Farrell, Mary Elizabeth Doyle and Margaret Mary Nugent. Their weight loss by 5 December ranged from 8 to 10lbs. They had been moved to one clean, furnished cell on 3 December, and had not fouled it in any way. They were receiving daily medical examinations, and their condition gave no cause for concern. The number of dirty protesters by 5 December was 468, and there were 15 prisoners refusing to work. At Armagh, 26 women prisoners remained on their dirty protest.

The seven male hunger-strikers remained in the Prison Hospital and continued to receive daily medical examinations. During this period they were also examined by a consultant physician. The condition of five of the strikers remained weak but satisfactory. The conditions of McKenna and McKearney, however, had deteriorated, and were giving some cause for concern. Both were having difficulty in holding down the water with salt that they had been taking. McKenna had not been well enough to take association with the others from 11 December, and it was clear that the time was approaching when he and possibly others would have to be moved to an outside hospital for more intensive medical surveillance.[28]

NOTES

1   TNA CJ4/3025 Atkins to Prime Minister, 15 November 1979.
2   PRONI NIO/12/153A Atkins to Penhaligon, 30 November 1979.
3   PRONI NIO/12/184A European Commission of Human Rights Partial Decision on the Application by 4 Republican Protesters at Maze, June 1980, A Summary.
4   Ed Moloney,. *Voices From the Grave: Two Men's War in Ireland.* (2010) Faber & Faber. p. 105.
5   O'Hearn *op.cit.* pp. 275–276.
6   TNA CJ4/3023 Report of visit to the Department of Justice, Dublin, 6–7 October 1980.
7   O'Hearn *op.cit.* p. 280.
8   PRONI NIO/12/189 A. S. C. Jackson to PS/Mr Alison Further letter from Father Reid, 20 October 1980.
9   TNA CJ4/3039 Secretary of State's meeting with Cardinal Ó Fiaich – 4.30 p.m. on 23 October in the Northern Ireland Office, London.
10 TNA CJ4/3039 Political.
11 TNA CJ4/3023 The Protestant Community.
12 O'Hearn *op.cit.* 285–287.
13 TNA CJ4/3039 Possible Developments on the Hunger Strike and Related Activity, 30 October 1980.
14 TNA CJ4/3039 The Maze Protest: A 'Political' Scenario, 30 October 1980.
15 TNA CJ4/3039 The Maze Protest, 3 November 1980.
16 TNA CJ4/3039 The Maze Protest, 4 November 1980.
17 PRONI NIO/12/196A The Republican Hunger Strikes: 27 October–19 December 1980.
18 TNA CJ4/3030 Note of a meeting held in Mr Davenport's Room, Stormont House Annexe at 11.00 on Friday, 7 November 1980.
19 O'Hearn *op.cit.* p. 290.
20 TNA CJ4/3039 Hunger Strike: SDLP Views.
21 TNA CJ4/3039 SDLP Conference and Hunger Strike.
22 TNA CJ4/3039 Bohill to Gee, 14 November 1980.
23 TNA CJ4/3039 For the record, 17 November 1980.
24 TNA CJ4/3041 Bishop Daly Bishop Daly, 20 November 1980.
25 PRONI NIO/12/196A The Republican Hunger Strikes: 27 October–19 December 1980.
26 TNA CJ4/3023 The Hunger Strike – Looking Ahead.
27 PRONI NIO/12/196A The Republican Hunger Strikes: 27 October–19 December 1980.
28 PRONI NIO/12/196A The Republican Hunger Strikes: 27 October–19 December 1980.

Chapter 4

The Collapse of the
First Hunger Strike

The NIO, in the meantime, continued to cultivate its relationship with non-violent Nationalism. As instructed, D. J. Wyatt met with John Hume in Derry. Hume said that this was in pursuance of his discussion with the PUS the previous week. Wyatt explained to Hume that the Secretary of State had it in mind to do three things at the end of the week. He would put out a summary of the ECHR findings, both those that supported the Government and those that were critical. He would publish a summary of the prison regime, regarding which there was still a lack of understanding concerning the facilities available to prisoners. He would make a statement of the Government's position that would state where HMG stood on political status; draw attention to the dangers of sectarian conflict; and place the Government's readiness to keep the regime under review in the context of the ECHR Report.

Wyatt showed Hume the draft that the NIO had prepared. Hume thought it 'very hardline', but after further discussion agreed that he would come out in support of it, though suggesting some minor amendments. Hume also announced that he would be visiting Dublin, on 3 December, to seek to get Charles Haughey and the leaders of the other main Irish political parties, Garret FitzGerald (Fine Gael) and Frank Cluskey (Labour), to make a helpful public response. This was important to him, his own position demanding that he did not permit himself to become politically isolated. Wyatt said that it should be understood quite clearly that if he spoke to his friends in the South he did so on his own behalf and not as an emissary of HMG. Hume entirely took the point, saying that his trip to Dublin was 'my business not yours'. He was very keen to get on the early evening television. He and Wyatt agreed on several important points that needed to be communicated clearly:

(a) He totally opposed the demand for political status.
(b) The Secretary of State had not promised him anything going beyond what would be in the Secretary of State's own statement following the meeting.

(c) In referring to calling off the strike 'to allow discussion', Mr Hume did not mean discussion with the strikers.

(d) The international aspect in relation to other governments facing terrorism was rightly important to the British Government.

They concluded by agreeing that 'our mutual concern was not with the problems the hunger-strikers had brought upon themselves but with the problems which might arise as between the two communities in Northern Ireland, and the Catholic community and the Government.'[1] Hume also wished to be reassured that the forthcoming meeting between the Taoiseach and the Prime Minister 'would not steal his thunder.' Wyatt thought that he was talking about the hunger strike, but on that he appeared to be relaxed. His concern was rather that there would be some breakthrough on politics. Wyatt said that Hume 'knew what we were about; we were engaged in reversing the 60 years of Ireland and Britain drifting apart.' This was not going to happen dramatically. The next meeting between the Taoiseach and the Prime Minster would merely be a step on the long road. At this point, 'Hume's Irishness became apparent; he commented that we would meet with opposition if we were trying to persuade Ireland to come back into the fold!'

The two men then spoke about the announcement on clothing on 23 October. Hume thought 'we had done well to bruise the feelings of Cardinal and Bishop Daly. This had brought them back in with the other Bishops who were more "conservative".' Wyatt commented that the Nationalist *Irish News* had taken a generally helpful line. Hume seemed surprised that Wyatt regarded this as worthy of remark. The reason was that Bishop Philbin was, through nominees, a substantive shareholder in the *Irish News*, 'and had given them their marching orders.' Hume implied that 'he had a hand in keeping Bishop Philbin on the path of reason.' Wyatt also spent some time emphasizing to Hume that it was important to keep the Protestant community calm since they, like the Catholics, could cause violence on the streets. HMG's difficulty was that there was nobody who spoke for the Protestant community who was prepared to exercise the right kind of influence. Hume thought that Andy Tyrie was probably better able than most Loyalists to see what was in his best interests and to deliver his followers. Wyatt said firmly that the Government could not be seen talking to paramilitary leaders from either side, which Hume accepted. They then had some discussion about politics. Hume felt that it was insufficiently appreciated that at the SDLP Conference he had taken political risks in advocating a ten-year limit on power-sharing and accepted that no institutional Irish dimension between Northern Ireland and the Republic could be brought about, except with the consent of a devolved government in the North. Since the Protestants had the majority, these two safeguards ought to have given them all they wanted. Wyatt recorded the point, not because it was new, but because Hume was concerned to emphasize that, once again, there were limits to how far he could go without losing his followers.[2]

Against this background, Humphrey Atkins made a significant statement on the hunger strike, to the House of Commons, on 4 December. He did so in order to set out the 'real facts' about the living conditions that were open to all prisoners in Northern Ireland, and explain the special measures that had already been taken on humanitarian grounds in respect of the living conditions of the protesting prisoners. The Secretary of State reiterated that the Government would not concede political status. The Government would not grant the five demands, 'since to do so would be to legitimise and encourage terrorist activity.' What the Government was committed to was to ensure that, for all prisoners, the regime was as enlightened and humane as possible. His statement clarified, in relation to the protesters' demands, how far this had already been achieved: under Prison Rules, prescribed under statute by the Secretary of State, prisoners were entitled to certain rights and might, if they conformed with the rules, enjoy certain privileges. Rights might not be withheld, although prisoners could – and the protesters did – choose not to take them up. Privileges, on the other hand, might be withheld if a prisoner was in breach of the rules. If prisoners abided by the rules, then the privileges were accorded as a matter of course.

The rights and privileges compared with the protesters' demands as follows. On clothing, the protesters wanted the right to wear their own clothing at all times. Prison Rules required prisoners to wear prison-issue clothing (or special clothes appropriate to their work) during normal working hours on weekdays (7.30 a.m. to 5.00 p.m.) As a privilege, though, prisoners might, unless they were engaged on orderly duties, wear their own clothing for the rest of the evening during the week and throughout the weekend. They might also wear their own clothing when receiving visits. For security reasons, colour and design of prisoners' own clothing was subject to the discretion of the Governor. 'It will thus be seen that a prisoner conforming with the rules may wear his own clothing for almost half the time he would expect to be outside his cell' noted Atkins. For the remainder of the time, the Government's decision of 23 October meant that conforming prisoners would be wearing civilian clothing issued by the prison authorities.

The protesting prisoners sought the right to refrain from prison work. Prison Rules required convicted prisoners to 'engage in useful work', and four main types of such work were undertaken. First, some prisoners undertook domestic tasks in the kitchens, dining areas, ablutions and wings. Second, an extensive range of industrial employment was provided in prison workshops. Third, vocational training was available to teach a wide range of skills. Fourth, education classes were provided during working hours (from two to twenty hours a week) to cover a wide range of prisoners' needs from remedial education to Open University courses. Classes in craft theory were given to complement the vocational training side, whilst tuition was provided in a wide range of subjects, enabling prisoners to study for Royal Society of Arts City and Guilds literacy and numeracy certificates, GCE O- and A-level certificates. In brief, while Prison Rules required a prisoner to engage in useful work, 'work' was interpreted to include orderly duties, industrial employment, vocational training and education.

On association, the protesters wanted the right to associate freely with one another. The Prison Rules provided, as a privilege, that each weekday evening for three hours, and throughout the day at weekends, prisoners had 'association', during which, within each twenty-five-cell wing, they might watch television, play indoor games, follow hobbies and exercise in the yard attached to each wing, and attend education classes. A wide range of evening classes was provided, and there was some dovetailing with daytime courses. Apart from textbooks, the Northern Ireland education and library boards provided well-stocked libraries. Books and newspapers could be taken to be read in cells. In short, said Atkins, there was already, as a privilege, association within each wing outside normal weekend working hours.

On recreation, the protesters demanded the right to organize recreational facilities. The prison regime already provided for the use of gymnasia and playing pitches in addition to the statutory exercise period of not less than one hour each day in the open air when practicable. During association periods, prisoners could use the Hobbies Room for supervised handicraft and artistic activities.

On visits, letters and parcels, the protesters demanded one visit, one parcel and one letter each week. Under Prison Rules, each prisoner enjoyed as of right one letter and one visit per month. The rules provided, as a privilege, seven additional letters per month at the expense of the prison, three additional visits and a weekly parcel. Special parcels were also allowed at Christmas, Easter and Halloween. Thus, the existing privileges were already more generous than the protesters demanded.

On remission, the prisoners demanded the restoration in full of the remission that they had lost while engaged in the protest. Prison Rules provided that a prisoner serving a term of more than one month received remission, subject to good conduct, up to one half of his sentence. This was a more generous rate of remission than was available elsewhere in the United Kingdom. Remission might be forfeited as a punishment for breach of Prison Rules, but it might be restored after subsequent good behaviour. The opportunity to regain lost remission already existed. The protesters had forfeited a substantial part of the regime described above. Nevertheless, the Government, acknowledging the injunction of the European Commission of Human Rights to keep under constant review their reaction to the protesters, had in the course of the year taken the following steps:

1. (i) On 26 March the protesting prisoners who by their failure to conform with prison rules have forfeited the privileges afforded to conforming

prisoners, were nevertheless offered exercise in sports gear, three letters in and out each month in addition to their statutory monthly letter, and two visits a month instead of one.

2. (ii) Since the later summer the protesting prisoners have been offered:
   1. *(a)* an hour's physical exercise a week;
   2. *(b)* one evening association a week in prison uniform;
   3. *(c)* access to books and newspapers (which are available in the cell blocks but not taken) in the rooms where masses are held on Sundays;
   4. *(d)* 'closed' visits (i.e. in which the prisoner is physically separated from his visitor) as an alternative to a body search; [and]
   5. *(e)* compassionate home leave on the same basis as conforming prisoners.
3. (iii) The protesting prisoners have never been denied their daily hour's exercise.

Thus, argued Atkins, the Government had shown themselves to be ready, despite the protest, to deal with the humanitarian aspects of the conditions that the protesting prisoners had imposed upon themselves.

> The Government take no pleasure in the sight of young men and women inflicting suffering on themselves and their families. We agree with the European Commission of Human Rights that, while there can be no question of their having political status, we should be ready nevertheless to deal with the humanitarian aspects of the conditions in the prisons arising from the protest.
>
> It is a matter of very great regret that changes made by the Government in response to the Commission have been rejected. We have always been and still are willing to discuss the humanitarian aspect of the prison administration in Northern Ireland with anyone who shares our concern about it.
>
> The Government remain determined that, subject always to the requirements of security and within the resources available, the progress achieved in recent years in the administration of Northern Ireland prisons should be continued to meet the legitimate needs of all concerned.[3]

In other developments, the prison chaplains, Fathers Toner and Murphy, met with NIO Deputy Under Secretary John Blelloch (alleged to have strong connections with the Security Service, MI5) to discuss the Secretary of State's statement. Blelloch began by stressing that the Government meant what it said in the statement. There could be no question of political status being granted. On this, there was no room for movement. The Government, however, was still committed to the amelioration of the prison regime, and the statement showed how far the five demands were already accommodated within the prison system. He went on to stress the immense difficulty for the Government of producing any further amelioration of the regime under the extreme duress created by the hunger strike. Fathers Toner and Murphy were left in no doubt about the Government's position. During the course of a 'rambling and sometimes confused' discussion, they made the following points:

i. the statement was an accurate presentation of prison conditions in the Maze.

ii. it would do nothing to get the prisoners off the hunger strike; if the Cardinal's and the Bishops' statement had been rejected out of hand, this would be treated in the same way.

iii. they believed that the statement was badly presented. What we needed to explain was how some movement could be found with which the existing prison rules could cope. Their specific suggestions were:

    a) Visits & Parcels: we were already going further than the demands; there was therefore no problem.

    b) Remission: the present system presented no problem.

    c) Clothing: we should allow prisoners to buy their own clothing to an approved pattern.

    d) Association: we should permit greater freedom of association in the evenings by allowing people to move around from one recreation area to another without having to seek permission each time.

    e) Work: this problem could be solved by permitting them to choose education instead of work; their choice would be guided by the Director of Education. We would find that prisoners would not be unwilling to do everyday chores such as cleaning, cooking etc.

iv. they stressed that we should not underestimate the determination of the men on hunger strike. At least five of the seven are prepared to die, and there would be others prepared to take their place. We argued that if they were so determined to die, it was unlikely that they would be bought off by such changes as the Chaplains were suggesting. They admitted that they could not guarantee that their package would have the desired affect. They merely believed from hints that had been dropped to them that it could work.

At the end of the discussion, Father Murphy said that he would be going to the Maze later that day, as would Father Toner on the following one. They would be discussing the Government's statement with the hunger-strikers. They expected the initial reaction to be very unfavourable, although the mood could change as the days went by. They asked whether they were right to keep their heads down and not to appear in the guise of mediators. The NIO officials assured them that they were right and there was nothing to negotiate about. The priests stated that they would, however, be prepared to come back to the officials with a further assessment of the mood of the hunger-strikers in the light of the Secretary of State's statement.[4]

Blelloch spoke to Father Toner again, telephoning him on 8 December. Father Murphy was with him. Murphy had been to the Maze, taking with him copies of both the Secretary of State's statement and the briefing on the ECHR findings. Toner had been to the prison separately, and both of them visited together on that day. Father Toner confirmed that the initial response of the strikers to the Secretary of State's statement had been 'hostile', and that it had, by the time of his own visit on the previous day, modified to the extent that it had become 'dismissive'. In elaboration of this, Father Toner said that, in the eyes of the prisoners, the Atkins statement was simply a recapitulation of the facts, and that while the reference to being ready to talk to those with a humanitarian concern was 'fine as far as it went', it was not of much interest to the strikers until such time as something came of these talks. Toner went on to say that the prisoners hoped that something *would* come out of them. Blelloch commented that he hoped that no one had encouraged the prisoners to think this way since the Government's position (denying political status, affirming commitment to a humanitarian regime, but no negotiations with the strikers) was absolutely firm. Toner said quickly that there was no question of him or Murphy doing any such thing; his function was to 'bounce' the statement off the prisoners and retell accurately what happened. They were 'not in a game of poker.' He said that the prisoners had entered the strike hoping that something of advantage would come out of it for them – after four years of protest that was hardly surprising – and that they were still hoping. He, for his part, had told the strikers that their action was a 'gamble', and moreover one that might not work. He had also said to them that, once the strike was over, the door would be open for further prison reform. The prisoners on the other hand wanted some evidence of this movement first. There were some signs of the prisoners' thought processes slowing up as a consequence of the strike, though there were no grounds for concern, except perhaps in the case of McKenna. He also said that, as the strike went on, there was more evidence of 'edginess and tetchiness' on the part of the prisoners, and of their becoming more short-tempered.

Father Murphy then came to the phone. In amplification of his solo visit to the Maze, he said to the strikers (in practice, Blelloch thought that this meant Brendan Hughes) that he had spoken to civil servants in the NIO who had given him the statement and the ECHR brief. He commented on the 'tenseness' he detected in the prisoners after forty days of fast. He had said that if the strikers came off the protest then the process of prison reform could begin 'reasonably quickly', but the strikers 'wouldn't listen'. On association, he had said to them that there was not much that could be added, but that he personally would support greater freedom of movement within the wings during association. Hughes commented that 'he wouldn't say "no" to that'. Blelloch asked whether he (Father Murphy) thought that such a change might be decisive in relation to the strike and the protest, but Murphy believed that what Hughes had in mind was that this might be sufficient to satisfy all of the demands rather than solely their demand on association. Blelloch pointed out, again, that there was no question of negotiation with the strikers. Father Murphy confirmed that he was quite clear about this, and indeed the prisoners would not accept either him or Father Toner as 'negotiators'. Hughes knew that that was not their present role. Reverting to his producing the statement, Father Murphy added that when it had been given to Hughes, he had read the opening passages and commented that these were simply 'a statement of fact'. Murphy had asked him to 'read on', but Hughes had made no comment on the concluding paragraphs of the statement. He had given the brief on the ECHR findings only the most cursory glance.[5] Afterwards, Blelloch reflected on the conversation:

> What I think the two Fathers were saying on this was that it might be sufficient, with regard to this one of the five demands, that prisoners be allowed to buy (or perhaps to make a contribution towards the cost of) the prison-issue civilian clothing. It is a thought which they said had only very recently occurred to them and therefore not one which they could say the prisoners would accept. Further, their language was not completely precise but they did speak of buying from 'the prison shop' and of the clothing so acquired being labelled so that the prisoners would get their own clothing back after laundering.
>
> This thought had occurred to us here as an engaging solution to this element of the five demands: it is of some interest that it has been put forward by the two chaplains.[6]

In a further effort to assess the state of feeling in the Nationalist community, Mike Bohill, of the Political Affairs Branch, met with Father Denis Newberry (whose parish was the Markets/Lower Ormeau area of Belfast) and Father Donnelly (Turf Lodge, Belfast) on 9 December to assess the mood within their parishes. Father Newberry's impression was that there was a not insignificant amount of sympathy for the plight of the hunger-strikers, and a general, and earnest, desire to see the strike ended without any loss of life. However, a variety of special factors had, during 1980, fostered a hardening of local attitudes towards the security forces – and in particular the police – so that many in the community, while holding no truck with the Provos' campaign of violence, supported the hunger-strikers out of an emotional 'herd' attachment, and as an expression of 'anti-establishment/anti-Brit' solidarity. It was this, rather than any real desire to support the Provos, which led many onto the streets, even though they suspected that it was all part of the PIRA's tactics. Father Newberry felt that the last thing the 'Provies' wanted was for HMG to give into their demands. He read the signs – the public nomination of individual 'acceptable' negotiators, the repeated calls for nothing less than 'Political status' – as all pointing in the direction of a plan to make it impossible for HMG to offer concessions so as to ensure that the hunger strike threat would go through to its inevitable conclusion. These deaths would herald the mounting of extensive rioting in Catholic ghettos, which the police would have to move in to control. At this point there would be confrontation between police and rioters, out of which would re-emerge local protectors 'to beat off the invading oppressors' and save the local Catholic communities.

Newberry was anxious that the NIO should not underestimate the explosive situation should a hunger-striker die, and be conscious of the need for it to be handled in an extremely sensitive way. He knew that the local police were worried about the prospects looming ahead, but said that he was also certain that the Provos would be putting everything into maximizing the tension of the situation to their best advantage. Newberry would be taking every opportunity to warn his parishioners against allowing themselves to be manipulated, but readily conceded that it would be an uphill task. His firm view was that support would remain limited up to the point where one striker died, but that after that the whole community would take to the streets and would demand – from both parties, but particularly HMG – some move that would save the remaining six from the same fate. If the situation were to remain unchanged, and others were to die, then Newberry had no doubt that 'all hell would be let loose'. Father Donnelly's assessment was 'much less sanguine'. The hunger strike had yet to mobilize any great practical support in Turf Lodge, despite the proliferation of H-Block posters in windows, and banners from (lightless) lighting standards. The area remained quiet, with the impetus on the H-Block issue coming from (mainly the female) relatives of people in the Maze and elsewhere. He did not offer new speculation on the scenario painted by Father Newberry, but merely felt that the die had been cast and the outcome was inevitable. He just hoped – and prayed – that the seven hunger-strikers and their families would come to their senses, stop the strike and leave the way open for HMG to look at ways of improving the Northern Ireland prison regime.[7]

Meanwhile, in Dublin, Mrs Thatcher arrived for a summit with her opposite number, Charles Haughey. The background to the summit was the establishment of a series of 'joint studies' between the UK and the Irish Republic. In the press conference following the summit, the Prime Minister made two points on the hunger strike. There could be no give on political status: 'Murder is a crime. Carrying explosives is a crime. Maiming is a crime. It must stay a crime in the ordinary sense of the word. Murder is murder is murder. It is not, and never can be, a political crime. So there is no question of political status.' Secondly, she referred to Atkins' 'very comprehensive statement the other day' setting out all of the rights and privileges that were already available for prisoners who conformed to the 'ordinary way of life' in a prison: 'I do not think they had ever been set out in full before.' It showed that some of the things that some of the prisoners were demanding were already available under ordinary Prison Rules:

> What we now have to do is to get over the full totality of that statement to those who are on hunger strike and those who are not conforming to the normal prison routine ... it is a question of getting what is already available home to those prisoners who are on hunger strike, because, really, most of the things, the ordinary things on humanitarian grounds which they had been asking for, are already available to all prisoners under ordinary prison rules.

When asked whether the Taoiseach agreed with her point that there could be no question of giving the hunger-strikers political status, she replied: 'There is no question. I do not ever ask anyone to agree with it, but I think he accepts that there is no question of our giving political status to people guilty of murder, explosions, maiming in Northern Ireland or anywhere else. There is no question of it at all!' The purpose of the Atkins document was to set out on humanitarian grounds what was already available, 'because I do not think that is fully known. I mean, you or I may know it, but I do not think it is fully known to those people in the Maze Prison ... what we have to try to get over to the people concerned is the extent to which many of the things they are asking for are already available to all prisoners.'[8] Subsequently, Mrs Thatcher pronounced on how what she regarded as the 'impressive list' of rights and privileges available to prisoners in Northern Ireland had 'amazed' people when they saw how humane and how extensive the list was. She thought that deaths during the hunger strike would be 'such a waste of lives, particularly when a number of things they are demanding are already available to ordinary prisoners in Northern Ireland.'[9]

In the summit meeting itself, at Dublin Castle – the seat of British rule in Ireland for 800 years – the Taoiseach told Mrs Thatcher that he thought the 4 December statement by Atkins had been 'very good'. The opening that had been left for further discussion of humanitarian issues was particularly important. The Irish Government was pressing very hard for this to be taken up. The hunger-strikers were still receiving relatively little support, the turnout at a march in Dublin on 6 December having been very disappointing for the organizers. The Irish Government, however, was still very anxious that a solution should be 'brought forward', feeling that there was still a need for some additional face-saving device. The Prime Minister explained that the statement was intended to be a 'final one', and considered that the British Government could not go on making offers. 'Everyone in the North' had said that there was no point in continuing the hunger strike, and the Catholic Church had come out strongly in this sense. Mrs Thatcher was delighted with the statement that John Hume had made. There was now 'nothing left to give.'

Haughey agreed that Hume could play a very important role, but thought that the next step should be for the Northern Ireland Office to talk 'quietly and unobtrusively' to the hunger-strikers about coming off the strike. Of course no more concessions should be made. When the Prime Minister asked who precisely the Taoiseach had in mind, he replied that the three prison chaplains in the Maze would be the best channel. The NIO should use them as intermediaries with the hunger-strikers rather than some other intermediary, such as more senior members of the Church or other prisoners. The more nearly there were direct talks between the NIO and the prisoners, the better. The Prime Minister, however, expressed some concern as to whether the presence of a representative of the NIO might not stiffen the resistance of the hunger-strikers. She asked whether, for instance, a representative of the NIO and one of the priests should see the hunger-strikers together. Haughey initially said that he was not sure, but on a subsequent occasion indicated that he thought that this might be the best formula. He considered that the priests were honest and direct. He trusted them.

Mrs Thatcher pressed the Taoiseach further, asking whether the priests knew that the Irish Government wanted a solution. Haughey replied, 'very much so'. His understanding was that the hunger-strikers accepted that political status was not achievable and that they were looking for a way of getting off the hunger strike. The Prime Minister asked whether the hunger-strikers themselves had the authority to abandon the strike. Haughey observed that the picture was not altogether clear, but he thought that they could decide for themselves. Brendan Hughes would probably take the decision, and it was through him that the effort to end the hunger strike would have to be made. Throughout the meeting the Taoiseach repeatedly stressed the great importance that he attached to ending the strike. Already the strike had enabled the PIRA to recover influence in Belfast. People who had not been seen there for years had recently been reappearing. Haughey warned the Prime Minister that if the hunger-strikers started to die, the scene in Ireland would change radically.[10] Despite this warning, and the general sense of impending crisis, there were lighter moments for the two premiers to share. The British Ambassador reported to London:

> ... just before lunch yesterday when Mr Haughey was showing the Prime
> Minister the throne in the main central Throne Room he invited her to

sit on it. She firmly disclaimed any intention of doing so but suggested he should do so if he wished. They both laughed and went off to lunch. Barney Smith, Head of Chancery, has now told me that after the press conference, which took place while we were going off in the helicopter to the airport, Haughey returned to the Throne Room, where a lot of his officials were still milling around and drinking. He then ascended the throne and sat on it, his feet not quite touching the floor, and told the company they should now all kneel. He has a good sense of fun, and we might as well take comfort from the fact that he clearly thought the day had gone well.[11]

Following the summit a decision was made to send in an NIO official to brief the prisoners on Atkins' statement. The Secretary of State himself met with Ian Paisley and James Molyneaux, leader of the main Unionist Party, the UUP, to warn them of this, but also to emphasize that this was to be an exercise in clarification, not negotiation. Molyneaux commented that the Secretary of State would have considerable difficulty convincing everybody that he was not negotiating with terrorists. 'Where would this stop?' wondered a concerned Molyneaux.[12] As instructed, John Blelloch went to see the seven hunger-strikers on the morning of 10 December at the Maze prison. The meeting lasted from 11.30 a.m. until 12.45 p.m. He was accompanied throughout by the Governor and a Prison Officer. The hunger-strikers were together: McKearney did most of the talking, although others took part, but Hughes summed up at the end. The atmosphere was calm and, Blelloch thought, attentive – and, in the circumstances, remarkably polite. Blelloch opened by referring to the Secretary of State's statement of 4 December, copies of which had been given to the hunger-strikers before the meeting. He said that the subject of the statement had been discussed by the Prime Minister and the Taoiseach in Dublin recently, and that he was there at the prison at their personal direction to explain the statement to them. Blelloch explained that the statement did three things. First, it set out what, by comparison with the '5 demands' was already available within the prison regime. Second, it made clear that the evolution of the regime had not stopped on October 27, but that the Government was prepared to listen to those who had a genuine humanitarian concern for prison administration and was determined that the process of improvement should continue as resources and security permitted (Blelloch was asked to amplify what he meant by this and took the opportunity to read out the last two paragraphs of the statement verbatim). Third, it left no doubt that the Government would not grant political status, differentiation by motive or affiliation, or the surrender of prison administration to the prisoners. In taking this stand it had the support of all democratic governments, who did not expect the Government to give way and would not support them if it did; of political leaders North and South of the border; and of the Catholic hierarchy in the North. Blelloch said, therefore, that if they pressed their claim for political status and what went with it, the claim would fail.

In the question and answer session that followed, political status 'simply did not arise as a topic', and a great deal of time was taken up with details of the regime in respect of clothing – the hunger-strikers wanted information about the style and colour of the civilian clothing now being procured – and association. They asked whether or not rooms were locked during association with other prisoners, and were told that they were at present. They further asked whether or not individual dining rooms in the wings would be big enough to accommodate all the prisoners simultaneously, to which Blelloch said that he thought that on his observation they probably would. In addition, questions were raised regarding work and education, where there was quite a lot of discussion about the arrangements for studying academic courses, and whether or not private study counted as 'work', or had to be undertaken at the expense of 'association' time. Blelloch was asked whether he could give some forecast of the timetable of events to be expected under the second of the three points in the statement (future progress), and replied that he could not speculate about that. He summarized what would happen when the strike and protest were called off: all concerned would be regarded as conforming prisoners at once, at which point letters, visits, parcels and personal clothing would become available; the new civilian clothing would be issued when it was available; there would be a period in which cells were cleaned, redecorated and re-equipped and work programmes sorted out; and the position on remission would be reviewed on a case-by-case basis for each prisoner. In general, the need was to exploit the potential *already* available within the prison regime, potential that had been untapped while there was not full co-operation between prisoners and prison administration. Finally, in his summing up, Hughes commented that there was nothing new in the statement. Blelloch answered that he thought that there were at least two respects in which the situation was new. The first was that this was the 44th day of the hunger strike, and what everybody said in that situation needed to be treated very seriously. The second was that, through the Secretary of State's statement, the position was now clear, in a way perhaps that it had not been before, about what was already available under the prison regime. Hughes then asked whether they could think about things and let Blelloch have 'some proposals'. Blelloch replied that of course they could think about things and that the Government was open to ideas from those with a genuine humanitarian concern, but it was not open to 'proposals' in any negotiating sense.[13]

After the visit, Sands was permitted to meet with Hughes. Sands revealed to Hughes information he had received about clandestine contacts between the British and the Republican Movement. He urged Hughes 'not to be fooled' by the morning's events, as there were 'better offers in the pipeline.'[14] Sands had been told, through Father Meagher, who was 'Haughey's man', of attempts by the Taoiseach to resolve the confrontation. John Hume, noted Sands, appeared to form part of this manoeuvring.[15] Hughes and Sands agreed that in future they would only talk to the NIO if both of them were together. Later Sands wrote to Gerry Adams that Hughes was 'very cool, except for one point' – he was 'jittery' about the situation as someone approached death. Sands told Hughes to 'dig in' regardless of any deaths if the British remained intransigent. Hughes was concerned, though, regarding how he was to judge whether the British were bluffing or unwilling to move. Sands was unnerved by this, as it seemed to suggest an unwillingness to push the hunger strike to its ultimate conclusion. When Hughes asked whether he should request to see Hume, 'This gave me a shock', Sands informed Adams. Sands immediately rejected this on the grounds that he could not permit Haughey or Hume to 'steal the show'. Sands interpreted Blelloch's visit as a possible attempt to undermine the hunger strike and the 'parallel talks' outside the prison with British Government elements. In the early evening Sands was visited by Father Toner, who brought 'guidelines' from Hughes stressing that any reaction to the NIO visit should not deter the British from returning to talk. This upset Sands, who felt that Hughes, who had confided this to Toner, might have undermined the hunger-strikers' position: neither considered the priest trustworthy. Sands told Adams that he feared the British would now be aware of the prisoners' stance.[16]

Father Toner telephoned Blelloch later that evening at 11.30 p.m. He said that he had been down to the Maze Prison since Blelloch's own visit and wanted to report back his impressions. He had seen both Hughes and Bobby Sands, and found them 'disappointed' and 'disillusioned'. They had questioned the object of the visit given the absence of any sign of movement on the Government's part. Blelloch had for example been asked whether he would consider 'proposals' ('which I had', observed Blelloch) 'and had said that I was not prepared to do so (though I had added which Father Toner did not mention) that the Government was prepared to consider "ideas" from those with a genuine humanitarian concern in prison regimes' – a concern which, as Hughes pointed out to Blelloch, and 'not without good humour, was something which prisoners were likely to have.' The prisoners' view was that the ball was now in HMG's court, and that they would be putting out a statement to that effect, no doubt emphasizing the unhelpful nature of the visit. Father Toner added that he had got the same reaction from Sands as he had from Hughes, the latter having debriefed the former. Sands had added that he had expected to be present at any meeting (Blelloch had heard from the Prison earlier in the evening that the meeting between Hughes and Sands had taken place. What they said was not overheard, but Sands did most of the talking.)

Blelloch commented only to Father Toner that 'I was slightly surprised at the account that he had given me since I had gone through what was available under the prison regime in some detail with them and they had seemed to understand that and the Government's position for the future.' Toner commented that at some point in discussing the regime it had been said, for instance, in respect of association, that the situation described was that applying 'at the present time', with the implication that things might change in the future if the hunger strike were to be ended. The prisoners had said to him that they were not prepared to end the strike on that basis. Blelloch replied that 'while I could – just – understand why a man might want to fast to death in pursuit of some great principle (which for some, though not for me, political status might be), I could not understand why someone would wish to do the same for a marginal change in the prison rules.'[17] The response of the prisoners was to issue a dismissive statement:

> We have no intention, despite our deteriorating condition, of abandoning our hunger strike. While accepting that the Northern Ireland Office had broken the ice we feel our position needs clarifying to prevent any misunderstanding by our supporters on the outside. To resolve the hunger strike without a death the following needs to occur:
>
> The Northern Ireland Office has got to approach the situation realistically and have to deal with the continuation of the hunger strike and the blanket protest through our representatives here.
>
> Nothing significantly has changed and the public should be made aware of this.[18]

While the prisoners were defiant, the rumour mill in the Protestant community led an irate Ian Paisley to telephone Roy Harrington of the NIO at about 12.30 p.m. on 11 December 'in some anger.' He asked whether it was true that Blelloch was at the Maze Prison, this time to negotiate with Sands. Harrington told him that was not true: Blelloch, as the senior official concerned with prisons, might have reason at any time to go into the prison, but he had explained to the seven hunger-strikers the day before the meaning of the Government's statement of 4 December, and the purpose of that visit was now complete. Paisley then asked Harrington to confirm that Blelloch had offered three new concessions to the hunger-strikers. Harrington told him this was 'nonsense': the Secretary of State had undertaken personally to Paisley only the day before that the sole purpose of Blelloch's visit was to ensure that the prisoners knew what was in the statement of 4 December, and his visit had of course been confined entirely to that. There was no question of any new concessions. Paisley then asked whether it was true that some of the hunger-strikers had taken food the day before. Harrington said that he had received no such information.[19]

There was a rather more sedate conversation with another Protestant clergyman the same day: Bishop Eames, the Church of Ireland Bishop of Down, rang T.

H. Gee of the NIO on 10 December, and asked him to call upon him the next morning. When Gee went to see Eames, he explained that he had been having talks with representatives of the UDA over the last fortnight. These had culminated in a meeting during the previous night with Andy Tyrie. Tyrie had told the Bishop that he was very worried about a potential UDA hunger strike. This was not something that the UDA had encouraged, but that had arisen from inside the prison. He was concerned on two counts. First, that he believed that at least three of the potential strikers were prepared to go through with it. Second, that Paisley, for whom he expressed extreme dislike and contempt, was going to try and make political capital and get people on to the streets. Tyrie himself professed to believe that the days of street rioting were over, considered that he could control the UDA, and 'did not want Paisley fishing in these waters.' Tyrie told the Bishop that he believed that he could get the UDA prisoners to abandon their proposed strike if only one of their conditions was met. Their chief concern was their proximity to Republican prisoners. Tyrie had reason to believe that there was quite a lot of inflammable material and the means of starting a fire in the H-Blocks. There was also, as long as the two sets of prisoners were close to one another, the chance of some sort of conflict. Therefore he believed that by moving the Loyalist prisoners further away from the Republican ones they could be induced to abandon their protest. The Bishop asked whether the NIO could advise him on how to reply to Tyrie.

Gee told the Bishop that he must stand firm on the Government's statement: 'We had made it clear that there was no question of political status. We were committed to a general programme of prison reform, but we were not going to negotiate on anything and we were certainly not going to do anything under duress.' On the specific issue of segregation, Gee was not prepared to comment in detail, 'but there would be no opportunity of even considering this while we were threatened with a hunger strike.' The Bishop said that he was grateful for this advice and that he would no doubt be seeing Tyrie later in the day after Tyrie had visited the Maze. He was convinced that Tyrie was doing everything in his power to stop the hunger strike going forward, but considered that he was unlikely to succeed unless he had something to offer. Gee reaffirmed that there was nothing that the Government was likely to offer, and certainly not at the present time.[20]

At Atkins' request, Harrington spoke to Tyrie. Harrington explained that the Secretary of State had made clear his willingness to discuss humanitarian aspects of the prison regime as it affected *all* prisoners and not just a particular section of the prison population. He had also made clear that neither he nor anyone acting on his behalf would contemplate negotiation or mediation with the prisoners. Tyrie 'took all this surprisingly quietly', although Harrington was asked to explain the argument about the risk of the appearance of negotiation two or three times. No reference was made to the visit to the Republican hunger-strikers by Blelloch. Tyrie explained that he was very concerned about the serious situation developing, because although he was using his influence to dissuade the Loyalist hunger-strikers from going ahead, the Government's unwillingness to accept that the UDA could carry messages between Stormont Castle and the prison meant that he had nothing to offer them. He thought that there was a considerable risk of a degree of competition between the different groups of hunger-strikers building up. He recognized that a Loyalist hunger strike could only make matters more difficult for the Government, but he would consider carefully the details of Atkins' statement of 4 December (Harrington arranged for him to receive a copy) and would consider urgently what he should say in a letter to the Secretary of State.[21]

On the morning of 12 December, six prisoners, all UDA, refused breakfast and declared themselves to be on hunger strike. This action was taken in support of the same demands for political status as expressed by the Republicans, to which was added a further demand – segregation from the Republicans. All six were located in H1 Block and had been participating in a 'clean' blanket protest for a considerable time. A smuggled letter, evidently from one of the prisoners, William Mullan, to his mother, was intercepted, which indicated that the proposed hunger strike was to highlight the Loyalist 'clean' blanket protesters, and was 'ostensibly a publicity stunt and that the participants have no intention of killing themselves.' Andy Tyrie twice visited the prison during the period and talked to two UDA prisoners. This was apparently to talk the prisoners out of their action. Tyrie in fact took little part in the visits. The running was made by John McClatchey (another UDA leader) who accompanied him. McClatchey offered no encouragement to the prisoners. It seemed clear to the NIO that this strike was sprung on the UDA leadership, who, together with the UVF, decided retrospectively to back it. The motives seemed to be frustration at the complete absence of support for and interest in the Loyalist blanketmen together with a characteristic opportunism. The prisoners wished to ensure that if any concessions were to be made, they too would be eligible 'without of course having had to carry matters to a conclusion. Although they are determined in starting their strike, as the Mullan letter shows, it very much remains to be seen how far they will carry it', noted the NIO.[22]

In the meantime, Mike Bohill's latest discussions, on 12 December, with his contacts in the Catholic community, involved the Parish Priest of St Paul's, Pulls Road, Father Montague, and the Parish Priest designate for Poleglass, Father Paddy McWilliams, who was a curate in the Republican Turf Lodge area, but who also knew the adjacent Whiterock/Ballymurphy area very well. Both men conveyed the same message: their local communities were far from totally committed to the H-Block campaign, and the activists had yet to secure any significant inroads.

Both men felt that, while no one wanted to see anyone die, the vast majority of their flock had no stomach for a fight for political status, no illusions about the 'evil intentions' of the H-Block Committee, and were not slow in contrasting the H-Block's call for 'humanitarian concern' to be exercised by the Government with a recent attempted murder in Strabane and the killing of a young UDR man in Belfast.

Both were convinced that the Government was right not to concede political or special status, and were fairly well aware that HMG had gone to considerable lengths to improve prison conditions. Father McWilliams was particularly sure that while there was general 'concern' about the strike, there was only limited active support in his area, pointing out that although every householder in Turf Lodge and Ballymurphy had been given a poster for his front window, perhaps only one in every four or five houses had put it up on public display. Again, as with Father Newberry in the Markets, both priests were nevertheless very worried about the extent to which some youngsters, particularly those in their early teens and who had never seen gunmen, or maybe even heard a shot fired in anger, were being sucked into the military-style marches and parades, and the effect this would have on them. On the other hand, Father Montague pointed out that only a tiny fraction of the pupils at secondary schools had joined a recent half-day 'strike'. He had checked this carefully, and conclusively refuted Ulster TV's statement that there had been school closures in West Belfast. Neither expressed any great concern about what might happen should a hunger-striker die. To some degree, both felt that if it happened it could turn out to be 'a seven-day wonder' and that, providing the security forces handled any rioting sensitively, it would, for the most part, all blow over fairly quickly without doing any serious long-term damage.[23]

The NIO also had to take account of the views of those who had to run the Maze: the Governor, his deputies and the Prison Officers. Blelloch asked E. N. Barry, of the Prisons Division, for a 'prisons view' on the analysis of possible bargaining counters available to the Government. In his reply, Barry stated that, because he was not free to discuss this with anyone, including Governors, the views he expressed were entirely his own, based on a close working relationship with Governors, his own headquarters staff, the Prison Officers' Association (POA) and prison officers. 'I recently addressed some 200 staff at Belfast Prison.' Regarding the attitude of staff: 'Implementation is dependent upon staff attitudes and there is no mistaking the strength of feeling through the Prison Service at the present time over the hunger-strikers and dirty protests at Maze and Armagh.' There had been a build-up of frustration over what prison officers regarded as concessions to the protestors, beginning with the package of minor changes in the prison regime announced in March, and culminating in the decisions to substitute civilian-type clothing for the old style prison uniform. Staff were never happy about any of these changes. They grudgingly accepted the various measures introduced on humanitarian grounds to ameliorate the regimes for the protestors, but in the process they had become increasingly suspicious of the Government's intentions, and they viewed the recent initiative on prison clothing as the last straw. Their present attitude was that 'enough is enough', and even at this stage it was by no means certain that they would agree to handle the new prison clothing when it became available, 'although a lot can happen in the three months before delivery is expected.'

Barry warned that: 'for the first time in my experience I am not sure that I could count on the full support of Governors in implementing any further changes in advance of the ending of the hunger strike and the dirty protest'. The whole picture could of course change if the hunger strike and protest could be brought to an end without the Government having to make any further changes in the regime. This would create an entirely new atmosphere and provide much greater scope for a liberal approach to humanitarian measures. Attitudes could change in the event that new circumstances arose, whether civil unrest, a serious upsurge of terrorist violence, renewed attacks on prison officers, the culmination of the hunger-strike in the death of one or more prisoners, Loyalist reaction or pressure of public opinion. But 'as of now, any further initiatives by the Government before the hunger strike comes to an end would outrage staff and cause morale in the Service to nosedive. It would also inflame protestant opinion and annoy the judiciary.'[24]

At Armagh Prison, the three female hunger-strikers continued with their fast. They were co-operating with prison staff, and were not fouling or damaging their cells. They continued to take daily exercise, and were given daily medical examinations, although their condition gave no immediate cause for concern. On 12 December, their individual weight loss was the same, within half a pound, at 15 lbs each. Farrell was visited by her parish priest and members of her family while Doyle was visited by her solicitor, Morgan. Nugent had so far received no visitors since she began her hunger strike. The number of dirty protestors, meanwhile, seemed to have levelled off at 466. The number of Republican prisoners refusing to work increased to eighteen. At Armagh Prison, the number of female prisoners on a dirty protest remained at twenty-six. Token three-day fasts continued at Belfast Prison.[25] Then, on the evening of Friday, 12 December, the NIO, as it recorded, was presented with the following four demands from within the prison:

(i)   Sands to meet Hughes;
(ii) McFarlane to see the other six hunger strikers;
(iii) Sands and Hughes to be visited by Mr Blelloch; and
(iv) Danny Morrison to have a special visit.

After consultation with the Secretary of State, numbers one and four were agreed. Quite apart from any other considerations, number three, following on from the hint of a hope of negotiation in a PIRA statement of the previous day, left the impression that the prisoners and some of their representatives might hope that the Government's refusal to negotiate or accept mediation was in itself a negotiation posture that could be changed by pressure. During the course of telephone conversations, the PUS, Sir Kenneth Stowe, emphasized to John Hume that such was not the case: the Government simply would not move from its declared position. Michael Alexander – Mrs Thatcher's Diplomatic Private Secretary at 10 Downing Street – also confirmed that there could have been no hint left in the minds of the Irish Government that the British Government was prepared to shift its position. Following Morrison's visit on the afternoon of Saturday, 13 December, reports were received from the prison that the meeting between him and Hughes had clearly been highly emotional. Subsequently Hume provided the NIO with an account of Morrison's meetings at the prison. According to Hume, Morrison told him that when he met Sands, he was told that the prison was 'about to explode'. The prisoners felt that Morrison and Hume were being 'taken for a ride by the Brits' and were wringing nothing out of the Government. The threat that thirty additional hunger-strikers might begin a fast on 15 December was mentioned. When he met Hughes, Morrison tried to plead with him to be patient for a little longer. Hughes lost his temper and threw Morrison out, throwing a food tray at him in the process, and telling him that McKenna was finding himself unable to take water, as a result of which the other six hunger-strikers might join him on a thirst strike in order to keep pace with him. Morrison thought, said Hume, that his role as a carrier of messages was now at an end. During the course of the morning, the consultant physician who had examined all the prisoners had warned McKenna that he was in urgent need of vitamin treatment by injection and by tablets to avoid serious, and potentially irreversible, damage to his sight. On orders from Hughes, McKenna refused all treatment.

Following the 'emotional' meeting between Morrison and Hughes, a request was made by Sands that a meeting should be permitted at the prison out of the hearing of prison staff between Sands, Hughes, Bernadette McAliskey and Gerry Adams. The Secretary of State was recommended to refuse the request, on the basis of public reaction if such a 'terrorist "Council of War"' were permitted, and that (as the NIO was warned during the morning by Hume) the purpose of such a meeting might be to draw the Government onto a path that, through small steps, could lead to a meeting of Adams and McAliskey with the Secretary of State. This would, in a sense, give them a form of political status. The fact that this special quadrilateral meeting had been asked for was made known to Hume soon after the request was received, and he was told of the decision soon after the decision was communicated to the Governor. In Dublin, the British Ambassador, Leonard Figg, was asked to pass on to the Irish Government precise details of the request that had been made, and the fact that it was being refused without any reasons being given publicly. He was asked to tell the Irish Government that, quite apart from public reaction to such a meeting, the consideration that the NIO had in mind was that to permit such a meeting would be to elevate the status of McAliskey. Roy Harrington agreed with the Ambassador that, after he had passed on this message, (which he did to O'Rourke, of the Department of Foreign Affairs (DFA)) Alexander at 10 Downing Street would be invited to discuss the whole matter informally with Nally of the Taoiseach's office. Both the Ambassador and Alexander subsequently confirmed that the Irish Government considered the message 'at the highest level'. The Irish were grateful for being kept informed, and fully understood the decision to refuse the request. They mentioned that there might be good reason to be more sympathetic to requests for a visit by Adams than to requests for a visit by McAliskey.[26]

On the morning of 15 December, there was a dramatic escalation of the hunger strike when twenty-three more Republican prisoners in HMP Maze refused breakfast and joined the fast. Meanwhile, there was a continued marked deterioration in McKenna's eyesight, and McKearney was developing similar symptoms, but the doctors had not recommended that any of the prisoners should be moved to Musgrave Park Hospital for nursing care. From the NIO's perspective, the determination of this new group of hunger-strikers was 'unknown at present.' Most of the names on the two 'reserve' lists, obtained previously by the NIO, had now joined the strike. In an assessment by the PUS's office, it was presumed that the new hunger-strikers had the intention of carrying the strike some considerable way; 'the remainder may be taking part in a more opportunist move.'[27] The dramatic escalation led the most senior civil servant in Dublin, the Cabinet Secretary-General, Dermot Nally, to contact Downing Street and request that the hunger-strikers be visited by Father Meagher. When asked whether there was any particular significance in his request for a visit by Meagher, Nally said that there was none beyond the fact that Meagher was known to be helpful and reliable. He would certainly do his best to 'sell what was on offer.' Nally added that the Irish authorities would be proposing, through the British Ambassador, that 'we should consider whether we would be prepared to accept phraseology on the clothing issue which would envisage the provision to prisoners of "clothes provided or approved by the prison authorities".' Nally said 'somewhat defensively "you probably won't look at it".'[28]

Attention was now focused on the approaching crisis in the health of the original seven, with McKenna causing most concern and McKearney not far behind. The other hunger-strikers refused to agree to treatment for McKenna, and on 18 December it was decided that his condition was so serious that he should be moved to the Musgrave Park Hospital. The other six hunger-strikers were told by the prison doctors that his condition was critical and that there was very little time before they too would be as close to death.[29]

Here it is appropriate to examine the external contacts between the British and the Republican Movement that Sands had referred to in his conversation with Hughes. Brendan Duddy, a Catholic businessman from Derry, had been a backchannel between the Secret Intelligence Service during IRA-HMG contacts in the 1970s. With close links to Martin McGuinness, 'of the Provisional Army Council', Duddy, in early December, had reactivated the link to SIS. The SIS officer concerned approached Sir Frank Cooper, at the Ministry of Defence, but formally NIO PUS, who put the officer in touch with Sir Kenneth Stowe. The current PUS drew up a paper suggesting some gestures that HMG might make. Stowe agreed that the SIS officer should take the paper to his contacts in Northern Ireland, and sought the Prime Minister's permission for the operation to go ahead. Mrs Thatcher, together with Atkins, was briefed by Stowe at a hastily arranged meeting in the House of Commons. The SIS officer, at this time, was sitting in Stowe's car awaiting the green light to dash to Heathrow Airport and fly to Aldergrove Airport outside Belfast. Mrs Thatcher endorsed the plan. Stowe's document was, according to him, 'a façade of concessions about the treatment of prisoners which gave them a ladder to climb down.' The gestures were presented as 'humanitarian' and applicable to *all* prisoners in Northern Ireland: civilian clothing from prisoners' families to be worn during visits and recreation; civilian-type clothing during the working day; free association at weekends; and the prospect of restored remission. The central issue on which HMG was unmovable remained control and authority.[30] There was nothing in the document that conceded the five demands, or undermined the Government's position in the dispute. Father Meagher took possession of the document at Aldergrove. Meagher took the document to the Clonard Monastery, where he showed it to Gerry Adams and other Provisionals. Described by Republicans as 'full of holes',[31] its relevance was academic. The hunger strike had, in the meantime, collapsed.

The dramatic ending of the hunger strike had begun when, according to Hughes, the 'authorities offered them their own clothes and free association at certain times of the day'. As this seemed to be 'close' to their demands, Hughes requested time for himself and the other hunger-strikers to consult among themselves. They all agreed, in principle, that the offer was sufficient. Hughes wanted the offer to be put into writing. McKenna, who was close to going into a coma, asked Hughes: 'Promise me that you won't let me die.' 'You have my word ... I won't let you die. We have the agreement here, we're just holding out for it to be on paper and to have a witness from the Republican Movement', replied Hughes. In Hughes' description of events, as evening approached Dr Ross informed him that McKenna had just hours to live. They were 'taking him to a real hospital.' Hughes got up and went into the corridor. Father Murphy and

Father Toner were supporting him by his arms. Hughes looked up the hallway and saw Dr Ross and the prison orderlies rolling McKenna out on a gurney. Hughes shouted to Ross, 'Feed him.' Sands arrived in his cell later that night with Father Meagher and the document from the British Government: 'They were really excited and we hugged each other. I couldn't read the document, my eyesight was gone, and I asked Bobby to read it' recalled Hughes, who felt the mood was 'fantastic.' Dr Ross was excited. Paul Lennons, a medical officer who was 'sympathetic to the hunger-strikers, was really excited. Best of all, "the screws were totally dejected because they seen it as, the Brits had given in and we'd won".'[32]

In the authorities' record of events, it was only after McKenna had been moved to the Musgrave Park Hospital that events moved quite rapidly: at 6.30 p.m., the prison authorities reported a dispute between Hughes and McFeely. Hughes wished to call off the hunger strike, but McFeely refused. Only then did Hughes request medical treatment for McKenna, which was granted, and the information was passed to the medical staff at Ward 18 in the Musgrave Park Hospital, who immediately began intensive treatment. Hughes asked to see Sands, and this request was granted.[33] Sands was taken to the prison hospital at 6.45. What he found there, as he later told Adams, shocked him:

> I saw Index [Father Toner] and Silvertop [Father Murphy] in the corridor as I walked down the wing. There were three cartons of eggs sitting in a doorway. My heart jumped. Dorcha [Brendan Hughes] came out of Tommy McKearney's room and went into Tom [McFeely]'s room in front of me. Tom was in bed. Raymond and Nixie were sitting beside the bed. They were all shattered. Dorcha said, 'Did you hear the sceal [news]?' I said, 'No.' He said it again. I thought Sean was dead. Then he said, 'We've got nothing, I called it off.' The MO was banging an injection into Tommy. Sean was en route to the hospital. Tom had been against it, wanting to wait and see what Atkins was going to say in the Commons. Dorcha was under the impression that Sean had only twelve hours to live.

Sands was angry that Hughes had 'usurped his authority', and ended the hunger strike, feeling that the 'whole thing had been a big waste of time and emotion.' He later told Adams: 'For what it's worth, comrade, we seen the move coming, but the boys just blew up. We were beat by a few lousy hours which were critical. Dorcha panicked when they rushed Sean to the hospital. If only he had realized that it was the sign that the Brits were moving. Well, that's that?'[34] In this, though, he was wrong: the Brits were not moving.

In the meantime, at 7.45 p.m. and onwards, in the presence of the Deputy Governor, the Prison Medical Officer, Fathers Toner and Murphy, the Prison Chaplains and Sands, each hunger striker in turn requested food and medical treatment. Sands asked permission to speak to each of the other mass hunger-strikers, and this was granted. At 8.45 p.m., Sands was returned to his cell. The hunger-strikers were reported to be stunned at the news, but gave no indication of their intentions at this stage. Fathers Toner and Murphy left the prison. At 10.00 p.m., it was agreed that Father Meagher could speak to Sands and Hughes together when he arrived at the prison at approximately 10.30 p.m. Meagher's request that Danny Morrison should visit Armagh Prison that same night was turned down, but it was agreed that Meagher could visit the hunger-strikers in Armagh the following day. It was also agreed that McKenna's family could visit him in hospital during the night.

Father Meagher was allowed into a prison hospital ward with Sands at 11.00 p.m., and they were permitted to speak to Hughes in the sight of prison staff but out of earshot. Ten minutes later Meagher was permitted to make a telephone call to a Belfast number, and spoke with an unidentified woman. He then rejoined Sands and Hughes at 11.45 p.m. Meagher asked to see the Assistant Governor on duty and requested an immediate meeting with prisoners McKeown from H6, McCallum from H4 and Walsh from H5. He also requested that Danny Morrison should be permitted to visit Sheila Darragh in HMP Armagh the following morning. His requests were noted to be passed on to the authorities; the immediate meeting was turned down, however, on the grounds of security, and Father Meagher was told that the earliest time that such a meeting could take place would be 7.45 a.m. the following morning. Meagher reported this back to Hughes and Sands. At 11.55 p.m., Meagher again asked to speak to the Assistant Governor with Sands. He made the following statement: 'Reference the blanket protest, Mr Morrison (editor of *An Phoblacht*) has a visit with Sands tomorrow and I request that Gerry Adams accompany Morrison to that visit to deal with the question of resolving the current blanket protest on the basis of the new proposals.' At this stage Meagher brandished two documents: a thick one entitled 'Regimes in Northern Ireland Prisons', and another two-page document, the title of which could not be made out by the Assistant Governor. Meagher's requests were noted, and he left the prison at twelve minutes past midnight.

The following morning, Friday, 19 December, at 7.45 a.m., Sands was allowed to speak to the spokesman of the other protesting blocks as Meagher had requested. The other male hunger-strikers took their breakfasts, indicating that they too had called off their strike. At 8.00 a.m., all protesting prisoners at the Maze and Armagh received the two-page document Meagher had brandished the previous evening, which was entitled 'What Will Happen When The Protests End.' This set out the Secretary of State's statement, which he proposed to deliver later that day in a TV broadcast of the step-by-step approach to be followed by the protestors if they wished to achieve the rights and privileges available to conforming prisoners.[35] Written before the end of the hunger strike, it stated:

> On the fourth of December the Government set out clearly what is available to all prisoners in Northern Ireland prisons.
>
> We hoped this would bring an end to the protests. Two more weeks have passed. The protests continue. Those on hunger strike are two weeks nearer death.
>
> Their demand for political status is not going to be granted. The European Commission of Human Rights has considered the case made to it by the protesters for political status, and has rejected it. The Commission asked the Government to keep the humanitarian aspects of the prison regime under continuing review. The Government responded positively to that request with the changes on nine specific points which I set forth in detail in my statement to the House of Commons on 4 December. It is our concern that these protests and the hunger strike should not lead to pointless deaths. To the protesters and those on hunger strike I want to say:
>
> There is no reason to go on. The Government has made its response. I want to spell out for you and your families what will happen when the protests end.
>
> First of all, any such prisoner will be put into a clean cell. If, as I hope, all prisoners end their protests, we shall have the task of cleaning up all the cells right away and this would take a week or ten days.
>
> Within a few days clothing provided by their families will be given to any prisoners giving up their protest so that they can wear it during recreation, association and visits. As soon as possible all prisoners will be issued with civilian-type clothing for wear during the working day. From then on, as I said in October, denim prison uniform becomes a thing of the past for all prisoners.
>
> They will also immediately become entitled every month to eight letters, four parcels and four visits.
>
> Prisoners who end their protest will be able to associate within each wing of the prison blocks in the evening and at weekends. If large groups of prisoners cease their protest simultaneously, a few days may be needed for cleaning up.
>
> We want to work out for every prisoner the kinds of available activity which we think suit him best — work (including of course the work of servicing the prison itself), vocational training and educational training. Again if groups of prisoners come off the protest together, getting this programme organised will take some time.

On the question of remission – and this will be of special importance to the prisoners' families – provision already exists for lost remission to be restored after subsequent good behaviour. We shall immediately start reviewing each case individually.

We do not want any prisoners to die: but if they persist in their hunger strike they will not be forcibly fed. If they die, it will be from their own choice. If they choose to live, the conditions available to them meet in a practical and humane way the kind of things they have been asking for. But we shall not let the way we run the prisons be determined by hunger strikes or any other threat.

Northern Ireland prisons are acknowledged to include some of the best in the United Kingdom. The boards of visitors will continue to play their part in maintaining this position. For our part we will, subject to the overriding requirements of security, keep prison conditions – and that includes clothing, work, association, education, training and remission – under continuing review.

It is the Government's earnest wish that, in the light of these possibilities, all prisoners now protesting in one form or another will bring their protest to an end. In particular, those on hunger strike have nothing to gain by fasting to death. The time to stop is now.[36]

Clearly there were no concessions in this document. Father Meagher, meanwhile, visited Armagh Prison and saw the three hunger-strikers, and Sheila Darragh, who was clearly the women prisoners' spokeswoman. After the strikers had taken exercise with those on the dirty protest (which provided association, and therefore an opportunity to confide), the three hunger-strikers declared their intention to begin taking food again. The Republican hunger strikes were over. A statement was issued on behalf of the seven hunger-strikers:

We the Irish Republican political prisoners in the H-Block prison hospital, having completed 53 days of hunger strike in demand of our just right to be recognised as political prisoners have tonight, December 18 1980, decided to halt our hunger strike action.

Having seen the statement to be announced by Humphrey Atkins in the British House of Commons and having been supplied with a document which contains a new elaboration of our five demands which were first enumerated upon by Humphrey Atkins in his statement to the House of Commons of December 4, we decided to halt the hunger strike.

In ending our hunger strike, we make it clear that failure by the British Government to act in a responsible manner toward ending the conditions which forced us to a hunger strike will not only lead to inevitable and continual strife within the H-Blocks but will show quite clearly the intransigence of the British Government.[37]

In its analysis of the reasons for the ending of the hunger strike, the NIO identified a number of factors that might have contributed, in varying degrees, to its end. The first of these was the fact that a lack of outside support for the strikers' cause 'must have contributed to a sense of futility among the strikers, whose only major firm constituency of support lay in the Republican areas in the North and mainly in West Belfast. Reports of the lack of support in the Irish Republic must have proved particularly disheartening.' The 'sensitive' handling of the H-Block protests by the security forces (mainly the RUC) avoided public disorder and 'contributed to the generally favourable view of the Government's handling of the issue.' A statement by Cardinal Ó Fiaich and the five Roman Catholic Bishops, on 28 November, appealing for an end to the hunger strike, 'must have provided another severe psychological blow, since before then the protesters had every reason to believe that their cause had the sympathy and tacit support of the Catholic hierarchy.' The unequivocal rejection of political status by the Government, and in particular the Prime Minister, 'offered the protesters no real hope of a capitulation by HMG. In particular, in the latter days of the strike it was becoming apparent that the Government was gearing itself up to deal with reactions to the first striker's death.'

A factor, the importance of which was 'more difficult to assess,' was the influence upon the hunger-strikers' determination of the various intermediaries who were 'probably carrying ambiguous and confusing messages in and out of the prison.' There were undoubtedly links to Sinn Féin and the Provisional IRA through families, the solicitor, Pat Finucane and Danny Morrison. There were links to John Hume through Father Toner, and there were probably links to the Irish Government via Hume and through Father Meagher. Some or all of these agencies may have persuaded the hunger-strikers that the Secretary of State's statement of 4 December and its supporting Prison Regime document held out the prospect of achieving the substance of their five demands, which would allow them to claim a triumph and give them a degree of control over their life within the prison. This, if true, would have vindicated the hunger-strikers and would have allowed them to call an end to the dirty protest. There could be little doubt that Father Meagher's visit to the prison during the evening of 18 December was for the purpose of showing the protesters the Prison Regime document and an advanced copy of the Secretary of State's statement of 19 December. Meagher 'probably intended to persuade them to read an offer of the substance of their five demands into these two documents and thus to end their strike.' However, the seven had decided to call off their fast before Meagher arrived. Nevertheless,

Meagher was 'probably able to help placate Sands and to provide the framework for a face-saving exercise by the protesters. The subsequent collapse of the face-saving exercise has probably finished Meagher as a credible intermediary in the eyes of the protesters.' However:

> Probably the single most important factor was that the seven hunger strikers just did not have the will to die. They may have been misled into thinking that their protest would succeed easily, and as it became increasingly clear that their deaths were going to be in vain, the fear of death probably became an increasingly significant factor. This effect was undoubtedly enhanced by the different rates of deterioration of health (in particular McKenna's distressing and rapid decline towards the end of the fast). By watching McKenna, the other six were given a preview of the fate which awaited them. Their death was clearly going to be painful and degrading and the leader Hughes was burdened with the responsibility of standing by and watching one of his subordinates die, probably in vain, while he still lived. When the decision was made to remove McKenna to the Musgrave Park Hospital, the doctors made it very clear to Hughes and the others that he was about to die and that the other hunger strikers would follow soon. This was undoubtedly the critical point for the strikers and it is evident from the reported argument between Hughes and McFeely that Hughes' determination had given way at this point under the double stress of responsibility for McKenna's death and the imminence of his own death. Once the group's leader had succumbed it was almost inevitable that the others would eventually follow suit.[38]

NOTES

1   TNA CJ4/3040 Note for the record, 3 December 1980.
2   TNA CJ4/3040 Meeting with John Hume, 2 December 1980.
3   TF Text of Parliamentary Answer by Humphrey Atkins (Maze Prison hunger strike).
4   TNA CJ4/3023 Record of a meeting with Fathers Toner and Murphy held in PUS's Office, Belfast, on Friday, 5 December 1980.
5   TNA CJ4/3040 Note for the Record, 8 December 1980.
6   TNA CJ4/3040 Record of meeting with Fathers Toner and Murphy held in PUS's Office, Belfast, on Friday, 5 December 1980.
7   TNA CJ4/3028 Main points arising from discussions with Father Denis Newberry (Markets/ Lower Ormeau) and Father Donnelly (Turf Lodge) on 9 December.
8   TF Press Conference after Anglo–Irish summit, 8 December 1980.
9   TF Radio Interview for IRN (Anglo–Irish Summit), 8 December 1980.

10 TNA PREM 19/507 Record of a Meeting Between the Prime Minister and the Taoiseach, Mr Charles Haughey, 8 December 1980.

11 TNA PREM 19/507 Figg to Alexander 9 December 1980.

12 TNA CJ4/3028 Note of meetings with Mr Concannon, Mr John Biggs-Davison, Dr Paisley and Mr Molyneaux, 10 December 1980.

13 TNA CJ4/3040 Note for the Record, 10 December 1980.

14 O'Hearn, *op.cit* p. 295.

15 *Ibid*, p. 294.

16 *Ibid*, pp. 295–296

17 TNA CJ4/3040 Note for the Record, 10 December 1980.

18 TNA CJ4/3028 Text of statement issued on Thursday, 11 December 1980.

19 TNA CJ4/3040 Note of a Telephone Conversation with Revd Dr Ian Paisley MP.

20 TNA CJ4/3040 Gee to Blelloch, 11 December 1980.

21 TNA CJ4/3040 Note of a Telephone Conversation with Mr Andy Tyrie.

22 TNA CJ4/3028 Maze Hunger Strikers (Loyalist).

23 TNA CJ4/3028 Catholic Community: H-Blocks, 12 December.

24 TNA CJ4/3041 E. N. Barry to Blelloch, 10 December 1980.

25 PRONI NIO/12/196A The Republican Hunger Strikes: 27 October–19 December 1980.

26 TNA CJ4/3040 Weekend of 13/14 December.

27 TNA CJ4/3028 Conclusions of a stocktaking on prison issues held in PUS's Office in Belfast on Monday, 15 December.

28 TNA CJ4/3028 Alexander to Hopkins.

29 PRONI NIO/12/196A The Republican Hunger Strikes: 27 October–19 December 1980.

30 Charles Moore *Margaret Thatcher. The Authorized Biography Volume One: Not for Turning* (London 2013) pp. 599–600.

31 O'Hearn, *op.cit.* pp. 300–301.

32 *Ibid*, p. 301.

33 PRONI NIO/12/196A The Republican Hunger Strikes: 27 October–19 December 1980.

34 O'Hearn, *op.cit.* pp. 299–300.

35 PRONI NIO/12/196A The Republican Hunger Strikes: 27 October–19 December 1980.

36 TNA CJ4/3040 'What Will Happen When The Protests End.'

37 PRONI NIO/12/196A The Republican Hunger Strikes: 27 October–19 December 1980.

38 PRONI NIO/12/196A The Republican Hunger Strikes: 27 October–19 December 1980.

Chapter 5

Stand-off

In the aftermath of the hunger strike's collapse, Gerry Adams informed Sands that he thought the key point was that the British had a sense that the prisoners had been broken, that:

> ... we've got them beat. Five years on the blanket and they tried the hunger strike and we beat them on that. So they probably thought that they had this thing in hand ... I would say that if I was a British strategist sitting back and intent on the implementation of what was then their strategy and if I had been concerned when the hunger strike started that this could escalate, I would be sitting back in January and saying, "Well, we have them now.[1]

The conclusion Sands took from his own assessment of the situation was 'very disturbing'. He wanted Adams to issue a statement, pointing to the 'inflexibility' of the British. The blanket and dirty protest continued, but, announced Sands, 'we embark upon another hunger strike! ... I don't believe we can achieve our aims or recoup our losses in the light of what has occurred. Sooner, rather than later, our defeat will be exposed. When I say, in the light of what has occurred, I mean not only the boys breaking but perhaps our desperate attempts to salvage something.' Sands was in a desperate situation with things 'so bad that in here men have left' the protest. When the 'situation fizzles out, which it indeed will, I will lose over three hundred men from this protest, perhaps more', he told Adams. On the next hunger strike Sands was determined to go the full distance: 'Someone will die. I know others told you this, but I am prepared to die and no one will call this hunger strike off, comrade'. With the Republican Movement and the prisoners having taken a blow, 'We need out of it and if it means death then that is accepted. We stand to be destroyed, comrade. You must realize once eaten up by the present penal system you don't come out a fighter, or very few will. When you're knocked down you get up and fight back. We can do it. We've created the proper conditions for it. If we've had luck, it's that we can go at them again.' Sands was 'not prepared to watch four and a half years of sheer murder be fritted into conformity and respectability.' He was not 'taking our failure personally' or blaming himself, but he was making a 'desperate plea' to Adams: 'I'm not so naive as to not accept that men will break again, but what we're heading for now is something so disastrous that I flinch thinking on it. I believe I can get five men, men who'll die. I think we have the right to stand up and fight back. I don't want to die, but I would prefer to die than allow what will take place here to occur.'[2]

What concerned Sands was that the Provisional Army Council (PAC) would veto a second hunger strike. On 20 December he wrote to Adams describing how: 'I'm still badly shaken, but what is killing me most and everyone here is if we get a refusal ... to have another go. We believe we have the ground to switch round the situation, hold what we have, and get at it again'. The H-Blocks were like 'morgues'. Another hunger strike was the only way forward. Sands had not 'eaten in days and I can't even sleep thinking about it all. If we hunger strike then that's sound. If not I will have to ask each block for their thoughts on future blanket protest, i.e. the best way to hold it together. When I say that, that's the ball busted (as they say)?'

In the evening, a comm from the PAC ruled out a second hunger strike. Sands replied to Adams: 'we accept army position on hunger strike, so that's out the windows. Now we are left with one feasible alternative – compromise'. But he complained: 'We lost seven men from the protest today. Time is not on our side. Brits know this. We'll have to work quick all round ... when we reach mid-next week I'm going to have to make a decision, because if I don't we'll have an exodus from the blocks'.[3] The options before the protesters were, as Sands told Adams, to test the 18 December 'agreement' and probe to see if more could be drawn from the prison regime, but: 'let's face it, comrade, Brits know they need only sit tight and most of us will go to them with our hands up. We have no banging power'. Adams acknowledged the prison regime was 'doggedly against any movement', yet urged that the system be tested.[4]

On Christmas Eve, Sands wrote to Adams setting out what he would accept: 'What we want is self-education and segregation. We must have both and a guarantee of self-education that will hold, that is Brits saying change in prison rules, work will be optional. We will be willing to concede clothing (so that's up our sleeve).' 'Work' included 'self-education'. During working hours, cell doors were to be left open for the prisoners to 'integrate and discuss'. The only other work they would consider would be self-maintenance of the block: 'We must not give on this at all ... No work', which included vocational training, cooking or laundry. 'So, to sum up, we'd wear their clothes during education periods, we'd want doors open to integrate.' Sands acknowledged that achieving this was 'going to be dodgy. Let me mention that in the conforming blocks four or five men congregating together is regarded as an illegal assembly. So, the point is they want to stop men mixing freely as this leads to discussion and politicising. We must break it, that is the point'.[5]

As the New Year began, Downing Street was informed that, since the hunger strike ended on 18 December, the dirty protest had continued, although the number taking part had fallen from 466 to 446. The twenty prisoners who had given up their protest had, as promised in Atkins' statement of 19 December, had all their privileges restored. All conforming prisoners in the Maze Prison, including the twenty who had given up their protest, had been issued with the new civilian-type clothing. But it was 'too early to say whether the "dirty" protest will now begin to crumble. The psychological barrier for men who have sustained such a protest for such a long time to conform even to a liberal prison regime cannot be expected, even at best, to be surmounted quickly.' In spite of clear statements by the Government of its position, there still seemed to be some uncertainty and confusion among the protesters, who might well in fact have been looking for some concession going beyond the position set out by Atkins, 'so that they may seek to turn the defeat of the hunger strike into a victory for the "dirty" protest'. Meanwhile, public opinion in Northern Ireland at large was calm, and there was now wide acceptance that the Government defeated the hunger strike without making concessions. Since the major battle had been won, there was less public concern with the lesser battle over the dirty protest.

'Scare stories' about a resumption of the hunger strike appeared in the press from time to time, but up to now such stories were not being given very wide credence in Northern Ireland in the aftermath of the failure of the last attempt. 'Secret sources' indicated that Republicans close to the protest, allegedly also reflecting opinion amongst the prisoners, were confused and disappointed that the dirty protest had not been brought to an end, effectively on their terms of no wearing of Government-issue clothing and no commitment to work. There was talk in such circles about calling a renewed hunger strike, not with the intention of carrying it through, but as a gesture designed to shake the Government's resolve. From the same sources, 'we learn that some Republicans are inclined to give the Government the benefit of the doubt on the basis that the holiday season has inhibited moves by the Government to make concessions.'[6] The Prime Minister was also informed, on 3 January, that Mike Pattison, from the NIO, had 'just rung to say that the National H-Blocks Organisation are meeting tomorrow and will probably be putting out a statement on Monday about future plans.' There had been some sign of activity from the people behind the dirty protest and hunger strikes, 'but the Northern Ireland Office don't regard it as particularly alarming, especially as there has as yet been no mention of a new hunger strike.'[7]

Back in Northern Ireland, Sir Kenneth Stowe chaired a meeting to assess the situation on the ground in the Maze. The civilian-type prison clothing issued to conforming prisoners was, he was told, 'varied and conveyed no sense of uniformity'. Orderlies wearing the new clothing worked in the blocks housing the protesters so that the civilian-type clothing would be seen by all prisoners.

Protesters wishing to receive visits would have to wear the new clothing during the visiting period. The protesters had been asked for their measurements so that the clothing would fit properly, but, by 6 January, only forty had complied. The dirty protesters, meanwhile, had been given two opportunities to accept clean accommodation and desist from fouling it; on 19 December some protesters had been moved into two clean wings, but had subsequently fouled them; on 5 January other protesters, including Sands, had been moved into another clean wing, but they had since fouled it. In both instances it had been made clear to the protesters by the prison staff that if the cells had still been clean after twenty-four hours, bedding and furniture would have been moved in very quickly. However, Sands had reacted to this in a hostile manner. Father Meagher saw S. C. Jackson, of the Prisons Branch, on 6 January, and said that Hughes and Sands had told him, on 3 January, that they needed a 'public statement of intent' from HMG or the prisoners would issue a public statement the following week threatening a further hunger strike. His version of their demands consisted of:

(a) Clothing. The protesters to be given prison clothing and their own clothing at the same time and to be allowed to choose what to wear from that.
(b) Work. Protesters would not do prison industrial work. They would do prison duties, vocational training and/or education.
(c) Segregation. This was the main demand of the loyalist protesters but they favoured this as well.
(d) Parcels. They would like to receive more than one parcel per month.
(e) Guarantor. They wanted a person of standing to supervise the implementation of the arrangements.

There had been no mention of association or restoration of remission, 'perhaps because these were already taken for granted by the protesters'. In general there did not seem to be a great deal of feedback on tension within the prison, 'but Sands was still working to gain movement from HMG.' Commenting on this, D. J. Wyatt told the meeting that there were two aspects of HMG's position to be both maintained and explained:

(a) There has been no deal; and there is nothing more on offer.
(b) Nevertheless, the Government does want to see an end to all protests and is anxious to bring about an early end to the dirty protest.

Blelloch pointed out the need to keep HMG's three objectives in sight:

(a) To maintain the position of HMG in the eyes of the community in Northern Ireland and to strengthen it if possible.

(b) To ensure that HMG honours its undertakings.

(c) To secure an end to the protests.

The third objective, he argued, 'should not be pursued at the expense of the other two. All of this was based on one crucial condition: there must be no move from HMG's stated position.' Stowe, summing up the mood of the meeting, decided that a submission should be prepared by Blelloch and E. N. Barry that would focus the Secretary of State's mind on the issues. It would set out the present position and then put two options:

(a) The first choice was for the Government to stand fast on its present position, adding nothing and taking nothing away from what we had done so far. This would put the proposition that the conditions available to the protesters were precisely the same now as on the day the hunger strike ended and it was put to them to conform and take advantage of what was on offer.

(b) The second choice was for HMG, without offering anything new, to make some pre-emptive moves such as offering clean furnished cells to some protesters at the next planned move to clean accommodation, at the same time making very clear how things would progress from that point if the protesters did not foul or damage the furnished cells.

It would be over-optimistic, thought Stowe, to expect the protesters to respond favourably to either option. The question was whether HMG had gone as far as it could in seeking to end the protests in the opinion of Parliament, the Northern Ireland community, the Taoiseach and international opinion, and whether that position could be sustained if the protests continued for the foreseeable future. The PUS noted that the next cycle of movement of protesters to clean prison accommodation was not to take place until the Secretary of State had decided on the course of action to be adopted.[8] Following this, the briefing to be given to the Prime Minister was along the following lines:

> You should know that lying behind this is our knowledge from intercepted letters that the hard men amongst the protestors in the Maze, led by Bobby Sands, intend to announce on Monday that there will be a further hunger strike commencing a few weeks hence. The letters make clear that Sands' object is to gain concessions on clothing, work and freedom of movement which go beyond the humanitarian regime on offer and would amount to recognising the protesters as political prisoners…
>
> Father Meagher is busted: he has been trapped by Sands into putting forward propositions which Sands (but not Meagher seemingly)

sees very clearly as conferring the 5 demands to these prisoners, ie political status. We cannot negotiate with Sands, via Meagher or anybody else. So we are continuing to use Toner and Murphy and other channels of communications (not negotiation).[9]

Atkins, after discussion with the Governor and officials of the Prison Service, approved the proposal to make another attempt to 'unwind' the protest early the following week by moving a small number of protesting prisoners into clean cells fitted out with furniture and bedding. This move would be carefully explained in advance to all the protesting prisoners, and to those who would be offered clean, furnished cells, as an initiative by the Governor to help to bring the protest to an end without requiring any prior commitment from them or any promise of a specific response. Downing Street was told: 'there is some reason to believe that it is the first step which is proving an insuperable barrier for the prisoners to cross. We are not confident that this move will work, but the Secretary of State is convinced that we ought to try it and be seen to be doing so, so that the Government's position remains positive and constructive even if we remain frustrated in our wish to bring the protest to an end.'[10]

On 10 January, however, the Republican mouthpiece, *An Phoblacht*, formally warned that British 'intransigence and inflexibility threatens to bring about the renewal of a hunger strike for political status by Republican prisoners. Today all supporters of the prisoners, particularly campaign activists, are once more being urged to go on the offensive, because of British inaction since the ending of the hunger strike during the week before Christmas.'[11] The prisoners, in a statement smuggled out of the Maze, declared:

We view the proposed move with acute cynicism, given the treacherous manner in which the British government has handled the protest, especially since the ending of the hunger strike. However, as a gesture of our sincerity in wishing to end the protest in a principled fashion, we have agreed that all the prisoners affected by the proposed move will not soil their cells for such a period of time as will facilitate the process which has been outlined to us.

The prisoners repeated that the ending of the blanket and no wash protest depended upon 'a sincere and responsible attitude from the British government.'[12] This was the background to Governor Hilditch's meeting with Sands, on 16 January, to inform him of his response to the latter's request for the protesters to be issued simultaneously with prison-issue civilian clothing and their own leisure clothing. The Governor told Sands that, having given careful consideration to his proposals, the implications were too serious and far reaching to give a decision that week. More time was needed for consideration. Reasonable progress, continued Hilditch, had been made so far with the first two moves of prisoners into clean, furnished cells. This was a suitable time to pause and to think very carefully again about what was available under the normal prison regime, remembering that the way forward had three parts to it, not just two: prison clothing and leisure clothing certainly, but also the activities that took place as part of the normal prison routine. The Governor added that he understood that the prisoners might find this delay frustrating and he understood that, as Sands told him, this would mean no more moves into clean, furnished cells for the time being. He was content to revert to the normal cycle for the moment. Hilditch explained that it was up to any protesting prisoner already in clean, furnished accommodation to ask for prison-issue civilian clothing if he wanted it. The Governor concluded by saying that he would see Sands again next week. Sands accepted the decision without any evident disappointment, and in the Governor's opinion seemed relieved that there would be no further moves into clean, furnished accommodation for the moment. He told the Governor that over the coming weekend he could expect ten prisoners from each of the two clean, furnished cells to ask to bath, shave and clean themselves up.[13]

Subsequently, Downing Street was informed, by the NIO, that the move, which included Sands, 'went smoothly, and we now have two wings of clean, furnished cells housing prisoners who, although they continue to refuse to wash, shave or wear prison clothing, are not fouling their cells or damaging their furniture.' Atkins was satisfied with the progress so far. He and NIO officials had been closely engaged in every detail of the winding down process, both with the prisons administration in Belfast and the Governor. The Governor had 'not put a foot wrong, and has handled a very sensitive situation with great skill.' The Governor, 'with our full backing, is quite clear that the protesting prisoners cannot be given the privilege of their own leisure clothing to wear at evenings and weekends before their intention to engage in the normal day-to-day activities of the prison has been demonstrated.' If they had it and then insisted – in breach of Prison Rules – on wearing it during the normal working day, it could precipitate a situation where prison officers would have to go into cells and forcibly undress the prisoners to take back their leisure clothing. 'We have evidence that some quarters would welcome such a development since it could give rise to allegations of assault on prisoners by prison officers.' It could equally have provoked the murder of a prison officer, potentially leading to subsequent outrage and disorder from both communities, including their paramilitaries: 'Our aim is to retain the initiative and so prevent the chain of events described above from taking place. In doing so, we shall continue our policy of explaining our actions clearly to the prisoners, prison staff, the media and all interested parties.' In keeping with this, the women protesters at Armagh would receive a note bringing them up to date with developments at the

Maze and encouraging them also to end their protest.[14] In Belfast, it fell to John Blelloch to contemplate the 'next moves', which had to be settled now because:

(a) the Governor's last meeting with Sands ended in acknowledgement that there needed to be a pause for reflection. We need to be clear whether or not it is in our interest to make the first move in ending the 'pause'.

(b) If it is in our interest, then we need to decide quickly because Sands may get in first and because, in any case, the Governor feels that he must see Sands again to follow up their last exchange in reasonably quick time (as further grounds for urgency, Mr Hilditch is due to commence ... a short period of leave that he has had planned for some time).

Blelloch described the possibilities to follow in terms of 'lateral' or 'vertical' moves. By 'lateral' moves, he meant moving more prisoners into furnished cells. By 'vertical' moves, he meant encouraging the prisoners to change from their 'blanket' or 'dirty' protests towards a 'no work' protest only. Both the number of protesters and the nature of their protest were to be considered and addressed. With regard to 'lateral' moves, Blelloch thought:

We could:-

(a) Say nothing and do nothing, leaving the initiative to the protesters. This would be inconsistent with a 'shutters up' policy and liable to misunderstanding, so it should only be adopted if it is clear there is no better course.

(b) Explain that there will be no further moves into furnished accommodation unless prisoners indicate that they want it. Better than (a) because it is clearer, (provided explained in a newsletter) and more positive, but to the extent that it relies on prisoners telling us their intentions orally it is vulnerable to misrepresentation should things subsequently go wrong.

(c) Explain, in a newsletter, that the routine of movement into clean cells will continue ... and that if, as in the second phase of the first move into a furnished wing, cells are clean after 24 hours, furnishings will be provided. Better than the other two because it avoids repeated questions and relies on what the prisoners do rather than what they say.

(d) Move another wing, or wings, or parts of wings, into clean cells already furnished, having given notice of intent to do so. In present circumstances this looks unnecessarily provocative.

On balance Blelloch considered that (c) looked the best bet: 'We look pretty secure against any charges of being either needlessly provocative or hesitant; and to the extent that those in furnished accommodation are now earning a reduced rate of lost remission, it applies just a little pressure.' With regard to 'vertical' moves, Blelloch thought that this must involve clothing, and was a much more difficult and important area than the 'lateral' moves already discussed. What would be done at this point depended on whether the authorities could actively seize the initiative, or merely react to a new move by the protesters. The chances were 'that we will be reacting. Sands has said what he wants', which was the simultaneous issue of prison and leisure clothing at a time when a conforming prisoner would be entitled to wear the latter. From a brief conversation with Father Toner, it looked as if that request would be repeated, but it would be reinforced by a prior gesture on the part of the protesters, of which the authorities had also had notice. The gesture was that a number of prisoners would volunteer to wash, shave etc. 'Our response needs to be selective', with the following main considerations in mind, argued Blelloch:

(a) we have got to have had sufficient indication of intent to conform before the privilege of leisure clothing is supplied. But in deciding what constitutes 'sufficiency' we have to bear in mind that this move might signal a return to a dirty protest, conceivably followed by a hunger strike. If so, then the Government's position must be seen to be reasonable as well as firm.

(b) We ought to select a move, or sequence of moves, which allows us to call a halt to the proceedings as easily and quickly as possible if we find that, whatever may have been said, prisoners are actually non-conforming.

(c) If we can devise a response which does not precisely match what Sands has asked for, but which it would be impossible for him reasonably to turn down, simply because of the mismatch, then that is much to be desired.

There were five possible things that the prisoners could do to demonstrate an intention to conform:

(a) they could simply say that this is what they intend;
(b) they could put on the prison-issue clothing;
(c) they could move to a conforming block;
(d) they could say they were available for work; [and]
(e) they could actually do some work that was allocated to them (which to be a fully credible indicator would need to be work other than that which we know they would be likely to settle for, i.e. light duties within the wings).

At the present stage of unwinding the protest, 'and with our present knowledge of what the protesters are really after, settling only for (a) above is surely not on', concluded Blelloch. The central question to be decided, therefore, was 'how many indicators do we need?' If it was only the first three, then it did not much matter when the process was initiated. If, on the other hand, 'we require four or five, then I think in practice we should have to insist that the process was initiated at the beginning, or at any rate early, in a working day.' There was one other implication of this central decision:

> If we require four or five indicators, then it becomes important that, in setting out this approach, that HMG should be seen to be offering a 'gesture' of its own at some point along what would otherwise be represented as a long string of 'gestures' by the prisoners. We have one available in that, once the prisoners are into prison-issue clothing, then extra exercise (one hour per day, making two in all) and one evening's association period of one hour (which we could presumably offer on the same day) would be available.

On this ('long winded') analysis, the balance of advantage, to Blelloch, did seem to lie with the four/five indicator approach. That conclusion was, of course, consistent with the line that was developing in a discussion of a sliding scale of punishment for prisoners, 'where our thinking links leisure clothing with work rather than with prison-issue clothing. If this is agreed, and if Sands, on seeing the Governor, says that a number of prisoners will wash and shave in return for which he is seeking the simultaneous issue of prison and leisure clothing ... then the line on which the Governor should respond would seem to be':

(a) to welcome the gesture as something that we have ourselves been looking for;

(b) to take Sands through the step-by-step approach making it clear that it will be operative on a weekday, which could be either Thursday or Friday – it seems best to react quickly to what Sands is saying rather than leave the weekend for reflection. If Sands refuses the offer, we are no worse off: at least the positive gesture will have been ours;

(c) we must have a newsletter ready, at the latest by the time that the Governor sees Sands, to show that the conclusions that we have arrived at independently, and for the record should this be the point when the prison slides back towards an expanded dirty protest and/or a hunger strike.

All this assumed that 'we are responding to a move on the protesters' part.' If, for whatever reason, Sands did not see the Governor, or said nothing that required a response, then the further question arose of whether or not a move should be made – even if unasked for – and if so, what it should be. There were two possibilities:

(a) the first is a low profile approach which would require us to do no more than issue this week as part of the newsletter dealing with furnishing, a recapitulation of what is available to a prisoner who elects to conform but adding the point that the wearing of prison issue clothing itself attracts certain benefits.

(b) We could ourselves select certain prisoners and put the proposition to them that if they accept prison issue clothing then the agreed sequence of events leading to the issue of leisure clothing would follow.

Because it seemed so overwhelmingly likely that Sands would be putting his own candidates forward, 'I have not had time to think through properly on what basis we might make the selection of prisoners, though this approach has the obvious attraction, if we can identify it, of making the offer to those who are believed to be the weaker brethren. I would like to consider this overnight.'[15]

After considering the options and then discussing the next moves with the Governor and Deputy Governor, it was decided that no difficulty arose on 'lateral' moves: they agreed that (c) was the best bet (explaining, in a newsletter, that the routine of movement into clean cells would continue and that if, as in the second phase of the first move into a furnished wing, cells were clean after twenty-four hours, furnishings would be provided). As expected, the problem arose on 'vertical' moves, regarding which the choice had to be made whether to adopt a high or a low profile. In terms of adopting a high profile, the following sequence would be followed:

(a) select (say) 10 prisoners: such a number would be significant for the purposes of a move, and manageable if things go wrong.

(b) Explain to this group that they were about to embark upon the following steps:
  (i) wash and clean up (if they have not already done so);
  (ii) select (or be issued with) prison-issue clothing;
  (iii) move to a wing in either a neutral or conforming block, be asked if they are available for work and, if so, given work to do; [and]
  (iv) when work was done, prison-issue clothing (if already in the prison) would be made available and could, of course, be sent for if not already in the prison.

The advantages of this course were, as pointed out by Blelloch, that it demonstrated who was running the prison, in that 'we can dictate the timing'; if there was a breakdown 'then it will be in response to a positive gesture by HMG that has been refused, and, finally, it is almost certainly not what Sands and the PIRA leadership want.' The Governor and Deputy Governor, however, advised strongly against it on the grounds that:

(a) it would fail (in the sense that the prisoners will not embark on this kind of course). This is because of the facts of the present [IRA] command structure in the wings whereby unless the prisoners had been selected by the CO and authorised to follow the course, they would have no choice but to refuse.

(b) Perhaps more seriously, any presentational gain that we might secure from such a refusal would have to be set against the possibility (to put it no higher) that such an initiative would be seen and represented to be forcing the pace and seeking confrontation, despite various protestations that we intend no such thing. Thus we would run a real risk of a step back into a dirty protest and possibly a hunger strike.

In the low-profile approach, 'we would stand on the present position as at present set out' on prison clothing, but adding that the wearing of prison clothing itself attracted certain advantages, such as extra exercise and an opportunity to associate. 'We must then expect to be tested, and we must assume that the timing and number of protesters used in the test will be inconvenient for us', warned Blelloch. As regarded timing, a possible sequence would be that a number of protesters would indicate that, as an earnest of their intention to conform, they were going to wash, shave, etc., in return for which they expected the issue of leisure clothing. The prison response would be on the following lines:

(a) once cleaned, prison issue clothing would be issued (issued rather than available for selection by them because that is what has happened to prisoners choosing to conform so far).

(b) The group would then if, say, 20 or less be moved to a 'neutral' or non-conforming block. If the group was larger than that we would say that we would have to proceed in stages.

(c) These moves would be made regardless of the timing of the original request.

(d) If by the time the prisoners were in the conforming block, it was not possible to allocate the prisoners to work and see the work done (eg because the process was initiated after lunch) then the prisoners would be told that the process would be resumed the following day (or the following Monday if the process started late on a Friday): but that, in the meantime, the privilege of association would be available, this being our response to the acceptance of prison clothing and movement to a conforming or neutral block.

(e) If the process was initiated early in the day, and work allocated and done, then leisure clothing, which we would have to assume would be available in the prison, would be issued.

As had been said already, as regards numbers, 'we should have to insist that we processed groups in sizes of our own choosing.' The advantages of this course were that it reproduced, as closely as possible, what happened with a conforming prisoner in normal circumstances, notably in the sense that it was he who initiated the process of returning to conformity: 'It absolves us from any charge of forcing the pace without removing any of the hoops that the prisoners must pass through. We have responses to the two most likely difficulties that we face, on timing and on numbers.' The disadvantage was that the main initiative passed to the 'other side.'[16] The decision was to opt for a 'lower profile' approach. The next stage was for the Governor to speak to Sands again, which he did on 21 January. Hilditch said to him:

> When we had our talk last week I said that there would be a temporary pause in the step by step approach and that I would have a further talk with you this week. It is in this connection that I am now here.
>
> In the first instance could I say that as I am talking to you a further Governor's statement is being circulated to protesting prisoners. I will leave a copy of this statement with you. This message is intended to update prisoners on progress so far. It contains information also about a reduced scale of punishment for those prisoners who are now on a clean form of protest.
>
> When we last talked, you expressed particular interest in a simultaneous issue of prison issue civilian clothing and own leisure clothing and as a first step towards this objective you mentioned the possibility of some prisoners washing and shaving which would serve as an indication of their willingness to move forward towards conformity.
>
> As you know the issue of leisure clothing is a privilege which is available only to conforming prisoners for wear outside working hours. The act of washing and shaving would however certainly constitute a first step in a sequence of moves which when completed would lead to leisure clothing being made available.
>
> What would happen next is that prison issue civilian clothing would be made available. Prisoners who put it on would be able to benefit from the opportunity to take daily exercise in the fresh air and for such prisoners I am prepared to double the exercise period to two hours a day. Limited association would also be available on one evening per week.
>
> The next step would be a move to a conforming wing. There prisoners would be assessed for and asked to undertake work. After the first work session was completed they would qualify for leisure clothing which would be issued as soon as it was available. In the meantime they would for the purposes of association be treated as conforming prisoners.

We shall implement this sequence as quickly as it practicable. The fewer the prisoners involved and the earlier in the working day the process begins the better chance of completing it in the same day. If it can be completed then leisure clothing (assuming it is available in the prison) will be issued. If it can not then, as an intermediate stage, the prisoners will be treated overnight, or over the weekend as the case may be, as conforming for the purposes of association: and the process will be resumed the next available working day.

It is up to you how to respond to this offer but I hope that what I have said and what is contained in my latest statement will be accepted as representing further positive stages in the step by step approach.[17]

Sands and the prisoners responded quickly. At approximately 9.45 a.m. on 23 January, E. N. Barry received a telephone call from Hayes, Governor Maze Cellular Prison. Ten protesting prisoners in H3 and thirty protesters in H5 had asked to see an Assistant Governor. It was believed that they intended to indicate their willingness to wash, shave and have their hair cut. Barry asked Hayes to do nothing until he gave him the necessary clearance. At 9.55 a.m., Barry spoke to Blelloch, who in turn spoke to London. At 10.00 a.m., Barry asked Hayes to arrange for an Assistant Governor to see the prisoners and to report back, through him, as quickly as possible. Because of the time factor, Barry asked that the Assistant Governor should provide an interim report after he had interviewed a few prisoners in each wing. At 10.25 a.m., Hayes phoned again. He said that four prisoners had been seen in each of the two blocks: H3 and H5. Their messages were identical:

1. they were prepared to wash, shave and have their hair cut;
2. they were prepared to clean their cells;
3. they were willing to have their photographs taken (this is a normal routine for a prisoner coming off the protest but prisoners do not always co-operate);
4. they did not wish to move from H3 or H5;
5. they were prepared to engage in full-time education;
6. they were not prepared to engage in prison work;
7. they were not prepared to wear prison issue civilian clothing unless own leisure clothing was provided at the same time;
8. they want to be regarded as non protesting prisoners; [and]
9. in taking this action they are having regard to the Secretary of State's statement of 19 December 1980.

Barry advised Hayes to await further instructions while he passed this information to Blelloch with a recommendation that they should:

i.   allow the prisoners to wash and shave and arrange to have their hair cut;
ii. make available in their cells on their return civilian issue clothing (because
     we do not have the prisoners exact measurements we will have to make
     an intelligent guess about sizes. If there are any obvious misfits these can
     be quickly rectified); [and]
iii. leave it to the prisoners to decide whether or not to put on the prison
     issue clothing. If they do not then the process comes to a halt. If they do
     then they are offered a move to a conforming block.

By 11.20 a.m., Barry received a phone call from the Governor. Eighteen parcels
of leisure clothing had now been delivered to the prison.[18]

Downing Street, in the meantime, was informed that these events at the prison
would 'involve our taking a stand to which the prisoners may well react adversely.
We therefore suggest that the nature of the stand, and the reasons for it, should be
passed on by you to Dermot Nally in Dublin, in order that the Irish Government
are forewarned. Our stand could become public quite soon' and be a subject for
discussion at a meeting of the National H-Block Committee Conference to take
place in Dublin the following weekend. The position at the prison was that some
100 prisoners had ceased to foul their cells and were housed in clean, furnished
cells. They had, though, continued their protest by refusing to wash and shave,
wear prison clothing or to undertake work. 'As we had expected, the prisoners
have today presented us with a renewed attempt to test the principles by which the
Government has always stood on this issue. They are trying to put us in a position
where either we grant a point which they can claim as a concession of principle,
or we take a stand on a point which they would represent as a minor one.'
    On Atkins' instructions, the Governor had told them that although they
could wash and shave and could have prison-issue civilian clothing, the regime
they were asking for was 'out of the question. There is no separate category of
"non-protesting" prisoners: if they conform with the full prison routine they will
be given the full range of privileges, including leisure clothing.' They would be
reminded that all of that was made quite clear by the Secretary of State's statement
of 19 December: 'We were always certain that a test of this sort would arise.
Given that we should in any event have had to stand on the declared principles
(no special regime for "political prisoners", no control by prisoners of the prison
regime) the timing is in two senses quite convenient.' First, the prisoners' request
was made early enough in the working day for the authorities to establish whether
they really were willing to conform, especially by accepting direction on work,
'before we had to give them their leisure clothing.' Second, following a number of
murders that week, the PIRA had 'reminded the general public of the shocking
nature of its members' crimes, and has provoked public figures (including some

who have a degree of sympathy for the protesters) into outright condemnation. We shall of course be making use of the latter point in meeting any suggestions that we should have conceded any of the prisoners' unacceptable suggestions.'[19]

Those killed were Ivan Toombs, a 42-year-old Protestant from County Down, a Major in the UDR and a customs officer, who was shot dead by the IRA at the office where he worked; Private Christopher Shenton, aged 21, of The Staffordshire Regiment, killed by an IRA sniper in Derry; Sir Norman Stronge, a former Speaker of the Northern Ireland Parliament aged 81; and his son, James Stronge, aged 48. The Stronge killings were particularly shocking: the two men were sought out and shot down by the IRA in their family home, Tynan Abbey, County Armagh. The home was then torched by the killers. The Provisionals stated that both men had been chosen as 'the symbols of hated Unionism.'[20] The Prime Minister wrote to Mrs Oliver, daughter and sister of the victims, to offer her personal condolences:

> I was deeply shocked by the news of the brutal murder of your father and brother at Tynan Abbey.
>
> You came with him, I remember, to the party here last summer for the Lord-Lieutenants, and the letter he wrote to me afterwards told me something of the courage with which he and your mother, while she was alive, had done their duty and faced the dangers around them. Words are not adequate, but I wanted you and the family to know that you have my deepest sympathy at this tragic time.[21]

The Stronge killings reinforced the fears of Protestants along the border that they were vulnerable to what they considered sectarian attacks by Republicans. In an effort to reassure one Unionist councillor, who wrote to the Prime Minister, Mrs Thatcher replied: 'I share your sadness and revulsion at the deaths of Sir Norman and his son. But I do not share your pessimism about terrorism along the border. As you say, I have been there. I know that groups of terrorists are still able to exploit the long stretches of lonely and isolated countryside through which the border runs, in order to murder, injure and cause destruction.' But the Prime Minister had also seen the 'skill, patience and grinding hard work' of the RUC and the Army, which were concentrated on preventing these attacks and on arresting those who had carried them out in the past. The Chief Constable and the GOC had the full support of the Government behind their efforts, and Mrs Thatcher was reassured that they were not wedded to particular operational patterns. They adopted varied tactics suited to the threat in particular areas. In the wake of the murders at Tynan, they were looking to see where they could make further refinements and improvements. In a last effort to reassure Protestants on the border, the Prime Minister wrote:

Let me, finally, assure you that it is no part of the Government's policy to encourage people in border areas to leave their homes. I know from Humphrey Atkins that he certainly did not advocate such a course of action when he met members of the Ulster Unionist Party during the Conservative Party Conference last autumn. What he did stress was the value of cooperation between neighbours and the importance of their keeping in touch with the security forces, for whom protection of those in border areas is a main priority, as problems arise.[22]

By this point, the apparent co-operation with the prison authorities had broken down. As *An Phoblacht* complained, the situation inside the H-Blocks had 'drastically reverted to square one' with the stubborn refusal of the British administration to follow a 'step-by-step' settlement, 'which they themselves' had proposed in December. The 'rising tide of militancy' in reaction to this by the blanketmen frustrated by lack of progress had resulted in the smashing of cell furniture, 'and has now brought the men to the brink of another hunger strike.' Over the previous two weeks, *An Phoblacht* reported, there had been a steady stream of grave reports from the H-Blocks, of prison warders verbally abusing prisoners, of a number of beatings and of other provocations, culminating in widespread assault upon and mistreatment of prisoners when they destroyed the furniture in their clean cells. This was a result of the 'insincerity' of the British administration when, by arrangement, the prisoners' relatives delivered clothes to the prison, on January 23; but after the men asked for these clothes they were refused them and were told by the prison Governor: 'Not until there is strict conformity and you agree to wear prison-issue clothes and do prison work will you get your own clothes.' This demand for the prisoners to 'crawl' was rejected out of hand by them, and 'shows that the Brits have learnt nothing about the tremendous strength of the Republican spirit of resistance' from the four-and-a-half-year-long struggle of the men 'on the blanket'.

But this, argued *An Phoblacht*, 'does not necessarily mean that the Brits are stupid. It shows that they are deliberately creating the conditions for another escalation of the prison protest, the defeat of which they believe will have adverse repercussions on the overall national liberation struggle.' By remaining intransigent and inflexible, HMG had taken a calculated political decision to ride out any criticism from those political and religious Irish leaders who were presently hiding their faces (those who called upon the hunger-strikers to 'give the British government a chance'), and to ride out the international criticism that the product of their intransigence – a second hunger strike – would inevitably bring. 'The Brits', meanwhile, had had a practice run in the psychological and physical isolation through which they put the last H-Block hunger-strikers. If there were another hunger strike, stated *An Phoblacht*, then it would be correct to assume that the gamble by the Brits of inflicting a defeat on the overall struggle through a defeat of the prisoners included not just going to the brink, as the last time, but also the temporary destabilization of the six-county State, which would follow in the wake of the death of a Republican hunger-striker, as the inevitable price to pay: 'It is on this count that the Brits are miscalculating.' Most Irish people, claimed *An Phoblacht,* viewed the British treatment of the prisoners and their attempts to criminalize them as being the 'traditional Brit response, which is as wrong today as it was in 1916 or with O'Donovan Rossa and Tom Clarke in the last century. People clearly understand that the republican prisoners are in jail under British lock and key because of their political motivation and the struggle for Irish Freedom: thus they are political prisoners and not criminals.' *An Phoblacht* then referred to Bobby Sands' explanation, smuggled out in a comm, as to what had happened when the men involved in the pilot scheme eventually applied for their clothes:

> So, on Friday 23rd January at 8 a.m., twenty men, as agreed, requested to wash, and to have their own clothes when the working day finished. By 11 a.m. (at which time the clothes were delivered to the jail by relatives) they were still waiting to be let out to wash. Shortly afterwards the prisoners told the Governor that they wanted to end the no wash/blanket protest and requested washing facilities and their own clothes. He hesitated and said he would answer this request later.
>
> At 2.30 p.m., six-and-a-half hours after the request for washing facilities was made, the governor returned and said they could wash and shave. However, he then said they would not get their own clothes until there was 'strict conformity'. Nevertheless, the prisoners went ahead and washed and shaved, and as the weekend started, requested again their own clothes.
>
> There is no legitimate reason ... why the prisoners should not have been allowed their own clothes, since after 4 p.m. on a Friday, except for orderlies, there is no prison work carried out and all prisoners are allowed to wear their clothes. None of these men were breaking 'prison rules' over the weekend, yet not only were they refused their own clothes, but they were threatened with being transferred to conforming blocks away from their comrades.

In a 'petty move', probably designed to distract attention from their overall intransigence, prison officials, when accepting the clothes from the relatives, 'made an issue of underwear and socks and refused to accept them!' Sands continued: 'The intransigent position of the British is in violation of a whole spirit of co-operation which followed the ending of the hunger strike, and which included talks between myself and the prison governor and the recognition of our command structure by the prison administration by allowing H-Block O/Cs to meet and discuss the settlement'. Through Sands' statement, the blanketmen pointed out that they had felt 'morally bound to explore all avenues which might have solved the H-Block crisis,' and that they had 'made genuine attempts to resolve the prison protest but have been exasperated and frustrated by the British administration. We have endured four-and-a-half years of the blanket protest, and were forced to escalate it when all else failed. We will not crawl now,' they asserted.

Shortly afterwards, reported *An Phoblacht*, prison warders moved in to the wings concerned, and moved the prisoners to other unfurnished cells. In H5 almost all of the forty-eight prisoners were assaulted in some fashion, some quite severely, 'according to initial reports seeping out of the prison.' Eddie Brophy (from Turf Lodge) 'may have suffered some form of heart seizure; and Eamon Digney (Andersonstown), who was also beaten, may have a fractured limb.' Neither of these men, nor any of the others injured, received any medical treatment throughout the night, it was claimed. In H3, men were moved to a wing, recently vacated by other blanketmen still on the 'no wash' protest, and consequently the cell walls were covered in excreta and cell floors in pools of water, waste and urine. The men were forced to remain in those cells throughout the night, naked but for a small hand-towel each and without blankets or mattresses. During the enforced wing-shift, men were assaulted by warders and in particular six men – Loudon (Unity Flats), Devlin (Ardboe), McKenna (South Derry), Gorman (New Lodge), and Lynch and McCloskey (Dungiven) were held over a table, the cheeks of their bottoms were forcibly parted by warders, and probed, 'in what can only be described as a disgusting act of humiliation and provocation.'[23] It was subsequently claimed by *An Phoblacht* that, in H5, prison warders came in at 10 p.m., about an hour after the 'smash-up'. A senior prison officer called Davenport led warders Alison, Mitchell, Howe and McAteer, among others, in the beatings. The warders, it was alleged, attempted to make Sean McPeake, from Bellaghy in South Derry, run, though he had an artificial leg, but he refused and sat down in protest. Davenport 'kicked and beat him and he was eventually dragged' to a recently vacated cell in A-Wing that was covered in excrement and pools of urine.[24]

As the countdown to the announcement of a second hunger strike continued, John Blelloch, at Cardinal Ó Fiaich's invitation, called on him at his house in Armagh on 28 January. Bishop Edward Daly was also present. After initial courtesies (throughout the hour and a half of the meeting the atmosphere was 'relaxed, friendly and low key – even in relation to the action of the prisoners at the Maze yesterday evening' following the destruction of furniture), Ó Fiaich asked Blelloch for his view of the situation. 'I said that I thought that we were dealing with a protesting population with two obvious components: the "rank and file", of whom a proportion (it was impossible to be precise how big a proportion) probably now did want to get off the protest, and "leadership", which undoubtedly contained a number of hard men.' The latter might themselves have felt that they were under conflicting pressures. There were those who might feel that, by the continued application of pressure, they could secure for themselves a privileged regime, or that privileges that were in prospect at the time the hunger strike was ended might be secured by such pressure, or both. As regarded the first of these two points, Blelloch hoped that he had succeeded in making it clear that the regime on offer was precisely the same as what had always been on offer, and would not be changed by pressure. The second was irrelevant, since the settlement of the hunger strike involved no deals. Acting in the opposite direction, the leadership may have been conscious of the difficulty of sustaining the protests given the number that were trickling from it, and, in particular, of sustaining a combination of a 'dirty', 'clean blanket' and 'no work' protest.

Blelloch noted that neither the Cardinal nor the Bishop had a lot to say about clothing. They indicated that they had said their say on October 23, and made no attempt to repeat what had been said. The Bishop asked why underwear and socks had been rejected when families brought clothing to the prisoners, and Blelloch explained that such items had never been part of the scope of leisure clothing. The Cardinal, 'interestingly', confirmed that this was the position on his own reading of the regime document given to the prisoners in December. Neither had any suggestions to make about routes that might be followed to ease the clothing impasse. The Cardinal had, however, spotted the ('no doubt deliberate') ambiguity of the prisoners' position about the simultaneous issue of leisure and prison-issue clothing: they had not actually said that they would not put the prison-issue clothing on.

Both the Cardinal and the Bishop were, in Blelloch's view, surprised by the stand that the protesters had taken on work, and both went a fair way to acknowledging that this now assumed an importance that they had not expected in the run-up to the hunger strike. Blelloch pointed out the full extent of the normal work routine from which the prisoners were seeking to be excluded: 'I think they recognised quite clearly that that is incompatible with the regime on offer', noted Blelloch. They both commented on the fact that there had been an enormous improvement in the relationship between prisoners and prison staff, at Armagh as well as at the Maze, in the immediate aftermath of the ending of the hunger strike, and that the position had subsequently deteriorated. Blelloch commented that he had, himself, sensed something of a deliberate attempt, in the words attributed to the prisoners, to blame any failure to maintain progress in winding down the protest on the attitudes of the Governor and his staff: 'I said simply that the Government rejected this line utterly: while prison staff (and prisoners) were human beings, and therefore not perfect, the former had done very well in managing a very difficult situation before and after the ending of the hunger strike.'

The three men then had some discussion about the 'step-by-step' approach. It was obviously desirable to move prisoners at least from a dirty to a clean protest: Blelloch suspected that both clergymen recognized the strength that had been lent to the Government's position by its attempts to achieve this. Nevertheless, 'could we do more? I replied, saying that we had explained in writing to the prisoners how they could indicate without, as it were, having to beg for it, that they wanted their cells to be furnished, and they knew that if they accepted "clean" status, then that attracted a revised scale of punishment. We could scarcely do more than that.' On the paramilitary leadership within the prison, the clergymen spoke of the need for good communication with all the prisoners and suggested that it would be advantageous if more time were available for prisoners to talk about things among themselves, for instance in a supplementary period of association (Bishop Daly's suggestion) or, if that were not possible, then before or after Mass at the weekend (Cardinal Ó Fiaich's). Blelloch noted this. With regard to 'compassionate' cases, Bishop Daly harked back to a parishioner of his who, as a lifer, had been refused compassionate leave for the death of his brother. Blelloch commented that this was a longer-term policy issue and that, in the meantime, 'we had acted upon agreement to treat protesting prisoners' for compassionate leave on a par with non-protesters. Blelloch added that in one case the privilege had been abused (the man addressed an H-Block rally). Cardinal Ó Fiaich also touched on the question of the return of the hunger-strikers to the main prison and the potential importance of this move. He believed that Brendan Hughes himself had hoped that the ending of the hunger strike would lead rapidly to an ending of all the protests, 'which would fit: it would have left Hughes' own position much less exposed', observed Blelloch, who said 'simply that we were giving thought to this ourselves.'

Cardinal Ó Fiaich, in summing up for his side, touched on the points above (step-by-step communication, and compassionate release). Blelloch replied by stressing that there was:

> … only one regime we were talking about and it was that set out in the Secretary of State's statement of last December, that we had been prepared to run risks in order to move protesting prisoners step by step towards that approach, and that while it remained our wish that this should happen, their action in vandalising accommodation and furniture had made the risks greater in future and the process correspondingly more difficult, and the difficulties had, in one sense, been compounded by the background of violence, from whatever quarter, against which the prison situation had now to be viewed.

As Blelloch left, the Cardinal said that Blelloch's coming to Armagh had been helpful in the sense that it was less conspicuous than he and Bishop Daly coming to Stormont. Blelloch noted: 'This may mean that this morning's exchanges were only the first of a renewed sequence. During the conversations the Cardinal has asked how he and the Bishop "might help". I avoided giving an answer. If so, then it will be necessary to consider with some care whether it is a road that [it] is in HMG's interests to go down.'[25]

One of the issues raised by the Cardinal, the paramilitary command structure in the Maze, was in fact already being considered by the NIO. E. N. Barry raised with Blelloch the question of HMG continuing to recognize Sands as spokesman for the Republican protesters at the Maze. Barry set out the issues involved:

The advantages of working through Sands are:

(i) It enables us to be sure of the prisoners' reaction at a very delicate time.
(ii) It allows us a very direct means of communication; there is no possibility of third parties misrepresenting either side.
(iii) It has been useful presentationally/politically up to now in facilitating some movement on the protest.

The disadvantages are:

(i) Such contact undermines the basis of our criminalisation policy; under this there is no such thing as a special terrorist prisoner or need for their spokesmen.
(ii) Governors strongly object to it as undermining their authority and having strong overtones of special category.
(iii) It is already leading to demands from other factions to have their spokesmen recognised; this will become increasingly difficult to resist the longer matters continue.

Clearly, argued Barry, the disadvantages would increase and would quickly become decisive 'unless we attempt to judge the issue as has been done in the Irish Republic, where they appear to recognise spokesmen when it suits them. This is not a course which I would advocate.' Nevertheless, it did raise the question of 'how we continue to communicate with prisoners; this has been one of our strong points so far and it is vital that we do not let something happen which could be propagandised as a break in communication on our part', warned Barry. The possibilities were:

(a) Continue to work through spokesmen as long as it suits us.
(b) Work directly with the prisoners – perhaps individual interviews with

Assistant Governors as were undertaken recently. We may of course only be referred to the O/C!

(c) Work less directly, but still individually, through the medium of 'governor's newsletters'. These are very valuable in safeguarding our position, though Governors are not enthusiastic about such an unorthodox means of communication.

(d) Work still more indirectly through, say, the prison chaplain (or even Father Meagher). Contact through the chaplain has presentational advantages over other forms in that he is likely to continue to be discreet. However it does place him in a difficult role and leaves open the chance of his being used by the prisoners.

Barry invited Blelloch to note the options discussed. His own preference was for the use of spokesmen to be phased out as soon as possible. However, as political considerations had, of necessity, been the deciding factor hitherto, it was clearly a matter of judgement in the weeks ahead as to when the political/presentational returns were insufficient to outweigh the objectives.[26] Barry had made this last point before the 'rampage' by the prisoners; now, following this, he noted: 'We are now back to square one as regards the dirty protest, and in the altered circumstances I think we should now revert to dealing with Sands as an ordinary prisoner and refuse to recognise him as a spokesman on behalf of a group of prisoners'[27] Blelloch, however, was of the opinion that 'much as we all disliked the practice of recognising paramilitary spokesmen among the prisoners, it was still necessary for the present to maintain certain channels of communications with the prisoners, bearing in mind the prospective new hunger strike.' He was not in a position, therefore, at this stage, to state categorically that there was to be no further dialogue with 'Sands and company', although he recognized that this might have to be much more tightly controlled in future. This was a 'purely temporary arrangement' aimed at getting over what could be a very sensitive period with important international and political implications. After further discussion with Barry it was agreed that:

(i) we should continue as necessary to make use of the news sheets to communicate with prisoners;

(ii) NIO should continue to brief prison chaplains on the background to what HMG is doing to resolve the issue;

(iii) if Sands, or whoever is acting as o/c of the dirty protesters asks to see the Governor he should be asked to indicate whether it is a personal matter he wishes to discuss or something affecting other prisoners.

(iv) The Governor may exercise his discretion and see Sands without reference to the [Prisons] Department, in which event headquarters will support his action.

(v) If however the Governor thinks that he should not grant Sands' request for an interview he should consult NIO (Mr Barry or Mr Jackson) before proceeding further.

(vi) If Sands asks to be allowed to speak to prisoners from other blocks, ostensibly for the purpose of de-escalating the protest he should be asked to produce clear evidence of his intentions and whether he would be agreeable to a discipline officer being present when such talks were taking place.

(vii) Applications for special visits will be granted sparingly.[28]

This compromise did not end the NIO debate about to do in relation to the paramilitary command structure. Another official, B. A. Blackwell, pointed out that, according to his contacts in the Home Office, there were three ways in which the Prison Authorities in Great Britain broke up prisoners' command structures within prisons to maintain control and discipline:

(a) The irregular movement of prisoners between prisons. This is used in particular with high risk prisoners to prevent the long term planning of escapes as well as a means of control.

(b) The use of Rule 43 of Rules for Prisons in England and Wales to segregate prisoners in the interests of good order and discipline.

(c) The use of Prison Circular No 30 of 1974 which allows a Governor to remove prisoners to designated cells in other prisons for periods of up to 28 days.

Clearly, within the geographical limitations of Northern Ireland, and also because of the administrative desirability of confining the dirty protest to one (male) prison, method (a) 'is not feasible.' Methods (b) and (c), however, were 'certainly applicable and relevant to the situation in the Maze.' Northern Ireland Prison Rule 24 was the equivalent of Rule 43, and with the authority of the Secretary of State there was no reason why the IRA O/Cs 'Sands, Hughes, McKeown and McCallum, Walsh et al should not be segregated in a wing separate from the other protesters. The Governor will then know only too well how to disrupt channels of communication between the segregated wing and the other dirty wings.' There was also no reason, argued Blackwell, why one wing in Magilligan or a few cells in Crumlin Road prisons could not be specially designed and used to take ringleaders at the Maze out of circulation for 28 days or so at a time. Admittedly the designated cells would be fouled, but administratively that would be manageable because of the small number involved. A further method, which Blackwell did not think would be so effective, would be to move a block or wing spokesman into a different wing or block from his cell- and wing-mates every time a move was made in the routine cleaning cycle. This would at least disrupt chains of command and channels of communication within the prison. Blackwell believed that methods (b) and (c) were relevant, and 'with ingenuity and the will to make things more difficult for the protesters the Prison Authorities could seriously disrupt terrorist command and control within the prison.' He recommended the use of some or all of the methods described to keep the Republican prisoner hierarchy unstable and thus to loosen their control over the main body of Republican prisoners: 'It goes without saying that the Prison Authorities must also refuse to recognise spokesmen – a direction I am sure they will be only too delighted to follow!'[29]

Barry, however, pointed out to Blelloch that 'the Home Office situation was quite different from ours. They have a total prison population of some 45,000, of whom not more than 200 are PIRA prisoners. Also they have numerous high-security prisons to which these prisoners can be moved.' The NIO's position was that any high-risk prisoner convicted of a terrorist type offence had to be held at either the Maze or Belfast prisons. Magilligan, in Derry, because of its isolated position and the response time by a rapid reaction force, was the only one suitable for accommodating medium-risk prisoners, and 50% of the population at Belfast were remand prisoners with only part of that establishment available for convicted prisoners. Barry pointed out that, as a result of their protest action, the non-conforming prisoners had achieved *de facto* segregation. Unless, therefore, 'we are to decide to house some of the protesters in Belfast Prison, the scope for movement of individual prisoners is restricted to internal transfers within the existing ... H-Blocks.' The movement of some of the protesting prisoners to Belfast Prison would be costly, disruptive, provocative, and would create serious managerial difficulties, including medical supervision, hygiene, cell cleaning, exercise, communication, etc. The structure and layout of the prison would not lend itself to this type of regime, and industrial cleaning of cells would be impracticable.

Barry acknowledged: 'We can move Sands around within the existing four protesters' blocks until he is dizzy but wherever he is located he will still be the recognised o/c of the protesters. Likewise, if we move the existing O/C s in the various wings to another wing or another block, a replacement will spring up overnight, and it is very doubtful if moves of this kind would serve any useful purpose such as disrupting the prisoners' channels of communication.' Since the phasing out of special category status, Governors had stamped down hard on any overt attempts by individual prisoners to represent themselves as spokesmen on behalf of particular groupings, and any such actions had been dealt with as offences under Prison Rules and punished. The authorities could follow any or all of the things suggested by Blackwell, but in the case of the protesters, any movements of prisoners would have to be within the existing H-Blocks. There might have been the occasional case where such a move would be justified, but

Barry was 'far from satisfied that anything would be achieved by chopping and changing prisoners around regularly within these narrow confines, particularly since we cannot say categorically at this stage that we will not need to recognise and consult with the o/c of the dirty protesters at some future date now that we are faced with the prospect of another hunger strike.'[30]

While apparently stuck with the PIRA command structure, the NIO proceeded to keep Downing Street informed regarding events in the Maze. The Prime Minister was told that the process of unwinding the dirty protest had, for the time being at least come to a halt, and: 'We have good reason to believe that there is now a significant risk of a renewed hunger strike'. If one were to begin:

> ... we could expect notice of it in the next few days, and the likeliest start date would be in the middle of February, ie so that the crisis was reached, for maximum effect, by Easter. It cannot be assumed that in this event PIRA would again maintain a tacit ceasefire: if they did not, we might expect to see a shift of emphasis in their intentions to attacks on eg members of the judiciary, civil servants and politicians, with further PIRA activity on the mainland and the continent.'[31]

This update was sent to Downing Street on 5 February. Two days later, *An Phoblacht* made the dramatic announcement that everyone had been waiting for of a 'New Hunger Strike To the Death'. A statement from the prisoners declared:

> We the Republican political prisoners in the H-Blocks of Long Kesh and Armagh prison, having waited patiently for seven weeks for evidence that the British government was prepared to resolve the prison crisis and having given them every available opportunity to do so, declare our intention of hunger-striking once more.
>
> Obstacle after obstacle was placed in our way, but we felt morally bound to explore every avenue before giving into exasperation and anger. The pettiness of the British administration was well demonstrated on January 23rd when the prison governor acting under orders refused a number of men their own clothes.
>
> It is a fact that ordinary prisoners in conforming blocks are generally wearing their own clothes unchallenged, and we were angered that the Brits were more intent upon humiliating us once again than on settling the prison crisis.
>
> Our last hunger strikers were morally blackmailed by a number of people and politicians who called upon them to end the fast and allow the resolution of the protest.

It needs to be asked openly of the Irish Bishops, of Cardinal Ó Fiaich and of politicians like John Hume, what did your recommending ending of the last hunger-strike gain for us?

We the blanket men, and we the women political prisoners in Armagh, have had enough of British deceit and of broken promises. Hunger-strikes to the death if necessary will begin commencing from March 1st 1981, the fifth anniversary of the withdrawal of political status in the H-Blocks and in Armagh jail. We are demanding to be treated as political prisoners which everyone recognises we are.[32]

Blelloch's response to the announcement, as he outlined to the Secretary of State, was that if a hunger strike started, it would do so in circumstances that differed in at least two important respects from the last. First, HMG had a well-established and generally well-understood position at the outset. Second, the background against which the hunger strike would be taking place was a good deal more uncertain and confused than it was four months ago: 'Thus we can afford to start with a low level public profile: how and when we decide to change that profile cannot be very positively debated in advance. Everything will depend on how the background I have referred to bears upon the issue of the strike itself'. Blelloch suggested, as the main elements of HMG policy in handling the strike, the following:

(a) to remember, at all times that the hunger strike is an incident (albeit an important one) in a wider campaign. The tactical handling of the hunger strike should always be consistent with our objectives in conducting that wider campaign.

(b) The Government's position rests squarely on the statements of 4 and 19 December 1980. There is within these statements ... some room for change. But, essentially, standing on those two statements means that, this time as last, what we are about is a confrontation with the strikers and their leaders and not a negotiation.

As regards detailed handling, in the short term, Blelloch considered that the key points were:

(a) We do not yet know that a strike will begin on 1 March and we do not want to promote the idea that we expect it, still less that we welcome or fear it.

(b) This time we have a position that is, by and large, well known and pretty well accepted.

Against that background, 'we need to decide, first of all, whether or not anything be said publicly before 1 March. My recommendation would be that it need not, but that we should prepare a brief statement of HMG's position for issue as a Press Notice as soon as we know that a hunger strike has started.' Secondly: 'What we do privately is another matter.' Here Blelloch thought that 'we must concentrate our efforts before 1 March only on those people and institutions likely to be directly influential. The usual round robin approach to "the great and good" should be resorted to only after a strike has begun.' The key people, not necessarily in order of importance, whom Blelloch suggested were:

(a) John Hume, whom either PUS or Mr Wyatt might see.
(b) The Cardinal, Bishop Daly and Fathers Toner and Murphy ... Any further action can be settled in the light of that meeting.
(c) The four Church leaders collectively have asked to see the PM (about unemployment) on 2 March. My recommendation would be that she should see them: and if she does should use that opportunity to convey our message about the hunger strike. If she does not they will need personal messages after the hunger strike has started.
(d) Dublin. Mr Wyatt is seeing Irish officials tomorrow. We should prepare a message from the PM to the Taoiseach in the light of that, before the hunger strike begins.
(e) PUS should write to Cardinal Hume [of the Roman Catholic Church in England and Wales] and Archbishop Heim [the Papal Apostolic Delegate to Great Britain] next week.[33]

As part of this process, Atkins, accompanied by Blelloch and Barry, saw Cardinal Ó Fiaich and the two prison chaplains (albeit at the Cardinal's request) on 18 February. The Cardinal had emphasized before the meeting that it was important that the fact that it was taking place should not be disclosed. At the beginning of the talk, he and the two chaplains underlined this point, Father Toner commenting that it would adversely affect their relationship with the prisoners, who would even be annoyed that the prison chaplains had discussed the hunger strike with the Cardinal, let alone with the Secretary of State. Ó Fiaich then explained that he had two suggestions to make to Atkins. He was glad to have an early opportunity to make them, because any action on the Government's part could be taken more easily and more effectively before the hunger strike began. Atkins, meanwhile, asked about the atmosphere in the Maze. He could not understand the attitude of those beginning a hunger strike in present circumstances, following the abject failure of the first. Father Toner replied that the atmosphere was frightening. There appeared to be a determination to have a 'sacrifice'. The prisoners' attitude was that the Government did nothing following the end of the hunger strike, though Toner himself acknowledged that the Government had done what they had undertaken to do. The attitude of the prisoners was more extreme than on the previous occasion. They did not really expect to succeed, although privately they probably had some faint hope that they might. Ó Fiaich added that he thought the intransigence of Sands as the leader of the hunger strike might not be typical of the rest. He, therefore, wondered whether the prisoners could be permitted to meet together to discuss what they were setting out on. Fathers Toner and Murphy immediately made clear that they did not think the Cardinal's suggestion could work: nobody would speak out against the hunger strike at such a meeting, and consequently no debate about the validity of the hunger strike could get going. They agreed with the comment by Atkins that the result of the sort of meeting that the Cardinal had in mind might be to strengthen the influence of the leaders within the prison rather than to weaken it. Barry pointed out the implications for prison discipline of allowing the prisoners' O/C to hold a meeting. Father Murphy, however, believed that the prospect of averting the hunger strike was not entirely hopeless. If there were negotiations on some points, which could be expected to result in a settlement of the protest within two months or so, that might end the hunger strike. (It was noted that 'he did not say that would prevent it from beginning.') The sort of points he had in mind, given that three of the original five demands had been substantially overtaken, was that the prisoners might adopt a lower degree of protest if they were permitted by the Government to wear their own clothes and refuse to work. Father Murphy recognized that the latter would be a breach of Prison Rules, which would merit punishment, though on a lower scale than the full-scale protest that was in progress.

Atkins reminded the two Fathers that the Government had made clear all along that there were no concessions on offer: the Government's stance had been very clearly set out and would remain unchanged. Father Murphy, nevertheless, suggested that to permit prisoners to wear their own clothing as of right might help, although he admitted that he could not guarantee that it would achieve any effect. He acknowledged that in their public statements the prisoners were asking for political status, but felt that by this sort of means the prisoners would be prepared to accept continuing their protest on a lower level: it was the sort of concession that would be seen both within the prison, as well as outside it, as a move in the face of which the prisoners would have to make some move in return. Father Toner then emphasized that, although he could understand that the Government did not see it in this way, the prisoners regarded any deviation from the full-scale dirty protest on their part as being in a sense a concession, and one that merited a balancing concession from the Government. That was how the prisoners saw it: he for his part acknowledged that the Government had complied with their undertakings, and had treated the prisoners reasonably. It was noteworthy that the seven who had been on hunger strike had, in Father Toner's view, been affected by the humane and considerate treatment that they received while in the prison hospital. Toner emphasized to Atkins that the Government should not expect full conformity from the prisoners; it would be appropriate to adopt a more limited objective. It was interesting that the prisoners had seen the immediate offer of prison-issue civilian clothing and a request that they should work as an immediate challenge to adopt complete conformity. As a result, they had reacted against it.

Atkins, though, emphasized that the Government had never expected complete conformity, and had made the important gesture of adopting a lower scale of punishment for a lower degree of protest. That was consistent with what had always been on offer. Other concessions were out of the question. Blelloch added that the Government had to take account not only of opinion within the prison, but its duty to the community at large, who expected the Government to abide by the principles that it had set out. After the end of the meeting Father Toner again stressed that he was in no doubt that the Government had stood by their undertaking: he made no complaint about that. The prisoners saw it differently because, as he had explained to the Secretary of State, they regarded moving to a lower level of protest as a concession that merited a move on the Government's part. Toner had not, in discussion with the Secretary of State, been endorsing that attitude; he had merely been describing it. His assessment of the prospects for the next few weeks was very gloomy. He believed that Sands had deliberately put himself in a position where he would be under maximum pressure to continue his fast to death, and he believed that he would do so. Toner for his part recognized that the Government's position had been very clearly set out, and he quite understood why they could not shift from it.[34]

D. J. Wyatt, of the NIO, then met with Irish officials, including Dermot Nally, and took the Cabinet Secretary-General through the sequence of events that had led to the renewed hunger strike. He emphasized that there had been no possibility of 'fudging at the edges.' The prisoners were not interested in anything except the regime for which they had begun their protest in 1976: a prisoner-of-war regime. Wyatt explained:

> We thought they realised that we would not give in … They were not prepared to surrender after 4 years. They were faced with a choice between continuing the dirty protest whilst they served out life sentences, or making yet another desperate doomed throw. They had taken the latter choice. The rationale for the renewed hunger strike seemed to me as simple as that.

Nally listened carefully and nodded assent throughout. In a separate conversation, Neligan, Assistant Secretary in the DFA, asked what HMG's tactics would be in handling the wider community. Wyatt said: 'we were keen not to raise the temperature before a hunger strike began' – Neligan said that was absolutely right – but once the hunger strike did begin, 'we would make our position clear on the record. We would then make sure that the people in the community were kept in touch with so that we maintained the impression of a caring government in charge of events.' Neligan, however, thought that HMG's 'long, boring statements perhaps did more harm than good.' Mike Moriarty (of the NIO) and Wyatt explained why it was necessary to get the facts on the record, and Neligan professed to be convinced.

Wyatt did not appeal for support from the Irish in the event of a hunger strike; the British Ambassador, Leonard Figg, had briefed him that he would prefer that the NIO did not do so on this occasion since the Irish would find this politically hard to give. Figg was keen that he should be authorized to give the Taoiseach a message from the Prime Minister before 1 March if HMG thought that a hunger strike was going to begin then. He thought it important that 'we should keep Mr Haughey on side ... an appeal for any public help from Mr Haughey would embarrass him.' Wyatt responded that he thought that, at the very least, the Prime Minister, in any message she sent to Haughey, would wish to appeal for 'support'.[35]

On 23 February, as the clock ticked down, Atkins formally warned the Prime Minister: 'We now expect that a second hunger strike will begin on 1 March, which would mean that the crisis would be reached over Easter.' Whether initiated by Sands alone, or by a small group at the Maze, 'we could expect further hunger-strikers, including some women at Armagh, to join in later on', he told her. The hunger-strikers themselves, and the leadership of the PIRA and INLA, probably realized that HMG would not grant these demands: 'Their belief must be that the Republican cause will be the better off for the addition of one or more martyrs. They presumably hope to win advantage for that cause from the strains that a hunger-striker, still more a death, would place on the community in Northern Ireland.' If a hunger strike did begin, then there were three main differences from the position last October, argued Atkins. First, this strike would take place in the aftermath of the failure of the first. The fact of that failure, and of its having occurred in the face of a Government position based on firm principles, 'is well understood in the community, and will be a source of great strength to us this time.' Second, the programme of street protests in support of the hunger-strikers could be expected to have small beginnings, building up to a climax at Easter, not least because the organizers recognized the difficulties they faced mobilizing mass support. But it was clear that, unlike last time, these demonstrations might seek rather than avoid confrontation. Third, the strike would be taking place in an atmosphere 'whipped up by the activities of Dr Paisley.' He had planned a programme of eleven rallies, two of which had taken place already, culminating in what he hoped would be a mass turnout at Stormont on 28 March.

It was against this background that Atkins considered how to deal with the hunger strike. First, the Government had already set out in some detail both the principles by which it was guided in dealing with the first hunger strike. Second, a great deal would depend, particularly in view of the character of the demonstrations forecast, on the sensitivity with which these were handled by the security forces: 'They learned a great deal from the last hunger strike and I have every confidence in them', declared Atkins. Third, 'notwithstanding our success in dealing with the earlier hunger strike,' a sustained effort would be needed again to put the Government's position across, and Atkins intended, with his Ministers and officials, to keep in close touch with community leaders. In the meantime, there were two items of immediate concern: 'The attitude of the United States is of great importance to us. Second, I think it is important that Mr Haughey should be aware of the Government's attitude before the strike begins.'[36] Mrs Thatcher duly sent a personal message to Haughey on 25 February:

> As you will know there is a renewed threat of a hunger strike.
>
> We are not prepared to concede these demands and we believe the prisoners know it. We think that their object now is to bring about one or more deaths of hunger strikers in order to inflame community passions. All the evidence is that community support for the protesters is at its lowest ebb. If there is another hunger strike we expect it to be accompanied by a campaign of Provisional IRA and INLA violence designed to provoke the Protestant community whose mood is more volatile than at the time of the last hunger strike.
>
> If there is anything you feel you can do to reinforce the actions we shall be taking to inform those who might have influence on the prisoners, this would be very helpful.[37]

In Dublin, the British Ambassador handed the message to Dermot Nally, who said that he would ensure that the Taoiseach received it that evening. He thought that the latter would certainly do what he could to help, per the last sentence of the message. Figg then took the opportunity to tell Nally that one of the ways in which the Irish Government could help would be in ensuring that the clear statement of the prisoners that they wished to be treated as political prisoners was properly known. For example, Figg had that morning received a letter from Bishop Cahal Daly in which he claimed to have reliable and recent information that a compromise would be possible on clothing and work. It seemed to Daly 'totally unjustifiable and inexcusable that the whole community be plunged into tension, probably accompanied by sectarian assassinations – merely because of quibbles over what qualified as "prison work", and what constitutes "prison clothes".' Figg did not, of course, know who the Bishop's informant was, 'but clearly he had made more impression than I had' – a reference to when the Ambassador had called on Daly on 6 February. It was in 'countering this kind of clever mischief in which we would like to look to the Irish for help' explained Figg.[38]

When the Ambassador later met with the Taoiseach, Haughey mentioned the message from the Prime Minister and said that he would certainly try to help if a hunger strike were to start. He desperately hoped, though, that it would not, and said, quite bluntly, that if he were in charge up in the North he could stop it without sacrificing any principles; what was needed was deviousness and cunning, seeming to make concessions without actually doing so. While there would probably be even less public support than last time, a new hunger strike would make things very awkward politically in view of the possibility of a general election in the Republic later that year. He thought that if a strike did start, those concerned would be bound to carry it through to death. Figg replied: 'I really didn't know. Last time the seven strikers were apparently chosen for their toughness and one wondered, if a strike were to start, how tough the next lot would be.' Haughey then commented that he had been much impressed with the explanation Ken Stowe had made at the time of the Dublin Summit when explaining how the Northern Ireland Office was handling the previous hunger strike. This had been a good mixture of ingenuity, subtlety and sensitivity. Figg assured the Taoiseach that just as much effort and thought was being applied in this new situation. Haughey was 'glad to hear it', and asked Figg particularly to pass on his remarks to Stowe, whom he held in high regard.[39]

As the British and Irish prepared their responses, *An Phoblacht* reported that the second hunger strike was backed by the seven participants of the preceding one. 'Firstly,' the seven stated, 'the hunger strike was ended only after we had received assurances, which, had they been adhered to, would have resulted in a just settlement to the problems here in H-Block and in Armagh jail. The detailed document which was presented to us and which accompanied these assurances could have satisfied our five basic demands', they declared. 'Initially it was hoped that an end to the blanket protest would follow in a matter of days. That this has not materialised is entirely the fault of the British government. The blanketmen were faced with such vindictiveness and intransigence that they were forced to call another hunger strike.'[40] On the eve of the second hunger strike, *An Phoblacht* declared: 'Force Thatcher to Turn Again', arguing that 'If the life of Bobby Sands, and the lives of those of this comrades joining him in the hunger strike, are to be saved, the British government must be forced to swallow hard on all of its deceit and on all of its intransigence, and to reverse its refusal to restore political status.' *An Phoblacht* was confident that 'It can be done.' It noted how, already, in the preceding ten days, Margaret Thatcher, whose 'arrogant boast' in her rigid pursuit of Tory economic policies was 'This lady is not for turning' had been humbled and humiliated by the organized strength of tens of thousands of coal miners in Britain, and forced to make a public U-turn in acceding to their demands to stop pit closures. Massive mobilization, co-ordinated protests, and growing confidence in 'our, and the hunger-strikers', ability to win, 'are the key ingredients which will shatter Thatcher's stone-walled heart again and force another U-turn, this time in her inhuman H-Block policy.' *An Phoblacht* called on all Nationalists to: 'Either stand with the prisoners or stand against them: there is no middle ground. Those who last time called on the prisoners to end their hunger-strike to allow a just resolution of the crisis have been swept away on the tide of their own insincerity and the British refusal to implement the December 18th settlement. Where are their voices now?'[41]

NOTES

1   O'Hearn, *op.cit*, pp. 307–308.
2   *Ibid*, p. 306.
3   *Ibid*, p. 308.
4   *Ibid*, p. 309.
5   *Ibid*, pp. 312–313.
6   TNA PREM 19/503 Hopkins to Pattison, 2 January 1981.
7   TNA PREM 19/503 Debbie Green to Prime Minister, 3 January 1981.
8   PRONI CJ4/3645 Notes of a Meeting on the Prison Protests held in PUS's Office, Belfast, on Tuesday, 6 January 1981.
9   TNA PREM 19/503 Speaking Note.
10 TNA PREM 19/503 Hopkins to Alexander, 9 January 1981.
11 *An Phoblacht*, 10 January 1981.
12 *An Phoblacht*, 17 January 1981.
13 TNA CJ4/3639 Report of Governor's interview with Sands – p.m., Thursday, 16 January 1981.
14 TNA PREM 19/503 Harrington to Alexander, 16 January1981.
15 TNA CJ4/3639 HMP Maze Prison Protests: The next moves, 20 January 1981.
16 TNA CJ4/3639 HMP Maze Prison Protest, 21 January 1981.
17 TNA CJ4/3639 Speaking Note used by Governor in talking to Sands on 21 January 1981.
18 TNA CJ4/3639 Note for the Record, Friday, 23 January 1981.
19 TNA PREM 19/503 Harrington letter to 10 Downing Street, 23 January 1981.
20 David Mc Kittrick et al, *Lost Lives: The Stories of the Men, Women and Children Who Died as a Result of the Northern Ireland Troubles* (Mainstream 2006), pp. 848–849.
21 TF Thatcher MSS (Churchill Archive Centre): THCR 3/2/48 f8.
22 TF Thatcher MSS (Churchill Archive Centre): THCR 3/2/49 f37, Prime Minister to Councillor Mrs Hazel Bradford, 6 February 1981.
23 *An Phoblacht/Republican News*, 31 January 1981.

24   *An Phoblacht/Republican News*, 7 February 1981.
25   TNA CJ4/3639 Blelloch Note for the Record, 28 January 1981.
26   PRONI NIO/12/196A Barry to Blelloch, 27 January 1981.
27   PRONI NIO/12/196A Barry to Blelloch nd.
28   PRONI NIO/12/196/A Note of Meeting in Mr Blelloch's Office on Friday, 6 February 1981.
29   PRONI NIO/12/196/A Attacking the Prisoners' Command Structure in the Maze, 10 February 1981.
30   TNA CJ4/3626 Barry to Blelloch, Attacking the Prisoners' Command Structure in the Maze, 11 February 1981.
31   TNA PREM 19/503 Harrington to Alexander, 5 February 1981.
32   *An Phoblacht/Republican News*, 7 February 1981.
33   TNA CJ4/3626 Blelloch to PS/Secretary of State, Handling of a Hunger Strike, 18 February 1981.
34   TNA CJ4/3626 Secretary of State's Meeting with Cardinal Ó Fiaich, Father Toner and Father Murphy – 3 p.m. on 18 February 1981 at Hillsborough Castle.
35   PRONI NIO/12/196/A. Wyatt to Blelloch, 20 February 1981.
36   TNA PREM 19/503 Atkins to Prime Minister, Hunger Strikes at HMP Maze and Armagh, 23 February 1981.
37   NAI D/T 2011/127/1050 Message from the Prime Minister to the Taoiseach of 25 February 1981.
38   TNA PREM 19/503 From Dublin Telegram number 48 of 25 February 1981.
39   TNA CJ4/3626 Dublin to FCO Telegram Number 51 of 26 February 1981.
40   *An Phoblacht/Republican News*, 21 February 1981.
41   *An Phoblacht/Republican News*, 28 February 1981.

Chapter 6

The Second Hunger Strike Begins

I am standing on the threshold of another trembling world. May God have mercy on my soul. My heart is very sore because I know that I have broken my poor mother's heart, and my home is struck with unbearable anxiety. But I have considered all the arguments and tried every means to avoid what has become the unavoidable: it has been forced upon me and my comrades by four-and-a-half years of stark inhumanity.

I am a political prisoner. I am a political prisoner because I am a casualty of a perennial war that is being fought between the oppressed Irish people and an alien, oppressive, unwanted regime that refuses to withdraw from our land. I believe and stand by the God-given right of the Irish nation to sovereign independence, and the right of any Irishman or woman to assert this right in armed revolution. That is why I am incarcerated, naked and tortured.

Foremost in my tortured mind is the thought that there can never be peace in Ireland until the foreign, oppressive British presence is removed, leaving all the Irish people as a unit to control their own affairs and determine their own destinies as a sovereign people, free in mind and body, separate and distinct physically, culturally and economically.

I believe I am but another of those wretched Irishmen born of a risen generation with a deeply rooted and unquenchable desire for freedom. I am dying not just to attempt to end the barbarity of H-Block, or to gain the rightful recognition of a political prisoner, but primarily because what is lost in here is lost for the Republic and those wretched oppressed whom I am deeply proud to know as the 'risen people'.

With these words, recorded in his diary on 1 March, Bobby Sands embarked on his slow and painful journey to martyrdom by beginning his hunger strike. On the following day, Republican prisoners ended, to the 'distaste of the screws' the no-wash protest. They were moved to B-Wing, which was 'allegedly clean' recorded Sands in his diary, adding that the prisoners showed 'considerable tolerance today.

Men are being searched coming back from the toilet. At one point men were waiting three hours to get out to the toilet, and only four or five got washed, which typifies the eagerness of the screws to have us off the no-wash. There is a lot of petty vindictiveness from them.' Sands saw one of the prison doctors, who recorded his weight at 64 kg (140.8 pounds). 'I've no problems', he noted. Father Murphy visited him in the evening for a short talk: 'I heard that my mother spoke at a parade in Belfast yesterday and that Marcella', his sister, 'cried. It gave me heart.'[1]

Outside the Maze, Bishop Edward Daly strongly condemned the new hunger strike in a hard-hitting sermon at a service in Derry on 2 March. He urged young people not to support the protest, which, he said, was not 'morally justified'. 'If you are invited to support a hunger strike, you must first ask the organising group if it has publicly made known its rejection of murder and bombing,' he said. 'If they are not prepared to do this, I urge you not to offer them your support,' continued the Bishop. 'You must not become involved with groups that have murder and destruction as their policy, in our society'. But he made it clear that, in his opinion, prison conditions could and should be improved, and that all prisoners should be allowed to wear their own clothes at all times.[2] Sands was 'very annoyed' when he heard of Daly's statement: 'Again he is applying his double set of moral standards. He seems to forget that the people who murdered those innocent Irishmen on Derry's Bloody Sunday are still as ever among us; and he knows perhaps better than anyone what has and is taking place in H-Block. He understands why men are being tortured here – the reason for criminalisation. What makes it so disgusting, I believe, is that he agrees with that underlying reason. Only once has he spoken out, of the beatings and inhumanity that are commonplace in H-Block.'[3]

By the next morning of his fast, Sands was 'feeling exceptionally well today. (It's only the third day, I know, but all the same I'm feeling great.)' He had a visit from two reporters, David Beresford of the *Guardian* and Brendan O Cathaoir of *The Irish Times*. 'Couldn't quite get my flow of thoughts together. I could have said more in a better fashion.'[4] Sands was adamant to the journalists that an agreement was reached at the end of the previous hunger strike. He said that, while being a practising Catholic, he rejected Bishop Daly's view that a hunger strike was not morally justified: 'If I die, God will understand' he reflected. He was carried forward by the 'spirit of freedom' and referred, in Irish, to the example of previous IRA Volunteers, such as MacSwiney, Gaughan and Stagg, who had died on hunger strike. Sands declared that 'after four-and-a-half years, the H-Block prisoners were not prepared to endure further torture'. He asserted that when negotiations with the authorities broke down in January, the protesters 'did not want to go back on the no-wash protest. But they moved us from clean to dirty cells'. He claimed that prisoners were still being kept waiting on the whim of a warder for permission to go to the toilet. Sands, who had now spent nearly one-third of his twenty-seven years in jail, did not want anyone to die, but he expected that he would have to sacrifice his life for the principle of political prisoner status. At the same time, he emphasized that the prisoners were prepared to accept undertakings on two issues before Christmas. These were that a blind eye would be turned on the matter of prison-issue clothing and that prisoners would be allowed to wear their own clothes; and secondly that study would be accepted as prison work.

Sands said that, having been ignored for more than four years, there was a flurry of activity before the last fast ended on 18 December: 'The unprecedented negotiations' involved the Northern Ireland Office, the Republican Press Centre in Belfast, prison authorities, the seven original hunger-strikers, a senior clergyman and himself. On that day, he said, the Governor came to him and asked: 'If you are playing a game of brinkmanship you had better call it off, as one of the hunger-strikers (Sean McKenna) is dying.' Sands claimed that he retorted: 'Thirty will die', and walked out. Later, a priest, whose identity he refused to disclose, brought two documents from the NIO, and it was on the basis of an interpretation of these that the fast was ended. The priest agreed to supervise the implementation of this agreement over an eight-week period. Sands told his visitors that he received thirteen visits from Danny Morrison in the course of a month; that he was given a room for private discussion with his O/Cs; and that in January the Governor came to his cell and asked for 'a week's grace' regarding settlement plans, which was 'granted willingly'. Then, as Loyalist pressure built up, Atkins introduced a six-point policy 'aimed at humiliating the prisoners.' Of this, Sands said: 'It included requirements which even conforming prisoners do not have to observe.' He had been replaced as O/C of the Provisional prisoners by Brendan 'Bik' McFarlane; they were united and determined to overthrow the 'criminalisation prison regime'.[5]

A table, meanwhile, was placed in Sands' cell, with food placed on it 'in front of my eyes. I honestly couldn't give a damn if they placed it on my knee. They still keep asking me silly questions like, "Are you still not eating?"' His reading material was a book of Kipling's short stories with an introduction of some length by W. Somerset Maugham. Sands took an instant dislike to the latter on reading his comment on the Irish people: '"It is true that the Irish were making a nuisance of themselves." Damned too bad, I thought, and bigger the pity it wasn't a bigger nuisance! Kipling I know of, and his Ulster connection. I'll read his stories tomorrow.' On 5 March, Sands read the statement Atkins had made to the Commons, reiterating the Government's position: 'It does not annoy me because my mind was prepared for such things and I know I can expect more of such, right to the bitter end.' He was inspired by some verse in Kipling's short stories: 'the extracts of verses before the stories are quite good. The one that I thought very good went like this':

The earth gave up her dead that tide,
Into our camp he came,
And said his say, and went his way,
And left our hearts aflame.
Keep tally – on the gun-butt score,
The vengeance we must take,
When God shall bring full reckoning,
For our dead comrade's sake.

'I hope not', Sands reflected. 'But that hope was not even a hope, but a mere figure of speech. I have hope, indeed. All men must have hope and never lose heart. But my hope lies in the ultimate victory for my poor people. Is there any hope greater than that?' He was saying his prayers: 'I believe in God, and I'll be presumptuous and say he and I are getting on well this weather'. Try as he might, Sands could not ignore the presence of food 'staring me straight in the face all the time.' He had a desire for brown wholemeal bread, butter, Dutch cheese and honey. He consoled himself with the fact that 'I'll get a great feed up above (if I'm worthy).' But then he was 'struck by this awful thought that they don't eat food up there. But if there's something better than brown wholemeal bread, cheese and honey, et cetera, then it can't be bad.' He was now 62 kg (136.4 pounds) and, in general, mentally and physically, 'I feel very good.'[6]

As Sands recorded this in his diary, his foremost adversary arrived in Belfast. As Prime Minister of the United Kingdom, Mrs Thatcher emphasised that her visit was to 'fellow citizens of that Kingdom and in a part of the same Kingdom – a most important part.' Of course Prime Ministers made regional visits to various parts of England, Scotland and Wales, she declared. In the past, though, visits to Northern Ireland had somehow been perceived to be rather different. There was, though, no justification for that perception, explained Mrs Thatcher: 'It ought to be as natural for the Prime Minister to visit this part of the United Kingdom as for her … to visit Lancashire or Kent, Northumberland or Cornwall, Anglesey or Caithness.' She stressed that the Government's first priority was to protect the people of Northern Ireland from the bullet and the bomb. The terrorists, whether they called themselves Loyalists or Republicans, had nothing to offer but heartbreak and bloodshed. They were the 'enemies of us all.' The Prime Minister highlighted how: 'We have come a long way in the fight against terrorism. We have made great strides in getting back to normal policing throughout Northern Ireland. The task is not yet done. But we can all have full confidence in the steadfast dedication of the Royal Ulster Constabulary and of the Army, including your own Ulster Defence Regiment, to carry it through.' The critics of the security forces should remember, stressed Mrs Thatcher, how many lives – since 1969 –

the police and the Army had laid down in order to protect the ordinary citizens of Northern Ireland.

'Our aim is to build a healthy and harmonious society in Northern Ireland', claimed the Prime Minister. She did not want the measures that the Government took to deal with the terrorist minority to damage the fabric of society: 'We must always be sure that we punish the lawbreakers, and not the vast majority of innocent people, Protestant and Catholic.' As to that terrorist minority, who would carry their determination to disrupt society to any lengths, she said: 'Once again we have a hunger strike at the Maze Prison in the quest for what they call political status. There is no such thing as political murder, political bombing or political violence. There is only criminal murder, criminal bombing and criminal violence. We will not compromise on this. There will be no political status.'[7] To emphasize this point, Mrs Thatcher told an interviewer on the following day: 'I am deeply sorry there is another hunger strike. It is to try to achieve political status for criminals. It will never achieve that status. Criminals are criminals. To me there is no such thing as political crimes. Murder is criminal. Violence is criminal. It will stay that way. That hunger strike will achieve nothing.'[8]

Back in the Maze, Sands complained that he had had no visit from a priest that night or the one before. He had also not seen his solicitor, which was 'another part of the isolation process, which, as time goes by, they will ruthlessly implement.' He had now noticed a 'loss of energy twice today, and I am feeling slightly weak. They (the screws) are unembarrassed by the enormous amount of food they are putting into the cell, and I know they have every bean and chip counted or weighed. The damned fools don't realise that the doctor does tests for traces of any food eaten. Regardless, I have no intention of sampling their tempting morsels.' He was sleeping well at night so far, and avoided sleeping during the day. Sands was even having pleasant dreams, and so far no headaches: 'Is that a tribute to my psychological frame of mind or will I pay for that tomorrow or later!' he wondered. There were:

> ... no doubts or regrets about what I am doing for I know what I have faced for eight years, and in particular for the last four-and-a-half years, others will face, young lads and girls still at school and thousands of others. They will not criminalise us, rob us of our true identity, steal our individualism, depoliticise us, churn us out as systemised, institutionalised, decent law-abiding robots. Never will they label our liberation struggle as criminal.

He pronounced himself 'amazed at British logic. Never in eight centuries have they succeeded in breaking the spirit of one man who refused to be broken. They have not dispirited, conquered, or demoralised my people, nor will they ever.' If he was going to die, he would die happy knowing that 'I do not have to answer for what these people have done to our ancient nation.'

Sands' twenty-seventh birthday was on 9 May. His weight was now 60 kg (132 pounds). He kept thinking of James Connolly, 'and the great calm and dignity that he showed right to his very end' when he was executed in 1916, his courage and resolve. 'Perhaps I am biased, because there have been thousands like him, but Connolly has always been the man that I looked up to. I always have tremendous feeling for Liam Mellowes' – the IRA leader executed by the first Government of independent Ireland – 'and for the present leadership of the Republican Movement, and a confidence in them that they will always remain undaunted and unchanged. And again, dare I forget the Irish people of today, and the risen people of the past, they too hold a special place in my heart. Well, I have gotten by twenty-seven years, so that is something. I may die, but the Republic of 1916 will never die. Onward to the Republic and liberation of our people', declared Sands in his prison diary.[9]

On 15 March, Sands was joined on hunger strike by Francis Hughes, an IRA legend, captured after a shoot-out with SAS troopers in which one of the British soldiers was killed. On 22 March, Raymond McCreesh, another PIRA Volunteer, and Patsy O'Hara, the INLA leader in the Maze, began fasts. But what changed the level of interest in the hunger strike was not the number of hunger-strikers but the fact that one of them was now a parliamentary candidate for the vacant seat of Fermanagh South-Tyrone. The opportunity arose following the death of Frank Maguire MP on 5 March and Sands' nomination as a candidate was completed on 26 March. Three days later, the SDLP, under severe pressure not to put up a candidate, stood aside. The by-election would now be a straight sectarian head-to-head between Sands and the Unionist candidate, Harry West, the former leader of the Ulster Unionist Party.

Initially, the NIO observed how Sands' candidature in the by-election had

> ... not so far produced any reaction within the prison. Indeed he has shown little or no interest in the affair, confirming our belief that he did not want to go forward in the first place but preferred to continue his strike. This interpretation – and the lack of prison reaction – is borne out by a conversation reported with a protesting prisoner who said that whatever the result of the election it would make no difference to the protests or the hunger strike; they would not stop 'until the Brits give in'.[10]

Officials, meanwhile, decided that almost unrestricted access to Sands would be granted to Owen Carron, his election agent, but no special concessions would be made with regard to correspondence or access to the media. It was again noted that Sands had not said anything about what his reaction would be if he were elected. Instead: 'It might be significant that he was still talking about "when" he died rather than "if".' In the meantime, Sands remained in the prison hospital. He had lost 1 stone 11 lbs, but remained remarkably fit. He was in much better condition than the pre-Christmas hunger-strikers had been at this stage, even though he had lost more weight than they had. It was noted: 'People differed however and some could be subject to a sudden deterioration. Sands might well be one of these.' At present his condition was causing no concern to the doctors.[11]

On 3 April, Atkins informed Mrs Thatcher that four prisoners were now refusing food and the remaining protesting prisoners had moved from a dirty to a clean form of protest – ostensibly to focus support on the hunger-strikers, but possibly also because they realized that the dirty protest was getting them nowhere. The 400 plus clean protesters were washed and shaved, but still wearing only a blanket; they were in clean, unfurnished cells, but had bedding. So far there had been little support for the hunger-strikers, 'but we expected that as deaths became imminent (probably around Easter – which is already an emotive time in the Irish calendar) some sympathy in the minority community in Northern Ireland and elsewhere, particularly in the Irish Republic and the USA, would be mobilised and increasing pressure brought on the Government to find a way out.' Responsible leaders of opinion, 'while supporting our stand on political status, are likely also to urge the Government to "find a way of avoiding deaths", but without, of course, saying how', warned Atkins. It was clear, he continued, from the outset that the psychology of handling this hunger strike must be different from the last:

> Then we were primarily concerned to establish in the minds of the minority community and informed opinion generally, in detail and with clarity, the eminently humane prison regime that was available to the protesters. This time we judged that there was very little real or latent support for the hunger-strikers in any civilised quarter, and since our position is firmly on the record and well understood, we must stand firmly on that ground. Our approach therefore is essentially 'quietist' – let the facts and the folly speak for themselves, but be ready to respond publicly as and when necessary.

This development would increase publicity for the H-Block campaign, and Sands' candidature posed the Prison Governor and HMG some delicate problems about his prison regime. Sands was a validly nominated candidate: by virtue of the Criminal Law Act 1967, convicted criminals (with the exception of those convicted of treason) were no longer disqualified from Parliament. 'It is our continued custody of Sands which would prevent him taking his seat', although it would be for the House of Commons to decide how to deal with that situation. Atkins added:

> We must avoid allowing Sands to exploit his position as a valid candidate, while at the same time avoiding the trap of so constraining his campaign as to make him a political martyr – especially since the legal limits within which I can operate to constrain him are untested by any precedent. The three immediate issues have been determined as follows:
>
> (i) I am allowing access to Sands by his election agent on a limited scale, consistent with the prison's capacity to handle visits without undue disruption.
> (ii) I shall consider personally any applications by other persons to visit Sands in connection with his candidature.
> (iii) I do not propose any relaxation in the present rules about correspondence.
> (iv) I do not intend to allow any media access to Sands ... (Others will, no doubt, speak on Sands' behalf).

Atkins admitted that it was difficult to forecast what effect all this would have on the security situation. The Provisionals might now take a relatively low profile until after the Fermanagh election, 'but we cannot be sure.' If the hunger strike continued – and Sands' candidature/election could be used as an excuse for calling it off – the likelihood of terrorist attacks within and outside Northern Ireland and of trouble between Paisley's and Sands' supporters still stood. The security forces were confident that they could contain any violence in Northern Ireland against the background of the known capabilities of the terrorist organizations and the limited extent of direct public support. It was, however, the strong view of the Chief Constable and the GOC, with which Atkins agreed, that HMG should not embroil itself in the Fermanagh campaign in any way. The best weapons against Sands were Harry West and the non-violent Catholic community themselves.[12] After reading Atkins' minute, the Prime Minister commented that she agreed with the course of action proposed in it.[13]

On 7 April, Roy Harrington, at the NIO, received a telephone call from Owen Carron, who read to him a document that Sands had signed, the gist of which was that he wanted access to television and press for the purpose of interviews connected with his election campaign. The document referred to the fact that the NIO had refused permission for a number of people, including Bernadette McAliskey, to go into the prison to discuss Sands' election strategy. After consultation with Michael Alison, the PUS, Blelloch, several other officials and then with the Secretary of State, Harrington telephoned Carron on Atkins' instructions.

He told him that the prison authorities were empowered to consider applications from Carron, as Sands' agent, to have access to Sands for purposes connected with the election, but there was no question of journalists being admitted to the prison for the purposes of interviews with Sands. Carron protested that Sands was a valid candidate and that the NIO were denying him his rights in connection with the election. He asserted that the Secretary of State's decision was in conflict with the Representation of the People Act, and said that he would be making immediate contact with his lawyers with a view to challenging the matter in the courts.[14]

By 9 April, Sands was clearly showing signs of deterioration; earlier in the week he complained of dizziness, tiredness and headaches, symptoms that might be expected by this stage. The prisoners' weights at this juncture were:

	Day of strike	Weight on first examination	Weight today	Weight loss during week	Overall weight loss
Robert Sands	40	10st 1lb (64kg)	7st 13½lb	4½lb	2st 1½lb
Francis Hughes	26	11st 3½lb (71.6kg)	10st 1½lb	3½lb	1st 2lb
Raymond McCreesh	19	9st 13lb (63.20kg)	9st	1½lb	13lb
Patrick O'Hara	19	12st 1lb (76.25kg)	10st 7½lb	5½lb	1st 7½lb[15]

As Hughes was moved to the prison hospital on 10 April, there was a noticeable deterioration in Sands' condition. Despite this, his condition was still not regarded as serious and the doctors treating him were of the opinion that he would not need to be moved to an outside hospital for another fortnight. As with the last hunger strike, arrangements would be made for the NIO and the security forces to receive prior notice of any move.[16] Meanwhile, in an eve of election statement, dictated to Carron, Sands was reported to have stated among other things that he was 'very angry' at the NIO's refusal to allow him direct access to the media:

I am being denied my rights as a candidate. This typifies the NIO attempts to play down what is happening in the H-Blocks and displays British bias with the Unionist camp.

It is obvious that Atkins has been in collusion with West before and since nomination day. The British Government are afraid of allowing a tortured prisoner the means of revealing the horrors of the H-Blocks.

He extended thanks to his supporters, and to all those working for the prisoners:

I place my life and the lives of my three comrades in the hands of the people of Fermanagh-South Tyrone. I ask you to vote for the prisoners tomorrow; to reject West and to keep the seat in Anti-Unionist hands.

I am confident that the people of Fermanagh-South Tyrone will not let the prisoners down. I can be your MP for approximately two weeks. Better that than Harry West for two years.

Inside the prison, the NIO noted a 'minor occurrence of interest': there was an unsubstantiated belief that McCreesh was strongly suspected of having eaten some custard. This 'might be a pointer to his likely staying power.' Outside, in the election campaign, the maverick Southern politician, Neil Blaney, crossed the border to give his support to Sands, and spoke at Enniskillen and Lisnaskea on 3 and 5 April respectively. In Lisnaskea he asserted that a vote for Sands was a vote against the (institutional) violence of which Sands and his fellows were the victims. A victory for Sands would strengthen Haughey's hand in talks with Mrs Thatcher, showing that local people wanted the British out of Ireland. Sands' supporters — especially McAliskey — tried to emphasize the personal as opposed to the Republican appeal: 'We are not asking you to take sides except in terms of the life of Bobby Sands'. However, from Sinn Féin, Richard McAuley's eve of poll statement spelled out the Provisional line quite clearly:

The prisoners believe, as do we campaigning on their behalf, that a successful outcome in the by-election will place so much pressure on the Thatcher Government that it may yet be possible to resolve the prisons crisis without a death ... a secondary aspect is the candidature of Harry West ... a vote tomorrow is not just a vote of censure against British penal policy but is also a vote against the sectarianism of Harry West.

Meanwhile, H-Block campaigners and Sinn Féin (in a statement from President Rory O'Bradaigh) tried to represent the murder of census enumerator Joanne Mathers in Londonderry on 7 April as a 'sinister attempt' to discredit Sands, the prisons campaign and the 'peaceful' census-burning campaign. O'Bradaigh claimed that the incident was part of an RUC smear campaign. However, a known PIRA gun killed Mrs Mathers;[17] she was shot as she was helping a resident fill in a census form. Joanne Mathers was married, with a young son. She was twenty-five years old.

An Phoblacht, meanwhile, devoted its front and back pages to Sands' election fight, saying that his would be a national household name and that popular opinion would be made more receptive to a 'wider publicity campaign'. Sands' election would invalidate British claims that 'the armed resistance in the North of Ireland is either a criminal conspiracy or without public support'. Sands himself was said in another article to be in very high spirits 'despite his isolation' in the prison hospital, although all four strikers were now suffering physically from their strike. The centre-page spread consisted of Sands' 'semi-autobiographical' essay written in 1978, which maintained that he would not be at peace until Ireland became a 'sovereign independent socialist Republic.' The essay included an imaginary sequence in which Sands was told by his wife that his mother was dead (she was still alive) and was then refused compassionate parole to attend her funeral. The NIO noted: 'Sands clearly likes to see himself as one of life's victims and admits that he suffers from chronic depression.' As the voters went to the polls, the NIO, internally, acknowledged that the election:

> ... is clearly a watershed in the overall campaign, and as support has otherwise been so low-key, many must regard the election as 'make or break'. There is still no indication of future policy after the election, but if Sands loses badly it is difficult to see how the campaign could continue with any credibility. If he polls well, but loses, or if he wins, then the organisers will consider themselves to have been vindicated and they will continue the campaign as actively as possible. Whatever happens outside, however, it now seems unlikely to affect Sands' own determination to die. In such circumstances the campaigners may now see the 'best' outcome as Sands to win but then die as an MP. If Sands loses, pressure to build up the terrorist campaign in the area will mount, but if he is successful, the local moratorium on attacks may be expected to continue.[18]

The result of the Fermanagh and South Tyrone by-election was announced on 9 April. The result was a stunning victory for Sands:

Bobby Sands (Republican H-block)	30,492
Harry West (Ulster Unionist)	29,046
Majority	1,446

There were 3,280 spoiled ballots in a total turnout of 86.7%. The NIO observed that though politics in Fermanagh was 'notoriously tribal', and there was a natural

Nationalist majority in the seat, the result 'surprised most observers, who had expected a larger proportion of Catholic voters to abstain (or spoil their votes) rather than vote for a convicted terrorist.' In particular, it had been expected that the murder in Londonderry two days before the election of the young housewife would have an adverse effect on Sands' vote. In the event, however, the NIO assessment was that the 'incentive' to vote against West proved too strong, 'and many Nationalist voters may also have been influenced by the implication in Sands' campaign that he would come off his hunger strike' and resign the seat if he won.

The result was greeted with outrage in the Unionist community. Harold McCusker (a UUP MP) described it as 'like 30,000 decent Catholics standing over the grave of Joanne Mathers ... and shouting three cheers for her killers'; while Ian Paisley's Democratic Unionist Party commented that the result 'explodes for all time the SDLP-Roman Catholic perpetuated myth that they have no sympathy for the IRA and its campaign of genocide against the Protestants of Co Fermanagh'. Oliver Napier, leader of the moderate cross-community Alliance party, called it 'a black day for Northern Ireland': 'we have seen the real evil of naked sectarianism ... The people of Fermanagh and South Tyrone are prepared to come out and vote for the tribal candidate, regardless of whether it is a decent guy, a politician or gunman ...'. Many Unionists renewed their criticism of the SDLP's failure to put up a candidate, and there was also some intra-Unionist squabbling – the DUP arguing that a 'Unionist unity' candidate could have won the seat, while Harry West said that the DUP had tried to scupper his campaign: 'if we had had the full support of Unionists of all shades, we would have taken it'. Loyalist paramilitary reaction to Sands' victory was predictable: UDA leader Andy Tyrie said that 'it is going to harden the Protestants and make them very frightened. No matter what way you look at it, the vote was a vote for the IRA'. There were media reports of a UDA commanders' 'emergency meeting' to discuss the situation.

Sands' victory produced a jubilant response from his campaigners, who emphasised its wider political implications for the British presence in Ireland and the fact that it put the 'prisons ball squarely in HMG's court'. McAliskey called it 'a victory for justice and humanity and against all that Unionism stands for'. Carron claimed that it had been achieved despite 'intimidation from the so-called security forces'. However, the need for further action was emphasized. Sinn Féin's Richard McAuley and Joe Austin warned that 'Bobby Sands' electoral victory, while a clear indication of massive popular support for the prisoners, does not mean the end of the hunger strike or of the campaign ... now is the time for us to redouble our efforts'. Inside the Maze, the authorities noted that Sands' election as an MP 'produced little reaction within the prison', where it appeared to have passed with 'very little comment'. There were no 'celebrations' to speak of. A statement from the Republican prisoners, however, said that 'this important victory must be built on and the breadth of political support achieved during the election should be spread throughout the country … only in this way can political status be won'. The result 'smashes Britain's criminalisation programme'. Sands himself appeared to have been largely unaffected by the result, and made no comment whatsoever regarding his victory to prison staff. The new MP's victory speech was made on his behalf by Owen Carron, who said:

> Despite intimidation from the so-called security forces, the voters of Fermanagh and South Tyrone stood by the prisoners and told Mrs Thatcher today that we, on behalf of the Irish people, will not accept the situation in the H-Blocks, and we demand an immediate end to the intolerable situation.

Sands' victory was welcomed by the Irish National Caucus (INC) pressure group in America; Congressman Mario Biaggi said 'we feel it could be very significant'. McAliskey paid a brief visit to the United States after the result was announced. Maureen Gibson, Kieran O'Hagan and a third H-Blocks campaigner continued a tour of Germany, but unlike a Western European tour during the first hunger strike, this event attracted very little interest. It was 'badly planned and hampered by internal wrangling amongst the hosts.' Kieran Nugent had been visiting Scandinavia, but again appeared to have 'aroused little enthusiasm.'[19]

In London, Sir Michael Havers, the Attorney General, had been asked by the Prime Minister to provide a legal opinion on the law in relation to parliamentary candidates who were serving a sentence of imprisonment. He informed her that such a candidate was not disqualified from election or from sitting and voting in the House of Commons (unless, as mentioned, his offence was treason). The Forfeiture Act 1870 disqualified any person convicted of a felony and sentenced to imprisonment for more than twelve months, but the Criminal Law Act 1967 repealed this provision as part of the process of abolishing the division of crimes into felonies and misdemeanours. 'Should Mr Sands be elected he would not be able to attend Parliament because he is lawfully detained in prison. It would be open to the House to expel him as a person who is unfit for membership.' Expulsion did not create any disability to serve again if he were re-elected. *Parliamentary Practice* by Erskine May, the authority on British constitutional convention, stated that it was customary to order the MP, if absent, to attend in his place before an order was made for his expulsion; if he was in prison, it had been the practice to order the Governor to bring him to Parliament in custody if he so desired. This custom had arisen in relation to members who had taken their seats, and the cases by May showed that even in such cases the custom was not invariable. 'I can see no justification for ordering the member to attend if he has not taken his seat', Havers told Mrs Thatcher.[20]

In the aftermath of the Fermanagh-South Tyrone result, when the Home Office contemplated how they would change the law to disqualify Sands, it found 'real difficulty in defining a straightforward change which could be announced' quickly. The officials there were worried about discrimination between those who were already MPs and those who were new Members; about categorizing criminals according to the seriousness of the crime; and about the probability that, whatever they did, someone just the other side of the boundary line would stand for the same cause they were seeking to outlaw. The Government was also warned that business managers in Parliament believed that they would not have a consensus, or sufficient latitude, to move a motion expelling Sands. The Prime Minister was told that time was against the Government: 'Tuesday is difficult, because it is the Transport Bill guillotine. That means that the earliest we could conveniently move an expulsion motion would be Wednesday. The Home Office do not see their way clear to recommending a change in the law which could be announced next Wednesday; and I doubt that they would be able to do it before it became possible to move the writ for the by-election again – which would be immediately after the Easter Recess.' All of this presented 'formidable difficulties.'[21]

From Washington, the British Ambassador, Sir Nicholas Henderson, warned, in a dispatch read by the Prime Minister, that the election of Sands 'will obviously be heavily exploited here' by 'pro-IRA commentators' such as Noraid, or the Irish National Caucus. With Bernadette McAliskey flying to New York to take part in a TV programme there: 'There is little or nothing which we can do to counter this effort in pro-IRA circles', lamented Henderson. But a more serious danger was that responsible mainstream opinion, and editorial comment in the major print and electronic media, would be adversely affected. The election result might be seen as 'demolishing our repeated assertions that the vast majority of Northern Irish people, Catholic as well as Protestant, abhor terrorism; that the IRA does not enjoy any numerically significant popular support; and that they have chosen violent rather than democratic methods for this reason'. These assertions had hitherto been generally accepted in responsible political and media circles, even by those critical of the pace or direction of HMG's policies. A shift away from acceptance of these fundamental premises would 'clearly be very damaging here', stated the Ambassador. Seen from Washington, therefore, it was essential to emphasize that this result did not reflect the political realities of Northern Ireland as a whole: 'I recognise the difficulty of offering on-the-record comment, and indeed I do not propose that we should do so. We will not seek to comment, and on the record we will decline any analysis or interpretation.' This was, however, sure to be a major topic of media coverage and comment in the immediate future: 'And I think it equally certain that we will be pressed, in the first instance by editorial writers, for some background comment.' A straight no comment would be taken as telling its own story. 'If, repeat if,' pressed by responsible and influential commentators, Henderson proposed to make the following points, off the record:

(i) The result, sadly, reflected an essentially sectarian voting pattern. West delivered the Protestant vote. There was no legitimate Catholic candidate: in his absence, Catholic voters opted for the only non-Protestant candidate.

(ii) There may also have been a humanitarian desire to avert Sands' death on hunger strike.

(iii) It is regrettable that the voters were not given a more representative choice, as in May 1979, and regrettable that sectarian considerations in these circumstances proved paramount. But it is not unprecedented in this particular constituency, which is known for intensity of hard-line Republicanism in the Catholic community: in the late 1950s another convicted Republican prisoner won an election in this same constituency (though under the then law he was debarred from taking his seat).[22]

In London, the Prime Minister met with John Hume, who had requested the meeting as he wanted to discuss with Mrs Thatcher his 'two points' for ending the hunger strike. He was told 'firmly' that a discussion on these lines with the Prime Minister would serve no useful purpose. Hume then proposed a general talk, citing the Prime Minister's invitation to him, during her visit to Northern Ireland in March, to come to see her whenever he was worried about the situation there, and it was on this basis that the meeting was to take place.[23] John Hoskyns, a key Thatcher economic advisor, had listened earlier to Hume on the radio when the SDLP leader said: 'If the Government could be a little bit more flexible, the problem could be resolved'. Although Hoskyns was wary of commenting on a 'subject right outside my remit, and about which I know nothing', that 'doesn't stop me dropping you a simple thought which can't possibly be new' he told Michael Alexander, in a note passed on to the Prime Minister. Hoskyns was 'struck by the illogical nature' of Hume's argument, 'no doubt presented in good faith.' He was saying that the whole business of the hunger-striking was really now 'about words'; in other words, a huge and tragic political problem all centring around whether or not the prisoners could wear their own clothes as women prisoners were apparently allowed to do. 'The point I am making is obvious' concluded Hoskyns: if the British Government was getting the whole thing out of proportion and showing 'intransigence' etc., by sticking absolutely to the letter of the rules, 'even though people are committing suicide in protest, are they really being any more unreasonable than the people who are prepared to commit suicide (or are prepared to instruct those people to commit suicide) over this same apparently trivial issue?' Hoskyns noted that: 'This obvious symmetry in the situation never seems to be picked up by the commentators and thrown back at the people they are interviewing. It appears reasonable to fast to the death in order to wear a checked shirt; unreasonable to refuse that request.'[24]

When he met with the Prime Minister and Atkins, Hume warned that the situation in Northern Ireland was the worst he had ever known. The Provisionals had planned the hunger strike well, choosing strikers who were from different regions of Northern Ireland and who represented different political strands of thought within the Provos and the INLA. Anti-British feeling in Northern Ireland was growing, as was support for the Provisionals. It was essential that there should be an initiative. There was no question of giving political status to the hunger-strikers, but something could and should be done within the five demands, which need not require any sacrifice of principle. Either the initiative would succeed, which would be a great victory for the Government, or it would fail, in which case the Government would still have won the initiative from the Provisionals. Hume recalled that before Christmas he had talks with the NIO about an initiative involving the prisoners being allowed to wear their own clothes and being given the right of limited association. He had been told then, by the hunger-strikers, that they would guarantee to call off the hunger strike if these concessions were made. Both concessions could be extended to all prisoners in Northern Ireland, and therefore need not imply special treatment. Women were already allowed to wear their own clothes, and conforming prisoners already had some rights of association. What was at issue, under the latter heading, was the prisoners' activities before breakfast and at lunchtime.

As evidence for his assertion that concessions on clothing and freedom of association would end the hunger strike, Hume cited his contacts with the hunger-strikers before Christmas; a message from a clergyman connected with the hunger-strikers' families to the effect that action along the lines he had been advocating would 'bring a definite response from the prisoners'; and a conversation he had had the previous day with Gerry Adams. Adams had asked what Hume would be proposing and, on being told, had said that if the substance of the five points was granted, the hunger-strikers would call off their protest. On being accused by Hume of always asking for more, Adams said that the Provisionals would make no demands beyond those already made as a price for ending the hunger strike. Adams stressed that the Provisionals were not interested in the suggestion that the ECHR, for example, might offer a way to end the hunger strike. He added that Hume should not try to be seen to be negotiating on behalf of the prisoners. Adams said, finally, that it was of no concern to the PIRA how HMG described any concession made. Hume argued to the Prime Minister that on the basis of his conversation with Adams, and of the other two pieces of 'evidence' he had cited, he was confident that action along the lines that he had proposed would do the trick. He was not seeking any credit from the affair. The Government could simply announce that it was renewing its efforts to implement the proposals made before Christmas with one or two additional features. There need be no intermediary or other involvement.

Mrs Thatcher's response was to point out that Sands, Francis Hughes and Hughes' brother, *An Phoblacht* and indeed Adams, as reported by Hume, were all asking that the five demands should be met in full. She resented the accusation that it was the Government that was being inflexible; everything recommended by the ECHR in its 1980 Report had been implemented. And beyond that, the decision to issue civilian clothing to conforming prisoners had been made: 'We had incurred criticism for that decision', she said, and it now formed part of what was a particularly humane regime. The media had been into the Maze more than once, and had been able to find nothing to criticize in the facilities. What the prisoners made of those facilities was, of course, their business. Contrary to Hume's assertion, the Government was not on a hook. Sands and Hughes had both been guilty of the deaths of innocent people. The Government's flexibility before the hunger strike began had not impressed them. Everyone had asked them to give up the hunger strike, and no one would be better pleased than the Government if the present hunger-strikers did so, but the Government was not prepared to be the victim of salami tactics (the process of eliminating opposition one slice at a time). They would not treat murderers as prisoners of war. Freedom of association would be merely a step towards that status. The people who had been killed by the PIRA had had no choice, but the hunger-strikers did.

In response, Hume asked whether the Prime Minister recognized the gravity of the situation and whether she was going to do anything about it. The emotional overtones of the hunger strike were enormous. The situation was the result of fundamental political instability, and was getting worse. Mrs Thatcher replied that the Government's job was to protect law-abiding citizens. Any wavering on the issue of political status would be to give a licence to kill. The present crisis was the result of the reluctance of some people to accept the ballot box as a means of resolving their disagreements. Hume commented that if this were all the Prime Minister had to say, the problems for Northern Ireland would be serious indeed. He did not expect to be around to help find solutions. He would be 'swept away' in the disturbances. The Prime Minister, though, repeated that the Government would place no obstacles in the way of the ECHR if it considered that it might provide a way forward. They would do everything to facilitate investigation of any complaint made under the Commission's terms of reference, and would do so in the same spirit as that in which they had allowed the media into the Maze and other prisons. The Government had nothing to hide. Hume said that the hunger strike was not about prison conditions; it was about a political problem. The PIRA held the stage. So long as they were allowed to do so, their support would grow. Eventually, the Government would not be able to control matters. Atkins interjected that Hume's argument was in effect that if six or ten people were tough enough, there was nothing the Government could do to stop them achieving their objectives. Hume countered that he had tried to persuade the hunger-strikers to desist, but had failed. The fact was that it was now more difficult for the hunger-strikers to end the strike than to proceed with it, and so it was essential that some political initiative should be taken. He had been campaigning for the following week's local elections; none of the electors was interested in anything but the hunger strike.

Mrs Thatcher repeated that she was willing to see the ECHR involved. She was not, however, prepared to see the hunger-strikers treated as political prisoners, which was what they wanted. Hume asked how political status should be defined, to which the Prime Minister replied that if the five demands were met, the hunger-strikers would have that status. It would be impossible for the prisons to be administered as at present; the prison staff would refuse to do so. She, like Mr Haughey, had never ceased to argue for peace and reconciliation, but she was not prepared to grant prisoner of war status. When Hume asked whether the steps he had proposed would be regarded as granting political status, the Prime Minister said that they would be steps towards that status. Hume commented that the Prime Minister should remember that the problem was one of nationalism, which was now on the increase. In the past, the Irish Government, under Éamon de Valera, had shot men convicted of IRA outrages. The British could never do this. To this, the Prime Minister complained that Hume was asking for total surrender. To give political status would be to act as a recruiting sergeant for the PIRA. Hume said that the Provisionals were in any case gaining support 'hand over fist'. They were winning the propaganda battle. If HMG were to take the initiative, they could reduce the hunger-strikers to their true status as men of violence. There would of course be risks in taking an initiative, but the cost of inaction would be greater. Polarization in the community was growing. The hatred of Dr Paisley in the Catholic community was increasing rapidly. Initially, his recent activities had not been treated seriously, but now the frustration was apparent. The divisions in the community would, of course, be shown up in the local elections the following week, he warned.[25]

While there was no agreement between Hume and the Prime Minister, there was at least some clarity emerging with regard to Sands' status as an MP. Sir Robert Armstrong, the Cabinet Secretary, reminded the Prime Minister that when the Cabinet considered that possibility of Sands being elected, she summed up the discussion by saying that, subject to further study of the legal position, the best course appeared to be for the Government to move a motion expelling him from the House as soon as the writ had been returned, and then to introduce a short Bill restoring the position on statutory disqualification substantially to what it had been before 1967. Since then there had been two meetings of the relevant Ministerial group, and the Chancellor of the Duchy, Norman St John-Stevas, had had discussions with (*inter alios*) John Silkin (Labour), David Steel (leader of the Liberal Party) and Enoch Powell

(Ulster Unionists). The clear view of all those he consulted was that the House of Commons should *not* take action to expel Sands. The argument was that the present law 'may well be an ass, but that Mr Sands was legally entitled to election and that those who voted for him knew that he was and would remain in custody.' As for the possible amendment of the law to disqualify felons from standing for Parliament, the Ministerial group established to deal with changing this had invited the Minister of State, at the Home Office, to put a paper to the meeting of the H-Committee on 15 April with a view to early legislation. The Chancellor of the Duchy's consultations had shown that there might well be general support for a change in the law, but, here again, there was a wish that the House should not take immediate action. It was worth noting, Armstrong pointed out to the Prime Minister, that if, as he himself predicted, Sands died later that month, the subsequent further by-election could hardly be postponed later than June or July. Unless, therefore, legislation were on the Statute Book before then, there would be nothing to prevent another convicted member of the IRA being nominated to succeed Sands.[26]

So it was made clear, on 13 April, that the Government would not – or rather, could not – seek to have Sands expelled from the House. The following day, John Hume suggested that Sands might use his newfound status to take the H-Block case to the European Commission on Human Rights; Sands subsequently dismissed his proposal as 'ridiculous'. Sinn Féin spokesmen also rejected the suggestion, challenging Hume to call on the British Government to grant political status. At a poorly attended press conference in Westminster on 14 April, Owen Carron called on the Government to 'negotiate an honourable settlement' with Sands and the other hunger-strikers, based on the five demands. While Sands' election won extensive coverage in local and national media, the issue faded rapidly in national terms after it became clear that he would not be expelled from Parliament, being overshadowed by the Brixton race riots and the launch of the American space shuttle. Coverage in the Irish press remained at a slightly higher level than before the election.[27]

In London, as he reflected on the situation with Michael Alexander, Robert Armstrong thought that there was reason to believe that the PIRA had been thinking seriously about an end to the campaign of violence, but felt that they needed a success, an avenue to pursue their aims politically, and something more on the prison regime. The Fermanagh by-election had given them the success, and a political opening, which there was reason to think they hoped to follow up in the local government elections. Armstrong noted that the Sands campaign was supported by a considerable amount of money from the Republic, and by Miss de Valera, who had previously been recommending a ceasefire. She was probably close to Haughey, 'and he probably sees the by-election result as a major success in steering the PIRA away from violence and towards politics', considered the Cabinet Secretary: 'There is reason to believe that the PIRA expect that, if enough of a push can be made in the next 10 days, it will be possible to bring the prison protests to an end.' The security assessment, Armstrong explained, was that, assuming no concession was made on the prison regime or the hunger strike, and Sands died, his by-election success would make the resulting violence sharper. Whilst it might last for some days, the security forces felt confident that they could contain it. Both communities in Northern Ireland would be watching from their different points of view what the Government's reaction was to the Sands by-election: 'The Catholics will be hoping and the Protestants will be fearing that the Government will offer some concession as a way out of the hunger strike. This cannot be given, but in the immediate aftermath of the by-election the Prime Minister's reaction should be very low key' Armstrong recommended to Alexander.[28]

In the Maze, on 14 April, all of the clean protesters requested that they should be issued furniture for their cells. Brendan McFarlane, the overall IRA OC, at an arranged meeting with the Assistant Governor, reiterated this request, and also stated that he would guarantee that the furniture, if provided, would not be abused. A statement was also made on behalf of the protesting prisoners by the Republican Press Centre that complained of how, despite ending the dirty protest six weeks before, they were still being forced to eat and sleep on the floor: 'The continual denial of cell furniture is completely unjustifiable ... We are demanding of the prison administration that we be given beds and chairs and lockers and we ask the public to monitor the British reaction to our demand.' It was agreed by the prison authorities that the prisoners' request should be granted. By 16 April, all four hunger-strikers were now housed in the Prison Hospital. Hughes was transferred there on 10 April, while McCreesh and O'Hara moved on 14 and 15 April respectively. While the condition of the three later hunger-strikers was giving no serious cause for concern at this point, Sands was beginning to show signs of a marked general deterioration in his condition. It now seemed probable that his condition would become critical within the next week to ten days.[29] The doctors treating him were now talking of his death in terms of days rather than weeks.[30] The prisoners' weights, on 16 April, were recorded as follows:

	Day of strike	Weight on first examination	Weight today	Weight loss during week	Overall weight loss
Robert Sands	47	10st 1lb	7st 10lb	3½lb	2st 5lb
Francis Hughes	33	11st 3½lb	9st 8lb	6½lb	1st 9½lb
Raymond McCreesh	26	9st 13lb	8st 9lb	5lb	1st 4lb
Patrick O'Hara	26	12st 1lb	10st 2lb	5½lb	1st 13lb[31]

At a meeting of senior medical prison staff, Professor Love and Dr Ross reported how Sands was 'now going downhill.' He complained generally of aches and pains; had a constant headache; was mentally sluggish; found it difficult to read, listen to the radio or watch TV; and was beginning to find even ordinary daylight a strain. On the other hand, there was no evidence of any organ failure and his biochemistry was stable. He had lost about 25% of his body weight. He was now (like the previous seven hunger-strikers) developing a distaste for water. The likelihood was that Sands would die in something like five to seven days. Before that, there might be a phase of coma, which could last from twelve to twenty-four hours, after which he would die. There was always a danger of cardiac failure, which would remain for a time even if Sands started to take food. He had refused treatment throughout, including the taking of vitamins. Dr Ross now authorized daily visits for close relatives. In terms of medical intervention, the Chief Medical Officer made the position clear:

(i) If Sands agreed that he should be treated – intervene.
(ii) If Sands said no, but after he had become comatose his relatives said yes – intervene. (If he were brought back to consciousness and repeated no, further intervention was unlikely.)
(iii) If both Sands and his relatives said no – no intervention.

The meeting agreed that if Sands did give up at the eleventh hour, every possible effort would have to be made to act quickly and effectively. The 'worst possible situation would be if he died after giving up.'[32]

Mrs Thatcher was, by now, on an overseas visit to India; her party was contacted by Alexander, who informed them that the NIO had told Downing Street they thought it likely that, if Sands' condition deteriorated quickly in the next few days, his family would ask Haughey to intercede with the Prime Minister: 'They think that this could happen at any time from now on. We will, of course, let you know immediately if we get an approach through any channel in London, but I thought you should be aware of the possibility', telegraphed Alexander.[33]

In fact, there had already been some indirect contact between the NIO and Sands' family. Father Rogan of Twinbrook rang Blatherwick of the Political Affairs Division, on the morning of 16 April, about Sands: 'I gather he is a reputable man and no friend of the Provisionals', noted the official. Father Rogan appreciated the Government's position, but thought that Sands was looking for some recognition of his status, which might come through a conversation with an official in which he was treated as an elected representative: 'X Could not an official call on him in his elected capacity?' was how the request was recorded in Blatherwick's minute of the conversation. Blelloch's 'answer to X was No.'[34]

The next move in the drama was unexpected. Alexander was informed by the NIO that three Irish Members of the European Parliament (MEPs), who were also Dáil Deputies (Teachta Dála, or TD), were going to see Sands. The request to see the three MEPs came from Sands himself, and was referred by the Governor of the Maze to the NIO. Atkins consulted Willie Whitelaw and the Foreign and Commonwealth Secretary, Lord Carrington, on 17 April. They decided that there was just a chance the three MEPs/TDs – who were Neil Blaney ('who was possibly involved in gun running some time ago'), Síle de Valera and Dr John O'Connell – might persuade Sands to come off his hunger strike. At the time it was thought the MEPs themselves did not know why Sands had asked to see them. There was, of course, strong reaction from Unionists. A telegram was sent to the Prime Minister from the UUP MP, Willie Ross, in the name of his party leader Jim Molyneaux, demanding that Atkins' decision to let the three MEPs see Sands be reconsidered, and that Irish MEPs should stop acting on behalf of HMG. The Unionist MPs had also said they wanted a meeting with the Prime Minster as soon as she got back from her overseas tour. The NIO issued a statement to reassure the Unionists that there had been no change in Government policy towards political prisoners, and that they had taken this opportunity of allowing the three MEPs to see Sands, who was deteriorating fast, in order to try to save his life.[35] Harold McCusker MP, however, remained 'disgusted and outraged by the decision': 'In no other country would a convicted terrorist be allowed to receive foreign sympathisers.' Together with James Molyneaux MP, McCusker had a meeting with the NIO Duty Minister (Mitchell) to argue against the visit, while Ian Paisley's DUP threatened to picket the Maze to prevent the Irish MEPs entering.[36]

To avert this, Paisley met with Mitchell allowing the former to register 'the very strong feeling of outrage' that had followed the announcement about the proposed visit. Dr Paisley recognized that it was probably not possible to rescind the decision, but he did want to make the Government aware of the consequences that would flow from it. He referred to the efforts that had been made by himself and fellow Unionist MEP, John Taylor, to influence MEPs prior to Christmas on the question of political status for the PIRA hunger-strikers. This had been done at the request of the Government, and now he felt betrayed that the same Government had given permission for '3 known IRA sympathisers' to visit Sands, especially as the three had all voted against the British Government and for political status in the European Parliament. He also felt particularly incensed as Northern Ireland political parties had recently had a planned visit to the Maze cancelled. Paisley felt that if Sands called off his strike, the same situation would recur again and again, and he felt that it would be in 'everyone's interest if he did die.' The violence of the last twelve years, Dr Paisley said, could not continue – it had caused serious damage to the economy as well as to the credibility of the Government, and the morale of the people and the Protestant community would not stand for it for much longer. Reverend Beattie, accompanying Paisley, added that he didn't believe that Sands intended to die, and that the Government should not underestimate the propaganda machine of the PIRA, or the use to which this visit would be put. This recent decision to admit the visit was further confirmation to the people of the North that the Government did not understand the situation in Northern Ireland, nor had they the ability to solve it. Paisley also reminded Mitchell that the IRA did not fight 'according to the rules of cricket', and that Sands alive would not save the lives of Protestants in border communities. He warned that if the elected representatives were ignored by the Government then the 'people would forsake them and take power into their own hands.' The Protestant people, he said, were angry to the point of being enraged, and this visit was the last straw.[37]

Reactions among Nationalists were, of course, different. John Hume called on the Government to 'act boldly' to resolve the hunger strike by sending officials to the prison to negotiate directly with the hunger-strikers. He argued that this would entail 'no sacrifice of principle'. As for the meeting between the MEPs and Sands, de Valera took very little part in the discussion while Dr O'Connell asked Sands a series of questions about his health. Blaney spoke about the position of the Republic's Government, stating that the Taoiseach would not want to be personally involved and that his 'hands were tied'. Sands repeated on several occasions during the visit that he did not want to die, but that he wanted to win something.[38] In the aftermath of the meeting, the Prime Minister's party, which had now moved on to Abu Dhabi, was informed that, at a press conference, the three MEPs had requested an urgent meeting with Mrs Thatcher to underline their fears for the life of Sands. They said that Sands was continuing his hunger strike in spite of pleas to call it off. They also demanded reforms in the prison system. Blaney said that the urgency of this meeting was absolute. They were prepared to see the Home Secretary if necessary. O'Connell explained that he had the impression that Sands was determined to die.[39] The three Irish/European deputies had also requested the ECHR to involve itself in the dispute. Signatures were also secured to a motion on the same subject for the next session of the European Parliament. Deputy de Valera sent a telegram to Mrs Gandhi, the Indian Prime Minister, seeking support and calling for her intervention. The three MEPs also sent joint telegrams to the President of the United States, Ronald Reagan; to each of the 'Four Horsemen' (senior Irish-American politicians in the US) – Senator Edward Kennedy, Senator Daniel Moynihan, Governor Hugh Carey of New York and Tip O'Neill (Speaker of the House of Representatives).[40]

In Downing Street, there was a discussion on how to respond to the request for a meeting with Mrs Thatcher: 'We need to send advice for the Prime Minister about the response to the Southern Irish MPs' request to see her about Bobby Sands.' It was noted that the Prime Minister had a press conference in Saudi before she departed for the UK: 'At that point she will play this away for a few hours on the grounds that she has not had an opportunity to get completely up to date on that point.' The recommendation to be sent to her was against agreeing that anyone should see the Irish MPs. The basis of their permission to visit Sands was that they would attempt to persuade him of the futility of his hunger strike. The coverage of their press conference suggested that their request for a meeting was on the basis that they wished to press HMG to do what was possible while there was still time in hand. This was, therefore, beyond the understandings on which their visit to Sands was allowed. The NIO took this view, noted Downing Street. There was, however, the question of how to say 'no'.[41]

From London, the Prime Minister was kept fully abreast of the situation in Northern Ireland: 'Weekend hooliganism – stone and bottle throwing – has been running in Londonderry for some months', she was informed. In the previous week it had taken a turn for the worse. A focus had been supplied by Sands' election – he was now a folk hero – the weather had been good and the schools were on holiday, which encouraged trouble on the streets. Added impetus was provided by an incident in which two youths were killed by an Army vehicle (Gary English and James Brown, both Catholics aged 19 and 18 respectively, were knocked down when a Land Rover ploughed into a crowd during rioting – the soldiers were subsequently acquitted of dangerous driving; four years later Gary English's brother, an IRA Volunteer, was killed when a bomb he was carrying exploded prematurely). The rioting during that week had included both stoning and the first use of petrol bombs in Derry for two years. The previous night, seven shots were fired, 'though this was probably opportunism on the part of PIRA' and not rioters with guns. Casualties suffered by the security forces had been very light, and damage to property had been very modest. The forecast was that 'there will continue to be trouble in Londonderry until Sands either dies or comes off his hunger strike. Both the RUC and the army are confident that they can continue to contain the situation. They regard it as significant that, apart from minor hooliganism, the trouble had not spread to other parts of Northern Ireland. The security forces do not wish to see any change in present policies.'[42]

On the more pressing problem of how to respond to the three TDs/MEPs, the Prime Minister was informed that their visit had to compete as news with the rioting in Derry. The visit had appeared in Northern Ireland 'as something of a damp squib' because it had no outcome of substance other than the proposal that the three should meet the Prime Minster. Unionist opinion was outraged, but the overall effect ('given that the Government's position remains, and is seen to remain, unchanged') had been to put HMG – particularly vis-à-vis the minority community, 'but also no doubt in the Republic and in the USA' – in the position of being seen to have taken 'every step short of surrender to save this man's life; and HMG has done this even at the price of a Unionist perception that the Government have been drawn into a Republican propaganda stunt (and one not unconnected with the likely forthcoming election in the Republic).' The NIO viewpoint was also presented to the Prime Minister:

> For the Prime Minister to accede to the request by the 3 TDs would infuriate Loyalist opinion in Northern Ireland because –
>
> a) it would be seen as treating with the enemy;
> b) it would be taken as a sign that the Government's resolve to withstand terrorism was weakening; and
> c) it would be regarded as confirmation that the visit to Sands was part of a back-door deal to which the British Government was a party.
>
> If the Prime Minister did see the TDs, the hopes of the minority community might be greatly buoyed up; but since HMG has nothing of substance to offer in such a meeting, beyond the prison regime already available, the subsequent let-down would be all the greater.

These arguments, Mrs Thatcher was told, were 'strong; there are countervailing benefits likely to flow from such a meeting which can be set against them. The same considerations apply in differing measure to any other Minister (eg Mr Whitelaw, as Deputy Prime Minster, or Mr Atkins) seeing the three members of the Irish Dail'.[43]

After considering all this information, Mrs Thatcher decided that the formal Government response should read as follows: 'The position of the British Government on the hunger strike is clear and on the record. Any solution to the strike has always been in the hands of those who are on strike. Those who wish to see an end to the strike should concentrate on persuading the hunger strikers to desist from their present course.'[44] The Prime Minister also delivered a public response at a press conference in Saudi Arabia:

> There is no question of political status for someone serving a sentence for crime. Crime is crime is crime. There is no possible concession on political status. To do that, in fact, would put many people in jeopardy.
>
> It is not my habit or custom to meet MPs of a foreign country about a citizen of the UK resident in the UK. If they wish to make representations, and if they wish to do so with speed, they should do so through their own Government in the customary way.

After the Prime Minister said no, the Chairman of the National H-Blocks Committee called on Charles Haughey to seek an immediate meeting with Thatcher and, if no response from her was forthcoming, to consider seriously breaking off diplomatic relations with Britain. Sinn Féin, in Belfast, also said that the Irish Government should reply to Mrs Thatcher's 'snub' to the three deputies by expelling the British Ambassador. John Hume confined himself to calling on the British to talk directly to Sands.[45] As these responses were delivered in Ireland, Downing Street, 'in view of the arguments about political status, which are continuing,' passed on to the Prime Minister the text of a letter from Gerry Adams, published in the *Guardian*:

> None of the hunger strikers is doing it for political status solely for himself. Mr Sands sought election as representative of all the political prisoners now on protest in the H-blocks and Armagh women's prison. Suggesting that he or the other hunger strikers be given 'some sort of political status' is comparable to suggesting that a member elected on a housing programme for example, would be satisfied if he were to be given a house.
>
> If one is to address oneself seriously to 'the question of the moment' which is 'how to contrive matters so that a prisoner with the political status of a Member of Parliament ... does not starve himself to death', then one has to examine the real politics of absurdity which create the present crisis.
>
> These are, put simply, that the British Government as part of a major propaganda campaign to project resistance to their presence in this country as criminal, attempted among other things to criminalise the Irish political prisoners. No one, despite British protestations to the contrary, presumes that any of these prisoners are criminal. An intricate network of secret police, British army and other crown forces, a conveyor belt of brutal interrogation centres, remand laws, special 'emergency' legislation and non jury courts has been contrived to deal with this essentially political problem.
>
> That the political prisoners refuse to accept their criminalisation is understandable, that they have widespread support and that the propaganda exercise of criminalisation has failed, is now obvious.
>
> Attempts to find a progressive, just and reasonable ending to the prison crisis, by the prisoners and their supporters have been persistently wrecked by the stupidity and high handed attitudes of the British Government which is more interested, as always, in protecting its own interests in this country than its alleviating the hardships and correcting the absurdities that its involvement creates.
>
> Bobby Sands and his comrades now face death, not because they are denied political recognition, but because they are denied the right to human dignity and to treatment as political prisoners. Five simple, just

and reasonable conditions can secure an end to the sufferings of the political prisoners who have endured a difficult protest for the past five years.

The British Government has to move only a little from its present position to that outlined above. That it refuses to do so is a great absurdity. That Irish people have to live and die despite and because of such absurdities is criminal.[46]

While these arguments carried little weight with Mrs Thatcher, in Dublin the Irish Government was beginning to feel the pressure as Sands' life ebbed away. The Minister for Foreign Affairs, Brian Lenihan, received, at their request, de Valera, Blaney and O'Connell. Blaney told Lenihan that each of them wished to convey their impressions of the situation and their ideas on how the impasse could be broken. He went on to say that Sands was 'not seeking by name "political status".' At the close of their conversation with Sands, he had remarked that he had never mentioned political status: 'Mrs Thatcher and Mr Atkins were harping on political status.' Blaney argued that it did not matter what it was called, political status or special category status, but there was an irrefutable case as to why Sands should get what the pre-1976 prisoners had, what Irish prisoners in Britain had and what they had 'down here'. The British, Blaney acknowledged, asked how could they be sure the prisoners would not ask for more. The answer to this was that the British had the prisoners inside the jail and could control them – they could if necessary take concessions back. The prisoners, however, needed to have concessions delivered to them. It had looked in December as if they would 'go to the end; they had given up and now felt welshed upon.' Blaney's impression was that there were many more prisoners ready to go on hunger strike – up to twenty more, who were very determined.

Deputy O'Connell added that he did not know why he had been asked to visit the prison. He did not believe that anyone should die for a principle. He did, however, feel strongly about the position of prisoners, and that loss of freedom was enough. He had found Sands remarkably strong, but other doctors he had met in the prison were very fearful and felt that he had six days at most to live. O'Connell then referred to the consequences in Northern Ireland of the death of Sands and the possibility of a spill over in the South. He said that Mrs Thatcher's intransigence was 'impressive', but that there was a formula that could get the British off the hook by concessions in the field of work and other areas. He referred to the fact that there was no trouble at present in Portlaoise. If something could be done, possibly behind the scenes, he and his colleagues would withdraw immediately. They would be delighted if the Government could solve the problem. O'Connell continued that, in his view, there was little public sympathy for the hunger-strikers, but if a solution were reached there would be great national relief. De Valera agreed with what the other two MEPs had said. The question of political status was being used as an excuse for not giving in by the British; there was a way out, and this would not involve any question of principle.[47]

Following this meeting, Haughey tasked Dermot Nally to approach his opposite number in London, Sir Robert Armstrong. Nally phoned the Cabinet Secretary to tell him that the Taoiseach and his colleagues were very worried that, if Sands died in the next five or six days, 'the whole area would go up in flames'. The Taoiseach had asked him to convey the message that he was extremely anxious to help in any way he could, and to ask whether there was anything he could do that might be helpful. Nally said that the Taoiseach would have to do something 'today or tomorrow' because of the political pressures in the Republic. He emphasized that the Taoiseach's concern was purely a humanitarian one. The Irish Government did not want HMG to meet the demands for political status. Nally wondered whether there was any future in getting the ECHR involved. He had heard Atkins on the television the day before that suggested that something in this area might be acceptable.

Armstrong replied that his understanding was that the ECHR had made it clear that there was no official locus for the Commission in the matter, because they had no complaint before them: 'I understood, however, that certain Commissioners had expressed a willingness to offer their good offices on a personal basis. I did not think that we should exclude the possibility of some of the Commissioners visiting Northern Ireland on a personal basis, so long as there was no suggestion that they were coming to mediate between Mr Sands or other prisoners and the Government.' Nally quickly disclaimed any idea of mediation. He said, however, that there were certain recommendations in paragraph 64 of the ECHR Report the previous year, which might provide a basis on which Commissioners could say that there was a continuing ECHR interest that they should be following up. Nally added that the Taoiseach would be sending a message 'through normal channels' later in the day, but in view of the shortage of time the Taoiseach was anxious to get this thought in to HMG at the earliest possible moment.[48]

The Taoiseach, meanwhile, asked Leonard Figg to call on him at 4.30 p.m. the same day, 22 April. He reiterated that he was very worried about the recent violence in the North and feared it could spill over into the Republic if Sands died. Matters had taken a turn for the worse because of the election of Sands to Parliament. He was under pressure to do something because the Prime Minister had been drawn into the affair by the telegram sent to her by the three Euro-MPs. He wished to consult HMG about what he might say. Haughey said that he had quite an open mind. A public statement seemed desirable, but he wanted to fit it into something 'we could do on our side.' A possible formula might be built on a visit to London by two European Commissioners for Human Rights, whom the Irish believed to be Nørgaard and Frowein. It might be possible to arrange for the two Commissioners to visit the Maze privately to see what improvements could be made in the prison administration. If this background could be arranged, then the Taoiseach thought he could appeal in a public statement to Sands to come off the hunger strike because of the interest and attention of the ECHR. Haughey believed that although Sands might be prepared to die, at heart he probably did not wish to do so: 'It was in our urgent interests to put our heads together and devise some formula … which might just possibly do the trick.' Haughey said that he would be available to see Figg at any time the following morning with any suggestions HMG might have: 'I should be grateful for urgent instructions accordingly', telegraphed Figg to London.[49]

There, Home Secretary Whitelaw and Atkins considered how the Government should proceed with regards to Sands and the other hunger-strikers, particularly in the light of the Taoiseach's conversation with Figg. They agreed that there could be 'no question' of European Commissioners for Human Rights visiting the Maze privately as suggested by Haughey. Rather, the Government should stand firm on the position that it first adopted some weeks before: that if the ECHR were to be involved it could do so only in response to a formal complaint, and that such a complaint could be made only by Sands or another hunger-striker, or someone with the necessary standing to act on his behalf such as a parent. If on receipt of such a complaint the ECHR decided to investigate, and formally asked HMG to facilitate its enquiry, the Government should agree to co-operate, including allowing one or more Commissioners to visit the Maze to inform themselves as to the circumstances giving rise to the complaint. Whitelaw and Atkins were firmly of the view that HMG must do nothing until the ECHR's formal processes had been activated in this way by a complaint being laid with them. They believed that if HMG were to be seen to be encouraging the submission of a complaint, the risk of a 'serious Protestant reaction' would be substantially increased[50] – Atkins judged it 'more dangerous' if the Protestant community should feel that the Government had bought off Sands' death than that others should criticize the Government for allowing him to die.[51] In the meantime, the Prime Minister was telegraphed the news that Sands' condition continued to deteriorate, and the latest forecast was that though he was still not in a coma, he was likely to die at the weekend. Whitelaw and Atkins let the Prime Minister know that, in their judgement, it was still more likely than not that he would die, and that 'we should continue to prepare ourselves for what would follow his death.'[52]

Figg was then informed that, after consultation between the Prime Minister, Whitelaw and Atkins, he should respond to Haughey as follows: 'We would not oppose an intervention by the European Commission for Human Rights … provided that the Commission's involvement is brought about in the only way in which it can be brought about, with the willing participation of HMG, namely by accepting and responding to a complaint made from one of the hunger strikers.' For Figg's personal information, the Ambassador was told by Lord Carrington: 'we have confirmed informally' with the ECHR ('and no doubt the DFA will similarly inform themselves') that such a complaint could be sent by telegram urgently to the ECHR Secretary in Strasbourg, that the ECHR would respond urgently by asking both HMG and the hunger-strikers to do nothing that would impede the Commission's consideration of the complaint, and the Commission would then ask HMG in these exceptional circumstances to facilitate a visit to the Maze by the Vice President of the Commission, accompanied by such other members as the Commission may wish so that the Commissioners could inform themselves about the circumstances giving rise to the complaint. The Commission would itself announce that it had made this request, which had been met by HMG. Carrington instructed Figg: 'It is important that in speaking in these terms to Mr Haughey you should emphasise that in HMG's view there is no other basis … for facilitating a visit to the prison by the Commissioners.'[53]

On 23 April, the family of Sands called on the Taoiseach at his home. As a result, an application was made by Marcella Sands on behalf of her brother to the ECHR under Article 25 of the European Convention on Human Rights against the Government of the United Kingdom.[54] The application complained under Article 2 (Right to Life), Article 3 (Prohibition of Inhuman Treatment) and Article 10 of the Convention (Freedom of Expression) about his conditions of detention. As already arranged secretly, in view of the urgency of the situation, the Acting President of the Commission (Carl Aage Nørgaard) informed the UK Government of the introduction of the application and indicated to the Government, under Rule 36 of the Rules of Procedure, that the necessary steps should be taken to enable a delegation from the Commission to meet Sands in prison with a view to obtaining his confirmation that he intended to make an application and, if so, discussing the contents and the handling of the application. The delegation on its way to the UK consisted of Nørgaard (a Dane) and Torkel Opsahl (a Norwegian).[55] The grounds for Marcella Sands' claim for intervention by the Commission were:

1. The British Government is in breach of Articles 2 and 3 of the Convention. My brother's life is in danger. He is now in the 54th day of a hunger strike which he had no choice but to undertake as a more conventional domestic remedy was not open to him to protest against prison conditions which he regarded as intolerable.

   No domestic remedies are available to him to enable him to have his present circumstances declared inhuman or degrading. There is no fundamental rights charter justifiable in Northern Ireland on which he can rely.

2. The conditions of my brother's imprisonment are in breach of Article 10 in that he is unable to give expression to the opinions of his constituents, despite the fact that he is a democratically elected member of the British parliament.

3. In the partial decision of the European Commission of Human Rights on application no. 8317/78 by T McFeeley et al against the United Kingdom the Commission at paragraph 64 expressed its concern at the inflexible approach of the state authorities which has been concerned more to punish offenders against prison discipline than to explore ways of resolving serious deadlocks in the Northern Ireland prison system. This inflexibility continues.[56]

Sands' condition, meanwhile, continued to deteriorate, 'but not just as quickly as recently.' He 'remained lucid and capable of taking rational decisions.' The consultant monitoring him now thought that he was likely to go into a coma around Monday 28 April and to die the following day. It was noted, however, 'that the doctors have been wrong before.' Sands was overheard by staff telling Carron, on 23 April, that he would go through with his hunger strike; Carron informed Sands that Gerry Adams and Tom Hartley had indicated to him in conversation that they did not see the granting of all five demands as a sticking point. Sands' reaction to this suggestion of a possible compromise was unknown.[57] It was known, however, that his solicitor Pat Finucane visited Sands, on 23 April, in order to make his will. By that day the prisoners' weights were:

	Day of strike	Weight on first examination	Weight today	Weight loss during week	Overall weight loss
Robert Sands	54	10st 1lb	7st 5lb	4½lb	2st 9½lb
Francis Hughes	40	11st 3½lb	9st 4lb	4lb	1st 13½lb
Raymond McCreesh	33	9st 13lb	8st 6lb	3lb	1st 7lb
Patrick O'Hara	33	12st 1lb	9st 10lb	5½lb	2st 4½lb[58]

On Friday, 24 April, two members of the ECHR obtained the formal agreement of the UK Government to visit Sands in prison. The object of the visit, it was stated, was 'to obtain Mr Sands' confirmation that he intends to pursue the application made on his behalf by his sister and to discuss the contents and handling of the application'.[59] It was shortly after 11 a.m. the following morning when the Commissioners were ready to start their proceedings. They first saw Dr Ross for about twenty-five minutes, followed by Sands' sister, Marcella, alone. Then Pat Finucane (who had been in the hospital from the beginning and had had a short visit with Sands) was called in. Finucane saw Sands again for five minutes from 12.20; he and Marcella came out from the Commissioners at 12.40. Some time after 1 p.m., the Commissioners asked to see S. C. Jackson of the NIO. Commissioner Nørgaard explained that they had reached an impasse in that Sands was not prepared to adopt the complaint made by his sister, and was unwilling to see the Commission's representatives unless Brendan McFarlane, Gerry Adams and Danny Morrison were all present. In the first place Nørgaard asked if McFarlane could be brought from the prison to see them. After final clearance with Blelloch, Jackson said that this would be done. At this point the Commissioners and NIO official adjourned to the Administration Block for coffee and sandwiches.[60]

In Qatar, the Prime Minister, who was about to embark on her journey back to the UK, was informed by Michael Alexander that the European Commissioners had a 'satisfactory meeting' with the FCO and NIO. The latter explained the British position in general, 'and in particular the point that we would not want Adams present at the meeting between them and Sands at the Maze.' The Commissioners fully accepted this, and explained that it was their normal practice only to see the complainant with the complainant's lawyer. The complainant in this case was in fact Sands' sister, with whom the Commissioners had agreed that Sands' lawyer should also be present at the meeting at the Maze. This was entirely acceptable to the NIO. Mrs Thatcher was told that the 'crunch' was likely to come when the Commissioners reached Belfast: 'Sands will then be told that they have arrived and that the meeting will be with the Commissioners, his sister and his lawyer only. Either he will accept this; or he will insist on Adams, and possibly MacFarlane [sic] ... and the PR man of the Sinn Féin [Morrison] being present.'

The NIO position remained that Adams and others should not be admitted. However, Mrs Thatcher was warned that the NIO were 'extremely worried about the prospect of Sands insisting on the others being present; and even now are showing some signs of wavering.' The Prime Minister was made aware that Whitelaw was in close touch with Atkins. If they were to decide to accede to Sands' demand that Adams etc. should be present, Alexander thought:

> ... that it would be as well for one of them to consult you on the telephone (if possible). However, once we take off we only have communications through the cockpit, and it will be difficult to have a sensible discussion. So, if there is to be a conversation between you and them, it would have to be before we leave at 3.00 p.m. (3.00 p.m. Qatar time will be 1.00

p.m. London). If we are in the air, and a decision has to be made, then presumably Willie Whitelaw and Humphrey Atkins will have to take it themselves without consulting you.

The Prime Minister scribbled her decision on the minute: 'I will have to leave the decision to HA and WW jointly. They will have the latest situation. MT'[61]

Back in the Maze, the Commissioners reassembled at 2.05 p.m. They saw Finucane again at 2.15 p.m., and after a few minutes the solicitor paid another short visit to Sands. Shortly before 2.40 p.m., the Commissioners saw McFarlane, alone at first and then with Finucane. At 3.15 p.m., McFarlane went to see Sands, and was with him for ten minutes. The Commissioners had a few final words with McFarlane and then with Finucane. At 3.35, the Commissioners asked to see Jackson again. Nørgaard explained that the impasse remained as it had been before lunch. They discussed, at first on a formal and then on an informal basis, the question of Adams and Morrison being allowed in to be present with Sands. Nørgaard said that the Commission did not wish to make a request to the NIO if it was clear beforehand that it was going to be refused. Jackson replied along the lines he had agreed with Blelloch earlier: if the Commission made the request it would be put to the Secretary of State, but Jackson's belief was that it would not be approved. At this point, Commissioner Opsahl volunteered the comment that it had been suggested to them that if Adams and Morrison were allowed to be present, it would be possible for 'real progress' to be made. Nørgaard added that he would like to speak to another NIO official, Marshall, to explain the situation that had been reached. Jackson talked further to Blelloch, who telephoned him back to say that he would speak to Nørgaard after he had discussed the matter with the Secretary of State. Shortly afterward, and before Blelloch telephoned, the Commissioners had a further short talk with Finucane. Marcella Sands had had a very brief talk with her brother shortly before 4.40 p.m. – he felt too weak to talk longer. When Nørgaard spoke to Jackson again it was just as Blelloch came on the telephone; the Commissioner said that they had decided not to make any request to the Government in regard to Adams and Morrison.[62] When Mrs Thatcher arrived back in the UK she was able to have a telephone conversation with Atkins, who briefed her on events:

Prime Minister: Hello, Humphrey.
Secretary of State: Hello, Margaret, welcome home.
Prime Minister: Thank you, but you've had a very difficult time.
Secretary of State: Yes it's been all go.
                       Sands is clearly determined. I don't know how much you
                       have heard about the line he is taking which is …

Prime Minister: No I haven't.

Secretary of State: To let Gerry Adams into the Maze Prison would have been something that would very seriously have upset a lot of people here. Well we were never actually formally asked to do so. And if we were I would have had to say no. But the Commissioners said look we either act formally on receipt of the complaint or we can't act at all.

So where we stand now is that anything may happen between now and tomorrow morning. It is probably that nothing will happen that will affect it – probably won't – and we are left then tomorrow with Sands determined to die.

Prime Minister: Yes and he's only got a few days.

Secretary of State: He's only got a few days. The doctors cannot be specific, they are talking of two or three but to be honest with you Margaret they don't really know.

Prime Minister: No because it's not a position with which anyone has very much experience. He's taking water presumably.

Secretary of State: He's taking water but he's not finding it very easy to keep down and I think probably it is only a day or two before he starts going into a coma and so forth but he has left the most clear and specific instructions and in writing that he is not to be given any medication or kept alive in any way. So my guess, although it is for the doctors to say and not me is that if he does go into a coma they will leave him alone. Now then there will be a good deal of flurry about all this I'm afraid.

Because there are two a fortnight behind him and another one behind that. And one hopes very much that we can prevent the thing going on week after week. I think there is bound to be a weak link later.

Prime Minister: Yes I think they will be getting worried after all if one died and then a second one died then a third one died and nothing happened.

Secretary of State: Yes it doesn't look very attractive.

Prime Minister: No it doesn't.

Secretary of State: That's right. But we will need to assess the situation if he does die shall we say, I don't know, Tuesday, Wednesday, that sort of thing, we'll have to assess it and work out how we handle the next one coming along and how we handle the situation that immediately develops and I'll have time to come and talk to you about it.[63]

Sands responded to the Commissioners' visit by issuing a statement through the Republican Press Centre. The NIO's assessment was that 'although it purports to be the work of Bobby Sands it is undoubtedly written by Gerry Adams … On Adams' instructions Marcella Sands has told the office of the Taoiseach that she will be going to be denouncing the cynical intervention in the hunger strike.' The statement said that Sands had not at any time requested the Commission to investigate the demands of the protesting prisoners. Despite this, and despite his lack of confidence in the Commission, he had been prepared to meet any European Commissioner, provided two advisers chosen by himself and a representative of the protesting prisoners were present, but:

These facilities were denied me. The legal submission and request to the European Commission was made in good faith by my sister Marcella, who was misled by Charles Haughey into believing that the Commission would deliver on the political prisoners' demands. Mr Haughey led my family to believe that the British Government wanted a way out of the dilemma in which they now find themselves, and that the Commission's intervention was the vehicle for getting the British off the H-Block–Armagh hook.

Because Mr Haughey gave similar assurances leading up to the confused ending of the last hunger-strike, and because Mr Haughey has in fact the means to put pressure and to call publicly on Britain to end the H-Blocks–Armagh crisis and has consistently refused to do so, I viewed his prompting of my family as cynical and a cold-blooded manipulation of people clearly vulnerable to this type of pressure.

The Commission's intervention has been diversionary and has served to aid the British attempts to confuse the issue.

The issue is basic and fundamental.

Four Republican political prisoners are on hunger strike on behalf of their 440 protesting comrades here in the H Blocks and Armagh. Our demands are reasonable and just. We on hunger strike are prepared to die for them. One of my comrades, Frankie Hughes, is in a steadily deteriorating condition. I am on the 56th day of the hunger strike. Patsy O'Hara and Raymond McCreesh are on the 35th day of hunger strike.

Now that the Commission discussion is out of the way and the confusion deliberately created by its intervention has cleared, we the political prisoners call once again for the people to support our demands.

The British Government has the ways and means to concede them. Until they do the hunger strike continues.

Signed, Bobby Sands, Prison Hospital, H Blocks, Long Kesh.[64]

To find out what had actually happened during the ECHR intervention, Martin Burke, of the Taoiseach's office, asked the Irish Ambassador to Britain, Dr Eamon Kennedy, to try and contact the Commission delegation at Heathrow Airport. Kennedy succeeded in making contact and spoke to Commissioner Kruger. The Ambassador expressed the disappointment of the Taoiseach in relation to what had happened at Long Kesh. Kruger replied that his delegation was just as disappointed. The main stumbling block had been Sands' refusal to confirm the application made on his behalf by Miss Sands. If Sands had been co-operative the Commission would have been inclined to press the British authorities on this matter, but felt, on balance, that they should not in the circumstances ask for a meeting on Sands' terms. In relation to the question of the Commission continuing to be involved on a formal or an informal basis, Kruger said that they did not wish to 'close any doors'. They were, however, inevitably restricted by the European Convention and the rules of procedure. They could only make progress or remain involved if Sands pursued an application. Kruger stressed that Sands' attitude had been 'central' to their consideration of the situation, and in view of his lack of co-operation they could not make progress.[65]

In the meantime, Mrs Thatcher was briefed, on 26 April, that: 'The doctors have seen Sands again late this afternoon. His condition continues to deteriorate, but they do not think that tomorrow is likely to be the crisis day.'[66] Monday 27 April saw Atkins personally brief the Prime Minister on the latest developments. He told her that he believed that it was only the day before that the PIRA had fully understood that the British Government was not prepared to change its position; meanwhile, Haughey would find himself in a dilemma if Sands died: he would have to choose between preserving the new momentum in relations between the United Kingdom and the Republic that had followed the Dublin summit and trying to outbid those extreme Republican politicians who would seek to capitalize on Sands' death in the period leading up to the forthcoming Irish general election. Atkins confirmed that Sands was now very close to death. He had given the prison authorities explicit instructions that the doctors were to do nothing to prevent his death. In practice, once he went into a coma, the doctors would ask his family if they wanted them to intervene. If they did, the doctors would revive him once and ask him whether he wanted them to treat him. If he said no, they would do no more and would let him die. Similarly, if his family said that they did not want the doctors to intervene, nothing would be done.

Atkins explained that if Sands died, there would be an enormous turnout for his funeral. There would be large-scale rioting, but the plans of the security forces for dealing with the situation were already laid. Their primary aim would be to stop Catholic demonstrators invading Protestant areas. There was already a certain amount of evidence that Protestant paramilitary organizations were getting ready to protect Protestant areas against Catholic rioters. If the security forces were unable to prevent intercommunity clashes, serious disturbances were likely to follow. The present assessment of Jack Hermon, the RUC Chief Constable, was that provided major intercommunity violence could be prevented, the Republican demonstrations would be likely to last two or three days and then die out, to give way to a resumption of the PIRA's campaign, which would be directed specifically at members of the security forces. Hermon believed that it might help to reduce the scale of the trouble if a small number of people who could normally be expected to be involved in directing the riots were arrested under the Prevention of Terrorism Act and taken out of circulation for a few days. Atkins proposed to sign the necessary orders for this purpose.

The Prime Minister agreed that this step should be taken. She thought it was likely that Sands' death would lead to a resumption of PIRA terrorism in Great Britain: 'We also had to look ahead to what would happen as the other hunger strikers moved towards a critical condition.' Atkins pointed out that the next hunger-striker, Hughes, was fourteen days behind Sands, with two others a week behind Hughes. One of the latter two was deteriorating rather faster than the others. If Sands died, a full assessment of likely developments would immediately be provided for the Prime Minister. His death would make it imperative to change the law to prevent prisoners serving sentences from being elected as Members of Parliament: otherwise Provisional Sinn Féin would put up one hunger-striker after another as candidates. The Prime Minister noted that further work on this problem had now been done, and the Home Secretary had told her that morning that it now appeared that the law could be changed relatively easily to make it impossible for prisoners serving sentences of more than a certain specified length to be nominated as candidates in a parliamentary election.[67]

Meanwhile, in a blow to those hoping for American intervention, President Reagan, in Washington, confirmed that he was not prepared to intervene in Northern Ireland, although he was concerned about the tragic situation in the North. In a statement the White House said that the President's 'sincerest hope' was that peace may come to Northern Ireland 'so that its young men will turn away from violence and turn their energies and idealism to the more difficult task of rebuilding their country.'[68] In Ireland, Cardinal Tomás Ó Fiaich made a last-minute appeal, in writing, to the Prime Minister to intervene and save Sands' life:

> Having appealed last week to hunger strikers to end their fast, I must continue efforts to save their lives. I therefore appeal to yourself and Cabinet to implement proposals on prison dress and work made several times last year by Bishop Edward Daly and myself for all prisoners in

Northern Ireland. These would have averted hunger strikes and brought prison protests to an end.

We do not ask for political status, but seek to save lives by recognising the unique situation here. We have a five-fold increase in prison population, of whom a vast majority are 1) very youthful, 2) first offenders, 3) from law-abiding families, 4) sentenced to long terms. To wear their own clothes does not confer political status. All prisoners in several countries, and here in Armagh Women's prison, are permitted to do so.

I urge you to send at once a representative of the Northern Ireland Office to talk to prisoners on the above basis, as was done during the last hunger strike. This now seems the only way to avoid deaths in prison and widespread violence outside.[69]

In Dublin, Haughey once more tasked Dermot Nally to contact the British. Nally rang up Sir Kenneth Stowe, the NIO PUS, to make two points, following discussion with the Taoiseach: the Irish, Stowe recorded, 'would be very interested in our view about how things were likely to develop'; and, with a hint of desperation, 'wondered whether we might simply let Sands go, on the ground that, as a Member of Parliament, he was unique.' Stowe discussed all this with Robert Armstrong on the telephone before and after lunch, and then rang Nally back. The PUS told Nally that, for various reasons, and in particular because of the electoral prospects North and South of the border, the situation now was more inflammable, and the flashpoint was lower than in December 1980. There was in any case a risk of an escalation of violence if and when Sands died:

We were determined that we must do nothing that might upset the precarious balance or de-stabilise the community, and that we must contain and control violence from either side even-handedly. If violence escalated it could spread across the border. It was in neither of our interests for that to happen. We much appreciated the continuing cross-border co-operation and looked forward to it continuing as effectively as ever.

Stowe explained that HMG now thought that, perhaps, the ECHR move had been misread by the PIRA as 'a ploy to get ourselves off the hook and as a sign of weakness. It was not that.' That being said, the ECHR was there and could be used again if, for example, another prisoner complained. The avenue was open, 'and we would facilitate it again if the occasion arose.' But there could be no question of negotiations between the British Government and the PIRA under cover of the ECHR Commissioners. Loyalist opinion was acutely sensitive and suspicious following the decision to let the three members of the Dáil see Sands, as well as the involvement of the ECHR:

> We had to be extremely careful if we were to avoid inflaming Protestant opinion to the point where we once again saw a recrudescence of Protestant violence. We were in no doubt that to release Sands now would have such an effect on Protestant opinion. We could not argue that he was unique because he was a Member of Parliament, because the Committee of Privileges was on record as saying that a Member of Parliament in prison should enjoy no privileges by virtue of being a Member of Parliament.

It was up to Sands at this point whether he lived or died, and his remaining time could be very short. Nally 'took note of all this.' He did not press further for the release of Sands; indeed, he implied that he accepted the strength of the arguments against it.[70] And with the Taoiseach rebuffed, the Prime Minister wrote to rebuff Ó Fiaich as well:

> Like all people who care for human life I hope very much that even at this late stage the hunger strikers will pay heed to your appeal.
>
> I recognise that in sending me your message you are seeking to save life and not the granting of political status.
>
> The fact remains that the hunger strike is in support of a demand for political status: the concessions which the hunger strikers are seeking on dress and work are in pursuit of that demand. The Government made its position absolutely clear on the questions of political status and the so-called five demands before the first hunger strike began last October. We are determined to stand firm on that position. To do otherwise would be to abandon sound principles in the face of the threat of violence.
>
> You also urge me to send an NIO representative to talk to prisoners. This was done last December in order that the hunger strikers should be in no doubt about what the prison regime afforded. I do not believe that there can now be any doubt about this, given the extensive efforts that have been made to publish the facts. I am afraid I therefore see no useful purpose that could be served in a visit of the kind you propose.[71]

On 29 April, Downing Street was again updated, by the NIO, on the situation in the Maze: Sands was now in the sixtieth day of his hunger strike, and was in imminent danger of death. There had been a slight, unexplained improvement in his condition on 28 April, but the doctors' present assessment was that he could not live much longer unless he accepted treatment. But: 'There is every indication that Sands is reconciled to dying if he cannot force us to concede.' Of the other three hunger-strikers, Hughes was reckoned by the doctors to be about one week behind Sands.

In Belfast, there had been frequent rioting by hooligans, sometimes drawn from the ranks of those who attended demonstrations, but the scale of the disorder had been both exaggerated, and to some degree encouraged, by the press. Despite the frequency of television and newspaper reports of stone-throwing incidents and hijacked vehicles, the disorder had not been widespread, had rarely involved more than 100 youths at a time, and had invariably lasted for only a few hours. There had been no repeat of the large-scale rioting, or the sectarian confrontations, that developed in 1969 and 1970. Both the capacity of the terrorists, and the number of terrorist crimes, had continued to decrease. The number of deaths, explosions and shooting incidents were all well down in 1981 compared with 1980 – but the influence of the hunger strike was shown in the fact that thirteen of the twenty-four deaths in the year had occurred since the beginning of the hunger strike – seven of them (including three rioters) during the last fortnight. The police had behaved 'admirably', and, closely supported by the Army, had succeeded in controlling not only outbreaks of disorder but also terrorist activity, with a minimum of irritation to the community at large.[72]

From Dublin, Figg telegraphed the Foreign Office with a dispatch, passed on to Mrs Thatcher: 'You may find it useful to have my assessment of the likely impact in Dublin of Sands' death.' The Ambassador recounted how, during the last hunger strike, 'we were repeatedly told that people's mood would change dramatically if there were to be a death. I do not think that that is likely to be true this time round because public indifference is much more marked now. (But I would be less certain of continuing apathy if Francis Hughes also died. Some parallel might be drawn with the way in which the execution of the 1916 leaders over a period aroused public opinion.)' While Figg did not believe that Sands' death would have much impact on Anglo–Irish relations, if reactions in the North to any death were violent and sustained there would be an inevitable knock-on effect 'down here. The Taoiseach told me last time I saw him that he feared a Protestant paramilitary campaign in the South. Also he would feel bound to make representations to us if the minority community in the North were to be attacked by the Protestants.' Short of serious problems on these lines, 'Mr Haughey has little option but to continue with the general line he had been pursuing up till now. Some of his critics might point out that his much vaunted "unique relationship" with the Prime Minister has not been able to save Sands. And of course what must bother him is that the hunger strikers have interfered with his election plans.'[73]

As all sides prepared for the death of Sands, a last-minute intervention by the Vatican seemed to offer the last opportunity for a breakthrough. The Irish received word from Rome, through Des Hanafin, a Fianna Fáil member of Seanad Éireann, that his wife, who was also in Rome, was a friend of Father John Magee, a native of Newry, County Down, and the Pope's Private Secretary; Hanafin's understanding was that if Sands requested the ECHR to intervene it was likely that Father Magee would be sent to see him on humanitarian grounds.[74] Early on 28 April the NIO was told that the Pope, as an expression of his humanitarian concern about the hunger-strikers, wished to send Father Magee to visit Sands in the Maze, having first met an NIO Minister. Magee was expected to arrive at Heathrow at about 2.30 p.m., and to take the next Shuttle plane (4.30 p.m.) to Belfast. Peter Blaker (FCO) and Michael Alison were tasked to meet him at Heathrow, accompanied if possible by Archbishop Heim, Apostolic Delegate to Great Britain. The visit was described as an unofficial one, 'and we do not know whether Father Magee, in meeting the Minister, will have any particular line to take', noted the NIO's Mike Moriarty. It was possible that, following the line taken by other Church dignitaries in recent days, he would represent that a little 'flexibility' on the part of HMG, without conceding any point of principle, would be sufficient to persuade Sands and others to give up the strike.[75]

When Blaker and Alison met Magee at the airport, the priest explained that his was a goodwill mission from the Pope, with the object of trying to defuse the violence that would erupt in Northern Ireland if Sands died. He hoped to talk to as many people as possible in Northern Ireland, but wanted to begin with a meeting with an NIO Minister, in the hope of receiving a message that he could deliver to Sands, which would provide a basis for securing time within which to make further explorations. Alison recalled the Pope's visit to Ireland the previous year, and reiterated HMG's desire to prevent violence. He explained that the strikers' aim was political status, embodied in a special prison regime. This HMG could not grant. The prison regime was a liberal one, and whilst there was scope for further development, this would stop short of handing over control to inmates. The best hope of avoiding violence lay in Sands ending his fast. Magee then referred to 'peripheral areas' where there might be scope for flexibility, for example prison clothing and work. There ensued a detailed explanation of the clothing regime, on which Father Magee appeared to be well briefed. He pressed the point that to offer all prisoners the option of wearing their own clothes all the time might be a gesture of goodwill that might make a difference in the present situation. Alison explained that such a change was desired by the protesters not for its own sake but as a symbol of a concession on political status: 'Nor had we any reason to suppose that any one change of that kind would make a difference to Mr Sands' position', added Alison. Magee picked up the references to the possibility of further developments on the prison regime and asked if this were something that he could hold out to Sands as a future hope. Alison said that it would be wrong for Sands to expect any specific and immediate change in regime, and Magee was also reminded that ambiguities in this respect at the end of the last prison strike had caused future troubles. In leaving for his connection to Belfast, Magee said that later in his visit he might ask to see the Secretary of State, and he was given the impression that this could be arranged.[76]

After Magee met with Sands he had a private discussion with Atkins, to whom he explained that he came as the personal, not the diplomatic, representative of His Holiness. He brought a message to the Secretary of State from the Pope. This was that he came on a mission of peace, goodwill and concern deeply felt by the Pope and especially where life was in danger. The Pope had spoken out very clearly against violence, for example at Drogheda, and his condemnation of violence included those engaged in violence against themselves. His Holiness wanted to offer his help in any way if it could avoid the loss of life. He had sent Magee not as a negotiator but as a personal representative to see whether there was any way of stopping this madness. Magee then gave a detailed account of his visit to Sands: he was surprisingly well, and asked Magee to thank the Pope for sending a representative. Magee explained to Sands at length the Pope's condemnation of violence, to which Sands responded by explaining his stand. With respect to Magee's plea to end the hunger strike, Sands response was 'do not ask me that'. Magee emphasized that this was a personal plea from the Pope, to which Sands responded that the Pope would understand that the people of Northern Ireland were a downtrodden people. Moving on, Magee asked Sands to provide time for possibilities to be explored by ending his hunger strike, if only temporarily – say for three days. Sands replied that he would end it immediately for five days provided that certain conditions were satisfied. Atkins here intervened to underline that while he was willing to hear what Magee had undertaken to pass on, he must re-emphasize that his meeting with Magee was taking place on the basis that there was no question of any form of negotiation. Magee stated that he recognized that, but Sands' conditions were:

a) An official from the NIO would visit him to discuss the whole question;
b) Two priests should be present as guarantors;
c) Three other prisoners (not the hunger strikers, but presumably the 'OCs' within the prison) should be present.

Sands emphasized that he was not demanding political status, but sought satisfaction on the five demands. If this were achieved, he would not begin his hunger strike again at the end of the five days. Sands realized that to set conditions for ending the strike was not the answer Magee wanted, but it would serve no useful purpose for Magee to come back again without a representative from the NIO. Magee asked Atkins whether there was any hope of movement on these well-known issues. He thought that there was not any great question of principle involved.

The Secretary of State emphasized his respect for the Pope's message and his personal respect for the Pope. It was quite clear, however, that Sands was setting conditions. He had explained that there could be no negotiation, which was what Sands was trying to initiate. The Government had no intention of conceding political status, but the excellence of the facilities at the Maze Prison and the Government's record of improving them (which they would continue even if Sands died) showed that HMG had acted humanely and compassionately. In particular, the Government had responded to responsible criticism, including the suggestions made by the ECHR. Improvement in conditions in the prison had largely overtaken three of the five demands. The response of the prisoners had been to intensify their demands. The Government would not grant demands made in this way, the effect of which would be to grant special status to special people, quite inconsistent with the Pope's message at Drogheda. The effect of giving in to the demands would be to create a regime within the prison in which a particular group made their own decisions as to what they wore, the nature of their work and whether they worked, and with which of their fellow prisoners they would associate. To concede that would be wrong – and would also provoke a violent reaction within Northern Ireland that would threaten innocent lives.

Father Magee thought that the prisoners would not be inflexible: they wanted evidence of goodwill because promises had been made to them at the end of the last hunger strike and had not been kept. Atkins stressed to Magee that no promises had been made at the end of the last hunger strike, and that fact was well known to Sands. The Secretary of State handed to Magee documents including the notices issued to the prisoners at the end of the last hunger strike, which would state the position quite clearly. At the end of the meeting Atkins explained, and Father Magee accepted, that the Secretary of State could not see him again because to do so would risk creating the impression that some form of negotiation was going on. There was no question of negotiation, and Atkins would need to continue to make that quite clear.[77]

Following the meeting, David Tatham, Counsellor at the British Embassy, contacted an Irish official and passed on Sands' proposition, stressing the confidentiality of the communication and stating that its contents would not be released by the British authorities. It was their understanding that Father Magee would not be making any statement in the matter either, although they recognized that Sands' proposition would probably become public knowledge at some stage. In their view, either Sands himself or his supporters would disclose the 'offer' at whatever time they considered appropriate. As regarded Sands' proposition, Tatham made it clear that 'this was not on. The British Government were not prepared to consider such a request.'[78] As promised, Magee did not make any further visits to the prison. Before leaving Northern Ireland, during the evening of 30 April, he issued a lengthy but uncontentious statement. This covered the background to his mission, which stemmed from the Pope's pastoral concern, and was in response to requests 'from both sides of the community in Northern Ireland to intervene directly at the present moment'. Meanwhile Owen Carron asked for a final meeting with Sands, also on 30 April, and was given this on the following morning, 1 May, when he saw him for the last time. In a subsequent statement Carron dwelt emotionally and at length on Sands' condition, which was correctly described as near death; Carron also confirmed that the prisoner was resigned to his fate. Sands gave him an account of Magee's visit, and thanked the three TDs, as well as all those who had helped him, 'but one message which Carron omitted to mention', according to the NIO, was that Sands also told him to 'burn everything'.[79]

In London, as news was awaited of Sands' death, the Prime Minister studied an Intelligence Assessment that showed how, towards the end of the period 1 to 29 April, the pace of terrorist activity, particularly the INLA's, appeared to quicken with a number of effective attacks. In all, four members of the security forces and two civilians were murdered. With Sands' death imminent, the Provisional leadership, Mrs Thatcher was informed, in contrast to their position before Christmas, 'seems still to be keener on achieving political status for the prisoners than saving Sands' life partly because they have been confident (particularly since his election) that HMG would eventually succumb. They have totally misread the situation throughout.' Their tactics had been determined on a day-to-day basis to take advantage of opportunities as they were offered, and it was unlikely that they had any clear policy on what to do next. Even with Sands dead there would still be three prisoners on hunger strike, and it could be that the 'Sinn Féin/H-Block' Committee would continue to concentrate their efforts on bringing political pressure to bear on HMG, for instance through large, peaceful demonstrations. However, a violent scenario seemed unavoidable, warned the assessment. There had been a good deal of intelligence in recent days of preparations by both Catholic and Protestant communities for severe civil disorder; and activity on both sides was provocative, with a poster war and plans for shows of strength. Rioting in Republican areas on Sands' death was inevitable and, with the prospect of attempts to erect barricades and no-go areas, likely to lead to confrontation with the security forces. Whether or not the Provisionals sought to provoke such disturbances – there would be no need for them to do so – they would undoubtedly take advantage of them, hoping to present themselves as protectors of the Catholic community. There was still little evidence, however, despite the Fermanagh vote, that Catholics on the whole had any sympathy for Sands or the demand for political status. Sinn Féin, it was claimed, 'came badly out' of the ECHR visit and had been widely criticized for their obduracy. Much would depend on security forces' success in controlling events in the early days, and on what the Loyalist paramilitaries did.

There were also 'undoubtedly' plans well advanced for terrorist activity. Decisions on whether and when to put them into practice were probably still to be taken. The Provisional leadership, whatever their preference, would inevitably come under pressure to give the go-ahead. Explosives (probably for use in car bombs) were available in Northern Ireland, a number of radio-controlled devices had been supplied, and there was an adequate supply of weapons, not necessarily modern, but suitable for the kind of 'defensive' activity principally envisaged at this stage. The Belfast IRA capability, with the presence there of Bobby Storey (recently acquitted at the Old Bailey), Martin Lynch ('recovered from a wound') and Tommy Gorman (recently released from the Maze) was 'greater than for some time'. But the pre-emptive arrest, in recent days, of a large number of active terrorists would temporarily have disrupted Provisional plans and made co-ordination more difficult for them. Though there was no recent, specific intelligence, it was to be assumed that the PIRA would also want to mount activity on the mainland. The INLA, meanwhile, continued with their targeting and, as their recent shootings and booby-trap bombings had shown, were capable of effective action, though on a limited scale. The INLA was also keen to foment disorder in support of the hunger-strikers. On the Loyalist side, Andy Tyrie, the UDA leader, had clearly decided that the moment had come to assert himself. Although, by extremist standards, he had been acting responsibly, for example ruling against confrontation with the security forces, he was behind the reactivation of the Ulster Army Council (likely to be the principal vehicle for UDA/UVF paramilitary co-operation). Tyrie 'certainly sees himself as the key figure. And while relations between him and Paisley remain distant, their objectives are essentially the same and the test, if it comes, will find them together for as long as their interests coincide.' Paisley's own plans remained obscure. There were rumours of 'another spectacular, but he may decide that things are running sufficiently his way at the moment for him to bide his time.'[80]

As part of this concern, Humphrey Atkins met with Paisley and his deputy leader, Peter Robinson, in Stormont Castle on 28 April, at the DUP's request, to discuss growing tension in the community. Paisley opened the meeting by saying that he was worried about the security situation, which would be exacerbated if the Government made any concessions to Sands. After Atkins confirmed that there was no question of the Government doing so, Paisley objected to the visit of the Pope's representative. The Secretary of State explained that he had no intention of refusing a visit from the representative of the head of Sands' Church. Robinson then pointed out that there was now real fear in Protestant communities. They were aware of the stockpiling of food, medicine and stores of weapons in Republican areas. There was a danger that the Protestant community would do likewise unless they were conscious of the readiness of the security forces to defend them. It would be essential to avoid the creation of no-go areas, and swift action would be needed against them. At this point Paisley asked whether the RUC were permitted to shoot petrol-bombers. Atkins explained that it depended upon the circumstances. Where such action would involve a threat to life, the police would be within the law in shooting. But the RUC's task – which they were carrying out most skilfully – was to act in an effective but unprovocative manner. There was a risk of sectarian conflict, which required great tact on the part of the police. When Sands died there would no doubt be a very large funeral, which might be provocative to many people. It was essential that law-abiding people should not take the law into their own hands. Dr Paisley made clear that he recognized and accepted that the funeral of Sands would be a large-scale affair. He did not expect it to cause too much trouble: the trouble would begin afterwards.[81]

Alongside the heightened level of activity in the North, North–South channels were active also. John Blelloch telephoned Assistant Secretary Neligan, of the DFA, on 30 April, to say that they were asking the British Embassy in Dublin to give the Government some further information later that day on what was happening in the Catholic quarters in West Belfast. Briefly, the Provisional IRA had for some days been operating what seemed to be an established plan to create a siege mentality and to have 'no-go areas' set up in those quarters.[82] For instance, the British claimed that Defence Committees had been set up, vigilantes had been appointed to individual streets, people were being panicked into stockpiling food if they had the money and forced to put up posters on their houses on threat of lacking food later on. Supposedly new Armalites were being shown around with the PIRA announcing openly that they would defend the community against the imminent Protestant attacks. There were plans to create flashpoints at Suffolk and Short Strand, which might be evacuated, and Turf Lodge had been designated as a safe refugee area: 'This information has come to us from people who are in the best possible position to know what PIRA are up to and are not likely to panic.'[83] The Provisionals were 'putting it about' that the Catholic areas would be attacked by Protestant paramilitaries and the SAS and were 'generally attempting to justify their own existence'. A campaign of 'vicious lie-spreading' was in progress. In this situation the authorities intended to rely on the Roman Catholic hierarchy and on their own information services to get across the truth to people in the areas in question in an effort to save lives. Their message would be, briefly: 'Don't be used. Don't be misled. Be careful who you're listening to. Listen to your clergy, listen to your radio. Don't listen to local thugs'. Blelloch hoped that the Irish might be able to help in efforts to prevent the 'deception of the people' leading to violence. Neligan reassured him that 'we would continue to deplore violence and to appeal for calm to all sections of the population whenever a statement by us seemed justified.'[84]

The Irish were alarmed indeed, so much so that on the Taoiseach's instructions, Michael Alexander was telephoned to inform him, for Mrs Thatcher's information, that Haughey intended to issue a statement shortly saying that he was asking the ECHR to intervene in the situation as a matter of extreme urgency, and asking him to convey to the Prime Minister the Taoiseach's wish that there should not be a negative reaction. Alexander commented that he did not think such a reaction would be forthcoming. The British view on intervention by the Commission had been given reasonable publicity and they were by no means averse to it. He would convey the Taoiseach's message immediately to the Prime Minister. Alexander was then told that the Taoiseach's action was being taken because of his view that, even at this late stage, there was some hope – however slight – of a way out of the present impasse; it was important that the authorities should understand the enormity of the consequences that might ensue on Sands' death. Alexander replied that they appreciated this and were deeply concerned. They had taken all measures they could think of to deal with possible eventualities.[85] However, on 4 May, the Commission replied to Haughey's request pointing out that it had 'no jurisdiction to consider any situation or make a recommendation without being seized of an application brought before it under the relevant provisions of the European Convention on Human Rights.'[86]

The Taoiseach's urgency was dictated by the fact that Sands' condition had become critical at the weekend when he lapsed into a coma on Sunday morning, 3 May. He did not regain consciousness before his death at 01.17 hours early on Tuesday 5, the 66th day of his fast. An hour later his body was taken from the prison to an outside hospital where a post mortem was performed later that morning.[87]

NOTES

1   Bobby Sands, *Writings from Prison* (Roberts Rinehart, 1997) p. 219.
2   *Belfast Telegraph*, 2 March 1981.
3   Sands, *op.cit.*, pp. 220–221.
4   *Ibid.* p. 220.
5   *The Irish Times*, 5 March 1981.
6   Sands, *op.cit.* pp. 223–224.
7   TF Speech in Belfast, 5 March 1981.
8   TF TV Interview for ITN, 6 March 1981.
9   Sands *op.cit.* p. 228.
10 TNA CJ4/3627 Protests and Second Hunger Strike – Weekly Bulletin 0900 hours on Thursday, 2 April to 0900 on Thursday 9 April.
11 TNA CJ4/3627 Note of a Meeting: Meeting to Discuss Development in Hunger Strike Protests in Prisons.
12 TNA PREM 19/503 Atkins to Prime Minister, 3 April 1981.
13 TNA PREM 19/503 Roy Harrington Note, 6 April 1981.
14 TNA CJ4/3627 Note for the Record Press Access to Robert Sands, 7 April 1981.
15 TNA CJ4/3627 Protests and Second Hunger Strike – Weekly Bulletin 0900 hours on Thursday 2 April to 0900 on Thursday 9 April.

16   TNA CJ4/3627 Security Implications of the Second Maze Hunger Strike – Note of Meeting held on Friday 10 April 1981.

17   TNA CJ4/3627 Protests and Second Hunger Strike – Weekly Bulletin 0900 hours on Thursday 2 April to 0900 on Thursday 9 April.

18   TNA CJ4/3627 Protests and Second Hunger Strike – Weekly Bulletin 0900 hours on Thursday 2 April to 0900 on Thursday 9 April.

19   TNA CJ4/3627 Protests and Second Hunger Strike – Weekly Bulletin No 7 0900 9 April – 0900 16 April.

20   TNA PREM 19/503 Havers to Prime Minister, 9 April 1981.

21   TNA PREM 19/503 Memo to Prime Minister, 10 April 1981.

22   TNA PREM 19/503 Washington to FCO Telegram No. 1177 of 10 April 1981.

23   TNA PREM 19/504 Hopkins to Alexander, 13 April 1981.

24   TNA PREM 19/504 Hoskyns to Alexander, 13 April 1981.

25   TNA PREM 19/504 Record of a discussion between the Prime Minister and Mr John Hume at 10 Downing Street on 13 April [sic] 1981 at 2200 hours.

26   TNA PREM 19/503 Robert Armstrong to Prime Minister, 13 April 1981.

27   TNA CJ4/3627 Protests and Second Hunger Strike – Weekly Bulletin No 7 0900 9 April – 0900 16 April.

28   TNA PREM 19/503 Armstrong to Alexander, 13 April 1981.

29   TNA CJ4/3627 Protests and Second Hunger Strike – Weekly Bulletin No 7 0900 9 April – 0900 16 April.

30   TNA CJ4/3627 Security Implications of the Second Maze Hunger Strike – Note of Meeting held on Thursday 16 April 1981.

31   TNA CJ4/3627 Protests and Second Hunger Strike – Weekly Bulletin No 7 0900 9 April – 0900 16 April.

32   TNA CJ4/3627 Note of Meeting on Thursday 16 April: Medical Aspects of the Current Hunger Strike.

33   TNA PREM 19/503 FCO to New Delhi Telegram Number 373 of 16 April 1981.

34   PRONI NIO/12/196/A Blatherwick to Palmer, 16 April 1981.

35   TNA PREM 19/503 SJ Pike to Alexander, 18 April 1981.

36   TNA CJ4/3627 Protest and Second Hunger Strike – Weekly Bulletin No 8 0900 16 April – 0900 23 April.

37   TNA CJ4/3627 Mr Mitchell's Meeting with a Deputation from the DUP to Register Objections to the Visit of the 3 TDs to B. Sands.

38   TNA CJ4/3627 Protest and Second Hunger Strike – Weekly Bulletin No 8 0900 16 April – 0900 23 April.

39   TNA PREM 19/503 Duty Clerk No 10 to Ingham, 20 April 1981.

40   NAI D/T 2011/127/1051 Diary of main events regarding H-Blocks Hunger Strike 21-4-81 to 27-4-81.

41   TNA PREM 19/503 Pattison to Saunders, 20 April 1981.

42   TNA FCO to Abu Dhabi Telegram Number 121 of 21 April 1981.

43   TNA FCO to Abu Dhabi Telegram Number 122 of 21 April 1981.

44   TNA CJ4/3627 Northern Ireland: Reply to the three TDs, 22 April 1981.

45   NAI D/T 2011/127/1051 Diary of main events regarding H-Blocks Hunger Strike 21-4-81 to 27-4-81.

46   TNA FCO to Abu Dhabi Telegram Number 123 of 21 April 1981.

47   NAI D/T 2011/127/1051 Note, 22 April 1981.

48   TNA PREM 19/504 Armstrong to Sanders, 22 April 1981.

49   TNA PREM 19/504 Dublin to FCO Telegram Number 116 of 22 April 1981.

50   TNA PREM 19/504 FCO to Salalah Telegram Number 7 of 23 April 1981.

51   TNA CJ4/3627 Note of a Meeting held on 23 April 1981.

52   TNA PREM 19/504 FCO to Flash Salalah Telegram number 7 of 23 April 1981.

53   TNA PREM 19/504 Telegram number 8 of 23 April 1981.

54   NAI D/T 2011/127/1051 Diary of main events regarding H-Blocks Hunger Strike 21-4-81 to 27-4-81.

55   TNA PREM 19/504 Communiqué to be issued by the Secretary to the European Commission of Human Rights (Rule 17 (3) 8 of the Commission's rule of procedure) at 1 p.m. our time.

56   NAI D/T 2011/127/1051 Sands to European Commission of Human Rights.

57   TNA CJ4/3627 Note of a Meeting on 24 April – Prison Protest.

58   TNA CJ4/3627 Protest and Second Hunger Strike – Weekly Bulletin No 8 0900 16 April – 0900 23 April.

59   NAI D/T 2011/127/1051 Diary of main events regarding H-Blocks Hunger Strike 21-4-81 to 27-4-81.

60   TNA CJ4/3627 Visit by Two Members of the ECHR to Maze Prison, Saturday, 25 April 1981.

61   TNA PREM 19/504 Minute to Prime Minister, 25 April 1981.

62   TNA CJ4/3627 Visit by Two Members of the ECHR to Maze Prison, Saturday, 25 April 1981.

63   TNA PREM 19/504 Prime Minister's telephone conversation with the Secretary of State for Northern Ireland on Saturday evening, 25 April 1981.

64   TNA PREM 19/504 From Northern Ireland Office Belfast.

65   NAI D/T 2011/127/1051 Contacts with Commission Delegation, 27 April 1981.

66   TNA PREM 19/504 Sanders to Prime Minister, 26 April 1981.

67   TNA PREM 19/504 Whitman to Harrington, 27 April 1981.

68   TNA CJ4/3627 Washington to FCO Telegram Number 1327 of 29 April.

69   TNA PREM 19/504 Ó Fiaich to Prime Minister.

70   TNA PREM 19/504 Stowe to Armstrong, 27 April 1981.

71   TNA PREM 19/504 Prime Minister to Ó Fiaich.

72   TNA PREM 19/504 Minute to Alexander, 29 April 1981.

73   TNA PREM 19/504 Telegram number 132 of 29 April 1981.

74   NAI D/T 2011/127/1051 Message taken by Brendan O'Donnell, 27 April 1981.

75   TNA CJ4/3627 Maze Hunger Strike – Visit of Father Magee (Vatican), 28 April 1981.

76   PRONI NIO/12/196/A Note for the Record Visit of Fr Magee, Papal Representative, to the Maze.

77   TNA PREM 19/504 Record of the Secretary of State's discussion with Father Magee – 29 April 1981 at 12.30 p.m. in Stormont Castle.

78   NAI D/T 2011/127/1052 Murray to Kirwan.

79   TNA CJ4/36329 Protests and Second Hunger Strike - Weekly Bulletin No. 10 0900 hours Thursday 30 April – 0900 hours Thursday 7 May.

80   TNA PREM 19/504 Monthly intelligence assessment (1 to 29 April 1981).

81   TNA CJ4/3627 Secretary of State's Meeting with Dr Ian Paisley MP and Mr Peter Robinson MP – 5.30 p.m. on 28 April 1981 in Stormont Castle.

82   NAI D/T 2011/127/1052 Neligan Note, 30 April 1981.

83   NAI D/T 2011/127/1052 Hunger Strike.

84   NAI D/T 2011/127/1052 Neligan Note, 30 April 1981.

85   NAI D/T 2011/127/1052 Hunger Strike Note.

86   NAI D/T 2011/127/1052 Response from European Commission of Human Rights to Taoiseach's further request of 4 May 1981.

87   TNA CJ4/36329 Protests and Second Hunger Strike - Weekly Bulletin No. 10 0900 hours Thursday 30 April – 0900 hours Thursday 7 May.

Chapter 7

Digging In

That evening, rioting broke out in Republican areas. Although these incidents made for dramatic pictures on television news bulletins, the assessment of the security forces was that the rioting was controllable. The Chief Constable, Jack Hermon, reported that Derry and the rural areas had been quiet overnight, but there had been orchestrated unrest in some areas of Belfast, with groups of 50–200 people causing disturbances (400–500 in New Barnsley). The disturbances were contained and normality restored quickly, but further violence was expected in the build-up to Sands' funeral, and there was a risk of attempts to break through the communal interfaces. There was little sign of deep feeling in the community about Sands' death. The head of the Army in Northern Ireland, General Sir Richard Lawson, reported that the Army had supported the police as necessary and was trying to ensure that the troops were properly rested when not required. Soldiers had had to shoot the ringleader of a rioting mob in the leg when they came under attack, but generally the violence had led to only few casualties.[1]

On the political front, Blatherwick, in the NIO Political Affairs Branch, told Wyatt that he found from 'our contacts with the Catholic community it is increasingly clear that a surprising number accept HMG's refusal to grant political status to the hunger strikers. But as we have reported before there is much criticism that the Government is "not doing enough" to solve the hunger strike, and this criticism is increasingly apparent from Protestants who fear inter-communal violence.' The danger (reinforced perhaps by the Prime Minister's Answers during Questions in the House the day before) was that 'we may suffer from the appearance of an intransigent hard-faced Government set in its ways and unable to get itself off the hook.' This danger would increase as the hunger strike continued, warned Blatherwick. The sort of things 'we can do are obvious', such as:

(a) Continue to emphasise regret over all deaths.
(b) Keep drawing attention to pleas by e.g. the Pope for the hunger strikers to desist.

(c) Emphasise that flexibility is not the issue because the Provisionals are interested in nothing except full political status.

(d) Point out that we have bent over backwards to give the Provisionals an opportunity to save their faces, by letting the 3 Southern MEPs, the ECHR and the Papal representative visit the Maze to talk to Sands.

(e) Re-emphasise the statement made by the Government at the end of the last hunger strike.

(f) Stress that the hunger strike is not about humane conditions in the prison, because prisons are already remarkably humane.

However, Blatherwick recognized that 'this may well not be enough.'[2] In the House of Commons, Mrs Thatcher's comment had been to point out that: 'In a democracy people can pursue their objectives by peaceful means. Only those people who reject democracy pursue their objectives by terrorist means. Terrorism is a crime and always will be a crime.' She was supported by the Labour Leader of the Opposition, Michael Foot, who stated that the concession of political status:

> ... cannot be done without the Government giving sure aid to the recruitment of terrorists. If political status were conceded, it would greatly increase the numbers who would be encouraged to join. That, in turn, would mean a great increase in the number of innocent people who would be killed. We believe that matters in Northern Ireland, as elsewhere in the country, should be settled democratically, and not at the point of a gun.

In response to one MP hostile to her handling of the situation, the Prime Minister was clear on her position: 'Her Majesty's Government are on the side of protecting the law-abiding and innocent citizen and we shall continue in our efforts to stamp out terrorism. Mr. Sands was a convicted criminal. He chose to take his own life. It was a choice that his organisation did not allow to many of its victims.'[3] In contrast, in their statement, the Maze prisoners countered that:

> No one, not even Maggie Thatcher, can justifiably dishonour Bobby Sands by robbing him of his political identity, for he died as he lived, a Republican, political prisoner and a man totally committed to the liberation of the Irish people. He is a symbol of freedom and truth and a lasting inspiration to those who struggle for justice.
>
> His death is yet another body blow for the Nationalist population throughout Ireland. It shows that their wishes are irrelevant and totally subject to the British Government's traditional policy of colonial oppression and of appeasing bigoted loyalists.

While responsibility lies, primarily, on the shoulders of the British Government, we feel that politicians and other leading people also share the blame for Bobby's death. The timidity and lack of courage in condemning strenuously the ruthlessness of the British Government allowed that Government to carry out this legalised killing. The time for diplomacy is over: those who lead the Irish people are duty bound to ensure that no other Irish political prisoner has to give his life in pursuit of his rights. The only way to ensure this is for those leaders to lead the Irish people in protest against England's inflexibility, and to take positive direct action against this callous Government.

To Thatcher, Atkins and the British Government we say: 'You have got your pound of flesh; now give us our rights. Do not for one minute think that we are going to allow you to rob us of our principles. There are many Bobby Sands in these blocks, and we will continue to die on hunger strike if needs be in order to safeguard those principles'.

Finally, we call on the Irish people and the freedom-loving people of this world to come out against British barbarity. The hunger strike goes on, and will go on until our demands are met, and the people of Ireland, and the people of the world, are the vehicles which will bring us to that achievement.[4]

From Dublin, Figg reported that so far there had been a muted reaction in the Republic to the death of Sands. On the morning of 5 May, 1,000 people gathered for a vigil outside the GPO in Dublin, headquarters of the rebels in 1916, and marched to the Dáil, where they held a rally. A statement was handed into the Taoiseach's office demanding Figg's expulsion. In the evening the crowd, which had grown to 2–3,000, moved off for a further rally at Parnell Square. A group of 200 youths broke away from this, threw stones at the Gardai, broke windows, and damaged a number of cars. Apart from this outbreak of hooliganism, the demonstrations were peaceful. A small picket on the Embassy gates was joined briefly by delegations of students, who handed in protest letters. In the Dáil itself no mention was made of Sands' death. The Dublin papers carried extensive reports of the demonstrations in both parts of the island, including many photographs. Editorial comment was generally critical of Britain's 'insensitivity in Irish affairs', and, in the *Irish Press,* of the 'mindless arrogance which the British decision-takers are showing towards the prison issue'. *The Irish Times* asked: 'Does no-one in Westminster read Irish history? Does not even Michael Foot remember what 1916 executions did to Ireland – and to England?'[5]

The leader of the main Opposition party in the Dáil, Fine Gael's Dr Garret FitzGerald, was concerned enough to ask Figg to call privately at his house. He thought that it would be useful to let the Ambassador know in advance of the general election (which he thought the Taoiseach would probably announce on 13 May) how he and his party saw recent events. He feared that the British had lost a propaganda battle with the IRA, and the position North and South looked very serious. Somehow 'we must get the hunger strikers off the hook.' While it was absolutely right not to negotiate with them under threat, the obverse of this was that some accommodation could surely be reached if the strike were temporarily called off. No doubt, thought FitzGerald, the hunger-strikers would be suspicious of a move of this kind because they claimed to have been conned in December. He mentioned John Hume as someone with enough skill to finesse this kind of difficult manoeuvre. FitzGerald added that, up till now, all main Irish parties had deliberately played the hunger strike in a very low key. This period would end, however, when the election was called. FitzGerald thought it likely that Fianna Fáil would again become a 'rather Republican party' in the run-up to the election and that the unique relationship with Britain might suffer somewhat, the reason being HMG's inflexibility on the prison issue. It would be difficult for Fine Gael to find the right line to take. In his comments to the Foreign Office, Figg suspected, if the hunger strike were still continuing, that FitzGerald and the Fine Gael leaders would probably feel obliged to do their share of criticizing British policy. Figg, in the meantime, had told FitzGerald that:

> … our position regarding prison administration was not rigid although we believed that the strikers were aiming for full political status and would not be satisfied with less. I was glad to hear he appreciated our position that we could not negotiate under threat. I then told him in very general terms of the possible role of the European Commission for Human Rights.

FitzGerald summed up his purpose in asking Figg to call by reiterating his grave disquiet about the apparent impasse at the Maze, 'and to beg us to look again at ways to break the deadlock. I said I would report our conversation.'[6]

In further comments to the FCO, Figg observed, disconcertedly, that from the Taoiseach's statements following Sands' death, it seemed that he still firmly believed that in some way the strike could be ended by manipulating the existing prison regulations: 'I am not sure to what extent he really believes this but I think it would be a mistake to suppose that he is not being sincere.' Assuming that this represented the Taoiseach's sincere belief, 'then it is very far from the way we see things, and indeed from what he was told at the December summit'. At that time he appeared to accept that the Provisionals were going for political status and nothing else. If so, it was no longer the case, 'and our differing views of what the Provisionals are aiming for could lead to a bit of a row.' Haughey had been under considerable pressure during the previous few days to be seen to be 'talking tough with us and I think we must give him credit for what is seen here as the calm line he has taken.' Figg thought, though, that the time had come to try and reconcile the divergent views as soon as possible. There was plenty of 'chapter and verse' showing that the hunger strike was aimed at political status. Giving the Taoiseach a 'piece of paper' on these lines, 'together with any new thoughts we may have,' would be better than nothing, recommended Figg.[7]

The Irish were indeed worried. When the Irish Ambassador in Washington, Sean Donlon, rang Neligan in Dublin on 6 May to enquire about the latest situation after the death of Sands, he mentioned that Senator Kennedy and Governor Carey had appeared jointly on television on 5 May and had spoken about the Northern Ireland situation in sensible terms. Kennedy was anxious to do whatever he could to show his concern about the present critical turn of events. The Ambassador then asked Neligan's views about the possibility of bringing pressure on President Reagan to 'say something' to Mrs Thatcher. He mentioned this because the conduct of business in Congress over the next 48 hours would put Speaker O'Neill in a very strong position to ask a favour of the President. Neligan reacted by saying that it did not seem appropriate from Dublin to try to get the President to question or criticize British Government policy on Northern Ireland prisons. Not a day passed that the London Government did not repeat, with emphasis, that they could not change that policy, and unfortunately they were supported in this attitude by the Labour Opposition. Moreover, the President would probably be reluctant to query an internal policy of an allied country directly.

It did seem possible to Neligan, however, that something might be suggested as appropriate material for a message to Mrs Thatcher based on the unprecedented interest of the American media in developments in Northern Ireland and the notable propaganda failure by the British Government in this context. In other words, it might be possible for the President to say that he felt he had to get in touch with Mrs Thatcher to comment on the very bad press that her Government was getting in the States arising out of Sands' death, and to wonder whether the British Government had given sufficient thought to this extremely negative publicity aspect when defining their policy. The President could possibly link his remarks with something along the lines used by him on St Patrick's Day, namely that it was not good for the Western Alliance to have within it an area of instability and violence such as Northern Ireland. The effects of the present crisis were not likely to reduce instability, in fact quite the contrary. Neligan was aware that there was, of course, no certainty that the President could be induced, even in the favourable circumstances described by Donlon, to make any démarche to Mrs Thatcher. He conceded, however, that it was possible that the proposal could be examined. Neligan then reminded the Ambassador that Reagan had already made a statement of regret on Sands' death through the State Department. Donlon replied that this would have been a low-level reaction relayed through the State Department but probably not even seen by President Reagan before being issued. In his view, that reaction did not preclude the possibility of the action now being considered.[8]

America was thus a vital propaganda battleground. Immediately following Sands' death the British Embassy was contacted by Kalicki (of Senator Edward Kennedy's office), who gave officials the text of a message that the Four Horsemen had telegraphed to the Prime Minister. The message was then released by them to the press. Kalicki emphasized that the message reflected the genuine concern of the Four Horsemen, and that they had made a real effort to strike a balance. He urged HMG to note their condemnation of violence, which he claimed would be very unpopular with the Irish–American community, who were exerting enormous pressure on the Four Horsemen. Kalicki claimed that the message was more moderate than most Irish–American reaction to Sands' death. He added that Senator Kennedy and his colleagues felt that some further concessions applicable to all prisoners in Northern Ireland on, for example, clothing, such as had helped to settle the last hunger strike, could now be made.

As a consequence, Sir Nicholas Henderson assured Lord Carrington, the Foreign Secretary, 'that we are doing our best here, in New York and in other parts of the US, through all means at our disposal,' to refute the view widely held in the US, and reflected in the Four Horsemen's message, that the issue was one of prison dress or prison administration: 'We are pointing out that what is at stake is whether someone who has been convicted of a crime of terrorism has the right to be given special treatment as though he had simply been involved in a political movement: we are rubbing it home that we do not have political prisoners any more than does the USA, which does not regard someone convicted say of assassination or the attempt of assassination as other than a criminal.'[9] The text of the letter to Mrs Thatcher read:

> We want you to know personally of our deep concern over the spectre of worsening violence and tragedy that threatened to engulf Northern Ireland after the death of Bobby Sands.
>
> In recent months, we have praised your hopeful initiative with Prime Minister Haughey of Ireland, and we have looked forward to further progress in securing a peaceful settlement of the conflict.
>
> Throughout these tragic years of killing and destruction in Northern Ireland, we have consistently and unequivocally condemned all violence from any source.
>
> But we question a posture of inflexibility that must lead inevitably to more senseless violence and more needless death in Northern Ireland.
>
> We urge you to act now, before additional lives are lost, to implement

sensible and reasonable requirements in the administration of the Maze prison – reforms that offer real hope of ending this violent impasse and achieving a peaceful and humanitarian settlement of the three hunger strikes that are now nearing the point of no return.

Surely it is possible to compromise on the practical issues of prison administration, without compromising in any way on the basic principle of opposition to violence. Surely the leaders of Great Britain have an urgent responsibility to do all within their power to end this tragic and unnecessary crisis.

Signed: Edward M Kennedy
United States Senate
Daniel Patrick Moynihan
United States Senate
Hugh O'Carey
Governor, State of New York[10]

Henderson's advice to London was clear: 'We should not leave the four horsemen's message unanswered. I recognise that the Prime Minister may not wish to reply personally. If so, the reply suitably amended, could come from me, on the Prime Minister's behalf.' Even so, a reply from the Prime Minister would have advantages. It would carry very much more conviction, and demonstrate the extent of HMG's concern. It would also disarm those US critics who, even while conceding the unacceptability of political status for terrorists, had fallen back on criticizing HMG, and the Prime Minster personally, for an allegedly aloof and inflexible attitude. It would additionally gratify the Four Horsemen. This was by no means an overriding objective, but that too had its advantages. They would no doubt ensure publicity for the reply (their own message had not so far attracted publicity in the US), and a reply that firmly shifted the argument to political status rather than details of prison administration deserved publicity; 'moreover, however irritating the public pronouncements of the horsemen may be, it is in our longer-term interest to maintain their (by Irish–American standards) relatively restrained attitude and their domestic influence above all in opposing any material assistance to terrorists, and thereby to diminish the rival claims of IRA-apologists', such as Congressman Mario Biaggi.[11]

Mrs Thatcher did reply personally. She welcomed the Four Horsemen's 'clear restatement of your unequivocal condemnation of all violence in Northern Ireland. I welcome too your efforts to discourage American support for the men of violence in Northern Ireland and to promote better understanding among all the people of Ireland.' As for the reference to a 'posture of inflexibility' that must lead inevitably to more violence and death in Northern Ireland, Mrs Thatcher insisted that this was not the British Government's posture and highlighted what had happened since the report of the ECHR. This showed that HMG had, in fact, acted with great flexibility: 'We have offered a series of improvements in conditions to all prisoners – most of which the protesters have rejected. We have also facilitated visits to the hunger strikers by the European commission of human rights, by members of the Dublin Parliament, by the representative of the Pope.' None of these actions had any effect upon the prisoners, whose sole purpose was to establish a political justification for their 'appalling record of murder and violence – murder and violence which deserve the same total condemnation in Northern Ireland as they would get in the United States.'

Political status would mean that the prisoners, not the prison authorities, would determine what the day-to-day regime within the prison should be. On this the Government 'will not compromise. It is not prepared, through the granting of political status, to legitimise criminal acts undertaken in pursuit of political ends. It is not prepared to surrender control of the prisons. It is not prepared to be coerced by protest action, in whatever form, into changes for which there is no justification on humanitarian grounds. We know from experience that to do so would not bring the protests to an end.' On the contrary, yielding to coercion would provoke further coercion, and would encourage more young people to follow the path of violence. It was the Government's profound hope that there would be no more deaths directly or indirectly due to the present hunger strike. Such deaths could serve no purpose. But if political status remained the protesters' objective, then it:

> ... cannot and will not be conceded. If they have other grounds for complaint against the prison regime, then further recourse to the European Commission of Human Rights remains available to them. The government has shown that it is prepared to respond to the Commission's findings and to facilitate in any way it can the Commission's conduct of its investigations.[12]

As part of the British propaganda effort, Atkins appeared via satellite on *Good Morning America* on 8 May to put the British point of view across. Afterwards, Henderson sent the Secretary of State a personal message of 'congratulations on your TV performance today. It will have been seen by 5 million Americans and struck exactly the right note.' The editorial coverage in the American press, on the other hand, 'over the last week or 10 days has been like the Curate's egg, but could I think have been worse in the circumstances', reported the Ambassador. But it was television that was making the biggest impact: 'I and my staff have been taking every opportunity across the country to put over the facts. But you carry special weight and what you said will be most helpful.' Although the purpose of Henderson's telegram was to thank Atkins for his television appearance, the Ambassador also took the opportunity of putting to the Secretary of State, 'given the tiresome importance of the American dimension', one or two impressions he had formed about coping with this problem at the present time.

What we are up against is not so much the traditional opposition of the American Irish who are deaf to argument and not open to any persuasion, but the atavistic, anti-colonial feeling that lies not far below the surface of so many Americans. They know nothing whatever of the history or problems at issue except insofar as they believe that those confronting the British authorities in Ireland today are in some way the heirs of their own revolution. We also have the problem of misunderstandings about the relevance of prison routine, as you will know from your questioning today; but I think that we may be making some inroads in getting the facts across on this. The much more difficult problem is coping with the national wish here to take an anti-colonial swipe at us.

The other feature that I should mention is the particular problem of television coverage. There are enormous numbers of American TV people in Northern Ireland at the moment and what is shown on American televisions is inevitably pictures of youths throwing bombs rather than people going about their lawful business. This is inherent in television, which feeds on drama and disaster rather than peace and reconciliation. Moreover, US news stories tend to be on matters of fashion: the past week's story has been deemed to be 'violence in Ulster', and US correspondents on the spot have done whatever they could to fulfil that order with the material available.[13]

Across the Atlantic, Northern Irish attention had soon begun to focus on Sands' funeral. His remains were taken by the undertakers to his parents' home in the Twinbrook Estate, Belfast, and from there, on the evening of 6 May, to his local church, St Luke's. Representatives of the NHAC called for a peaceful protest and many shops and businesses closed for the day on 7 May. Derry was almost completely closed. Alongside the obvious sympathy for the loss of a life in trying circumstances there were numerous allegations that shop owners had been intimidated into closing their premises. Sands' funeral Mass took place on the afternoon of 7 May at St Luke's; Father Liam Mullan, the celebrant, appealed to the mourners to help stop any violence that might follow the burial, saying: 'People should not use the occasion of the death of Mr Sands as an excuse for violence and sectarian strife'. His call for prayers for Constable Phillip Ellis, killed by the IRA on 6 May at a Protestant–Catholic interface, as well as Sands, did not go unnoticed. Some 30,000 people – according to the RUC – joined the funeral cortège, including at least 300 who had arrived in Belfast from Dublin by train and twenty-eight busloads from throughout Northern Ireland. The Provisional IRA provided a uniformed escort for the coffin, and masked gunmen fired volleys over the grave. At the funeral, Gerry Adams warned: 'the organisation to which Bobby Sands belonged will make its own response in its own time'. At the conclusion of the ceremony the crowds dispersed peacefully. That night, however, there were riots at many places in Northern Ireland, but especially in Belfast. The security forces were attacked by stones, acid bombs, petrol bombs and bullets. Rioting again occurred on the following night. Dr Paisley, meanwhile, held a memorial service at Belfast City Hall for 'the innocent victims of IRA terrorism', which coincided with the start of the funeral. He deplored the unjust focus of world attention 'on the burial of an IRA man who took his own life in prison. Those whom we remember today had no choice'.

The funeral also attracted considerable overseas attention. Four MEPs attended Sands' funeral. On the day of the funeral, several hundred demonstrators marched on the British Embassy in Lisbon, but were stopped a hundred metres from the building by police. The crowd was addressed by a member of Sinn Féin. On 9 May, seventy people demonstrated outside the British Chancery building in Reykjavik and handed in a statement announcing that 'British Imperialism has once again savagely attacked the ranks of Irish Freedom Fighters'. Lech Walesa, leader of the Polish trade union Solidarity, described Bobby Sands as 'a great man who sacrificed his life for his struggle'. The slogan 'Long live the IRA' was painted on a wall in Oslo alongside the route that was being used by the Queen during her visit to Norway. In India, Opposition MPs in the Upper House of Parliament stood for a minute's silence in honour of Sands. Iranian Muslim Students in Manila demonstrated outside the British Embassy on behalf of the hunger-strikers, and a street alongside the British Embassy in Tehran was renamed Khiyaban – E Bobby Sands. Indeed, Iranian Embassy staff from London attended Sands' funeral, which was also marked by demonstrations, marches and vigils in a number of towns and cities in the Republic. At a demonstration in Dundalk, effigies of Mrs Thatcher and Haughey were burnt. A number of services were held to commemorate Sands, some with paramilitaries in attendance. According to the trades unions, there was a poor response to a call for a day of industrial action in the Republic to mark Sands' death, but several border towns closed down completely in the afternoon of 7 May. That night, gangs of youths threw petrol bombs at the Gardai in Dublin.[14]

Although seriously ill and confined to bed, and despite reports to the contrary, Francis Hughes, in the meantime, remained fully conscious. The brainstem deficiency (observed with Sean McKenna), however, was now well established. He still had some vision, and his fluid balance was now being maintained. By 7

May, the likely crisis in his condition was thought to be just over a week away, though prognosis in this context continued to prove difficult.[15] On Saturday 9 May, Joe McDonnell refused breakfast and announced that he was joining the hunger strike as a PIRA replacement for Sands. McDonnell was considered, by the NIO, 'a hardened and dedicated individual who must be expected to go through with his fast if called to do so.' He was 30 years old and was serving 14 years for possession of firearms and ammunition with intent. He was a co-defendant of Sands, having been arrested in the same car after the bomb attack on a suburban store in Belfast. For now, McDonnell remained in H-5.

Despite continuing disturbances, the Chief Constable and the GOC remained satisfied that the security situation was better than might have been expected. The evening violence, on 7 May, was relatively low-key. There had also been a notable success on the border: two brothers were arrested (one in the North and one in the South) carrying firearms. Gardai co-operation had been excellent, and the follow-up search was now going on: it was possible that there was a wounded terrorist still in the area. A possible bombing 'own-goal' in Carrickmore was also being followed up. The RUC had made some good arrests, and the charge rate remained high. The intelligence about the PIRA's intentions was thought to have been accurate, but a number of factors had contributed to the relatively low level of violence. The weather had helped, and a statement by Atkins and comments by the Chief Constable had had a calming effect. Hermon believed that violence over the weekend would not have the same impact for the PIRA as it would have done the previous night. It was likely that the focus of any violence would now move to the rural areas and to County Derry (where Hughes came from). The GOC decided to maintain his troops in readiness for whatever sort of violence was forthcoming, but the people and tactics would be different for the events such as street disturbances compared with shooting attacks. He would provide the Chief Constable with whatever support he wanted, and he hoped to maintain flexibility over the location and use of the Army's Spearhead Battalion that would be used as backup.

When Hermon and Lawson briefed Atkins and Stowe on 8 May, there was some discussion as to how the Government's message on what the prison issue was all about could be got across simply to the 'man in the street'. It was agreed that briefing was taking place at many levels and the expression of the message depended to some extent on the audience. Official statements by HMG had to be precise as they were scrutinized very closely by those hostile to the Government. In general, the PR position appeared stable, both within the UK and internationally: 'But we would undoubtedly have to keep plugging away day by day at our message' along the lines of:

- every death is a matter for compassion
- the issue is who controls the prison
- it is not us who are inflexible
- the ECHR route is still open
- we are not giving up on political development.[16]

The following night witnessed more disturbances, but, as the Chief Constable and the GOC reported, the security situation continued to be better than might have been expected, although there had been several 'ambitious' attempts to kill. 'If we were careful, the situation should not get worse', commented Hermon. He predicted that the pattern of violence would continue to remain the same for that night and the following one also. It would be necessary at planning level to be ready to 'shift our posture as circumstances dictated.' To date, the need for change had only risen in some individual cases. The RUC still expected that the pressure would now move to the rural areas. The PIRA's capacity had been limited, and it was possible that they would move to the more spectacular action of using petrol bombs in Protestant towns, which could lead to counter-demonstrations by Loyalists. It was known that the view held by the PIRA, before Sands' death, was that the security forces would contain the violence, and they had looked for political success. There had not been a controlled terrorist response. The Provisionals would attempt a more controlled response following Hughes' death. Hermon felt that the minority community was content with the way the security forces had handled the demonstrations and violence, but they were feeling the pressure in their own areas. There had been no increase in complaints against the police, 'and the general feeling was – keep it going as it is.' The Catholic communities had not turned on the PIRA, and it was felt that if this were to happen it would be a limiting factor on the PIRA. They were hesitant to turn against the PIRA 'as there was a slight fear that they might need them.' It was also felt that if some encouragement could be given to the communities to turn against the Provisionals, and if they could be reassured that the security forces had the resources to protect them, this would be constructive, reflected Hermon.[17]

By 11 May, the RUC judged that a 'degree of stability' had now been established. The Provisionals were not managing to get large numbers on the streets, and their activities appeared partly counter-productive. The interfaces remained quiet, and the Loyalist paramilitaries passive. Contact with the local community had frustrated attempts to reactivate a PIRA group in Ballymena. The RUC were looking at recent attacks against property and industry to see if any pattern could be discerned. Although there had been little community unrest there, Fermanagh remained sensitive. There was evidence, thought Hermon, that the PIRA was orchestrating a PR campaign focussed on baton rounds and arrests of suspects. The GOC, meanwhile, hoped that the military profile could be lowered a little while violence subsided so that troops would be 'mentally relaxed' when disturbances reoccurred. Although there was an increase in sniper activity, it was important that troops were deployed in a way that did not set them up as targets. Hermon and Lawson agreed between them that a balance had to be struck between an adequate preventative profile throughout Northern Ireland (to pre-empt incidents and reassure the community) and keeping manpower fresh.[18]

More trouble was soon to follow, for Francis Hughes' condition deteriorated quickly. He started to go into a coma on Monday 11 May, and by the following day was described as 'deeply unconscious'. He died on the same day at 17.40 in the prison hospital; it was the fifty-ninth day of his fast. Rioting again erupted in Belfast. Hughes was described in a statement issued by the Provisional IRA as 'one of this struggle's bravest soldiers'. Gerry Adams accused the British Government of murdering Hughes 'in the face of overwhelming public opinion in Ireland and abroad'.[19] News of Hughes' death promoted a further anti-H-Block demonstration outside the GPO in Dublin, which later resulted in petrol bombs being thrown at the Gardai. The sisters of hunger-strikers McCreesh and O'Hara demanded that Haughey must 'now call publicly on Mrs Thatcher to implement the five demands of the prisoners'. During the week, the residences, in the Republic, of Sir James Comyn, a British judge, and Lord Farnham were burnt in arson attacks. On 13 May, in London, the Queen opened Wood Green Shopping Centre. As the royal car drove along High Road, Wood Green, a banner was raised bearing the legend, 'Bobby Sands, MP, Political Prisoner Murdered by HM Government'. Two persons were detained by the police, but later released without charge.[20] Of more concern was the mysterious explosion as Her Majesty officially opened the Sullom Voe oil terminal on Shetland the day before. The IRA claimed that a seven-pound bomb was planted in the terminal's main power station to coincide with the official opening ceremony, although the police claimed that no evidence had been obtained to establish the cause of the explosion. The IRA stated: 'Had we managed to place Saturday's bomb close enough to the British Queen then she would now be dead.' The statement continued: 'Members of the British ruling class and administration will continue to be subject to IRA attacks.' The explosion was centred on the waste heat boiler in the power station, which was not in commission at the time of the incident. At first, BP said that it was a routine mishap affecting switchgear, but later said that it could have been caused by an explosive device or a mechanical malfunction.[21]

The fallout from another hunger-striker's death meant that the British had, once more, to cast an eye over international reactions. In Italy, a group of Italian left-wing terrorists bombed a British Leyland showroom in Milan in protest at Hughes' death. Of more seriousness was the reaction in Paris, which the Prime Minister followed with interest. There the British Ambassador, Sir Reginald Hibbert, gathered that there were indications that the families of hunger-strikers might try to appeal to President-elect Mitterrand for sympathy and/or support. Hibbert called, on 13 May, to Madame Neiertz, the Secretary for International Affairs of the Socialist Party and a member of Mitterrand's Inner Political Council. At the end of their talk she herself raised the question of Northern Ireland, reminding Hibbert that she had led a PS (Socialist Party) delegation to the British Embassy recently to highlight the Bobby Sands case. This enabled Hibbert to take the opportunity to tell her that there were no political prisoners in Northern Ireland, and to warn her that there was no question of political status being given to IRA prisoners. The Ambassador reminded her that Northern Ireland was as much 'part of Great Britain' as Corsica and the *Départements D'outre-Mer* were parts of France, and that Northern Ireland had been 'part of Great Britain' for longer than some of the provinces of mainland France had belonged to France. He asked whether she thought it was conceivable that a French Government would grant political status to Corsican, Breton or Basque terrorists. Neiertz commented that France ought perhaps to set an example, but 'she said this in a way which made it clear that she did not imagine that the incoming Government would be making concessions on this front.' Hibbert told her that as long as France offered none of its prisoners political status, no one there had any right to press for political status for anyone in British prisons. She did not disagree. The Assistant Secretary, who was with Neiertz, objected to the fact that the British Embassy had claimed publicly that those who protested about the Sands case belonged to the French Communist Party. Hibbert replied that what:

> ... we had said was that over 90% of the protests which the Embassy had received had come from members or organs of the FCF and CGT. The statistics were irrefutable. I remarked that it was perhaps very foolish of the IRA to have sought or accepted Communist Party sponsorship in France, but it showed what bad company they were. He and Mme Neiertz agreed with this aspect of the argument.

In the circumstances, Hibbert concluded in his dispatch to the FCO, 'we have done enough to ensure that those close to M. Mitterrand are aware of the dangers of becoming sucked into the Northern Ireland problem.'[22]

Two days later, Petrie, a member of Hibbert's staff, followed this up by speaking to Mitterrand's Presidential Transition Team (*Antenne Présidentielle*). The Secretary General, Beregevoy, being absent, he spoke to a member of his staff (Boulard) and said that the Embassy had heard that members of the family of one of the hunger-strikers would be in Paris that day (the information was carried on French radio) for a meeting with Mitterrand: 'I did not of course know whether the second half of this information was correct but I wished to point out urgently the importance of the possible implications.' The question of Northern Ireland was one of close and immediate concern to the British Government and public opinion, who found it difficult to understand that third parties should give any encouragement to those who were associated with violence and illegality in Northern Ireland. The hunger-strikers and those speaking on their behalf clearly belonged to this category. No foreign Government had supported the hunger-strikers, pointed out Petrie. At the moment the new Presidential authority was preparing to take over in France, it was of the 'greatest importance for our future relations that they should allow for full discussion with Britain before adopting any public position on the important and complex issues in Northern Ireland.' Boulard would neither confirm nor deny the information, but said, several times, that he fully appreciated the delicacy of the question. He would ensure that the points Petrie had made were brought urgently to the attention of M Beregevoy, and would seek to ensure that a reaction (*un retour d'information*) was received as soon as possible. Petrie said that he hoped this would be before any decisions were taken, if indeed decisions had to be taken, on the application for an interview. Boulard again said that he would do his best, but would not comment further.[23]

The British response overseas was thus to marshal, where it could, its tremendous diplomatic capacities to counter the enormous emotive potential that the hunger-strikers had in the minds of those unfamiliar with the intimacies of Northern Ireland. But the most challenging international situation remained that on Britain's doorstep. In the aftermath of Hughes' death, Figg began to feel less sanguine about the mood in the Republic. The BBC's Dublin correspondent, Philip Whitfield, reported on *From our own Correspondent* on 9 May his impression that Sands' death 'had had relatively slight impact here. I am not sure this is right', Figg telegraphed London. Certainly demonstrations had been poorly supported, but moderate political opinion in the Republic 'is beginning to reflect the view that, however good our case for refusing political status, HMG is being unimaginative'. Figg noted that the H-Block Committee's decision the day before to run candidates in the border constituencies in the forthcoming general election would have the effect of profiting Fine Gael at the expense of Fianna Fáil: 'The Taoiseach told me that he feared this might happen. Now that it seems likely he will be even more anxious that the strike should end.'[24] In assessing the problems facing Haughey, a dispatch from Figg giving impressions of the mood in Dublin immediately after Hughes' death was particularly useful for the Prime Minister: 'I believe it would be a mistake to think that public opinion in the Republic will remain unmoved by further deaths' cautioned the Ambassador. The demonstration that turned up outside the British Embassy – within three hours of the news of Hughes' death reaching Dublin – had seen, for the first time, demonstrators turn violent while the Garda were forced to baton-charge them. While it was true to say that public opinion was not yet strongly aroused, there was increasingly a mood that two deaths were enough.

Brian Lenihan had told Figg that he thought that the Irish Government could cope with Hughes' death, but that something then had to be done to prevent any further deaths: 'The Irish see our current policy as an unwillingness to consider any course of action other than the one we calculate to get complete surrender by the strikers. They see this as just one more occasion when British political sense and acumen are switched off when faced with Irish problems.' In this there was, of course, the feeling that HMG's area of political manoeuvre was much too restricted by consideration of what the Protestants might do. Almost all sections of opinion were longing for some initiative by HMG quickly to avert any more deaths: 'For us to make no move will, I fear, lead to widespread criticism', warned Figg. There would be a corresponding strain on Anglo–Irish relations, 'and we naturally cannot be sure that the Taoiseach would still be able to hold a moderate line.' In the circumstances, Haughey 'has so far done us very well.' His public utterances had been restrained, but the present situation was causing more and more difficulty. There were now loud murmurings within his own party against the line that he was taking. This was reflected in the warnings, 'which even our most well-disposed contacts here are now giving us. They also say that PIRA will receive more sympathy with each new death.' The hunger strike had also thrown Haughey's electoral plans into disarray. The longer he left an election, the worse the economic position got (the banks had just announced a 1% increase on lending rates). The expectation was that the election would be called immediately after a Fianna Fáil parliamentary party meeting already arranged for the morning of Thursday, 14 May, but it was now suggested that Hughes' death could cause a further postponement.[25]

The anxiety in Dublin was reflected, on 12 May, when Dermot Nally rang Michael Alexander to say that the Taoiseach had asked him to convey to London his genuine and deep concern about the situation in Northern Ireland. Haughey believed that the Catholic population in the North was now completely under the control of the IRA, and feared that the population in those areas of the Republic close to the border was also being increasingly influenced by the IRA. There was now a possibility that, in a general election, as many as six seats in the border areas might be won by IRA sympathizers. If this were to happen, it was not inconceivable that IRA-inclined members of the Dáil would hold the balance of power after the election. This would obviously be a thoroughly undesirable situation. Nally explained that the Taoiseach had tried to get the hunger-strikers to associate themselves with a further appeal to the ECHR, but they had refused since, according to Nally, 'they knew they were on a winner.' The Taoiseach was, therefore, wondering whether it would be possible for HMG to take steps to involve the Commission: 'Could we, for instance, take as our starting point the document issued by the Northern Ireland Office on 18 December and invite the Commission to investigate the claim that undertakings given in that document had not been carried out.' But Alexander, as he explained to Nally, was sceptical about the merits of this suggestion, both from the point of view of its acceptability to HMG and from the point of view of its impact on the hunger-strikers. Nonetheless, he undertook to convey the Taoiseach's message to the Prime Minister. Nally expressed his gratitude, going on to say that if HMG thought it would be helpful, the Taoiseach would be 'very ready' to meet with the Prime Minister to discuss the situation. Failing that, Nally himself was ready at any moment to come to London to talk matters over. Alexander took note of the offer.[26]

Some of these concerns were put directly to the Prime Minister and Atkins by Dr Eamon Kennedy, who visited Downing Street on 13 May. The Irish Ambassador later described the atmosphere as 'courteous and friendly but a little tense at the beginning.' He had marshalled the Irish Government's arguments on small cards instead of reading them from a written text. The Prime Minister listened carefully to what Kennedy said, without interruption.[27] Kennedy told Mrs Thatcher that there would soon be an election in the Republic. It was conceivable that IRA candidates might, for the first time, stand, and could win considerable support. Against that background, the Taoiseach considered that the time was ripe for a political initiative. Two hunger-strikers had died. There would now be a pause before any more 'candidates for martyrdom' lost their lives, and this pause should be exploited. It would, of course, be risky to make a move. It would be equally risky not to move. The Irish Government recognized that political status for the hunger-strikers was 'not on'. But within the five demands, would it not be possible to move on clothes and on association outside work periods?[28] Kennedy revealed that 'our contacts had given us to believe that if there were satisfactory movement on clothes and association it might be possible to reach an end of the strike without granting political status.'[29] There was also the possibility of making use of the ECHR or its Secretary-General; or to consider appointing an outsider to review the situation. The Irish Government had reason to believe that if movement could be secured on the two issues that Kennedy mentioned, the strike would collapse. There could be no certainty about it, but that was their assessment. The collapse of the strike would, of course, have an enormous impact on Anglo–Irish relations. The Taoiseach would want to come to London to signal the opening of a new chapter in the bilateral relationship.

In her reply, the Prime Minister recalled that the last thing Bobby Sands had said before lapsing into a coma was that he wanted all five demands. Nothing less would do. Hughes had taken the same position. So had his brother, on television the previous evening. The fact was that the hunger-strikers wanted political status[30], 'and they can't get it.' She referred to the Ambassador's call to Number 10 in October, just before the first hunger strike began, and said that she regretted any suggestion that she was inflexible then or now; it was the hunger-strikers who were being inflexible. The previous October the Government had made a genuine effort to help on clothing, but this had been rejected by the prisoners as not enough. Atkins made the point that there seemed to be very little difference between a sweater supplied by Marks and Spencer and a sweater supplied by a prisoner's family. It seemed hardly worth dying for – which proved that the real point at issue was not the sweater but political status.[31] Mrs Thatcher concurred. The rules in the Maze were those appropriate to the running of a prison. They did not give the inmates prisoner of war status. There could be no question of HMG submitting to salami tactics leading to political status. Hughes had been a murderer, not a prisoner of war. Freedom of association was not possible. Anything that was made available to prisoners in the Maze would have to be made available throughout prisons in Northern Ireland.

Atkins interjected to call attention to a recent article in *An Phoblacht*, which had stressed that nothing less than the five demands would end the hunger strike. Kennedy had said that the Irish Government had reason to believe that meeting two demands would end the hunger strike. The hunger-strikers themselves denied this.

Kennedy's comment was that if Atkins was right about the reality, there was no hope of breaking the deadlock. But the relatives of the hunger-strikers had led the authorities in Dublin to think that it might be possible to sway them. He repeated that there could be no certainty, but he hoped that if there were some give in the British Government's position, a way out might be found. To this, the Prime Minister said that the ECHR were 'welcome to come in'. 'We had nothing to hide. But we could not invite the Commission in.' Someone had to make a complaint; the Commission could not accept an invitation from HMG. Kennedy then recalled that the Commission had said in its previous Report that in one or two respects the prison regime was inflexible. Atkins' response to this was that it was for this very reason that nine different changes in the regime had been introduced in 1980. Kennedy, though, stressed that he had only mentioned the point because of the need to find a mechanism to reintroduce the Commission into the situation. Atkins wondered whether the ECHR was relevant given that Sands had refused to endorse the complaints made by his sister. If any of the other hunger-strikers or their relatives complained, HMG would give the Commission every facility. The Prime Minister then commented that if Kennedy's account of the prisoners' frame of mind was correct, they ought themselves to be willing to complain. Kennedy acknowledged the point, adding that his Government was trying to 'get the hunger strikers into that frame of mind'. He thought that the fact that there were hundreds of prisoners who still enjoyed special category status while serving out their sentences was bound to affect the outlook of those prisoners who did not have that status. The case of Sands was particularly relevant: he was a prisoner who had had special category status during a previous period in prison.[32]

The only reply Kennedy got ('which illustrates a total lack of a sense of urgency', he later reflected), was that the two classes of prisoners would be segregated later the following year when a new prison would be ready.[33] Kennedy, though, did not wish to lay too much stress on the issue of the existing special category prisoners. This was just another ingredient in the situation. He warned that support for the IRA in the South and in the North was growing. In the North they now appeared as the natural leaders of the Catholic community, a role previously held by the SDLP. Polarization was increasing. The men in the middle were being left without a role. In a an effort to be positive, Mrs Thatcher repeated that if a role could be found for the ECHR, acting within its terms of reference, no obstacle would be met from HMG. On the broader situation, she asked Kennedy to convey to the Taoiseach her appreciation of his attitude in recent days. Like him, she had tried to keep alive the search for peace and reconciliation. She did not want to give up the progress that had been made. Kennedy replied that the Taoiseach was well aware of what the Prime Minister had done. He also did not wish to be blown off course.[34] The Ambassador went on to make the point that 'we only have about ten days from now to the next deaths and that it was essential that both governments keep in touch in order to find a way out of an intolerable crisis.' The Prime Minister concluded by sending good wishes to the Taoiseach, 'and agreed we should keep in touch as suggested'.[35]

Kennedy's point was indeed correct that there was only to be a temporary respite before the next hunger strike death. Hughes, meanwhile, was laid to rest, although not without some controversy. His remains were removed to an outside hospital for the post mortem, but were not finally taken away by the family until late on 13 May. This delay was caused by the family's reluctance to comply with the RUC requirement that the body be taken straight to Bellaghy and not via the receptions organized on the Falls Road or at Toomebridge.[36] The Chief Constable had decided that the RUC could not afford to let the plans for Hughes' removal from Forster Green Hospital to his home in Bellaghy to take their course. A 'very dangerous' situation might develop, quite outside the control of the police. Hermon could not have the procession parading past Protestant areas. The PIRA had already taken over St Agnes' Chapel in Anderson town, for the body to rest at the beginning of the procession, against the wishes of the priest in charge. Accordingly, the RUC arranged for the transit of the body themselves. This meant taking the hearse in a police convoy. Hermon informed the NIO that this was a police operational matter, from which the NIO should stand back. Hermon was 'less certain than one would like' as to the powers under which the RUC would conduct the removal, lacking family co-operation. He later decided that the best way to do this was in acting in discharge of his responsibility for keeping the peace under the Common Law.[37]

On 14 May, Hermon reported that the security situation had improved slightly, although rioting had continued the previous night with seven shooting incidents and one explosion. The decision to re-route the movement of Hughes' body had proved successful. Crowds that had gathered to see the arrival of the coffin had dispersed without any disturbances when it did not come. The Chief Constable noted, however, that should there be future deaths it would be necessary to repeat this exercise to avoid possible confrontations in mixed areas and to prevent the PIRA from taking complete control of the preliminaries to the funerals. As far as Hughes' actual funeral was concerned, the funeral route had been drawn up to minimize the risk of confrontation. Hermon noted that the indications were that the PIRA was showing signs of frustration, having been unable to provoke a Protestant backlash, which had been their objective. He thought that it was felt that there would be some merit in making the PIRA's strategy known to strengthen Loyalist resolve not to be provoked.[38]

By the next day, 15 May, Hermon observed that while the diversion of Hughes' funeral route had been accepted – albeit under protest, and although the situation remained delicate – he thought that the funeral itself would now pass off without any trouble. As far as the general situation was concerned, despite a rocket attack on a police Land Rover the previous night in West Belfast (in which Constable Samuel Vallely, aged 23, was killed), he did not think that there was any need for a change of tactics. The GOC agreed with this assessment. Lawson did not think that the rocket attack marked the start of a new PIRA offensive. He warned, however, that they had the capability to launch some sort of offensive, which would probably be against three types of target: civilian and political targets in Great Britain; military targets in Britain and Germany; and 'spectaculars' in Northern Ireland. Against this background he stressed the importance of matching the security force profile to the conditions on the ground, and of lowering it as quickly as conditions warranted it.[39]

The police estimated that approximately 15,000 people attended the funeral of Hughes. At the Requiem Mass the Parish Priest, Father Michael Flanagan, told the congregation that the ways of violence that had been tried over the past twelve years were the 'wrong ones'. In an appeal for reconciliation he said that there had to be forgiveness and trust, one towards another. As at Sands' funeral, the Provisional IRA provided paramilitary trappings to the ceremony. The RUC, as planned, diverted the funeral cortège away from the Protestant areas of Bellaghy. Some youths began throwing stones and bottles at the police, but they were stopped by stewards who were supervising the mourners. Martin

McGuiness, 'Chairman of PIRA's Provisional Army Council', declared that Francis Hughes had sacrificed his life to deny the policy of criminalization and described him as 'an unconquerable man, part of a cause that can never be broken'. Gerry Adams criticized Haughey for encouraging the hunger-strikers to seek the intervention of the European Commission of Human Rights. According to Adams, the Commission's intervention 'was doomed to failure … unless it can proceed on a clear understanding that the British Government are committed to achieving a settlement based on the prisoners' just demands. Mr Haughey knows this'.[40]

Of the two surviving original hunger-strikers, McCreesh's condition continued to deteriorate: he was seriously ill and now bedbound. The deterioration continued to follow the same pattern as Hughes', and his vision was seriously impaired. His fluid level remained satisfactory, and he was no longer suffering nausea. The prognosis was that his life expectancy might be some seven to ten days. O'Hara's condition was not quite as serious, though his deterioration was following the same pattern. He was no longer sick, and his vision was still satisfactory. He was able to take association in a wheelchair on 13 May, but otherwise was effectively bedbound. McDonnell's condition was not giving any cause for concern. The prisoners' weights on 14 May were:

	Day of strike	Weight on first examination	Weight today	Weight loss during week	Overall weight loss
Raymond McCreesh	54	9st 13lb	7st 3lb	5lb	2st 10lb
Patrick O'Hara	54	11st 3½lb	8st 7lb	7lb	2st 10½lb
Joseph McDonnell	6	11st 4½lb	11st 1½lb	3lb	3lb

Proof of the prisoners' determination was shown when, after Hughes' death, two of his relatives appealed to McCreesh and O'Hara to end their strikes, as the other deaths had obtained nothing. McCreesh was reported to have cried, but said that he would continue; O'Hara laughed.[41] On Saturday, 16 May, a miniature camera was discovered in McCreesh's bed. Only one shot had been taken. It was not known if it was the same camera that took the poor-quality picture of O'Hara later published by the *Irish Press* on 20 May. On Tuesday a pocket tape recorder was found in O'Hara's bed, but it did not have a battery and there was nothing on the tape. Although staff had suspicions as to how these items were introduced, there was no concrete evidence.[42]

As both men neared the end, there was a controversy concerning McCreesh. On Saturday, 16 May, McCreesh was on day fifty-six of his hunger strike. He was confined to bed and was described by the doctors as being in a confused and disorientated state of mind as to time, place and person.[43] Hospital Senior Officer Nolan was in charge of the Prison Hospital on 16 May when Hospital Officer Lennon told him that he was of the opinion that McCreesh might wish to stop his protest. At this time, McCreesh was being visited by the Prison Chaplain, Father Toner. When the visit was completed at approximately 18.25, Nolan entered the ward accompanied by HO Lennon. Having asked McCreesh how he was feeling, Nolan explained to him the folly of not taking water to drink, and also told him that there had been no urine passed all day. Nolan gave McCreesh a drink of water, which he took slowly, and pointed out if he wanted milk, or any sustenance, all he had to do was ask for it. McCreesh expressed a desire to pray, and he was left alone to do so.

On coming out from McCreesh's ward, Nolan was told that Dr Emerson wanted to speak to him on the telephone. During the course of conversation, Nolan mentioned that there was a possibility that McCreesh may wish to end his hunger strike, and Dr Emerson advised him that he would arrive in the prison shortly. Dr Emerson went to see McCreesh escorted by Lennon. Some minutes later, Lennon asked Evening Duty Principal Officer Orr, who had arrived in the hospital, and Nolan, to go to McCreesh's ward. When they arrived in the ward, according to Nolan's account, Dr Emerson said to McCreesh: 'Do you want me to try to save your life?' McCreesh replied '"Yes" in a strong voice.' When the staff came out of the ward, Emerson said that he wanted to phone his superiors. He also wanted to phone McCreesh's family. Principal Officer Orr spoke to the Duty Governor by telephone. At 20.30, McCreesh's visitors arrived and were interviewed by Emerson. At 21.15, Dr Bill arrived at the hospital and, after being introduced to McCreesh's relatives, they went to visit McCreesh. The visit ended at approximately 22.15 when the visitors left the hospital block, after having expressed to Doctors Bill and Emerson, in Nolan's presence, that the wish of McCreesh, which was expressed some weeks before, should be respected, and he should be allowed to continue his hunger strike with dignity.[44]

HO Paul Lennon gave a similar account of events. He was Night Guard Hospital Officer on duty on the evening of 16 May in South Wing in the Prison Hospital. He was aware that McCreesh was considering ending his hunger strike, and was present earlier with Nolan when Dr Emerson asked the hunger-striker if he wanted to end his fast, to which McCreesh 'answered a definite "Yes".' Lennon, together with another Night Guard Hospital Officer, McAleavey, reported on duty at 20.30, and accompanied him to McCreesh's ward. Nolan recalled: 'We offered him a drink of water, he drank a little, and then asked "Is this milk?". He was told "no" and was asked if he would like milk, to which he replied "Is my family here yet?". We told him "yes" and he then said, "I'll wait till I see them first".' At 21.20, McCreesh's visitors entered the wing, these being his mother, sister and two brothers (one of whom was a priest). McAleavey and Lennon were told by Nolan that the McCreesh family could have their visit, 'In sight out of hearing'. Whilst standing outside the ward door, 'we could both clearly overhear parts of the conversation, probably due to the fact that McCreesh's hearing was affected and the visitors had to speak loudly.' Lennon recalled hearing Father McCreesh repeatedly telling his brother to be strong and to remember where he was: 'You are in Long Kesh Concentration Camp, being looked after by prison warders. Remember O'Hara, he is strong and on hunger strike the same number of days as you'. Raymond McCreesh asked about Francis Hughes, to which his brother (Father McCreesh) replied, 'He is in Heaven with Bobby Sands'. Both brothers 'told of how proud they were to have carried Hughes' and Sands' coffin at their funerals.' At 'one stage his mother said "Now Raymond, you are going back on your word".' McCreesh was repeatedly told to remember where he was, not to get confused and not to listen to anyone but his family. At 22.00, his visitors left the ward to see Dr Bill, reminding McCreesh not to get confused and that they would see him the next day (Sunday). Later, Lennon learned that the McCreesh family said that he had made the decision whilst he was of sound mind, and the decision to remain on hunger strike stood.[45]

Lennon's story was corroborated by his colleague McAleavey. When McAleavey came on duty he was detailed Hospital Wards. Dr Emerson was in the hospital, and when McAleavey arrived on duty he was told that McCreesh was considering ending his hunger strike and wished his life to be saved if possible. McAleavey was detailed to the hospital wing with Lennon. At approximately 21.00, Doctors Bill and Emerson visited McCreesh. Dr Bill asked him if he would like to have medical treatment etc. in order to save his life – McCreesh replied, 'I never wanted to die in the first place'. Dr Bill asked him if he would he take some food. McCreesh replied, 'Aye … I would take food if I could'. Both doctors then left. Lennon and McAleavey were present during the doctors' visit. At approximately 21.00 also, McAleavey recalled, the McCreesh family arrived at the Prison Hospital having been sent for by Dr Emerson in light of what was happening. At 21.15, McAleavey offered McCreesh a drink of water in the presence of Lennon; he drank a sip, 'then asked me "Is this milk?" McAleavey told him it was not but asked him would he like milk – McCreesh then asked if his family had yet arrived. When McAleavey told him they were with the doctors and would be in to see him soon, he then replied "then I'll wait to see them".' McAleavey took this to mean whether or not McCreesh would drink milk etc. At 21.20, McCreesh's family entered the wing. McAleavey was instructed by Nolan to place four chairs in the prisoner's ward for visitors, to close the door with the observation flap up and to remain outside. McAleavey and Lennon did this, but the former also claimed, probably because the prisoner's hearing was affected, that:

> ... the visitors spoke rather loudly and we could easily overhear some of the conversation. We heard the brother of McCreesh, Fr McCreesh tell his brother to be strong and remember where he was 'In Long Kesh Concentration Camp, being looked after by Prison Warders'.
>
> 'You are doing this for a cause'.
>
> 'Remember O'Hara, he is strong and on hunger strike with you for the same amount of time'.
>
> The prisoner asked his family where Francis Hughes was, to which the brother (priest) replied, 'He is in Heaven with Bobby Sands'.
>
> Both brothers went on to say about the funerals of Sands and Hughes and how proud everyone was of them.
>
> We overheard his mother say 'Now Raymond you are going back on your word'. But I don't know what she meant by this.
>
> The prisoner was repeatedly told to remember where he was in Long Kesh and to listen only to his family and not the medical or prison staff.
>
> He was told that they would be in to see him tomorrow (Sunday) and to be strong and listen to them and everyone was proud of him and asking for him.

At 21.55 approximately, Dr Bill asked to see the family. At 22.00 the four members of the family left the hospital wing and spoke to the doctors. As she was leaving, his mother asked McAleavey to help McCreesh drink some water, particularly because he could not see very well. McAleavey replied that 'we would and had been doing that.' A short time later, the family left the hospital complex, and McAleavey learned that the family believed the prisoner had made up his mind to remain on hunger strike several weeks ago and this decision still stood.[46]

Although the McCreesh family subsequently refuted any allegation they intervened to keep Raymond on the hunger-strike, claiming the reports were falsified, at the time the Prime Minister was given a precis of these events. Mrs Thatcher was informed: 'We can not, of course, refer to this conversation in public; nor can we admit to its existence in private.'[47] The McCreesh family was angered by alleged leaks from the NIO and, on 20 May, the family issued a statement demanding:

> ... an independent inquiry by experienced legal and medical personnel into all aspects of Raymond's care and condition in the Maze Prison

hospital between 4.00 pm and 9.00 pm on Saturday 16 May 1981, to include:

(1) his medical condition with special reference to his sudden and marked deterioration to his mental state within that period;

(2) the alleged dialogues which were carried on with him;

(3) why certain questions were put to him;

(4) why certain interpretations were put upon his alleged answers;

(5) why the family was summoned in the way they were;

(6) why certain statements were issued to the news media after Saturday;

(7) why certain leaks were conveyed to the news media before Saturday to expect a certain event.

The inquiry must ask whether this whole affair was deliberately contrived to meet political expectations.[48]

As time ticked away towards the deaths of McCreesh and O'Hara, the Taoiseach's determination to involve the ECHR in the dispute saw the Irish European Commissioner in Strasbourg, Michael O'Kennedy, meet with the Irish member of the ECHR Council and the Secretary General of the Council of Europe before directing the Irish Permanent Representative there to contact Kruger, the Secretary to the Commission. O'Kennedy also had contacts with Douglas Hurd, the Minister of State in the FCO, in the margins of the European Committee of Ministers meeting. Three options to involve the ECHR were discussed with all concerned. As David Neligan, recalled, these were:

i) An inter-State case. It became apparent that, although we know this option was seriously looked at by the Commission (with the idea that a third power, perhaps Austria, might initiate a case against Britain non-contentiously and for the purpose of establishing facts and making recommendations), it was not going to be acceptable to the British Government or to the Human Rights Secretariat who disliked the precedents that would be set.

ii) Action by the Secretary-General (Article 57). The Secretary-General readily accepted the [Irish] Minister's suggestion that, given the gravity and urgency of the case, he should create precedent and enlarge his role by acting to demand an account of the situation from the British authorities, but made it clear that he would only do so if the British concurred, even tacitly or informally. However Mr Hurd indicated British objection to this option.

iii) Action by the Human Rights Commission either on foot of a new petition or revival of the existing one (McFeely et al...). In the event this option was adopted by the Commission which decided during the course of the day to reactivate its consideration of the McFeely case. At a later stage, the way was cleared for very early action through communication from London that Britain was waiving its right to submit observations on the Commission's decision which as a party it was entitled to do. Without exercise by the British of this waiver, action would have been held up for, at least, several days.[49]

Under the provisions of the ECHR, the Commission, acting under Article 28, would (a) examine the complaints and ascertain the facts and (b) would subsequently place itself at the disposal of the parties with a view to securing a friendly settlement. The British Government had an obligation to facilitate (a), but did not have a similar obligation to facilitate the subsequent step at (b). If this procedure did not lead to a conclusion satisfactory to both parties, the Commission would proceed to arrive at a judicial decision on the complaints. The Commission now wanted to enter upon the procedure at (a). The question for decision by the British was whether the Government should indicate a readiness to take part in the procedure under (b), or should make it clear at this stage that it would not participate because it had nothing to offer.

In London, the Prime Minister, Atkins and the Attorney General, Sir Michael Havers, met to discuss the ECHR position. Atkins revealed to the Prime Minister that the PIRA had been in touch with the NIO through a known channel and had indicated that they wished to see the Commission follow the Article 28 procedure. They still believed that the Government was on a hook and was looking for ways of getting off it. Atkins explained: 'If we did not facilitate an inquiry by the Commission under Article 28, the Provisionals would claim that all we had said in the past about being ready to facilitate the involvement of the Commission in attempts to solve the hunger strike had been false and that the British were as inflexible as they always had been.' There was a major risk that the Government would suffer a substantial public relations reverse, especially in the United States and the Republic. He therefore proposed that HMG should facilitate the Article 28 procedure. Atkins added that the PIRA's perception of the issue of the hunger strike was 'different from ours.' They believed that the deaths of Sands and Hughes had strengthened their position and that the Government was in difficulty. They appeared to think that if the ECHR applied the Article 28 procedure this would give them the substance of what they wanted. J. A. Marshall, of the NIO, confirmed to the Prime Minister that the Provisionals were pressing strongly for an indication of the Government's attitude: 'If we did not reach a decision within the next few hours, they would assume that our view of the Article 28 procedure was negative and they would begin to make this clear in their propaganda.'

Mrs Thatcher voiced her concern that the Article 28 procedure was the start of a very slippery slope. The fact was that the Government was not on a hook: 'We had always said that we would give the Commission facilities to conduct an investigation provided a proper and specific complaint was laid with them.' It seemed to her that the danger of the Article 28 procedure was that 'we would appear to be negotiating,' and that she was not prepared to do. Moreover, it would be 'disingenuous of us to allow the Commission to embark upon this course if we had no intention of accepting a friendly settlement.' It would be better if the Commission examined the complaints and ascertained the facts and then proceeded to a decision, omitting the stage of attempting to secure a friendly settlement. She did not feel able to reach a final view on the basis of the information before her, even though the matter was urgent.

The mood changed significantly, however, at the later stage when Atkins informed the Prime Minister that he had received word that the Provisionals had come to realize that the Article 28 procedure was not a route by which they were going to see their five demands met. They were, therefore, no longer interested in proceeding in this way and were not pressing the Government to make a statement setting out its own views on the Article 28 procedure. It remained the advice of his security advisers, though, that it was important that the Government avoid appearing as the party that prevented the ECHR from trying to help to resolve the hunger strike. He still proposed, therefore, that the Government should go along with the first part of the Article 28 procedure and that, 'even if we eventually said that we had no proposals for a friendly settlement to offer, we should not make this clear at the very outset, since to do so would effectively bring the procedure to an immediate halt.' Mrs Thatcher, summing up the discussion, said that the gathering agreed that the Commission should examine the complaints and that the Government should facilitate their efforts to ascertain the facts.[50]

The problem with following this route was that ECHR involvement would take a considerable amount of time to manifest itself, which was of little help in the short term. Against this was the grim reality that the hunger strike might, as the Cabinet Secretary warned Mrs Thatcher, be a very long, drawn-out affair. The Provisionals, Armstrong pointed out, claimed that they had got seventy potential hunger-strikers lined up, so that as current strikers died there would be a steady stream of replacements. Public opinion in the United Kingdom and in Parliament had not so far shown much reaction to the deaths that had taken place to date. Abroad and in Northern Ireland the effects had been greater. Armstrong was blunt: the ECHR looked 'like a dead duck' as a means of bringing the hunger strike to an end, at least unless and until the Provisional IRA changed their minds and abandoned their insistence on the five demands.

In the meantime, the ECHR's only conceivable advantage was as an instrument in the propaganda war: 'if we stick firmly to the line that we shall not stand in the way of but facilitate the Commission's pursuit of any complaint which is admissible under the Convention it is difficult to fault that position, and we have a reasonably good defence against the charge of inflexibility on this score.' But hunger-strikers 'will, it seems, go on dying. We ought to try to assess the effects of this on the two communities in Northern Ireland, and on the security forces. It will presumably harden the polarisation of the two communities', he warned. The Protestant community would no doubt be reasonably content to see the British Government standing firm, and their paramilitaries would hold off. But would continuing deaths weaken the strength and support of the SDLP in the Catholic community, and incline them to turn back to the Provisionals? It would be a serious development in security terms if a growing sense of despair in the Catholic community increased their readiness to offer safe havens and other assistance to the PIRA terrorists. And the price of standing firm might be – perhaps already was – increased casualties in the security forces: 'Do we have to do any more in political terms to maintain their morale in the face of these attacks?' asked Armstrong. The other question was that of long-term political development. The apparent absence of a policy on long-term political development represented a real weakness in the Government's present position, he warned the Prime Minister.[51]

If Mrs Thatcher had any doubts as to whether she should stay on the path not to yield to the hunger-strikers, then they were swept away on the same day that she received Armstrong's memo. On 19 May, five British soldiers were blown to pieces, in a Saracen armoured vehicle in South Armagh, by an IRA bomb. Claiming responsibility, the Provisionals warned the British Army: 'You are fighting a war which you cannot win'. Commenting on the murder, Father Faul asked: 'How can people put forward the value of non-violent protest in the prisons when all their good work is negatived by a savage deed like this? One lesson from Long Kesh in recent weeks is the superiority of the sacrificial fast over the violence of the paramilitaries. That lesson has now been lost'.[52]

The GOC regarded the bomb attack as being in tune with others on the security forces – they were largely opportunistic: the attack had made use of a previously prepared ambush position and not one specially prepared to mark McCreesh's imminent death. He also expressed concern about the fact that terrorists in Belfast were making use of the civil disorder to practise and improve their sniping techniques.[53] Speaking the day after the attack, at the fifty-first Annual Conservative Women's Conference at Central Hall, Westminster, the Prime Minister said:

> Yesterday, in Northern Ireland, part of the United Kingdom, five of our soldiers, three of them under the age of 21, were murdered by the Provisional IRA.

They were doing their duty, faithfully, responsibly, loyally. They were there to protect the lives and the property of the law-abiding people of Ulster – and they gave that protection, impartially, to every citizen alike.

I hope that when their murderers have been tried and convicted, no one will claim that they are entitled to special privileges – which is what political status means – when they serve their prison sentences.

But it is not just in Northern Ireland that the terrorist casts his cruel shadow. The international scene is disfigured by violence.

The [assassination] attacks on President Reagan and the Pope; terrorist outrages in Spain, Italy and Germany. The world is daily assaulted by those who seek to impose their views upon us through violence and fear.

Terrorism is an attack upon the whole community. It undermines everyone's confidence in the security of their families and the stability of their society. Where will the gunman strike? Whom will the bomber choose?

This is the tension that induces cold fear – the atmosphere which the terrorist seeks to create. If he can destroy our trust in a well-ordered society, if he can spread consternation and provoke retaliation – then he is on the way to achieving his ends.

Even more – if he can gain some recognition for his cause and some sympathy for his aim – then he can strike a body blow at society's efforts to defeat him.

That is why TV and Press have so great a responsibility. They must, of course, report the facts. Nothing would be more damaging than misinformation and lack of balance. Yet the line is hard to draw for terrorism needs publicity. Newspaper and television coverage can provoke the very reaction the terrorist seeks.

It can give the convicted criminals on hunger strike the myth of martyrdom they crave, but the true martyrs are the victims of terrorism.

Government, too, has a great responsibility. Terrorism can only be beaten if terrorists know they can never win. If the bomber is seen to succeed then he has beaten the ballot box. In a democracy our determination to defeat the terrorist is based on our commitment to freedom. It is the Government's first duty to protect its people from attack. To that duty, this Government is wholly committed.[54]

Later Mrs Thatcher and Atkins met to discuss the latest information from Northern Ireland. Atkins warned that a time of considerable difficulty lay ahead. The next hunger-striker (McCreesh) would probably die the following day, and the fourth (O'Hara) by the end of the week. An interval of three to four weeks was then likely before the fifth striker would be near death, unless he chose to accelerate the process by refusing water as well as food. Given the continuous strain to which the security forces were subjected, Atkins was worried that there was always the risk of a mistake on their part leading to an accidental death, which could spark off even more serious trouble. But, he reassured the Prime Minister, they were so far coping well with the situation, and there was beginning to be some scope for shortening their exceptionally long periods on duty.[55]

The Prime Minister received better news from Sir Nicholas Henderson, who reported from Washington that the 'decline of US media attention … continues. Northern Ireland remains a prominent story, but by no means the dominant one'. Major developments such as Hughes' funeral and the murder of the five British soldiers had received full but factual coverage. Editorial coverage continued at a lesser rate: it remained the case that no influential US newspaper had called for the granting of political status. Indeed, editorial comment, though by no means uniform, was increasingly favourable.[56]

Meanwhile, in a last attempt to save his brother's life, Father McCreesh made an appeal directly to the Prime Minister to intervene and grant the hunger-strikers' demands. Mrs Thatcher replied that, while she and her colleagues regretted as much as anyone the conditions in which a number of prisoners at the Maze had lived: 'you must be aware that these were conditions which the prisoners chose to impose upon themselves.' So far as the hunger strike was concerned, the Prime Minister was emphatic: 'the aims which your brother and his fellow-strikers declared, or which were declared on their behalf, are simply not in any responsible Government's gift. If that was not clear at the outset of their action, it must surely be clear now.' It was Mrs Thatcher's 'profound hope that those to whom your brother listens and whom he trusts will explain this to him so that even now a chance can be taken to save one life at least'.[57]

It proved to be too late. By Monday, 18 May, Raymond McCreesh was virtually unconscious. Subsequently, he rallied somewhat before the final rapid decline on Wednesday 20 May[58]. John Blelloch reported that day that although the forensic reports on McCreesh had not yet been received, the indications were that he had not received external nourishment. He was now thought likely by the doctors to die sometime the next day, with O'Hara following twenty-four to twenty-eight hours later.[59] McCreesh died the following morning, the sixty-first day of his strike, at 02.11. Shortly afterwards the body was removed to Daisy Hill Hospital, Newry (a deliberate choice as Newry was only a few miles from Camlough, the family home).[60] O'Hara died the same day. His mother, Peggy, recalled:

My son explained to me long before there ever was a hunger strike, that once a man from the Republican movement goes into prison, even if he is a [INLA] leader on the outside, once inside he is in a new situation where prisoners choose their own leader and make their own decisions.

Decisions made by the prisoners are accepted totally by the leadership outside.

So ... the leadership are in no position to order the hunger strikers to come off their fast.

Peggy recollected how, when her son decided to be the next in line, the INLA leadership outside sent him a message asking him to step down and let another Volunteer take his place, but he refused. He told Peggy about it in one of his smuggled notes written on toilet paper. He wrote: 'Mammy, I am committed to the hunger strike and no way would I stand down and say to the next man: you go first.' Peggy and 'Patsy ... were very close and he could always talk to me like a friend, so that I knew and understood every move of him, and I knew at that point there was no way I could talk him out of it, so I didn't try.' Her 'understanding and awareness of the situation helped me to face the most tragic experience in my life, but it did not relieve the soul-searching agony I was to go through. No words of mine could express what I felt on my lonely vigil watching my son's life ebb away'. But: 'From the day my son went on hunger strike, I knew he was absolutely resolute about what he was doing, but he was always full of hope and told me not to worry. I too was full of hope, and in the back of my mind I was determined that my Patsy was not going to die.'

Unknown to anybody else, however, at that stage Peggy had decided that when her son was in a coma she would sign for medication to save his life. In the light of that, 'I was very careful to avoid making any promise to Patsy, so as not to be bound, as the other families had been, to their sons.' Each day a meal was brought to O'Hara and left there all day on show, 'even though he was unable to take a sip of water and the smell of dinner made him vomit. I requested them to take it away but they refused. I brought a local councillor to witness this, but the dinner was still there when he was dead.' Two days before O'Hara's death, every effort had failed. His sister Elizabeth had been to France and Dublin. Charles Haughey had raised her hopes the day before – as Peggy recalled:

> ... when I say that Mr Haughey gave Elizabeth hope I should have told you how much our hopes were raised, because the words that Mr Haughey used were 'Elizabeth I promise you that Raymond McCreesh and your brother Patsy are not going to die'. When Elizabeth phoned me from Dublin I couldn't wait to get telling Patsy and when I did his face lit up with pure joy.

But the next day that 'hope was dashed and everything looked black.' She decided that the time had come for her to intervene: 'It was then that I made it known to the leadership of the movement outside that I was going to sign for medication to save Patsy's life and that I wanted to tell them first.' Her decision was met with sympathy and understanding: 'They said I had a right to make that decision if I so wished and that just as they had stood behind the prisoners in their decision to go on hunger strike so also would they stand behind me in mine. We won't desert you, they said.'

The next time Peggy went to visit her son, 'he looked terrible and I felt heartbroken but determined that I was not going to let him die.' When the warder came to tell her that her half-hour was up, 'I was so distraught I put my arms around my son, and I said to him: "Patsy, at this moment I don't care about Ireland or the whole world, you are the only thing that matters to me – everything has failed and now I'm the only one who can save you and I am going to do it".' She then dashed out without looking back. She stayed in Belfast, but O'Hara's father had to go back to Derry to attend to some urgent business. He had only just arrived in Derry when he received the word that his son had taken a heart attack and he returned immediately. He arrived at the prison at 10.10 p.m. Peggy was already in there waiting for him, but at this point was not aware that he had arrived, or that he had been refused admission:

I was standing by Patsy's bedside wetting his lips and tongue with moistened cotton wool as he could no longer take water. His eyes were open but he could not see. He was very weak and seemed unable to speak but I knew when I held his hand that he was still conscious.

There I was, myself alone, consumed by grief, and torn by this dilemma. Then, as if he was reading my mind, he suddenly turned to me and spoke loudly and firmly.

He said, Mammy, I'm sorry we didn't win but please, mammy, let the fight go on.

Those words gripped my heart like a vice, and only then did the reality of his dying hit me. I could never explain the torment of my mind and the pain in my heart in those last lonely hours. I thought this must have been the way Mary felt when Jesus told her: I must be about my Father's business. I prayed for strength, I prayed for help, it was so lonely.

Just about then, a warder came in and informed me that my husband had arrived ten minutes late and was refused admission, and I thought: Dear God, must I bear the burden of this alone. I asked the warder if I would be permitted to go to the rest room to sit with the McCreesh family for a while. I just wanted somebody to share this awful moment with me, but he said No.

So I just continued to wet Patsy's lips and hold his hand. I knew I had to wait until he was unconscious before I could carry out my intentions.

My mind was racing: I knew that if I signed for medication he would continue his fast when he became conscious again. I asked myself, would I, by trying to save him, only prolong his agony and his suffering?

My mind argued with itself, and I thought: I don't care if he hates me for the rest of his life, I just want him to live. Each time when I wanted to cry out loud I want to save my son, his last words gripped my mind and I froze.

The night seemed like years, and in the morning Elizabeth, my daughter, came with her father. I told them everything as it happened through the night.

My husband told me then how he had been refused admission, and he had sat in the car for some hours outside the prison gate. He said it was hard to watch the twilight lady friends of the security forces go in and out of the gate after midnight, yet he was forbidden to see his dying son because the law says the gates close at ten.

Elizabeth took over from me at Patsy's bedside and continued to moisten his lips. As she did so she said to him: Patsy, I'm going to save you. At that moment he sealed his lips and pushed away the moist cotton wool as if he feared that what she was now doing was giving him medication.

Elizabeth continued to try and moisten his tongue which was now greatly swollen, but he still rejected the drops of water.

By now his eyes had rolled to the back of his head, and showed only the blood-shot whites of his eyes. There was an unbearable smell of death in the over-heated cell.

Patsy was blue in the face and moaning with pain. I thought I would go mad. Around this time his brother Tony had arrived under guard. We were ordered to leave, and to go to the rest room during Tony's ten-minute visit. Some hours later Patsy died.

On looking back, I realise that my being left alone was an extra agony imposed by the prison authorities. I am convinced that this was completely deliberate because having heard the words I said to my son on the previous visit they felt that had broken me, and if let alone with Patsy, I, in turn, would break him.

But Patsy was unbreakable, either by me or anybody else, but at least now he is free for all the beatings, the torture and degrading naked body searches which brought the prisoners to the desperation of hunger strike in the first place.[61]

As for the other hunger-strikers, by the time of McCreesh and O'Hara's deaths, Joe McDonnell's condition was not giving any cause for concern and he remained in H-5. Brendan McLaughlin, an IRA Volunteer, though only a week into his fast (he replaced Hughes on 14 May), was moved to the prison hospital on 20 May. This reflected concern at the significant weight loss he had suffered in a very short time (around one stone), coupled with frequent vomiting. He had been vomiting blood, evidently from an ulcer, and was described as acutely ill, although he had no history of this type of complaint. McLaughlin required urgent treatment, but so far had given no indication that he would accept this; McCreesh's death, however, was reported to have shaken him. If the internal bleeding continued, death could occur within a matter of days.[62]

On 22 May, the Chief Constable reported that there had been a violent overnight reaction to the death of O'Hara. There had been some difficult encounters, and one rioter had been killed with a plastic bullet in Derry (it was subsequently disputed whether the victim, Harry Duffy, a 44-year-old widower who left seven children, was involved in any disturbances). Hermon said that the violence was within the capacity of the security forces, however, and pointed out that his total riot casualties over the period were only a quarter of the Metropolitan Police casualties during the recent Brixton riots. The movement of McCreesh's body to his home had passed off without incident. O'Hara's body was currently at an undertaker's in Derry and was due to be moved to his home that afternoon for burial. The GOC agreed that there had been some 'sharp encounters' overnight. His personal observations in Poleglass, in Belfast, however, had been that actual violence had only been caused by a very small number of young people, and that the bulk of the people there, after they had come out on the streets to express their anger and concern, had taken no further part in the incidents. He felt that this could well reflect the mood of the Catholic community at large in that they were concerned, but they were not as a group prepared to express their concern in terms of violence. Hermon, however, wanted action on the political front, and urged that some response to the ECHR question should be made as a matter of extreme urgency as a means of reassuring Catholic opinion.[63]

On the following day, approximately 12,000 people joined McCreesh's funeral cortège at Camlough, South Armagh. Two days later a maximum of 10,000 people attended the funeral of O'Hara in Derry. Both were given paramilitary trappings. Rory O'Bradaigh, of the PIRA Army Council, described McCreesh as 'a great Irishman who was moulded in the Republican traditions of South Armagh'. Father Brian McCreesh had already appealed for people not to react violently to his brother's death, and the Belfast H-Block Committee called for twenty-four hours of mourning in commemoration of McCreesh. The town of Newry practically closed for the day. At O'Hara's funeral (which was followed by rioting), a uniformed INLA member read out a statement declaring that the hunger-striker had been 'murdered by the British Government and the Haughey administration in the South'. The speaker continued: 'We will be highly disciplined and while we do not intend to engage in wild acts of violence, what we have done in the past will be bettered in the future'.

Earlier in the week, Sinn Féin's Richard McAuley had admitted: 'The prisoners now accept that the Tories were more inflexible and intransigent than they had envisaged', but the protest would continue. Anti-H-Block campaigners joined the controversy surrounding the use of plastic bullets against rioters, the Chief Constable having made a statement on 26 May defending their use as a 'minimum-force weapon'. Following the death of Carol Ann Kelly, an 11-year-old Twinbrook schoolgirl killed by a plastic bullet, Gerry Adams wondered if Hermon was suggesting 'that Carol Ann Kelly, for example, was carrying an RPG or a petrol bomb?' In the Republic, small-scale picketing was staged outside the British Embassy in Dublin after the hunger-strikers' deaths, but the NAHC cancelled a black flag protest outside the Taoiseach's home on the day of McCreesh's funeral as it feared that street violence would follow. Instead, a black flag vigil was held outside the GPO building in Dublin. However, anti-H-Block protesters did force Haughey to curtail one of his election campaign walkabouts in Dublin (he called the vote on 21 May with polling day set for 11 June) and, in Navan, Dr Rose Dugdale shouted 'murderer, murderer' at him. Garret FitzGerald was also jeered at during an election meeting by H-Block demonstrators.[64] As the British Embassy explained to the FCO:

> Outside Dublin the picture is less encouraging. There has been intimidation and a number of incidents, not all of which have received publicity. These include an unsuccessful attempt of burn the Sligo Church of Ireland Cathedral and the successful burning in Leitrim of a bus being used by a group of British anglers. It is scarcely surprising that the Irish tourist industry's prospects for this season are bleak.

Haughey had a pot of paint thrown at him on 22 May, and he was jostled by a crowd the following day. However, reported the Embassy, 'he has continued to be robust on the question and is said to have told the Fianna Fáil Parliamentary Party that he would not ask for concessions on the five demands because he would not act as the spokesman of the Provisionals. There is no division between the two main parties on the hunger strike and indeed Dr Fitzgerald [sic] in a moment of candour admitted that the Taoiseach had handled the issue as well as anyone could have done.'[65]

Unfortunately for the Taoiseach, it appeared that little help would be forthcoming from London. A key factor in limiting how far the Government could move on the hunger strikes remained the reaction of the Protestant community to events. A paper on the prisons protest, considered by Ministers on 20 May, contained the following paragraph: 'For the Protestant community, HMG's handling of the prisons is seen as a measure of its resolve against the IRA. Concessions to Republican pressure would be interpreted as weakness and would have consequences for the security situation'. But, as the NIO informed Mrs Thatcher, 'the picture in the Protestant community is complex.' Unionist politicians, the NIO explained, were unanimous (though with differing degrees of vehemence) in protesting against anything that suggested that HMG might be in the process of making concessions of any sort to Republican prisoners, whether as a result of international or Church opinion, the Irish Government, a terrorist campaign, but above all if concessions might result from the hunger strike. Every reiteration of HMG's firm stance was 'music to their ears.' This general attitude, 'so far as we can judge from our contacts,' was shared by the Protestant community as a whole. Even very moderate Protestants would insist on the necessity not to give in to the IRA, and they believed that the Provisionals, if HMG stood firm on this issue, would eventually capitulate. The Protestant community as a whole would, however, have preferred to accept any changes in the present situation that resolved the prisons issue and its accompanying violence, provided that this was not tantamount to the acceptance of political status or a concession that the prisoners could have control over how they spent their time, and that it did not amount to a charter for an eventual amnesty. A touchstone of Protestant reaction would be their assessment of what weakness the Government had shown towards the Provisionals.

Thus, while the UDA would not support political protest against concessions with either paramilitary or terrorist activity, they would feel bound to react if they thought that the Provisionals had won a major confrontation with the Government, and might be drawn into violence through the reaction of the Protestant community as a whole. Other bodies representative in some ways of Protestant opinion and important in this context were the UDR, the RUC and the prison officers. The GOC and the Chief Constable had already told the Secretary of State that they would not expect the two former bodies to react adversely to movement forward under the ECHR procedure, for instance under Article 28. Because of their close involvement in dealing with the prisons protest, prison officers were more sensitive to changes that could be interpreted as concessions to protestors. Subject to the provisos already outlined, though, some movement, for example under the ECHR, could be achieved without causing an unacceptable reaction from these quarters. The NIO concluded that the Protestant community's attention was presently focussed on the prisons and the hunger strike, but its mood was dependent on issues going far wider. Its need, which remained much the same as had been identified in December during the first hunger strike, was for reassurance that:

a) the security situation is under control;

b) HMG has made no plans in association with Mr Haughey for radical moves in the political or institutional field; and

c) intends to stand firm on the position that while we will continue to operate a humanitarian prisons regime there is no question of concessions which would be tantamount to political status.[66]

As for attitudes within the Catholic community, the Prime Minister was informed that while the present hunger strike evoked little interest at its outset, attitudes had been changing with the deaths of the hunger-strikers. What was true chiefly in West Belfast applied also in Londonderry and, to a lesser but increasing extent, in other parts of Northern Ireland, and applied to all sections of the Catholic community: they feared that the current rioting could lead to a major confrontation between the security forces and the Catholic community. They were also anxious that, with the community polarized, there were dangers of inter-sectarian violence. At the same time, many Catholics, even those who did not support militant Republicanism, instinctively sympathized with the H-Block protestors, 'who strike a deep chord in nationalist sentiment.' Candidates in the local elections standing on an H-Block ticket, some with Provo connections, did well. Gerry Fitt, the former leader of the SDLP, who spoke out against the hunger strike, was defeated:

We have detected no great upsurge of popular support for the Provisionals. Catholics resent PIRA attempts over the past few weeks to manipulate them. They are deeply worried about the trouble which PIRA can bring to their communities. But though they blame PIRA too for the stalemate in the hunger strike, they have no illusions that PIRA will prove flexible and this accentuates their tendency to look to Government to make a move.

The necessary actions of the security forces in containing riots were inevitably exploited by PIRA sympathizers; the longer street confrontations continued, the more tempting it became for those Catholics caught in the ghettos to blame them on the security forces. Familiar allegations were already circulating about Army and police brutality, and were widely believed. It was clear, not least from intelligence sources, that the shift of Catholic opinion described above had been a major aim of the PIRA's policy: 'We have evidence of an organised campaign to stir up anger over the security forces' activities for example', Mrs Thatcher was told. As the hunger strike continued, Catholic frustration was turning increasingly to bitterness and anger. Alienation of the community posed difficulties for everyday government and put at risk the return to normality in Northern Ireland. The task of the security forces in policing Catholic areas had become more difficult, and the growing acceptance of the RUC by the Catholic community was being checked. Intelligence confirmed stories that PIRA terrorists were finding the population of West Belfast more ready than they were a few weeks earlier to give them the passive support they needed to operate:

> We have succeeded in getting through to PIRA, to the Protestants and the Catholics the important message that Government cannot yield on the five demands, or on political status. That message must not change. Our problem is, at the same time, that we must not allow those seeking the alienation of the Catholic community by exploiting their fears to achieve their aim.[67]

The Prime Minister was also provided with the latest security assessments: she was told that terrorist activity in Northern Ireland had been characterized by periods of relative calm alternating with outbursts of violence, but the Provisional IRA's main targets had remained unchanged. The RUC and the Army continued to be the prime targets, but there had been attacks on property in an effort to disrupt the life of Northern Ireland. The terrorists were undoubtedly capable of mounting attacks using powerful weapons, particularly on 'soft' targets, and had been particularly doing so along the border with the Republic recently. The level of violence in Northern Ireland had nevertheless declined substantially. There was less violence in 1980 than at any time since 1970. The level of violence earlier in the year continued its downward trend. Indeed, the level of violence in the first four months of 1981 was lower than in the same period the previous year.

There had, however, been an upsurge in both violent attacks and street disorder since the death of Sands on 4 May. So far there had been seventeen deaths (eight security forces; nine civilian, two of which were known to have been terrorists), but the level of violence was still somewhat below the average for 1980 as a whole. In the first four months of 1981, 220 persons were charged with serious terrorist type offences by comparison with 200 during the same period the previous year. The regular Army strength in Northern Ireland was currently about 11,000 men, in addition to which there were about 7,500 (full- and part-time) members of the UDR. They were deployed in support of the 7,000-strong police force. The size of the Army's presence was determined principally by the RUC's requirement for military support, and as this had declined, so had troop levels (from 13,000 at the beginning of 1980). It had, however, always been recognized that at times of tension additional reserves might be necessary, and this was the reason for the recent deployment to Northern Ireland of the Spearhead Battalion of 600 men. Troop levels since January 1980 had been:

Date	No. of major units	No. of men (approx)
Jan 1980	13	13,000 +
Feb 1980	12	12,500
July 1980	11	11,900 (by Oct 1980)
Nov 1980	10	11,300
Apr 1981	9	c11,000
May 1981	9 +	c11,650

Spearhead [Battalion to be deployed from Great Britain][68]

These briefings formed the background for a meeting, on 27 May, that the Prime Minister held at Chequers with the RUC Chief Constable and the GOC NI, where, in response to the Prime Minister's invitation, Jack Hermon outlined how the situation in Northern Ireland had been developing rather rapidly since mid-April. Prior to that, the security forces had succeeded in stabilizing the situation. Following the deaths of the four hunger-strikers, however, there was a growing tendency for the Catholic community to display sympathy for the 'martyrs'. He confirmed to Mrs Thatcher that Catholics were also becoming alienated from the Government's policy. There was little sympathy for the PIRA as such, and no pressure for the granting of political status or the five demands, but the continuing violence and the activities of Paisley were giving rise to unease and dissatisfaction. There was increasing support among the young for the PIRA. The police were being forced to abandon foot patrols and to remain in their vehicles. In sum, there was some doubt as to whether the level of security achieved in the recent past could be maintained, and a risk that some of the ground won, for instance in terms of the Catholic community's confidence in the security forces, would be lost. If the Government could dispel the impression of inflexibility, and could get over instead that its policy was magnanimous and caring, these risks might be reduced.

General Lawson supported Hermon. He agreed that the security threat could be contained. Neither the riots nor the scale of terrorist activity were as substantial as in the past. The Government was in no danger of defeat. Nonetheless, the population was becoming alienated. The PIRA had succeeded in obscuring the fact that they were responsible for the present troubles, and the Catholics were looking to HMG for movement of some kind. The Prime Minister was also told that the PIRA recognized that they could not win through terrorism. Their thinking was concentrated on the need to find a way to win back the support of the Catholic community, which they had lost in recent years. They saw the hunger strike, about the launching of which they had had grave doubts, as a way to drive a wedge between the Catholic community and the Government. They knew that the situation was delicately balanced, and that their effort might already have 'peaked' in PR terms. It was possible that there would be an opportunity in the weeks that followed for the Government to attempt to reassure the Catholic community.

The Prime Minister asked whether there were any specific proposals aimed at securing the objective that had been outlined. It was not easy to envisage a proposal that would be substantial enough to satisfy the Catholic community and, more particularly, the hunger-strikers, while being sufficiently limited in scope to avoid alarming the Protestants. Hermon answered that the precedent of the Bennett Enquiry into allegations of police brutality during interrogations might be helpful. He believed that there would be value in setting up a similarly expert enquiry to investigate prison conditions in Northern Ireland. The enquiry might be tasked to consider whether the types of crime, the motives of the criminal and the purpose of imprisonment in Northern Ireland were the same as those in the rest of the United Kingdom. The terms of reference would include no promise of change in prison conditions, nor indeed any acknowledgement of a need for change. A principal objective of setting up the enquiry would be to remove the question of prison conditions from the political arena. Sir Kenneth Stowe, also in attendance, interjected that the need for an investigation into prison conditions in Northern Ireland had been apparent for some months. He had, for instance, been struck by the absence of specialized psychiatric and psychological advice. There were no penologists in Northern Ireland. The gulf that divided the Protestant prison officers from the largely Catholic prison population was a problem peculiar to Northern Ireland: it had been largely responsible for the breakdown of the situation in the Maze in the weeks after the collapse of the first hunger strike. If it were agreed that there was a case for an initiative on prison conditions, the next four weeks – before the next hunger-striker was expected to die – could be the time to launch it.

In subsequent discussion it was confirmed that an enquiry of the kind proposed would cover all prisons and prisoners in Northern Ireland. It was recognized that if the idea were to be pursued it would need to be worked out in considerable detail and would have to be considered by Ministers. Clearly the enquiry could not be mandated to enquire into the five demands or to consider the question of special status for the hunger-strikers, but any enquiry would be forced to deal with the question of existing special category prisoners. It was argued that, even if it were agreed to launch an enquiry into prison conditions, this would not of itself reverse the present trend towards the alienation of the Catholic community. A sustained effort, which would have to involve the Prime Minster herself, would be required, which would have to continue for some weeks. This would, in effect, be a major hearts-and-minds campaign aimed at the Catholic community. In the timing of any initiatives, it was suggested that the PIRA would attempt in the days and weeks immediately ahead to intensify the street rioting and to raise the level of terrorist activity. They would also engage in more political activity with the objective of broadening their support in the Catholic community and, perhaps above all, of capitalizing on the forthcoming election in the Republic. They could also be expected to renew their efforts to move a writ for a further by-election in Fermanagh. All of this suggested that the Government, if it were to take any kind of initiative, should move sooner rather than later.

Mrs Thatcher, though, warned that the Government must be 'rock solid' against any concessions to the hunger-strikers or the Provisionals. She doubted whether the answer to the present situation could be as simple as a statement by her or an announcement of an enquiry into prison conditions. However, she agreed that the suggestion of an enquiry into prison conditions should be analysed further. She also agreed that a gesture towards the Catholic community should be made, and that it should be made by her in Northern Ireland. If she were to go to Belfast, her visit must have a purpose and should encompass a meeting with religious leaders. She would be prepared, if necessary, to visit in the very near future and to make a statement or be interviewed on TV while there. The Prime Minister requested, therefore, that urgent consideration should be given to the timing of her visit and to the programme for that visit.[69]

In fact, the urgency of what the Prime Minister had just heard led her to decide to visit Northern Ireland the very next day. Operation TUSSORE was put into immediate effect. TUSSORE was the operational codeword, passed to the NIO, the receipt of which meant: 'Visit of the Prime Minister to Northern Ireland'. Knowledge of the codeword and its meaning was controlled on the strictest possible need-to-know basis. The codeword was changed after each visit, whether or not it had been compromised by 'incorrect use, unauthorised communication of its meaning, or through a security breach.'[70] Thus, Mrs Thatcher arrived in Belfast, on 28 May, and delivered a major speech at a Stormont Castle lunch. She said:

> The security forces are the targets of PIRA terrorism; the Protestant community of their threats, the Catholic community of their intimidation.
>
> Faced with the failure of their discredited cause, the men of violence have chosen in recent months to play what may well be their last card. They have turned their violence against themselves through the prison hunger strike to death. They seek to work on the most basic of human emotions – pity – as a means of creating tension and stoking the fires of bitterness and hatred.
>
> In doing so the PIRA have put the Catholic Community on the rack ... People say that something must be wrong when such things can happen. They are right. But the present situation is not of the Government's choosing. It is a tragedy that young men should be persuaded, coerced or ordered to starve themselves to death for a futile cause. Neither I nor any of my colleagues wish to see a single person die of violence in Northern Ireland – policemen, soldier, civilian or prisoner on hunger strike.

The PIRA take a different view. It would seem that dead hunger strikers, who have extinguished their own lives, are of more use to PIRA than living members. Such is their calculated cynicism ... Some people argue that the Government could make the problem go away. We can of course maintain and improve an already humane prison regime. But there is no point in pretending that this is what the PIRA want. They have remained inflexible and intransigent in the face of all that we have done because what they want is special treatment, treatment different from that received by other prisoners. They want their violence justified. It isn't, and it will not be ... the Government cannot bring peace and tranquillity. These things are not in our gift. The necessary will, desire and understanding can only come from the hearts and minds of men and women here in the Province. No Government can make people thoughtful and considerate towards one and other. Only they themselves can do that.[71]

Afterwards, in an interview, Mrs Thatcher confirmed that she would not bend on the hunger strike: 'You can't compromise with violence, ever. You have to beat it.' The fast could be ended at any time: 'I don't wish a single person to die that way. It could be ended any time by those who are in charge saying "Look, enough". It is up to them. I am not going to compromise with what is right. They want political status. That is to say they want to be treated differently from other prisoners. That they can never have. Murder is murder – whatever the motive.' There could be no compromise for that, 'and if there were I should be putting the lives of hundreds and thousands of men, women and children at stake. It is for them to end it. It is they who are being inflexible, intransigent, coldy, brutally cynical in the way they are carrying it out.' Asked if she was inflexible, the Prime Minister was emphatic: 'In upholding the rule of law, in defending people impartially, in standing out against violence, I am inflexible. Remember that is the same thing as saying "I am resolute".'[72]

While decrying publicly the level of support that the Provisionals enjoyed, the Prime Minister was prepared in private, as for instance in a meeting with Protestant Churchmen, to admit that 'whatever view might be held of the PIRA or the hunger strikers, there was a good deal of sympathy on the Catholic side for republican principles.' But Mrs Thatcher believed that good relations between the two communities could only be built if the Government were successful in implementing the 'fundamental duty imposed upon Government of enforcing the law and preserving order.' The Prime Minister also confided to the Churchmen that, while she realized that the long-term aims of many members of the two communities were irreconcilable, she 'would like to be able to hope that people's desire to improve the lot of their children and families would prove to be an obstacle to widespread support for disorder, but she feared that her hope would not be realised in Northern Ireland.'[73] As she prepared to leave Northern Ireland, Mrs Thatcher penned a note to Cardinal Ó Fiaich, who had been unable to attend a meeting with her at such short notice, and offered a talk with her in London.[74]

When the Prime Minister returned that evening to London, she was furious at what she found had developed with the ECHR initiative. At a meeting with Atkins on 18 May, the Prime Minster had indicated that she had no wish to see the Government involved with the 'friendly settlement' procedure that was one of the steps normally gone through by the ECHR in dealing with complaints under the Convention. The Commission had now written formally to inform the Government that it had declared admissible the complaints in the Maze case under Articles 8 and 13, and had invited the Government to submit any proposals HMG wished to make with a view to arriving at a 'friendly settlement'. In this connection, they also invited HMG to send someone to an informal meeting with them (they were inviting representatives of the 'other side' to meet them separately). These steps were part of the normal procedures of the Commission. Atkins had been considering how to respond to this invitation. It was essential, in his view, that HMG handle the ECHR's involvement in the Northern Ireland prisons issues as one of the many strands in the presentation of the Government's case, at home and abroad, over the weeks leading up to the next series of hunger strike deaths: 'The substance of our case is firmness (of course), coupled with a reasonable approach to all who share our concern at the futile loss of life in Northern Ireland' he told the Prime Minister in a minute. It was with this overriding consideration in mind that he assessed the Government's options as follows:

(a) to turn it down flat. This would give the other side the opportunity (which they would be sure to exploit) to blame us publicly for having killed any possibility of ending the prison impasse, and would have a damaging effect on the Catholic section of the Northern Ireland community. It would also, in the view of the FCO, be bad for our general relations with the Commission (with whom we have a wide range of dealings going far beyond NI);

(b) we could seek a postponement of the ground that we need more time to think. That would give the impression that we were contemplating proposals to put forward, and, since we are not, it could only generate later disappointment; and

(c) we could seek a way of responding positively which will nevertheless avoid any danger of our being sucked into any kind of negotiation or give the impression that we were seeking a friendly settlement.

(d) above seems the best course, not because we are in the game of looking for a compromise, but in the interests of maintaining good relations with the Commission and, more crucially, because of the need to counter the main thrust of PIRA's propaganda.

Atkins, therefore, proposed to the Prime Minister that 'we should send one or more officials' to Strasbourg, briefed to speak on the following line – a line to which they must adhere strictly. It would run as follows:

> The Government has from way back been very flexible in its readiness to improve the regime for all prisoners in the interests of being humanitarian. (At this point they would offer the Commission a 'bout de papier' ... which would set out the various steps taken over the last 18 months (most in response to the Commission's own criticisms of last June) to make available better conditions to both conforming and protesting prisoners). However, although flexible, there are certain points of principle on which the Government, for moral and practical reasons, has not been, and will not be, prepared to budge, viz no differentiation for particular groups of prisoners; and no ceding of control by the authorities to the prisoners over day-to-day life in the prison. (Here it would be pointed out that the first half of the 'bout de papier' consists of a statement of these principles). Thus the Government, while standing firm on certain important issues, has in fact gone far to meet the case for improved conditions, whereas the protestors have not moved one inch from their demands. [Here Mrs Thatcher scribbled: 'This implies that if they moved we would move.']
>
> We have no proposals of our own to put forward, but we should – subject always to our points of principle – be prepared to consider anything the other party may put forward. ['No No No' was the Prime Minister's comment here.]

In this way Atkins believed that it would be possible to:

(a) maintain our good relations with the Commission;
(b) strike the right balance between firmness on points of principle and a readiness – which we have already stated publicly – to consider proposals from responsible bodies (although we have none of our own to offer); ['It doesn't strike a balance at all', wrote Mrs Thatcher]
(c) demonstrate how far we have already moved to improve the prison regime in Northern Ireland, and how inflexible the other side have been; and
(d) reassure the Catholic population in Northern Ireland (and many others abroad – eg the Irish Americans) that we are not dismissive of the interests of the prisoners with whom they have natural sympathies.

As time was short, Atkins hoped that he could be informed by early the next day whether the Prime Minister was content with this proposal. She was not: Mrs Thatcher's parting broadside on it was that: 'This letter must have been written and the policy decided before we left Belfast today. I am utterly dismayed and very angry that at no time today was it raised with me', even though Atkins 'knew how strongly I felt about it.'[75] Instead she made a number points that were then written up and passed on for Atkins to implement:

(a) The representative who goes to Strasbourg ... – or one of the representatives – should be a legal expert fully conversant with the relevant law;

(b) It must be made clear that, as the Attorney General said during the meeting with the Prime Minister on 18 May (Clive Whitmore's letter to you of 19 May refers), we regard our position on admissibility as fully preserved and that we shall, if necessary, be prepared to argue our case at a later date;

(c) ... HMG are of course prepared to facilitate the work of the ECHR in examining complaints under Articles 8 and 13 of the Convention and in ascertaining the relevant facts. However, as far as we are concerned, the only complaint at present extant is that under Article 8, relating to correspondence. In the absence of any other complaint, the Prime Minister assumes that action under Article 13 will relate to Article 8;

(d) As far as the friendly settlement procedure is concerned, HMG have no proposals to bring forward. We assume that if anyone else has proposals to make these will be submitted to the ECHR in the normal way;

(e) The Prime Minister has no objection to the points set out in the 'bout de papier' ... being put across provided it is made crystal clear that our making them in no way implies that they are the subject of negotiation;

(f) You may think that, in the light of (d) and (e) above, the final two sentences of the brief summarised in your letter should read as follows:
'The Government, while standing firm on these issues, has of course made major improvements in prison conditions. These are summarised in the attached "bout de papier". We have no proposals of our own to put forward under the friendly settlements procedure. We assume that proposals which any other party wishes to put forward will be submitted to the Commission in the normal way.'

Mrs Thatcher wanted it made it clear to Atkins that while she was prepared to see the ECHR carrying out their duties in the manner outlined above, she was not prepared to appear to be seen to be negotiating about prison conditions through the ECHR. She 'would regard it as particularly damaging for this impression to be created in the immediate aftermath of her visit to Belfast.'[76]

While the Prime Minister may have been upset with how the NIO were handling the ECHR initiative, there were plenty, in Nationalist Ireland, who were dismayed by her performance in the North. In Dublin there was anger at the tone and content of Mrs Thatcher's speech. Following discussions with Dermot Nally, Neligan instructed Dr Kennedy: 'we are of opinion that having regard to the timing and content of PM's statement of 28 May you should seek very early opportunity' to see Sir Kenneth Stowe; the Ambassador was to base his remarks on the notes Nally jotted down concerning the speech. The Secretary General to the Cabinet complained that the speech made:

1. No recognition of the damage being done in the way of IRA recruitment, sympathy for their cause amongst the Catholic population (eg 70,000 at Sands funeral) and in the middle of an election here, where this sort of hard line attitude only creates support for the H-Block sympathisers.
2. The more fundamental lack of appreciation of where the fault and its remedy lie. The short-term answer may be in an humanitarian prison regime or in security or law and order measures, but the long-term answer can only come from a recognition of the cause of the trouble and from policies to remove that cause.
3. From certain contacts we get the impression that the H-Blockers may be looking for a way out. If they are a solution is not being made any more easy – and may in fact be put further off – by the repetition of the line in the speech.

Regarding paragraph 1 above, Neligan added to Kennedy:

… you will know of the hostile reception given to T[aoisech] yesterday in Bundoran and Ballyshannon and the intensifying pressure on him in domestic political terms. Neither in this respect nor in his personal relations with Mrs Thatcher is he at all helped by hard line clumsily timed British Government statements.

A further point was the Prime Minister's reference to the avoidance of the legitimation of the hunger-strikers' cause by word or deed. This was an understandable concern, 'but what do the British authorities consider that the granting (and the present maintenance) of special category status did for the "cause" of those convicted between 1972 and 1976? Did it legitimate it? Does it not still do so? The situation is not black and white and absolutist statements will not make it so. More politics and less morality might be recommended.'[77]

NOTES

1 PRONI NIO/12/197A Meeting with the Chief Constable and GOC held in PUS' Office Belfast on 5 May 1981.
2 PRONI NIO/12/197A Blatherwick to Wyatt, 6 May 1981.
3 TF House OF Commons PQ, 5 May 1981.
4 TNA CJ4/36329 Protests and Second Hunger Strike - Weekly Bulletin No. 10 0900 Hours Thursday 30 April – 0900 Hours Thursday 7 May.
5 TNA CJ4/36329 Dublin to FCO Telegram Number 142 of 06 May 1981.
6 TNA CJ4/36329 Dublin to FCO Telegram Number 144 of 07 May.
7 TNA PREM 19/50 Dublin to FCO Telegram Number 141 of 5 May 1981.
8 NAI D/T 2011/127/1053 Neligan Note, 6 May 1981.
9 TNA CJ4/36329 Washington to FCO Telegram Number 1409 of 6 May.
10 TNA CJ4/36329 Washington to FCO Telegram Number 1410 of 6 May.
11 TNA CJ4/36329 Washington to FCO Telegram Number 1430 of 7 May.
12 TF Letter to Senators Kennedy and Moynihan, Congressman O'Neill and Governor Carey (Northern Ireland), 14 May 1981.
13 TNA CJ4/36329 Washington to NIO London Telegram No. 001 of 8 May 1981.
14 TNA CJ4/3630 Protests and Second Hunger Strike – Weekly Bulletin No 11 0900 Hours Thursday 7 May – 0900 Hours Thursday 14 May.
15 TNA CJ4/36329 Protests and Second Hunger Strike - Weekly Bulletin No. 10 0900 Hours Thursday 30 April – 0900 hours Thursday 7 May.
16 TNA CJ4/36329 Note of a meeting with Chief Constable and GOC held in PUS' Office Belfast on 8 May.
17 PRONI NIO/12/197A Note of a Meeting with the Chief Constable and GOC held in PUS' Office, Belfast on 9 May.
18 PRONI NIO/12/197A Note of a Meeting with the Chief Constable and GOC held in PUS' Office on 11 May 1981.
19 TNA CJ4/3630 Protests and Second Hunger Strike – Weekly Bulletin No 11 0900 Hours Thursday 7 May – 0900 Hours Thursday 14 May.
20 TNA CJ4/3630 Protests and Second Hunger Strike – Weekly Bulletin No 11 0900 Hours Thursday 7 May – 0900 Hours Thursday 14 May.
21 *Daily Telegraph*, 12 May 1981.
22 TNA CJ4/3630 Paris to FCO Telegram Number 356 of 13 May 1981.
23 TNA CJ4/3630 Paris to FCO Telegram Number 364 of 15 May 1981.
24 TNA CJ4/36329 Dublin to FCO Telegram Number 149 of 11 May 1981.
25 TNA PREM 19/504 Dublin to FCO Telegram Number 153 of 13 May 1981.
26 TNA PREM 19/504 Alexander to Harrington, 12 April 1981.
27 NAI D/T 2011/127/1056 Call on Prime Minister.
28 TNA PREM 19/504 Record of a conversation between the Prime Minister and the Irish Ambassador, Dr Eamon Kennedy, at 10 Downing Street on 13 May at 1805 Hours.
29 NAI D/T 2011/127/1056 Call on Prime Minister.
30 TNA PREM 19/504 Record of a conversation between the Prime Minister and the Irish Ambassador.
31 NAI D/T 2011/127/1056 Call on Prime Minister
32 TNA PREM 19/504 Record of a conversation between the Prime Minister and the Irish Ambassador.
33 NAI D/T 2011/127/1056 Call on Prime Minister.
34 TNA PREM 19/504 Record of a conversation between the Prime Minister and the Irish Ambassador.

35 NAI D/T 2011/127/1056 Call on Prime Minister.

36 TNA CJ4/3630 Protests and Second Hunger Strike – Weekly Bulletin No 11 0900 Hours Thursday 7 May – 0900 Hours Thursday 14 May.

37 TNA CJ4/3630 Note for the Record: Removal of Francis Hughes' Body to Bellaghy, 13 May 1981.

38 PRONI NIO/12/197A Note of a Meeting between the Chief Constable and the CLF held in PUS' Office, Belfast on 14 May.

39 PRONI NIO/12/197A Note of a Meeting with the Chief Constable and the GOC in PUS's Office, Belfast on Friday 15 May 1981.

40 TNA CJ4/3630 Protests and Second Hunger Strike – Weekly Bulletin No 12 0900 Hours Thursday 14 May – 0900 Hours Thursday, 21 May.

41 TNA CJ4/3630 Protests and Second Hunger Strike – Weekly Bulletin No 11 0900 Hours Thursday 7 May – 0900 Hours, Thursday 14 May.

42 TNA CJ4/3630 Protests and Second Hunger Strike – Weekly Bulletin No 12 0900 Hours Thursday 14 May – 0900 Hours, Thursday 21 May.

43 PRONI NIO/12/197A Note for the Record Hunger Strike 2 – Raymond McCreesh.

44 PRONI NIO/12/197A L Nolan, Hospital Senior Officer 96 to the Governor.

45 PRONI NIO/12/197A Paul Lennon, 628 to the Governor.

46 PRONI NIO/12/197A J McAleavey 747 Hospital Officer Statement, 18 May.

47 TNA PREM 19/504 Ingam to Thorne, 19 May 1981.

48 PRONI NIO/12/197A Statement on behalf of McCreesh Family, 20 May.

49 NAI D/T 2011/127/1053 Ministers visit to Strasbourg (13–14 May 1981).

50 TNA PREM 19/504 Note by the Principal Private Secretary, 19 May 1981.

51 TNA PREM 19/504 Armstrong to Prime Minister, 19 May 1981.

52 TNA CJ4/3630 Protests and Second Hunger Strike – Weekly Bulletin No 12 0900 Hours Thursday 14 May – 0900 Hours Thursday 21 May.

53 TNA CJ4/3630 Notes of a Meeting with the Chief Constable and GOC held in PUS's Office, Belfast, on Wednesday 20 May 1981.

54 NAI D/T 2011/127/1054 News Service: The Prime Minister The Rt Hon Margaret Thatcher MP (Barnet, Finchley) Speaking at the 51st Annual Conservative Women's Conference, 'Women and Employment' at Central Hall, Westminster, London SW1.

55 TNA PREM 19/505 Clive Whitmore to Stephen Boys-Smith, 21 May 1981.

56 TNA PREM 19/505 Telegram number 1577 of 20 May 1981.

57 TNA PREM 19/505 Whitmore to McCreesh, 20 May 1981.

58 TNA CJ4/3630 Protests and Second Hunger Strike – Weekly Bulletin No 12 0900 Hours Thursday 14 May – 0900 Hours Thursday 21 May.

59 TNA CJ4/3630 PRONI CJ4/3630 Notes of a Meeting with the Chief Constable and GOC held in PUS's Office, Belfast, on Wednesday 20 May 1981.

60 TNA CJ4/3630 Protests and Second Hunger Strike - Weekly Bulletin No 12 0900 Hours Thursday 14 May – 0900 Hours Thursday 21 May.

61 *An Phoblacht,* 12 June 1981.

62 TNA CJ4/3630 Protests and Second Hunger Strike – Weekly Bulletin No 12 0900 Hours Thursday 14 May – 0900 Hours Thursday 21 May.

63 PRONI NIO/12/197A Note of a Meeting with the Chief Constable and the GOC held in the PUS's Office, Belfast on 22 May 1981.

64 TNA CJ4/3630 Protests and Second Hunger Strike – Weekly Bulletin No 13 0900 Hours Thursday 21 May – 0900 Hours Thursday 28 May.

65 TNA CJ4/3630 Dublin to FCO Telegram Number 172A of 25 May 1981.

66 TNA PREM 19/505 Northern Ireland: The Protestant Community Northern Ireland Office, 26 May 1981.

67   TNA PREM 19/505 Northern Ireland: The Catholic Community Northern Ireland Office, 26 May 1981.
68   TNA PREM 19/505 Security Brief A.
69   TNA PREM 19/505 Michael Alexander to Stephen Boys-Smith, 27 May 1981.
70   TNA PREM 19/503 Visits to Northern Ireland by the Prime Minister – Instructions for Use of Codeword, 11 March 1981.
71   TF Speech at Stormont Castle lunch, 28 May 1981.
72   TF TV Interview for ITN, May 28 1981.
73   Prime Minister's Meeting with Northern Ireland Church Leaders: 3.00 p.m. Thursday 28 May 1981, Stormont Castle.
74   Mrs Thatcher to Cardinal Ó Fiaich, 28 May 1981.
75   TNA PREM 19/505 S. W. Boys-Smith to Alexander, 28 May 1981.
76   TNA PREM 19/505 Note of Prime Minister's comments.
77   NAI D/T 2011/127/1053 For Ambassador from Neligan: Mrs Thatcher's speech yesterday.

Chapter 8

Persuading the British

At his own request, John Hume called on Sir Kenneth Stowe on 29 May. Hume's first theme was that the SDLP had fought the recent local elections in the most difficult of conditions – under attack from former members Gerry Fitt and Paddy Devlin on the one hand and from Republicans on the other, and without any help from HMG – yet they had held the Roman Catholic community. The SDLP had 3,000 more first-preference votes than in 1977, more seats than when the elections were called and control of two councils. This underlined the SDLP's identity with the Catholic community and gave him a mandate to speak on their behalf. He emphasized that the SDLP vote had held up particularly well in those areas – Derry and West Belfast – where the community had been most exposed to the reality of the hunger strike issue. On the hunger strike, he argued that the Government (exemplified by the Prime Minister's remarks) had completely failed to comprehend the minority community's complex attitude of disapproval and understanding towards PIRA terrorism and the hunger-strikers. If the situation were not 'switched off', the bitterness in the minority community would grow.

The decision of Brendan McLaughlin to end his hunger strike – his ulcer meant that he would have died very quickly – provided a 'window' before the next death, which gave HMG the opportunity to do something. Hume's main point was that HMG's interests would be advanced if the ending of the hunger strike were associated with the moderate, democratically elected leaders of the minority. It would also be in his own political interests – the Catholic 'protest' vote would return to the SDLP and double its strength – but it offered substantial and tangible benefits to HMG. Hume repeated an earlier suggestion of his that the occasion of Governor Hilditch's replacement might provide an opportunity to end the hunger strike, and suggested that HMG publicly exhort the new Governor to interpret the prison regime flexibly. He did not pursue this too far, however, once Stowe had demonstrated that the possibilities for liberalization only covered the surface of the main struggle for control within the prison.

Hume's main proposition was that HMG should make the two adjustments to the prison regime that he had been advocating, and should do so as the culmination of a series of meetings between HMG and the SDLP (and Cardinal Ó Fiaich), which was likely to build up speculation about a possible solution and enable the point to be reached at which, when the adjustments were announced, they had the public endorsement of Hume and the Cardinal. The hunger-strikers would either take the excuse to give up, without HMG having sacrificed any principle, or would – by being made to appear intransigent – lose their support in the Catholic community and internationally, and thus be forced to give up later. Hume also reported a suggestion from Mrs Lynch, mother of the third current hunger-striker, that the hunger-strikers' mothers should meet the Prime Minister. Stowe, however, held out no hope that this suggestion would be taken up. Hume explained that he had spent the previous evening with Lynch's parents, who were 'typical decent anti-IRA people', who would disown their son if ever he were released, but were understandably willing to do almost anything to prevent his death.[1]

Just in case the Government had not got the message from the Irish or the SDLP, when D. J. Wyatt of the NIO called on Edward Daly in Derry on 29 May, the Bishop made it plain that he 'resented our attempts' to persuade him and Cardinal Ó Fiaich to endorse (as he put it) the Prime Minister's speech in Stormont Castle the day before. The speech, and the subsequent interviews, had merely repeated the Prime Minister's disastrous line of 'no surrender'. She had been entirely negative and cold. Her attempts to distinguish between the Provos and the Catholic population were pointless when nearly every family in the Bogside and Creggan, and in West Belfast, had relatives in the Maze, or had friends with relatives there. It was simply not true to say that the Provisionals had no support, and to state that their cause was discredited was a significant error: it was their means, not their goal of a united Ireland, which were unacceptable. 'And so on.' Neither Daly nor the Cardinal could risk being present on such occasions. He still smarted from being similarly conned (in his words) some time before. Moreover, the NIO could not simply summon the Cardinal to a meeting at a few hours' notice: 'and when we tried, we might at least have the decency to tell him, and the Bishop himself, that it was to meet the Prime Minister. A confidential message could be passed if necessary through the local RUC chief. Did we think him not trustworthy?'

Bishop Daly nevertheless thought that it might soon be time for a *private* meeting between him, the Cardinal and the Secretary of State in order to run over the ground. Things were 'not well' in Derry. Active support for the Provos was growing, and men released from the Maze who had hitherto kept out of trouble were slipping back into the Provisionals. People were bitter, frustrated and longing to get the hunger strike over with. There was a dangerous feeling that the Troubles had gone on too long, and so 'let's get it all over with', either way, once and for all. Wyatt and Daly then spoke about the hunger strike, on familiar lines. The Bishop thought that the only way forward might be for an international body of impeccable standing (the ECHR might best fit this bill) to make recommendations (for example that *all* prisoners should be allowed to wear their own clothes all the time), which the Government could implement without compromising on political status. He accepted that the Provisionals might not be ready for a compromise, but thought that the Catholic community would put such pressure on them that at best they would settle and at worst would range Catholic sentiment firmly against them. The important need was for some move by the Government. Despite their differences, Wyatt found that Bishop Daly was friendly throughout and seemed anxious to talk.[2]

In his assessment of the Prime Minister's speech, the NIO's Blatherwick acknowledged that it:

> ... has gone down in the Catholic community like a lead balloon. Anyone I have told – Catholic or Protestant – that the chief purpose of the Prime Minister's visit was to reassure Catholic opinion, has been incredulous. All they have seen or heard is the Prime Minister repeating a policy of no surrender to the IRA, and saying again in interviews that a crime is a crime.

The result of the Prime Minister's visit had been further to alienate Catholics, and to cause even more moderate Protestants to 'wonder what we are at.' When people of influence read in full what the Prime Minister said (and her speech had been widely circulated), 'we may be able to claw back some of the ground lost – though the vast majority of Northerners will not read it, and unfavourable initial impressions will stick. We can hope to exploit the "softer" parts of what the Prime Minister said, for example by amplifying them in public statements.'

A major aim, thought Blatherwick, must be to try to get the Catholic hierarchy on board again. Bishop Daly seemed to be in favour of a meeting between the Secretary of State and the Cardinal, which would need some groundwork before it could be set up. Wyatt hoped that a message to the Cardinal, even at this late stage, might offer a way both to set the ball rolling for a meeting and to get the message of reassurance to the Catholic community across in more explicit terms:

> This is all very well so far as it goes. However, virtually all my contacts agree that though impressions of concern for the Catholic community might well slow the process of their gradual alienation from Government in the short term, only the end of the hunger strike will stop it and enable us to begin reversing the trend; and that unless the hunger strike ends soon, probably before the next hunger strikers die and certainly before the beginning of the marching season, the situation will then begin to deteriorate rapidly.

Blatherwick noted that the hunger strike and security problems had mesmerized everyone (including, in popular opinion, HMG). Many people would have liked to see the Government start some political process in order to give the community something positive to think about in the future and to show that politics, not violence, offered a way forward. Few would advocate launching an initiative at this time, 'but it is perhaps not too soon to start talking about the need for political movement', thought Blatherwick.[3]

What that might be remained unclear, but outside the political bubble of the NIO and Whitehall, one suggestion, on 3 June, was raised by a Catholic lay organization, the Irish Commission for Justice and Peace (ICJP). It suggested:

(i)   that prisoners in the Maze, who are at present permitted to wear their own clothes for a great part of the time should, like the prisoners in Armagh, be allowed to do so at all times;

(ii)   that some moves might be made to increase opportunities for association while making it clear that military training, or any other activity which would be illegal in society at large, would not be tolerated in the prisons; and

(iii) that the question of prison work should be reviewed both in order to ensure that the work is of the greatest possible cultural and educational value and that no work of a demeaning nature is demanded.

If these reforms were implemented *throughout* the Northern Ireland prison system, this would not constitute the granting of 'political status', to which the Commission had already indicated that it would be opposed.[4] The ICJP was also keen to emphasize that it had no political leanings and that: 'The most fundamental human right is the right to life. The Irish Commission for Justice and Peace in no way condones crimes, like those of which many prisoners in the Maze have been convicted, which violate or endanger that right.'[5] The ICJP proposals were seized upon by the Roman Catholic Hierarchy: on 17 June, at the Irish Catholic Bishops' Conference, in Maynooth, Co Kildare, they (including Ó Fiaich) issued a major statement on the 'evils' blighting lives in the Troubles and the hunger strike:

> Many of these evils spring from the existence of private armies or paramilitary organisations which claim the right to wage war. Not only have they sent out their members to carry out cruel and murderous deeds, but they have been responsible for leading young people into evil by urging them to acts of violence. We make our own the appeal which our Holy Father made in Drogheda to the young people of Ireland.
>
> If you have been caught up in the ways of violence, even if you have done deeds of violence, come back to Christ, whose parting gift to the

world was peace. Only when you come back to Christ will you find peace for your troubled conscience and rest for your disturbed minds.

We are not unmindful, however, of the injustice in Northern Ireland over the years which created a climate for easy recruitment by paramilitary organisations...

We appeal also to politicians and Governments and we remind them of the solemn words of the Pope in Drogheda:

'To all who bear political responsibility for the affairs of Ireland, I want to speak with the same urgency and intensity with which I have spoken to the men of violence. Do not cause or condone or tolerate conditions which give excuse or pretext to men of violence. Those who resort to violence always claim that only violence brings about change. They claim that political action cannot achieve justice. You politicians must prove them to be wrong. You must show that there is a peaceful, political way to justice. You must show that peace achieves the works of justice, and violence does not.'

At this critical juncture we welcome the recent statement on the hunger strike from the Irish Commission for Justice and Peace and we commend it to both sides as a positive effort to find a way out of the impasse. Like the Commission we call on both sides to give an indication of their willingness to move towards a solution. We ask the prisoners and those who speak for them to make it clear that the Commission's proposals on clothing, association and work would, if implemented, provide the avenue for a solution. We ask the Government to show a corresponding openness on these issues.[6]

For now though, Atkins was entranced by the need for some urgent political initiative alongside one for the prisons. On 12 June, Atkins circulated, to the Prime Minister, two papers for discussion; they were also to be distributed among colleagues on the OD Committee. One dealt with the political situation in Northern Ireland; the other with the prisons. The two groups of problems, although set out separately, were closely interrelated, Atkins argued. Each, within its own field, proposed a new development in the policies HMG had pursued so far. It seemed to Atkins essential that, in reading these papers, his colleagues should have before them an explanation of 'why I think the time for movement has now come':

On politics, we have said for two years, in two White Papers, that we were looking for the agreement of the local parties, and could not move without that agreement – any move had to be 'acceptable' to both sides of the community. I am now convinced:

(a) that the prospects of such agreement, never good, have receded in recent months;

(b) that we cannot stand still for the remainder of this Parliament on political development in the North while continuing to pursue – as we are committed to doing – the development of relations with Dublin; and

(c) that we must therefore contemplate taking a unilateral step now, looking for support to Westminster.

On prisons, we have over the last eight months stood firm against the hunger strikers and their demands. And I am quite clear that on our points of principle (no differentiation; and no loss of control) we must continue as firm as ever.

But there was both room and, Atkins believed, need for movement. He was, therefore, proposing the setting up of a Committee to advise on some difficult medium- and long-term problems that HMG faced, which could also, if they so chose, be charged with the more urgent role of providing a possible way of easing the short-term impasse. These two moves were linked: 'We have not been wrong in seeking the agreement of local political parties to constitutional change. We have certainly not been wrong in standing firm on the prisons issue.' But:

(i) I believe there is increasingly a mood in the country that if we cannot do something about the Northern Ireland problem, we should consider withdrawal. The message which I get loud and clear from every contact I have with broad public and political opinion – including particularly backbench Conservative opinion related by the officers of the Party's Northern Ireland Committee – is that the time has come for us to be seen to be making moves, on both fronts, political and prisons, since they reinforce each other. We are not winning friends by doing nothing.

(ii) On the political front it is clear from all our efforts of the past two years that acceptability is a chimera. We were right to try to find it. We should be foolish to refuse to acknowledge that it is not to be found. If by the next election we wish to be seen to have made some progress, we must be bold enough to proclaim and pursue a course in spite of local disagreement.

(iii) On prisons, apart from the longer term problems (which we have to face in any case), I now feel strongly that a continuing, apparently endless, series of deaths from hunger strikes will cumulatively lose us both the Catholic population of Northern Ireland and the sympathy of the world opinion. We may outface the hunger strikers; but we shall pay a heavy price for doing so. In my view we must be seen at least to have tried to facilitate a lessening of tension, perhaps leading to a way of ending the strikes. In the perception of the outside world the line between firmness and intransigence is a narrow one.

With these considerations in mind, Atkins proposed the appointment of some kind of Departmental Committee to consider and advise on the problems in Northern Irish prisons. On politics, it was as impracticable as ever to set up without the agreement of the parties to any new body exercising *executive* powers: 'I am therefore proposing that we should establish an elected advisory body, being an arrangement which we could, if necessary, impose.'[7]

Atkins was anxious for some feedback on his proposals, and asked Leonard Figg for his comments on the prison review when the Ambassador paid a brief visit to Belfast on 16 June. As he informed the FCO later: 'I said I thought the mood in the Republic about the hunger strike was hardening against us following the surprisingly high vote for the H-Block Committees candidates in the recent elections.' The rights and wrongs of the matter were beginning to be obscured there by the fear that 'we are perhaps allowing the strike to get out of control and failing to recognise or counter its dangerous side effects – polarisation in the North and hostility to Britain and possible turbulence in the South.' Before the election it was hoped that HMG's 'open and enlightened' attitude to moves by the ECHR would – if not resolve the question – at least isolate the Provisionals from their 'humanitarian' fellow travellers ('who are now clearly more numerous than we thought and whose numbers are still growing'). The ECHR initiative was now seen to have run into the sand. 'What I think is wanted is some new way of drawing in respectable and well-known foreigners, perhaps from within the European Community, in any new initiative we may contemplate', concluded Figg. The proposed prison review might be a convenient way of doing this, argued the Ambassador, who warned that, in the present emotional state generated by the hunger strike deaths:

> ... we must try and get out of our present difficulty whereby Irish men are seen to die in British prisons and the British can't or don't want to stop them. A review in which well-known foreign legal luminaries participated would help internationalise our difficulties, and, provided of course that the foreigners played their proper part, might at last turn the tide in our favour.[8]

In a minute to Mrs Thatcher, Sir Robert Armstrong offered his thoughts on the situation. He pointed out that while the security forces did not doubt that they could contain the terrorists, they were concerned that the hunger strike deaths were now associated with street violence, which was no doubt well orchestrated, but involved people well beyond the hard core of terrorists: they were apprehensive about the reappearance of 'no-go' areas in Belfast. If the street violence continued, there was a possibility of the security forces being 'goaded' beyond endurance and becoming involved in 'another "bloody Sunday" type of incident', which would alienate international opinion, particularly in the Republic of Ireland and the United States. The difficulties would increase when, as seemed likely, a regular series of strikers' deaths began to take place every ten to fourteen days, starting early the following month and continuing into the indefinite future. In the Irish election, the H-Block candidates did better than anyone had predicted, polling over 42,000 first-preference votes and getting two members elected in border constituencies. This suggested that the Fermanagh by-election was 'not a passing phenomenon', warned Armstrong. The questions posed by Atkins' memoranda presented an acutely difficult balancing of political judgement. Either way, 'a little bad luck could bring us on to a slippery downhill slope in relation to our entire policy towards Northern Ireland.' Progress down this slope might be accelerated by further hunger strike deaths, and a growing 'troops out' movement in Great Britain. But it could also be accelerated (if the Chief Constable and the GOC were right) by the lack of any modification in the Government's stance: 'If we get the balance wrong, we might be forced into thinking in very different terms from the limited sorts of initiative now under discussion', cautioned Armstrong. Ministers must take seriously the view of the Chief Constable and the GOC that the setting up of a Departmental Committee on the prison system would reassure the Catholics of the Government's sense of concern, and would thus ease the burden of maintaining law and order. But it would probably enrage the Protestants: it would be seen by them and by the PIRA as a sign of weakness, and it seemed unlikely that it would persuade the hunger-strikers to give up, even if it did not actually strengthen their belief that they were winning. It could all too easily be seen as a move towards arbitration, and thus as a sign of the Government losing political control.

As regarded political progress, Atkins' proposal for an elected advisory body had been under consideration for a long time, Armstrong reminded the Prime Minister; it had been discussed and rejected in 1979. It might, however, be welcome initially to international opinion, as an indication of political movement. But in Northern Ireland it could be a 'damp squib: and it could end all too easily as a "talking shop" which would be a source of damaging criticism of Government policy but would not accept any responsibility for constructive action.' In judging the balance between action and inaction, the essential criterion must be the need not to jeopardize the very real assets that HMG still retained. The improvement in the general security situation had been maintained. In the Irish election, although the H-Block candidates may have done well in the border areas, the overall result was certainly not a victory for the extreme Republicans. It was significant that Síle de Valera lost her seat in Dublin South. Much international opinion had been broadly sympathetic to British policy. Other countries had similar problems, and the West Germans, for example, let their Baader-Meinhof hunger-striker die. The Anglo-Irish joint studies remained a useful link with Dublin that both Haughey and FitzGerald were anxious to preserve. Armstrong's conclusion was thus: 'I find it difficult to believe that this is the right time for launching a proposal for a Departmental Committee in the prison system.' If that view were to be accepted, then the question would be 'whether we could sit still and do nothing, – at least until the autumn – and whether, if it is felt that some move must be made, the political initiative proposed is credible and sufficient on its own.' The Cabinet Secretary also suggested to the Prime Minister that: 'You will also wish to have at the back of your mind the possibility that you may wish to appoint a new Secretary of State before long.' The appointment of a new Secretary of State would itself be an important political event and gesture in Northern Ireland. A new Secretary of State would 'need shots in his political locker', and to launch a political initiative now would, 'to put it at its lowest,' diminish his options.[9]

This was essential advice for the Prime Minister, for Armstrong was someone she trusted and who had considerable experience of dealing with the Northern Irish problem from his days working with Edward Heath during his premiership. Armstrong also forwarded the latest intelligence-based analysis, prepared by the NIO, to Mrs Thatcher. It raised some disconcerting issues. Written by Mr Ronson at the NIO, it recalled how, from time to time and in particular at the beginning of 1981, 'we have considered whether and under what circumstances the Provisionals might switch the focus of their efforts to the political front'. It had, sometimes, been thought that a consequence of this might be a reduction in the amount of energy and effort they put into their terrorist campaign. 'The reality is of course that they have for some months been devoting increasing effort to political action, while continuing the "military campaign" at the lower level which their now limited capabilities permit.'

An important part of the Provisionals' political activity, pointed out Ronson, consisted of seeking to broaden out their support through the H-Block campaign, thus involving uncommitted members of the minority community in peaceful protest in support of Sinn Féin objectives. In a short space of time the Provisionals had demonstrated great skill in manoeuvring cynically and adroitly to attract a significant spectrum of support. The Fermanagh by-election and the Dáil elections were the best illustrations of this: 'We have tended to regard the involvement of the Provisionals in political activity as a development to be encouraged. But it is a development that requires a response from Government, as their terrorist activities receive a response'. There was 'very general' agreement that the Catholic community had been disturbed by the hunger-strikers' deaths, that it blamed the Government, that there was a degree of alienation and that the Provisionals were getting more support. Unless their political exploitation of the hunger strike situation – and the resulting recrudescence of support for the PIRA – could be countered, 'then the Provisionals "going political" can succeed, where their terrorist activity has failed, in reversing the progress of recent years towards "normality" and renewing for them a base from which a revitalised terrorist campaign could be launched.' It was this process that the suggested Prisons Review and a further round of political activity were presumably intended to counter: 'If we could find less controversial and more certain means to achieve the objective no doubt we would do so, but all options are difficult and can, and no doubt will, be criticised.' If it were argued that to have a review of the prisons was to signal that the Government was wavering and if Ministers, on this score, were inclined to reject the proposal, there was surely a counter-argument: 'To take no action in the face of the Provisionals effective political campaign centred on the hunger strikes is not standing firm, but is admitting defeat in the political arena. This will be proved to be so as the Provisionals gather wider support with serious implications for security and law and order.'[10]

If this proved to be accurate, it meant that the entire basis of British strategy towards militant Republicanism since the 1970s of getting them to abandon armed struggle in favour of participation in the political process was under threat: the Government was faced with the possibility of a joint Republican political and military campaign instead. The British Government's immediate options, as suggested by Atkins, suddenly got a lot narrower as Armstrong's concerns, voiced to the Prime Minister, were echoed elsewhere in Whitehall. The OD Committee, composed of senior Ministers, including the Prime Minister, had originally invited Atkins to lay before Cabinet, for consideration on 25 June, a paper that would:

a) consider the composition and terms of reference of a body to advise on the special problems of managing Northern Ireland prisons; and

b) contain a proposal for the establishment of a non-elective political advisory body.

After consulting the Home Secretary, Willie Whitelaw, though, Atkins concluded that he must recommend to the Cabinet that it would be 'inappropriate' to establish, at this moment, the sort of enquiry on prisons that was envisaged by the OD Committee. OD concluded that there would be objections to setting up a Committee related in any way to the hunger strike. Atkins was now persuaded, on the basis of his further examination of the matter, that there were serious objections to announcing *now* the establishment of a committee explicitly unrelated to the hunger strikes and their security implications. The Home Secretary agreed. The reasons were:

a) Either it would be regarded as incredible that we should set up such a body unless it was to concern itself with the immediate problem – we should be suspected of creating a route to give concessions – or it would be seen as fiddling while Rome burns.

b) The international reaction would be especially severe. It would be likely to convict us of precisely the inflexible and inhumane attitude which we are trying to pin on the other side.

c) It would impose an impossible responsibility on the Committee's members. They would be established as a committee to examine the prison regime, but to ignore the hunger strike deaths which would go on around them.

d) An announcement in the terms proposed would have to say that the Committee was not to concern itself with the hunger strike, and so would imply that we were concerned only with getting the special category prisoners into cells. That would be especially provocative to moderate Catholic opinion. We would be seen by them as saying that we were indifferent to the hunger strikers' deaths, and the troubles on the streets.

Atkins regarded those arguments as 'particularly compelling' at a time when the Irish Catholic Bishops, in their statement of the previous week, had 'come out in support of so much of our cause.' They, like the statement of American Bishops also made that week, commended to *both* sides the statement of the ICJP issued on 3 June. Announcing a committee so emphatically unrelated to the hunger strike or these important statements by Catholic opinion 'would be seen as a deliberate rejection of their moderation, even though in several points they support the Government's position.'[11]

From Haughey's perspective, things were looking no better. Two H-Block prisoners – Paddy Agnew and the hunger-striker Kieran Doherty – were elected in the Irish general election, run under a proportional representation system, with the result that Fianna Fáil had been deprived of an overall parliamentary majority in the Dáil. The success of the two H-Blocks TDs coincided with the introduction of a Bill at Westminster designed to disqualify from the UK Parliament convicted prisoners, and providing for disqualification at nomination stage. The prisoners' election, together with the polling of over 42,000 first-preference votes (11% of the total) for NHAC candidates, far exceeded the expectations of the pundits, and David O'Connell, Sinn Fein's Director of Elections (and on the IRA Army Council). The Foreign Minister, Brian Lenihan, felt that there was 'an emotional content' in the vote for the H-Block candidates, adding that: 'There are people who feel seriously about this issue. We in Government regard their stance as in many ways to be ill-advised.' John Hume concluded that it was clear from the results that the North was a serious issue in the minds of Southern voters: 'This is reflected not simply in the H-Blocks votes but in the votes for all the parties', he added. In the general election the prisoner candidates received greatest support in the border areas, generally at the expense of Fianna Fáil. The results enabled NHAC spokesmen and women to renew their pressure. Gerry Adams remarked: 'The considerably weakened incoming Dublin Government, regardless of the composition, has been given a clear warning to move on the prisoners' demands before more hunger strikers' lives are lost'. David O'Connell announced that he was seeking a meeting with the three main political parties in the Republic. His aim was to 'point out that their policies previously pursued were wrong and that a message has come through from the electorate that they expect decisive action on what is a very critical situation.' A statement from the Republican prisoners smuggled out of the Maze declared: 'There can be no doubt now in anyone's mind that the political prisoners have widespread support'.[12]

In his analysis for the FCO, Figg described the achievement, by the NHAC, 'as the biggest surprise in the election.' Before polling, David O'Connell predicted between 2,500 and 3,000 votes for prisoner candidates, which he said would be a credible performance, and the pundits 'all said' that the H-Block candidates would have no significant effect in the outcome of the election. As it was, there could easily have been a third success. In the border constituency of Sligo-Leitrim the hunger-striker Joe McDonnell came close to being elected as a result of high support from young voters in Sligo Town. He might well have been elected but for the burning of a bus belonging to a party of British anglers in Leitrim, which seemed to have alienated support in that part of the constituency because of a decline in the tourist trade caused by the incident. The Cavan-Monaghan seat, considered Figg, could be regained by Fianna Fáil in the event of a by-election caused by the death on hunger strike of Kieran Doherty. But assuming that Paddy Agnew did not go on a hunger strike, the Louth seat would be lost to Fianna Fáil unless an accommodation with the NHAC was reached and Agnew resigned his seat. This outcome, concluded Figg, vindicated Bernadette McAliskey's view that more H-Block candidates should have been fielded: 'It is a sad fact that the H-Block question has now become an active political issue in the Republic and a gloomy version of North-South dimensions.'

The Ambassador thought it was predictable that the highest level of support for the H-Block candidates should have been in the border constituencies, where the level of support for the H-Block movement had been consistently higher than elsewhere in the Republic. Paddy Agnew had the additional advantage that he was a native of Dundalk, which helped explain why he topped the poll in Louth. The H-Block candidates seemed to have received a large measure of support from young voters (14% of the electorate had not voted before) whose subsequent transfers crossed party lines. They may also have profited from the vote of those who, for ideological reasons, had not participated in Dáil elections before because they did not recognize the State.

An interesting feature of the election was that despite the unexpectedly large support for H-Block candidates, sitting Deputies with Republican views did not do well. Síle de Valera lost her seat in Dublin South where Fine Gael won three out of the five seats. In Donegal North-East, Neil Blaney's share of the vote was less than expected, and he was elected on the third count, whereas in 1977 he reached the quota on the first. In Clare, Fianna Fáil deputy Dr Bill Loughnane nearly lost his seat to Fine Gael. This prompted some commentators to suggest that there had been a rearrangement of the traditional Republican heartland: 'but the truth is probably that some deputies lost out because of a combination of poor tactics', concluded Figg (in Clare and Dublin South there were too many Fianna Fáil candidates chasing too few quotas) and insufficient constituency work (Síle de Valera and Neil Blaney were both MEPs and therefore absent much of the time).[13] The seriousness of the political situation was, of course, clear to the decision-makers in London. The day after Figg's dispatch, the Prime Minister responded to a letter from Edward Daly and mentioned, specifically, the ICJP. Mrs Thatcher wrote:

I very much appreciate the full and frank way in which you wrote in your letter of your anxieties about the current situation in your area. I fully share that anxiety, and sought in my recent speech in Belfast to express it clearly and unambiguously. I admire and respect the courage and devotion of Church leaders such as yourself and other leaders who seek in these difficult times to reassure the community and to hold it together. You know that I and my colleagues care deeply about the sufferings of the Catholic community arising from the hunger strike and the disturbances to which it has given rise. The Government is determined to do all that it can to alleviate them and to resume progress towards tackling the wider problems of Northern Ireland.

We will weigh carefully what you say, and what is contained in the document drawn up by the Irish Commission for Justice and Peace. But the Provisionals have made clear what they are after. There must be the gravest danger that any changes made now would simply encourage the Provisionals to press harder. The hunger strike would then be reinforced and with it the continuing distress in the Roman Catholic community.

The next step must be for the hunger strike to end. The pointless waste of young lives, the anguish of relations and friends, the effect of the disturbance in the wider community – all this is of the keenest concern to the Government. The Government has already demonstrated its flexibility in dealing with the prison protests. It is committed to keeping the regime for all prisoners in Northern Ireland under review. We remain ready to facilitate any investigation that the European Human Rights Commission may wish to make in the course of considering the presently outstanding application or any fresh application which may be made.

I realise how the Provisionals are seeking to exploit the issue, and I realise how difficult the resulting situation is for community leaders, as for Government. We must all keep explaining what we are trying to achieve clearly, openly and with the fullest sympathy for what so many are having to bear.[14]

As the Prime Minister dispatched her letter, Paddy Quinn (PIRA) refused breakfast the same day, Monday 15 June, to become the sixth member of the hunger strike. He had been captured alongside Raymond McCreesh as they attempted to ambush an Army patrol in 1976.[15] On the day before Quinn joined the hunger strike, Richard McAuley, of Sinn Féin, announced that the most likely campaign strategy in future would be for one prisoner to begin a hunger strike every seven to ten days. The aim would be to maintain constant pressure on the British Government instead of allowing a respite between the deaths of one wave of hunger-strikers and the next. Father Faul was dismayed by this threatened escalation of the hunger strike. He remarked: 'The new tactic of putting on one new hunger striker a week could lead to a serious loss of life and that was a matter of grave concern … While we deplore the extreme irresponsibility and cruelty of Mrs Thatcher and her Government let us not show the same cruelty and irresponsibility on our own side'. This tactic was soon reconsidered, as announced by Gerry Adams on 17 June. Adams also indicated that Paddy Angew TD would not be one of the two new hunger-strikers.[16]

The Sinn Féin Vice-President was angered, in particular, by the statement issued by the Roman Catholic Bishops' meeting at Maynooth pushing for the ICJP to become involved in the dispute. Adams complained that the Bishops failed to mention the presence of a British Government and its military forces as being in any way instrumental or responsible for the 'serious and deteriorating situation'. That the Irish Bishops, in making comment about political instability in Ireland, had omitted to do this or to examine the effects of the 'British-imposed partition of our country cannot but be regretted by many Irish people. One could speculate that English Bishops if faced by an Irish imposed partition of their country would at least take cognisance of this fact when enumerating the sources from which "many of these evils" spring.' On the issue of the H-Block/Armagh crisis the Bishops were 'less than honest' when they referred to the hunger-strikers and 'those who direct them' and 'the evil of their actions and consequences'. The hunger-strikers, pointed out Adams, only resorted to the hunger strike as a last desperate attempt to win their five reasonable and just demands. The Bishops 'know this, Bishop Daly and Cardinal Ó Fiaich in particular'. Adams urged the Bishops to use their good offices to encourage the British Government to deal directly with the prisoners in an attempt to break the deadlock, and to do so on the basis of the prisoners' five demands. The prisoners were the 'weaker force' in the prison conflict. They deserved the support of all influential people, and of the Church to which many of them belonged, if the British Government's 'death policy' was to be thwarted: 'Such a forthright demand by a powerful body, like the Irish hierarchy, would restore the confidence of many Irish people in the integrity of those in positions of power in Irish religious and secular life. It would also go a long way to save the lives of the present group of hunger strikers', he concluded.[17] On the specific issued of the ICJP, David O'Connell commented that the statement of 3 June by the Commission made reference to only three of the five demands, and that the Commission had 'clouded the issue in verbiage and fudged it.' He continued: 'perhaps they assume that if the 3 items were dealt with these two (ie visits and full remission) could then be solved, but with our experience we must not make that assumption at all'. He expressed a wish, however, to meet the Commission in order 'to inform them of the facts of the matter'.[18]

It was at this point that the ICJP now emerged as a possible way forward. The British Embassy had forwarded, to the FCO, a recording of a call that its counsellor, Tatham, had made to the ICJP on 9 June. It was clear to the Embassy that the Commission had not consulted the Provisionals on their proposal of 3 June, and this was borne out by O'Connell's subsequent remarks. The Commission had told Tatham that their 3 June proposals were simply intended to improve the general climate, 'but they could pass messages if we wished them to.' Tatham had stressed that he was calling without instructions, and said that HMG regarded the hunger strike as a political trial of strength, not an industrial bargaining session: 'We believed any concession would be pocketed and fresh demands made.'[19] Then, on 18 June, in the Ambassador's absence, Tatham was asked to call on the Commission, where he met the Chairman, Brian Gallagher, Bishop O'Mahoney plus Hugh Logue and Father Crilly from Northern Ireland. The last two did most of the talking. They wanted HMG to know that, from contacts they had had with prisoners' families over the weekend and from visits by Father Crilly and a Mr McGill to the Maze on 16 June, they believed that there was genuine interest among prisoners and their families in resolving the hunger strike impasse on the lines of the ICJP statement of 3 June. They claimed to be reinforced in their belief by two telexes they had received that day from the Republican Press Centre in Belfast, which as far as they knew had not been released to the press, and which seemed conciliatory.

The ICJP maintained that the present lull of ten days before there was imminent danger of another death should be used to end the strike. They pointed to the disastrous side effects of the hunger strike in the North, the gains H-Block supporters had made in the Dáil elections and the possibility of violence in the South at a time of a weak or unstable Government in Dublin. HMG should not see this approach as a sign that the strikers or the hardliners were cracking, but rather as a chink of sanity among the less committed, which could provide an opening and might enable HMG to separate Catholic opinion from the hardliners. It was vital that some expression of British interest should be received within twenty-four hours, otherwise the hardliners could tell the families that the British were not interested and bring them back to the Provisional camp. Tatham explained that, while he would pass on this approach, the issue was a hot subject in London and there was no chance of a substantive reply within twenty-four hours. He also pointed out that if HMG wanted to follow up the question they might prefer not to do so in Dublin; they accepted this. Tatham later learnt that Logue had been also been in touch by telephone with Wyatt, of the NIO, in Belfast.[20]

The same day as Tatham's report of his contacts with the ICJP were sent to the FCO, Mrs Thatcher was told by her Cabinet Secretary that his opposite number, Dermot Nally, had rung from Dublin at 3.45 that afternoon. He said that he had been asked by Haughey to speak to Armstrong on the following lines: the situation in Dublin 'is difficult, and is going downhill. The more things are suppressed in the North, the more they break out elsewhere. Contacts are being established and systems are being set up which are destabilising and make the situation not a happy one.' Against this background, the Taoiseach felt that the present lull before the next death of a hunger-striker might be a time to get other things moving. He had two factors particularly in mind:

(a) there is at present some tension in relations between the parents of hunger strikers, the hunger strikers themselves and the Provisional IRA controllers outside, which could be exploited;

(b) if there is a change of Government in Dublin, the new Administration may not be as apparently sympathetic as the present, and that may [not] make the Provisional IRA more amenable.

Nally's suggestion was that HMG should consider whether there was any possibility of 'getting back to what had been talked about last December', not so much in substance as in presentation. The suggestion was that the British should once again find some way of drawing attention to the fact that what was already on offer was not very far removed from what was demanded, perhaps by issuing a comprehensive restatement of the position, of the kind issued by Atkins in December. Nally suggested that if London thought there was something in this, Dr Kennedy (the Irish Ambassador) would be prepared to come and see the Prime Minister (or Armstrong, or anyone else she named) to discuss it; or the Taoiseach would send across Nally himself. Nally added that he thought that this suggestion was made in a spirit more of opportunism than optimism; there was a lull in the procession of deaths of hunger-strikers, 'and we ought to see if we could use it'.[21]

Haughey was desperately searching for some initiative that might salvage his Government, but his time as Taoiseach was passing for now. On 21 June the man who was likely to be the next Taoiseach, the leader of Fine Gael, Dr Garret FitzGerald, called on the British Ambassador at his home. FitzGerald explained that his talks with the Irish Labour Party had been going well, and it was probable that he would form a Government on 30 June. If the hunger strike had not been resolved by that date, he said that, assuming he was Taoiseach, he would be asking for an urgent meeting with Mrs Thatcher. It did not appear that any new moves were in train since the last deaths to resolve the strike, and another death would make the situation worse. He and other politicians had seriously underestimated the support for the H-Block campaign. Opinion after the next death might create such a further extension of this sympathy that the democratic process in the South could be affected. As for the present situation in the H-Block, Dr FitzGerald said that, according to his sources, there was a definite difference of view between the present relatives and the IRA, 'and we should exploit it.' The next set of relatives might well have been less inclined to keep an independent line. On association, he made the point that the prisoners not on hunger strike felt that the atmosphere in the prison was now better than before the strike started, and they were no longer being abused by warders. In some way, they felt that the right to associate within the whole block would give them a kind of protection in this respect once the strike was over.[22]

In his appreciation, for the FCO, of the developing situation in Dublin, Figg explained that a new Irish Government was bound to rely on independent support and was 'likely to take a more publicly critical line on our policy in Northern Ireland.' The likely death of the hunger-striking Deputy, Doherty, in mid-July would once again focus attention (and possibly world media attention) on the strike. Irish opinion, 'which the election shows more sympathetic to the hunger strikers than we had imagined, is increasingly moving in their direction, less out of sympathy for the Provisionals than from concern at the penalty HMG's policy is believed to be imposing North and South of the border.' If Fianna Fáil moved into Opposition, they were likely to tap this anti-British feeling (as they did when they were last in Opposition). Haughey's present policy of co-operation between the two Governments was, by definition, not available to the Leader of the

Opposition, pointed out Figg.

The Ambassador then took up the point that the 'slight softening' in the stance of some prisoners and the families of the present hunger-strikers, which both Dr FitzGerald and the ICJP claimed to detect:

> ... could offer scope to prevent a further deterioration. If we take no steps publicly during the present lull in strikers' deaths, either through changes in the prison administration or via the European Commission for Human Rights or by some international device, to be seen to be doing something about the strike, we will appear here to be in a worse position a few weeks from now than we are at present. It seems that each death will lessen our room for manoeuvre and that the likely background of serious public disorder will make an end to the strike more difficult.[23]

The ICJP option was becoming increasingly the only one available. Mrs Thatcher, for example, had noted that the failure of the hunger-strikers to complain to the ECHR 'made it clear that they in fact had no genuine complaints about the prison regime. Their objective was quite different. They would not be diverted by concessions.' She felt that the 'difficulty with the approach advocated by the Taoiseach was that it went along with the salami tactics of the IRA leadership.'[24] But criticism of HMG's policy was not confined to those outside Whitehall – in Northern Ireland both the RUC Chief Constable and the GOC voiced their concerns. While Hermon assured the Government that the police were ready for further disturbances, he stated strongly his view that HMG's present course:

(i)   Would demand sacrifices by the security forces with little justification.
(ii) Would aggravate the sectarian divide in the community.
(iii) Would enhance the terrorists' base in the community.
(iv) Would prevent the security forces getting the intelligence they needed to control terrorist activity.
(v)   Demonstrated the historic attitude of Westminster towards Ulster which had had such unfortunate consequences in the past.

The community, thought the Chief Constable, was looking for a lead from the Government that was *not* forthcoming. The Catholic Church, on the other hand, was pointing a way forward, and the Loyalist community was indicating quietly that they accepted that something had to be done. But it was clear that these feelings were not communicating themselves to those who took the decisions on these matters. To proceed on the political front without any token or gesture on prisons would be 'courting disaster', warned Hermon. The GOC also complained of the low profile that was being taken by HMG in Northern Ireland. It appeared that HMG was not interested, and there was a need for a much more keenly felt Government 'presence' during this difficult time. HMG should keep talking to the community about the problem and not stay quiet having stated a fixed position. There should be scope for the Secretary of State to take his own initiatives within the Cabinet's broad policy; there was now a feeling that there was no executive arm of Government in Northern Ireland itself.[25]

It was with these pressures as background that a delegation from the ICJP called, at their request, to see NIO Minister of State, Michael Alison, in Stormont Castle on 22 June. The Commission delegation consisted of Bishop O'Mahoney, Jerome Connolly (Secretary), Brian Gallagher (Chairman), Father Oliver Crilly and Hugh Logue (also an SDLP member). Alison was accompanied by John Blelloch. At the beginning of the meeting Alison told the delegation that in his view there were certain concessions that a responsible Government, pursuing justice dispassionately, could not make: it could not surrender responsibility for seeing that the rule of law was, in the fullest sense, upheld without negating the principle of government. The three areas – clothes, association and work – that the ICJP had identified as offering prospects for adaptation in the prison regime were areas in which the Government had already made much progress: it already ran a more advanced regime than in the rest of the UK, and in many other countries in the western world. To this, Logue replied that the resolution of the impasse would require substantial movement on prison regimes. Until recently he had had the impression that neither side wished to indicate any sign of movement because each feared that any sign of weakening would encourage the other side to 'tighten the screws'. But he now sensed among various groups, particularly the prisoners' relatives, a real desire to resolve the situation before any more deaths occurred. Time was therefore very short. He outlined what he saw as the 'triangle' of the prisoners, their friends and relatives outside the prison and the 'propagandists'.

A long discussion on the details of the three proposals put forward by the ICJP then followed. Alison explained which opportunities were available in all three areas to those prisoners who conformed to the prison regime – opportunities of which the protesters were not availing themselves. Dealing first with association, he pointed out the loss of control that would result from prisoners, many of whom were convicted of serious crimes of violence, being allowed complete free association in the wings, let alone the blocks that might contain up to 200 men. It was possible to envisage that the existing hours of association, which in a sense mirrored the pattern of outside life with a working day and evening and weekend recreation, and which were already generous, might be extended to a degree, but this would not happen within a predictable timescale. Logue thought that any progress on this front would have to be made in the very near future (seven to eight days) if it was to contribute to a resolution of the current dispute. He and Bishop O'Mahoney suggested that association within the whole of the H-Block, rather than in each wing, might be a significant factor. Alison was willing to consider the possibility of more association between wings within a block, on the present supervised basis of association, for conforming prisoners but this, he said, was a technical point, and no dramatic change – of the sort that might dissuade a man from starving himself to death – was likely to emerge. Blelloch warned that there were serious risks in effectively opening up an H-Block to free movement. There had to be supervision during periods of association.

On the question of work, the existing types of prison work were outlined and Alison assured the delegation that there were no circumstances in which prisoners were made to work for prison officers. He was not clear exactly what the ICJP had meant by 'work of a demeaning nature', as in any community there would always be certain chores and 'orderly' duties that had to be done (such as cleaning cells and work in the kitchens). In the other areas of work, for instance industrial, vocational and educational training, the preferences of the individual prisoners were taken into account as far as possible within the limitations imposed by resources and availability. It was essential, though, that the prison authorities should ultimately decide who should do what work. The authorities could not surrender control. Alison emphasized that any reform in this area would have to apply to *all* prisoners, and not to particular groups. Public opinion would not tolerate a situation in which a select group of prisoners was in effect being maintained by the rest.

On clothing, Alison drew attention to the Government's record of flexibility, but pointed out the practical difficulties of prisoners wearing their own clothes all the time. Apart from the fact that some prisoners may not want to wear their own clothes, there was a serious question of maintaining security within working hours when large numbers of prisoners were moving about. It was not a question of principle, but of practicality. Logue then summed up his understanding of the position, set out by Alison, as follows:

(i) On association, for conforming prisoners there might perhaps be scope for investigating ways of providing longer periods, and wider movement within the blocks;

(ii) On work, a certain amount of cleaning etc had to be done, but prisoners had some discretion over what courses or types of work they pursued; however, because of the logistical problems, the ultimate decision would lie with the authorities;

(iii) On clothing, there would be no objection in principle to all conforming prisoners wearing their own clothes all the time provided that they dressed in a manner that the authorities approved.

Father Crilly felt that in present circumstances, as a particularly tense time of the year was approaching (the Orange marching season), there would be justification for a 'quite extraordinary' effort to resolve the current situation. His impression was that, although the prisoners wanted to reach a solution, they were determined to die on hunger strike if nothing acceptable to them was put forward. He thought that there was no likelihood of a resolution of the problem on the basis of telling prisoners what would be available to them if they conformed. This had not worked in the past, and it would take something very radical to achieve anything now. However, Logue and Crilly felt that now was a better time than ever before – in terms of the attitude of the families of the prisoners – to try and resolve the issue. If this opportunity were missed, the propagandists would take a much firmer hold on the families.

Alison, however, reminded the Commission that this meeting was not a negotiating forum; he could not lead the delegation to believe that they should convey messages back to the 'other side'. The delegation declared that they accepted this fully. It was then agreed that the foregoing discussion of the prison regime had been based on the presupposition that prisoners conformed to the regime. Alison said that, while it had been of value to have a discussion of the Commission's statement and the prison regime as between reasonable and responsible people, that discussion had nevertheless been unreal. He did not believe that men who had committed dreadful crimes outside prison, had then inflicted years of suffering on themselves in prison and ultimately had committed suicide in pursuit of changes in the prison regime which the Government could not make, were reasonable. They were after bigger game. What was at issue was a challenge to the authority of the State. He hoped he was wrong, but he did not believe so. Before the Commission left they were given copies of the Secretary of State's letter to Cardinal Ó Fiaich, as Chairman of the Conference of Irish Bishops, which reinforced the point that 'the next step must be for the hunger strike to end'.[26]

In that letter, Atkins wrote to the Cardinal expressing his admiration for the Bishops' statement on the hunger strike. It was difficult to see, he wrote, how anyone could remain unmoved by its compassion, its urgency and its directness: 'We must hope and pray that those who direct that violence, together with the hunger strikers themselves and their families, will follow your clear lead. It will be a tragedy if they fail to do so and force the minority community in Northern Ireland to suffer again as they did last month.' The letter was made public and received extensive media coverage.[27] Two days later Cardinal Ó Fiaich responded to the Secretary of State – also in an open letter: 'I trust our words will make a notable contribution towards the restoration of peace and particularly towards the resolution of the prison deadlock.' The letter then went on to expound again the view that it was the Bishops' belief that the proposals of the ICJP would provide the avenue for a solution: 'To achieve this it is essential therefore that there should be movement from both sides.'[28]

On the diplomatic plane, following another telephone call from Nally on 25 June, Sir Robert Armstrong telephoned his opposite number at 5.00 p.m. the following day. Armstrong explained that he had conveyed the Taoiseach's message to the Prime Minister, who had been grateful for it and would ensure that it was carefully considered. He explained London's preliminary reaction on the six points made in the message (drawing on points made by Sir Kenneth Stowe in a letter to the Cabinet Secretary):

(a) We were fully seized of the present situation and of the significance of the present lull.

(b) We accepted that in practical terms it was the prisoners themselves who had the final choice. But others still exerted influence on them and their decisions.

(c) As for the channel of communication, there already was an effective channel to the prisoners through the Governor. This had proved successful so far on a number of other matters. This remained the most natural channel to use and it would avoid any confusion. But we were of course prepared to be in touch with any responsible body which wished to put views to us.

(d) The Government would be making a statement … (almost certainly the Secretary of State for Northern Ireland) containing a restatement of what was currently available to prisoners and Her Majesty's Government's commitment to a humanitarian regime. It would be on the lines of the 18th December statement. It would be shown to the Irish in advance … through the normal channels. It would also be circulated to the prisoners.

(e) On the suggestion of a settlement phased over six months, perhaps involving guarantors, Sir Robert said that he had no wish to leave any doubts in Mr Nally's mind. We were not looking for a method to concede the five demands surreptitiously. We welcomed the recognition that any changes inevitably take time. We believed that if there were changes, the question of guarantors would be less relevant since any changes would be self-policing.

(f) Sir Robert said that as for the search for a 'final settlement', we would be glad to see progress now if it could be made. We remained committed to a humanitarian regime in the prisons. The Government could not change its position on the basic principles: no differentiation in the conforming prison regime and no loss of control. We were pleased the Irish were not asking for this and were willing to go on talking.

Nally was grateful for this response. While he would of course now have to see what reaction there was to the Secretary of State's statement (which he would show to the Taoiseach as soon as he received it), he thought that what Armstrong had told him 'looked slightly hopeful'. Armstrong then emphasized that it was important not to overstate HMG's room for manoeuvre: 'We had already gone a very long way and it was difficult to see how much further we could go without compromising our basic principles.' Nally thought that the process of setting down clearly on paper what was currently on offer would be a great help: it would demonstrate that there was little between what was being demanded and what was already on offer. Nally added, however, that he thought that it was now a question of 'percentages'. If there could be some slight movement – not a major step – that would help to resolve the problem. Armstrong replied that he would see what scope there was for a further move, 'but it would be idle to pretend that it was not difficult for us to envisage any further movement.'[29]

While Downing Street remained resolute, the Foreign Office voiced its frustration and concern through the Lord Privy Seal, Sir Ian Gilmour. He wrote to Atkins on 29 June, reminding the Secretary of State that at a meeting at Number 10 'about a month ago, I raised the possibility of feeding the hunger strikers intra-venously.' Gilmour accepted:

> We cannot make concessions to the demands of the IRA and their sympathisers, since to do so would almost certainly lead to further demands. All that a concession would probably do would be to bring us closer to granting political status. On the other hand any more deaths will do great damage both in Ireland and abroad, with consequences that cannot be fully foreseen. Hence a continuation of the hunger strike carries considerable dangers for us in Ulster and elsewhere, yet any concessions to bring it to an end are impossible.

The only way out of this impasse, it seemed to Gilmour, was to stop the hunger-strikers from killing themselves. This could be done either by intravenous feeding or by further restrictions on those whom the strikers were allowed to see, a point that he raised at Cabinet the previous week. Indeed, a combination of these things would probably be necessary since any relations and priests allowed in might well be 'fanatical' enough to wrench out 'the drip' and smash the equipment. Force-feeding was abandoned, 'as I remember, partly because it was dangerous and repulsive, and partly because it was thought that if people wanted to die they should be allowed to do so.' These reasons had now lost their force. Intravenous feeding was not repulsive – 'many of us have undergone it – nor I think is it dangerous: and the avowed political objectives of these hunger strikers remove their cases from the realm of purely personal decision.' The Irish Roman Catholic Bishops referred to 'those who direct them' and to the 'contempt for human life, the incitement to revenge, the exploitation of the hunger strikers to further a campaign of murder, the intimidation of the innocent'.

To interfere with the (partly) self-imposed martyrdom of these people would not infringe any principle 'that I know of.' The IRA would certainly be enraged by 'our stopping their supply of martyrs, and would undoubtedly cause trouble in the prisons and outside. But I think that any such trouble would be far less than the difficulties caused by a further succession of deaths in prison, renewed violence and greatly increased tension on both sides of the border.' The decision could be easily justified as the logical extension of:

> ... our present policy: we have been thoroughly reasonable throughout and have produced a remarkably liberal prison regime; but, as this has had no effect on the intransigence of the IRA, we have no alternative but to stop the strikers dying. In doing so we would surely have the support of the Irish Bishops and most other reasonable people.

Of course, accepted Gilmour, if the relatives of the present strikers really were more sensible than their predecessors:

> ... and you are able to reach an agreement with them, none of this will be necessary. Or there may be insuperable technical objections, in which case I apologise for intruding. But, if no such agreement is likely and the technical difficulties can be overcome, then I think what I have suggested is preferable both to surrender, which is unthinkable, and to a continuing series of deaths, which will be highly dangerous.[30]

Despite this frustration, there was to be no change in policy.

Instead, Alison, on 30 June, wrote to Bishop O'Mahoney to make sure that the ICJP was certain of the Government's position. The Minister stated that the three specific suggestions concerning clothing, association and prison work made in the Commission's statement of 3 June did not, in the form in which they were expressed, conflict with the Government's principles. Equally, though, the Commission's expressed proposals might be interpreted as embracing in full the corresponding demands of the prisoners. It was, therefore, of vital importance that there should be no ambiguity in the Government's position, all the more so as the prisoners were alleged, twice, in the past ten days to have said that the Commission's proposals fell short of what would bring the protest to an end; 'we must be clear that what we are talking about is the bringing to an end of the protest and not merely the hunger strike', emphasized Alison. It was for this reason that the Secretary of State was once again making the Government's position in general clear in a statement that day. A comparison of the Government's position with statements attributed to the prisoners, on 19 June and again on 28 June, showed clearly that these attitudes could not be reconciled, which was why the Government believed that it would be wrong to make moves in advance of the ending of the hunger strike and simply in the hope that they would have this effect. In other words, the Government was not prepared to give the protesters something on account in the hope that 'they would not present the rest of the bill later.' The Government nevertheless wanted to set down for the record the specific questions O'Mahoney put to it in the two previous meetings.

The Government, explained Alison, could not concede the principle that prisoners should decide with whom they mixed or that they be segregated according to religious denomination or other factors. In practice, common sense would dictate how the Prison Authorities would deploy prisoners day to day. It would be for them to decide what at any time would be the overriding consideration. O'Mahoney had asked whether, subject to the necessary considerations of control and security, prisoners in adjacent wings might be allowed to associate together during the period when association was normally permitted to non-protesting prisoners in the evenings, at weekends and during recreation in the exercise yard. This did present practical problems of controlling and supervising more movement and larger groups of prisoners, wrote Alison; the considerations mentioned would mean that such movement could not be through the central control areas of a block. Otherwise, the problems need not be overriding in the situation of normality, 'which we assumed as the context of our discussions. But this assumption is important, since there is obvious scope for misuse of the increased association involved.' O'Mahoney had also asked whether it would be possible, from unlock to lock-up, normally to leave cell doors unlocked. Alison had considered this and had to say that 'we would not find this possible in view of the men we are dealing with and the need to protect prison officers.' In addition, many prisoners preferred the privacy afforded by the present arrangements:

> You asked whether ex-protestors would be required to contribute in the same way as presently non-protesting prisoners to orderly work in the blocks and to analogous duties in the central facilities (such as kitchen and laundries) which serve the whole prison. You also asked whether ex-protestors would in practice have to engage in 'productive' work in prison industry. In principle we regard all prisoners as liable to allocation by the Prison Authorities to some prison activity. But I went on to explain that prison activities embraced a spectrum from the essential functions

needed to maintain the prison through 'productive' activities and activities which benefit primarily the prisoners, and that there are areas where the one shades into the other. There are obvious attractions in increasing the proportion of time which prisoners spend in useful activities that are also congenial to them, and to offering the widest practicable choice. But we cannot agree that any group of prisoners should as of right opt out of a particular form of activity, since what matters to us is that in practice the Prison Authorities decide what prisoners actually do.

The Government, though, was prepared, in accordance with its previous statement, to be generous about restoring lost remission on an individual basis and subject to continuing good conduct in circumstances in which the whole protest had come to an end. It would be wrong, however, to imagine that the restoration would immediately be total, or given without an appropriate period of evidence of continuing good behaviour. The problems involved in letting the prisoners wear their own clothes all the time related to security and control. As such, they were of a different order from those considered under the other heads above in that they were not, in the Government's perception, problems of the prisoners' status or the day-to-day authority of the Prison Governor.[31]

Alison's letter, as he mentioned, was co-ordinated with another statement of the Government's position, by Atkins. He highlighted how, in the three aspects picked out by the ICJP, and in other aspects, the Northern Ireland prison regime was generous, had been and 'will be administered flexibly by the authorities. There is scope for yet further development.' Whilst the protesting prisoners might have been reluctant to abandon their protest because they did not trust the Government's commitment to continue to improve the prison regime, Atkins stressed:

> ... that our commitment is declared in this and similar statements, and is there for all to see. What we said publicly in December would happen to those giving up their protests has happened to the 89 who have since done so. But it must be emphasised that this improvement is not something that can all be accomplished overnight.

Prisons were complex institutions. The requirements of security, and the particular characteristics of the inmate population, added to their complexity. They were run by staff doing a difficult and hazardous job, whose interests had to be given proper consideration. All of this meant that proposals for change would have to be fully and carefully weighed, and their implications explored, before they were adopted. This process could not proceed further while the hunger strike placed the authorities under duress, declared Atkins.[32]

As the respective positions were being outlined, Mrs Thatcher prepared to meet the most substantial critic of her policy: Cardinal Tomás Ó Fiaich. When the Prime Minister had visited Northern Ireland on 28 May, it was hoped that Ó Fiaich would be among those that she met, but the shortness of the notice, compounded by inhibitions (for security reasons) about disclosing the visit in advance, meant that the Cardinal was unable to attend any meeting. These events produced at the time some feeling on his part that he had been discourteously treated.[33] Thatcher wrote to Ó Fiaich on 28 May, suggesting that they meet when convenient. The Cardinal replied on 2 June, informing the Prime Minister that he would be in London from 30 June to 1 July:

> ... but I should point out that the reason for my visit is an invitation from the Parish Priest of Balham to commemorate with his parishioners the third centenary of the execution of a former Archbishop of Armagh, St Oliver Plunkett. The execution took place on 1st July 1681. You might not consider this the most auspicious occasion for a meeting.

In addition, having read her speech at Stormont, and being aware that two events would be pending: the death of more hunger-strikers, unless something happened to persuade them to end their strike, and the Protestant marches leading up to the twelfth of July celebrations commemorating the Battle of the Boyne in 1690, Ó Fiaich wondered at the wisdom of having a meeting at that time, 'which will undoubtedly become public. We both have a common concern to keep normal life going and to work unceasingly for peace and reconciliation', stressed the Cardinal.[34] The Prime Minister was eager to meet regardless, and arrangements were made for Ó Fiaich to come to Downing Street on 1 July. Officials stressed to Thatcher that her objectives in the meeting should be:

1. To assure the Cardinal, and through him his fellow-bishops and priests and the Catholic community, of HMG's continuing care and concern for that community, especially at a time when it is subject to stress resulting from the prisons crisis.
2. To express appreciation of the efforts of the Cardinal and other leaders to rally and reassure moderate Catholic opinion, especially as regards the hunger strike and PIRA violence generally, and to urge the continuance of those efforts.
3. To welcome the constructive approach to the hunger strike of the Irish Commission for Justice and Peace – and the Bishops' Conference, and to explain HMG's position.
4. To assert that HMG is not wholly preoccupied with the prisons crisis. It is concerned also with political development in NI; with the development of

the unique relationship with Dublin; and with making economic and social provision for NI on a healthy foundation. In pursuing all these policies, HMG is at pains to be even-handed as between the two parts of the community.[35]

Cardinal Ó Fiaich was accompanied to Downing Street by Bishop Lennon of Kildare and Leighlin; the Prime Minister was joined by Humphrey Atkins. When they sat down together, Mrs Thatcher remarked on how, during her visit to Northern Ireland, there was nothing she could do to make people kind, considerate and thoughtful to each other. There was no role for legislation here. She prized reason and fair play; but she recognized that reason could not always overcome deeply held feelings. She hoped that the Cardinal would be able to tell her things about the feelings of the minority community of which she was unaware, or that he might be able to express to her in a more vivid way what she already knew about their feelings. To her it was appalling that people should go on hunger strike, and she was the first to want to see it ended. The conditions in the Maze would stand comparison with prison conditions anywhere else in the world, and she did not think that they could be the driving force behind the hunger strike. Perhaps, she speculated, the hunger-strikers were protesting in this way because they had been ordered to do so by people outside.

Cardinal Ó Fiaich answered that he did not believe that the hunger-strikers were acting on external instructions from the IRA leadership; the impetus for their protests was coming from within the prison. He was at one with the Prime Minster in wanting to see an end to the hunger strike. He had felt a glimmer of hope when the ICJP had produced their statement a fortnight earlier, thinking that the prisoners might see the Commission as an independent group who were interested in their future and might therefore be ready to listen to them, but that would require them to be allowed access to the hunger-strikers. The Cardinal recognized that this request was difficult for the Government to accept because it would look as though the Commission was becoming involved in negotiations between the Government and the prisoners, but he thought that it would be helpful if the Commission could see Michael Alison again and then visit the prisoners. He wanted to suggest that Father Crilly, who was a relation of one of the hunger-strikers, and one or two other members of the Commission should be allowed in. They would not be conducting a negotiation, but they could explain to the hunger-strikers what the position was. There would be trouble if the hunger-strikers were allowed to die just because prison regulations said that certain types of person could not visit prisoners – the Government had, after all, allowed three members of the Dáil to go into the Maze some weeks before. The Cardinal believed that there was, barely, a hope that the Commission could find a solution, and so he urged the Government to allow them access to the prisoners.

Atkins agreed that there was no problem about allowing Father Crilly to see the prisoners, whether as a priest or as a relative of one of them, but he could not let the Commission as a body go into the Maze, otherwise a lot of other organizations would ask for the same facilities. There were many people who wanted to see the hunger-strikers, and it was essential that the Government adhered to the practice of allowing access only to prisoners' relatives, lawyers and priests. In any case, if it were thought that the Government was negotiating with the strikers, or using the Commission as negotiators by proxy, this would be likely to produce a strong reaction in the Protestant community, and thus put at risk Catholic inhabitants of Northern Ireland. The Cardinal commented, at this point, that such an argument could be pushed too far. He recognized that a balance had to be preserved vis-à-vis the hardline Protestants, but it should be remembered that there were Protestant prisoners in the Maze as well as Republicans. The central question was how he and the Prime Minister and the Secretary of State could help each other to bring the hunger strike to the end that they all so much desired. The longer the strike went on, the more beneficial it was to the PIRA, to which the strike was undoubtedly bringing recruits. The middle ground in Northern Ireland was evaporating. Bishop Lennon supported this analysis, pointing out that he had a number of nephews who had hitherto not been involved in the Republican Movement, but he was distressed to see the shift of opinion among them since the hunger strike had started. Young people like this were put in an impossible position: if they criticized the PIRA, they were dubbed as Unionist quislings; if they criticized the British Army or the RUC, they were labelled as members of the PIRA. The problem of the hunger strike was too urgent to quibble about whether someone was allowed to see prisoners as a priest or as a relative or as a member of the ICJP. Replying to a question by the Prime Minister, Bishop Lennon added that the hunger-strikers were taking the action they were because they felt – however misguidedly – that they and the community from which they came were suffering injustices.

In response, Mrs Thatcher declared that she could not agree to sanctify crime by giving those on the protest political status, for to do so would be tantamount to saying that they had a licence to kill for political reasons. It was, of course, true that there were prisoners in the Maze who already had special status, but that was for historical reasons and she could not change that situation. Cardinal Ó Fiaich, though, stressed that he was not asking for special category status and he had made this clear in a telegram to the Prime Minister. He wanted to draw her attention to the facts in the North as they were, 'whether we liked them or not.' For example, some of the prisoners were very young when they began their sentences, and many of them were long-term prisoners. He was not describing these points as special factors, but he believed that they did make for a different situation. The prisoners were using that different situation in their own interests:

'We all wanted to bring the situation to an end', Ó Fiaich declared, and he had offered many suggestions for doing so. He believed that 'we had had a solution in our grasp last year, a solution which he and Bishop Daly had brought about by working through the priests and the prisoners' relatives.' The prisoners had wanted to get off the hook of the protest, and so had the Government. If all prisoners in Northern Ireland had been allowed to wear their own clothes, the whole protest would have ended. He had thought that the Government was going to agree to this, but of course what the Government had conceded was that the prisoners could wear civilian-type dress supplied by the prison authorities. 'If we could now only get back to that stage where a solution had been so close, everybody would be glad', argued the Cardinal.

Mrs Thatcher replied that she did not believe that this was possible. The Government had decided, before last autumn's strike had started, that civilian-type clothing should be allowed. More generally, the Government had got into a position where the prison conditions were very good and were better, for example, than those in United States prisons. This position had then been made clear to the hunger-strikers, who had in due course called off their protest. There was no reason why the present hunger-strikers should seek better conditions. Here Cardinal Ó Fiaich agreed that the conditions in the Maze were potentially among the best in the world, but the fact was that the atmosphere in the Maze was one of very deep hostility between the prison staff and the inmates, in respect of which it contrasted sharply with Magilligan and Armagh prisons. Atkins observed that the prisoners were not on strike against the atmosphere in the Maze; they were on strike to win special category status and not to secure a change in the prison conditions. The ICJP had offered some ideas for resolving the situation, but the PIRA's reaction had been negative. To this, Bishop Lennon pointed out that the decision to go on a hunger strike was a very difficult one to take. The strikers were young and did not want to die, and did not embark upon this course lightly – he was not, of course, saying they were forced to take it. The Prime Minister, however, said that she doubted whether the hunger-strikers understood the prison regime that was on offer. They were chosen to go on the hunger strike and had to 'carry the cross for the cause.' They dared not refuse to do so.

Cardinal Ó Fiaich repeated that the hunger strike must be brought to an end. He did not know what special category or political status was; to him, it meant nothing. One could take any five conditions and call them political status. He accepted that the Government had many constraints on the action open to them. The Church similarly had very little room for manoeuvre, though he wished to point out that it had condemned the use of violence consistently. The ICJP had made proposals for bringing the situation to an end, and he wanted to know what alternative way forward there was. If the present situation were allowed to continue indefinitely, moderate people would become hostile to the Government.

If another hunger-striker died, tension would build up again; and if eight died, there would be chaos in Northern Ireland. It was essential to establish for what the hunger-strikers would come off their protest: their reasons for going on the protest were for now irrelevant. The Prime Minister, though, emphasized that she believed that the hunger strike could be brought to an end tomorrow if those taking part in it were given the necessary orders. She was not prepared to barter. She could not accept the prisoners' argument that their crimes were committed for political reasons and were, therefore, different from ordinary offences. Murder was murder, whatever its motive. All criminals, whatever their religion or political beliefs, had to be treated in the same way in prison. The law was the same for everybody. It had to be applied justly and impartially to all sections of the community.

Bishop Lennon tried to highlight the minority's grievances: there was a strong feeling amongst the young Catholics in Northern Ireland that the law was not applied fairly, and there was a great deal of resentment of which the hunger strike was only a part. The Catholic community's sense of injustice went back for many, many years. They had been treated unjustly by the Stormont regime, and Westminster had done nothing about it. This was the background against which the hunger strike had to be seen. Mrs Thatcher, however, commented that if the Republican community really believed that what it was fighting against was the accumulated wrongs of 400 years, she had to make it clear that there was nothing she could do about it. In any case, she doubted whether this was really so. Cardinal Ó Fiaich answered that much of Northern Ireland's problems sprang from the fact that the border was the 'most artificial division ever created.' The whole of Northern Ireland was a 'lie' from start to finish. At root, what the hunger-strikers believed they were striking for was a united Ireland. Bishop Lennon added that he thought that 'we were seeing the beginnings of an eventual solution to the problem.' What was required was a British declaration of intention to withdraw from Northern Ireland, though he accepted that withdrawal could not be immediate and that no timetable should be attached to such a declaration. Atkins, however, pointed out that this was to ignore the one million Protestants who formed the majority. The people of Northern Ireland must seek to solve their problems by persuasion and not by violence, whether against others or, as with the hunger-strikers, against oneself. The Republicans should try to persuade the Protestants that the unification of Ireland was a desirable objective. The people of Northern Ireland should sit down and work out their own future. In the meantime, all the British Government could do was to maintain the absolute impartiality of the law.

Cardinal Ó Fiaich asked when the time would come when the British Government would say that its presence in Northern Ireland was divisive – as it was. The Catholic community did not regard itself as British and did not want

British government. There was no hope for British policy if the Government believed that the ordinary people of Fermanagh thought of themselves as being as British as the people of Yorkshire did. Rather, British policy for the future should be stated as a strong desire to bring together all sections of the Northern Ireland community in peace and harmony as a step to bringing all parts of Ireland together in peace and harmony. The only solution was to bring together all the Irish people under a government of Irishmen, whether in a federal or a unitary State.

Mrs Thatcher retorted that the course advocated by the Cardinal could not become the policy of the British Government because it was not acceptable to the majority of the population of Northern Ireland. There was no point in complaining about partition: the border was there, and she could not change that fact. She wanted to see the United Kingdom, of which Northern Ireland was just as much a part as was England or Scotland or Wales, live in peace and co-operation with the Republic. Those who sought a united island of Ireland must learn that what could not be won by persuasion would not be won by force. Bishop Lennon responded that he did not believe that the hunger-strikers would be persuaded to give up their protest. Prison conditions were irrelevant. The prisoners were not on hunger strike because of physical conditions; they had embarked on the strike because they believed – rightly or wrongly – that they were being treated unjustly. As the meeting drew to a close, Mrs Thatcher remarked that their discussion had been valuable because it had been frank. She felt that they understood one another better as a result. She regarded the meeting as a private one and she did not intend to reveal that it had taken place, but if it leaked, she would not be able to deny that there had been a meeting. In that event, she proposed to say that they had had a wide-ranging and very open discussion of the situation in Northern Ireland. Cardinal Ó Fiaich agreed to proceed in this way. He did not want the meeting to become public knowledge. He thought the fact that they had all spoken 'so bluntly and openly' could only be a good thing.[36]

Cardinal Ó Fiaich had pushed hard for the ICJP to be admitted to the Maze, as now also, in Dublin, did the newly elected Taoiseach, Dr Garret FitzGerald, who told Sir Leonard Figg that the hunger strike was now at a very critical stage and that there was probably no better moment to solve it. The strikers' families were standing up well against IRA pressure: 'We simply must give the Irish Commission for Justice and Peace what help we could', he said to Figg. FitzGerald asked HMG 'most earnestly' to see that the ICJP would meet again with Alison with the least possible delay and then have access to the strikers and prisoners. He also made the point that the strikers were well aware of what they regarded as brinkmanship on HMG's part when the last strike ended: 'We must get the Commission moving again before McDonnell deteriorated much further.' The Taoiseach made two further points of interest. First, that the statement by Sinn Féin that Atkins' statement the day before was insufficient did not reflect the prisoners' views. Second, that it was important that Gerry Adams should remain on the scene for the next few days (the significance of this was not explained). FitzGerald, Figg reported to London in a telegram also read by the Prime Minister, had made 'a very strong approach to us on behalf of the Commission. While we may not agree with him about their importance we should not refuse what he asks. If we turn down his request we shall get off to a bad start here', warned Figg.[37]

Pressure continued on the British to take some sort of initiative. By 2 July, Joe McDonnell's condition was beginning to give cause for concern. The brainstem deficiency was now becoming more marked, with both his sight and hearing suffering from deterioration. He was not bedbound, however, as he had been the previous week, and was able to sit up. On his present course, death could be expected from the following Wednesday, 8 July (day sixty-one). Neither Kieran Doherty nor Kevin Lynch had yet displayed the first major symptom of deterioration: vomiting. Martin Hurson's condition had, relatively speaking, improved. His vomiting had stopped completely, and he was now able to hold down water. Thomas McElwee was expected to be moved to the prison hospital on 3 July for purposes of closer observation. The next set of hunger-strikers, Quinn, Devine and McKeown, were giving no cause for concern at this stage and remained in the blocks. The prisoners' weights on 2 July were:

	Day of strike	Weight on first examination	Weight today	Weight loss during week	Overall weight loss
Joseph McDonnell	55	11st 4½lb	7st 12½lb	8½lb	3st 6½lb
Kieran Doherty	42	11st 11lb	9st 2½lb	6½lb	1st 8½lb
Kevin Lynch	41	9st 7lb	7st 6½lb	4½lb	2st 0½lb
Edward Hurson	35	10st 13lb	8st 9lb	3lb	2st 4lb
Thomas McElwee	25	10st 8lb	9st 1lb	7lb	1st 7lb
Michael Devine	11	9st 8½lb	8st 13lb	5½lb	9lb[38]

To emphasize the seriousness of the situation, FitzGerald telephoned Mrs Thatcher at Downing Street. After thanking the Prime Minister for her message of congratulations on his appointment as Taoiseach, he said that he was looking forward to co-operating with the Prime Minister and to continuing the work that she had started with his predecessor, and that nothing but good could come from this process. In the meantime, he was anxious to have an early word with the Prime

Minister on one particular matter: the H-Block situation. He had seen Sir Leonard Figg about it earlier in the day, and there were two points he wished to put to her. First, speed was very important. The first hunger strike had been resolved at a very late stage indeed, and he did not believe that this way of proceeding could operate again on this occasion. The work that had been done already should be pushed ahead. He did not know the details of the contacts between the Northern Ireland Office and the ICJP, but he believed that the Commission was working along useful lines. The second point that he wanted to make was that the Commission should have the opportunity to explain to the prisoners in the Maze what was proposed so that there was no misunderstanding. He hoped that if the Commission could be allowed access to the Maze, the prisoners would end their protest on the basis of various arrangements, which he believed were desirable in order to improve their conditions.

Mrs Thatcher commented that Alison had already met the Commission and had had a useful exchange of views with them. He could certainly have another meeting with them, although he probably would not be able to do that in the next twenty-four hours since he would almost certainly be attending an important debate on Northern Ireland in the House of Commons the following day. She could not agree that the Commission should be allowed to meet the prisoners. Prisoners were allowed to see only their relatives, their solicitors and their priests. If the Commission were given access to them, it would look as though they were acting as intermediaries in a negotiation between the British Government and the prisoners, and this was something that she could not accept. It remained her earnest hope that the hunger-strikers would end their protest, and she thought that the statement issued by Atkins the previous day might be sufficient to encourage the families of the prisoners and the clergy to try to persuade the hunger-strikers to end their protest. While FitzGerald saw the difficulty of letting the Commission have access to the prisoners, he hoped that the Prime Minister would be prepared to consider further her position on his request. Another meeting between Alison and the Commission would be very helpful, but it would need to be held quickly. Friday (this conversation was on Wednesday) might be too late: he was concerned about the deteriorating condition of the hunger-striker McDonnell. He wondered whether there was any possibility of Alison meeting the Commission later that evening. Mrs Thatcher, however, did not believe that Alison should rush into a meeting with the Commission as quickly as that – and there was the Commons debate to take into consideration:[39]

Dr. Fitzgerald [*sic*]: When does the debate end, Prime Minister[?]

Prime Minister: The debate tomorrow, about 10.00. 10.00 tomorrow night – it's our annual debate. And it is an important day for Northern

Irish affairs and it is our annual debate and of course the Secretary of State – I'm not quite sure whether Michael Alison is winding up but we have most of our Ministers there tomorrow because it is our very important annual debate. But I will certainly see if we could arrange something for Friday.

Dr. Fitzgerald: Well it worries me a little because of the state of the … morning earlier or something like that. I'm sorry to press this but …

Prime Minister: Yes well I do think. Taoiseach, it's 6.15 on Wednesday night. We have a major debate tomorrow. It does seem to me to be reasonable to try to fix it up early on Friday morning. Because you see Michael Alison will have to get over here for the debate tomorrow.

Dr. Fitzgerald: He could have seen them this evening …

Prime Minister: I don't think we should dash at it quite like that but he will naturally wish to prepare himself. I will see how early we can arrange, Garret, but I think early Friday morning is reasonable. But I have not spoken to him, obviously I didn't know of the suggestion.

Dr. Fitzgerald: Yes I understand. But perhaps you can look and see if it is possible. There is just this danger that all that has become possible might no longer be possible …

Prime Minister: I just hope that everyone will try to urge all of the prisoners on hunger strike to come off it because it is a futile waste of their own lives. A futile waste of their own lives.

Dr. Fitzgerald: You don't have to convince me of that, Prime Minister. I'm not new to the subject as you probably know. But …

Prime Minister: Yes I know. Everyone is trying to get them off the hunger strike and absolutely I don't wish them to waste their own lives in any way at all. I will get in touch with Michael Alison straightaway.

Dr. Fitzgerald: Thank you very much Prime Minister.

Prime Minister: Thank you for phoning. I look forward to seeing you. Goodbye.[40]

The Taoiseach, together with his Labour Party coalition partner Michael O'Leary, met with relatives of the hunger-strikers on 3 July as there appeared to be a continuing lack of urgency from the British. Unknown to the Taoiseach, though, London was about to make a significant shift in direction – not least because of Dublin's pressure. On 2 July, Atkins wrote to the Prime Minister, informing her that he had considered, in the light of their discussion at Cabinet that morning, 'whether we could find some way of resolving the situation in the Maze Prison before any further deaths of hunger strikers occur (McDonnell, the prisoner who has fasted longest, will probably reach a critical point early next week), or at least of vindicating our present stand.' When the OD (Cabinet) Committee had discussed the prisons situation on 18 June, 'we came down against action which, while appealing to the Catholic community, would appear to be a weakening of the Government's resolve to resist the prisoners' demands for political status.' Atkins had, therefore, issued a long and carefully considered statement of the Government's position only two days before, making clear that, 'while we were prepared to make improvements in the general prison regime for all prisoners, this could not be done while we were under the duress of the hunger strike.' While the pressure of Catholic opinion in Northern Ireland, in the Republic, in Great Britain and in the US favoured some concession by the Government, any move of that kind would provoke a strong adverse reaction among Northern Ireland Protestants, who would read it as the beginning of a sell-out. This reaction would only matter if the move failed to bring an end to the strike.

Unless the hunger-strikers lost their nerve, Atkins wrote, 'we shall only resolve the impasse by shifting our ground in the hope of inducing the strikers to give up, even against the will of the Provisionals. There is no reason to believe that the ICJP proposals alone would do the trick as regards the Provisional leadership.' On the evidence available, only the granting of the five demands, in full, could be certain of doing that. Lesser moves would involve a change of stance for HMG, if declared, before the hunger strike ended. 'We have so far followed a very hard line, arguing that any weakening could only encourage the strikers to hold out for their full demands. A move by us now would be seen – in Northern Ireland by Protestants and Provisionals – as a signal that we were cracking.' 'If we go for a compromise,' argued Atkins, 'there are two further risks we run':

(i) The prisoners – or those who control them – could accept the concessions offered, end the strike, and three months later repeat it to get the rest of their demands.

(ii) They could reject them and hold out for their full demands. In that event we shall be seen – depending on the point of view – either as having weakened to no useful effect, or as having made a reasonable offer and thus put the prisoners clearly in the wrong. Some moderate Catholic opinion, eg in the States, may tend to the latter; but it could be a high price to pay for a PR gain.

In considering how a resolution of the hunger strike might be achieved, 'we have three broad options available to us', stated Atkins:

(a)   We can continue to stand firm and make no concessions, in which case we would be accepting the consequences of further deaths and relying on the hunger strikers' nerve breaking to avoid them.

(b)   We can call in some outside body of standing (eg the International Committee of the Red Cross) to look at our prison regime and say whether it is not – as we believe – humane and reasonable, (in which case we shall be powerfully placed to counter hostile propaganda).

(c)   We could ourselves exploit the general commitment we are already on record as having given, to maintain and improve the prison regime.

If the Government wished to pursue the third of these three options, 'we can proceed by direct negotiations with the Provisionals or the prisoners. I reject this.' But, if his colleagues agreed, there were four possible channels open to the Government. These were listed below, but Atkins was clear that, given the time constraint under which the Government might need to operate, (a) below was the only practical one:

(a)   We could use the ICJP. They have the merit that they are active and on the doorstep. They could be allowed to see the strikers and would willingly act as mediators if we wished. As a Catholic body they are likely to be trusted by the prisoners (but per contra to use them would be suspect among the Protestants).

(b)   We could revive the idea, rejected by OD, that a suitably prestigious Committee (which we shall need to set up before long anyway to advise us on some medium and long term problems we face in NI prisons) should be set up now and charged additionally and as a matter of urgency to examine and report on the current regimes for all prisoners, conforming and protesting, and on the scales of punishment appropriate for persistent breaches of prison rules. Since this body does not yet exist, it would not be possible for it to operate immediately – it would take some time to set it up.

(c)   We could invite the International Committee of the Red Cross (ICRC) – who have already indicated their willingness to do so – to undertake the task at (b). The ICRC has the merit – as against the ICJP – of being an international and non-sectarian body; but it is connected in the public mind with POW camps. However, it has a well-established role in dealing with civil unrest, and has previously been involved in Northern Ireland at the invitation of Unionist Governments.

(d) We could without difficulty resuscitate the interest of the European Commission on Human Rights (ECHR), whose procedures under Article 28 of the Convention to arrive at a 'friendly settlement' are still available. This would however take time.

If the Government was prepared to contemplate, suggested Atkins, some further movement, it would be only sensible to do this before McDonnell died – which could be within a week or even less. The ICJP was the only readily available independent channel of communication with the strikers, 'and we could instruct Michael Alison to engage with them tomorrow' on the possibility of resolving the issue on the basis of his previous discussions with them as summarized in his letter to them and as reflected in Atkins' statement. However, 'I think we must recognise that it may be necessary for him to be more specific about measures and timing than in his letter if the hunger strikers are to be persuaded that they can safely abandon their protest', Atkins told Mrs Thatcher. There was one further point: 'whatever course we pursue, there would be some serious disadvantages in bringing to an end the current dialogue with the ICJP. They are on the stage; they are trusted by the prisoners; their support is valuable.' Any other organization would be viewed by the prisoners with great reserve. A hard-line statement issued the day before, on behalf of the protesting prisoners generally, (but not by the strikers themselves, who appeared to be more amenable, thought Atkins) suggested that they were no longer insisting on a differentiated regime for terrorist prisoners, but would be content if their five demands were conceded for *all* prisoners. 'That would mean we had surrendered control to all prisoners: we must instead look for an outcome which does not infringe the principle that we cannot concede control over how the prisons are run to groups of prisoners', stressed Atkins. In addition:

… if we are to move quickly we may well have to concede via the ICJP something specific 'on account' to be introduced as soon as the hunger strike ended (eg restoration of more lost remission; the right to wear own clothes all the time) while further exchanges about the continuing regime continue. We should not assume that a mere promise to consider, eg, the ICJP proposals (which would need very detailed examination in the light of practicalities) without something on account would bring them off.

Once a process of this kind had been authorized, Atkins stressed the need to follow it through and for the Government's spokesman to have wide discretion about a final settlement.[41]

The Prime Minister held a meeting to discuss Atkins' minute. William Whitelaw, the Home Secretary, the Lord Privy Seal, the Chancellor of the Duchy of Lancaster, Atkins, Alison, Sir Robert Armstrong, Sir Kenneth Stowe and Philip Woodfield were also present. Mrs Thatcher began the meeting by stressing that she felt that no concession could be made to the hunger-strikers in any way. There was, however, something to be said for meeting, at least in part, Dr FitzGerald's wish for the ICJP to be allowed into the Maze Prison. She had been confirmed in this by her discussion with Cardinal Ó Fiaich: her initial view was that Alison could allow the Commission to see the hunger-strikers to explain their proposals, but not to negotiate. It was for consideration whether the Commission should be represented by a single spokesman, perhaps Father Crilly, who had a distant relative among the hunger-strikers.

Discussion then concentrated on the basis on which the Commission would be allowed to visit the hunger-strikers. Alison had already explained to the Commission that the Government must stand by the principle that the Prison Governor must retain control and authority over conditions in the prison. He had, however, indicated to the Commission the flexibility in the Government's position on their three proposals on association, work, and clothing. Alison had also 'hinted', on clothing, that the Government did not see this as an issue of principle, but one of security and control. Outside working hours, the prisoners were already free to wear what they liked, subject to certain guidelines laid down by the Governor. There was some possibility of extending this regime to working hours. It might also be possible for the Commission to persuade at least one of the hunger-strikers to give up his protest by exploiting this flexibility. A possible formula on clothing would be to allow the prisoners to wear their own clothes, subject to the Governor having a veto on the choice. On the other hand, it could be argued that any concession, even of this marginal kind, would become the 'top of a slippery slope'. Such concessions were unlikely to bring a permanent end to the hunger strike. The hunger-strikers were 'the pawns of the Provisional IRA.' While it was true to say that 'offering flexibility on clothing would not strictly speaking be a concession', the Provisionals would exploit it as a symbolic victory. They might call off the hunger strike temporarily while exploiting this victory, but they would probably return to the strike when they felt the time was right. If the Government's purpose was to persuade one or more of the hunger-strikers to give up their protest, then the option of prolonging their life by intravenous feeding ought to be considered. If such options were pursued, however, the Government would inevitably be accused of force-feeding. The British Medical Association's Rules of Ethics, and a similar international declaration of ethics made in Tokyo in 1975, both prohibited doctors from taking such action. It might have been possible to persuade doctors in the Maze to introduce force-feeding in the last stages of a hunger strike, but the Government could open itself to international criticism by taking this path. The Home Secretary had recently been asked for assurances by the German Government that the UK would not reintroduce force-feeding. It was, however, agreed that this option should not be ruled out, and the Prime Minister asked for information on the practice in the United States on force-feeding.

The gathering then considered how, if the Government's purpose was to reduce criticism of its policy, the emphasis should be to lay the blame for lack of progress on the hunger-strikers themselves, and to show that conditions in prison were excellent. This, it was suggested, might be achieved in two ways. First, the ICJP could be asked to urge the hunger-strikers to direct their complaints to the European Commission on Human Rights. If the hunger-strikers refused, 'they would condemn themselves.' If they accepted, the Government had already made plain that it was happy for the ECHR to respond. The second option was to invite the Red Cross to look at the present regime in Northern Ireland and to say whether it was humane and reasonable. The ICRC had been into the Maze in each of the years from 1971–1974, though this had been to examine the conditions for handling internees, 'who had of course not been convicted by a court and who in the public mind were more akin to prisoners of war.' However, the advantage of this option was that the ICRC could be invited in by the Government, whereas the ECHR, because of its terms of reference, could not. Moreover, the ICRC was often active in countries not in a state of war but only in conditions of 'internal disturbance or tension'. Since there could be no question of the ICJP's negotiating with the hunger-strikers and the Government, it should be made clear that the Commission would not be able to see Ministers after they had visited the Maze. They would, however, be free to discuss their visit with officials.

The Prime Minister, summing up the discussion, said that it was unlikely that the ICJP could persuade any of the hunger-strikers to call off their fast. The Government's main aim should be to demonstrate that the blame for the hunger strike lay with the strikers themselves rather than with the alleged inflexibility of the Government. There should be no change in the Government's position on clothing, but the ICJP should be allowed to visit the strikers. The Government should make a statement before the visit took place. The statement should first explain the Government's position, as set out in Atkins' recent statement and Alison's letter to the Commission. It should also say that the Government hoped that if the hunger-strikers had any complaints about their treatment, the Commission would explore and encourage the possibility of an approach to the ECHR. In such circumstances the Government would at once contact the ECHR, and start making arrangements to enable it to act on the complaint without delay. The statement should emphasize that, in taking up the Government's offer to visit the Maze, the ICJP stood by the absolute necessity for the control of the prison to vest in the Governor. It should also welcome the statement by the Conference of Irish Bishops. If, following the Commission's visit, the hunger-strikers refused to make any approach to the ECHR, the Government would invite the ICRC to report on the conditions in the prison.[42]

NOTES

1   PRONI NIO/12/197A Note of a Meeting with John Hume on 29 May 1981.
2   PRONI NIO/12/197A Wyatt to Blatherwick, 1 June 1981.
3   PRONI NIO/12/197A Blatherwick to Wyatt, 1 June 1981.
4   TNA PREM 19/505 Statement on Hunger Strike in the Maze Prison Northern Ireland, 3 June 1981.
5   TNA PREM 19/505 Statement on H-Block.
6   TNA PREM 19/505 Irish Catholic Bishops' Statement, 17 June 1981.
7   TNA PREM 19/505 Atkins to Prime Minister, 12 June 1981.
8   TNA PREM 19/505 Dublin Telegram to FCO Number 199 of 17 June 1981.
9   TNA PREM 19/505 Armstrong to Prime Minister, 17 June 1981.
10 TNA PREM 19/505 Armstrong to Alexander, 17 June 1981. The Provisionals – Political Activity, 16 June 1981.
11 TNA PREM 19/505 Cornick to Alexander, 22 June 1981.
12 TNA CJ4/3631 Protests and Second Hunger Strike – Weekly Bulletin No. 16 0900 hours Thursday 11 June–0900 hours, Thursday 18 June.
13 TNA CJ4/3631 Dublin to FCO Telegram Number 195 of 14 June.
14 TNA CJ4/3631 Note, 15 June 1981.
15 TNA CJ4/3631 Patrick Joseph Quinn.
16 TNA CJ4/3631 Protests and Second Hunger Strike – Weekly Bulletin No. 16 0900 hours Thursday 11 June–0900 hours, Thursday 18 June.
17 TNA CJ4/3631 Belfast Republican Press Centre, 17 June 1981.
18 TNA CJ4/3631 Dublin to FCO Telegram Number 201 of 18 June 1981.
19 TNA CJ4/3631 Dublin to FCO Telegram Number 202 of 18 June 1981.
20 TNA CJ4/3631 Dublin to FCO Telegram Number 203 of 18 June 1981.
21 TNA CJ4/3631 Armstrong to Prime Minister, 18 June 1981.
22 TNA CJ4/3631 Dublin to immediate FCO Telegram Number 206 of 22 June 1981.
23 TNA CJ4/3631 Dublin to FCO Telegram Number 208 of 22 June 1981.
24 TNA CJ4/3631 Alexander, 23 June 1981.
25 TNA CJ4/3631 Note of a meeting with the COC and CC held in PUS Office in Belfast on 22 June 1981.
26 TNA PREM 19/505 Meeting with the Irish Commission for Justice and Peace – Tuesday, 23 June 1981.
27 TNA CJ4/3631 Note of a meeting with the COC and CC held in PUS Office in Belfast on 22 June 1981.
28 TNA CJ4/3631 Note of a meeting with the COC and CC held in PUS Office in Belfast on 22 June 1981.
29 TNA CJ4/3631 Note for the Record, 26 June 1981.
30 TNA CJ4/3631 Gilmour to Atkins, 29 June 1981.
31 TNA PREM 19/505 Alison to The Most Reverend Dermot O'Mahoney, 30 June 1981.
32 TNA PREM 19/505 Extract from Secretary of State's statement of 30 June 1981.
33 TNA PREM 19/505 Brief for meeting of Prime Minister and Secretary of State for Northern Ireland with Cardinal Ó Fiaich.

34   TNA FCO 87/1261 Ó Fiaich to Thatcher, 2 June 1981.
35   TNA PREM 19/505 Objects of Meeting.
36   TNA PREM 19/505 Meeting, 1 July 1981.
37   TNA PREM 19/505 Telegram number 223 of 1 July 1981.
38   TNA CJ4/3632 Protests and Second Hunger Strike – Weekly Bulletin No. 18 0900 hours Thursday, 25 June–0900 hours Thursday, 2 July.
39   TNA PREM 508 Whitmore to Fall, 2 July 1981.
40   TNA PREM 19/508 Telephone Conversation between the Prime Minister and Dr Garret FitzGerald on Wednesday, 1 July 1981.
41   TNA PREM 19/505 Atkins to Prime Minister: Northern Ireland: the Hunger Strike, 2 July 1981.
42   TNA FCO 87/1261 From the Private Secretary Stephen Boys-Smith, 4 July 1981.

Chapter 9

Deal or No Deal?

In Norther Ireland, Michael Alison began a marathon series of meetings with the ICJP at which the Government's prison regimes were 'clarified again – and again.' The first took place at Hillsborough Castle on Friday 3 July, and lasted some eight hours from 14.30.[1] The Prime Minister was informed that 'unfortunately no real progress has been made. The main topic for discussion was the clothing aspect. The subject was "talked round" at great length with Mr. Alison stressing the Government's position as stated in Mr. Atkins' 'statement'. Mrs Thatcher was reassured that the problem as to what was regarded as duress by the Government was broached, and it was discussed whether, with the hunger strike ended, the Government would still consider itself to be under duress.[2] The next morning, at the same venue, Alison and the ICJP had another three-hour meeting.[3] Mrs Thatcher phoned Alison to find out the latest news:

PM: You have had a terrible time?

MA: No we've had a good time but I just need to take your mind on a couple of points. First I should report that the Irish Commission have now asked officially for permission to go in and see the hunger strikers and that they want to go in to persuade the hunger strikers to desist from their hunger strike unconditionally, but on the basis that we have a moral obligation to pursue the course of development that we've outlined in our public statement. In other words they are going to say to the hunger strikers that there's no hope of securing any objective whilst we are under duress.

PM: But I think that we have to agree to that Michael. Is Ken Stowe listening. No he isn't. Whose [sic] listening from your end.

MA: It's just you and me at the moment. That was the line we've agreed hitherto and so if they do persuade them to go off the hunger strike they will do so unconditionally. But the Commission will then say in the light of what the Secretary of State said in his public statement we really do think the Government have got an obligation to move ahead on all those three areas.

PM: Yes. Please let it be absolutely firmly understood that we do not have a moral obligation to give in to the five demands. It must be understood that control and security remain with HM[G].

MA: Right, absolutely and that is clearly understood and they are themselves going to say that. Now there is, this is really what I need to take your mind on Prime Minister. There was a draft statement prepared and it has four paragraphs, the last two of which the Commission would much prefer us not to make.

PM: The last one I remember was the control and security point.

MA: Yes, they say they would much prefer to make that in their statement, that they regard that any moral obligation that may be upon us must be reflected by a moral obligation to reflect the fact that the Governors have got to govern the prison; and we would rather prefer it to come from them in their statement.

PM: I still think we must nevertheless put it in ours. We don't necessarily put it as we don't necessarily attach it to them. But in our statement we say we have made it clear to the Commission that control and security must remain and continue to remain with the authorities.

MA: Yes, that will be fine. As the statement stands I welcome the acceptance by the Commission they would much rather they made that themselves.

PM: You can say we have made it clear to the Commission that in any future arrangements control and authority must remain with the authorities of the prison. And that principle cannot be compromised.

MA: We can certainly say that coming from us and they will reiterate it for their own side. The only other paragraph …

PM: I hope they will reiterate it Michael

MA: They are committed to doing so and I will get a further committal [*sic*].

PM: They must reiterate it otherwise it's not fair and I can't go ahead.

MA: The other paragraph in the statement they would much rather we did not make at this stage is the reference to the Conference of Irish Bishops which has called for an end to the hunger strike. Because it was such a fierce statement from the Commissioners' point of view and they are going to have such a rough time with the prisoners that they think it would be unhelpful to refer to the Irish Bishops at this stage or indeed to the European Commission.

PM: Oh in that case Michael they haven't got anything left in that statement.

MA: It would then simply be a bland statement about my authorising them to go into the hunger strikers on the basis on our public statement and on the basis that we retain full control.

PM: Yes, but I think we then can say, that is a statement, then we HM adds our rider, not riders our fundamentals, the one on control and authority that has been made clear; secondly that we have urged the Commission on the European Commission of Human Rights. And what was the third one – well the Bishops have already been made and I thought in the end it was a bit compromising in the end – so we've dropped the Bishops.

MA: OK. I will take that back and proceed.

PM: Right, Michael you are doing a super job.[4]

As the Minister and ICJP met, Brendan McFarlane, in a smuggled comm to Gerry Adams, dismissed the ICJP initiative highlighting how the hunger-strikers believed the Commission 'has absolutely nothing in their so-called clarifications. The lads don't expect much to come of their efforts and proposals so perhaps we'll get some sort of condemnatory statement from them against the Brits which would help us'.[5] On the back of this the protesting prisoners issued a lengthy statement, also on 4 July, in response to the Secretary of State's statement of 30 June. In it they made a fundamental concession. The prisoners argued it was 'wrong for the British Government to say that we are looking for differential treatment from other prisoners. We would warmly welcome the introduction of the five demands for all prisoners. Therefore, on this major point of British policy, there is no sacrifice of principle involved.' The protesters believed that the granting of the five demands to *all* prisoners would not in any way mean that the administration would be forfeiting control of the prison, nor would their say on prison activities be greatly diminished; 'but the prisoner could have his dignity restored and cease to occupy the role of establishment zombie'.

Atkins had outlined the present work routine under the title 'Prison Activity'. The prisoners described this as 'a crude system which Mr Atkins disguises with flowery jargon. Yet, it should not be a major point of contention between the administration and ourselves.' What the British Government recognized as '"prison work" we do not. Therefore, with goodwill, "work" and the achievement of a compatible arrangement, should be available without loss of principle.' Besides self-education, which would be the main prop in any agreement, the prisoners declared themselves prepared to maintain their cells, wings and blocks, and engage in any activity that they defined as self-maintenance. Atkins, they stated, was either misinformed or exaggerating the free association demand: free association meant that there would be freedom of movement within the wings. Supervision need not be restricted; that was a matter for the regime's discretion. There would be no interference with prison officers, who would maintain their supervisory role. It had to be remembered that H-Blocks were control units and each wing was built to accommodate twenty-five prisoners: 'So it is rather a red herring to speak of the regime losing control of the prison if the prisoners had freedom of the wing.' Equally, it was misleading to quote figures of 100 prisoners presumably associating together: 'We believe there should be wing visits but we do not envisage ourselves (although Mr Atkins does) running around the block as we please in large numbers.' It was unrealistic to expect Loyalists and Republicans to integrate satisfactorily together. The forced integration of, or the deliberate creation of a confrontation between, those who bore arms in respect of their highly conflicting political ideologies was wrong and could only lead to trouble: 'If studied carefully it will be seen that our definition of free association is far removed from what seems to be Mr Atkins's.'

With regards to clothing, the protestors contended that the concessions made would have only minimal effect. It was illusory to restrict the wearing of prison clothes to half the week; prisoners, like everyone else, slept, and for most of the rest of the time would be forced to wear prison clothes. The women in Armagh prison wore their own clothes, and there was no objective reason why all prisoners should not be allowed to wear their own clothes, declared the protesters. As for lost remission, this was a result of the protest and was not connected with the cause of it:

> As the British Government says, the machinery exists to reclaim it – yet, for some reason the British Government is being ambiguous on this matter. What constitutes a 'subsequent good behaviour period?' What does one fifth return of remission mean? This should not be an area of

disagreement for it does not directly affect the running of the system. But it is of mutual benefit to all whom it affects that full remission is given back to we prisoners.

In giving their views on what Atkins said, the protesters stressed:

... we have outlined what should be the basis of a solution, without loss of principle to either side in this conflict. By asking the British administration to come in to discuss a resolution we ask nothing unreasonable. It is common for officials from that administration to visit this prison and converse with prisoners. It has been done before.

The prisoners acknowledged: 'It could well be that Mr Atkins has been misinformed about our demands. It certainly appears from his June 30th statement that this is so. We ask all parties involved to study this statement closely. We particularly ask the British to study it. It should not be taken lightly.'

Naturally, the Government pored over the statement to see if there was any movement in the Republican position: the answer was not clear-cut for, as far as the NIO was concerned, the statement 'was evidently produced outside the prison and was very carefully phrased', noting it was conciliatory in tone and accepted that 'special treatment' was not being sought. However, the 'measured phraseology' was such that it could be 'interpreted as either a continued insistence on the substance of the 5 demands or a significant watering down of these. The ambiguity is such that it would not be unreasonable to assume some change in PIRA thinking', noted the NIO.[6] The NIO's assessment that the statement had been constructed outside the prison was incorrect – it came from the prisoners and it was a significant concession from them: by agreeing that the five demands could be applied to *all* prisoners in Northern Ireland they had effectively conceded on special category status. But that did not meet the Government's criteria that it would not make any concessions under duress, or that the prison authorities were the ones who would make the decisions and retain control.

The same afternoon, the ICJP was admitted to see the fasting prisoners all assembled together in the prison hospital. The meeting ended after some two and a half hours, following which the hunger-strikers had a short discussion among themselves (as did the Commission) before asking to see Bik McFarlane. The latter was given permission and met the strikers for some forty-five minutes.[7] The ICJP informed the prisoners of the clarification given by Alison in response to its statement of 3 June, of their meetings with him and his letter to the ICJP. Having regard to the substance of these clarifications, they told the hunger-strikers that in the event of the hunger strike coming to an end, the British Government would, in their considered view, be morally obliged to take action on the areas suggested by the ICJP in their 3 June statement within a reasonable timescale, which they could suggest. In particular, in the event of the hunger strike coming to an end, the British Government would be morally obliged to allow all prisoners to wear all their own clothes at all times as of right (unless such clothes resembled prison officers' uniforms, constituted a form of paramilitary uniform and were manifestly outlandish), whether or not the blanket protest would come to an end. In the ICJP's opinion, a reasonable timescale to implement this (including embodying prison regulations) was two weeks from the ending of the hunger strike. In the event of the hunger strike coming to an end, the British Government would be, in the ICJP's considered view, morally obliged to increase opportunities for association by the prisoners in an open-handed and flexible manner, and in particular:

(1) to allow movement by all prisoners during daily exercise time between exercise yards of every two adjacent wings in each block;

(2) to allow movement by all prisoners of every two adjacent wings in each block during the daily recreation periods.

These concessions would be subject in the final analysis to the principles of security, maintenance and of overall control by the prison authorities. In the ICJP's opinion, a reasonable timescale for the implementation of these measures was four weeks from the time the protest came to an end. Furthermore, the ICJP believed that in the context of the new situation, which would be created were the protest to end, the British Government should seriously consider, as part of the generous and flexible approach to prison improvement referred to in the statement by Atkins on 30 June, allowing an extension of the daily period of association within individual wings (such as between the hours 7.15 to 8.30 and 5.00 to 5.30 p.m.) However, this would be under supervision. The ICJP believed that the Government should also increase to the maximum the range of useful activities prisoners might engage in during the week, to offer each prisoner the widest choice of activity, which, as far as possible, should be congenial to him within the broad and visible framework of prison management, excluding work that might be regarded as demeaning in particular circumstances and subject in the final analysis to the principle that all prisoners were engaged in some form of activity. The following was a list of proposals made by the ICJP, which they claimed the British Government considered compatible with the above:

(1) provision should be made for prisoners with an acceptable level of skill, knowledge and expertise in the areas of cultural education and practical living, including arts and crafts, to pass on such skills, knowledge and

expertise to other prisoners as part of the range of useful activities in which prisoners might engage;

(2) prisoners may wish to work for charitable or voluntary bodies on condition that if necessary the body concerned will provide material free of cost to the prisoners, to enable such work to be done. There would be no remuneration for prisoners in the case of the above conditions. (Prisoners may opt for work of a remunerative nature).

(3) The prisoner who fails to find accommodation within the choices provided may in the last analysis be required to do manual work though he may refuse remuneration. Such work may include work by prisoners on the construction of a church or equivalent facilities for relevant work within the prison.

The British Government, claimed the ICJP, indicated that this list need not be exhaustive and that other proposals would be considered. It was the Commission's view that personal laundry could be accommodated within the prison. In its opinion, a reasonable timescale for the implementation of these measures would be four weeks for No. (1) and eight weeks for No. (2) above, and six months for the type of activity outlined at (3) above. The timescale for increasing the range of useful activities available to prisoners to an acceptable level would be eight weeks from the time of the ending of the hunger strike. The ICJP also believed that it had obtained clarification that, in addition to the aspects of the prison regime outlined above, on the ending of the protest, prisoners would be entitled every month to receive four visits and eight letters, and send back a proportionate number. Prisoners serving sentences of over two years would be allowed to have a radio in their cells.

It was 'clearly understood' by the ICJP that if the protest were to come to an end, a new situation would be created. The prisoners who had come off the protest received a restoration of full remission for the unexpired portion of their sentence, and restoration of 20% of the amount forfeited because of their protest. If and when the protest ended, the British Government had said that it would be 'imaginative and dramatic'. The ICJP interpreted such words to mean, at the very least, the restoration of the great part of the remission already forfeited, and that total remission should be sympathetic in the spirit of magnanimity. As the ICJP understood it, the Government was prepared to grant the cultural aspirations of the prisoners and to facilitate them as far as possible. This meant that the Government was morally bound to allow Irish literature and textbooks and cultural classes on a comparable basis. The ICJP noted that the Government had already allowed a copy of an Irish language book to be presented by the Commission to the prisoners.[8] While this was being presented to the prisoners, Alison updated Mrs Thatcher:

PM: Oh Michael what a marathon, whatever happened?

MA: They do like talking. You know we were motoring on the three demands for three areas of change, so we had to spend a good deal of time going over them all. On two of them, namely association and work as you know we were indicating areas of …So that needed a good deal of plotting over. But then we spent a long time on clothing; then of course its all or nothing. And following your instructions I stone-walled and said there were no circumstances in which the Government could be seen or actually effect the buying-off of the hunger strike by openly and directly conceding a change in clothing. So that's where they were pressing us. And I did indicate that the only way forward in this area is for the hunger strike to stop inequivocally [*sic*] … and this would bring into play paragraph 19 of the Public Statement which amongst other things said that improvements the general prison regime are a different matter, there is scope yet for further development.

PM: Yes, with in the control and security clause.

MA: But above all without any explicit and automatic link with the ending of the hunger strike. So they went away at the end of the day having, I think, registered finally that there was no way in which they could go into the prison and say if you do this then this will happen. But the formula is that if the hunger strike stops then it will create an environment in the prison and outside in which it will be possible for the Government to consider moving forward on the general lines of improvement. That's where we are at present, they went away to think about that over night. I think they are coming back now at 11.00 hrs and I think they are going to say to me – OK, it's just possible that that formula will work but only if we can have some idea as to how soon improvements will begin to materialise. We are reflecting on that but I am so far saying that there is no possible means of giving them any time.

PM: They do realise to do this that control and security must remain that's the absolute principle?

MA: Oh yes, I've used your formula. The effect is choice effectively remains with the Governor, in other words total control over the … which can be brought in.

PM: Michael what a terrible time you must have had.

MA: It's all very engaging and friendly and we have a good atmosphere and a good spirit.

PM: It tries one's patience doesn't it.

MA: I don't mind it, I'm quite happy to do it. I'm used to it now. I think its all part of the process.

PM: I think you are marvellous and I am very grateful to you.

MA: We are not by any means through yet and my own feeling is that we haven't got anything like enough on offer in relation to their demands to stop the strike, but I may be wrong. I tend to be pessimistic.

PM: On the news this morning they said that there was a meeting in Dublin too?

MA: I think that's quite possible, in the middle of our meeting yesterday the Taoiseach rang up from Dublin to speak to Hugh Logue (?) probably I think to say to him that the families were with him and what was the atmosphere like.

PM: I rather gathered it was a meeting in Dublin with the families. They are anxious to get it off aren't they.

MA: There is one area which is going to be a little sensitive in a way Prime Minister. That is the difference between the hunger strikers and the back-up of 400 men who are on the protest. Now I think our objective is to get the hunger strikers off the hunger strike.

PM: That would stop the deaths.

MA: Yes, I don't think we should get the protesters off the protest at the same time.

PM: You cannot get everything Michael.

MA: Right. Now it follows from this if I can just elaborate slightly. That if we then within a fortnight or three or four weeks began to do something about own clothing in an atmosphere of calm and not under duress then we might find that the protesters were still on protest and would then find that they were benefiting from a new regime of clothing in their protest if you see what I mean?

PM: But surely any new regime available to full conforming prisoners.

MA: Well the point is that prison clothing is not a privilege, its automatic to all prisoners who will actually put on clothing; so you would then find that the protesters were able, because clothing is not a privilege but a right to have own clothing while still on protest. But actually if we can live with that because that is exactly the situation which prevails in Armagh Jail where the women wear their own clothing. So I think we can get round that one without too much trouble and this lies some way behind.

PM: I think we will meet that one later.

MA: So we deal with the hunger strike.

PM: I think that's the main objective.

MA: So you confirm to me that I am to stand firm on this position?

PM: Oh indeed Michael.

MA: ... under any circumstances [will I] yield own clothing under duress.

PM: Oh indeed yes...[9]

The ICJP, however, was not the only show in town. In the aftermath of the prisoners' statement, the British Government reactivated a secret backchannel between it and the Provisionals. The intermediary, or contact, between the two was the Catholic businessman, Brendan Duddy, from Derry, known as 'Mountain Climber' to Republicans, reflecting his passion for hill-climbing. On this occasion the British had given him the codename 'SOON' (they had given him different ones over the years). The Prime Minister was provided with an account of the contacts. At 22.00, on 4 July, SOON phoned his British Government contact and reported that a great deal of confusion had arisen in Provisional circles from the impression, given by the ICJP, that there was every indication of movement by HMG. Since no confirmation had been issued on the SOON channel, the Provisionals tended not to accept this. SOON then described the circumstances of the issue of the prisoners' statement of 4 July. He said that the statement had been issued independently by the prisoners in the Maze, and that the timing came as a surprise to senior Provisionals outside. The content of the statement represented a line previously agreed between the prisoners and the Provisionals. Unfortunately, the timing of the release of the statement had caught the Provisionals unaware. The Movement's senior members, and SOON claimed there were eight, were widely dispersed. Only Gerry Adams and Rory O'Bradaigh were readily available. They were regrouping, and SOON's Provisional contact had instructed him to stand by. But SOON saw two immediate problems. Firstly, in the period from Saturday afternoon (4 July) to Monday morning (6 July), the Provisionals would be out of contact with the prisoners. Normally this would not matter, but it now became important when rapid action was required. Secondly, if the Provisionals made contact through the SOON channel it would be beneficial for a generalized response to be available.

SOON had rung his British contact prior to a request from the Provisionals to do so in order to prepare HMG for this situation. Firstly, he asked whether any way could be found of getting communications in and out of the prison in the period between Saturday afternoon and Monday morning. Secondly, he stated that a meeting of senior Provisionals had taken place on 28 June at which they considered realistic conditions for the ending of the hunger strike. SOON believed that the thinking of the Provisional leadership was as follows: immediately following the ending of the hunger strike, concessions would be required on parcels, visits and the wearing of prisoners' own clothes.. This, he said, would provide the Provisionals with a face-saving way out. The remaining demands dealing with work and association could be subject to a series of discussions *after* the ending of the hunger strike. He stressed that the Provisionals' position was, in his opinion, represented by the prisoners' statement. Thus, if the arrangements detailed in this statement were acceptable to HMG and immediate concessions could be made on clothing, parcels and visits, he was optimistic. Since the prisoners' statement had caught the Provisionals 'on the hop', they would be suspicious that this had been arranged in some way over the weekend to aggravate the position. He warned that if the Provisionals should ring and ask for clarification, and no answer was available, this would heighten their suspicions. He left HMG with two questions: would it be possible for a visit to be arranged to the prison by the Provisionals over the weekend, and why had the SOON channel not been activated to clarify the situation?[10]

At 02.00 on 5 July, SOON called again, and began by restating the Provisionals' disorganized position. He pointed out that to take a decision of this magnitude – to engage in finding a solution – required the presence of 'all eight senior members' of the Provisionals concerned. They would be unwilling to take any decision without a full complement. The issue of clothing would be the one area where a testing of HMG's intentions would take place. The majority of the remainder of the conversation was taken up with SOON's views on how the mechanism for issuing of clothing should occur. He produced two or three scenarios over a period of an hour, none of which, HMG observed, were compatible with the principle that the hunger strike must be called off before any action could be expected: 'We repeatedly stressed this point'. After a 'long and generally unrewarding' discussion over the minute details of the issue of clothing, HMG representatives suggested that the probable line would be that the eight hunger-strikers would be issued with their own clothes immediately on terminating their protest. The remaining protesting prisoners would receive their clothes at some time in the future.

This led SOON to point out what he considered to be a genuine misunderstanding by HMG. He said that it was not possible to separate the hunger-strikers from the remaining protesting prisoners: there was an agreement that the hunger-strikers were standing as representatives of all the protesting Republican prisoners in the Maze and that they should not receive preferential treatment. If it were only practical to issue clothing to a small group at first, this should not be totally comprised of hunger-strikers. SOON added that one of the major difficulties over the implementation of the agreement at the end of the last hunger strike had been the attitude of some of the prison officers. He pointed out that the Provisionals believed that HMG had been sincere in trying to implement their side of the agreement in December 1980. The breakdown had occurred because some of the prisoners had been harassed by some of the prison officers. SOON, therefore, requested that in HMG's proposals there should be an instruction to the Governor of the prison to encourage flexibility in the implementation of any agreement. In response to his two specific questions raised in the first phone call:

> ... we said that HMG would have no objection in principle to a visit to the prison but that we hoped that the Provisionals would propose a representative who would be acceptable. In response to his question about communications on the SOON channel we explained that we had only ever initiated calls in response to queries or requests for clarification.

The call ended at 05.00.[11] At this stage there was no offer on the table from the British – this would have required Ministerial approval; but what seems to have been discussed between SOON and HMG contacts can be envisaged from Duddy's diary entry of 5 July:

> Clothes = after lunch tomorrow and before the afternoon visit.
> As a man is given his clothes he clears out his own cell.
> Pending the resolution of the work issue which will be worked out [illegible] as soon as the clothes are and no later than 1 month.

> Visits= [illegible] on Tuesday. Hunger strikers + some others
> H.S. to end 4 hrs after clothes + work has been resolved.[12]

It is important to note that the British rejected any scenario, as outlined by Duddy, unless the hunger strike ended first. SOON rang again, at 10.45, to say that the Provisionals were rapidly regrouping and that he expected that they would meet between 12.00 and 15.00 that afternoon. He then returned to the subject of the prison visit, stating that the number of senior Provisionals with a full grasp of the situation, including knowledge of the SOON channel and the status to enable them to act authoritatively, was very limited. He added that if the key to accepting any agreement was persuasion, education and knowledge, then that was not available outside the very upper echelons of the Provisional movement. It was not even available as of right to the entire Sinn Féin leadership. This, SOON claimed, posed a problem. In response to HMG's request for suggestions of Provisionals who would fit this description, SOON produced Danny Morrison, Gerry Adams and Martin McGuinness as the only three candidates. After consultation, HMG said that it would accept Morrison but would on no account accept either Adams or McGuinness. SOON understood this, but then warned that a problem with this was that Morrison was rumoured to be in the USA. The Provisionals were, however, taking steps to try and find him.

SOON then proceeded to offer the Provisionals' view of the ICJP. He said that determination still existed not to let the ICJP act as a mediator. As a consequence, there was a body of opinion within the Provisional leadership that was unaware of the SOON channel and, therefore, took a destructive view towards any current proposals since they believed that these would involve the ICJP. SOON's Provisional contact had led him to believe that the Provisionals would compare the statement of the Secretary of State and the prisoners to find common ground. There would then need to be considerable attention given to detail, and SOON said that this would be very difficult through his channel because of the nature of the communications. He added that it might be a good idea to consider ways around this, either via some written communication delivered to SOON or via a meeting. SOON then revealed that, at 08.00 that morning, he was faced with the statement by the Provisionals that HMG was insincere. He had replied that unless that belief was totally dispelled he was 'going on holiday.' He added that if he had not maintained his independence from the Provisionals, this would not have been possible. The strength of his reply had, he said, won the day. SOON concluded by saying that the next contact would be between 16.00 and 18.00 that day at the earliest, and this would be for preliminary comments only. The call ended at 11.25.[13]

At 14.05, SOON made a short call to HMG to say that Morrison had been located and had agreed to visit the prison, but that it was important that this should take place as quickly as possible. SOON also said that it was essential that Morrison should be allowed to see the hunger-strikers, McFarlane and any other prisoners. After rapid consultation, HMG representatives rang back at 14.30 to say that this was acceptable provided that Morrison understood that he would not be allowed to see McFarlane and the hunger-strikers together. This was agreed. SOON then indicated that Martin McGuinness had just arrived at his location. He said that time was of the essence and asked what the current HMG position was. HMG explained that it was important, before drafting any document for consideration by Ministers, that 'we should possess the Provisionals' view. SOON then undertook to seek clear views on their position, which would be relayed to us later after discussion in the light of Morrison's visit.'[14]

Then, in the middle of a British discussion concerning a possible clash of visits by Morrison and the ICJP to the Maze, SOON rang back at 15.00. HMG began by trying to get him to delay Morrison, but he said that it was now too late to do so. He made the point that HMG was considered to have been very, very helpful in allowing the visit. SOON then said that, in the opinion of his Provisional contact, the Provisionals would be working from the prisoners' statement in terms of association, remission, visits, parcels and work. It would be all important, he said, to get the clothing and timing right. SOON believed that he had now been able to persuade the Provisionals that HMG was not interested in any settlement unless the hunger strike was called off first. He was fairly confident that this would be acceptable. He said, however, that a major problem was that 'if panic sets in, this will be the first point to be abandoned.' Therefore, it was essential that there should be 'backup systems'. When HMG queried what this meant, SOON said that he believed that if a further statement were to be produced, it would be very helpful if the Provisionals could see it before publication. He suggested that this could best be achieved by a handover at a meeting between the two ends of the SOON channel. He added that, given the Provisionals' wariness of HMG's position, even trivial setbacks could result in major disasters. He then asked what contingencies were being considered about the implementation of clothing after the hunger strike was called off.

HMG's representatives replied that, although it would be useful to have some idea of what would be acceptable to the Provisionals, there was little point in considering this while their view on the nature of a settlement was unclear. Nevertheless, SOON insisted on suggesting the following possibility: would it be possible for a small number, such as ten to twenty parcels of clothes, to be delivered to the prison in advance and stored by prison officials so that when the hunger strike was called off these could be immediately issued to an appropriate number of prisoners? He added that it was very important that the implementation of clothing should be seen to be operating as soon as possible after the hunger strike was ended. In this way, the Provisionals and the prisoners would be reassured of

HMG's motives, and this would prevent disillusionment at an early stage. SOON then said that it would be extremely helpful if there could be some mention in HMG's proposals of the prison authorities allowing a gradual return to normal conditions. He then referred again to the harassment of prisoners.[15]

In the meantime, Danny Morrison had been to the prison. According to an account provided by Morrison, the proposals sent through the backchannel 'goes further than ICJP's understanding of government position.' Morrison met Brendan McFarlane and explained the 'Mountain Climber' proposals (there is some confusion as to whether Morrison believed this was the codename for the British Intelligence link with Duddy rather than Duddy himself). McFarlane met subsequently with the hunger-strikers. Morrison was allowed to phone out from the doctor's surgery. He told Gerry Adams that the prisoners would not take anything on trust, and that they wanted 'offers confirmed and seek to improve them.' While waiting for McFarlane to return, Morrison was ordered out of the prison by a Governor.[16]

Richard O'Rawe, the IRA public relations officers in the Maze, claimed that he and McFarlane then discussed the 'offer' and agreed there was enough there to accept it: 'We spoke in Irish so the screws could not understand,' O'Rawe later claimed; 'I said, "Ta go leor ann" – There's enough there. He [McFarlane] said, "Aontaim leat, scriobhfaidh me chun taoibh amiugh agus cuirfidh me fhois orthu" – I agree with you, I will write to the outside and let them know.'[17] McFarlane later denied that any such discussion took place. Meanwhile, at the outset of the next call between Duddy and the British, at 17.50 on 5 July, SOON indicated, by a prearranged code, that he was accompanied by a representative of the Provisionals. He had previously suggested that in this situation HMG 'should adopt a hard line.' SOON indicated that a major problem had been the monitoring of the position in the prison currently being carried out by Morrison. He explained that since the Provisionals' representatives were trying to convince the prisoners, the Provisionals' supporters and the relatives, this could cause problems when delegated to one man alone. In order to ease this situation and to enable all parties to be sure that the position taken by Morrison was correct and properly interpreted, SOON considered it important that a second representative should accompany Morrison. HMG representatives answered that 'we would have to consult on this matter and we asked who the Provisionals had in mind.' SOON immediately replied that McGuinness should be allowed to enter the prison. HMG representatives replied that 'we were absolutely certain that the position of HMG would be that this was unacceptable' and pointed out that they had been as helpful as possible at short notice to allow Morrison to enter, 'and we explained to SOON that while senior Provisional personalities could be acceptable, there was absolutely no chance of senior PIRA personalities being allowed access.' This was 'not received well. After establishing that if a second representative were to be allowed this would not apply to the visit taking place that afternoon, HMG representatives allowed SOON several minutes to consult with McGuinness: 'To his credit, he managed to persuade McGuiness [sic] of our point of view ... We said that there was no urgency involved and that we would consult the appropriate authorities', noted the British.[18]

By this point, the ICJP had returned to the Maze, where they spent about four hours talking to McFarlane. The Commissioners also met with the prisoners, including the hunger-strikers. They wanted a senior official from the NIO to explain to the hunger-strikers what was on offer. As Hugh Logue recalled, the hunger-strikers 'were all saying that we had to square any settlement we had, even if it was acceptable to them, with Bik.' McFarlane was in a bed in the hospital wing, so he was available for consultation with the Commissioners. Logue and O'Mahoney talked to McFarlane, who listened to the Commissioners 'for about two minutes' before, remembered Logue, he 'turned around and went back to sleep and Joe McDonnell was going to be dead within thirty-six hours and I never forgave him for that. He was not in the business of trying to get a solution.' Before the Commissioners departed, Oliver Crilly talked, in Gaelic, to Kieran Doherty. Crilly told Logue that Doherty had said 'that if somebody came in and read the terms out to the hunger strikers, they would accept them.'[19] While the Commissioners had argued that their proposals contained the principle of the five demands, and the British would not offer anything else, McFarlane pushed the prisoners' 4 July document. He protested that parts of the Commissioners' offer were 'vague and much more clarification and confirmation was needed to establish exactly what the Brits were on about.' As McFarlane subsequently communicated to Adams: 'I told them the only concrete aspect seemed to be clothes and no way was this good enough to satisfy us.'[20]

When SOON next rang the British, at 23.00, he warned that there had been a series of alarming reports relayed by Morrison from the prison: the situation was now so bad that the possibility of any settlement was seriously in doubt. There was a complete feeling of hostility among the prisoners towards the ICJP, who had been in and out of the prison during the day. The role of the ICJP had created an alarmist view of the sincerity of HMG, and every type of neurosis imaginable was surfacing within the Provisionals' leadership. The British asked what had caused this sudden deterioration in the position. The answer was that, from an apparently enthusiastic position, SOON had been called into an angry and hostile meeting of the Provisionals, almost verging on a complete breakdown. The Provisionals' view of the situation was that the prisoners' statement had been totally ignored by the ICJP. There had then been 'many incoherent abuses' aimed at the SOON channel, with the implication that the time spent in discussion on the SOON channel had been a front by HMG to enable the ICJP to manoeuvre the prisoners into an impossible position. When SOON asked the Provisionals what their position was he was told that all consideration of work and association was being ignored. There was a deep resentment in the Provisional leadership at what they thought of as the pressuring of the prisoners by the ICJP. SOON was told that the prisoners would give a very firm 'no' to the ICJP proposals and that the abuse of the channel had created a predisposition to disbelieve anything that SOON said.

SOON had, therefore, been told that the Provisionals' view was not available because they were extremely upset at the 'bully-boy' tactics of the ICJP. HMG pointed out that the ICJP had volunteered their services independently and that they had met the Provisionals, the Dublin Government, the prisoners and their relatives as well as HMG: 'We asked why HMG was now being asked to shoulder all the blame for the ICJP's proposal? No answer was provided.' In order to attempt to 'brighten what we saw as a depressing situation, we reverted to the question of whether a second representative would be allowed in the Maze.' SOON replied that he would keep this in reserve for the time being. At this point, SOON indicated that a considerable number of Provisionals had arrived. HMG representatives said that time was pressing 'and it was now imperative that we have a statement of the Provisionals' position.' SOON undertook to try and obtain this, and rang off at midnight.[21] At 01.00, SOON rang back to say that he had managed to persuade the Provisionals to provide their view, which he then dictated. It was as follows:

> The Provisionals fully accept the position as stated by the prisoners, and that is the only basis for a successful draft proposal by HMG. When HMG produces such a draft proposal it is essential (last word underlined) that a copy be in the Provisionals' hands before it is made public. This is to enable the Provisionals either to approve it or to point out any difficulties before publication. If it were published without prior sight and agreement they would have to disapprove it.

Having delivered this, SOON said that the Provisionals were very worried about the timescale now involved. He added that the situation would be irreparably damaged if a hunger-striker died, and he urged HMG to act with the utmost haste. At this stage the assessment of HMG representatives was that: 'While we appreciate that it has taken a long time to obtain the Provisionals' view we are convinced' that SOON 'has performed his task as well as possible'. They also found that there was little difference between the final view and that which SOON predicted earlier in the weekend. SOON had stressed that time was running short: 'We believe that he will probably ring some time in the night of 6 July for, at least, a progress report. We will await further instructions.'[22]

The ICJP hat, meanwhile, was still in the ring. Michael Alison met the ICJP for a fifth time at 7.00 p.m. in Stormont Castle that evening. The five members of the Commission (Bishop O'Mahoney, Gallagher, Logue, Father Crilly and Connolly) were present, and Alison was accompanied by Blelloch, Wyatt, Jackson and Blatherwick from the NIO. It was the scene for a major row between the two sides over what had been agreed between them. In the Commissioners' view, the hunger-strikers saw the ICJP's clarification of its discussions with Alison as the basis for a settlement. There were two main difficulties:

(i)   the 'skeleton' described … by the ICJP needed filling out; and
(ii) the prisoners deeply distrusted the Government; largely because of what had happened in December.

The Commission had decided that it was important that they should make a statement following their many hours of discussion with Alison, and they had prepared one, which they wanted the Minister to study. They told Alison that the prisoners were insistent that someone from the NIO should go into the prison to clarify the position. The hunger-strikers had expressed 'extreme gratitude' to the ICJP for trying to obtain clarification of the Government's position, and the relatives of the hunger-strikers had also told the ICJP how grateful they were for its efforts. The Commission was convinced that precise details of what the Government could offer were very important; the prisoners read two meanings into everything. Father Crilly commented that the view that the Commission had held at the outset of their meetings with Alison had been reinforced, and they were more than ever convinced that now was the time to come to a settlement. The feedback from the prisoners themselves, the statement issued on 4 July on behalf of the prisoners and the attitudes of the hunger-strikers' families all contributed to the view that a new willingness to accept the prison regime existed. What would be accepted at this point, however, might not be accepted two days later – if Joe McDonnell died. The prisoners were very committed people who would not give in on the off-chance, and this was why precise details, rather than general principles, were so important. Father Crilly thought that the Government's handling of the issue of clothing at the time of the last hunger strike had disturbed both parts of the community, and it was important that misunderstandings should not occur again.

Alison's reaction was that it was ludicrous for prisoners to bring about their own deaths for the sake of 'nuts and bolts' issues in a prison regime that the Government was already committed to administering progressively. The Government could not, in the environment of a continuing hunger strike (that is, under great duress) list in detail the changes that might be made in due course. Nor could it send an official into the prison to expound on the position that the Government had set out. In the areas of work and association, the spectrum embraced an infinite number of variations: the Government had made it clear in public statements that there would be movement within the spectrum. Guarantees of specific moves could not be given under the duress imposed by the hunger strike. On the question of clothing, there were no degrees of movement. It was clear that only one move remained. The Commission, though, repeated that a very deep distrust existed on the part of the prisoners. Their statement of 4 July, however, had been widely recognized as conciliatory. The prisoners appreciated the work that the ICJP was doing, but realized that the Commission could not explain in detail what they were conveying. They therefore wanted an official of the NIO to go to the prison to provide some clarification. The statement that the Commission proposed to make was then examined and discussed.

After examining the ICJP's proposed statement, Alison responded that, while he did not envisage a redrafting of it — which would probably be profitless and impertinent — he had some comments on it. The statement referred to the Government's 'moral obligation' to take action — in the event of the hunger strikes coming to an end — in the three areas of association, work and clothing. Alison said that it should be made clear that it was the *Commission's* view that the Government was under a moral obligation. When he had spoken of this obligation at the last meeting, he had done so in the context of the Secretary of State's statement of 30 June, and of his letter to the Commission. The Commission's proposed settlement went beyond the range of the discussions that had taken place; these discussions had not entailed a commitment to specific details. They had been private discussions and not negotiations; areas of possible movement had been illustrated, but it could not be said that the Government was under a moral obligation to implement certain changes purely because they had been discussed. Alison emphasized that the scope of the earlier discussions had been an open and sincere attempt at clarification of the extent to which — in general terms — the Government might be able to make changes in the prison regime. This had not given the Commission an entitlement to tell the prisoners that there was a fixed offer from the Government, and he did not think the Commission had believed that they had such an entitlement. If the statement prepared by the Commission were issued, it would be necessary for the Government publicly to repudiate it.

Logue replied that the Commission had considered at length the content of their statement. They had tried to keep as closely as possible to the text of the Secretary of State's statement of 30 June in order to accommodate the Government's position. Logue did not believe that they could have arrived at a more helpful wording in their proposals relating to prison work. Father Crilly added that the ICJP had been leading the hunger-strikers to believe that goodwill existed on the part of the Government. It was necessary to clarify, immediately, the details of the actual changes to be implemented; otherwise the Commission might need to withdraw from the scene. They had accepted throughout their talks with Alison that they were not negotiating, but if the Government had not expected them to produce something on the lines of their proposed statement, then it had misled them, and the Commission in turn had misled the prisoners and the prisoners' families, and would have to make a public statement – on the eve of McDonnell's death – to make this known. Crilly continued that the Government had created an illusion of movement, which suited it at this time, and he was sorry that the Commission had been used as a vehicle for this illusion. If the illustration quoted on clothing could be transferred into reality, he did not see why the same could not be done in the other areas that had been discussed. The Commission had already been accused of confusing the situation, and people would say that they had hindered rather than helped.

Alison told the Commission that he *had* expected them to convey to the prisoners what had been discussed, but the discussions had been an illustrative exchange, not the drawing up of an exclusive 'shopping list'. He had tried to put into perspective the kind of changes that *might* be made, while remaining compatible with the need for the prison Governor to maintain control of the prison. He had no objection to the ICJP referring to the matters that had been discussed, but he did not accept that they were in a position to state that the Government had a moral obligation to implement specific changes. Blelloch then reminded the Commission that the Government's position had been set out in the Secretary of State's statement of 30 June and in Alison's letter of 30 June – and obviously this position could be quoted. He thought that the points at issue in the ICJP's draft statement were capable of resolution. On the question of the Government's moral obligation, he thought that the Commission accepted that it must be clear that this was *their* view.

The Commissioners answered that they saw the text of Alison's letter as a moral obligation, although they could not insist on it, since the Government could always renege. They – and others – had begun to become suspicious when Alison had delayed the third meeting with them until Friday, instead of meeting them on Wednesday as they had requested. Since then there had been a growing distrust that the ICJP was being used. If they were not in a position to regard the modest proposals that they had drawn up as binding on the Government, they would have to say publicly that they had been misled, and had misled everyone else, and they would have to withdraw because they were creating confusion. The Commission had entered into these discussions in good will and with commitment as an independent body not employed by either the Government or the prisoners.

They had genuinely believed that the illustrations described during their talks with Alison would be put into practice when the hunger strikes ended. To persuade the hunger-strikers to believe them, they needed more concrete information on the practical detail. To quote the metaphor used by the hunger-strikers, it was necessary to 'put some flesh on the skeleton'. The Commission intended their statement as the first stage, and they reserved the right to publish it, while acknowledging that the Government might decide to contradict it.

Alison objected that it was one thing for the Commission to say that *in their view* the Government was under a moral obligation to do certain things, and quite another for them to state categorically that there was such an obligation on the Government. The ICJP was transposing what had previously been said. For example, any fair reading of the section relating to controlled association in Alison's letter of 30 June could not be reconciled with what the Commission was saying about a moral obligation to implement reforms in this area. S. C. Jackson added that the passage on work in the Commission's proposed statement seemed in his opinion to be quite at variance with what had been discussed on the previous Friday. Alison told the Commission that he realized that there had always been a danger, in the kind of free and frank exchange that he had had with them, that the Commission might feel that they had to make a statement that the Government could not endorse. It might be that they would have to agree to differ. He had genuinely attempted to give illustrations – indeed, he might have given more – and he was quite happy for the Commission to publicize what had been discussed, but he could not accept that the Commission should say that this was an offer that the Government had a moral obligation to implement. On the question of clothing, the issue was simple: it was all or nothing. In the other two areas – association and work – there was a gulf between what the prisoners had asked for and what realistically might be available. In the discussion with the Commission, Alison had touched on some possible changes, but he did *not* have a list of specific proposals, and was *not* in the business of negotiation.

Logue replied that the Commission had set down what they regarded as a minimum of what was reasonable. The prisoners were anticipating a response to their statement of 4 July. He urged the Minister to send an official to the prison and to communicate to the prisoners the precise details of the changes that could be made. Blelloch asked the Commission what, in view of the distrust of the Government that had been expressed, they believed had happened in December when the first hunger strike ended. The Commission replied that they could not have a view on this since they did not know what had happened. Blelloch wondered whether the Commission would accept that the Government might distrust the prisoners. He thought that the difficulty over the Commission's statement was one of language and presentation; Alison then offered to discuss changes to it. The Minister was concerned that if the Commission's statement were issued in its present form, and countered – as it would have to be – by a Government statement, the position would be confused for the prisoners, and the possibility of them ceasing the hunger strike in such a situation would be removed. But the Commission's statement could not be allowed to stand unqualified; it did not set down the position accurately, and it would not be fair to let the prisoners think that it did.

The Commissioners accepted that it was true that the hunger strike would not end in such circumstances. Many were disposed to accept what the ICJP had set out, but they would not come off the hunger strike in response to illustrations. Suspicion was the single most important factor in this, and it was essential that someone from the Government went to the prison to clarify the situation. The Commission had shown Alison's letter of 30 June to the hunger-strikers and had recommended that they should desist from the hunger strike and accept what was set down in the Commission's proposed statement. They understood that the prisoners saw this as a considerable move on the part of the Government, but were afraid that Alison's letter admitted of differing interpretations. The prisoners wanted an NIO official to make clear its meaning, and they wanted to see something in writing. This needed to be done within a matter of hours.

Alison repeated that the Commission had no right to commit the Government to specific actions that had been discussed merely as illustrative examples, and it had no right to expect the Government to deliver now in these areas, even though it was not inconceivable that what had been discussed might be implemented at some stage. When Logue asked the Minister what he would do in the absence of the Commission's statement, Alison replied that he must stand by the Secretary of State's statement of 30 June and his own letter. The prisoners would have to decide whether they trusted what these documents contained. On clothing, the meaning was clear; in the other two areas it was not possible to be more specific. The Commission countered that to prolong the present situation would be to prolong an illusion, and the hope that they had held out for the last eighteen days. They again urged that the NIO should speak directly to the prisoners. The meeting then adjourned, at the Commission's request, for twenty-five minutes.

When it resumed, Bishop O'Mahoney suggested that two people – one of the Commission and one of Alison's advisers – might be nominated to work on redrafting the ICJP's statement. Alison made another suggestion. Since the key to the problem was the need to make clear to the hunger-strikers exactly what was on offer, he could ask an official or the Governor to see the hunger-strikers to explain that the Secretary of State's statement, and the letter to the ICJP providing the context within which progress could be made in the absence of duress, who would be prepared to answer questions from the hunger-strikers. However, as in the case of the discussions with the ICJP, nothing very concrete could be said, since real, practical complications existed. If the Commission agreed to publish

Alison's letter, their own statement could be very brief, simply referring to the topics discussed and making no commitments. A statement might then be produced that the Government would not need to qualify. Upon hearing this, Logue thought that there was now 'some light at the end of the tunnel'. He considered that Alison's suggestion should be implemented forthwith, and that meanwhile work on the statement – perhaps an agreed one between the ICJP and the Government – should begin. After a further adjournment, of about ten minutes, Alison asked the Commission to suspend their statement until the following morning. It would not have been helpful for it to be issued sooner, and meanwhile he would need to consult and take advice. He assured the Commission that there was nothing devious in this request.

Logue felt that this was reasonable, but urged Alison to send in one or two officials to the prison as early as possible – by 7.00 a.m. the following morning. Alison insisted that he would have to be allowed flexibility on this, but he assured the Commission that he was apprised of the need for urgency. After yet another adjournment, the Commission agreed to hold back their statement. They requested permission to telephone the prison chaplain to explain why they had not been back to the prison and to inform him that an NIO official would be coming to the prison. Alison, however, stressed that they could not state categorically that an official would go in. He had undertaken to let the prisoners know the Government's position, but had not made a commitment as to how this would be done, which was something for the Government to decide. The Commission once again suggested that a redrafting of their statement should be commended. There was a clear need for a written document.

Alison thought that it would be time-consuming and wasteful to attempt to redraft the statement immediately; there might have been no need later for such a substantive statement. The basis of the clarification provided by the Government would be the Secretary of State's statement of 30 June, and (if the Commission agreed) the letter of 30 June, to which would be added a clear exposition. Wyatt warned that it was quite likely that the prisoners would find some of what the Government said unacceptable; there was no point in trying to deceive them. Bishop O'Mahoney said that the Commission's document had been prepared very carefully in the light of the need to safeguard the position of the Government and the prison governor, and in the context of enlightened prison reform. He asked that whoever went to speak to the hunger-strikers should do so in the spirit of this document. Alison observed that the clarification for the prisoners would be carried out rather in the spirit of his talks with the Commission, in an attempt to keep to reality. As the meeting concluded, at around 10.30 p.m., the Commission agreed not to issue their statement for the time being.[23]

What was revealing about this meeting, and the previous conversations between Alison and the Prime Minister, is that the former did not go beyond his brief and give the ICJP the impression that he had agreed a package to be presented to the prisoners – only for the 'lady behind the veil' to repudiate it – the Commissioners never challenged Alison's repeated assertions that any options on work or association were merely illustrations of what might be, not offers of what would be carried out by HMG. The Commissioners were nevertheless frustrated with the British Government's position because, by the time they met with Alison, they knew that HMG was already in contact with the Provisionals: earlier in the day Crilly and Logue were called out to see Gerry Adams, who complained that the Commissioners were undermining the prisoners' position and that the prisoners actually had a better deal on offer than the ICJP option. Adams did not reveal that the British were in contact, but this was the inference that Crilly and Logue took from the meeting.

Adams' position, as he later outlined, was that it was a 'disgraceful episode' in which the Commission was involved:

> An SDLP politician, a bishop and a couple of other people were involved in … raising families' expectations, of playing on the prisoners' emotions … The ICJP were a diversion and not only because of their political antagonism to Republicanism. There was, one, the actual substance of what was being talked about; two, the wrong signal was being given to the British by the ICJP; three, the ICJP's own selfish political concerns overrode the issue, and then finally there was the whole time problem.

Logue's anger with the Government was that it undermined the position of the hunger strikers' families who, on 5 July, had moved from a position of being 'weak and timid towards the Provos' to a point where, on 5 July, they had 'thrown the Provos out' of a meeting:

> … and said they only wanted to talk with us. The families had got very tough with Morrison and with Adams and Jimmy Drumm [of Sinn Féin] … Our sense of betrayal by the British was much more a sense of the families being marginalized … We had gotten the Provos to an extent sidelined and gotten the families to the point of demanding that the hunger strike be ended; 'they were putting pressure on the youngsters in the prison. We were well on the way there and they [the hunger-strikers] were ready to accept what was on offer … We had shaken the families free of the tentacles [of the Provos]. They were still grappling with them but they had by now said they were going to run the thing. We were in the driver's seat at that stage and our primary concern was that having taken the families that far with us and having got to a stage of the Brits

making a proposal, the families were being forced back into the Provos' arms by what the British were doing.[24]

So, with the Duddy channel to the Provos still open, the next move in the drama was up to HMG. At 7.30 p.m. Mrs Thatcher met with Atkins, Whitelaw, Sir Ian Gilmour, Francis Pym, Philip Woodfield (who had just succeeded Stowe as NIO PUS) and another, unnamed official, presumably an Intelligence Officer. Atkins introduced a draft statement that might be issued, and updated the Prime Minister on events in the Maze, pointing out that the hunger-strikers and the ICJP accepted that there was to be no negotiation with the Government and that HMG's position was that it would only seek to improve the regime if the hunger strike were called off. Atkins explained that the prisoners' latest statement contained a significant concession in that they had given up their claim for preferential treatment. He concluded, however, that the Government should continue to stand firm. There was a chance, albeit faint, that the hunger strike would collapse of itself. Atkins pointed out that the disadvantage was that if the hunger strike were to end on terms that were not acceptable to the Provisionals, an end to the current terrorist campaign would be unlikely. In discussion, the following main points were raised:

(a) There was some evidence that some Provisionals favoured a ceasefire. There were practical difficulties for the PIRA in maintaining a terrorist campaign. The Provisionals had gained considerable success through political, rather than terrorist, activity, following the death of Sands. However the Provisionals would never call a ceasefire from a position of weakness ...

(b) There had been recent indications that the hunger strikers were willing to consider an end to their protest, but their resolve was now stiffening in the face of apparent inaction by the Government. The ICJP had been depressed by the commitment of the hunger strikers to their protest. Unless the Government took some action before the death of McDonnell ... there could be no prospect of an early end to the protest.

(c) There was a danger that if the Government indicated that it was willing to move on one or more of the five demands, it would immediately be drawn into negotiation. Once an offer of movement had been made to the hunger strikers, it could not be withdrawn. On the other hand, too firm a stance by the Government would only strengthen the criticisms of inflexibility levelled at Ministers. It would also condemn the Government to facing further deaths of hunger strikers, with all that that entailed. There was no way of further involving the European Commission of Human Rights unless one of the prisoners or a foreign Government made a formal complaint to the Commission. The initiative therefore rested with the Government.

Summing up this part of the discussion, the Prime Minister said that it was agreed that the Government should issue a statement within the next twenty-four hours. This should not make concessions to the hunger-strikers, but should express the hope that the protest would now end so that improvements in the prison regime could be pursued. The meeting then moved on to consider the draft statement presented by Atkins. In discussion, the following points were made: the second paragraph on the second page referred to the Government's commitment to improvements in the prison regime. Atkins explained to Mrs Thatcher that the Government was constantly improving the prison regime, and was ready to continue these improvements, as he had indicated in his statement of 30 June. Recent examples of such improvements were the introduction of new workshops, more courses and more educational facilities. It was agreed that the statement should not refer to the Government's commitments, but to the Government's actions, and should say that Ministers were ready to continue the programme of improvements in the prisons once the hunger strike was over.

The meeting also agreed that the statement should not give the impression that the prisoners' demands were minor details, nor should the statement refer to 'threat or blackmail' on the part of the prisoners. The meeting recognized that, of the five demands, remission and parcels presented few problems. The issues regarding association were more difficult; too much freedom of movement within the wings of the Maze could put the prison officers at risk. On work, the Government would have to stand by the principle that it was for the Prison Governor to decide what work was acceptable. On clothes, the meeting considered that it might be possible to indicate that the Government was willing to agree that men should enjoy the same privileges as women in all Northern Ireland prisons.

In conclusion, it was agreed that the Government should only make a statement on the lines discussed if there was a chance that it would end the hunger strike. The crucial decision at the meeting was now made: the 'statement would therefore have to be shown to the PIRA before it was made; otherwise there was no possibility that they would allow an end to the hunger strike.' If successful, the statement would also have to be made within the next twenty-four hours, or at least before the death of McDonnell.

Mrs Thatcher suggested that Atkins should reconsider his draft statement in the light of the comments made at the meeting and of any statement by the ICJP. His statement, added the Prime Minister, should say that the Government was willing to continue with its programme of improvement of prison conditions if the hunger strike were called off. It should offer no concessions on association. On work, it could offer only marginal improvements and must maintain the principle that the Prison Governor had the final decision on what work was acceptable: 'In short it could report Atkins' comments on work and association in his 30 June statement.' It should mention that the statement could offer to put all male prisoners on the same basis as the female prisoners in Armagh. Atkins:

> … should clear his draft with the Prime Minister before communicating it to the PIRA later that night. It should be communicated to the PIRA on the basis that it would only be made public if they indicated that the hunger strike would be called off. If the PIRA could not accept it, the Government would either deny any knowledge of it or consider whether it should be issued as a response to the ICJP.[25]

And so, on the evening of 6 July, Mrs Thatcher personally approved the text of what was to be offered to the prisoners and sent down the SOON channel to the Provisionals. She also made a number of amendments to the text, shown below in italics. The message read:

> The British Government is prepared if, but only if, it would lead to an immediate end to the hunger strike and protest to issue a statement which would include the following points:
>
> (i) The clothing regime in Armagh Prison would be applied to all prisons in Northern Ireland (ie own clothes subject to approval) *of the Prison Governor.*
> (ii) Parcels, visits and letters would be made available on the same basis as for conforming prisoners at present;
> (iii) On work, association and remission the Government's position will be as set out in the Secretary of State's statement of 30 June. However, emphasis will be laid on the Government's record of its readiness to administer the regime flexibly, and on the 'scope for yet further developments'.
> (iv) *On work the Prison authorities must retain the right to decide what work shall be done.*
> (v) *On association******[left blank]**** *30ᵗʰ June.*
>
> If we receive a satisfactory response to this proposal by 9.00 a.m. on Tuesday 7 July we shall be prepared to provide you with an advance text of the full statement.
>   If the reply we receive is unsatisfactory and there is subsequently any public reference to this exchange we shall deny that it took place. Silence will be taken as an unsatisfactory reply.
>   *Within this fundamental role further* ******of work are added to the schedule from time to time.*[26]

Now there was a British offer on the table. However, in its essentials, it did not go beyond previous *public* statements by HMG. No additional commitments were made except a further hint that the British would be generous – there was no movement on work or association. However, in Duddy's diary, the offer he records from the British is the same as that agreed by the Prime Minister except with regard to work, where he noted: 'On work – the prison administration must maintain the right to decide what work should be done. Within that rule, further kinds of work are added from time to time, i.e. Open University, Build a Church (Ó Fiaich's idea), Toys for spastic children.'[27] But this addition was not approved by Mrs Thatcher, and the reasons for its appearance are unclear, but probably a result of the various conversations he was having with HMG representatives. The Provisionals dealing with the backchannel discussions provided their response to the British offer in the early hours of 7 July. As recorded in Duddy's diary, it amounted to an attempt to open negotiations with the British:

To assist us in taking a ... decision on your proposals, elaboration on Point C – Remission, Point D – Work, Point E – Association is necessary. These are obviously the major points of contention which need to be resolved if the prison protests are to be permanently ended. The position outlined by you is not sufficient to achieve this.

When this present phase of exchanges was initiated, we were informed
1. That you sought agreement on a document which would have our endorsement.
2. That you sought agreement on a mutual public position.
3. That your interest centred on the prisoners' statement of 4/07/81

In this statement, the prisoners outlined their definition of work as Quote 'Self education would be the main prop??? We are prepared to maintain our cells, wings and blocks and to engage in any activities which we define as self-maintaining' Unquote.

On Association, the prisoners' position is that 'there would be freedom of movement within the wings. Supervision need not be restricted. There would be no inference with prison officers who maintain their supervisor's role. We believe there should be wing visits.' Unquote.

The prisoners then outline reasons fundamental to the harmony within the prisons, for continued segregation of prisoners (as presently exists in protest blocks)

On Remission, the prisoners outline reasons for the restoration of full remission and argue that the ending of the protests should surely lead to this restoration.

The prisoners also state Quote 'We would warmly welcome the introduction of the five demands for all prisoners'

If prison protests are to be ended, these points need to be resolved.

If it your intention, as outlined in the Atkins statement of 30th June 81 'To improve the prison regime'....on these points (following the ending of the Hunger Strike) then we and the prisoners need an outline of the specific improvements envisaged by you.

We also require your attitude to the detailed proposals outlined by the prisoners.

Because of this unsatisfactory method of exchanges, we request acknowledgement on receipt of this communication from you and request approximate time of a reply. We also request access to prisoners.[28]

On the afternoon of 6 July according to O'Rawe, a comm came in to the prison from Adams saying that he did not think that the Mountain Climber's proposals provided the basis for a resolution and that more was needed. The message said that the right to free association was vital to an overall settlement, and that its exclusion from the proposals, along with ambiguity on the issue of what constituted prison work, made the deal unacceptable. There was hope, though, that the Mountain Climber could be pushed into making further concessions.[29] McFarlane's reply was to caution Adams:

I don't know if you've thought on this line, but I have been thinking that if we don't pull this off and Joe dies then the RA [IRA] are going to come under some bad stick from all quarters. Everyone is crying the place down that a settlement is there and those Commission chappies are convinced that they have breached Brit principles. Anyway we'll sit tight and see what comes...[30]

The British response, through Duddy, was angry: 'Mag', presumably Mrs Thatcher, could not move from the position of 30 June that 'went to the limits' of HMG's position. By 'suggesting that we do more, the SS [Shop Stewards – code for Provisionals outside the Maze] are inviting us to abandon our principles.' This 'we cannot do. We are appalled by this decision.' The discussions had 'come to an end' and the backchannel would 'have no further parts in our efforts to resolve the problem.'[31] Another communication, however, was sent down the channel, from the Republicans:

> We are fully aware of Joe McDonnell's position and his commitment to the prison demands. We have stressed this on many occasions. We cannot and will not intervene in the Hunger Strike unless satisfied [the prisoners' demands] are met to their collective satisfaction.
>
> Joe's life and the lives of his fellow Hunger Strikers can only be saved and the consequences altered by a common sense movement towards the conditions required by the prisoners.
>
> That is now being done at the last possible moment and through the worst possible channels is not our fault, nor our responsibility.
>
> We are always prepared to facilitate a more practical and confidential means of conducting this dialogue.[32]

The Provisionals' position, as they set out in another communication passed on to the British, was that they had 'no false impression' and had not been influenced by the ICJP: 'If false impressions are given, they are contained in in the very parameters set down by you when this dialogue was initiated.' The Republicans complained: 'We outlined our position in relation to these. You have not and in our dialogue with us you have to satisfy your own criteria for the dialogue.' The prisoners, they continued, had principles: 'It is within the British Government's power to concede the conditions required by the prisoners without loss of principle by any side.' Did the last communication, from the British, mean 'that you are breaking with the original criteria you set or do you wish to continue?' Joe McDonnell, they stressed, was 'pledged to die unless he achieves the conditions required by the prisoners for a settlement.'[33] But the initial British response to the Provisionals' attempt to negotiate was to close down the backchannel: Atkins wrote to Mrs Thatcher to tell her that, following 'the sending of the message which you approved last night, we have received, as you will know, an unsatisfactory response. That particular channel of activity is therefore now no longer active.'[34]

The Government's immediate attention was diverted back to dealing with the ICJP, which was threatening to issue their statement outlining their proposals; the Commissioners also continued to insist that HMG send a senior official into the Maze to outline, to the prisoners, what was on offer. Alison telephoned Bishop O'Mahoney shortly before 12.00 noon on 7 July to explain to him where the Government now stood. He explained that he had had consultations in the interval and had concluded that, whatever happened, the Commission would wish to issue their statement and that it would not permit of any modification. The key point was that some clarification of the Government's position was needed for the prisoners. There would need to be a Government statement complementing the ICJP's statement; taken together these could amount to realistic clarification for the prisoners.

Bishop O'Mahoney replied that, when Blelloch had telephoned him earlier, he had expected to be told that an official was on the way to the prison. It had been his clear understanding the previous evening that this would happen by midday at the latest. He was deeply disappointed. Alison answered that it had become clear that there must be no obscurity about the Government's position and a very careful statement was therefore required; something had to be on the record to avoid accusations later on of bad faith. The statement was at this time being finalized. He had asked the Commission the previous night not to expect him to be explicit about how the necessary clarification was conveyed to the prisoners. He was now asking them to publish their statement as soon as possible, as this would make it easier for the Government to publish its own.

O'Mahoney pronounced himself shocked at such brinkmanship. The Commission was unanimously agreed that it could not see Alison again and, since McDonnell's life was at stake, it felt bound in conscience to state publicly that the undertaking it had been given, that officials would talk to the hunger-strikers that morning, had not been honoured. He accepted that the Commission's statement needed further clarification, but he did not think it would be helpful to issue it now. After consultation with his colleagues, the Bishop confirmed that the Commission would not be issuing a statement, but if they had not heard by 12.20 p.m. that an official was on the way to the prison they would call a press conference and reveal that the Government had broken its undertaking. Alison insisted that this was impossible. There was no point in the Commission holding a pistol to the Government's head. If the ICJP was not issuing its original statement, this would delay the issue of the Government's statement because it would need amendment. When it was ready, someone would take it to the prison, but he could not say when, except that it would be as soon as practicable. O'Mahoney insisted on an assurance that someone would go to the prison immediately. Alison repeated that he could not give such an assurance. A clear and unambiguous Government statement would be made available to the prisoners as soon as possible. It was the Commission's right to set up a press conference if they wished, but this would serve no useful purpose, and would cause unnecessary alarm and despondency.[35]

At 4.00 p.m. Alison had a short meeting with the Chief Constable and the Commander Land Forces (CLF) – the second senior Army officer in Northern Ireland after the GOC – in Stormont Castle, where the Minister explained that the Government was about to produce a statement that would be read to the hunger-strikers (he hoped within an hour). Alison's judgement was that this would not prove acceptable to the prisoners and that McDonnell would die. He believed that the prisoners had been told that what was 'on offer' was not enough. The CLF observed that the degree of trouble resulting from McDonnell's death would depend on the public perception of the situation. The Chief Constable was confident that the RUC was geared for the next death and had made contingency plans. He was very happy with the Government's position at present. It was seen to be one of caring concern, showing a willingness to move but not departing from principle. The PIRA, on the other hand, was looking for capitulation by the Government and was seen to be intransigent. Hermon saw the ICJP as a well-meaning, somewhat naïve group, probably slanted in their outlook, given their origins. The police were prepared for violence and prepared to accept it; they were in a strong position. From the point of view of PR, the Chief Constable felt that the ICJP – as well-intentioned, energetic people desirous of a solution – should be protected. The ball should not be put back into the PIRA's court. From the Loyalist point of view, there was a need to see the Government standing firmly by its principles in the face of pressure.

Alison explained that so far it had been possible to bring the ICJP along with the Government's position, but they had an obsession about an NIO official going to the prison by lunchtime, and were ready at any moment to accuse the Government of brinkmanship. He described briefly what had occurred at his meeting with the ICJP the previous night. He hoped to hold them 'at bay'. John Blelloch added that the ICJP had overstated the case when they went to the prison to see the hunger-strikers. They had hoped that the Government would endorse their proposed statement and were now in a difficulty because they did not want to issue it without a Government imprimatur. He realized that a chance had been taken in entering into discussion with the ICJP; on balance it had been thought better to take the chance than not to.[36]

Atkins, in the meantime, informed Mrs Thatcher that the ICJP had decided, contrary to their earlier intention, not to issue a statement to the press about their talks with Alison. There were, however, 'two good reasons why we should issue an early statement.' One was to correct a rich crop of rumours circulating in the press about possible deals. The other – and the more important – was 'to straighten out the prisoners themselves who may have been misled by the zeal of the ICJP for turning general statements into particular examples.' Atkins, therefore, attached for the Prime Minister's approval the draft of a statement that he proposed to issue that evening. It was in two sections, and his intention was that the second part in particular should be given by the Prison Governor to each of the protesting prisoners, including the hunger-strikers, in an attempt to ensure – 'yet again' – that they were in no doubt about HMG's position and about the regime that was available to them when they started to conform. In drafting this document Atkins paid close attention both to the views 'you yourself expressed last night and to the need to safeguard Michael Alison's position with the ICJP, with whom he has spent many hours in detailed discussion. The words are therefore carefully chosen. I should be glad to know if you would be content with this.'[37]

A few hours later, just after 7.00 p.m., Alison telephoned O'Mahoney again and asked the Bishop to maintain his 'exemplary patience' a little longer. The Government's statement was awaiting approval and would be delivered as soon as possible. He must ask the Bishop to refrain from saying anything in public. There was nothing to be gained from doing so, and he hoped that the harmony that had so far existed between the Commission and himself would be maintained. O'Mahoney insisted that he must have an answer to the question of whether an official would be present when the statement was handed to the prisoners. He was convinced that, if not, it would be almost impossible to achieve anything. Alison told the Bishop that he had taken this point on board, but could not give a specific answer. He undertook to keep in touch with the Commission and said that the statement would be issued as soon as possible.[38]

It was not until 00.15 in the morning on 8 July that Mrs Thatcher was able to meet with Atkins to discuss the latest developments; Philip Woodfield and an unnamed official were also present. Atkins recounted how the message, which the Prime Minister had approved the previous evening, had been communicated to the PIRA. Their response indicated that they did not regard it as satisfactory and that they wanted a good deal more. That appeared to mark the end of this development, and this had been made this clear to the PIRA during the afternoon. This, explained Atkins, had produced a very rapid reaction, which suggested that it was not the content of the message to which they had objected but rather its tone. The question now for decision was 'whether we should respond on our side.'

Atkins concluded that 'we should communicate to the PIRA over night a draft statement enlarging upon the message of the previous evening but in no way whatever departing from its substance.' If the Provisionals accepted the draft statement and ordered the hunger-strikers to end their protest, the statement would be issued immediately. If they did not, this statement would not be put out but instead an alternative statement, reiterating the Government's position as Atkins had set it out in on 30 June, and responding to the discussions with the ICJP, would be issued. If there were any leak about the process of communication with the Provisionals, his office would deny it. The unnamed official said that it was thought that the revised statement, based on the previous night's message, would be enough to get the Provisionals to instruct the prisoners to call off the hunger strike. He then outlined the procedures that would be followed if the PIRA said that they would call off the hunger strike. The meeting then considered the revised draft statement that was to be communicated to the Provisionals. A number of amendments were made, primarily with a view to removing any suggestion at all that the Government was in a negotiation. Mrs Thatcher, summing up the discussion, said that the statement should now be communicated to the PIRA as Atkins proposed. If it did not produce a response leading to the end of the hunger strike, Atkins should issue at once a statement reaffirming the Government's existing position as he had set it out on 30 June.[39]

Duddy recorded in his diary, during the early hours, the message from the British:

> The management [Government] will ensure that as substantial part of the work will consist of domestic tasks inside and outside the wings necessary for servicing the prisoners, such as cleaning and in the laundry and kitchen, construction work for example on building projects or making toys for charitable bodies and studying for Open University or other courses. The factory authority [prison management] will be responsible for supervision. The aim of the authority will be that prisoners should do the kind of work for which they are suited. But this will not always be possible and the authorities will retain responsibility for decisions.

However: 'Little advance is possible on Association. It (Association) will be permitted within each wing under supervision of factory staff [prison staff].'[40]

Once again it appears that Duddy's contacts within the Government were verbally elaborating what would be on offer in terms of work. It did not satisfy the Provsionals as it would not form part of any statement. Hence, at 4.00 a.m., Republicans made a request for Gerry Adams to be admitted to the Maze.[41] An hour later they suggested a new proposal for a private document to be given to them, to back up any agreed public document between themselves and the British. The message sent down the Duddy channel, from the British, was that: 'The management [Government] cannot contemplate the proposal for two documents set out in your last communication and now therefore the exchange on this channel [is] to be ended.'[42]

Whilst these communications were taking place, Joe McDonnell's condition had deteriorated significantly, and he died at 04.45 (he was certified dead at 05.11). He had become semi-conscious early on 7 July and unconscious after 04.00 on 8 July. Death came unexpectedly quickly after unconsciousness – it had been up to forty-eight hours in the cases of the other hunger-strikers.[43]

In the aftermath of McDonnell's death, Atkins' statement was finally given to the protesting prisoners early in the morning and read to the strikers by the Governor, accompanied by a senior NIO official. The latter was on instructions only to elucidate questions of fact and, as none were put, he played no part in the proceedings. The hunger-strikers showed little reaction, though Mickey Devine (INLA, joined hunger strike on 22 June) and Tom McElwee (IRA, joined on 8 June) did ask for officials or the Governor to come and discuss the document after they had read it. The prisoners were given an opportunity to discuss the document among themselves, and also saw Bik McFarlane for a time. Kevin Lynch (INLA, joined hunger strike on 23 May) and Doherty – 'the 2 most determined strikers' – said afterwards that there was nothing in it for them. The statement was also given to the ICJP before publication. The statement issued by Atkins declared that he, despite all the efforts made by the Government since October 1980, and despite the ICJP's own efforts, was 'persuaded by the Commission that there is still doubt in the minds of prisoners about what in practice would happen if they gave up the hunger strike.' Some, he continued, might doubt the Government's intention to be flexible and humane in applying the existing regime; some might 'delude themselves that the flexibility is infinitely extendable into a mirror of the regime for special category prisoners. Both are wrong. I have therefore set out in very simple terms what we can and cannot do.' In doing this 'we are setting out to the prisoners what is already available to conforming prisoners. The regime is administered flexibly. There is scope for further development but not under duress.' The protestors' action, far from bringing about changes, had in fact rendered movement impossible. The only key to advance was for them to end the strike.[44] The statement was essentially a reaffirmation of that on 30 June, and emphasized that no moves would be contemplated under the duress of a hunger strike and that the ICJP were not in any sense negotiators. The second part of the statement – 'what happens when the protest ends' – was aimed at making sure that the protesters were aware of what was available. Little expansion of association was contemplated, but the suggestion of association by adjacent wings (made by the ICJP) was taken on board. On clothing, the 'possibility of further development' was not ruled out. On work, no one would be excluded as of right from liability to allocation to workshops, but the commitment was given to add to the range of activities.[45]

In response, the prisoners issued another statement, on 8 July: Joe McDonnell, they complained, 'need not have died. The British Government's hypocrisy and their refusal to act in a responsible manner are completely to blame for the death of Joe McDonnell and the deep sorrow that accompanies his death.' The prisoners claimed that the British had, for a considerable period of time, stood on ceremony, asserting again and again that they would not talk to the prisoners in order to find a solution. Yet, 'after Joe's death, they decide to send an official into Long Kesh to talk to us: or rather talk at us.' To say the least, that amounted to criminal negligence and typified the insensitivity and ineptitude of the British Government's mishandling of this issue. A lack of urgency, 'pomp and ceremony' should not enter into such a serious and distressing crisis as this, the prisoners continued. They referred to their July 4 statement, 'in which we outlined the substance of a solution.' In drawing up that statement:

> ... we went to considerable trouble and pains to take into account the British Government's dilemma and to provide a principled and practical solution for all concerned ... we were led to believe that the British Government received it very favourably. Yet the only definite response forthcoming from the British Government is the death of Joe McDonnell.

Now, Atkins had issued the prisoners with yet another 'ambiguous and self-gratifying statement. Even had we wanted to respond by ending the hunger strike it would have been too late.' That statement, even given its most optimistic reading, was far removed from the prisoners' July 4 statement. At face value it amounted to nothing. The prisoners finished by calling on everyone, especially the British Government, to make a careful and unprejudiced appraisal of the July 4 statement: 'This very carefully composed statement can, and must, provide the basis for a just, principled and practical solution for all sides.'[46]

The ICJP, meanwhile, acting under pressure to tell its side of the story, finally held a press conference – also on 8 July – in which it accused the Government of 'clawing back' from the peace formula allegedly drawn up between them. Bishop O'Mahoney's statement that 'we feel very, very disappointed and saddened and let down' was indicative of the tone of their views, while their description of the Secretary of State's statement as 'not a serious attempt' to solve the deadlock reflected how far they felt it fell short of what was needed.[47] The ICJP also accused the British Government of causing a breakdown of the Commission's initiative by not sending an NIO official into the Maze Prison as agreed (by mid morning of 7 July at the latest). The Irish Government, in a statement, commented that 'the facts disclosed and the outline of an agreement given by the ICJP ... call for the most serious consideration by the British Government.' In a statement on the death of Joe McDonnell, the Taoiseach, Garret FitzGerald, added in an unconcealed criticism of London: 'I have repeatedly said that a solution can be reached through a flexibility of approach which need not sacrifice any principle. The onus of responsibility for showing this flexibility rests on both sides ... But the greater responsibility must, as always, rest on those with the greater power'. John Hume accused Mrs Thatcher of showing 'a disastrous failure to understand the seriousness and urgency of the situation in Northern Ireland arising out of the prison crisis', and called on the ICJP to continue its efforts.[48] Alison, speaking at a press conference earlier the same day, defended the Government's handling of the issue and repeated that if the prisoners called off their action the Government could get on with developing prison reform. But he insisted that this could not take place while a pistol was being held to the Government's head, and categorically rejected earlier allegations by Ian Paisley that the Government had been negotiating, even indirectly, with the prisoners.[49]

On the following day, 9 July, the NHAC, Sinn Féin and the IRSP held a joint press conference and demanded that Alison, FitzGerald and Haughey should meet them. Bernadette McAliskey, of the NHAC, maintained: 'It is only on the basis of the five demands that a solution which will last can be found.' A final settlement could only be achieved if the NIO agreed to discuss matters directly with the prisoners. Jim Gibney, of Sinn Féin, endorsed these views, and added that the British Government had 'abused' the ICJP. Gerry Adams, meanwhile, called on the Republic's Government to tell 'governments worldwide that Britain is wrong.' He continued that Cardinal Ó Fiaich should 'give a direction to his flock on an issue which senior Churchmen see as the responsibility of the British Government,' and called on the SDLP to withdraw its representatives from Northern Ireland's local councils.[50]

As Adams spoke, the condition of Kieran Doherty was showing the first significant signs of deterioration, with some eye trouble and vomiting; he was also complaining of neuritis in this right leg. However, his condition had not deteriorated to the extent shown by other hunger-strikers at this stage of their strikes. Similarly, Kevin Lynch was still remarkably well, despite having lost 25% of his body weight. His urine had remained clear and he had no significant symptoms. There was some NIO speculation that he might have had a small amount of nourishment or vitamin supplement given to him. Paradoxically, the condition of Martin Hurson (IRA, joined hunger strike on 28 May) was actually the most serious; it was worse than any of the previous strikers at the same stage. He was quite ill, was vomiting a lot and evidently had bleeding in his mouth and throat. He already had marked signs of eye deterioration. McElwee and Quinn were both moved to the hospital on 3 July; neither had any symptoms so far, nor had Devine or Laurence McKeown (IRA, joined hunger strike 29 June). The prisoners' weights on 9 July were:

	Day of strike	Weight on first examination	Weight today	Weight loss during week	Overall weight loss
Kieran Doherty	49	11st 11lb	8st 10lb	6½lb	3st 1lb
Kevin Lynch	48	9st 7lb	7st 2lb	4½lb	2st 5lb
Martin Hurson	42	10st 13lb	8st 2lb	7lbs	2st 11lb
Thomas McElwee	32	10st 8lb	8st 7lb	8lb	2st 1lb
Michael Devine	18	9st 8½lb	8st 8½lb	4½lb	1st 0lb[51]

In the aftermath of the ICJP press conference, and with a seemingly never-ending procession of prisoners joining the hunger strike, D. J. Wyatt sent a minute to Blelloch pointing out that the NIO actually had to focus on what it was prepared to accept in a final settlement with the prisoners rather than the nebulous hints it had been sending out: 'We have a very short time until the next hunger striker dies to decide where we go from here. We have come rather better out of the ICJP exercise than we might have expected.' The prisoners had moved quite a bit on association and differentiation without yet giving up the substance of the regime they sought; the Government had managed to float the idea of the wearing of the prisoners' own clothes as a reward rather than a bribe for giving up the hunger strike, and the clothing issue had now ceased to be the stumbling block it was; the hunger-strikers and families were presumably no less anxious to see an end to the hunger strike if they could get one; and there were growing signs that Sinn Féin were less than happy with its continuance.

'It would be wrong to be in the least optimistic but I do not feel despite the outcome of the ICJP negotiations that we are in any way further from a solution', argued Wyatt. Nevertheless: 'We need to clear our minds well in advance of the next hunger strike death which will undoubtedly bring disagreeable pressure on us from Dublin.' He then made an attempt to identify some questions. Wyatt did not see any real problems in the area of visits, parcels, letters and remission that could not be overcome in the context of an end to the hunger strike. Clothing was not a problem of principle: 'We accept that we are going to have to give it. The prisoners accept that we are going to control it.' The two difficulties were:

(a) Timing, since the prisoners would expect their own clothes within a very few days of giving up the protest whereas we would need time to formulate the rules, consider the security and control problems and peripheral questions like laundry.

(b) Assurances. We are not prepared to commit ourselves to clothing in advance of the ending of the hunger strike and the prisoners are not prepared to commit themselves to end the hunger strike in advance of an assurance in terms of own clothes.

Wyatt thought that these modalities could be overcome in one way or another:

As I read it the prisoners accept that free association is out. They are going to be confined to their wing (and in principle the adjacent wing) for periods of controlled association. There is endless scope for argument about the severity of control and the period of association but the prisoners are on a slippery slope to accepting our terms.

However: 'Segregation is a problem.' The prisoners were only going to accept HMG's terms of association under a segregated regime. Common sense would dictate that these very committed men were not easily going to be integrated with Protestants, and the probability was that:

> ... we shall have to leave them more or less as they are for the immediate future. But we cannot give a commitment to do that because if we did all the other Republican prisoners, on whose behalf also the protesters have protested, would demand segregation and we would end up with a wholly segregated prison. I do not at the moment see any way around this. In short, the real problem is work.

Secondly, 'we need to hammer home the unreasonableness of the Provisionals. We have some good material to put out in the shape of well produced pamphlets dealing for example with':

(a) the regime available which provides so much in each of the areas the Provisionals say they care about.
(b) The reality of a 'free association' regime.
(c) The crimes for which the hunger strikers have been committed to prison – some of which are horrific.

Wyatt saw nothing inconsistent in putting out a 'soft line about our own attitude and a hard line about that of the Provisionals. It all contributes to the pressure.' Wyatt's conclusion was very simple: 'that our first and most urgent ask is to clear our minds on what sort of a work regime we think is in fact obtainable which we could live with.'[52]

Before that process could begin, the prisoners issued another lengthy statement on Saturday 11 July in which they complained that the ICJP, while undoubtedly feeling that they were doing what was for the best, had been 'used by the British against us and if they were to continue being involved in this issue we feel that they would be used against us again.' In the first place the ICJP's proposals were an 'unacceptable dilution of our five demands as stated in our July 4 statement and therefore the Commission would have been undermining our five demands.' Secondly, intermediaries by nature invariably looked for a solution 'at any price and while we share as no one else can their great concern that a solution be obtained, we feel that there is no room for intermediaries of any sort for the British will use them to try to sell us short.' Thirdly, the prisoners thought that it must be painfully obvious in the aftermath of the British 'double-dealing' with the Commission that there was only one way in which this issue could be solved: 'and that is direct talks between the British and ourselves.' The prisoners called on the Commission to forfeit their role in the dispute and called on it 'to support our five demands and demand direct dialogue between the hunger strikers, Brendan McFarlane and the British. We call on them also to repeat their belief in public that our July 4 statement is a just solution for all concerned in this issue.'[53]

While the NIO remained hard-line on how the hunger strike should end, within the Foreign Office concern continued to grow as to the impact the issue was having on Britain's international position: one official, P.K.C. Thomas, complained to another, Patrick Eyers, that there was 'an enormous gulf between the generally accepted perceptions of the hunger strike in Dublin and London. I think this gulf may be the cause of misunderstandings between HMG, the ICJP and the Irish Government.' Put simply, the significant element in the difference in perception was that, in London, the hunger strike was seen as an unjustified protest by convicted criminals who had stepped out of line, and that it was up to them to resolve it. In Dublin, however, the 'extraordinary' lengths to which the protesters were prepared to go and the suffering that they were prepared to inflict upon themselves conferred on the protest a justification that made it incumbent on the other side of the dispute to compromise in order to find a solution: 'This is not logical for an Englishman. But I nevertheless think that this is how the Irish see the matter and I am sure that this difference is widely misunderstood on the British side.' It explained why the ICJP (and the Provos and the Irish Government) held as a basic assumption that HMG was looking for a compromise and were prepared to negotiate, 'and why they feel let down, and accuse us of "clawing back" when they find out that we are not.' As Thomas commented, the basic problem was that 'HMG are I think prepared for some (further) compromise; but not to negotiate. That is difficult to understand and adds to the problem you have identified.'[54]

The fallout from the ICJP initiative travelled across the Atlantic as Bishop O'Mahoney and Michael Alison took to the airwaves and were interviewed on *Good Morning America*, ABC's coast-to-coast television show, for about six minutes each. O'Mahoney, who was speaking by satellite from Belfast, said that on 6 July the Commission had a document regarding essential points of prison reform following sixteen hours' negotiations with Alison. This was accepted by the prisoners as a basis for a settlement of the hunger strike, but on the next day, Tuesday, there was gradual withdrawal by the British Government and a clawing back. A real opportunity was lost, he said. Asked specifically what the British backed away from, the Bishop said that the Government was giving a firm commitment that all prisoners could wear their own clothes at all time. This meant that there was no question of granting special status to some prisoners. Alison, who was interviewed from Washington, explained that he could understand the Bishop's disappointment, but 'the good Bishop has one weakness, he doesn't understand the inside of a prison'. Asked whether wearing one's own clothes was really an issue, Alison commented that this was important for Irish terrorist prisoners. In principle the Government could go down that road, but it had to accent the negative side. Strict control had to be adhered to. Alison said that there was a parallel with the Pacific War with the kamikaze or suicide pilots: 'The Irish terrorists die but they also kill.'[55]

Alison next attended a meeting of the 'Friends of Ireland', where there were twelve members of Congress; Senators Laxalt, Kennedy, Moynihan, Dodd and Speaker O'Neill sent aides. From speaking to aides afterwards the Irish Embassy gathered that there seemed to be a general consensus that the meeting did not go well for Alison. With one exception, Mrs Fenwick, those members attending presented a united front in criticizing British intransigence on the hunger strikes and in forcefully pointing out its effects on moderate opinion in the US. Congressman Shannon, who had been well briefed by Kennedy's aides, closely questioned Alison on (a) why he was in the US at this critical stage, and (b) why it had taken the NIO thirty-five hours to respond to ICJP. In response to (a), Alison said there were others who could deal with the issue in his absence. In response to (b), he indicated that he had acted in good faith and had endeavoured to move with all speed, but, under close questioning, did admit to some delay in processing the matter in London. Congressman Dougherty forcefully made the point that in his opinion the British did not understand the nature of the pressures on Irish-American politicians. He said that British intransigence on the hunger strike issue had lost them (the British) the sympathy of Americans, had isolated moderate Irish-American opinion and had spurred a growth in support for the PIRA's position. Dougherty spoke at length about his recent visit to Ireland, and gave many examples of the polarization between the two communities. Other members complained that there appeared to be no progress in British policy since their briefing from the British Ambassador recently, at which time they had strongly indicated the dangers in the United States for the British viewpoint.[56]

Back in Europe, pressure was mounting on HMG from another source: the Irish Government was becoming increasingly frustrated by the apparent rigidity of the British. To defend their position the British dispatched a document to Dublin in which they explained that, while it was agreed with the ICJP that the best way to proceed was for the Government to clarify its position to the prisoners, HMG was surprised that the Commissioners 'now seem genuinely to have believed that in accepting the obligation to clarify our position we had accepted the method they suggested.' The method of clarification, however, though important in the view of the Commission:

> ... was not the prime issue for us. What we had to do was to find a
> very precise form of words which a) reflected the movement we were

prepared to make after the hunger strike ended (inter-wing association; expansion of the range of prison activities to include things like building a chapel, mutual self-education, and work for charity; and by implication own clothes) but b) also reflected the realities of a prison regime which would remain – in particular that no prisoner would be allowed to opt out of work which the prison authorities required him to do and that segregation is not a right.

The appropriate text required extensive consultation between Belfast, where Alison and the responsible officials were, and London, where Atkins, whose authority was needed, happened to be. But, from the British point of view: 'The reality is that on at least one important point of substance (work) we and the Commission are not at one. This and not the mechanics of conveying our views to the prisoners is what stood in the way of ending the hunger strike, even if the Commission are right that their formulation set out what the prisoners would settle for.'[57]

Dublin was not convinced. In their analysis of the different positions between the British and the Commissioners, it was noted how the ICJP made clear in their statement that Alison suggested, on the night of 6 July, in response to the urging of the ICJP, that one of his officials be sent with the Governor of the Maze to the hunger-strikers by mid-morning at the latest on Tuesday 7 July. This was because it was essential that clarification of the Government's position be made so that there could be no doubts in the minds of the prisoners. The British, in a document of 9 July handed over to the Irish authorities, claimed that while accepting the obligation to clarify their position, they did not accept the method or the timing suggested by the ICJP. For Dublin, the ICJP version was borne out by the facts that:

(a) in view of the assurance given by Mr Alison at the meeting on Monday night (6 July) that an official would go in on Tuesday morning the ICJP postponed publication of their document;

(b) the ICJP telephoned the prison Chaplain at 10.15 pm on Monday 6 July from Stormont Castle to say they would not be going to the prison that night but that an NIO official would be going to the prison in the morning. The Chaplain so informed the prisoners on Monday night;

(c) Mr Logue at his meeting with the Taoiseach on Thursday 9 July quoted Mr Alison as saying at the Monday 6 July meeting that as 'clarification is of the essence' we will send in an official. Furthermore, the ICJP suggested that the official should be one of the people involved in all the discussions and who knew the mood and spirit of the process. This was accepted by Mr Alison at the Monday night meeting according to Mr Logue;

(d) the ICJP were asked by the NIO at 11.40 am on Tuesday 7 July to come to Stormont Castle.

They refused to do so when they ascertained that no official had yet gone to the prison. The ICJP threatened to hold a press conference and release their statement unless reassured that an official would go to the prison immediately. Just before 1.00 pm on Tuesday when the press conference was about to begin the NIO told the ICJP that an official would go in that afternoon. The press conference was cancelled. Several further promises were made on the evening of Tuesday 7 July by Mr Alison and the NIO to the effect that an official would go in to the prison that night;

(e)   at the late night meeting at Stormont on Tuesday 7 July between Alison plus Blelloch and Bishop O'Mahoney plus Hugh Logue, Mr Alison was asked why he had gone back on his promise to send in an official. He had responded that he was 'not a sufficient plenipotentiary';

(f)   the Taoiseach and Mr Nally contacted the British authorities on Tuesday afternoon and were given assurances that an official would go in.

The other major concern for the Irish rested on the question of British acceptance of the ICJP document containing its understanding of the areas of agreement reached. The ICJP said in its statement of 8 July that it showed its statement of understanding to Alison on Monday 6 July, and that he accepted that the statement reflected a true picture of what Alison had indicated to be the position of the British Government except for two aspects:

(a)   Mr Alison suggested that the phrase 'in the considered view of ICJP the British Government would be under a moral obligation' be substituted for 'the British Government would be under a moral obligation'. The ICJP accepted this amendment to their text;

(b)   Mr Alison stated that apart from the clothing reform which he accepted as an absolute commitment, his understanding was that the specific details of the other reforms were meant to be illustrative only.
     The ICJP reject this understanding and stand over their statement in full except for the amendment at (a) above.

On the clothing issue, Alison gave an 'absolute commitment' that prisoners would be permitted to wear their own clothes at all times at the meeting of 6 July. Yet the Secretary of State's statement, which was given to the prisoners on the morning of 8 July, did 'not rule out the possibility of further development' on the clothing issue. 'Why did the British authorities change their position on this?' In the document given to the Irish authorities by the British, the latter stated that the prime issue for them was to find a very precise form of words that would reflect the movement that they were prepared to make, after the hunger strike ended, on association, work and 'by implication own clothes'. According to

Logue, the ICJP was told at Stormont by Alison on Saturday 4 July, after he had consulted London, that the change regarding clothing was fully accepted. Alison also indicated, according to Logue, that even if the blanket protest continued, the clothing concession stood once the hunger-strikers began to eat again.

If the ICJP's understanding of the agreement on association was 'illustrative' only, then why, wondered the Irish, did Atkins in his statement to the prisoners say simply that 'it would take time to arrange the necessary physical facilities for this' (the ICJP proposal)? The 'clear implication is that the British had agreed to the ICJP proposal on this issue.' On work, there was a clear difference of approach between the British authorities and the ICJP. The ICJP felt that the British had agreed to a range of measures that would maximize the choice and congeniality of 'useful activities' that the prisoners could undertake, excluding work that could be regarded as demeaning in particular circumstances. The ICJP made the point that a prisoner who failed to find accommodation within the new choices provided 'may in the last analysis be required to do remunerative work'. The British started off from the position that no one would be excluded as of right from the liability to work in prison workshops. Atkins also made clear in this statement to the prisoners that while he would consider the 'examples' given by the ICJP, it would 'at the end of the day' be for the prison authorities to decide what jobs a prisoner did. The British saw the 'degree of choice and congeniality in a much more restrictive light than that proposed by the ICJP.'

The Irish analysis also noted that, in his statement to the prisoners, Atkins rigidly repeated that one fifth of remission was restored to protesting prisoners who subsequently behaved normally. On the other hand, the British had said to the ICJP (in writing to Bishop O'Mahoney in December) that if the protest ended they would be 'imaginative' and 'dramatic' on this matter. In addition, Atkins, in his letter of 30 June to the ICJP, said that the British Government would be 'generous' subject to continuing good conduct, 'but it would be wrong to imagine that restoration would immediately be total'. 'Why was this aspect of the dispute presented in such a negative fashion to the hunger strikers on 8 July when the British Government has something much more generous to offer?' asked the Irish. The change in tactics and behaviour outlined above clearly supported the ICJP's assessment in its statement of 8 July that they could not regard the statement (given to the hunger-strikers) as a serious attempt to seek a resolution (of the hunger strike) in the light of the discussions they had and of the position clarified to them by the Minister.[58]

The Irish Government now turned up the heat on the British. Dermot Nally informed Figg that, in the conversation the Taoiseach had the day before (9 July) with Gallagher and Logue of the ICJP, the difficulty about prison work was discussed. The Commission thought that the prisoners' position that they would do no work that supported the prison system 'may not be as difficult to overcome as it seems.' They thought that something close to the formula that they proposed in their statement of 3 June would be acceptable provided it was explained in a document; this would mean an official going into the prison and being prepared to answer questions if only on a yes and no basis. Among the other points made by Nally was that it was the Irish Government's understanding that, unlike the hunger strike before Christmas, the imminence of a striker's death hardened the resolve of the others; secondly, political status no longer seemed to be an issue and was not mentioned; and thirdly, the effects of the deaths amongst the young in working-class areas in Dublin had led to considerable recruitment for the IRA.[59] This last point was reinforced to Figg by the Irish Director of Military Intelligence, who told the Ambassador's defence attaché that all the evidence available to him suggested that if the next hunger-striker – Doherty – died, the security situation in the Republic would deteriorate markedly. According to the Director's information, recruitment into the IRA in the Republic was now much greater than recruitment into the Irish Army, even though the latter paid a salary.[60]

All of this Figg communicated to the Foreign Office. Figg himself informed London that he was becoming 'increasingly worried at the way in which our handling of the hunger strike is being seen in Dublin. The Taoiseach, Mr Haughey and responsible officials no longer see the hunger strike problem in terms of dangerous criminals with whom it is not right to negotiate.' This was not to say that any responsible opinion had an excuse for IRA crimes, but the fact that men were prepared to go on dying 'are making a lot of people wonder whether we have got things right.' Figg had been doing what he could to correct the 'misunderstanding' with the ICJP: 'But I don't think we need be too concerned about what has happened. It is what will happen that matters.' Both Haughey and FitzGerald had said that it was up to the more powerful side in the dispute to show flexibility: 'And many here would agree and fear that we may be boxing ourselves into a corner without room to manoeuvre.' They saw Atkins' statement of 8 July as not differing at all in substance from the statement of 19 December: 'Meanwhile we have had five deaths.' The next death would probably be Doherty, a member of the Dáil. If he were to die 'without our having been seen to make a much greater effort to end the strike than we have done hitherto, the consequences for our relationship will be extremely damaging', warned Figg.[61]

On 10 July, an exasperated Dr FitzGerald wrote to Mrs Thatcher expressing the Irish Government's deep concern about the impact of recent developments in the hunger strike 'upon the situation in our country.' Since the first deaths in the hunger strike 'we have had to contend with the political problem of rising levels of sympathy for the prisoners', explained the Taoiseach. The general election results showed this growth very clearly when two imprisoned candidates were elected to

Dáil Éireann: 'This is a development which directly threatens the ability of our state through the intrusion of interests which would never have been lent such formal authority but for the propaganda effects of the confrontation in the Maze.' But there was now an additional major problem. People in Ireland found the 8 July statement of the ICJP to be a credible account of the Commission's meetings with Alison on the one hand and with the hunger-strikers on the other. As a Government 'we too are persuaded by this account and so are unable to do or say anything to counter the lack of public confidence in the British Government's handling of the situation. We are thus faced with the danger of a serious and progressive deterioration in bilateral relations', warned FitzGerald. Up to this point, the Irish Government had always supported the position that political status should not be given to prisoners duly sentenced for serious crimes, and so had avoided any appearance of taking the side of the hunger-strikers; in the preceding few days, however, the 'deplorable' situation had been reached that the points of view of the Irish Government and the Commission 'are seen to converge with that of the Provisional IRA in criticism of your authorities' handling of these events. This is naturally the last position in which we would wish to find ourselves.'

The state of public opinion now emerging 'could only have a bad effect on our internal security situation, though we are determined to maintain an undiminished effort in this area.' British security forces in Northern Ireland had, up to now, been able to rely on the effective co-operation of Irish security forces, as had been acknowledged from time to time by British spokesmen. As both Governments knew, the effectiveness of security measures depended on the prevailing climate of local public opinion. Even before this latest development, FitzGerald had to face a broad spectrum of IRA propaganda, which proved sadly effective in appealing simultaneously both to those who were inclined to violence and to people of humane sympathies genuinely moved by the loss of life and bereavement of families.

Looking into the immediate future, 'we face the prospect of the death of a hunger striker who is a member of our parliament. As you know from the case of Mr Sands, the propaganda potential of such a death would be immense, in our society, in Britain and throughout the world', the Taoiseach informed Mrs Thatcher. It was against this background 'that I urge you, without any more loss of time, to accept the detailed description of a possible future prison regime set out by the ICJP on the basis of contacts with the NIO as a foundation of a solution of the crisis.' In this connection it was important to recall that, in their last statement issued, the prisoners said that they were not seeking differentiation from other prisoners or concessions that would involve surrender by the authorities of control of the prison. While FitzGerald would not wish this message to be interpreted as in any way suggesting that the difficulties created by the hunger strike should ultimately be laid at any door other than that of the IRA, he believed that 'an end to the hunger strike will deprive them of their most potent weapon and restore a climate in which our efforts can again be directed to more positive and constructive endeavours' in pursuance of the process initiated in Dublin in December, 'to the continuance of which I attach great importance.'[62]

In the light of these concerns, the Irish demanded, and secured, an urgent meeting between Michael O'Leary, the Tánaiste (Deputy Prime Minister), and Professor James Dooge, the Irish Foreign Minister-Designate (he had yet to be appointed to Seanad Éireann); and on the British side Atkins and Gilmour. The Irish pulled no punches in referring to the ICJP 'fiasco' and asking:

> Why, if no real advance is possible, had the British Government encouraged the ICJP over several days of intensive discussion to believe that it was?
>
> Why had the British Government delayed their first contact with the ICJP until July 3 despite the Taoiseach's personal call to Mrs Thatcher on July 1?
>
> Why had the British delayed in sending an NIO official into the Maze until after McDonnell's death on the morning of July 8 despite an undertaking on the evening of July 6 to send someone in on the morning of July 7?
>
> Why had the NIO official eventually selected not fulfilled the conditions agreed with the ICJP of full involvement in the discussions from the beginning? The Minister also mentioned the impression of the ICJP that the person concerned (Jackson) was notoriously unsympathetic in his attitude to the prisoners, however excellent an official he might otherwise be.
>
> How did the British see the crisis ending?

Both Irish Ministers rejected the suggestion that the British attitude had displayed sufficient understanding of the seriousness and urgency of the problem. Atkins, who did most of the talking on the British side, said that he had done little else since last October except try to solve the crisis. It was the prisoners, not the British Government, who had shown 'inflexibility'. Until the previous week the prisoners had not been prepared to accept the same category of treatment as other prisoners. It had become clear to them that their demand for separate treatment enjoyed no support in the UK, Ireland or the US. A close reading of their statement of 4 July, however, showed that the prisoners would not be satisfied by anything less than control of the prisons, and this the British Government could not and would not concede. On the ending of the crisis, Atkins made a 'pat and unoriginal' statement on the need that the prisoners should accept the principles of control of the prison regime by the prison authorities and of identity of status with other prisoners.

A despairing Dooge described Atkins' proposed solution as 'hopeless'. He said: 'our object should be to recreate the conditions which made it possible to attempt such a solution. We should not get bogged down in minutiae of "principle" which have been elevated into unalterable conditions.' Prisoners in Portlaoise were not, for example, required to do prison work. Professor Dooge thought that the problem might admit of a solution in practice, which seemed feasible, rather than arguing over the incompatibility of principles. But both Atkins and Gilmour replied that principles in this case were non-negotiable. Dooge countered that the prisoners, however fanatical, however demented, had their own 'principles', and that any solution would have to take that fact into account. He stated repeatedly that the ICJP had impressed on the Irish that the predominant attitude in the prisoners' minds was 'suspicion'. Any approach to them that smacked of brinkmanship, such as approaching them only when one of their members was near death, only intensified suspicion and diminished the chances for success. A serious and open approach by the British was essential. 'Our conviction is that the problem can be solved on a basis and in words other than those of the "5 demands"', explained Dooge, adding that a resolution might be achieved were the British to look at the differences as differences of emphasis rather than of principle, for instance on the issue of work. Such an approach would show that there was more compatibility between the two sides than the British supposed. He urged the British to get back to that basis for a solution and to renew contact with the ICJP. Atkins said that he would consider doing so. Reflecting afterwards, the Irish regarded the interventions from their side as 'insistent and frank. The British responses were non-committal and defensive. At a number of points one had the impression that the British side, in particular Mr Atkins, were somewhat shaken by the intensity as well as the extent of information shown in the Irish presentation.' Nevertheless they felt that the British responses were for the most part 'pro forma and added very little to our information.'[63]

On the following day, the Duddy channel was once again activated and a message dispatched down it, at 4.00 a.m. on 11 July, to the Provos:

> The management is reassessing its position with a view to offering a settlement through their best option ie The Church or Garret Fitzgerald, or both.
>
> A section of the management still believes that the shop stewards [Provisionals] are the best long-term hope but this section of management has lost ground, If face is to be saved for this section of management, they would need assistance. Only the shop stewards can do this.[64]

The Provisionals' reply stated that the 'shop stewards, being aware of the present management moves and intentions for ending the conflict on the factory floor to the management's satisfaction,' were concerned that 'it was impossible for the present conflict to end unless the management grant in full the shop stewards and trade union terms for settlement in clear, unambiguous terms. If a settlement cannot be reached to the shop stewards satisfaction, then escalation will surely follow.'[65]

As this exchange ended, Martin Hurson's condition declined unexpectedly rapidly and he became unconscious by midday on 12 July. Death followed at 04.30 on the following morning, the forty-sixth day of his hunger strike, the result of the same brainstem disorder as in previous deaths, but occurring some two weeks earlier than predicted.

NOTES

1   TNA FCO 87/1262 Northern Ireland Office Protests and Second Hunger Strike – Weekly Bulletin No. 19.
2   TNA PREM 19/506 Memo to Prime Minister, 3 July 1981.
3   TNA FCO 87/1262 Northern Ireland Office Protests and Second Hunger Strike – Weekly Bulletin No. 19.
4   TNA PREM 19/506 Prime Minister Talking to Michael Alison, 4 July 1981.
5   David Beresford, *Ten Men Dead: The Story of the 1981 Irish Hunger Strike* (Harper Collins 1986) p. 216.
6   TNA FCO 87/1262 Northern Ireland Office Protests and Second Hunger Strike – Weekly Bulletin No. 19.
7   TNA FCO 87/1262 Northern Ireland Office Protests and Second Hunger Strike – Weekly Bulletin No. 19.
8   NAI D/T 2011/127/1056 ICJP Statement.
9   TNA PREM 19/506 Prime Minister Talking to Michael Alison, 4 July 1981.
10 TNA PREM 19/506 Call No. 1 – 2200–2312, 4 July.
11 TNA PREM 19/506 Call No.2 – 0200–0500, 5 July.
12 UCG Pol35/166 Duddy Archive The Red Book Manuscript 5 July 1981.
13 TNA PREM 19/506 Call No. 3 – 1045–1125, 5 July.
14 TNA PREM 19/506 Call No. 4 – 1400–1405, 5 July.
15 TNA PREM 19/506 Call No. 5 – 1500–1620, 5 July.
16 *Daily Ireland*, 7 June 2006.
17 http://sluggerotoole.com/2011/11/23/the-smoking-gun/comment-page-2/ (accessed 15 January 2013)
18 TNA PREM 19/506 Call No. 6 – 1750–1817, 5 July.
19 OMalley, *op.cit.* pp.92–93.
20 Beresford, *op.cit.* pp.226–227
21 TNA PREM 19/506 Call No. 7 – 2300–2400, 5 July.
22 TNA PREM 19/506 Call No. 8 – 0100–0117, 6 July.

23   TNA CJ4/3632 Further meeting with the Irish Commission for Justice and Peace: Monday 6 July 1981.
24   O'Malley, *op.cit.*, pp.94-97.
25   TNA PREM 19/506 Letter from Private Secretary, 7 July 1981.
26   TNA PREM 19/506 Hunger Strike – Message to be Sent Through the Channel, 6 July 1981.
27   UCG Pol35/166 Duddy Archive The Red Book Manuscript Reply 6 July 11.30 p.m.
28   UCG Pol35/166 Duddy Archive The Red Book Manuscript 3.30 a.m.
29   O'Rawe, op.cit. p. 184.
30   Beresford op.cit. p.227.
31   UCG Pol35/166 Duddy Archive The Red Book Manuscript Reply 6 July 11.30 p.m.
32   UCG Pol35/166Duddy Archive The Red Book Manuscript 2nd Note 7.50pm, 6 July 1981.
33   UCG Pol35/166 Duddy Archive The Red Book Manuscript 1st Note, 7 July 1981.
34   TNA PREM 19/506 Atkins to Prime Minister: Northern Ireland: the Hunger Strike 7 July 1981.
35   TNA CJ4/3632 Telephone conversation with Bishop O'Mahoney, 7 July 1981.
36   TNA CJ4/3632 Meeting with Chief Constable and Commander Land Forces on Tuesday 7 July.
37   TNA PREM 19/506 Atkins to Prime Minister: Northern Ireland: the Hunger Strike, 7 July 1981.
38   TNA CJ4/3632 Telephone conversation with Bishop O'Mahoney, 7 July 1981.
39   TNA PREM 19/506 Whitmore to Boys-Smith, 8 July 1981.
40   UCG Pol35/166 Duddy Archive The Red Book Manuscript 8 July 1981.
41   UCG Pol35/166 Duddy Archive The Red Book Manuscript 4.00 a.m., 8 July 1981.
42   UCG Pol35/166 Duddy Archive The Red Book Manuscript 5.00 a.m., 8 July 1981.
43   TNA FCO 87/1262 Northern Ireland Office Protests and Second Hunger Strike – Weekly Bulletin No. 19.
44   TNA FCO 87/1261 Statement by the Secretary of State for Northern Ireland, July 8, 1981,
45   TNA FCO 87/1262 Northern Ireland Office Protests and Second Hunger Strike – Weekly Bulletin No. 19.
46   TNA FCO 87/1262 Northern Ireland Office Protests and Second Hunger Strike – Weekly Bulletin.No. 20 09.00 hours Thursday 9 July – 0900 hours Thursday 16 July.
47   TNA CJ4/3632 Protests and Second Hunger Striker – Weekly Bulletin No. 19 0900 hours Thursday 2 July – 0900 hours, Thursday 9 July.
48   NAI D/T 2011/127/1057 Developments in the H-Block: Prisoners protests since 30 June 1981.
49   TNA CJ4/3632 Protests and Second Hunger Striker – Weekly Bulletin No. 19 0900 hours Thursday 2 July – 0900 hours Thursday 9 July.
50   TNA FCO 87/1262 Northern Ireland Office Protests and Second Hunger Strike – Weekly Bulletin No. 20 09.00 hours Thursday 9 July – 0900 hours Thursday 16 July.
51   TNA CJ4/3632 Protests and Second Hunger Striker – Weekly Bulletin No. 19 0900 hours Thursday 2 July – 0900 hours Thursday 9 July.
52   PRONI CENT 1/10/52 Maze Prison Protest Wyatt to Blelloch, 9 July 1981.
53   TNA FCO 87/1262 Northern Ireland Office Protests and Second Hunger Strike – Weekly Bulletin No. 20 09.00 hours Thursday 9 July – 0900 hours Thursday 16 July.
54   TNA FCO 87/1261 Thomas to Eyers, 10 July 1981.
55   NAI D/T 2011/127/1056 To HQ from CGNY.
56   NAI D/T 2011/127/1056 From Embassy Washington, July 1981.
57   TNA FCO 87/1261 FCO to Dublin Telegram Number 541 of 9 July 1981.
58   NAI D/T 2011/127/1056 Major differences between ICJP and Minister of State Mr Alison.
59   TNA FCO 87/1261 Dublin to FCO Telegram Number 232 of 10 July 1981.

60 TNA FCO 87/1261 Dublin to FCO Telegram Number 239 of 14 July 1981.
61 TNA FCO 87/1261 Dublin to FCO Telegram Number 231 of 10 July 1981.
62 TNA FCO 87/1261 FCO to Dublin Telegram Number 108 of 13 July 1981 Text of a message from the Taoiseach to the Prime Minister delivered on 10 July.
63 NAI D/T 2011/127/1056 Meeting at Foreign and Commonwealth Office, 10 July 1981.
64 UCG Pol35/166 Duddy Archive The Red Book Manuscript 10.50 p.m., 11 July 1981.
65 UCG Pol35/166 Duddy Archive The Red Book Manuscript 10.50 p.m., 11 July 1981.

Chapter 10

A Final Push

On Friday 10 July, Pat McGeown refused breakfast despite his previous denials that he was the next candidate for hunger strike. Matthew Devlin also refused breakfast on 15 July. He was a 31-year-old single man from Coagh, East Tyrone, serving seven years for attempted murder and possession of firearms. Devlin's fast marked a return to the PIRA's established pattern – he was replacement for Hurson on a geographical basis; he was also single, 'unimportant in the organisation' and took part in the mass hunger strike of 15/16 December. Of more immediate concern was the fact that Kieran Doherty's condition had worsened considerably in the past few days; he was receiving daily visits from his family. He was 'somewhat stupefied' with vision severely affected and hearing diminishing, but was not yet quite bedbound. Doherty had said 'goodbye' to the Chaplain. Kevin Lynch, on the other hand, remained rather better than might be expected, but had begun to deteriorate more rapidly. He was now having definite visual problems and his urine was affected. Barring any sudden collapse in his condition, death was considered unlikely before day sixty. He was still able to walk and associate, but his morale had now sagged; on 15 June he had told the doctor 'I'm finished'. Thomas McElwee had not shown any signs of deterioration so far, though signs were shortly expected to occur. Devine, McKeown, McGeown and Devlin were also unchanged. Quinn was, however, showing signs of early deterioration, and already had some eye disturbance.[1]

McDonnell, in the meantime, was buried with full IRA military honours at Milltown Cemetery; the British Government was attacked by the presiding priest who declared that 'Joe McDonnell did not want to die. His wife and relatives did not want him to die. Like all of us, they hoped the mission of the Commission would lead to resolution and peace. But the integrity and honest endeavour of the Commission was not seen to be matched by the British Government'. John Hume added to the criticism of the Government, maintaining that a real opportunity still existed to 'resolve the hunger strike and give massive relief to community tensions'. He claimed that the prisoners' 4 July statement offered a real basis for a settlement and urged the Government, if it had either the will to solve the problem or any appreciation of the urgency of a settlement in community terms, to 'grasp the opportunity which now exists by talking directly to the prisoners.' The call for direct negotiations with the prisoners was taken up, on 13 July, by both Cardinal Ó Fiaich and the Irish Government. Ó Fiaich said: 'I repeat the appeal, which I have made on a number of occasions to Mrs Thatcher, to send a Government representative to talk to the prisoners without delay. With equal urgency I call on the prisoners and those who speak for them to build, in a conciliatory fashion, on the Commission's hard-won achievements'. In a significant development, the Taoiseach now publicly urged the British to heed what they had been told by the ICJP and negotiate directly with the prisoners following the death of Hurson, while Professor Dooge made a similar public appeal in Brussels, where he had a meeting with Lord Carrington. Dooge said afterwards:

> Every death in the Maze is a potential propaganda victory for the IRA and they take good care to convert it into such. If we are going to have a death a week from now on, including possibly the death of a member of the Irish Parliament, in my view the IRA will be the only beneficiaries and the British and Irish Governments will be the sufferers.'[2]

This was the same as what Dooge had urged upon Carrington in their private discussion, where the former stressed the urgency of action to resolve the hunger strike. The resulting growth of world sympathy for the IRA threatened to internationalize the situation, he warned, which was what both Governments had been seeking to avoid throughout. He asked that the Foreign Secretary pass on what he had to say without delay to Mrs Thatcher and Atkins. The Irish Government was asking for a prompt and considered reply to the Taoiseach's 10 July message to the Prime Minister. The easiest reply would of course be to stay put, as Atkins had done the previous week, but this would be potentially disastrous. The Irish Government had believed that there was a possibility of a settlement a week before, though the two subsequent deaths would have hardened the position of the strikers (in an earlier private conversation with Carrington, Dooge said that Hurson was the most obdurate of the strikers, and that his death might actually improve the prospects for a settlement). It was important, argued Dooge, for the British Government to distinguish between the prisoners themselves and their external IRA manipulators, to whom each death bound them more firmly. The British should be prepared to exploit this distinction by 'dealing' (though not negotiating) directly with the prisoners. The Irish, noted Carrington, 'were not asking us to abandon our fundamental principles – that there should be no special status, and that our prisoners should remain under the control of our own prison authorities.' These principles did, however, leave room for some flexibility, as had been indicated in the ICJP statement of the previous week. The Irish Government understood that HMG might fear that a settlement on these lines might come unstuck, as had happened after the first hunger strike the previous December. This was why the Taoiseach had asked Dooge to suggest that the European Commission on Human Rights play a monitoring role after a settlement. In addition, the Irish did not exclude a further role for the ICJP, though Dooge accepted that this role would have to be a passive rather than an active one.[3] In a further move to put pressure on the British, FitzGerald wrote directly to President Reagan on 14 July:

Dear Mr President

On the happy occasion of your visiting the Embassy of Ireland today, I wish to ask your help on a matter of great urgency and importance.

Since its inception our State has had to fight an almost continuous battle against terrorism which is now at a critical stage.

My Government deeply appreciate your firm opposition to support for terrorism in Ireland by Americans. We also appreciate the courageous leadership shown in this matter by prominent Americans of Irish extraction notably Speaker O'Neill.

The hunger strike crisis in Northern Ireland has increased support for terrorist organisations, is benefiting them and is now seriously threatening our security.

The hunger striker next expected to die, Kieran Doherty, is an elected member of our own legislature. It is expected that he will die on Friday next.

I beg you to use your enormous influence with the British Prime Minister within the next 24 hours to implement immediately an already existing understanding mediated by the Commission of Justice and Peace of the Irish Catholic Hierarchy to avert his death so preventing the very dangerous consequences which would inevitably follow.

With my best wishes

Yours sincerely
Garret FitzGerald[4]

Ambassador Sean Donlon handed the Taoiseach's message to Mike Deaver (Deaver, Baker and Meese 'are the triumvirate that run the White House' he informed the Taoiseach) at 2.30 local time. Donlon, on arrival at a function at the White House at 7.00 p.m., was taken aside for forty minutes by Meese who had, among other functions, been Governor Reagan's head of correctional facilities in California. This 'proved to be something of a disadvantage in the Ambassador's efforts to explain the political dimension of the problem to him.' Donlon had, he thought, more useful exchanges with Baker and Deaver, but feared that, given the issue, the President might rely more on Meese.[5]

John Hume, in the meantime, telephoned the NIO from Derry to say that he had returned from a one-day visit to Co. Donegal some hours earlier to find the atmosphere in the city's Catholic community very unsettled because of the Hurson death – more so than on earlier similar occasions. He also found the SDLP under very severe pressure across Northern Ireland to withdraw from local councils and to take a posture very hostile to the British Government. Hume also telephoned Atkins and requested a meeting with Mrs Thatcher. Atkins indicated that he did not think that it could be arranged, but asked Hume to come to see him within a few days. Hume warned Atkins of the likelihood that the SDLP would have to withdraw from local councils etc. and gave no commitment on going to see the Secretary of State. Atkins replied that pressure was coming from all sides to intervene before Doherty's death to 'solve the problem.' He specifically mentioned the Taoiseach's letter to the Prime Minister and the Ministerial meeting at the FCO. As a result, he stressed that the whole problem was under reconsideration in London.[6]

Hume spoke of increasing tension within the Catholic community, and described the present situation as 'pretty desperate'. He and his party were under pressure, if not to state publicly their support for the hunger-strikers, then at least to be seen to be pressuring the Government to talk to them. Hume was anxious for an official to go into the prison and talk to the hunger-strikers on the basis of their 4 July statement, which he suggested was not dissimilar to what he had said to the Prime Minister at their recent meeting. Atkins pointed out that since 4 July the prisoners had issued a further statement that repeated their more familiar hard line and clearly implied that they, rather than the prison authorities, should be in control of the prison. The Secretary of State nevertheless felt that, whilst this latest statement was disappointing, there was still hope for a resolution of the problem. Hume re-emphasized his concern and said that the strength of feeling, particularly in the Republic, aroused by the hunger strike was greater than ever. Action was required with the utmost urgency. Atkins undertook to report to the Prime Minister what Hume had told him, and said that he would be in touch with him again at the end of the week. It was noted that Hume, whilst anxious throughout the conversation, was neither aggressive nor belligerent, and appeared to be grateful for having had the opportunity to speak to the Secretary of State.[7]

The reconsideration to which Atkins had referred concerned the possibility of involving the International Committee of the Red Cross (ICRC) in the prison dispute. Atkins was shown a Foreign Office telegram from Geneva; it outlined how, in May, the ICRC had made an offer to 'to visit on a regular basis, all persons incarcerated as a result of the events in Northern Ireland, in order to submit, confidentially, its reports and suggestions on material and psychological conditions of detention to the competent authorities.' The offer went on to say: 'as is known to the British authorities the sole aim of such visits is to improve, if necessary, the detention conditions and they can in no way affect the legal status of the prisoners visited.' The ICRC had previously paid half a dozen visits, at HMG's invitation, to Northern Ireland prisons between 1971 and 1974 to inspect and report on the conditions under which internees and detainees (being held pending trial, or during the trial process) were held. They had not at any time visited convicted prisoners, special category or otherwise. Between 1974 and 1980, the ICRC had approached HMG tentatively once or twice to ask whether there might be a role for them to play in Northern Ireland prisons. At the time the NIO concluded that there was no such role, but during a meeting with NIO and FCO officials in December 1980, Miss Simonius of the ICRC made a 'rather more forceful' approach in which she said that a series of visits could be presented as a regular part of ICRC activity, and that, assuming after their visits they could give the Northern Ireland prison regime a clean bill of health, this could strengthen the Government's propaganda armoury. HMG had pointed out that any visits to the Maze by the ICRC might be interpreted as an exercise in mediation and, given the ICRC's well-established reputation in the prisoner of war field, it might appear that prisoners were implicitly being given prisoner of war status. The ICRC had never, for example, visited convicted prisoners in any part of the United Kingdom.

At the end of April, the three TDs (Blaney, O'Connell and Síle de Valera) who visited Sands had asked the ICRC to intervene under the Geneva Convention. In its reply, the ICRC said that it remained prepared to visit Northern Ireland prisons if authorized to do so by the British Government. As it pointed out to the TDs, and in its recent message to HMG, the ICRC was 'wholly clear' that it would be operating *outside* the various Geneva Conventions that applied to international and non-international armed conflicts. Over the years the NIO and FCO had seen to it that the situation in Northern Ireland was 'not caught' by conventions affecting these conflicts. The ICRC's constitution did, though, permit it to offer protection and assistance in situations not covered by international humanitarian laws. The ICRC's reports, which would be confidential, would be addressed to HMG, and would not be intended for publication. The Government could, however, publish them if it wished. 'Quite rightly', the ICRC would not permit a Government to get away with publishing favourable extracts: in that event the ICRC usually responded by publishing the entire report. In May, NIO officials considered the attractions and risks in taking up the ICRC's offer:

Arguments for

(i) The ICRC is a well respected international body with experience in this field.
(ii) Publication of reports would be a matter for HMG. If we decided to publish, we should be able to demonstrate that our house was very substantially in order; insofar as the ICRC suggested improvements which we could accept, we could pray in aid the recommendations from an impartial body when explaining why we have made further changes in the prison regime.
(iii) There would be no question of negotiation or mediation.

Arguments against

(i) Despite its extra-Conventional role, the ICRC is popularly associated with investigating the conditions of prisoners of war. The Provisionals would exploit this.
(ii) Once we let the ICRC in, it could be very difficult to get them out again ...
(iii) It seems that they would want to talk to many if not all the prisoners. No doubt some sensible formula could be found but periodic visits could nevertheless be disruptive.
(iv) We would be under pressure to publish the ICRC reports. There is a risk, which is difficult to assess, that the reports would be unhelpful ...

Recommendations

There are significant political risks in taking up the ICRC's offer, but as PUS has said we should not rule out visits at some stage. However, the time is not yet ripe.[8]

By mid-July, though, the feeling was that the situation demanded another initiative. Atkins approved a telegram to the British Embassy in Geneva asking for the Red Cross' intervention in the prison dispute:

We should now like to take up that offer. We should be grateful if the ICRC could visit NI prisons urgently on the basis which it has suggested and let HMG have in confidence the benefit of its advice as soon as possible. We recall that in their note the ICRC said that 'the sole aim of such visits is to improve, if necessary, the detention conditions and they can in no way affect the legal status of the prisoners visited.'[9]

From Dublin, Figg commented: 'I understand we are now enlisting the help of the International Red Cross. With respect, I think it is too late to do so.' A few weeks earlier this would have 'stood a fair chance' but, with the failure of the intervention of the ICJP, the Ambassador believed that the evidence was that the prisoners and hunger-strikers would not deal with any more third parties. He warned: 'If Doherty dies the consequent by-election will probably make the Irish Government's position even more precarious. We shall be blamed. The consequences, here and internationally may cause us grave difficulties.' His conclusion was to overturn previous policy:

These risks seem far greater than the one represented by talking directly with the hunger strikers. This need not cut across the Red Cross initiative. Both might proceed together. But with time so dangerously short I recommend in the strongest possible way that we should delay no longer in explaining directly to the hunger strikers what is on offer.[10]

Figg's views were ignored: Philip Woodfield phoned the Ambassador at 5.10 p.m. on 15 July to tell him that an official was to go into the Maze to explain the Government's initiative on the ICRC to the hunger-strikers and, if they raised it, to answer any questions they might have about Atkins' statement of 8 July. Copies of a statement (as in the telegram from Geneva) about the ICRC would be given to the hunger-strikers and simultaneously released to the press. The ICRC would arrive in Northern Ireland the following day and visit the Maze. The PUS explained that Atkins thought it desirable for the Taoiseach to be shown the statement and told about the official's visit a short time (about half an hour) before it was issued to the press and given to the prisoners. Figg agreed that he would say that he might wish to see the Taoiseach or Dermot Nally urgently. It was further agreed that Woodfield would telephone Figg again when all was ready to proceed in Belfast.

At 6.10 p.m., Woodfield phoned Figg again to say that John Blelloch had left for the Maze, and the way was clear for the Taoiseach to be told.[11] Figg delivered the message to FitzGerald, and stated that the NIO official at the Maze would be ready to clarify or explain the Atkins statement of 8 July. FitzGerald commented that he would have to reflect on the wisdom of saying anything in response to the initiative. The prisoners, to say the least, were not supporters of his; he 'would not like them to be able to claim that we were involved in something directed against them. The prisoners were now deeply suspicious.' The Taoiseach, though, wished to express appreciation of the British Government's action. Its success would depend on the extent to which the clarifications offered by the official went to meet the position reached in the statement of the ICJP;[12] obviously he would have to suspend judgement on its worth until he saw its result. Whatever happened it was clearly worth doing, but it would be much more worthwhile if it were crowned with success. The Taoiseach also stated that when he had met the families of the hunger-strikers, he had been impressed by their apparently sincere wish to urge the hunger-strikers to cease their fast on the basis of the ICJP proposals, even though at that time the families had not known what those proposals were. He thought that it might be useful to give the families facilities for visits again at this time.[13]

Figg's other task was to deliver Mrs Thatcher's reply to FitzGerald's earlier personal message to her. The Prime Minister acknowledged that the ICJP had worked hard to find a solution; indeed, 'HMG admires the Commission's determination and dedication to its task and I do not wish in any way to denigrate their efforts.' But they had, in their statement, implied that Alison was guilty of bad faith in that he gave assurances that he later failed to fulfil. 'You say in your letter that you, as a Government, quote are persuaded by this account unquote', noted the Prime Minister:

> This is not the place to go in detail over precisely what was and was not said in some 16 hours of talks ... but I must say plainly that I totally repudiate the charge of bad faith. It may be that in such prolonged talks misunderstandings arose: but I must ask you to accept my word that Mr Alison, and through him the British Government have acted honourably throughout.

The truth was that the Commission had all along underestimated the constraint laid upon HMG by the need to retain proper control of, and apply a common regime within, a prison containing some 1,000 convicted criminals, many guilty of the most heinous crimes and drawn from all the paramilitary groups; and they had seriously overestimated the possibility of persuading the hunger-strikers (and, equally importantly, the Provisionals who controlled them) to accept their own compromise proposals. This last point had been amply demonstrated by the latest statement issued in the name of the hunger-strikers in which they rejected the Commission's proposals as an 'unacceptable dilution' of their five demands.

Mrs Thatcher went on: 'I do beg of you not to be misled into thinking that this problem is susceptible of any easy solution, wanting only a little flexibility on HMG's part. It is not.' The protesters had abandoned their claim for differential treatment, and that was helpful 'because it was totally unacceptable. But they still, it seems, hold to their five demands. In our attitude to these demands we are not seeking to be difficult for the sake of saving face', stressed Mrs Thatcher. 'We have to grapple not only with a serious problem of prison control but also with issues going to the standing of the Provisionals.' Of course the regime could be modified in various ways (as it had been already), 'and we have consistently maintained that we are prepared – once the hunger strike is over – to make yet further improvements on humanitarian grounds.' Nevertheless, it was important to appreciate that the aim of the Provisionals, ('and this is why they see no role for the ICJP'), was not merely – or mainly – to get easier prison conditions for their members. It was to achieve within the Northern Ireland prison system a regime originally for themselves, but now apparently for all prisoners, in which the prisoners and not the prison authorities determined what went on. If they achieved this, it would confer a kind of legitimacy upon the acts for which those prisoners were convicted. If, in addition, the Provisionals were to be drawn into direct negotiation with the British Government on the terms of settling the hunger strike, that would confer upon them a status that they would value.

'I am sure that these aims are as unacceptable to us as they would be to you', commented Mrs Thatcher. Furthermore, 'we are not prepared to subscribe to forms of words which by their generality can mean all things to all men.' That course could only lead to subsequent recrimination and to yet a further round of strikes at a later date. 'We know that you recognise the importance of ensuring that any settlement is a lasting one', she told FitzGerald. Finally, Mrs Thatcher noted what the Taoiseach had said about co-operation between the British security forces and those of the Republic:

> As you know, we value that co-operation highly. As I have observed above, terrorism is our common enemy. It recognises no borders. I cannot believe your Government will wish in any way to diminish the scale or intensity of that co-operation. I appreciate the importance of local opinion; but the reaction of public opinion here to any suggestion that the authorities in the Republic were offering less than full co-operation in the detection and apprehension of terrorists would be sharp and bitter and there must be a risk that it would have an adverse effect on wider Anglo-Irish relationships.[14]

Simultaneously with the delivery of the Prime Minister's message, Atkins announced that a three-man team from the ICRC would visit prisons in Northern Ireland. He made it clear that the Red Cross was not acting:

> ... on the basis of the Geneva Conventions of 1949 which dealt with the conditions of prisoners of war but in exercise of its right to take

humanitarian initiatives: The ICRC have made it clear to the Government that the sole aim of their visit will be to assess and, if necessary, to make recommendations to improve the conditions of imprisonment in Northern Ireland.[15]

When Gerry Adams gave his initial reaction to the ICRC visit he accused Britain of 'once again trying to abuse an international organisation for its own ends in order to create an illusion of movement during a critical phase of the hunger strike.'[16]

Across the Atlantic reaction was more favourable. In Washington, the British Embassy telephoned its principal contacts within the Administration and in Congress to inform them of Atkins' statement. The immediate reaction was 'one of relief that we have found a way of involving a reputable body which could help bring the hunger strike to an end', reported Sir Nicholas Henderson to London. 'Our initiative with the Red Cross will help here. But Congress will continue to see the hunger strike essentially as a problem which is up to the British Government to solve, even if we invoke the aid of an outside body to help us do so.' This meant that if the hunger strike was not settled before the next death occurred: 'our action in bringing in the ICRC may be turned against us and presented by the Friends of Ireland and others as another example of prevarication on our part and of unwillingness to move quickly and decisively to save human life for fear of losing face', warned Henderson. As far as US opinion was concerned, the expected date of the next death (at the weekend) did, therefore, set an uncomfortably close deadline for the ICRC's activities, 'and for our ability to make the wholly positive use of their involvement which we are doing at the moment.'

As for the general mood in Washington, Henderson found that there was no sign of weakening in the Administration's desire not to intervene, although they were coming under increased pressure to do so: 'Our principal difficulty (apart from harassment of our staff, particularly in New York and Boston, which is a growing problem) remains the enhanced standing of Noraid and the attitude of Congress.' Irish-American politicians 'are not just angry with us because they themselves are under pressure (O'Neill has had a sit-in at his office in Boston and Kennedy is also being barracked.) A number of them seem to feel that they must take some action which will hurt us in order to make us pay heed to their point of view.' The Embassy had been informed by one staff member of the Chairman of the House Foreign Affairs Committee that such action could take the form of an attempt to block the annual renewal of certain Government-to-Government defence contracts.[17]

Henderson also learned, from White House staff, of the message from FitzGerald to the President on 14 July. The message, he understood, asked the President to intervene with the Prime Minister to urge the British Government to implement the understanding reached with the ICJP. Reagan, reported Henderson, was due to go to the Irish Embassy later that evening to attend the conferral on his father-in-law of an honorary fellowship of the Irish College of Surgeons. The President, Henderson was informed, had been briefed by the White House to tell the Irish Ambassador that it was doubtful whether direct US intervention would be helpful at this point. Subsequently Henderson reported: 'We do not know if the President spoke to the brief, but the White House press office appear to be speaking to journalists on these lines. The Irish Embassy are under instructions from Dublin to make no comment to the Press.' The White House was saying that there had hitherto been no suggestion that the President should mention Northern Ireland when he was due to see the Prime Minister, soon, in Ottawa. In a speech, at the dinner in honour of his father-in-law, the President had made a passing reference to the continued tragic situation in Northern Ireland, but otherwise said nothing of substance.[18]

The White House was true to its word. The Irish Ambassador, Sean Donlon, was seated close to the President at dinner in Decatur House following a reception. They had a private conversation for about fifty minutes about Northern Ireland generally. The President showed goodwill and concern, but not a great deal of close understanding about the general problem. In the 'classical mould of an Irish-American', he wished to know what 'we could do' to solve the situation. He seemed convinced that the problems would ease were Church leaders on both sides to co-operate more closely and were Eastern European influences to cease their machinations. The Ambassador informed him 'bluntly' that unhelpful American influences had done more harm in this case than Eastern European infiltration. The President was concerned about this. On the prisons, Reagan said that he had a difficulty in that he did not wish to aid prisoners detained for crimes of terrorism. He did not, however, rule out an intervention on his part. Reagan revealed that he had in previous days sent a message to Mrs Thatcher conveying the concern of Speaker O'Neill and Senator Kennedy on the hunger strikes.[19]

While events in Washington were proceeding well from a British point of view, in Dublin a mini-crisis occurred following Figg's assurance to the Taoiseach that the visit by a senior official to the Maze Prison to explain about the ICRC would also provide an opportunity for the official to make clear any points the prisoners might wish to raise arising out of Atkins' statement of 8 July. Governor Hilditch and John Blelloch saw the hunger-strikers during the evening of 15 July.[20] Blelloch went in to see the hunger-strikers at 7.00 p.m. All eight were there. Doherty could not read, but appeared to comprehend generally. The Governor delivered the statement on the Red Cross. The strikers listened closely. Blelloch then highlighted the prestigious, impartial, international nature of the body, and made a point about follow-up visits by the ICRC. The prisoners conferred among themselves for ten minutes. They then asked two questions. The first was whether the ICRC required their permission to visit. Blelloch answered that this was a matter for the ICRC; they were coming to try to help, and it would be surprising if they did not feel that seeing the hunger-strikers was helpful. The second question was when would the ICRC come to the Maze. Blelloch was not certain, but thought that it could be as early as the next day.[21] It was commented on, by the prisoners, that the last time an official was present they were not allowed to ask questions ('which was, of course, the brief at that time'). Blelloch explained that he was there and could answer, 'but I made it very plain that I was neither there to negotiate nor to substitute for the authority of the Governor.'[22]

The prisoners then asked to see McFarlane. The Governor agreed to a limited session. Blelloch asked the prisoners whether they had reflected on Atkins' statement of 8 July. They said that they had, and had one or two points; but then did not pursue this and seemed to be much more interested in the ICRC. The Governor and Blelloch then left, and McFarlane was fetched. Hilditch's 'feel' was that the atmosphere was one of 'deathly calm'. The hunger-strikers realized the seriousness of their situation, but were unlikely to act without Sinn Féin orders. They would probably decide nothing that night, but would want to hear the radio and possibly receive 'messages' via visitors. At 8.45 p.m., Blelloch phoned the NIO to say that McFarlane had returned to his cell and the hunger-strikers had dispersed without requesting a further meeting.[23] Blelloch was also asked, by Hugh Logue, to telephone him in Dublin (twice). He did so at about 10.15 p.m. Logue, as Blelloch recalled, had three main questions/points:

(a) How had the meeting gone? I told him, fairly firmly, that I did not think it would be helpful for me to speculate on that since any views attributed to the British Government and its officials on this sensitive matter were hardly likely to be favourably received, whatever those views, by the prisoners. I also refused to be drawn on what questions they had put and what answers I had given;

(b) he commented that my presence was 'more important' than the request to the ICRC. I said that if my presence were to prove helpful towards the outcome that we all wanted, ie that the hunger strike should end then no-one would be happier than I: but that I did not see my presence as a first event in a 'negotiating spree';

(c) he asked about the Committee's movements and stressed the urgency in view of Doherty's condition. I said that the Committee's movements were a matter for them, that I believed they would be coming on Thursday, that they would be likely to be well aware of the need for speed and that they would find no impediment placed in their way by the British Government.

Logue was, Blelloch suspected, 'considerably put out at what he may have felt to be a distinctly unhelpful – a favourite word of his – conversation', and it was possible that he, or another member of the ICJP, spoke to the Taoiseach under the influence of the conversation.[24]

Later that evening, Figg informed the Irish by telephone in broad terms how the visit had gone, and that the hunger-strikers seemed to have paid little attention to the 8 July statement. Then, at 1.15 a.m., the Taoiseach telephoned ('when I was fast asleep', recalled Figg) and complained that his information was that the official had made no attempt to explain the 8 July statement, 'and that I had misled him into believing that this would be done.' Figg pleaded that this sounded most unlikely, but he would seek a proper explanation in the morning.[25] Figg telephoned Woodfield at 9.15 a.m. to say that an 'irate' Taoiseach had telephoned to say that he had been misled. The PUS and Figg agreed that, as had been explained the previous evening, Blelloch's object in going into the Maze was to explain the statement about the ICRC and answer any questions about the 8 July statement if the prisoners wished to pursue such questions. The prisoners had in fact shown more interest in the ICRC than in following up the statement. Woodfield and Figg agreed that the Ambassador might tell the Taoiseach this and say that, if the prisoners asked to see an official again to make comment on the ICRC visit, then there would be a further opportunity for them to ask questions about the Secretary of State's statement if they so wished. In discussion of how FitzGerald might have known what happened at the prison, Figg said that he had told Kirwin, at the Taoiseach's office, at 10.30 p.m. that the prisoners had shown little interest in the 8 July statement. Blelloch later told Woodfield on the telephone that the Taoiseach might also have got a message to this effect from Logue.[26]

The Ambassador phoned Dermot Nally on the morning of 16 July, 'in a state of considerable anxiety', to say that he had been phoned in the night by the Taoiseach. In view of his anxiety and clear wish to get the record straight urgently, Nally said that he would see him immediately. Figg was particularly concerned that the visit to the prison by Blelloch, which he had brought about by his personal intervention, appeared, in the Taoiseach's eyes, to have gone badly wrong. This distressed him greatly. The Ambassador then gave an account of what had happened, after which Nally said that, from Dublin's point of view, 'our basic point was that, somehow, what was on offer to the prisoners must be brought as close as possible to what had been the position of the Irish Commission for Justice and Peace when their intervention had been suspended.' Nally thought that, on all indications, there was the basis for an honourable settlement in their proposals.[27] From Figg's of view it seemed that Nally 'clearly' accepted the visit as a serious attempt by Blelloch to focus the strikers' attention on the 8 July statement and to elicit questions on it. Figg commented that he very much hoped that the Taoiseach would accept it in the same way.[28]

Professor Dooge then asked Figg to call at 12.30 p.m. He wanted to make clear what the Taoiseach had said at the previous meeting. This was that the success of the present British initiative would depend on the extent to which the clarification offered of the movement the British Government was prepared to make after the strike ended would meet the position set out by the ICJP. He realized that, of course, there was no possibility of all this being taken into account when the official visited the Maze the day before. But the Irish very much hoped that another visit could be paid very soon. They were naturally disappointed 'as no doubt we were' that the hunger-strikers had not taken the opportunity to ask questions about the 8 July statement. This made a further visit necessary and urgent, especially as they thought that Doherty might not live through the night. Figg commented that the question of a further visit to the hunger-strikers would probably depend on how a request was made. He did not think that there was the slightest possibility of a further visit happening before the Red Cross arrived at the prison, 'and we would not wish to get the two exercises mixed up.' On being specifically asked whether a further official visit might be made if the strikers wished to ask questions they failed to put the previous night, Figg admitted: 'I really did not know. But if the request for further clarification were clearly genuine, I thought it might be favourably received.'[29]

Following on from this, in the late afternoon, Dooge contacted Mike Hopkins, of the NIO, and pressed for a discussion on the telephone with either Atkins or Ian Gilmour. Hopkins asked his superiors for instructions on what line should be taken on the question of an official going back to the Maze to talk to the hunger-strikers. After discussions with Woodfield, Hopkins was told that the line to take was as follows:

i) the ICRC are in the Prison at the moment and it would not be appropriate for us to send an official into the Prison while the ICRC were thus operating;

ii) should the hunger strikers, however, request an official goes back in the context of the ICRC's visit, we would consider that request sympathetically;

iii) if an official went to the Prison it would be on the same basis as yesterday evening that if the hunger strikers wanted to raise points on the statement of 8 July, the official would be prepared to answer questions.[30]

In the event, Gilmour telephoned Dooge at about 4.50 p.m. Dooge explained that he had asked to speak to Atkins, but was very happy to speak to Gilmour, knowing that his message would reach the same destination. Dooge wished to refer first to the state of health of hunger-striker Doherty. The latest information he had was that he might die that night. Gilmour said that, privately, the assessment available to him was much better: that Doherty was holding his own. Professor Dooge responded that he had received similar information earlier in the day: that Doherty was stable and looked better. The later information was that there was instability that could prove dangerous. The latest evaluation that they had was that Doherty would not last in any event beyond the evening of the following day.[31]

The ICRC delegation – consisting of Dr Frank Schmidt, Philippe Grand d'Hauteville and Dr Rémi Russbach – arrived in Northern Ireland the same day, 16 July. They went straight to the Maze, where they first saw the Governor and then had a lengthy meeting with the hunger-strikers and McFarlane. They also selected seven prisoners from the conforming blocks; six agreed to see them and one refused. Four protesters were also chosen, but three refused, saying that McFarlane would speak for them. After leaving the prison later in the evening, meetings were held with senior officials[32] including Woodfield and Blelloch.

After the usual pleasantries, the ICRC explained that their basic interest was in prison conditions and not specifically to persuade the hunger-strikers to end their fast – but they realized the urgency of the situation. In their talks with the hunger-strikers and McFarlane they had been asked to pursue the question of prison conditions with the NIO. The prisoners felt that in the past there had not been sufficient opportunity for constructive discussion on these questions. The ICRC would be willing to help as a 'moderator' or 'mediator', but they did not feel that it would be particularly helpful for them to act as a 'go-between'. The ICRC explained that the prisoners would like a round-table discussion with the NIO, with the ICRC, McFarlane, Gerry Adams and Danny Morrison all present, on the basis of their 4 July statement. The ICRC had made it quite clear that they were not prepared in any way to depart from matters of prison conditions to 'political matters'.

Woodfield explained the very grave difficulties that this proposal held for HMG: that the five demands appeared to be about prison conditions but were in fact the substance of political status; and that the Government could not enter into negotiation with representatives of the IRA to discuss the particular regime that their members should have in prison. 'Our position was that we were only prepared to explain on humanitarian grounds to the hunger strikers themselves statements that the Government had already made.' Blelloch elaborated on the fact that the five demands were identical with political status, and explained why the prisoners wanted the Government to be drawn into negotiations with their commanders outside – thus bypassing the prison authorities and in effect negotiating through a 'council of war'. The ICRC asked whether it was not a fact that discussions had already taken place between officials and the hunger-strikers and whether there was any leeway for negotiation between what the prisoners wanted and what the Government was prepared to offer. Woodfield accepted that it could be said that there was an element of negotiation in any communication between two people, but this was different to 'trading and dealing terms' with the prisoners. He explained to the ICRC the circumstances of Blelloch's visit the previous evening: 'we were prepared for Mr Blelloch to return and answer questions on the 8 July statement if that would be helpful.' The PUS then explained what Blelloch would be authorized to say on the various points in question.

The ICRC asked about whether further moves were dependent on the hunger strike ending or the hunger strike and the protest ending, and Woodfield replied that because of the complexity of the question of work, the issue could not be looked at simply in these terms. On work, he explained that it was essential that if prisoners refused to do certain types of work then they would suffer appropriate penalties. Dr Schmidt asked whether it would not be possible to enable prisoners to earn remission for prison industry work (as prisoners in some Spanish prisons could). The officials explained that the 50% remission scheme in Northern Ireland was already extremely generous. While explaining all this, the PUS stressed that the Government could not concern itself entirely with the situation of the prisoners – the reaction of the Loyalist community and the question of the prison system and public opinion in Great Britain all had to be taken into account. There was then discussion of how matters might be taken forward.

The idea of Blelloch going into the prison to clarify the 8 July statement with the ICRC present was suggested, but the ICRC felt that such a discussion would not be constructive without McFarlane present, and the NIO officials explained why that was not possible. After further discussion, which in particular took account of the urgency of the whole matter, it was suggested that the ICRC might act as an 'honest broker'. They could clarify the points in the statement of 8 July to the hunger-strikers and McFarlane, and if there were points on which the ICRC needed further clarification, it might be possible for them to make separate contact with the responsible officials. On the question of sincerity, the ICRC could highlight the final paragraph of the its statement, which indicated that they might make further visits. The ICRC said that they had already arranged to start their routine work at 9.00 a.m. in the prison the next morning, and they could then ask to see the hunger-strikers if that seemed appropriate. At this stage it was agreed that the meeting would adjourn so that the PUS could consult the Secretary of State. The ICRC then returned to the Stormont Hotel.[33]

Woodfield telephoned Atkins at 11.00 p.m. and explained what had taken place during the discussion with the ICRC. They were clearly a very sophisticated body of high calibre who were very willing to help and were fully aware of HMG's position on principles, but also of the desirability of getting the hunger strike called off. Woodfield put to Atkins the proposal that the ICRC might clarify the statement of 8 July to the prisoners along the lines of Blelloch's original steering – the relevant parts of which PUS had read to the Committee on a confidential basis. The ICRC could seek further discreet clarification from officials if necessary. It was Woodfield's judgement that the ICRC would behave responsibly, even if at the end of the day the gap between the prisoners' demands and what the regime offered could not be bridged. Atkins agreed that 'we should now proceed as proposed but that it should be stressed to the ICRC that the room for manoeuvre was very limited.'[34]

With the green light having been given, Woodfield and Blelloch headed for the Stormont Hotel to inform Dr Schmidt that Atkins had agreed that the Committee should proceed as proposed. Woodfield stressed that he was not optimistic of the outcome and that the statement of 8 July indicated the limited movement possible in the areas concerned. At the ICRC's request, Woodfield and Blelloch then explained the complexities of the various issues in question: on segregation it was essential that the prison authorities retained the right to decide how prisoners should be deployed in the prison. The current penological objective was to integrate the prison population so as not to facilitate the paramilitary command structure and to encourage coexistence. (Some conforming Catholic and Protestant prisoners already shared cells and mixed in recreation and sport.) The Governors were passionately committed to this concept. It was accepted that there was a need to segregate some classes of prisoner for security reasons, but the prisoners should not be led to believe that they had the right to determine where they were put and with whom they mixed. This was an important point, but one that bore on the longer-term development of association in the wider context. The officials then explained the position on clothing and the intention to implement the changes in the regime as rapidly as the practical arrangements could be made, although there were difficulties, which mainly centred on the question of laundering of clothes.

Any decision on which arrangement should be made could not be taken in advance, though Blelloch's view was that the prisoners initially might wear their own clothing throughout the day on the same basis as the conforming prisoners could during part of the day. This would mean that they initially wore prison-issue undergarments. With regard to association, conforming prisoners already received about forty hours' association a week – three hours per evening and all weekend. Arrangements for association between adjoining wings might be implemented, and would be practical where the number of prisoners per wing was moving towards the one prisoner per cell target. This problem had to be considered in terms of four different locations:

a. the exercise yard – association of around 50 people would be acceptable.
b. recreation rooms: association here would similarly be acceptable.
c. hobbies room: commonsense restriction would be necessary because of the size of the room.

d. Cells: it was essential that only the occupants of the cells were allowed inside them. This was a measure of protection for the occupants themselves (who could be pressurised or bullied by others entering their cell) and for the occupants' contents. Association inside a cell would be very difficult for prison officers to supervise effectively.

Letters and parcels, as had previously been discussed, did not create a problem. On work, educational courses were open to suitable prisoners, but the authorities could not allow 'self-education', where prisoners would seek to instruct each other. There was then some discussion on censorship of books. It was admitted that rather restrictive censorship might have been practised hitherto, and there may be scope for relaxation in this field with prison security being the prime influencing factor. With regard to remission it was important that the prisoners should not be misled into thinking that the Government was prepared to be more generous than in fact it was in restoration of lost remission. Other prisoners would want remission restored, and the issue was a very sensitive point publicly. Since December the authorities had been expecting a three-month period of good behaviour before remission was restored, but this was not immutable. This period was to ensure that the prisoner was really coming off the protest properly: 'We had to be careful that prisoners did not abuse the system by coming off and then going back on the protest', explained the officials.

It was finally agreed that the ICRC would go into the prison as planned at 9.00 a.m. the next morning. They would then ask to see the hunger-strikers. They could ask to see anyone they wished in the prison, but it was quite impossible for the Government to allow Gerry Adams into the Maze, and it would be extremely difficult for Morrison to be allowed in. Woodfield explained the extreme anxiety about Doherty in the Irish Republic and the reasons why his death would destabilize the Government there. He said that there would be continuing pressure from the Irish Government for HMG to send an official in, and it was agreed that 'we would take the line that "the ICRC thought that it would not be helpful for their continuing visit to the Maze to be interrupted by an NIO official as this would only confuse the prisoners".'[35]

So, on Friday 17 July, the ICRC again saw the hunger-strikers and McFarlane, as well as individually making tours of different blocks and the working parts of the prison; in the course of this they again spoke to a number of prisoners.[36] At noon Dr Schmidt telephoned Woodfield to say that that the prisoners still wanted direct contact with the NIO because they were worried that when discussion centred on the finer details there was a risk of misunderstanding through 'honest brokers'. The prisoners wanted an agreed and witnessed written document. Schmidt suggested that the ICRC could publish this, but he was thinking in terms of publishing it as an agreement between the NIO and the prisoners rather than recommendations to the Government by the ICRC. On the five demands, the prisoners had said that there seemed to be nothing very new in what the ICRC was telling them. Schmidt felt, however, that they were more interested in what was going on than they were letting on. The prisoners wanted Danny Morrison to be allowed to visit McFarlane and another man, Flynn, to visit Micky Devine. The ICRC wanted a meeting with the Secretary of State as soon as this was convenient. The ICRC also asked to see the families of the hunger-strikers. Woodfield said that the idea of a published agreement was unacceptable, to which Dr Schmidt replied that they had not exhausted the possible modalities. Woodfield concluded the conversation promising he would telephone Schmidt back on the question of the visits.[37]

Woodfield telephoned Atkins at 12.30 p.m. and briefed him on the call from Schmidt. Atkins agreed that a visit by Morrison ('who however we understand is unwell') and Flynn should be allowed. It was agreed that the ICRC would see Atkins at Hillsborough Castle at 4.45 p.m. (officials would arrive at 4.30 for a pre-briefing).[38] At 12.45 p.m., the PUS telephoned Dr Schmidt. He agreed to the visits and said that the prison chaplain would put Schmidt in touch with the families. The arrangements for the meeting at Hillsborough were also agreed.[39] After this, arrangements were made to brief Michael Alexander at Downing Street. Dr Schmidt telephoned the PUS at 1.55 p.m. Woodfield asked whether it was still his view that it would not be helpful if an official went into the prison to clarify the Secretary of State's statement of 8 July. Schmidt asked whether the prisoners were still making this request. Woodfield replied that there was still an outstanding approach from the prison chaplain, and pressure from the Republic was continuing. Schmidt agreed that such a visit would be acceptable given that it was unconnected with the talks that the ICRC was having with the prisoners about 'possible negotiation'. Woodfield said again that 'we had made it clear that a visit by an official could only be for clarification not for negotiation; that clarification being the clarification of the statement of 8 July on the lines that the Committee had been told the previous evening.' He asked whether there was any additional news from the Committee's further talk with the hunger-strikers; Dr Schmidt said that there was not.[40] There followed a call from Carl Jackson of the NIO at 3.45 p.m., to say that the prisoners had now asked if Gerry Adams could go and see McFarlane as Morrison was unavailable. The message passed back was that this was impossible and that Adams, as the Committee would understand, was 'only a "totem figure".'[41]

At 5.00 p.m., Atkins met with the ICRC at Hillsborough Castle, the Secretary of State's official residence. Dr Schmidt began by explaining that, in discussion with the hunger-strikers, during the course of which McFarlane had been present and had done most of the talking, he and his colleagues had explored possible ways in which a more satisfactory dialogue between the Government and the protestors could be established. The ICRC had drawn on the information given to them in the previous evening's discussion with officials. They had suggested that it might be valuable to seek to produce a document to which both sides would be party, or to produce an ICRC document recording the basis of an agreement. They remained ready in the meantime to talk to the prisoners' families, although they did not think at the moment that the time had arrived for them to do so. The hunger-strikers had shown some interest in these ideas, but had not reacted favourably to them. They had indicated that in their view the intervention of the ICRC was no more likely to produce a satisfactory outcome to the dispute than that of the ICJP. Moreover, they did not think that the ICRC offered anything that the ICJP had not offered. The hunger-strikers did not believe that the clarification of the Secretary of State's statement would advance discussion, or provide a basis for a solution. The preparation of documents of any kind would have to be preceded by discussion that would be open to misunderstanding, whether or not the ICRC was involved as a go-between. They had also expressed their apprehension that, even if an agreement were arrived at, the Government would renege on it. They noted, however, that Dr Schmidt and his colleagues would be ready to pay a series of visits, during which an agreement could be monitored.

In these circumstances, the ICRC was not clear what steps could be taken to move to an understanding in the light of which the hunger strike could be ended. The ICRC noted that the Government was ready to send in an official to clarify statements to the hunger-strikers, but not to do so in the presence of McFarlane or the PIRA Command, and not to enter into negotiations whether under ICRC auspices or not. They understood too that the hunger-strikers were unwilling to seek clarification without McFarlane being present. The ICRC was used to meeting representatives of prisoners, although not those claiming a position as political leaders within the prison establishment. They wondered whether the Government would be ready to meet with a group of prisoners of which McFarlane was a member but not the spokesman. The ICRC did not find it easy to offer a judgement on the substance of the five demands because of their highly political nature, but they did not think that the entitlement to wear one's own clothes was vital. They were, however, satisfied that more important than the content of the demands was the need to establish a dialogue between the Government and the protestors. In the light of this, they wished to impress two points upon the Secretary of State, which they felt were necessary if progress were to be made:

(i)   there was a large element of mistrust on the part of the hunger strikers which would have to be dispelled;

(ii) a means of establishing more efficient dialogue should be sought. They recognised the wider context of the dispute and the political problems facing the Government, but these did not detract from the desirability of establishing better communication in some way.

It was pointed out to the ICRC representatives that McFarlane wanted to be present to establish formally the position he claimed in the prison – as OC – and to seek to ensure that any talks were substantive negotiations, not simply a process of clarification. The Government remained adamant in its refusal to enter into negotiations over the dispute. If the protestors wished to use the process of settlement as a means of obtaining more than the Government was now ready to offer then a dialogue would be bound to fail. Devices such as the ICRC had proposed, like keeping both parties in separate rooms and using Red Cross representatives as go-betweens, amounted to negotiation. The Government felt that it had shown its good faith in the past, and the experience of those who had come off the protest was evidence of it. They were not prepared to give formal recognition to the PIRA Command structure in the prison. The production of an agreed document could give such recognition, and it could be seen to indicate that the discussions with the Government had effectively been negotiations.

After a break in the discussion, Atkins told the ICRC representatives that he had taken full note of their view that it was important to establish better communication. It remained his view that the Government could not meet the hunger-strikers in the presence of McFarlane and that there could be no negotiation. But any prisoner, acting in his own right and not as a representative, could make an application to the Governor for clarification of aspects of the regime, and it was open to the Governor to be accompanied by an official of the NIO. If McFarlane were to make such an application for clarification of the Government's position, he might expect that it would be granted speedily and that a senior official would be present. Such an interview should not take place in the presence of the ICRC; it was important that it was seen to be as orthodox a move as possible. Nor could the hunger-strikers be present. Atkins still believed, however, that McFarlane would wish any such application to lead to negotiation. The Governor could not enter into discussion of the prisoners' statement, but would have to confine himself to matters for which he had a responsibility; this would not prevent McFarlane from referring to the prisoners' statement. Atkins agreed that a message to this effect might be passed to McFarlane by the ICRC representatives on the visit they were proposing to pay to the prison later that evening.[42]

At 12.30 a.m., Schmidt and his colleagues visited Woodfield at his flat in Stormont House to inform him that the proposal that McFarlane might apply for clarification from the Governor (at which a NIO official would be present) as an individual prisoner was unacceptable to the prisoners. They thought that this demonstrated HMG's unwillingness to move to find a constructive dialogue of quality with them. The prisoners felt that the ICRC was being used by the authorities to repeat the exercise already carried out previously (by the ICJP), and this was wasting valuable time, which could instead be devoted to constructive dialogue. The prisoners saw no point in entering into any sort of 'negotiation' with the ICRC. The ICRC had, therefore, concluded that it would not be helpful for them to pursue this aspect further at this stage. They would instead continue their routine work of assessing 'detention' conditions. They had only become involved in the hunger strike because the five demands appeared to be closely linked to prison conditions, and they could not merely ignore it. They would aim now to produce a report in the usual way. In the event, of course, that there was a new initiative, or they perceived a further way to help in the hunger strike later, this would be possible. There was then some discussion of what might be said about the proposal that McFarlane might individually have applied for clarification. The ICRC made clear that they had only conveyed an offer to clarify in this way; not to negotiate. It was concluded that it might not be in HMG's interest to reveal the McFarlane proposal. Woodfield then asked whether the ICRC would like to say 'off the record' whether they felt HMG's attitude was unreasonable. Dr Schmidt said that it would be 'presumptuous' of them to answer that. Woodfield then explained why it was in the IRA's interests for Doherty to die.[43]

By this point, Dublin had delivered a formal note to the British, on 18 July, renewing their request that HMG send in a senior official to the Maze and 'in a positive way to give whatever clarification it could to its position'.[44] The British, however, were cool in their response. Carrington instructed Figg to use the eight points below as the basis for his reply to the Irish aide-memoire:

a) We agree that only paramilitaries would benefit from any bad effect in Anglo-Irish relations of any further deaths of hunger strikers.

b) Those who wish to avoid such a situation should advise the hunger strikers to end their action.

c) The latest statement from the protesters calls for negotiations. That is not possible.

d) We have always understood the Irish Government to be opposed to all forms of negotiation with subversive organisations.

e) The British Government have made clear their readiness to clarify to the hunger strikers the Government's position as set out in the statement of 8 July.

f) That statement reflects what was said to the ICJP about the areas in which movement is and is not possible.

g) The ICJP statement did not make clear the limits to Government action and as such is not a basis on which a Government official could speak to the hunger strikers.

h) There is no solution already arrived at.[45]

Having read the British note, Dooge commented to Figg that the Irish Government hoped that HMG did not see Dublin's note as being an appeal to negotiate with the hunger-strikers. He had particularly stressed this to the Lord Privy Seal in their recent telephone conversation. The second point Dooge wished to make was that, for the past twenty-four hours, HMG had hesitated to send in anyone to talk to the prisoners, apparently on the grounds that the hunger-strikers 'wished to have someone else present' (Bik McFarlane), which was unacceptable to the British. This appeared to be a sticking point. Figg stated that, so far as he knew, the hunger-strikers were asking that McFarlane should be present, 'and that if we agreed to this we should in fact be agreeing to negotiation.' McFarlane would be 'acting as a chairman of a negotiating committee.' Dooge agreed that McFarlane's presence might not be helpful, but the hunger-strikers wanted someone with them, which seemed reasonable, and if there were no way forward unless this person was McFarlane, 'we should agree.' His presence need not mean negotiation; the British 'very strict' interpretation of words was quite unjustified in the urgency of the moment. If HMG could not do better than this and get over its 'imagined difficulty' of talking with McFarlane present, relations between the Governments would suffer, warned Dooge. In the circumstances, Figg did not wish to deploy the argument about McFarlane being part of the command structure, 'which I am sure Professor Dooge would not have understood and would have made our position look to him even more difficult. I said that I did not consider it would be useful to continue our conversation and that it would be best if I passed his remarks on immediately. We parted perfectly amicably.'[46]

There was clearly growing momentum for yet another visit by an official to the hunger-strikers. Adding to it was a statement from the Provisionals, in the afternoon of 18 July, on the need for an official to meet the prisoners. This, and the ICRC's participation, led to Philip Woodfield travelling, in the evening, to Downing Street to brief Mrs Thatcher on the events of the last thirty-six hours. He told the Prime Minister that Atkins felt that the Government had to respond to the PIRA's statement, either with a statement of its own 'along the usual lines' refusing any negotiation, or by sending in an official to clarify the position to the hunger-strikers yet again. The official would set out to the hunger-strikers what would be on offer if they abandoned their protest. He would do so along the lines discussed with the Prime Minister the previous week and communicated through 'the channel'; he would say that the prisoners would be allowed to wear their own clothes, as was already the case in Armagh prison, provided those clothes were approved by the prison authorities; he would set out the position on association; on parcels and letters; on remission; and on work. On this last point he would make it clear that the prisoners would, as before, have to do the basic work necessary to keep the prison going: there were tasks that the prison staff could under no circumstances be expected to do. But insofar as work in the prison workshops was concerned, it would be implicit that the prisoners would be expected to do this; if they refused to do it they would be punished by loss of remission, or some similar penalty, rather than more severely.

Woodfield emphasized that the official would not be empowered to negotiate; he would simply be making a statement about what was on offer to the hunger-strikers if they abandoned the hunger strike. The statement would be spelling out what had been implicit in the Government's public statements and explicit in earlier communications on the channel: 'We would aim to avoid argument on the conditions under which the meeting had been arranged. We would simply say that we had done it on our own terms.' There could be no guarantee that acting in this way would end the hunger strike; however, explained Woodfield, there had been one or two indications that the hunger-strikers were hoping to come off their strike. Woodfield added that, from a purely parochial, Northern Ireland, point of view, there might be a good deal to be said for letting the hunger strike continue. In the Secretary of State's opinion, though, the broader view, taking account of the situation in the Republic and the United States, 'argued for a further effort to end the hunger strike.'

Mrs Thatcher's response was that she was less concerned about the situation in Dublin than about that in North America: 'If we were to act along the lines envisaged by the Northern Ireland Secretary, there would be obvious arguments, notably the possibility of Doherty's early death, for acting soon.' She agreed that a further effort should be made to explain the situation to the hunger-strikers. The official who went in should stick closely to the statement that had been drafted the previous week and communicated down the channel to McFarlane. He should go into the prison early the next morning. Meanwhile, the channel should be activated that night and informed of the Government's intentions. The Ambassador in Dublin needed to be put in the picture, while the Home Secretary should be briefed in the morning.

Following further discussions, however, it was drawn to the Prime Minister's attention that any approach of the kind outlined above would inevitably become public, whether or not it succeeded. Mrs Thatcher reviewed the proposal on the telephone with Atkins, who confirmed that it would not be possible to keep the initiative quiet once it had been communicated to the hunger-strikers. The Prime Minister said that she had thought that the approach could be made on the same basis as before, and that therefore nothing would be lost by trying, however it now seemed that this was not the case. She was more concerned to 'do the right thing' by Northern Ireland than to try to satisfy international critics. Atkins observed that, considering matters only with regard to Northern Ireland, he would rather do nothing. Mrs Thatcher asked whether it would not be sufficient for the official to repeat the Secretary of State's previous statement. Atkins said that he 'did not think this would do the trick.' The Prime Minister then asked whether, if a detailed offer along the lines set out above were made and failed, he could hold the prison officers. Atkins thought that this would be just about possible. Mrs Thatcher pointed out that once an offer of the freedom to wear their own clothes had been made public, it would have to be implemented whether or not the hunger-strikers called off their strike. Atkins agreed. After further discussion, the Prime Minister decided that the dangers in taking an initiative would be so great in Northern Ireland that she was not prepared to risk them. The official who went into the prison could repeat the Government's public position, but could go no further. Atkins agreed, but added that he would have to make sure that no steps had been taken to activate the channel. Despite this, Downing Street was informed on the morning of 19 July that, contrary to the decision just taken, the channel had in fact been activated.[47]

A flurry of activity ensued, through it, on 19–20 July. Atkins had made yet another statement, on the first day, insisting that there would be no talks with the prisoners, but the backchannel witnessed further attempts, by the British, to convince the Provos of their sincerity that the Government would be flexible. At 3.55 p.m., Duddy received a call from the British in which the Government stated that it 'deeply regrets the tragic loss of life brought about by the decision of some prisoners to embark upon a Hunger Strike.' In the conviction that the prisoners would see no further point in their action, the Government reiterated 'its firm intention' to improve the prison regime. The details of this were set out as follows:

When the Hunger Strike in support of the prison protest is brought to an end, the Government will:

Extend to all male prisoners in Northern Ireland the clothing regime at present available to female prisoners in Armagh prison.

It will be important that the prisoners and the prison authorities know precisely how the regime will be applied in the different circumstances of male prisons.

It will take time to formulate new prison rules to cover for example the following points

1. The need for clothes not to resemble those of prison officers.
2. The need to prevent prisoners adopting a form of uniform clothing.
3. The exclusion? Of forms of clothing which are offensive? And unsuitable.
4. The scale of clothing including underwear, socks and shoes.
5. Laundry arrangements.

Meanwhile, any prisoner who wishes to send for other clothing which is of the kind presently issued as prison wear, (that is to say a shirt, a pullover and slacks) may do so, and will be allowed to wear it.

Prisoners who choose to go on wearing prison-issue civilian clothing may do so immediately.

All Northern Ireland prisoners would receive the allowance of letters, parcels and visits at present given to conforming prisoners, who could send and receive one letter weekly, and receive one weekly visit and one weekly parcel containing fruit and toiletries. Remission would be restored as indicated in Atkins' 30 June statement, subject to a satisfactory period of good behaviour. The aim of the authorities would be that prisoners should do the kinds of work for which they were suited: 'But this may not always be possible.' Control and supervision would remain within the ambit of the prison authorities. Little advance, however, was possible on association. If there were no protests, the only reason for segregation of some prisoners from others would be for the judgement of the prison authorities, 'not the prisoners.' It was emphasized that this statement 'is not a negotiating position. It is further evidence of the Government's desire to maintain and improve an enlightened and humane prison regime. The Government hopes the Hunger Strikers and the other protestors will cease their protests.'[48] At 8.45 p.m., however, Duddy recorded in his diary: 'Crisis! Danny Morrison took suddenly ill ...'. No one else was acceptable to the British to go into the Maze. He lamented:

The position has gone dead. Neither side can or will move. Everyone is tired. Time is running out. It is 1:33am July 20th 1981. I am almost defeated. I can't move forward. The British are asking for their plan to be accepted ... I am so tired, I can't save Kieran Doherty's life. It is so tragic. It is regrettable that a solution does not seem to be possible. 2.25am July (20th).[49]

NOTES

1   TNA FCO 87/1262 Northern Ireland Office Protests and Second Hunger Strike – Weekly Bulletin No. 20. 0900 hours Thursday 9 July – 0900 hours Thursday 16 July.
2   TNA FCO 87/1262 Northern Ireland Office Protests and Second Hunger Strike – Weekly Bulletin No. 20. 0900 hours Thursday 9 July – 0900 hours Thursday 16 July.
3   TNA FCO 87/1262 Brussels to Immediate FCO Telegram no 2657 of 13 July 1981.
4   NAI D/T 2011/127/1056 Letter handed over to President Reagan, 14 July 1981.
5   NAI D/T 2011/127/1056 Memo to Taoiseach.
6   NAI D/T 2011/127/1056 Note, 13 July 1981.
7   TNA CJ4/3632 Note for the Record, 14 July 1981.
8   TNA CJ4/3632 NC Abbott to Moriarty, 19 May 1981.

9   TNA CJ4/3632 Note for the Record, 15 July 1981.

10   TNA CJ4/3632 Dublin to FCO Telegram Number 241 of 15 July 1981.

11   PRONI CENT 1/10/52 Note of Conversation with Sir Leonard Figg, 15 July 1981.

12   NAI D/T 2011/127/1056 Andrew O'Rourke Memo, 15 July 1981.

13   TNA FCO 87/1262 Dublin to FCO Telegram number 244 of 15 July 1981.

14   TNA FCO 87/1262 FCO to Dublin Telegram number 112 of 15 July 1981.

15   TNA FCO 87/1262 Northern Ireland Office Protests and Second Hunger Strike – Weekly Bulletin No. 20. 0900 hours Thursday 9 July – 0900 hours Thursday 16 July.

16   TNA FCO 87/1262 Northern Ireland Office Protests and Second Hunger Strike – Weekly Bulletin No. 20. 0900 hours Thursday 9 July – 0900 hours Thursday 16 July.

17   TNA FCO 87/1262 Washington to FCO Telegram number 2148 of 15 July 1981.

18   TNA FCO 87/1262 Washington to FCO Telegram number 2162 of 15 July 1981.

19   NAI D/T 2011/127/1056 Memo to Taoiseach.

20   TNA FCO 87/1262 Northern Ireland Office Protests and Second Hunger Strike – Weekly Bulletin No. 20. 0900 hours Thursday 9 July – 0900 hours Thursday 16 July.

21   PRONI CENT 1/10/52 Mr Blelloch's visit debrief.

22   PRONI CENT 1/10/52 ICRC and the Maze, 16 July 1981.

23   PRONI CENT 1/10/52 Mr Blelloch's visit debrief.

24   PRONI CENT 1/10/52 ICRC and the Maze, 16 July 1981.

25   TNA FCO 87/1262 Dublin to FCO Telegram number 245 of 16 July 1981.

26   PRONI CENT 1/10/52 Note for the Record, 16 July 1981.

27   NAI D/T 2011/127/1057 H-Blocks: Hunger Strikes, 16 July, 1981.

28   TNA FCO 87/1262 Dublin to FCO Telegram number 245 of 16 July 1981.

29   TNA FCO 87/1262 Dublin to FCO Telegram number 247 of 16 July 1981.

30   PRONI CJ4/3632 Note for the Record, 16 July 1981.

31   NAI D/T 2011/127/1057 Note of telephone conversation between the Minister-Designate for Foreign Affairs and the Lord Privy Seal, 16 July 1981.

32   PRONI CJ4/3632 Protests and Second Hunger Strike – Weekly Bulletin No. 21 0900 hours Thursday 16 July – 0900 hours Thursday 23 July.

33   PRONI CENT 1/10/52 Record of discussions with the ICRC on the evening of Thursday 16 July 1981 in PUS' Office Belfast.

34   PRONI CENT 1/10/52 Telephone Conversation between the Secretary of State and PUS.

35   PRONI CENT 1/10/52 Meeting in Dr Schmidt's room, Stormont Hotel at 11.40 p.m.

36   PRONI CJ4/3632 Protests and Second Hunger Strike – Weekly Bulletin No. 21 0900 hours Thursday 16 July – 0900 hours Thursday 23 July.

37   PRONI CENT 1/10/52 Telephone Call from Dr Schmidt at 12 noon on 17 July.

38   PRONI CENT 1/10/52 Telephone Call to the Secretary of State at 12.30 p.m.

39   PRONI CENT 1/10/52 Telephone Call to Dr Schmidt.

40   PRONI CENT 1/10/52 Telephone Call from Dr Schmidt at 1.55 p.m.

41   PRONI CENT 1/10/52 Telephone Call from Carl Jackson at 3.45 p.m.

42   PRONI CENT 1/10/52 Meeting with the International Committee of the Red Cross, Hillsborough Castle, 5.00 p.m. Friday, 17 July 1981.

43   PRONI CENT 1/10/52 Note of a meeting held in PUS' Flat Stormont House at 12.30 a.m. on the night of 17/18 July.

44   TNA FCO 87/1262 Dublin to FCO Telegram number 248 of 19 July 1981.

45   TNA FCO 87/1262 FCO to Dublin Telegram number 115 of 19 July 1981.

46   TNA FCO 87/1262 Dublin to FCO Telegram number 248 of 19 July 1981.

47   TNA PREM 19/506 Whitmore to Fall, 18 July 1981.

48   UCG Pol35/166 Duddy Archive The Red Book Manuscript 3.55 p.m. 19 July 1981.

49   UCG Pol35/166 Duddy Archive The Red Book Manuscript 8.45 p.m. 20 July 1981.

Chapter 11

A War of Attrition

In Dublin, thoughts turned to how the Irish Government might deflect accusations of not doing enough to resolve the crisis. The latest idea doing the rounds was to release a chronology of the Government's efforts in the diplomatic field, but this could prove to be a double-edged sword: Liam Hourican, FitzGerald's press secretary, warned the Taoiseach that, on reflection:

> I am concerned about the decisions taken this morning regarding our possible reactions in the event that Mr Doherty dies before a British official has gone into the prison. I feel that the publication of a detailed chronology of our efforts to end the strike, or even the extensive use of such a chronology for background briefing could be counterproductive.

If used on its own (without overt diplomatic action, or without a strong public statement from the Taoiseach or the Foreign Minister), 'it might serve merely to illustrate the extent of our failure to influence the British Government.' The more activity 'we point to over the past fortnight, the more remarkable will seem our inability to change the British approach.' If then the chronology was revealed without accompanying action or political comment, 'we may find ourselves in a weak position. We will seem to have expended massive effort without effect.' Moreover, by 'opening the books', while eschewing further action (even for the moment) 'we will be seen to be closing the incident and declaring ourselves to be losers on a grand scale.' Hourican suggested, therefore, that any disclosure of the Government's actions over the past fortnight should be accompanied by a 'strong, unapologetic assertion of the rightness of our point of view, and the error of the British position.' Precisely because the Government's words had gone unheeded they should now become public and insistent. To do less would be to appear to accept defeat, 'and this I suggest we cannot afford.'

Hourican appreciated that there were compelling reasons for the postponement of diplomatic action. Pending such action, however, the line needed to be held by means of a strong statement criticizing Britain's handling of the whole affair, not just from the time of the Government's first public involvement, but from the beginning of the ICJP initiative. As to the most recent British excuses 'for not going in, they should, I feel be condemned as unacceptable.' By listening – through the Governor – to McFarlane's conditions for a meeting, and then refusing those conditions, the British Government was in effect negotiating with the prisoners. It was, at least, responding to conditions imposed by the prisoners. It was quite possible that McFarlane was misrepresenting the views of the hunger-strikers, but apart from that 'the British Government again shows bad faith towards us by treating McFarlane's conditions as more compelling than our demands.' There was nothing to prevent the British now ignoring any difficulties thrown up by the prisoners or their spokesmen, and going into the prison to explain what was on offer in the event of the hunger strike ending. By acceding to McFarlane's pressure they were in effect giving a stronger role to Sinn Féin than to the Irish Government.[1]

This kind of talk unnerved Dermot Nally, who warned FitzGerald that there 'is a real danger of getting too close to the IRA on all this. Our demands are becoming indistinguishable from theirs – in the public press. There are real and urgent dangers for us in this identification. What do we do if Portlaoise erupts?' he asked. Furthermore, Nally urged caution on the grounds that: 'Whatever we may think about them, the British are nearer the ground in dealing with the strike. They have their faults and undeniably made mistakes. But we should not compound them by trying to say what exactly they should or should not do. Our advice must always be based on second hand information and can not be tactical – only strategic.' Though it might seem irrelevant at this point, 'there are larger issues, and any mistakes of emphasis made by us in relation to the hunger strike can endanger relations – just as much as mistakes made by them – to the ultimate loss of both our countries.'[2]

As this debate raged in Dublin, Northern Ireland Office officials visited the Maze Prison at 2.00 a.m. in order to clarify, once more, previous Government statements to the hunger-strikers. Father McEldowney, a priest from Lynch's parish of Dungiven, phoned the Duty Officer on Monday evening, 20 July, and Blatherwick, of the NIO Political Affairs Bureau, rang him back. He said that he had earlier that day seen Lynch, one of the hunger-strikers, whose parish priest he was. Lynch had shown him a letter from the Prison Governor received the day before (enclosing the Secretary of State's statement of 19 July), and asked that an NIO official be sent into the prison to clarify to him the Government's position. He understood from Doherty's relatives that Doherty had a similar wish. Blatherwick questioned Father McEldowney specifically on whether Lynch wanted McFarlane to be present. He replied that Lynch had not mentioned McFarlane, but had said that the official's visit should take place on the same basis as when officials had spoken to hunger-strikers in the past. Blatherwick reported this to Wyatt, the NIO Under-Secretary.[3]

The Duty Governor at the Maze was then asked to speak to Lynch and Doherty as well as their families. All denied making any request, but the two hunger-strikers said that they were content for an official to see the group of strikers. Doherty also specified that McFarlane must be present.[4] In the light of the priest's request and of the fact that the relatives (Doherty's father and mother and Lynch's brothers) were at the prison, it was decided that Blelloch and Blackwell, the Home Office Prisons Specialist, would make a visit. The NIO officials started operating at the prison at about 2.00 a.m. They offered to meet the relatives who agreed to meet them together. The relatives themselves asked for clarification of one or two points. Doherty's father raised the problem of trust, which Blelloch tackled head-on as the official who had explained the Government's statement to the hunger-strikers at the end of the last hunger strike. The relatives then raised the matter of McFarlane, and Blelloch said that this was a problem. The Prison Officer present said that all five hunger-strikers in the prison hospital (except Lynch) were insisting on McFarlane being present. Blelloch explained the difficulty of this to the relatives. He then went to speak to each of the five hunger-strikers individually.[5] It was explained that they were present to help and to ensure that the prisoners had a true picture of prison policy; the prisoners could be seen singly or as a group, and could have relatives or local priest present if they wished.[6] Each of the five made clear that they did not wish for clarification unless McFarlane was present. (Blelloch noticed that one of Lynch's brothers had spoken to him in the meantime, 'presumably to ensure that he also asked for McFarlane' – who was not his O/C.) Blelloch told the hunger-strikers and the relatives that he regretted the hunger-strikers' attitude and was disappointed with this response, and was ready to return to the prison at any time if asked to do so to clarify the Government's statement.[7]

Father McEldowney phoned again on the morning of 21 July; he asked Blatherwick that 'we should reconsider our insistence that McFarlane could not be present; if we did, he and the other priests concerned would put every pressure they could on the families of strikers to end the strike.' Blatherwick phoned back in the evening to say that 'we could not change our stance, and explained why':

(a) we could not deal with a paramilitary structure in the prisons, for practical as well as moral reasons;
(b) McFarlane had no standing in our eyes and was an unhelpful influence on the hunger strikers;
(c) McFarlane had made it clear that he was interested only in round the table negotiations on the 5 demands.

Father McEldowney accepted this. He asked about a wireless report that some new initiative was under way as the result of a call by Nationalist councillors, from Dungannon, on Michael Alison. Blatherwick explained that the councillors wanted to pursue the possibility that the hunger-strikers might receive an official in the presence of relatives and priests. This would be acceptable to the authorities, but had in fact already been turned down in the past by the prisoners. McEldowney said that he would go away and think again.[8]

Following this burst of activity there was a rather unusual occurrence, on 22 July, when Lord Elton, Parliamentary Under-Secretary of State at the NIO, visited the Maze with the Duke of Norfolk – the senior Roman Catholic peer of the United Kingdom (the Norfolks had remained loyal to the Papacy since the Reformation) who had represented the Queen at the installation of Pope John Paul II. In the prison hospital Elton avoided contact with the hunger-strikers and their families in view of the risk of misleading publicity resulting. The Duke, however, talked to Patsy Quinn and to relatives of Kieran Doherty. He afterwards told Elton that he had identified himself as unimpeachably Roman Catholic and that this had been accepted in each case. It also seemed to be accepted by all concerned that the hunger strike had been condemned as sinful, and he pointed out that it could achieve nothing. It became clear, however, that there was a 'fixed dedication' to achieving the death of the hunger-strikers in question. Doherty's mother in particular made it clear that if her son came off the strike it would be a personal defeat for him. In spite of obvious emotional distress, she was committed to supporting him to the end. His girlfriend on the other hand appeared to be much less enthusiastic, and said little. Elton spoke to the doctor on duty. He 'clearly had lively' suspicions that members of the family were bringing in some sort of sustenance to Doherty, who had been at death's door over the weekend and had sat up in bed reciting poetry after it.[9]

The parents of Kieran Doherty, in the interim, requested the Taoiseach and the Tánaiste to visit their son. FitzGerald dismissed this in a statement, pointing out that 'such a visit would serve no useful purpose'. The statement continued:

> ... following prolonged representations the Northern Ireland Office sent officials into the prison to offer clarifications to the hunger strikers of the conditions which would apply in the event of the strike ending. I greatly regret that the offer was not accepted and hope that the resultant deadlock can still be resolved.[10]

Bernadette McAliskey subsequently telephoned Liam Hourican to say that press reports regarding the Government's reaction to the visit by officials to the Maze suggested that the Irish Government was now 'going to side with the British Government when Kieran Doherty is about to die'. Hourican protested that this was a quite unreasonable construction to put on what had been said: there had merely been an expression of limited satisfaction at the belated acceptance by the NIO of *one* request, which had been made from Dublin. There was no general approval of the British Government's handling of the affair. But, Hourican pointed out, the Taoiseach had regretted the failure of the recent morning visit, which seemed to be attributable to unreasonable preconditions demanded by the prisoners. McAliskey asked how the Government knew what had happened. Hourican replied that this was the account it had received, and that it had not been seriously contradicted in any quarter. This did not impress McAliskey, who thought that it must have been difficult for the Government to know what went on when it would not talk 'to the people who have the information'. Hourican commented that if she wished to convey any information on to him informally, he would undertake to pass it on.[11]

The hunger-strikers then issued a statement branding the officials' visit as 'not a serious attempt to end the hunger strike'. 'It was a propaganda stunt to try to shift the onus from the British Government to us.' They protested that only meaningful talks – not one side dictating to the other – based on a principled and practical foundation as outlined in their July 4 statement cold breach the impasse. They made it clear that 'our protest and our actions represent not just ourselves but the 450 men and women who have been on protest for the five demands some for nearly five years.' The hunger strike was not the only issue in need of resolution; the five-year-old protest had to end simultaneously. This could only be done by the British Government agreeing to tackle the prison dispute in a common-sense manner:

> Brendan McFarlane is the representative of all the protesting prisoners. He, in conjunction with wing and block representatives, speaks for us in everyday dealings with the prison administration.
>
> This is a fact of political life inside the prison and has been for years. Before now on numerous occasions the prison administration have recognised his status by involving him in meetings. [12]

By this point according to O'Rawe, a comm had come to the prisoners from Gerry Adams on 22 July, stating that talks with the Mountain Climber had broken down once more and that nothing new was on offer. Adams outlined the view that the prisoners were facing two options: to end the hunger strike immediately without accepting the Mountain Climber's proposals, or to stay on hunger strike. He then repeated the 'opinion that the Mountain Climber's proposals did not provide the basis for an honourable settlement.' The reason given was that 'there was too much distance between the Mountain Climber's offer and what was needed to validate the deaths of the six hunger strikers.' Adams also contended that, if the prisoners opted to continue with the hunger-strike strategy, there was no telling how many men would die. There was no guarantee that the British would eventually cave in. It was made clear that the Republican Movement would respect any decision the prisoners made, adding that no damage would be done if they decided to end the strike. Adams believed that the Mountain Climber was being honest with him, and described the last communication from the British as a 'very frank statement' that outlined their policy position. The Mountain Climber indicated that he was sad that it had come to this, and had informed Adams that, at some time in the future, circumstances might change and the British Government might be forced to go further, 'but no politician in England could afford to gamble his political future on that assumption'.[13] McFarlane's response to Adams was that this was:

> Quite a revelation I must say. I lay on my bed for a couple of hours, trying to weigh up everything. Almost dashed out of my cell once or twice. I even toyed with the idea that their 'very frank statement' was a master-stroke linked to a super brink tactic. It was then that I wised up and started looking to the future (immediate and distant) and began moving to a positive line.

Firstly, McFarlane wanted to let Adams know that he believed he had done:

> ... a terrific job in handling this situation and if we can take the opposition's 'frank statement' as 100% (which it does appear to be) then in itself it is quite some feat, i.e. extraordinary such an admission from them. Then again I suppose it is something we have all known already (or at least suspected).

He fully agreed with the two options outlined: 'It is either a settlement or it isn't. No room for half measures and meaningless cosmetic exercises.' McFarlane acknowledged that the hunger strike looked 'like a costly venture indeed.' After careful consideration of the overall situation, however, he believed that it would be:

> ... wrong to capitulate. We took a decision and committed ourselves to hunger strike action. Our losses have been heavy – that I realize only too well. Yet I feel the part we have played in forwarding the liberation struggle has been great. Terrific gains have been made and the Brits are losing by the day. The sacrifice called for is the ultimate and men have made it heroically. Many others are, I believe, committed to hunger strike action to achieve a final settlement. I realize the stakes are very high – the Brits also know what capitulation means for them. Hence their entrenched position. Anyway, the way I see it is that we are fighting a war and by choice we have placed ourselves in the front line. I still feel we should maintain this position and fight on in current fashion. It is we who are on top of the situation and we who are the stronger. Therefore we maintain. In the immediate this means that Doe [Kieran Doherty] and

Kevin [Lynch] will forfeit their lives and as you say the others on hunger strike could well follow. I feel that we must continue until we achieve a settlement, or until circumstances force us into a position where no choice would be left but to capitulate. I don't believe the latter would arise. I do feel we can break the Brits.

Adams had asked McFarlane to consider what the price was to be. McFarlane thought that it was a matter of 'setting our sights firmly on target and shooting straight ahead. It's rough, brutal, ruthless and a lot of other things as well, but we are fighting a war and we must accept that front-line troops are more susceptible to casualties than anyone.' They would just have to steel themselves to bear the worst. McFarlane was now going to comm all O/Cs and give them a general outline of things. He would impress upon anyone who forwarded his name for hunger strike that he would only have two months to live. In the meantime, McFarlane was concerned that the INLA prisoners were wavering: one of them was talking of 'pushing his people outside to call a halt to the hunger strike. This is bad crack and could cause problems.' They had one volunteer left as replacement for the hunger strike.[14]

So the impasse continued and time began to run out for the hunger-strikers: by now the conditions of Lynch and Doherty were essentially the same. Yet again the clinical progression had been erratic – particularly in the case of Doherty, who had seemed likely to die during the previous weekend. Both prisoners had been largely stable for the past few days; they were lucid and able to converse freely. Their fluid balances were positive. By 23 July, unconsciousness and death were considered to be at least forty-eight hours away if the present pattern continued. None of the other hunger-strikers were giving any cause for concern. McElwee, although on day forty-six, had not entered the vomiting phase exhibited by most other strikers. Quinn was deteriorating rather faster. McKeown was admitted to the prison hospital on 23 July; the prisoners' weights were at this point:

	Day of strike	Weight on first examination	Weight today	Weight loss during week	Overall weight loss
Kieran Doherty	63	11st 11lb	NA	-	*3st 6lb
Kevin Lynch	62	9st 7lb	NA	2½lb	¥2st 12½lb
Thomas McElwee	46	10st 8lb	7st 0lb	5lb	2st 13lb
Michael Devine	32	9st 8½lb	7st 13lb	4½lb	1st 9½lb

* Last weighed on 14.07.81
¥ Last weighed on 19.07.81

On 24 July a new avenue appeared, from Dublin's perspective, to open up – it centred around the news that Father McEldowney had mentioned to Blatherwick. Liam Hourican informed the Taoiseach that Jimmy Canning and other Nationalist Councillors from Coalisland had telephoned him that morning. He was one of those chiefly involved in a meeting between Alison and Dungannon Councillors. This meeting was also attended by Blackwell, who had gone to the Maze with Blelloch on 21 July. Canning explained to Hourican that it was the British who had proposed the idea of a conference or seminar to involve the hunger-strikers, the relatives, parish priests and NIO officials. He and his colleagues seized on this as a useful suggestion, but pointed out that McFarlane would have to be present as well. This was rejected. Canning was aware of the difficulties created by McFarlane recently setting preconditions, but he now believed that all of these had been discarded. McFarlane had let it be known that he would now settle for a silent observation role at the conference. He would, naturally, prefer to be allowed to ask questions, but he was no longer insisting on negotiations in any form. The only other variation posed by Canning to the NIO formula would be to bring in certain priests who were close to the prisoners (such as Fathers Faul and Murray) in addition to the parish priests who, in some cases, had no knowledge of the situation, but he would not insist on this.

Hourican said that he would convey Canning's views and call him back later in the day. Hourican told the Taoiseach: 'It strikes me that, provided that McFarlane['s] retreat from his ... position, is clear and unambiguous, the British could not reasonably resist his inclusion in the Conference, and should now be pressed to accept him.' Canning was convinced that the conference formula was the only viable one left. The Taoiseach was informed that support for Canning's reading of the situation had come, in the night, from Mary McElwee, a cousin of Father Oliver Crilly and sister of the hunger-striker Tom McElwee. She told Hourican, after a visit to her brother, that the hunger-striker was extremely anxious for a meeting with the British authorities, provided that the hunger-strikers were accompanied by McFarlane. McElwee was not unduly concerned by the format or conditions of such a visit once McFarlane's participation was assured, but he had expressed interest in the conference proposal.[15]

As part of a new diplomatic push, Neligan, as the Head of the Anglo-Irish, Information and Cultural Division of the DFA, telephoned Wyatt the same day and raised with him the reports that McFarlane had said that he was prepared to play a minor and apparently passive role in a meeting between British officials, the hunger-strikers, their relatives and spiritual advisers. Neligan said that 'we found this more conciliatory position interesting and expressed the hope that it would be followed up by the British authorities.' Wyatt answered that HMG approached with caution remarks of this kind, which were floated by IRA spokesmen and often denied later.

One had to be watchful and not take these statements at their face value. Neligan remarked that when the ICJP had been in contact with the hunger-strikers, contacts with McFarlane had also been facilitated, and he had been in an adjoining room or in the corridor outside and easily accessible at various times during those talks. This suggested an approach that might well prove fruitful if followed again, particularly in association with a large meeting of the kind proposed by Jim Canning. Wyatt replied that the positions of the ICJP and that of the Government were very different. It was necessary to steer a line between withholding concessions on a major matter such as recognition of McFarlane's 'supposed status' and allowing progress to be made. The NIO felt that they were steering such a line in letting McFarlane talk for an hour with the hunger-strikers after Blelloch's visit (he did not stipulate which visit, 15 or 21 July); while letting McFarlane talk directly to the hunger-strikers, relatives and priests together was potentially useful, they felt that Canning himself made a point when (as quoted in the *Irish News*) he said that the arrangement would only serve a purpose if the British authorities had something different to say. 'There isn't anything different to say', said Wyatt, and a fundamental gulf on the essential issues of work and association remained.

Neligan repeated 'our fundamental point that McFarlane had now apparently taken up a more conciliatory position.' There were periodic swings in the attitudes expressed by the IRA spokesmen and the prisoners. Hard-line positions were regularly succeeded by suggestions of a softer line: 'We were now in the presence of what looked like a softer line and the opportunity could surely not be neglected to see whether or not it was genuine.' The existence of the slightest opportunity of this sort 'was of great interest to our Government given the gravity of the problem and its effects. We would be very reluctant to believe that this opportunity should be ignored.' Wyatt replied that the main consideration in the British view was the outcome of any approach to the hunger-strikers. In the case of failure, the British would be left just as they were now except for having given a status to McFarlane that had never up to now been accorded to him. Neligan commented that status was surely a question of degree. Diplomatically, people could be and frequently were admitted to talks without their being accorded the full status of participants. Perhaps McFarlane could be admitted to the passive role with which he would now apparently be satisfied, while the NIO would make it publicly clear that his presence did not represent recognition by the fact that he held any particular position. Something could surely be 'fudged' so that the chance of success, which now seemed to exist, would be taken up; Wyatt assured Neligan that the British Government was not going to ignore any opportunity. They would look for evidence that what he had described as a 'swing' in this case was genuine. In conclusion, he had to say, however, that they did not see from all the contacts they had pursued that the hunger-strikers and their supporters saw the strike as ending otherwise than on the basis of the five demands been conceded.[16]

The Irish, however, were not going to let this lie. Professor Dooge met with Figg to push for the Canning proposal. Before all the points that the Irish wished to make had been expressed, though, the Ambassador intervened to say that the British authorities felt that McFarlane knew exactly what was on offer, that there was no need to clarify anything to him and that he wished to be there for quite another purpose, namely to ensure refusal by the hunger-strikers of any proposal short of the five demands. The Minister-Designate stressed in reply that an opportunity nonetheless might exist to make progress, and that it should not be ignored. Continuing with his points, he emphasized the importance of the matter, which should be positive, of a British clarification of a new regime to the prisoners. The Ambassador quoted Canning's remark, in the *Irish News*, that the success of the conference meeting would depend on the authorities presenting something new, and associated this with McFarlane's quoted dismissal of the ICJP document as being a dilution of the five demands and therefore unacceptable. Dooge referred to the swings of opinion that appeared to be reflected in various IRA statements, and put it that the more positive swings, such as that of 4 July, should be promptly utilized in the search for a solution. Figg said 'a little sharply' that it was now 24 July, and wondered whether McFarlane had really said what was attributed to him in the papers. Dooge said that efforts to explore and use the apparent opportunity must be made very rapidly. The Taoiseach had asked him to say that the Government was hard pressed on this issue.[17]

Dooge and Figg met again on the following day, 25 July. The Ambassador's dispatch concerning their meeting had reached London in time to be considered at an NIO-FCO meeting, and Atkins had been consulted in Belfast about the terms of reply. The following points, as recorded by the Irish, were made by Figg in response to the points by Dooge the previous day:

- McFarlane's alleged statement of his willingness to participate passively in a meeting of the 'conference' (hunger strikers, relatives, priests, NIO officials) had not been 'confirmed' as we [Dublin] suggested by the NIO whose only information came from press reports.
- No request had been received from the prisoners for a meeting on the basis proposed (that McFarlane should be present as an observer). In regard to McFarlane the British authorities made the following points:
   a) they did not feel that they had taken account of McFarlane's statements in the way we had suggested they had. They did not accord any status to McFarlane in practice or otherwise. Having him present but apart would not meet their position;
   b) if McFarlane were admitted to a conference meeting on the understanding that he would remain silent, as now purportedly proposed, the British would have to break off the meeting if he

> spoke, thereby giving him the power to cut short the discussions at
> any time, which would be intolerable;
>
> c) if the hunger strikers really wished for clarification then the presence
> of McFarlane would be unnecessary.

Dooge offered some brief comments. On McFarlane's willingness to accept a
role as observer, he enquired whether someone in the prison could not approach
McFarlane directly and seek confirmation of the attitude that had been attributed
to him. Such confirmation might enable everyone to advance, even if only
slightly. On the matter of withholding any status from McFarlane, Dooge recalled
an NIO statement that it was no use having a discussion because the prisoners
were only willing to talk on the basis of the five demands. On that occasion the
NIO accepted McFarlane's word as expressing the prisoners' views. No action
was taken by the NIO because of what McFarlane had said – he was accepted
as representing the prisoners. Any modus operandi that did not go beyond that
degree of recognition should be used to make progress. On McFarlane having
the power to disrupt the proposed wider forum simply by speaking, Dooge
considered that, if McFarlane were present, a limited number of questions from
him should not be judged sufficient to bring about closure of the proceedings.
Argumentative and disputatious questions tending towards negotiation could
be ruled out. Alternatively, the device of having McFarlane available nearby for
contact by either side might be resorted to – this would not delay the proceedings.
On the point that McFarlane's presence would be unnecessary if the prisoners
really wanted clarification, the Minister-Designate put it that the weakness of
the hunger-strikers precluded long discussions on their part, even if only for
purposes of clarification. Dooge hoped that the British Government would not
obstruct the wider type of meeting by insistence on McFarlane's absence. The
Irish Government desired to see a solution if at all possible. If McFarlane could
be present as an observer or available nearby, 'this should be done in view of
our strong desire, the consequences of no solution being found and the physical
state of the hunger strikers.' After Figg said that he would report to London the
next day, Dooge mentioned the names of Fathers Faul and Murray to say that
'while we know the NIO were opposed to their inclusion in the "conference",
our understanding was that this was no longer a factor for the prisoners and
their relatives who were asking only for the attendance of parish priests.' The
Ambassador commented that Father Faul would not be unwelcome and that his
presence would not be a decisive objection if it were the only objection. He then
took his leave.[18]

Meanwhile, the determination of the hunger-strikers appeared solid. Bishop
Daly had planned to go to the Maze and urge the hunger-strikers to give up.

He intended to point to the possibility of a helpful judgement by the Red Cross and suggested that the British should now be pressed to carry out their implied commitments to introduce reforms after the hunger strike. Daly sounded out this idea with the hunger-strikers through the Prison Chaplains, but received a flat rejection. The Lynch family, meanwhile, reported that, in the early hours of Sunday morning, their brother heard footsteps outside his room. He said: 'that might be the officials but they'd better have McFarlane with them'.[19] With this as background, Neligan was informed (on Saturday evening 25 July) by Hourican (who had received the information from Jim Canning) that Father Toner had a piece of paper signed, by McFarlane, as follows:

> If NIO officials were to talk to us we will talk to them (meaningful dialogue) ie if their purpose is to clarify we will listen and post questions. If they rule out negotiations for a settlement then it is blatantly obvious that negotiations will not take place.

> (Signed)   B McFarlane
> Witness   T Toner
> (Text may not be completely accurate).

Neligan conveyed this to Figg at 10.30 p.m. The Ambassador's reaction was that it was 'totally phoney'. Asked to convey the information to London, Figg was reluctant, in view also of the late hour. Neligan argued him out of this line and told him that 'we wished him to stress the importance of the development'. The Ambassador, however, regarded McFarlane's method of communication as 'weasly': McFarlane could communicate through the Governor. Figg would, however, pass on the message and report the Taoiseach's interest. In the course of the conversation the Ambassador expressed considerable resentment at the fact that Canning had told the NIO that he (Figg) had said (possibly in a conversation with Dooge) that McFarlane could be accommodated at talks with the prisoners. He had not said this.[20]

As the Irish awaited the British response, Charles Rushing, Chargé d'Affaires at the United States Embassy, called on the Taoiseach to deliver a copy of a letter from President Reagan to him replying to FitzGerald's letter to the former on 14 July.[21] The President informed FitzGerald that: 'While the US does not intend to intervene directly in the current situation in Northern Ireland, US policies and my own personal feelings … are well known to the British Government.'[22] There was no surprise in Reagan's message, so FitzGerald remarked to Rushing that his Government had had reasons for making the approach to the President, in particular the known influence of the Administration with Mrs Thatcher. Replying to questions from Rushing about the differences between the ICJP and British positions on prison work, which seemed to be the only outstanding issue, the Taoiseach said that he did not himself appreciate that any substantial difference existed. He added that the British position on the McFarlane issue was in fact dishonest given that the British had already negotiated with him and had, indeed, accepted his statement as representing the position of the hunger-strikers on issues on which the hunger-strikers had not themselves been consulted by anyone, even McFarlane. FitzGerald lamented that the British seemed to want a complete victory: 'We are dealing with "impossible people" in London, notably Mrs Thatcher.' The Taoiseach added that there had been a direct British negotiation with the Provisional IRA 'since our efforts began and of which, of course, we were not officially aware.'

FitzGerald was frustrated because this group of hunger-strikers, 'as far as we know,' want to live. They would accept a modified form of the five demands, but they would need to be satisfied that such a form of the demands would be implemented. The Taoiseach felt that there had been an opportunity to destroy the current extensive IRA campaign of propaganda. The opportunity had been lost, complained FitzGerald:

> For us the consequences were at present unknown. It was not a question of us being soft on terrorism; we want to destroy it. Support for the IRA is now higher than since the thirties and the British are in effect fermenting this. Meanwhile, we are being impeded from developing good relations with the British Government.

FitzGerald added that the Garda Síochána in Dublin had only just managed to hold off an 'attack' of Republican demonstrators: 'The British don't seem to care a great deal about the security of our State, given their lack of response to our representations. Despite our difficulties and the limitations on our security forces, we will hold the ground.' The Taoiseach noted that in the period from May 1979 to December 1979 it was very clear that the British were acting energetically with regards to the North under pressure from Washington and President Carter on Mrs Thatcher to do so, but British responsiveness declined when Senator Kennedy's chances of becoming the Democratic Party candidate began to fade. Lord Carrington had told FitzGerald this when the Taoiseach was in Opposition. His own assessment was that the Anglo-American relationship was a critical factor in British thinking, a substitute for Empire.[23]

The problem for the Irish, in trying to persuade the White House to become more involved, was set out by Sean Donlon, who reported from Washington that the US Secretary of State, General Alexander Haig, 'is a great admirer of the British role in Northern Ireland and in various conversations with him I have found him to be neither well informed about or sympathetic to our position.' Donlon remained of the view that the H-Block situation 'is not one on which we can hope to secure a significant US Administration support.' The most influential officials in the White House clearly saw it as simply another prison problem and a purely internal British matter. Even on the broader Anglo-Irish political question, it was not going to be easy to secure significant US support:

> We are up against a particularly close relationship between President Reagan and Mrs Thatcher, a Secretary of State here who, despite his Irish Catholic background, has shown no signs of taking even a minimal interest in Irish affairs and a national security advisor to the President who is possibly even less sympathetic to our interests than the traditional state department bureaucracy.[24]

If the American route was a diplomatic dead end, the Irish soon had an opportunity to put their concerns, once more, forcibly and directly to the British. A high-level meeting of senior British and Irish civil servants met in Sir Robert Armstrong's office on 27 July. Accompanying the Cabinet Secretary, on the British side, were Wade-Gery (Cabinet Office) and Eyers (Foreign and Commonwealth Office). On the Irish side were Nally (Secretary of the Irish Government); Kirwan (Department of the Taoiseach); and Neligan (Department of Foreign Affairs). Opening the conversation, Nally did not propose to talk about the details of the situation, but rather to air its wider aspects. Tremendous damage was being done in the South, and not only in the security field. A few months earlier, no one would have expected that two Maze prisoners would be elected to the Dáil, nor that demonstrations of the scale and violence seen in Dublin on 18 July would occur, but these reflected the advances being made by the IRA, both as regarded recruitment – which would do incalculable damage – and as regarded the propaganda battle, which they were winning in the South, in the United States, and indeed, though less importantly, elsewhere in Europe. The general attitude had been that the hunger-strikers, given their criminal records, should be left to die if that was what they wanted; now the emphasis was on the incidents that had led them to take up arms. Meanwhile, the hunger-strikers' demands were moving away from 'political status' involving differentiation from ordinary prisoners. The Irish recognized that the prison authorities had to retain control in the prisons; however, mistakes made on timing (implicitly by the British) had aggravated the difficulties. Could not the flow of information to the Irish Government be improved? The Taoiseach had been about to make a strong speech, but had cancelled it when he learnt through his own channels that the Duke of Norfolk and Lord Elton were intervening in the Maze. The Irish quite understood that certain matters, such as contacts with the IRA, might need to be kept under wraps, but they were very well aware of those contacts. They were bound to be suspicious if they were given what purported to be a full account of transactions going on when they knew this not to be the case. That suspicion could be removed if they could be given, confidentially, a full account of all that was occurring.

Kirwan added that what was at stake for Ireland went beyond propaganda and electoral considerations; if the IRA succeeded in bringing down the Government, this could bring about a state of instability in Ireland that would have an international impact on the country's standing. Neligan cited the prisoners' statement of 4 July as an example of a missed opportunity. Admittedly, they had since made hard-line statements, and so the caution of the British authorities was understandable, but the Irish wanted to see the UK Government act quickly in response to the softer statements: it was important, in propaganda terms, to demonstrate the intransigence of the IRA. He recognized that the Irish Government might appear to fuss over minutiae, but this was a reflection of their concern to find ways of demonstrating that it was the hunger-strikers who were being unreasonable.

In reply, Sir Robert Armstrong explained that the British Government shared the apprehensions of the Irish about the propaganda effect of the present situation, especially in the United States and Northern Ireland. Ground had been lost among the Catholic community in Northern Ireland, which was becoming more alienated again. Further sectarian violence in the North had been avoided, but there had been trouble on the streets, which was leading to instability. Like the Irish, the British wished to see the situation resolved. As regarded the flow of information, he noted the Irish concern, and would look into the matter, with a view to seeing what, if anything, could be done to improve channels of communication. As for the points made by Neligan, he agreed that the hunger-strikers' position had changed in successive statements. The Government had been trying to show some degree of flexibility, while maintaining control in the prison and refusing political status. Armstrong accepted that they might not have gone as far or as fast as the Irish would have wished, but he did not think that the Irish Government would want them to depart from their stand of principle. An official had gone into the prison; but HMG was apprehensive about being sucked point by point beyond what was acceptable. There had been no developments during the weekend over McFarlane's involvement, but it was difficult to see what more could be done so long as the five demands were maintained.

Nally admitted that the Irish had no solution to offer; they were not urging the granting of political status, but from a delicate source they had an inkling that there might be movement on the part of the prisoners. Neligan said that the British side would be aware of the arguments the Irish Government had put concerning the participation of McFarlane, and the Irish side understood the differences of approach regarding the ICJP proposals. They supported the

British Government's 'negative bottom-lines' – for example they agreed that it was for the prison authorities, not the prisoners, to decide what tasks should be undertaken, but there was still room for improvements in presentation, for example by widening the area of choice of work to be undertaken, though not to the extent envisaged by the ICJP. From their contacts with HM Ambassador, they understood that there was now less of a problem over free association between the prisoners. As for McFarlane, the Irish had the impression that his views had on earlier occasions been accepted by the NIO as representing those of other prisoners. Was there not room now to fudge this point, for example by allowing his presence on the grounds of the physical feebleness of the hunger-strikers? The Irish had noted with satisfaction the NIO officials' approach to the prisoners, and seen its negative outcome. They hoped that the British would not allow themselves to be discouraged by this.

Armstrong, however, commented that anything that gave the impression of direct negotiation with the Provisionals would have severe political consequences. Kirwan acknowledged that it was unsatisfactory for a government to have to explain its policy to convicted prisoners; unfortunately, this was necessary given the prisoners' suspicions of what had happened between the lifting of the previous hunger strike in December 1980 and its renewal in February 1981. Would it now be possible for the British Government to provide further clarification to the prisoners, knowing that this would become public, on the basis of the additional information contained in the British Embassy's note to the Irish on 9 July? Armstrong replied that there was really very little left to give away. Nally accepted that the British Government was on quite strong ground, but the more it produced offers that were then turned down, the stronger its position would be. It was certainly difficult, though, to extract a consistent answer from the four parties engaged on the other side: the prisoners, the hunger-strikers, the IRA and the INLA. Kirwan added that it was clear that Michael Alison had gone further in talking to the ICJP than Atkins had been prepared to go in his 8 July statement. He recognized the difficulty of making offers in the absence of any sign of a solution, but it was important to bear in mind the influence of such an offer on the United States and opinion elsewhere.

Armstrong, though, objected that there was no end to the small additional concessions that might be asked of the British Government, but the room for manoeuvre was in fact extremely small. The Government had to take account of opinion in Northern Ireland; the views of prison officers there; and the limits to the creation of further disparities between the treatment of prisoners in Northern Ireland and those in Great Britain. Nally interjected that there were suggestions that Northern Ireland prison officers were not averse to the continuation of the hunger strike because of the resulting overtime earnings. Unionist criticisms of concessions to the hunger-strikers would be softened by the fact that UDA members would also benefit. Kirwan commented that, just as there was an interaction between the Unionists and the British Government, so was there was interaction between the Catholic community and the Government of the Republic. Emphasizing that he was speaking personally, Kirwan suggested that it might be possible for the Irish Government to give a lead by establishing, with the British, parameters of action, and then making known their support for those agreed limits.

Nally continued that the IRA would be certain to reject any proposal that they believed to be the result of agreement between the Irish and British Governments. Concluding for the British, Armstrong observed that a proposal of this kind would be very difficult for the United Kingdom too, although the discussion had served to emphasize the need for good channels of information between the two Governments; meanwhile the Prime Minster had welcomed the Taoiseach's statement to the effect that it was now up to the prisoners themselves how the hunger strike ended. Kirwan commented that he was not sure that the Taoiseach had used the actual words ascribed to him in press reports.[25]

Irish frustration with the British reached exasperation levels once again on the following day when FitzGerald was forced to fire off a letter to the Four Horseman on 28 July complaining about Mrs Thatcher's own letter to them published that morning. In her letter the Prime Minister had expressed surprise that:

> ... you should feel that there is a lack of commitment by the Government to reach the earliest possible settlement of the strike. We have facilitated the efforts of the Pope's personal representative, the European Commission of Human Rights, the Irish Commission for Justice and Peace, and now the International Committee of the Red Cross.

All had foundered on the intransigent adherence of the prisoners to the five demands that they had formulated five years before, and which had not changed in substance since: 'The responsibility for additional deaths rests firmly on the shoulders of those who are ordering these young men to commit suicide in the cause of subverting democratic institutions in Ireland North and South.'

In answer to the Four Horsemen's request for the Prime Minister to send a representative into the Maze, she stressed that repeated efforts had been made to explain directly to the hunger-strikers 'that it is up to those who are being ordered to die, what will happen when the protest ends.' The hunger-strikers had refused to listen on the orders of the prisoner they regard as in charge of them: a man who made clear to the Governor on 19 July that he was prepared only to engage in negotiation on the basis of the prisoners' demands and not to listen to any exposition of the Government's position. Mrs Thatcher pointed out to the Horsemen:

You will no doubt have seen that a spokesman for the Prime Minister of the Irish Republic said Dr. FitzGerald believed that the British Government had met his suggestion that an official speak to the hunger strikers, that he deeply regretted the hunger strikers had rejected the offer from officials to clarify what conditions would apply if the strike ended, and that in his view responsibility for finding a solution now rested with the prisoners.

Mrs Thatcher stressed that she had thought very carefully about the hunger strikes in recent months, and had in particular taken account of the Horsemen's representations and those of others at home and abroad who, like the Government, wanted to see the hunger strikes brought to an end as quickly as possible: 'I am convinced that we have acted honourably throughout, and that we have shown great flexibility while adhering to principles which no responsible Government could abandon.' The Government's commitment to the further improvement of the regime had evoked no constructive response from the protesting prisoners. She continued to hope that the hunger-strikers and 'those who direct them will recognise that we shall stand by that commitment when the hunger strike ends, but that to continue their action will bring only further suffering to themselves, their families and the whole community in Northern Ireland.'[26]

In response, FitzGerald wrote to Senator Kennedy, furious that the Prime Minister's:

> ... latest letter to you misrepresents my position and that of my Government in regard to the H-Block hunger strike. Her letter refers to a press report of Wednesday, July 22 which purported to indicate my Government's position following a visit by British officials to the hunger strikers at 2.00 am on July 21. The letter suggests that the Irish Government is now satisfied with what the British authorities have done to solve the crisis.

The Taoiseach set the record straight: 'Last Friday, Jim Dooge ... told the British Ambassador that this press report, amongst others, should be ignored and drew attention to Irish newspaper reports of Friday July 24, as reflecting the true position of the Irish Government.'[27] The Taoiseach also summoned the British Ambassador the same day. He told Figg that he found it 'difficult to see how the British Prime Minister could represent a version of our position to US Politicians and to world opinion which was based on an inaccurate press report.' The Thatcher letter, complained FitzGerald, was undermining the credibility of his Government in the USA to the advantage of the IRA and its supporters: 'If Mrs Thatcher's version of our position were believed in America by many people, and we must assume that it might be, that would undermine our efforts to counter the IRA and this would have as an after effect the weakening also of the British position in American public opinion.' The Taoiseach was 'astonished that the British Prime Minister should give an account of our position'. Three aspects were emphasized by FitzGerald: firstly, that it was not for one Prime Minister to present publicly the views of another; secondly, that this should not be done on the basis of press reports; and thirdly, that this should not be done given the fact that those reports had been specifically repudiated by the Irish Government. A unilateral statement issued without consultation was very unusual, and all the more so since it was based on press reports, the unreliability of which had been the subject of an official indication to the Ambassador two days earlier. The Taoiseach commented that 'our relationship with Britain was, as we knew, unique and he had to say that there was certainly something unique about Mrs Thatcher's approach in this case although not in the sense in which the word had been used up to then.'[28] A few days later Figg reported to FitzGerald that the Prime Minister was entirely unaware that she was in any way misrepresenting his views and would regret it if any difference between the two Governments should arise in consequence.[29]

Mrs Thatcher's attention, meanwhile, was occupied by the Royal Wedding of Prince Charles and Lady Diana Spencer on 29 July. The occasion did, though, allow the Irish ambassador to raise the matter of the hunger strike informally when he attended an evening reception hosted by Lord Carrington. Kennedy met and spoke to all the members of the Government present, including the Prime Minister, Whitelaw, Sir Geoffrey Howe, the Chancellor of the Exchequer and Sir Ian Gilmour, as well as Carrington. All spoke with concern about the hunger strike. The Prime Minister 'seemed in a very tough mood, indeed.' She was certain that the hunger-strikers now wanted to come off the strike, but were being manipulated inside the prison by the Provos outside. Kennedy had hoped that, because of the euphoria generated by the wedding, there might be some sign of 'give' in her attitude, 'but I have to say I could not detect any. She seemed in a belligerent mood. Mr Whitelaw, though much relaxed, took the same line.' Carrington said that he fully understood the concern of the Taoiseach at the efforts by the IRA to 'destabilise our political system', and that he would 'very much want to avoid our two countries drifting apart' over the H-Block situation. Sir Ian Gilmour, though, 'surprised me', recalled Kennedy. He said that 'we should make our representations through the Foreign Office rather than through the NIO because (he implied) the latter would not receive them as sensitively as the former. He seemed to feel our two countries might be approaching a breakdown in relations.' Kennedy pointed out to him that 'we have been making our representations through the FCO and that he would recall I had presented our last and very grave démarche on Saturday evening 18 July to the FCO addressed to him.'[30]

That there might be divisions within Whitehall over the hunger strike seemed to be confirmed, to the Irish, during a discussion between the Taoiseach and the British Ambassador about the London meeting: it emerged that there was considerable friction between the NIO and the FCO. FitzGerald was informed that the recent letter from the Prime Minister to the Four Horsemen had, in fact, been drafted and submitted by the NIO without, apparently any FCO participation. Certainly Figg had not seen the draft or known of the proposal to send the letter, and it was noted in Dublin that: 'If he had he would immediately have seen the dangers of picking on the reference in the press, to the inaccuracy of which his attention had already been drawn here.'[31]

On the British side, the NIO had noticed another set of apparent divisions: amongst the relatives of the hunger-strikers. Father Faul had been a significant figure in attempts to persuade the relatives that the protest was hopeless and that the Government would not give in. The relatives in turn had put pressure on the Provisionals and IRSP leadership to order an end to the fast.[32] On 28 July, D. J. Wyatt met with John McEvoy, Chairman of Newry & Mourne District Council and a fellow SDLP Councillor, Savage, who brought Lawrence and John Quinn to see him. They were brothers of Patsy Quinn, who was the next hunger-striker expected to die after Doherty and Lynch. McEvoy asked Wyatt where the Government stood on the issues, which he enumerated. Wyatt said that there were three kinds of issues:

(a) Procedural: The question of how one dealt with McFarlane's desire to be in on the act raised real problems for us of giving a toehold to the Provisional command structure which could be exploited later and of legitimising the Provisionals outside the prison. But the real point was that we were not going to make concessions in this area when there was no sign that the prisoners had moved from their 5 demands. Some of these demands raised questions of principle and some did not.

(b) No principle involved: The restoration of lost remission, visits, parcels and letters were areas where the Government had the room for manoeuvre. The issue of principle on clothing was whether uniform was worn or was not worn. Provided that the rules were tightly drawn there was no issue of principle in deciding whether the Government or the prisoner paid for approved civilian clothing.

(c) Principle involved: Where principle was involved was in the area of concession and work. The Government would not allow free association even within wings. It would not accept that prisoners could refuse to do work allocated to them without punishment.

McEvoy urged strongly on Wyatt the view that the prisoners now had a sufficient sense of reality to be ready to accept a written statement of precisely what would happen when the protest ended, and to give up their hunger strike even with the refusal to concede on association and work that Wyatt had indicated. It would have to be guaranteed in some way, however, because the prisoners did not trust the Government. Wyatt noted that the Quinn brothers were a good deal more doubtful about this, and thought that it was not necessary to concede the five demands. They agreed with McEvoy that precision was needed. The hunger-strikers would not give up on the basis of phraseology like 'We would not rule out the possibility of further development'. What was needed was 'A day in the life of Paddy Quinn' from unlock to lock-up. They agreed that the issue of a guarantee was important. If someone like Cardinal Ó Fiaich believed that the Government would do what it had said and would monitor its performance, they thought that would satisfy the prisoners, but they considered that the sticking point on association and work was really one of segregation. The prisoners might accept that they would not have freedom of association in their wings, and might accept that they would have to go to prison workshops and do domestic chores in the central services, but they would never accept that they had to do these things in common with Loyalist prisoners and 'ordinary decent criminals'. The Government would have to find some way of guaranteeing continued segregation, which the Loyalists wanted too, and which was already a fact of life for the protesting prisoners. Wyatt found this much more convincing than what McEvoy had said.

The Quinn brothers asked why such a document should not be prepared and given to all prisoners, which would obviate the need for McFarlane to get into the act vis-à-vis the Government. Wyatt said that the answer was quite simple. The Government believed that the Sinn Féin figures controlling the hunger strike were determined to squeeze it for all it was worth, and would pocket such an offer and order the hunger strike to continue, saying 'three demands down, two demands to go'. The Quinns 'shook their heads sadly.' Wyatt added that he would report their views to the Secretary of State. He could promise no more, and warned them that although:

> ... I had listened to all the arguments in favour of putting such a document before the prisoners in what they had reported to me to be the hunger strikers 'desperation' to give up and although I saw the force of those arguments, it did not mean that there were no arguments against doing such a thing. I had indicated what some of those counter arguments were.

Wyatt would report the common view that any such document would need to be 'guaranteed'; McEvoy's view that it would be worth trying 'even on the basis of our hardest position'; and the Quinn brothers' view that the hunger strikes would not end unless the prisoners were satisfied that they would not be forcibly integrated with Loyalists and common criminals. At the end of the meeting, McEvoy emphasized that he did not wish it to be known publicly that the conversation had taken place.[33]

Inside the Maze, McFarlane was informed, by Paddy Quinn, who had a visit from his brother, about the contact with Wyatt and, as Adams was informed, 'we could get clothes, something on remission and something on segregation, but that work remained the same. A load of balls as you can see.' However, Quinn said that, while he could not speak for everyone, he would be interested to hear what the 'SDLP boys actually had.' Tom McElwee also had a visit, from Father Crilly, who put a proposal to him: as it stood now, he said, both parties were almost at the peak of a mountain, but neither wanted to make the first move: 'We should make that move, he says, and terminate the hunger strike, thus moving directly to that peak. From there we can enjoy universal acclaim and support which would insist in ensuring that a settlement is arrived at.' McFarlane 'tore it to shreds', and pointed out that the moment the hunger strike stopped then cosmetic reforms would be the order of the day: 'I told him straight that the decision was theirs – either we pursue course for five demands or we capitulate. No in-between solutions.' McElwee then pointed out to McFarlane that he was not talking about 'half a loaf', but just a possible change in tactics to secure the five demands. McFarlane replied that 'we should keep firmly on our line and not deviate in the slightest, because to do so spelt danger.' Quinn and McElwee expressed concern about saving Kevin Lynch and Kieran Doherty's lives if a way could be found through a change in tactics, although they accepted that the offers 'floating about were of little or no relevance at all. They all say they are strong mentally and determined to carry on. They say they realize it could mean all of their deaths, but they understand this', reported McFarlane to Adams.

The hunger-strikers expressed concern about the pressure 'swinging towards us', and the British using McFarlane as an excuse for not talking. They were thinking of a way to 'turn the tables on the Brits' and expose them as having nothing to offer. They proposed that McFarlane should take a back seat and allow them to see NIO representatives so they could 'get rid of this red herring for good. I explained the position about my presence being essential at any negotiations and that a break in the line now would hammer us for the future. Also, that keeping firmly on line weighed far heavier in the balance than a propaganda exercise.' McFarlane added that Adams and his companions outside were doing their utmost to ensure that bad propaganda was warded off 'and that you'd counteract Brit moves. The boys said you were making heavy weather of it this last week. I then explained how you were on the ball' every day, pulling FitzGerald back into the firing line, 'and that we'd gone through periods of unfavourable press coverage before.' He told them that:

... we could always expect things to run this way, but that we'd managed to get above the situation alright. I said that you lot were in the best position to advise and to read the situation and that you had agreed that my presence is a must at any talks. Also that you'd ensure 100% effort and more to steering the propaganda in the right direction.

Quinn expressed the opinion that, once Doherty and Lynch died, then 'we couldn't really expect further pressure to build on the Brits, even if they were all drawing close to death.' He felt that there would come a time when 'we'd have to make a move.'

McFarlane clarified 'our position' to Adams. Firstly, cutting him out to gain a propaganda victory was dangerous, and that it in itself 'would not save the boys' lives.' Secondly:

... we had two options – 1. pursue our course for five demands, or 2. capitulate now. I told them I could have accepted half measures before Joe died, but I didn't then and wouldn't now. I told them that the price of victory could be high and they might all die before we get a settlement. I said the Brits took a firm stand last week, but had also acknowledged that somewhere along the line they may be forced to meet our terms. I then asked them for an opinion and they each told me that they'd continue and maintain the line. They are strong.

Meanwhile, when McFarlane visited Lynch and Doherty, he found that the former could not talk or see, while the latter was delirious, although able to tell McFarlane that 'he's strong and determined and maintains the line'.[34]

On the following day, there was a dramatic development when a request for Gerry Adams to be allowed to visit the hunger-strikers was granted – a significant relaxation in policy by the NIO. This followed an approach by Father Murphy on 29 July, who had asked the Duty Officer at the Maze to get hold of an NIO Prisons Official. He passed on a request by Cardinal Ó Fiaich for a visit to the hunger-strikers and McFarlane by Adams, another member of Sinn Féin and of the IRSP. The visit had to take place that day before another death. The Cardinal had expectations that this visit would result in the hunger strike being called off. B. D. Palmer, the NIO official concerned, made it clear that there could be no question of any Government involvement in such a meeting, nor could the Governor be involved, and he would need to know the names of the other two visitors before any permission to visit could be given. Father Murphy took these points and went back to Cardinal Ó Fiaich. Palmer then spoke to Woodfield and Alison, and it was agreed that such a visit could go ahead. Palmer confirmed this to Father Murphy after he had told him the two other names: Owen Carron and Seamus Ruddy (IRSP).[35]

McFarlane, McElwee, Laurence McKeown, Matt Devlin, Pat McGeown, Paddy Quinn and Micky Devine were assembled in the canteen of the prison hospital when Owen Carron, Seamus Ruddy and Adams arrived. Quinn was in a wheelchair, and sat with the others around two tables, which had been pushed together in the centre of the room. McFarlane, McGeown and Devlin had been taken from their cells to the prison hospital while the others, dressed in prison-issue pyjamas and dressing gowns, had been brought from their cells in the prison hospital itself. Kevin Lynch and Kieran Doherty could not attend the meeting, but McFarlane made arrangements for the visitors to see them later. 'It had taken us an hour to pass through the various security checks from the main gate of Long Kesh to the prison hospital, as the screws, sullenly resentful of our presence, quizzed our escort and driver' recorded Adams. The hunger-strikers 'all looked rough, prison-pale skin stretched across young skull-like faces, legs and arms indescribably thin, eyes with that penetrating look which I have often noticed among fellow prisoners in the past.'

The visitors outlined the clergymen's proposal to them. The 'lads were fully aware of all developments, but we persisted in detailing in a factual and harsh manner, everything which had happened over the past few weeks. They sat quietly, smoking or sipping water, listening intently to what we had to say.' Occasionally Paddy Quinn, who sat beside Adams, used the spittoon, which he held on his lap. Quinn, heavily bearded, was by far the worst looking of the hunger-strikers. As Adams talked, or listened to Owen Carron or Seamus Ruddy talking, he 'couldn't stop my eyes straying below the tables where the scrawny legs of the hunger strikers were stretched. We smoked in relays, in the absence of matches keeping our cigarettes alight by ensuring that somebody was always smoking, thus avoiding having to ask the screw for a light.' But: 'There was no basis for a settlement. The British government were still persisting in their refusal to move meaningfully on work, association, or segregation.' The prisoners' 4 July statement outlined their position:

> Yes, they knew they could come off the hunger strike at any time. Yes, they knew the Movement would have no difficulties in explaining the end of the hunger strike. If there was an alternative to the strike, they wouldn't be on it. Five years of protest was too much. A reasonable and commonsense approach by the British would end permanently, all the prison protests.

The hunger-strikers stated that they 'weren't motivated by a personal loyalty to Bobby, Raymond, Francie, Patsy, Martin or Joe. They knew the score, they didn't want to die.' But they needed a settlement of the issues that caused the hunger strike before they would end the hunger strike. 'No, they weren't driven by a personal loyalty to each other. Regardless of what the others did, each was personally committed to the five demands and to the hunger strike.' They weren't under any duress. Apologetically, at first, because 'I knew all those things myself,' Adams:

> ... told the lads that I felt duty bound to satisfy the clergymen and all those who were pressurising their families. I painted the darkest and blackest picture possible: between ten and twenty prisoners dead, nationalist Ireland demoralised, and no advance from the British government. 'You could all be dead. Everyone left in this room when we leave will be dead'. 'Sin é,' [that's it] said somebody. 'They won't break us. If we don't get the five demands, then the rest of the boys and the women will.'

McFarlane arranged for the visitors to go and see Kieran Doherty. Adams:

> ... told the lads that I wouldn't tell Doc of their position. 'He knows it anyway,' someone said. 'We saw him last night after Fr Crilly's visit.' 'Gerry A, Failte.' He greeted us all his eyes following our voices. We crowded around the bed, the cell much too small for four visitors. I sat on the side of the bed. Doc, who I hadn't seen in years, looked massive in his gauntness, as his eyes, fierce in their quiet defiance, scanned my face.

Adams spoke to him quietly and slowly, 'somewhat awed by the man's dignity and resolve and by the enormity of our mission.' '"You know the score yourself," he said. "I've a week in me yet. How is Kevin (Lynch) holding out?"' Adams said: 'You'll both be dead. I can go out now Doc, and announce that it's over.' Doherty paused momentarily, and reflected, then said:

> We haven't got our five demands and that's the only way I'm coming off. Too much suffered for too long, too many good men dead. Thatcher can't break us. Lean ar agaigh. I'm not a criminal ... For too long our people have been broken. The Free Staters, the Church, the SDLP. We won't be broken. We'll get our five demands. If I'm dead ... well, the others will have them. I don't want to die but that's up to the Brits. They think they can break us. Well they can't.

He 'grinned self-consciously'. As the visitors left, Doherty said: 'Don't worry, we'll get our five demands. We'll break Thatcher ...'.

Outside Doherty's cell, the prison officer led them in to speak to Kieran's father and brother, who had just arrived to relieve his mother. They then went in to speak to Kevin Lynch's family. The prison chaplains were with Kevin, and the prison officers had advised McFarlane that Lynch should not be disturbed. They spent a few minutes with Lynch's father and older brother. Lynch, they were told, was totally determined to continue his fast unless the five demands were conceded. Lynch's father, broken-hearted at his imminent death, 'told us of his anguish in the face of British intransigence. "To rear a son and see him die like this…"' the party left, unable to speak with Lynch.

Back at the canteen, Paddy Quinn, by now restricted to his cell, was absent. The remaining hunger-strikers asked about Lynch and Doherty's condition. Adams scribbled out an account of the visit and read it to the hunger-strikers. They suggested that Adams include two paragraphs calling upon the Catholic hierarchy, SDLP and Dublin Government to publicly support and pressurize the British Government into moving towards the 4 July statement. 'And tell them to get off our families' backs', demanded the prisoners.[36]

Following the high hopes the visit had generated in some circles, it seemed that a number of the hunger-strikers' relatives had, however, indicated that they were not satisfied that Gerry Adams had done all he could to persuade the prisoners to give up. Recent public statements by Lynch and Doherty's relatives suggested, thought the NIO, that Adams may have been able to reassert his influence over them. A new suggestion that emerged, however, from a meeting involving the families at Toomebridge on 30 July, was for the setting up of a 'Help the Prisoners Committee' to monitor the implementation of promised prison reforms. Father Faul, involved in setting up this committee, also called for other groups in society such as bankers, stockbrokers and businessmen to realize the importance of resolving the dispute and to make their own protests according to their own conscience.[37]

The Irish seized on the developments at Toomebridge. Liam Hourican reported, on 31 July, to the Taoiseach that: 'Last night's decision to set up the Monitoring Committee represents an important victory for the Priests, Councillors and a number of the relatives over Sinn Féin.' It came unexpectedly towards the end of a long and difficult meeting, which saw recriminations on many sides. For example, the division within the families was more marked than ever with the Lynchs and Quinns vigorously criticizing the tactics of the Provisionals, while being attacked by other families for promoting splits. Bernadette McAliskey 'remained hard-line', while other members of the H-Block Committee wanted to call for an end to the strike. Adams' handling of the visit to the prison was attacked by some as a cosmetic exercise that did not fulfil the request made after the first meeting. Those present included Joe Austin of Sinn Féin (but not Adams), Seamus Ruddy (IRSP), most of the families, McAliskey, Canning and Fathers Faul and Murray.

According to Hourican's information, the Monitoring Committee was first proposed to Sinn Féin at an early morning meeting in Belfast on Wednesday, 29 July. Adams 'turned it down flat.' He subsequently claimed that the hunger-strikers rejected it too: 'Now the tables have been turned on the Provisionals. The creation of the Monitoring Committee must have the effect of reducing their control over what happens in the prison', reported Hourican. The British, though, were unlikely to view the committee with much enthusiasm either. They could quibble about allowing it access or giving it official recognition, but, even if this were withheld, the committee should be able to function in some fashion. This was because a number of its members (the priests) already enjoyed regular access to the prison for pastoral reasons. Hourican suggested to FitzGerald that the Government should give an early indication of support for the committee. Fathers Faul and Murray were reported to be 'extremely helpful last night.' They were openly critical of the Provisionals. Two nights before, Adams agreed to meet the relatives only after Faul had threatened to invite the NIO and the media to Toomebridge so as to expose the Provisionals' behaviour. Seamus Ruddy also made one helpful suggestion. He said that even in advance of a cessation of the hunger strike, the British should be asked to implement their promised reforms immediately for the conforming prisoners. There were a substantial number of these, even on the Republican side – mostly short-sentence men. Hourican thought that it might be necessary to be quite severe with the relatives about steps that the Irish Government could or would take. The hard-liners had been justifying their stand with the argument that intense pressure on Dublin would result in pressures being mounted from there that the British could not resist. McAliskey, for example, had outlined the following scenario:

> Dublin withdraws its Ambassador and expels British Ambassador.
> The Punt and Sterling immediately fall.
> The business community takes fright and demands surrender by the British Government.
> The strikers thus win their five demands.

Some relatives scoffed at this version of what might happen, 'But clearly there are credulous people who believe in something like this', observed Hourican.[38] After being informed of the latest developments, Figg spoke to the NIO, and reported back to the Irish that the NIO was quite ready to talk to any group, including a monitoring committee, to verify the eventual implementation of reforms in Northern Ireland prisons. The concept of monitoring was one to which the NIO had no objection. For instance, they had hoped that the ICRC would carry out that role in regular visits to the prison in the future. The NIO would, however, have to look carefully at what was being proposed. In this connection Figg mentioned that

Father Des Wilson, a priest associated with severe criticisms of the security forces, had been mentioned as a member of the Monitoring Committee, and implied that he would not be acceptable.[39]

On 31 July there was a major setback for the hunger strike when Patsy Quinn's family authorized medical treatment for him. Whether or not Wyatt's meeting with the Quinns was the significant factor in convincing them that the Government would allow him to die, it was the 'most obvious and publicised breaking of ranks.'[40] Kevin Lynch and Kieran Doherty were not so fortunate. Lynch died on day seventy of his fast. His condition was critical, and he had already been unconscious for a number of preceding days. He died on Saturday, 1 August at 01.00. His body was moved to Coleraine Hospital later that day, and subsequently to his home at Dungiven. He was buried on Monday, 3 August. Doherty died on 2 August after seventy-three days on hunger strike.

A cortège of about 1,500 followed Doherty's coffin to the city cemetery in Belfast along a route lined by a further 2,000 or 3,000 people. Jimmy Drumm gave a funeral oration in which he dismissed the idea that the hunger strike continued only because the prisoners were confused as to what was on offer:

> It is not a matter of clarification ... the prisoners have said that so far there is no basis for a settlement. It is common knowledge that the British Government will allow prisoners to wear their own clothes, more visits and reinstate lost remission. But the Government need to be moved on the issues of work and segregation.

The Tricolour over Leinster House flew at half mast to mark the death of Doherty, as a member of the Dáil, but there was no official Government representation at the funeral. Neil Blaney and Niall Andrews (a Fianna Fáil TD) attended the funeral.[41]

The week, from the NIO's perspective, had been one of significant developments on the prison front, though these had not pointed in any one direction. Quinn's removal from the strike at his mother's request represented the first break not sanctioned by the PIRA; it was assumed that he would not rejoin the strike. It was also evidence of the rift widely reported to exist between some of the relatives and the PIRA/INLA leaderships. Although the pressure on the prisoners to come off was maintained, this did not produce any evident weakening, as shown by the deaths of Doherty and Lynch, the 'approaching demise' of McElwee and the continued hard line of attributed statements. Also of significance were the reports – borne out by developments that week – that hunger-strikers would now be going on weekly and not on a replacement basis. It was possible that this might 'reflect difficulty in drumming up volunteers for suicide' – there was now in fact a deficit of two replacement strikers – though it might only have been an attempt to ensure that fewer gaps occurred in the chain of prospective deaths. Lynch's replacement by Liam McCloskey followed the established PIRA patterns, though he was INLA. It was also noted that although previous hunger strike deaths had been followed by rioting and attacks on the security forces, the Northern Ireland-wide bombing of commercial targets during the early evening of 5 August did represent an apparent change in the PIRA's policy. The attacks, it was felt, might well reflect the feeling of the Provisional leadership that such violence was the only way to maintain the pressure on the Government in a situation that appeared otherwise to be an impasse.[42]

While the NIO remained confident that a significant shift had occurred in the prison dispute, it was in the FCO that British concerns were crystallized. Figg returned to London on 5 August to call on Woodfield to brief the NIO PUS on the continuing anxieties of the Dublin Government. There were indications that a by-election in the Cavan/Monaghan seat would not be contested by the H-block supporters, but if Fianna Fáil won this seat, forcing a general election, there were rumours that H-Block candidates would then be fielded in every constituency. There seemed to be good cause, therefore, particularly in order to keep moderate opinion in the Republic on-side, for HMG to make public exactly what would happen when the hunger strike ended. During the discussion, Woodfield made the following points:

(i) there was very little more on offer for the prisoners and it was well known what this was (we had indicated what was on offer in clarification to eg the relatives and the ICRC). The only value of a public statement was to give the hunger strikers a ladder to climb down when they wanted to come off. There was no indication that this was the case at the moment.

(ii) if HMG issued a clarification statement and it failed to end the hunger strike, the Republic's Government and others would very soon be pressing HMG for further concessions, and there would then be absolutely nothing left to give.

(iii) at present the pressure to move was in the UK context and particularly in NI, not on HMG directly. The other elements in the situation (Churchmen/ PIRA/relatives/SDLP) were engaged with each other – with no sign of cohesion – and anything HMG might do in this situation would certainly not be effective.

(iv) there were very reasonable cards already on the table which had not yet been picked up: ie our offer to clarify Government statement to the hunger strikers and (separately) to MacFarlane [sic]. The last card should be kept until there are indications it will take the trick. It might be that some restatement of our present position would be necessary before then.

Figg took these points, but was still a little concerned as to why it was so difficult to say publicly what was well known already privately. There was a feeling in the Republic that 'we were looking for "total surrender".' The PUS acknowledged that it was difficult to please all the 'audiences' in this situation: 'we might consider whether it would be helpful for Sir Leonard to speak informally to the Irish making the points above', he thought. After Figg left, R. L. Smith, Private Secretary to the PUS, went through the discussion with Peter Thomas of the FCO's Irish Department. He let Smith know, informally, that he understood that Sir Ian Gilmour intended to write to Atkins along the lines of Figg's arguments. Just then David Tatham telephoned, from the Dublin Embassy, to say that John Kelly, the Acting Minister for Foreign Affairs, had just called him in to suggest that HMG should let the conforming prisoners have what was on offer to the hunger-strikers if they ceased their fast. The Irish intended to make this suggestion public.[43] Kelly felt that HMG did not understand the seriousness of the current H-Blocks crisis as it appeared to Dublin. He personally thought that the appearance of a formerly moderate Fianna Fáil deputy (Niall Andrews) at Doherty's funeral was a depressing sign of the way things were going. If HMG believed that the wavering among two families (Quinn's and Lynch's) was the start of a trend, they were wrong; these two had always been the weak links. The Irish Government believed that there was a long queue of volunteers to take their place in the strike.

Kelly then made his 'constructive suggestion': Michael Alison had said, at the beginning of July that if the strike ended, 'an advance' in the prison regime was possible. The Irish proposed that this advance should be put into effect now for conforming prisoners. This would enable HMG to demonstrate their good faith and short-circuit problems of communication with the prisoners. No face or ground need be lost. He added that this suggestion did not detract from the Irish Government's broader view that an opportunity had been lost at the start of July in the discussions between Alison and the ICJP. They believed that a small degree of flexibility then could have solved the problem. In reply, the British official undertook to pass on this message to London, but said that HMG was dealing with an unscrupulous adversary:

If we made the concession he suggested, it could simply be pocketed and the strike continue. Our aim was to end the protest in the prisons and any clarification of our views should be calculated to achieve that end. At the moment, we simply did not believe the IRA wanted a solution. We could clarify some points but if we did not therefore end the strike we and the Irish would be much worse off. Mr Kelly said he appreciated this but he thought the most pressing need was to end the present crisis at once.[44]

Upon his return to Dublin, Figg telegraphed to the FCO his view that Kelly's remarks 'show how really worried the Irish Government are about the hunger strike and their ability to deal with the security and other side effects.' Following his talk with Woodfield, Figg wrote:

> I understand the undesirability of making any new move just at the present moment. But in view of Mr Kelly's approach to us I hope we will not delay too long before making a move of some kind. Frankly to do nothing until after the Fermanagh by-election [following Sands' death] would put us in a very bad posture with the Irish Government. And whatever we may think of the Irish Government's suggestion about implementing prison reforms before the hunger strike ends we must try and give Mr Kelly sympathetic and reasoned reply soon which can be made public.

As Figg had said to both Sir Ian Gilmour and Woodfield, a continuation of the hunger strike for more than about another six weeks could cause serious parliamentary consequences in Ireland: assuming Fianna Fáil won the by-election there, Agnew, the H-Block prisoner who was a TD in the Louth constituency, would be told to resign, and in the subsequent by-election Fianna Fáil would gain another seat. This would mean a tie in seats in the Dáil between the Government and Opposition, and would almost certainly mean a general election. The H-Block Committee could then be expected to put up candidates in all constituencies. The issue would be central in the election, and judging by their previous performance the H-Blockers might well gain seven or eight seats. The new Government would be bound to take their views into account, assuming the H-block candidates took their seats, 'and the consequences for us could be very serious.'[45]

The Foreign Office response disappointed the Ambassador. It told Figg to seek an early opportunity to speak to Kelly on the following lines:

> We note that the Government of the Republic's objective is to end the hunger strike. There is nothing between us on this – that is also HMG's aim. We do not, however, have any grounds at all for believing that, if we did what the Government of the Republic is now proposing, that move would cause the strikers to end their fast.

Kelly would appreciate that the relatively minor changes that HMG stood ready to make were a long way from the five demands of the protesters. That the protesters stood by those demands was made all too clear in the oration by Jimmy Drumm of Sinn Féin, on 4 August, at the graveside of Kieran Doherty. HMG's difficulty was this: 'if we are to retain control of the prison (and that is for HMG a responsibility they cannot and will not abandon) there are only very limited improvements indeed which can be made in the regime at the Maze (and it is worth noting that Jimmy Drumm discounted in advance any movement on "own clothes").' It might be that at some point in time the strikers would be looking for some movement, however minor, to provide them with a 'colourable' reason for coming off their strike; if so, it would be important at that juncture to have something to offer: 'If we use up our limited supply of powder now, with no reason to think it will do the trick, it will have been wasted and our locker will then be bare when something is needed. We therefore take the view that we should husband what little we have.' One further point to be made was that Kelly's suggestion that the move he proposed might end the strike was hardly borne out by his own belief that there was 'a long queue of volunteers' to replace strikers who died. Finally, Figg was asked to make it clear to Kelly that 'we are giving him the reasons for our decision not to act as he suggested in strict confidence. These reasons substantially give away our tactics vis-à-vis the hunger strikers and it would do great harm if they became known.'[46]

It was not that there had been an absence of discussion within Whitehall between the FCO and NIO. Just before he went away on holiday, Lord Carrington saw a telegram from Figg in which the Ambassador recommended that HMG should spell out more clearly what would happen when the hunger strikes ended; the Foreign Secretary thought that the suggestion seemed a good one. Sir Nicholas Henderson's telegrams, from Washington, argued in a similar sense. With these concerns in mind, Ian Gilmour wrote to Humphrey Atkins pointing out that these descriptions of the damage that the hunger strikes were causing to 'our interests' tied in closely with the warning from Sir Anthony Parsons, the UK's Ambassador to the UN (in his letter of 7 July to FCO, a copy of which was sent to NIO) of the dangers that HMG faced in the United Nations, specifically the possibility of the passing, in the Human Rights Commission or the Third Committee of the General Assembly, of a hostile resolution on Northern Ireland. Such a resolution would be an important coup for the Provisionals, and a serious humiliation for the Government:

> I know that you are considering the very difficult problem of how to handle the hunger strikes daily and that there are many arguments for and against the various possible courses of action. However, I am becoming more and more firmly of the view that the Government's handling of the hunger strike campaign or, rather, foreign perceptions

of our handling of it, are doing serious damage to the United Kingdom's wider interests and that this damage will increase if the hunger strike stretches on into the coming months. I am well aware of the risk that if we make a clear statement of our final position the Provisionals will leap on it as a basis for negotiation and try and force us into further concessions. I am nevertheless of the view that the advantages in our making a forward movement, either in the form of such a statement or in the form of an actual change to the prison regime, are now beginning to outweigh the possible disadvantages. It would show our flexibility and sincerity to moderate world opinion. It would strengthen the hands of the moderates in Ireland and increase pressure on the Provisionals. It might not bring the hunger strikes to an end. But if it is the case that the hunger strikes would only be brought to an end by our conceding principles that there can be no questions of our conceding, then it seems all the more important that we give careful consideration to minimising the dangers that a prolonged hunger strike campaign poses to our wider interests.[47]

Gilmour sent copies of the letter to the Prime Minister and Sir Robert Armstrong. Atkins, however, rejected the idea of a public statement. Crucially, Mrs Thatcher accepted the Secretary of State's advice that 'there is no case for any initiative by the Government at present.' On the ICRC, she hoped that 'we shall cross-examine the Committee on their views, when these have been amplified', although she considered their views, generally, 'totally irresponsible.' In view of the Prime Minister's comments, Downing Street thought that the NIO would wish to consider setting up a 'diplomatic dialogue' with the ICRC.[48]

Within the FCO, debate continued as to trying to find a way forward: Peter Thomas wrote to his colleague Ewan Fergusson, on 7 August, accepting there was force in Atkins' arguments for not making a public statement: 'Furthermore the Prime Minister supports them', he noted. The Lord Privy Seal might, therefore, be rebuffed if he suggested a further public move by HMG as a means of improving the international climate: 'But I think there is an alternative', argued Thomas. The key element seemed to him to be the Dublin Government. Their statements had of late been more helpful to HMG, not because of any effort on HMG's part ('indeed despite us'), but because the hunger-strikers' supporters had alienated public opinion in the Republic by, for instance, the violence against the Garda and by a sit-in at the Taoiseach's office: 'We should encourage the already existing trend of the Irish Government to become more helpful.' They had asked to be kept more closely informed about developments; Thomas thought 'we should be forthcoming in our reply to this. We cannot undertake to inform them of every twist and turn and of every visitor to the Maze.' But they still held to the opinion that HMG could accept the ICJP's recommendations.

The Foreign Office, believed Thomas, should persuade the Northern Ireland Office to put all their cards on the table to the Irish Government, in strict confidence, and explain to them, with all the technical details about position of grilles and numbers of warders and so on, 'just why it is that we cannot go any further than we can.' The NIO would take a lot of persuading of the merits of this, although the instructions that they drafted for the reply to Kelly's latest suggestion went some way towards it. As Thomas urged Ferguson:

> Our position is reasonable and we stand a chance of gaining the Irish Government's support for it. If we could get a commitment from them to support these limited moves, the resultant Anglo-Irish cohesion would do a great deal to remove the international pressure upon HMG. You will recall the tremendous success of the Dublin summit in Irish America. If we make a positive effort to get the Irish Government on our side rather than repeatedly rebuff their admittedly tiresome continual interventions, I do not see that it can do us anything but good.[49]

As the Foreign Office debated a way forward, another encounter between Sir Leonard Figg and Kelly saw the latter ask the Ambassador 'how we saw the strike ending. I said that I did not think anyone could see that at the moment.' Kelly dismissed Figg's answer by complaining 'we were not making enough effort to end it and that we seemed to be expecting a complete surrender by the strikers.'[50]

With two prisoners having just died, and the condition of another, Thomas McElwee, deteriorating, the protesting prisoners issued another statement. They stated that there was a vast difference between prison conditions and the prison system. Prisoners could be held in decent conditions, but still be treated as subhuman: 'What in essence we seek is the uplifting of the present Victorian prison system. We are convinced that all prisoners are entitled as human beings to retain their dignity and self-respect. The present system, virtually unchanged from the 19th century, denies prisoners both.' It was noted, by the NIO, that at no time in the 2,000-word statement, which the prisoners said was issued to elaborate on certain aspects of their earlier July 4 statement, was there any reference to 'political status' or any demand for negotiations with Government officials. Instead, the prisoners argued that the British refusal to settle:

> ... leaves us with absolutely no alternative but to continue with this strategy. Their defiance, in the face of reason based on the reality that an obvious and principled solution exists, challenges the authority of every

concerned body in Ireland. It is our opinion that every authority has pursued a moderate approach which the British have treated as weakness and dismissed contemptuously.

If further deaths were to be avoided, more vigorous pressure would have to be applied to the British by the 'offended' Irish authorities, which the prisoners primarily pinpointed as the Dublin Government, the SDLP and the Catholic Church: 'We have already said that what the regime regards as work we do not. Also an examination of what we propose will reveal that a high level of compatibility exists.' The Government's 'what happens when the protest ends?' statement had compounded the prisoners' point that the prisoner was an 'unopinionated robotic object in their eyes, something whose entire life is totally programmed.' This Government attitude was wrong and could only lead to more deaths.

As pointed out in the prisoners' 4 July statement, 'we are prepared to clean wing and blocks. As well as that we are willing to do any maintenance work within our capability such as painting our blocks. We are prepared to do our own laundry if facilities are made available for us within our blocks.' Also, given the facilities, which would not amount to much, 'we are prepared to do our own cooking within our blocks.' The term 'self-education', continued the prisoners, seemed to have caused some confusion: 'Basically we define self-education as the right to choose how you feel you should be educated and what subject you should pursue in your education.' The prisoners argued that it was almost impossible to participate in cultural or academic education during the prison working day: 'Usually a prisoner has to forfeit his association to attend a class. Daytime education is available usually only for the educationally subnormal', the statement said. 'But the machinations for an education system as envisaged by us already exist. We envisage an education system where prisoners of proven outstanding tutorial ability can blend with outside teachers to provide an excellent educational system.' It was a fact that the Irish language, which originally was limited to only a few prisoners, had been taught by some of the aforementioned prisoners to 50% of all blanketmen. So successful has this self-education system been that Irish had virtually replaced English as the principal language in the protesting blocks. Likewise, there were blanketmen who from experience were exceptionally adept at handicrafts, and blanketmen who were accomplished musicians – all of whom would be willing to pass on their knowledge.

As the prisoners saw things, there was also no reason why they should not have the freedom of the wing for association between the hours of lock-up. It would be of benefit educationally, and, with prison officers guaranteed immunity from attack or rebuke, their supervisory roles would not be diminished, argued the prisoners. Segregation was a must if any degree of harmony was to exist within the prison. Wing visits should not present any problem to the authorities.

Letters, visits and parcels were at present a privilege to conforming prisoners to be withdrawn as the regime saw fit: 'We would like them to be a prisoner's right', stated the prisoners. They also failed to see why prisoners at one end of the camp should receive a substantial food parcel and they should receive only four pounds of fruit: 'We want our food parcel increased to the amount available at the other end of the camp. The only reason for this particular piece of inequality is punitive.' To achieve all this, the prisoners called on all concerned: the British, the Dublin Government, the SDLP, the Church and all bodies who were involved in this issue to respond to this statement: 'It should not be disregarded solely because we wrote it.'[51]

In his reply, Humphrey Atkins noted that the statement indicated that the protesting prisoners now accepted that in their own best interest they should bring the protest and the hunger strike to an early end. Even so: 'To my profound regret I can see nothing in this latest document which represents any change of substance from their statement of 4 July, and nothing to suggest that they have understood the Government's reasons for refusing to concede their five demands.' The Secretary of State welcomed (as he did in his statement of 8 July) the fact that the protestors were:

> ... no longer claiming a privileged regime to set them apart from the other prisoners. That claim was always totally unjustified. Equally I deplore the protestors' apparent inability to understand the inevitable consequences which flow from the need for the prison authorities to retain proper control over the daily life of a prison. What the prisoners' statement calls 'the present Victorian prison system' is in fact in the Maze, a complex of physical facilities of the most up-to-date kind, coupled with a regime which is not only one of the best in the UK but which stands comparison with the most enlightened systems in the western world.

It was of the greatest importance, continued Atkins, that the protestors, their families and others who either influenced their thinking or claimed to speak for them should understand clearly that the protestors' demands, as elaborated in their latest statement, 'cannot be met unless the Government agree to the abandonment by the prison authorities of their proper responsibility for control within the prison. This the Government will not do, now or at any later stage.'[52]

NOTES

1   NAI D/T 2011/127/1057 To An Taoiseach from Liam Hourican, 21 July 1981.
2   NAI D/T 2011/127/1057 Nally to Taoiseach, 21 July 1981.

3   PRONI CENT 1/10/52 Blatherwick to Blelloch, 22 July 1981.
4   TNA CJ4/3632 Protests and Second Hunger Strike – Weekly Bulletin No. 21 0900 hours Thursday 16 July – 0900 hours Thursday, 23 July.
5   PRONI CENT 1/10/52 Brief of Mr Blelloch's visit to the Maze Prison, held in PUS' Flat at Stormont House at 3.45 am on Tuesday, 21 July 1981.
6   PRONI CJ4/3632 Protests and Second Hunger Strike – Weekly Bulletin No. 21 0900 hours Thursday 16 July – 0900 hours Thursday, 23 July.
7   PRONI CENT 1/10/52 Brief of Mr Blelloch's visit to the Maze Prison, held in PUS' Flat at Stormont House at 3.45 am on Tuesday, 21 July 1981.
8   PRONI CENT 1/10/52 Blatherwick to Blelloch, 22 July 1981.
9   PRONI CENT 1/10/52 Note for the Record by The Lord Elton, 24 July 1981.
10   NAI D/T 2011/127/1057 Developments in the H-Block: Prisoners protests since 30 June 1981.
11   NAI D/T 2011/127/1057 To Taoiseach from Hourican, 22 July 1981.
12   TNA CJ4/3632 Protests and Second Hunger Strike – Weekly Bulletin No. 21 0900 hours Thursday 16 July – 0900 hours Thursday, 23 July.
13   O'Rawe, *op.cit.* pp. 200–201.
14   Beresford *op.cit.* pp. 253–254.
15   NAI D/T 2011/127/1057 To Taoiseach from Hourican Hunger Strike – The 'Conference' Proposal 24 July 1981.
16   NAI D/T 2011/127/1057 Note, 21 July 1981.
17   NAI D/T 2011/127/1057 Call by British Ambassador to Department, 24 July 1981.
18   NAI D/T 2011/127/1057 Minister-Designate's conversation with British Ambassador on 25 July 1981.
19   NAI D/T 2011/127/1057 To Taoiseach from Hourican nd.
20   NAI D/T 2011/127/1057 Note to Secretary, 27 July 1981.
21   NAI D/T 2011/127/1057 M Lillis Memo, 27 July 1981.
22   NAI D/T 2011/127/1057 Ronald Reagan letter, 23 July 1981.
23   NAI D/T 2011/127/1057 M Lillis Memo 27 July 1981.
24   NAI D/T 2011/127/1057 From Neligan from Ambassador US Administration and H-Block.
25   TNA FCO 87/1263 Record of a Discussion on the Situation in the Maze Prison held in Sir Robert Armstrong's office on 27 July 1981.
26   TF Thatcher letter to Senator Edward Kennedy, 27 July 1981.
27   NAI D/T 2011/127/1057 Letter to Horsemen, 28 July 1981.
28   NAI D/T 2011/127/1057 Interview between Taoiseach and British Ambassador, 28 July 1981.
29   NAI D/T 2011/127/1057 Call by British Ambassador on 31 July 1981.
30   NAI D/T 2011/127/1057 For Secretary from Ambassador.
31   NAI D/T 2011/127/1057 H-Blocks Joint Studies, 30 July 1981.
32   TNA FCO 87/1263 Protests and Second Hunger Strike – Weekly bulletin No. 23 0900 hours Thursday 30 July – 0900 hours Thursday, 6 August.
33   PRONI CENT 1/10/52 The Hunger Strike: Meeting with Families, 28 July 1981.
34   Beresford *op.cit.* pp. 335–37.
35   PRONI CENT 1/10/52 Note for the Record – Wednesday, 29 July 1981.
36   *An Phoblacht*, August 1981.
37   TNA FCO 87/1263 Protests and Second Hunger Strike – Weekly bulletin No. 23 0900 hours Thursday 30 July – 0900 hours Thursday 6 August.
38   NAI D/T 2011/127/1057 To Taoiseach from Hourican Second Toomebridge meeting: Monitoring Committee, 31 July 1981.
39   NAI D/T 2011/127/1057 Neligan Note, 31 July 1981.

40 TNA FCO 87/1263 Protests and Second Hunger Strike – Weekly bulletin No. 23 0900 hours Thursday 30 July – 0900 hours Thursday 6 August.
41 TNA FCO 87/1263 Protests and Second Hunger Strike – Weekly bulletin No. 23 0900 hours Thursday 30 July – 0900 hours Thursday 6 August.
42 TNA FCO 87/1263 Protests and Second Hunger Strike – Weekly bulletin No. 23 0900 hours Thursday 30 July – 0900 hours Thursday 6 August.
43 TNA FCO 87/1263 Note for the Record: Call by Sir Leonard Figg, 6 August 1981.
44 TNA FCO 87/1263 Dublin to FCO Telegram number 281 of 5 August 1981.
45 TNA FCO 87/1263 Dublin to FCO Telegram number 282 of 6 August 1981.
46 TNA FCO 87/1263 From FCO Telegram number 132 of 6 August 1981.
47 TNA FCO 87/1263 Gilmour to Atkins.
48 TNA CJ4/3624 Rickett to Hopkins, 6 August 1981.
49 TNA FCO 87/1263 PKC Thomas to Ferguson, 7 August 1981.
50 TNA FCO 87/1263 From Dublin to FCO Telegram Number 284 of 7 August 1981.
51 TNA FCO 87/1263 Prisoners' Statement, 7 August 1981.
52 TNA FCO 87/1263 Atkins Statement.

Chapter 12

The End

On 8 August, the ninth hunger-striker, Thomas McElwee (aged 23) died after sixty-two days on hunger strike. In the aftermath of the latest death, FitzGerald's deputy premier, the Tánaiste Michael O'Leary, gave an interview to the Irish broadcaster RTÉ, in which he stated that, since his Government had come into office, he had:

> ... been struck by the intransigence of the British Government at various points. I'm not saying that there hasn't been intransigence on the part of others. I believe that the Provisional IRA leadership have played headline politics throughout, but I believe the major responsibility rests with the British Government. After all, this is their prison, these are their prisoners.

O'Leary also thought that the British Government lacked the will to get a settlement: 'That's why I believe they bear major responsibility and I believe that the proposals of the ... Commission of Justice and Peace ... had all the elements of settlement in them, had there been a willingness on the part of the British Government to get a settlement.' It was O'Leary's 'personal opinion that this matter would have been settled had there been any other Prime Minister in Britain.'[1]

Following O'Leary's outburst, the Irish Government moved quickly to rectify the suggestion that it was putting the British and the Provisionals on the same level of intransigence. The next day, John Kelly made a statement observing that a 'new feature' in the Northern Troubles was that the Dublin Government was being called on daily, by someone or other 'in what may roughly be called the IRA camp, to exert pressure in a direction which suits that camp's purposes.' So, it was time that a 'few plain words' were spoken about this development, and that all possibility of misunderstanding was removed:

> The reason why we have urged upon the British the need to settle the
> H Block situation quickly is that we see it as obstructing and delaying

the achievement of an overall settlement and reconciliation between the people of the North and between them and ourselves. We have expressed disappointment that our urgent words to London have not had a better response.

But what was to be said of the stance of the IRA, asked Kelly. They and their satellites tried to harangue the Government into attitudes and gestures that they thought would advance their aims. The reason they took this trouble with the Government was that they knew that it was recognized and seen, in the outside world, 'as the lawful Government of this state, and its Taoiseach as the Government's lawful leader. In other words, they wish to exploit for their own purposes the legitimacy of the Dublin Administration, whose acts and gestures will command abroad a respect which no other body in the country can command.' But when that same Government condemned their violence, their 'crude contempt for human life, their ruthless indifference to the wishes of most Irish people, suddenly the Government's legitimacy counts for nothing, and its authority is the subject of insult. People cannot have the amenities of civilisation, of which ordered government is the greatest, on terms like these', stated Kelly. The Government said to the IRA: 'call off your campaign of violence; cease the shooting and the bombing and the intimidation; halt the wicked cruelties that have shamed and disgraced the name of Ireland and its flag.' When that call was heeded, 'at least it will become logical to invoke the diplomatic aid of the Government of Ireland in pursuit of a compassionate end. But as long as it goes unheeded, the attempted exploitation of the Government's legitimacy will remain just another piece of hypocrisy.'[2]

Figg reported to London, in the aftermath of O'Leary's 'unhelpful' statement and Kelly's strong condemnation of the IRA, that the Irish Cabinet had met to consider policy towards the North. From what the Embassy had been able to discover (and many of its normal senior official contacts were on leave during the summer recess), it was decided:

i) that any future statements on Northern Ireland by Government Ministers would be cleared with the Taoiseach first;
ii) a meeting to review policy on Northern Ireland would be held on 24 and 25 August, and officials and Ministers have already been told to return from leave.

This was reasonably satisfactory, concluded Figg. It would be politically impossible for the Taoiseach to slap down his senior Labour coalition partners publicly, but he had at least restrained O'Leary – a Labour TD. Kelly's allusion on the BBC earlier in the day to 'the possibly unconsidered remarks of a Minister who does not have responsibility for the North' was also an oblique disavowal. But 'we cannot rule out further' Labour Party statements, warned Figg: the hunger strike was becoming the main political issue in Dublin and the party would wish to pronounce on it just as, during the last Fine Gael-Labour coalition, Conor Cruise O'Brien held forth on Northern issues to the irritation of his Fine Gael partners.[3]

Kelly, though, had not finished his attacks on the Provisionals. On 13 August, he commented on how it was reported that H-Block activists throughout the Republic were beginning a campaign to demand the early recall of the Dáil 'in an effort to force a solution to the H Block crisis'. Just as the 'IRA's front groups' tried to mobilize in their own interests the authority of the legitimate Government, yet ignore that Government's leadership when it did not suit them to respect it, so too the Dáil itself was 'treated as a pawn in their sinister game.' Kelly complained that Republicans were 'perfectly happy to concede prestige to the Dáil just so long as they can usurp its natural publicity value for some of their own operations; but they show, by their other actions, that they hold the status and authority of the Irish nation's legislature in brutal contempt.' The very same Dáil, about whose recall they now showed such 'pious diligence, had, not once but repeatedly, and without a single dissentient voice, condemned violence as a means to Irish unity.' Kelly continued:

> Again – and I make no apology for citing the law of our constitution – the Dáil is declared by Article 28 to be the sole authority for the declaration or waging of war by Ireland.
>
> Yet the very people who now pretend such an urgent respect for the Dáil have ignored its sole authority by their belligerent acts ostensibly committed in the name of the people who elect the Dáil members.
>
> Finally, by Article 15 the sole right to raise and maintain an armed force is vested in the Oireachtas, of which the Dáil is the most important component; and the Article states that 'no armed force other than one raised by the Oireachtas shall be raised or maintained for any purpose whatsoever'. When the groups now sanctimoniously demanding an early Dáil recall show willingness to respect this clear and definite law, they may perhaps expect to be taken seriously; but not before.[4]

The public distancing of the Government from any suggestion of sympathy for the hunger-strikers' situation continued when FitzGerald gave his first interview as Taoiseach to RTÉ TV on the evening of 14 August. The bulk of the interview, which was broadcast during the *Today Tonight* programme, dealt with the Irish Government's attitude to the H-Block strike. The interviewer began by asking the Taoiseach whether his Government was not sympathetic towards the position of the British Government on the H-Block dispute. Dr FitzGerald replied: 'as far as the Government is concerned, any question of granting political status is something which we haven't ever pressed and wouldn't ever press.' Asked who was being inflexible, the prisoners or HMG, the Taoiseach answered:

> ... insofar as a solution was arrived at between Mr Alison and the ICJP, and we believe that it effectively was, and that it wasn't carried through, and the visit to the prison that was promised on Tuesday morning didn't take place ... there was a change of policy of inflexibility there which prevented the visit taking place. But the basic inflexibility lies on the side of the Provisionals themselves, and the answer really lies there primarily.

FitzGerald went on to say that, although the intervention of the Irish Government had so far been unsuccessful, 'what we have done is to raise the consciousness of British public opinion on this subject, especially political opinion'. He noted that there had been reports in the British newspapers 'of divisions in the (British) Government and the fact that many Government Ministers were unhappy at the situation arising from the failure to carry through what had been effectively agreed.' When the interviewer asked FitzGerald whether there would be an increase in pressure on the British Government by his administration as forecast by O'Leary, the Taoiseach replied:

> Well it's our job to keep other governments informed of the position as we see it ... The British Government may have been sustained in taking up a position of some inflexibility by a belief that it was supported by one or two other Heads of Government who perhaps didn't understand that the whole thing was a bit more complex than had been put to them. Our job is to ensure that the complexities are understood ... But I don't want to start a major propaganda campaign against the British in other countries. It would not help the situation; indeed, it could only lead to a hardening of attitudes.[5]

The Tánaiste's vexation with the British was a timely reminder as senior NIO and FCO officials met to discuss the differences between them. J. A. Marshall and Roy Harrington represented the NIO, and Ewan Fergusson and Peter Thomas the Foreign Office. Fergusson described the international repercussions of the hunger strike, and in particular the implications that these had for security in Northern Ireland and HMG's policies there. Marshall agreed that this was a matter of increasing concern. The risks in the Republic were more important than those in the United States. He thought that there was a lot to be said for a letter from the FCO at ministerial level, which would point these dangers out. To have most effect, the letter might be from the Foreign Secretary to the Prime Minster once both were back from holiday at the beginning of September. Fergusson suggested that, on the scope of the changes in the prison regime that could be made available, he detected a change in tone between the statements of Atkins and Alison of 8 July and the instructions that had been sent to Dublin to reply to Kelly on 7 August.

Marshall explained that there was a worry that the impression was growing that the Government had a package ready that could bring the hunger strike to an end without conceding its principles. This was not the case. The changes that the Government could make to the prison regime fell well short of the five demands. He was anxious that the FCO 'should do all we could to begin to minimise expectations on this front.' Harrington added that in their latest statement the prisoners had in fact moved further away from compromise by detailing what they wanted on work. For Marshall, while it was not possible for tactical reasons to spell out what changes the Government was in fact prepared to make to the prison regime, he saw advantage in the idea of a piece of paper explaining in detail why the Government could not give the prisoners what they wanted. The NIO was considering the possibility of such a document, which might include pictures of the sort of items that special category status prisoners had manufactured in the past.[6]

The background to the meeting was that Lord Carrington, shortly before leaving for his holiday, had expressed some concern about the adverse effect on Anglo-Irish relations of the hunger strike. Following on from Ian Gilmour's comments that the stance adopted by HMG remained the right one, Carrington acknowledged 'the tone in which we are presenting our position may be seen by the Irish as being very harsh. If so, it makes it difficult for them to be seen to stand alongside us.' The Foreign Office was 'just as aware as we are that we have a great deal to lose. In the present unstable political situation in the Republic, pressure could well mount for an end to the valuable security co-operation which we at present receive.'[7] Fergusson was keen to follow up this point, and contacted Moriarty at the NIO to emphasize that HMG's present policy over the hunger strikes, however logical and tenable viewed from the point of Northern Ireland's needs, was in fact based on the assumption that the external environment would remain constant, 'or at least that no pressures would build up overseas with which we would not be able to cope. I fear that matters have turned out differently.' These factors posed considerable risks to the Government's Northern Ireland policies: 'I realise that what I am saying will not come to you as a complete surprise; nor will you be surprised if I stress how important it is that full notice should be taken of the international aspects in the formulation of tactics.' It was, of course, 'for you, not us,' to weigh these risks against all the other arguments involved: 'If you continue to judge that it would be unwise for the Government to explain precisely what changes they are willing to make to the prison regime, the FCO will continue, of course, to accept your assessment.'

Even so, argued Fergusson, there appeared to be a good deal of misunderstanding outside about the breadth of the gap between what the Government was prepared to do and what the protesting prisoners were demanding, and a widespread belief that the ICJP's proposals were reasonable and would not breach HMG principles. This was a presentational point: 'If we cannot set out what we are prepared to do, I should nevertheless see advantage in the Government explaining as clearly as possible, and in detail, in a public statement, just what the implications of the prisoners' demands are and why they – and the ICJP's proposals – are unacceptable.' Fergusson envisaged a statement that explained precisely why 'free association', for instance, would give the prisoners the freedom to organize military training, manufacture weapons and intimidate other prisoners. The hunger strike campaign might well drag on for several months. If it did, FCO Ministers might consider that presentational changes would not be enough to prevent the very serious potential dangers that could arise later in the year: 'One could not exclude their proposing that the Government review how far it is desirable, or even possible, to stay on the present course!' For the time being, however, there appeared to be scope for 'neutralising some of the widespread external misunderstanding of our policies ... without making any shift in substance and I hope that we shall be able to make full use of this.'[8] This was clearly a warning that, although the FCO was agreed that the NIO's policy was the correct one, it did so, with serious concerns, only for the present.

The NIO, though, fought its corner. In his reply to Fergusson, Moriarty accepted that if Ministers judged it right to issue a further statement in the near future:

> I believe that we could usefully build on that guidance. We have thought a lot about this in recent days but our judgement for the moment remains that as we have nothing new in substance to say it is better to avoid re-statements which run the risk of suggesting to the majority community that we are 'wobbling', and to the minority community that we are intransigent. Clearly we carry the same risk outside Northern Ireland.

As the NIO saw it, 'our present policy was arrived at collectively by Ministers on the basis that it was right to stand up to the hunger strikers, for reasons which are not narrowly confined to Northern Ireland considerations.' They might decide to change the policy either because it had ceased to be right or because it was expedient to change it, whether it was right or not. In the meantime:

> ... the tactics that we have adopted in pursuing that policy have certainly tried to take full account of the international dimension, and with that dimension in mind we have taken what are very considerable risks in Northern Ireland terms – for example, in the access that we have offered

individuals and bodies to visit the Maze and the hunger strikers, and in the public commitments we have given to improving the regime for men who many people think (not altogether without reason) are well served already.

If the international factors at this point or in the future suggested to FCO Ministers that a change of policy was needed because of growing pressure abroad, then the best – indeed the only – course was for them to put their views to their colleagues for collective discussion. Meanwhile, if there were 'any concrete proposals which you would like us to consider, we should be happy to do so', Moriarty told Fergusson.[9]

What the NIO did do was put together a comparison of the differing viewpoints between the various parties: the prisoners, the ICJP and the Government. This would also be helpful for the FCO in terms of disseminating information to various British Missions around the world. Even for those involved in the minutiae of the dispute, it was not easy. Harrington found it 'a surprisingly difficult task, for several reasons. First, it is difficult to set down concisely but accurately the position of the non-government parties, who sometimes use grandiose but imprecise jargon such as that in the prisoners' statement of 6 August (our statements, by contrast, are no doubt crystal clear).' Second, 'though we must be accurate, we must not go into such detail that it is incomprehensible to the laymen. (Even so, we must not leave out the details which explain practical limitations on our freedom of action.)'[10]

The document produced was probably the first time that the authorities' position was actually set out in detail regarding why the prisoners' position remained unacceptable. The Government's position was, in principle, 'quite straightforward. It is publicly committed to making whatever improvements in the regime at the prison may be practicable.' Such changes would apply to all prisoners; would be made regardless of the protest; would not be introduced under the duress of a hunger strike; but would be subject overall to the two guiding principles that the Government would not concede a special or differential status to a particular group of prisoners merely because they claimed a political motive for their crimes, and that the Government would not abandon control of the prison. In terms of the substance, it was true that the protesting prisoners seemed, in their statement of 4 July, to have withdrawn their insistence on differential status. It was also noteworthy that their major statement of 6 August made no reference to political status, although a spokesman of Provisional Sinn Féin, commenting on this, said that there was no significance in the omission and that the five demands amounted to political status. In fact, the gaps between the positions of the Government, the ICJP and the prisoners were 'crucial, and relate in particular to control of the prison. The improvements in the regime which the Government could make without conceding control are relatively small.'

According to the statements issued in their name on 4 July and 6 August, the prisoners demanded the right not to wear prison uniform, that prison clothing should be abolished and that all prisoners should be allowed to wear their own clothing as of right. The Government's position was that prison uniform had already been abolished. Prison-issue civilian clothing was required to be worn only during the working part of the day. At other times prisoners could wear their own clothing, but for security reasons colour and design were at the discretion of the Governor. The Government did not rule out further development. On prison activity, although the prisoners demanded the right not to do prison work, there were things that they were prepared to do:

i)   Clean cells, wings and blocks;
ii)   Perform maintenance work within their capability;
iii) Do their own laundry and cooking within their blocks if facilities were provided (at present they are centralised);
iv) Have the right to choose how they should be educated and what subjects to pursue including recognised academic qualifications;
v)   Be instructed by suitably qualified fellow prisoners;
vi) Undertake handicrafts and music lessons under instruction of fellow prisoners; and
vii) Organised sport and recreation.

These work demands 'would result in the prison authorities losing control over the prisoners' day to day activities.' The 'so-called "officers commanding" (OCs)' of the wings and blocks would draw up rotas for the carrying out of essential duties such as cooking, cleaning and laundering, and further rotas for other activities, such as education and handicrafts. '"Prisoners choice" in this scheme is a euphemism for paramilitary control.' The use of prisoner tutors, which was unexceptionable in controlled circumstances, would be a further extension of Provisional IRA control as the OCs would appoint education officers to oversee the teachers and the curriculum. The Government's aim was to give each prisoner an activity best suited to him, subject to the basic maintenance demands of the prisons as a whole being fulfilled – cooking, cleaning, laundry and such like. In the last resort, however, the allocation of the activities and control of the working day had to remain with the prison authorities. The range of educational and other activities was already wide and imaginative, and the Government would add to these as quickly as possible.

The prisoners demanded free association with 'fellow political prisoners', but no 'running about the block in large numbers' and 'no interference with the prison officers who may retain their supervisory role'. They also demanded freedom of movement within the wings, including between the hours of lock-up at night and opening in the morning, wing visits and segregation from Loyalists. This was 'the very nub of the prisoners' undiminished demand for political status.' Free association – the unrestricted access of all prisoners to all cells and rooms within a wing – 'means the end of effective physical control over whatever size or group of prisoners is involved.' Once twenty-five to fifty prisoners could assemble at will, staff were inevitably intimidated by the sheer number, whatever the guarantees the Provisional IRA might purport to offer. Loss of control meant that paramilitary instruction, indoctrination and punishment could be carried out without hindrance.

'Wing visits' were a further manifestation of loss of control. These were clearly aimed at facilitating the movement of the wing OCs – or block OCs – between the four wings of a block. This would help maintain the paramilitary command structure. Moreover, if movement across the central bar of the H-Block were granted, the integrity of the blocks as secure units would be internally destroyed. Segregation – newly expressed in the prisoners' statement as a Republican demand – ensured a homogenous area of control, within which the maintenance of 'discipline' would be untrammelled by prisoners of another political affiliation. The Government's position was that 'normal' association was already generous. Association was allowed for three hours each evening and at weekends. Prisoners also mixed at various other times, such as during exercise, games and meals. Supervision was vital to maintaining control and good order; the Government had a duty to protect not only prison officers but also individual prisoners and their property, although the Government's position was 'not immutable and some properly supervised association between wings may prove possible with some structural modifications'.

Prisoners demanded the right to one weekly visit and to one letter in and out each week. These demands were 'surprising because what is already available matches or exceeds the protesting prisoners demands.' They could send one statutory and seven privileged letters at the authorities' expense and receive a commensurate number of replies. Conforming prisoners already received one statutory and three privileged visits a month. The prisoners demanded the right to receive one 'special category type parcel' each week. To the prisoners, the acceptance by the authorities of this demand would be seen as the granting of a part of special category itself. The Government's position was that one parcel a week was already given to conforming prisoners. The prisoners demanded the restoration of full remission, which was lost as a punishment for protesting. Their objective was 'obviously to get their people out of prison as quickly as possible, particularly as many are now faced with the prospect of serving their sentences in full having effectively lost all their remission'. Prisoners in England and Wales serving sentences of more than one month were entitled to one-third remission of their sentences. Prisoners in Northern Ireland were entitled to one-half remission. But, as in England and Wales, remission could be forfeited for misconduct, although it could be restored after subsequent good behaviour. Prisoners who had abandoned their protest had had up to one-fifth of remission lost for non-violent protest action restored to them. Once the protests came to an end, though, there could be scope for improvement in this.

In the end, the differences between the prisoners and the Government 'are of principle and are not easily resolved. The prisoners want a special category type regime not because it is "better" but because it is plainly not an ordinary prison regime, but one appropriate to "political prisoners" or "prisoners of war" and which would facilitate maintaining the paramilitary structure.' If the Government conceded this it would be a 'great gain for the Provisional IRA' because it would confer a degree of legitimacy on their methods as well as on their aims, and therefore prejudice the fight against terrorism by reducing the deterrent effect of sentences and encouraging prisoners to expect an amnesty. Moreover, it would be 'very risky for the Government to go ahead with improvements hoping that it was dealing with prisoners who did accept the regime, and very foolish to do so knowing that they did not.' Any improvements the Government could make would fall well short of the five demands, so making them while the five demands in full were still on the table 'seriously risks prolonging the hunger strike if the strikers hoped that they could secure the balance. A lasting resolution of the protest will be reached only when the prisoners accept that control – applied intelligently and with restraint – is a matter for the prison authorities and it is the latter who must in the end decide how much control is enough.'[11]

This position did not mean that the NIO was unconcerned with the impact and the length of the hunger strike. There was also a growing concern within sections of the NIO with the shockwaves it was having on community relations within Northern Ireland. On 17 August, Blatherwick sent Blelloch a paper, based on the Political Affairs Bureau contacts in the community, on the social and political costs of the hunger strike. It did not attempt to assess the economic costs (for example to inward investment), nor the consequences for HMG's relations with the Republic or the US. Nor was it designed to be a 'concealed recommendation that we should change our stance on the "five demands".' But: 'The picture it paints is not a happy one. Even if the hunger strike were to end tomorrow, its consequences will be with us for a long time to come', warned Blatherwick.[12]

The paper began by describing the direct financial costs of the hunger strike and its consequences as roughly quantifiable. It was less easy to assess its political and social effects. Of these, the most important had been a sharp increase in the influence of the Provisional IRA in Catholic areas, the alienation of much of the minority community in Northern Ireland from the Government and the disruption of political life. Minority reactions to the hunger strike, however, were by no means uniform. Middle-class Catholics might not be directly affected, but they were concerned at what was happening to their co-religionists. Feelings had run highest in West Belfast, the Bogside/Creggan and localities in which the hunger-strikers' families lived. Even in these areas, surprisingly few (say 10%) seemed to take an active, concerned interest. Except among the under-20s, where recruiting was said to have prospered, active sympathy for the IRA was remarkably low. Most Catholics condemned them for their obduracy over the hunger strike and for cynical manipulation of the hunger-strikers, their families and minority sentiment. They criticized them for bringing trouble onto the streets, and for the wide moral gap between their alleged ideals and their methods. The minority community was conservative and religious, and even in the Falls and Turf Lodge many could see through the Provos' rhetoric to the unpleasant reality beneath.

Nevertheless, the fate of the hunger-strikers aroused atavistic sympathy. Few Catholics remained entirely unaffected. Out of a community of some half a million, nearly all knew families with members in the Maze. Many protestors were from decent homes, and their neighbours found it hard to accept that they were the criminals described by 'the Brits'. The Provos and their friends had played cleverly on Irish history and tradition to show that the strike was the latest phase of a noble cause, and that at bottom the British were responsible. Many Catholics, while giving no support to the Provos, found it increasingly difficult to refute this line. They found themselves under increasing tribal pressure at least to acquiesce in a cause they knew was wrong. They believed that the Government, far from trying to help them find a way out of their dilemma, was making things worse by demanding a total and humiliating surrender by the hunger-strikers and the Provisional leadership.

Most dangerously of all, they inclined increasingly to the view that the Government did not understand the dilemma they were in, or care about it, and that if the Government would not help them, they would soon have no option but to side against the British. This was probably what people meant when they spoke of a new '1916 complex', or what John Hume meant when he spoke to the Secretary of State about a possible coming 'explosion'. 'This is however for the future': the effects of the strike so far were bad enough. The Provos and INLA had gained a new pool of recruits: 'The feeling of alienation, bitterness and frustration we detected in Catholic areas in May has grown steadily stronger. People are becoming anti-British and less ready to give the system their support.' The Provisionals and their allies had succeeded in exploiting this background. They had engineered confrontations with the security forces in which the latter had inevitably made mistakes. These had been used in order to engineer further confrontations, on the familiar pattern of the early 1970s. The consequence was a widespread distrust of the RUC, and outright contempt and hostility for the Army, in particular the UDR. Because of this public hostility to the security forces, the Provisionals and their friends had been able to establish a hold in parts of the community, not least by threats and intimidation. They were unpopular, and people resisted them strongly – especially the clergy. But they were there. Thus, minority politics had been seriously disrupted. The local elections showed a swing of opinion in rural areas to 'green' parties like the IIP, and a swing in West Belfast towards candidates standing on an H-Block ticket. This proved to be a continuous process. The IIP had withdrawn from politics until the strike was over. Though the SDLP had so far resisted pressure to do likewise, they were losing members and influence to their 'greener' rivals, and had been brought to decide (rightly or wrongly) to opt out of the Fermanagh/South Tyrone by-election. On the Nationalist side, the Provos and their allies were making the running and outflanking the moderates.

At the same time, the gap between the communities had widened. Catholics were retreating in upon themselves. Many Protestants were dismayed at Sands' election, and were angry at Catholic sympathy for the hunger-strikers and at what they saw as the treachery of minority politicians who bowed to 'green' pressure while the IRA murder campaign continued. The increased polarization, reflected in the local election results in May, had led to a sharper sectarian divide and a sharper tone in many District Councils. The prospect of agreement on the political future of Northern Ireland seemed further off than ever. The Government's plan for a new advisory Northern Ireland Council seemed unlikely to get off the ground: the SDLP had said they would not take part in present circumstances, and the UUP's opposition to it had hardened. Even the Alliance party was depressed and wary of taking part.

In this atmosphere, the hunger-strike had become a test of the Government's credibility. So long as it failed to resolve the issue, its standing and the standing of Catholic moderates would continue to decline. On the other hand, any movement on the Government's part was apt to be seen as a sign of weakness of resolve to maintain law and order and uphold the Union. Many people throughout Northern Ireland believed that public morale was at an all-time low. Before the spring there had been guarded optimism about the future, but the hunger strike had revealed that attitudes were as entrenched as ever. It had also coincided with a sharp increase in unemployment. There was now deep uncertainty and doubt in all parts of the community, and no light at the end of the tunnel. For the moment this mood was masked by summer weather and holidays, but the mask could slip rapidly in the autumn. The end of the hunger strike would of course bring an immediate improvement. Pressure on the minority would be sharply reduced as the Provos' grip on minority life and politics loosened, but it would take a considerable time for fences to be mended between the communities, and between the minority and the Government. Resentment at Government 'intransigence' over the hunger strike, and at the security forces' activities in West Belfast, would take a long time to clear. A new generation of children had been 'infected with rampant Anglophobia. New heroes and myths had been created, and new wounds opened which would take years to heal.' For their part, Protestants would not easily forgive or forget Sands' election, or the trimming statements by Catholic leaders, lay and clerical. And, concluded the report, whatever the circumstances in which the hunger strike ended, Protestants were likely to find some confirmation of their suspicions that the IRA had won something.[13]

For the Government, this was depressing reading, but crucial to its strategy of preventing increasing alienation within the wider Catholic community were relations with the SDLP, for whose leader, John Hume, it was essential to try and find a way of ending the hunger strike in order to prevent his party haemorrhaging support to the Provisionals. Hume had also been asked (according to his account) by Gerry Adams to intervene to see what could be done to end the hunger strike. Following a meeting with Atkins, on 10 August, Hume spent a further 1½ hours with Blelloch and Blatherwick. They went over the hunger strike ground in some detail. Hume admitted that he had wondered whether Adams wanted him to try and fail, in order to destroy the SDLP's credibility further. Hume put forward tentatively the idea that HMG should grant '4½' demands and call them something else, for example a regime for high-risk prisoners. Blelloch explained why this was not possible, and made it clear that though the Government was ready to make changes in the prison regime, there was no prospect of the introduction of anything resembling a compound system, as the prisoners appeared to wish.[14] Hume telephoned Blelloch the following afternoon, seeking confirmation of three points that he recollected the Secretary of State as having made in their meeting. They were that:

(a) a 'suspension' of the hunger strike by the prisoners was one example of the kind of signal of good faith on their part which we would need before acting in the areas we had indicated in which further development was possible;

(b) there were three such areas (clothing, association and work);

(c) the other two, (though one of them – parcels, letters etc – was not a problem anyway) that correspond with the balance of the 5 demands might be covered by the forthcoming report of the ICRC.

Blelloch did not see (b) and (c) above being so tidily distinguished: 'and that further we did not know what the ICRC might say about any or all of the 5 areas.' Hume said that he fully understood this. He also asked about HMG's intentions on clothing, and Blelloch explained that the Government's position on this was not an area in which a point of principle was involved, and that further development was, accordingly, not ruled out, though such development did have real, practical problems associated with it (such as the need to control the type of clothing). Blelloch made it clear that Hume could not commit the Government on this, though if he chose to say that in his view this was not a problem area he was of course free to do so. Hume later rang Blelloch and took the opportunity to explore the word 'suspension' at (a) above. Blelloch thought that the Secretary of State, in using it, had in mind the realities of the situation: whatever the circumstances in which the hunger strike ended, it was always possible for a fresh one to be started up. There would be great dangers if the Provisionals tried to be 'clever' over suspension. Hume fully took this point also, but went on to say that he had informed his contacts that 'he had got nowhere' and was not going to be drawn into a negotiating process.[15]

With the Fermanagh/South Tyrone by-election imminent on 20 August, contested by Sands' electoral agent Owen Carron and Ken Maginnis of the Ulster Unionist Party, Hume telephoned the Irish Government, from Brittany, and was 'obviously well-informed on the situation on the ground in Northern Ireland and said that he believed this opinion among the minority had begun to shift heavily against the Provisionals on the hunger strike issue because of the efforts of the Lynch and Quinn families. He felt his party could now go on the offensive in the bye-election.'[16] Hume was preparing 'to issue a "major statement" on the SDLP's position on the hunger strike.' The National Armagh and H-Block Committee had issued repeated calls for the intervention of the SDLP, the Catholic Church and the Dublin Government on the H-Blocks crisis, which implied that the continuation of the crisis was somehow the fault of these bodies. Hume's response was to be as follows:

> The SDLP ... wish to point out that its point of departure so far as the prison crisis is concerned is completely different from that of the H-Block Committee.
>
> The campaign of violence of the IRA places a secondary value on human life.
>
> The approach of the SDLP is based on the principle that human life has a sacred primary value.
> We find it difficult to understand the position of the British Government. The British Government has ignored the advice which it has received repeatedly from the SDLP and the Irish Government. The intervention of the British Prime Minister is unfortunate in that it has made the crisis seem to be a personal issue so far as she is concerned.
> We say to the National H-Block Committee and its 'constituent paramilitary groups' that the best contribution they can make is to use their influence to end the violence.

Hume's reason for issuing the statement now was because Cardinal Ó Fiaich had given an interview to the *Sunday Press* that was very anti-British and 'revealed' in detail his meeting with Mrs Thatcher.[17] He telephoned Michael Lillis, in the Irish Government, on 18 and again on 19 August, revealing that he had received a visit from the McCloskey family, whose son Liam was on hunger strike, and Father McEldowney. The latter said that the mood of the prisoners whom he had visited the day before, and who included hunger-strikers and non-hunger-striking protesting prisoners, reflected a greater realization that they 'were getting nowhere'. At the same time, the determination of the hunger-strikers to continue with their protest was undiminished. McEldowney's private assessment was that the hunger strike could be solved, or at least suspended, at this point on a pretext that could involve less substantial concessions than the prisoners had originally demanded. McEldowney made the following proposal to Hume, which emanated, he said, from a prominent member of the Provisionals in the H-Blocks:

> The British Authorities would separately inform Mr Hume and the Irish Government of the details of what reforms they would implement in the event of the hunger strike ending (or being suspended);
>
> Mr Hume would personally inform those on hunger strike of these details and would confirm that the Irish Government had been given the same information as he had.

Hume told McEldowney, however, that he would not take any action unless he had a specific authorization from Brendan McFarlane to proceed. He asked McEldowney to take this matter up with McFarlane. Hume also mentioned another proposal, which emanated from Conradh na Gaeilge (Gaelic League), a non-governmental body that promoted the Irish language. The President of Conradh had met with the prisoners, including the hunger-strikers, on a number of occasions. The proposal was that the hunger strike would be suspended on the British concession of the right of prisoners, including hunger-strikers, to communicate orally and by letter with outsiders, including visitors, through the medium of the Irish language. Hume's view was, though this proposal might seem somewhat bizarre, that it reached the heart of the symbolic element in the hunger strike protest.[18]

Hume also contacted Blelloch to say that he had been contacted by McEldowney and mentioned a proposition – without going into detail as he had with the Irish – which he believed 'should not cause the NIO too much difficulty'. Blelloch took note. Hume telephoned again to say that he had secured the confirmation that McFarlane would accept the plan, and requested the approval of the NIO for McEldowney to make a special visit to the IRA OC. Blelloch consulted Liaison Staff and the Prisons Department, who agreed that there was no possible objection to this. Hume and the Maze were accordingly informed, and the visit duly took place. Hume telephoned Blelloch again in the afternoon to say that Father McEldowney had seen McFarlane; the priest repeated that the attitude of the prisoners was now more realistic in that they were getting nowhere with their hunger strike: they were still bound very tightly, however, by a feeling of solidarity among themselves and with the dead, and had a major psychological problem in giving up.

Blelloch noted that the proposition – unspecified the previous afternoon – now appeared to be that the prisoners wished to obtain from Hume and the Irish Government ('an angle Hume did not mention yesterday evening') an indication 'in private' of what was on offer, which, if provided by these guarantors, would be sufficient for them to 'suspend' (Hume quickly added that he was not sure what word they would actually use) the hunger strike and the protest action. McFarlane had apparently been less immediately receptive that day than had the prisoners, and Hume told Blelloch that he was now pondering the matter. He was ringing simply to keep Blelloch informed, and would phone when there was anything further to say. Blelloch thanked Hume for the information and made two comments: first, Blelloch said that 'we did indeed acknowledge the psychological problem and added that it was not part of our policy to work for outright victory of which we could make much future display. We sought an end to the protest for everybody's sakes.' Second, Blelloch said that 'we had, in our view, gone a very long way to spell out in public and in advance of the ending of the strike what was in our minds. But that there was a very great difficulty in going any further than that i.e. the difficulty that the prisoners would pocket what was offered and simply hold out for more. Hume noted the point.'[19]

Despite Hume's efforts to conjure up some solution, it was increasingly clear to the Department of Foreign Affairs in Dublin that there was now little way out of the impasse. The DFA's assessment of the position, on 20 August, took the view that: 'When one considers the H-Blocks hunger strike issue at this stage as compared to when it began it seems as if the problem and the cause have now been reversed and the focus of our policy may therefore need to be changed.' When the hunger strike campaign commenced, the cause of the problem was the fact that prisoners were in the process of self-immolation, and were likely to make significant gains in terms of IRA propaganda. The problem was that the British Government could not see its way to recognizing the dangers and dealing with the situation appropriately. The Irish Government's policy was rightly, therefore, directed at the British Government in these circumstances. As of now, however, the situation was reversed. The problem was not so much the fact that there were prisoners involved in self-immolation – 'the impact here in any event may be reducing' – or that the British Government was refusing to yield to their demands (although both these points were of course of concern), but that the Provisional IRA might in fact already have made the substantial gains that were threatened, 'and now pose a stronger challenge to our institutions than for many years.' The cause of this happening (which at this stage was secondary) was the unwillingness of the British Government to face up at an early stage to the prospect of this becoming the reality that it now was. Neligan made the point that the Provisionals had succeeded in setting back the assertion and acceptance everywhere of the cause of a united Ireland on a basis of reconciliation and consent. In Northern Ireland the Provisionals now occupied the centre of both the military and political stages, and this relatively advantageous position was not something that an organization like the PIRA was likely to yield easily. Further action by the Provisionals when the hunger strike ended could be contemplated in order to occupy this centrality of position in Northern Ireland's political scheme. In this respect Neligan made the point in his note that the prison protest would continue indefinitely, and it would be in the form of a hunger strike for as long as the IRA so decided.

The DFA paper recognized that the Provisionals had made considerable gains, both domestically and possibly internationally as well, although the full extent of these gains in the latter context and particularly in the US would take some time to become apparent. The rise to prominence and centrality of the PIRA was now the real problem, and the solution to the H-Blocks hunger strike issue, when it eventually came, would not be a solution to this. The Irish Government would have to consider for their part how they were going to counteract these gains, and a determined effort would sooner or later have to be made in this regard. It had maintained a consistently critical approach to the British authorities' handling of the issue: 'It must be considered whether this is getting us anywhere, whether it may be causing damage to the good relations between the two countries and whether this issue and the circumstances behind it is one on which we would wish to let our relationship founder.' It was obviously difficult to strike a balance between ensuring the need to maintain good relations with the British (which was obviously essential in the long term) and yet encouraging the British Government to face up to the situation and effect a solution. Neligan made the point that the limits of ingenuity and persistence had been reached, and indeed the limits of prudence exceeded, in Irish efforts so far to point the way towards an honourable compromise. In saying all this, however, one should not exaggerate the extent of the British Government's sensitivity. There was an understanding on their part of the Irish Government's delicate situation and the peculiarity of the circumstances of the moment. It might well be regarded that 'our activities on this front are nothing less than consistent with the well founded fears of a country that has been affected by this issue and indeed the whole Northern Ireland issue for a long time.' There was the point that the 'more legitimate our interest in this issue is seen to be by the British Government and the harder we exert it, the more legitimate will be seen to be our interest and involvement in the broader dimensions of the Northern Ireland problem.'

On balance it might well be that 'we could yet go a long way in subjecting the British Government to pressure without in any way seriously damaging our relationship. What we may have to be careful about however is the means by which further pressure on the British Government is exerted.' The more public pressure that was put on the British Government, coupled with public criticism of the Provisionals, the more likely there was to be public confusion about the issue nationally and internationally, and the more likely also that Mrs Thatcher's standing on the issue would harden. According to most observers, Mrs Thatcher became more rigid as the public criticism of her became more audible. Consideration had also to be given to the future effects of Government policy on attitudes domestically and whether, through overt and active criticism of the British Government, the Irish Government might unwittingly generate sympathy for the hunger-strikers and ingrain in people's minds a suspicion of the British Government, which might be difficult to counteract. These latter points were also of importance:

> ... when one speaks of internationalising the issue. If this means simply keeping friendly governments well informed this is hardly objectionable and indeed is a self-evident function of the Government's diplomatic services. If on the other hand it means using Third Parties to exert pressure on the British Government this may not only be getting Ireland's relative importance to these countries vis a vis Britain out of proportion but also further harden Mrs Thatcher's resolve.

It also called into question the uniqueness of the relationship that existed between Britain and Ireland:

> The answer to our concern regarding the problem of the H-Blocks does not lie in internationalising the issue but lies (as we would maintain in respect of all other issues concerning Northern Ireland) between the British and Irish Governments and through our bilateral dealings. The more we seek to involve others the more inadequate will be seen to be the uniqueness of our relationship and the realistic prospects of our acting in concert to solve the Northern Ireland problem generally.[20]

As the DFA completed its assessment, the Fermanagh/South Tyrone by-election result, on 20 August, was announced: it was won by Owen Carron (Anti H-Block) with a majority of 2,230 over Ken Maginnis (UUP). On a high poll (88.6%), Carron slightly improved the majority achieved by Sands in April. The poll result was:

Owen Carron (Anti H-Block Proxy Political Prisoner)	31,278
Ken Maginnis (UUP)	29,048

Carron's victory was widely deplored by non-Nationalists. The DUP said that the 'Unionists of Northern Ireland as a whole can only view with alarm and disgust the fact that over 31,000 people came out to vote for Owen Carron who has consistently supported the actions of the convicted terrorists in the H-Blocks'; while the moderate Alliance Party commented that 'those who voted for him carry a share of the responsibility for continued violence and death'. Maginnis called Carron's supporters 'fellow travellers of the IRA murderers who have gunned down innocent people in this constituency and who murdered our helpers after the last election'.[21]

As Republicans celebrated Carron's win, the mood was dampened by the news of the death of Michael Devine (aged 27) after sixty days on hunger strike. Devine's sister Margaret's husband Frankie McCauley, and his uncle Patsy Moore, were with him when he died. McCauley recalled: 'We wanted to make sure there was always somebody at the hospital near the end and that Micky would not die a lonely death, the way the prison didn't contact the McElwees and Tom McElwee died alone.' His family was told that Devine had twenty-four hours to live, but then he passed twenty-four hours, and then Father Murphy (the assistant prison chaplain), on the following night, said to McCauley that he could not see him passing six o'clock the next morning: 'Micky was not in a coma and though he was slipping into unconsciousness he could hear us because he would move his head to let us know. You couldn't have understood what he was saying as his teeth were sort of locked and his mouth paralysed.' He was in some pain, had not been able to take water and had not been to the toilet for four days. His bladder was full up and, when he drank, water and acid would just come out of his mouth. Earlier, Theresa, his aunt, had wanted to put Vaseline on his mouth to ease the pain from Devine's chapped lips, which he was constantly biting, but he said 'No'. When lying in bed 'he was always sliding down and would need pulling up so that he could just lie in the centre of the bed with his hands outspread and balancing his frail body.'

McCauley remembered:

> We were coming back and forth to the cell and at about one o'clock in the morning when we were waiting in a room we could hear Micky roaring in pain. We then went to him and he was freezing. The medics were changing him where he must have vomited over himself and asked us to give them a few minutes. We sat with Micky and felt his feet. They were freezing. I went up his leg a bit, if you could call it a leg, it was thinner than my wrist.

Father Murphy had explained to McCauley that 'when death was creeping up on Micky coldness would set in. His knees were stone cold, I felt his forehead and his ears and nose and they were turning cold.' They sat and prayed, and at about six o'clock in the morning Devine lost consciousness. The doctor pressed his heel and said something about it being the weakest part of the body:

> There was no response from Micky … the next thing the priest walked in – the authorities must have known it was nearly over and sent for him. This was about ten past seven. I said to Fr Toner, 'were you sent for?' and he said, 'Yes'. He started to say the Rosary and Patsy and I sat there praying.
>
> I was watching the monitor which registered Micky's pulse and heart and the next thing I saw it go flat and bleep and I knew Micky was dead. They told us to get out of the cell; we would have to wait on the RUC and identify Micky's body.
>
> Micky died at exactly twelve minutes to eight because I looked at my watch. The authorities must have taken two minutes to confirm him dead and that's why they said he died at ten to eight.
>
> A cop came in and Patsy went in and identified the body.

Father Toner then said that he would get Devine's personal belongings. These were his suit and shoes, which he wore in court when he was sentenced in June 1977. There were letters that people had sent in to him when he was on the strike, and his glasses. His sister Margaret had been exhausted at the vigil, and she had left the prison at seven on the night before his death. Devine's last request was that, if he went into a coma, Margaret was not to sanction medical intervention. 'The bond between them, she being seven years his elder, and his only sister (both their parents are dead), was very strong', recalled her husband. Devine had said to Margaret: 'Now, there's to be no needles (injections). You are going to come under a lot of pressure because you're the only one belonging to me.' He always called Frankie:

> … McCauley, and he said to me: 'McCauley, look, you go with her, everywhere she has to go in here and watch these bastards. Sign nothing. They'll say to you they want to give you something for my eyes.' Michael hadn't very good eyesight and he knew they'd go first. He said to me: 'They'll say to you sign for something for my eyes or pains in my head. Just say, "No". I don't want anything. I'm depending on you to pull that through.'

The doctor had come in to McCauley and Devine's uncle Patsy, and said that 'he could bring Micky round before he went into a bad condition. I said we were standing by his last wishes.' A local priest, from the Creggan, told Margaret that he had something to tell her that she should always remember if she ever had any doubt in her mind about what she should or should not have done: 'Micky had told him that he was worried about Margaret signing to get him treatment. But, according to the priest, Micky had told him that "if Margaret signs to get me treatment she'll only be prolonging my agony, because as soon as I come round again I'm going back on the hunger strike."' The priest told Margaret that she had nothing to worry about as those were Devine's very words to him. He said that 'he hadn't told her before because he didn't want to influence her at the time; it was her decision. But she should know that Micky was totally determined to go back on hunger strike.'[22]

With no end of the strike in sight, Owen Carron wrote and asked to meet Mrs Thatcher. Instead he was offered a meeting with Michael Alison in Stormont Castle on 28 August. Alison was accompanied at the meeting by officials such as Blelloch. Carron came alone (as had been agreed with him previously). Alison began by saying that he felt bound to ask at the outset – having read Carron's election address – whether he intended to take his seat in the House of Commons and to take the Oath of Allegiance. Carron replied that he could not consider going to Westminster while the hunger strike continued, and he had been elected on a non-attendance basis. He could not commit himself to what his position might be when the hunger strike ended. Alison explained that, while he would do all he could to be helpful, this made it necessary for the Government to reserve its position a little in its dealings with him. It was necessary to bear in mind those of Carron's constituents who would not in effect be represented. Carron accepted this, but did not wish to pursue the point further. He had come to see the Minister in order to impress on him the urgency of a settlement of the hunger strike issue. He believed that a vast amount of support for and goodwill towards the prisoners existed in the community. There was also tremendous pressure on the Government to resolve the issue, internationally and from the broad stream of nationalist opinion in Northern Ireland. He believed that the prisoners were willing to be flexible and that there should be some movement on the part of the Government. Alison assured Carron that the Government fully understood the immense emotional feeling generated by the hunger strike, and that the last thing that he, or the Prime Minster or the Secretary of State, wanted was for the unnecessary deaths to continue, but the hunger strike was an extreme form of pressure. A democratic government was not a free agent, but was answerable and responsive to the electorate and could not be 'hijacked' by this form of duress. Nevertheless, the gap between the respective positions of the Government and the hunger-strikers did appear to be somewhat less than it had seemed at one time, now that the prisoners had claimed that they were not seeking a differentiated regime.

Carron stressed that the protesting prisoners saw themselves as being different from other criminals because they had been convicted under special legislation, and because of the motivation behind the deeds for which they had been convicted. The hunger strike was the culmination of the protest; they saw it as something to which they had been obliged to resort rather than a means of exerting duress. They were, however, prepared to see the regime that they were seeking extended to all prisoners. Alison then explained the difficulties that arose over the prisoners' stated wish only to do work in their own H-Blocks or wings. Cooking, for example – which the prisoners had said they were willing to do – was done in central facilities outside the blocks. It would be far-fetched, even if it were considered desirable, to build separate kitchens in each block. Various other activities, such as laundry, vocational training and industrial work, took place outside the blocks. The protesting prisoners' claim that they wanted the same regime for all prisoners was not compatible with their desire to work only in their own blocks. The prison could not be run on such a basis, with no prisoner being required to go outside his own block. Carron, though, wondered if this was then a purely practical problem and whether the Government saw a special arrangement for some prisoners, to enable them to remain in their own blocks, as the answer. Alison acknowledged that Northern Ireland prisoners were of a different type to those in Great Britain or elsewhere in Europe because of the exceptionally high proportion of young prisoners serving very long sentences. He believed that this difference was already reflected in the Northern Ireland prison regime – with, for example, 50% remission and the freedom to wear their own clothes outside working hours. There could, though, be no differentiation for a particular group within the Northern Ireland regime itself. In any case, he understood that the prisoners were no longer seeking differentiation.

Carron added that the prisoners saw segregation from Loyalist prisoners as the basic issue; they did not want to be desegregated as in the conforming blocks. The authorities were able to exercise control within the compounds, but even so there was a better atmosphere there and a system agreeable to everyone concerned – both prisoners and prison warders. There were statistics, he claimed, to show that prisoners who were released from the compounds were less likely to be convicted again than those emerging from the H-Blocks. Alison replied that integration was a policy that the Government believed was valid. It made good, practical sense in terms of running prisons efficiently and economically, and it was obviously valuable that prisoners should learn to live together. The Gardiner Report had criticized the compound system as being a regime that did not allow for the proper exercise of the sentences imposed by the courts, such a regime not acting as a sufficient deterrent to those contemplating crime. The statistics on which Carron based his proposition that prisoners leaving the compounds were less likely to re-engage in crime could not be regarded as overriding.

Carron then asked whether the Government could not state, even privately, what changes it was prepared to make in the prison regime. The H-Block issue had to be grappled with; the Government had to agree that the campaign had alienated people from authority. The problem was that the Government would not be specific. Alison replied that the Government had already set out its position publicly. Its position on remission, as he had told the Irish Commission for Justice and Peace, was that there was already 20% restoration of lost remission for those who ceased protesting, and in an environment of conformity the possibility of further change was not ruled out. He did not believe that remission was a significant issue between the Government and the protesters. On clothes, the Government had already introduced civilian clothing, and out of working hours the wearing of prisoners' own clothes was allowed. Further improvement could only mean one thing, but it could not be used to 'buy off' the hunger strike. There was no reason to believe that it would do so. The important issues were, in reality, association and work. Here again, the possibility of developments was not ruled out.

Carron explained that the prisoners saw work, association and segregation as intertwined, and as the real problem. Why could the Government not spell out precisely what it would do? Alison clarified the impossibility of producing a detailed schedule of what work each prisoner could be expected to do. There was a wide range within each type of work; the ICJP had made some suggestions about other types of work, such as charitable work, and the Government had no objection in principle to this; indeed, it was always seeking ways in which to extend the range of work available, but this did not alter the need for the Governor to retain the right to decide who should work where. Carron thought that the prisoners were concerned about the principle of being able to choose, at least in the first instance, to do what they felt they were suited to. Alison emphasized that the system could not function if the Governor did not retain control over the disposition of prisoners, but nevertheless, every effort was made to 'fit round pegs into round holes'. Given the endless permutations in the work regime, it was not possible, while the protesters were not prepared to work, for the Government to be specific about what it would do. Carron felt that the Government, being in a position of strength as compared to the prisoners, could afford to show some generosity.

Turning to association, Alison pointed out that, although the term 'association' referred to specified periods of time when prisoners could mix with a relative degree of freedom, there was also association in practice at other times of day, during work, exercise and so forth. A prisoner ceasing to protest would find himself with a much greater degree of association than before. Carron asked whether the fact that the Government was considering allowing the mixing of prisoners from the wings of a block did not invalidate the argument about loss of control. In a desegregated, conforming situation this sort of mixing could create control problems. Alison replied that the question of control had been very carefully examined and it had been decided that, subject to some physical adjustments in the block, association between two wings would be acceptable in a conforming situation. Desegregated prisoners already mixed satisfactorily in the conforming blocks. Carron replied that the hundreds of prisoners who did not accept segregation saw it as inseparable from the issues of work and association. The policy on segregation created an unnecessary problem in the prison system. Alison repeated that it was a policy to which the Government adhered, was accepted by conforming prisoners, and that it was not in fact one of the 'five demands'. Even without the hunger strike, prisoners who were refusing to work and thus not conforming were in any case segregated. It was certainly not worth their dying over this issue. Carron's response was to repeat his request that the Government should spell out what would be allowed and what would not; he did not believe that the exercise of control by the authorities was really an issue. When Alison reminded him of the incompatibility of the prisoners' claim that they were not pressing for a differentiated regime with their refusal to work outside their own blocks, Carron suggested that their statement that differentiation was not being sought was made so that the Government would not make an issue of the request for a separate status. The meeting, 'which was calm and friendly throughout,' came to an end after about one hour. Alison expressed the hope that a situation would arise when Carron felt that he could attend the House of Commons.[23]

The importance of the exchange was that it was the first time a British Minister had communicated, as far as he could, personally to a Republican the flexibility that the Government was prepared to show after the hunger strike was over. Even so, it seemed as if there was to be no end to the stand-off between Mrs Thatcher's Government and the hunger-strikers. In fact, the crucial point in the hunger strike was about to be reached.

At approximately 14.10 on Friday, 4 September, on the fifty-second day of his fast, Matt Devlin's consciousness became clouded and his family was summoned. His mother and brother duly arrived at 16.05. After seeing Devlin and the doctors, they then gave the necessary written approval to effect medical treatment. This was instituted immediately, and he left the prison hospital at 16.45 on transfer to the Intensive Care Unit (ICU) of the Royal Victoria Hospital. The following day he was moved to Ward 18, Musgrave Park Hospital, and was soon eating normally. Lawrence McKeown's fast condition had also worsened considerably towards the end of the week, and his family accepted prison facilities on 5 September to enable them to stay in the prison hospital overnight. On the seventieth day of his fast, the doctor examined McKeown at approximately 11.35 on Sunday 6th September, concluding that McKeown had largely lost mental and physical control. His mother signed the necessary document to save his life. He was transferred to the ICU of the Royal Victoria Hospital at 12.35, and the next day to Musgrave Park Hospital. He was also soon eating normally.

This was the turning point in the hunger strike. The NIO noted that the 'first major setbacks have occurred in the campaign.' Firstly, the impact of further deaths was diminished by the likelihood that relatives would ask for resuscitation. Secondly, there was now a major gap in the chain of deaths. The weakening of the INLA's commitment to the hunger strike – which was running out of volunteers – posed a threat to Republican unity within the prison. Finally, the intervention of Father Faul as the 'champion of the relatives' rights' had posed the campaigners with definite problems since it was impossible to brand him as a 'tool of British Imperialism'; nevertheless, it was clear from a number of indications that the strike was not over so far as the PIRA was concerned. A weekend H-Block Conference also envisaged preparations for a long campaign, with its election of a new committee and prolonged talk of future policy and by-elections. The appeals for Republicans to register for voting purposes – an entirely new departure in recent history – 'must be seen in the same light',[24] noted the NIO.

The fissure in the hunger strike coincided with the arrival of a new Secretary of State in Northern Ireland: on 14 September, James Prior took the hot seat at Stormont Castle, moving from Employment, while Mrs Thatcher shifted Atkins, who became Lord Privy Seal, effectively the deputy Foreign Secretary. Prior was joined in Northern Ireland by Lord Gowrie, an Anglo-Irish peer, as Minister of State replacing Alison, who moved over to Employment.

In the aftermath of the new appointments, Blelloch discussed with D. J. Wyatt and other officials (Doyne-Ditmas and Miss MacGlashan) 'where we might be going on the hunger strike.' On 21 September, Wyatt replied with their conclusions. Wyatt pointed out that the impetus that was keeping the hunger strike going clearly now came from within the prison. All the evidence pointed this way, 'even though we are uncomfortably ill-informed on the thinking of the protesters and the undercurrents which may exist there.' The Provisional leadership outside the prison was apparently content to let the prisoners make the running, taking what propaganda and political advantages they could, but neither directing nor controlling the protest. The protesters themselves did not appear yet to be in the least ready to settle for anything short of their five demands. Every 'do-gooder who has tried to persuade us that there is a half-way house has succeeded only in proving that the prisoners will settle for all or nothing.' In these circumstances, 'there seems literally nothing that we can do directly to bring the protest to an end.' It was likely that the end would come for 'reasons over which we have no control' (Wyatt thought that it might be because the influence of families meant that more people were giving up the hunger strike than were continuing it; because McFarlane lost his authority; because the Provisional leadership decided to take a different view; or because the propaganda value of the protest was seen to be a declining asset). When the moment came at which the prisoners were prepared to settle for something short of the five demands, 'we shall need to be very ready to produce the necessary face-saving devices to enable them to claim that they have gained something by their sacrifice.' This of course was 'postulated on the assumption that we remain unwilling to give them their 5 demands which is the only other way of ending the strike.'

Meanwhile, explained Wyatt, he and the other officials concerned:

> ... asked ourselves what should the Government's posture be. From our point of view it is quite ridiculous that all political debate should be dominated by the issue of the 400 protesters in a Province which is plagued by terrorism, whose industry is collapsing, whose political institutions are in abeyance, and whose constitutional future is under question.

In other words, 'we concluded that the major requirement in dealing with the hunger strike was that Government should be seen to have priorities different from those of the Provisionals and their allies.' The difficulty was that the level of emotion in the Catholic community, North and South, about the hunger strike was sufficiently high for it to need a rather large distraction to make them think about anything else; the larger issues were difficult to deal with whilst the Catholics were in their present mood. Nevertheless:

> ... we concluded that the hunger strike whilst making it more difficult also made it much more desirable to make progress on the twin roads of the Government's policy, namely political development within Northern Ireland and a rapprochement between London and Dublin. We should make a great mistake if we were to conclude that both these should be put on the long finger because of the hunger strike since to do so would merely enhance the value of the hunger strike to its supporters.

The new Secretary of State's expressed intention to make a determined effort to reverse Northern Ireland's economic decline fitted wholly into this thinking and could only be helpful. The officials discussed other aspects of the administration of Northern Ireland, 'at which we might take a fresher look in the context of finessing the hunger strike', but concluded that there was insufficient scope for the sort of major Government activity that might put the hunger strike into its proper perspective. Meanwhile, the Information Services aimed to switch argument away from questions about 'who buys the clothes which convicted criminals wear on to why they are in prison in the first place and a booklet about acts of Provisional terrorism which should help to set the humanitarian argument in context is now ready for printing.'[25]

Reflecting on this, Blelloch put his own thoughts down on paper for Prior.[26] Philip Woodfield had sent a minute to the Secretary of State, on his arrival, summarizing the present position on the hunger strike. It suggested that there were three possible future courses of action: to sit tight, to make a gesture, or to finesse the issue. Wyatt's minute discussed the third of these: the object of Blelloch's note was to provide a basis for discussion of the second. Blelloch considered that there were four points worth registering by way of background. The first was the nature of the issue between HMG and the prisoners. In a sense, argued Blelloch, HMG and the prisoners had, to date, been addressing two quite different things. HMG based its position on the existing prison regime and on a broad commitment to maintain and *improve*, as resources and the requirements of security permitted, what it believed was already a good and enlightened system. The prisoners rejected the system and wished to substitute something else. Thus HMG and the prisoners did not, at the moment, share, as common ground, a single spectrum of possibilities, with each taking its stand at a different point of the spectrum and with the possibility, therefore, of finding some common point along it. The importance of this point was simply that actions taken by HMG consistent with its commitment to improve the existing regime might be irrelevant to the solution of the prisons dispute until such time as the prisoners acknowledged that the existing prisons regime (however improved) was all that was on offer.

The second background issue was the likely outcome. The logic of Blelloch's first point above was that in theory it:

> ... requires unconditional surrender by one of the two parties: either the prisoners give up their ideas of special category status or HMG accepts that it has to re-introduce it, at any rate for a proportion of the present prison population. In fact our own thinking has always been that 'unconditional surrender' by the prisoners is an outcome that is neither necessary to HMG or even very desirable.

Five years of a protest culminating in the hunger strikes were going to have to be claimed to have produced something; for some prisoners it might be necessary to serve their sentences in a form of protest that allowed them to claim, de facto, a kind of special status: 'Our own view has been that the most likely level of stable non-conformity was that of a no-work protest of the kind at present sustained in Armagh, where the prisoners are clothed, refrain from prison work, and, for that, lose some remission and association.' Such a form of protest was manageable in prison terms, and was of no propaganda value to the Provisional IRA. The two problems had always been how to get the prisoners clothed, and then to determine what level of punishment for refusing to work was sufficient to deter all but the hardened minority from pursuing this form of protest on the one hand, but on the other was not so harsh as to provide propaganda value and perhaps invite the attentions of bodies like the ECHR. Blelloch concluded that 'one thing we have gained during the course of the strike is widespread acceptance that our own clothing will be introduced.' Given the controversy surrounding the previous autumn's decision to switch to civilian-style clothing, this acceptance was a considerable plus, and did open the way to the 'no-work' protest that the NIO envisaged.

The third background point Blelloch identified was the multiple audiences: 'Throughout, we have tried to take account of the fact that whatever HMG says or does is going to be studied, and responded to, by a number of audiences, notably the prisoners, the Provisional IRA outside the prisons, the two communities in Northern Ireland, British and Irish public opinion, and opinion overseas.' A course of action that may be appropriate to one or more of these might also be highly inappropriate to the rest. In particular, 'we have had to try to reconcile the need to be very firm with the prisoners (in order to bring home that there really is no chance of their securing all they want) with being very reasonable in the eyes, say, of the Catholic population in Northern Ireland.' It followed that gestures designed to ease the position of the latter could actually be counter-productive in terms of ending the hunger strike by encouraging the hunger-strikers to hold on in the belief that by doing so they would secure more than was already on offer.

Finally, Blelloch turned to the present position. Much was made of the 4 July statement: the claim for political status as such was dropped, as was the demand to be treated differently from other prisoners. The language was moderate, and important concessions appeared to be made on both association and work. In practice, the differences remained wide: 'There is no present evidence that the prisoners are ready yet to settle for something short of the "5 demands".' Within the last fortnight, for example, the prison chaplains had told the NIO that 'the prisoners' leadership still see things in all or nothing terms.' The Provisional IRA for its part did not seem to be much interested in settling the strike: it would exploit its propaganda value while it lasted, but had no ideas of its own about how it might be ended short of the five demands. In the Northern Ireland community, there was probably widespread acceptance that the Government meant what it said about not conceding the five demands at all and not being forced to act under duress – though of course opinion would differ about the wisdom of the Government's stand on these matters. The full weight of the Catholic hierarchy seemed now to be behind the efforts to persuade the families successfully to intervene. Turning to future possibilities, Blelloch observed that, obviously, in considering fresh action, Ministers would want to distinguish between their impact on the prisoners (who alone could bring the hunger strike to an end) and on opinions and attitudes other than those of the prisoners.

In fact, the end of the hunger strike was aided by a crucial meeting in the afternoon of Monday, 28 September, when the new Minister of State, Lord Gowrie, had a meeting in Stormont Castle, at their request, with relatives of five of the remaining six hunger-strikers. The request for the meeting had been received the night before via Independent Councillor Jim Canning acting on behalf of Father Faul, who had convened a meeting of relatives of the same families the day before. It had not proved possible to contact the Devine family, so they were not represented at the meeting. The following were present:

Lord Gowrie	Mr Eddie Carville	-	Brother and sister of [Hugh] Carville
Mr Blelloch	Mrs McElroy		[IRA, joined hunger strike 31 August]
Mr Brooker	Mrs Pickering	-	Mother of [John] Pickering [IRA, joined strike 7 September]
	Mrs Hodgins	-	Mother and sister of [Gerard] Hodgins
	Mrs Quinn		[IRA, joined strike 14 September]
	Mr McMullen	-	Father of [Jackie] McMullen [IRA, joined strike 17 August]
	Louise and Ann Sheehan	-	Sisters of [Patrick] Sheehan [IRA, joined strike 10 August]
	Mr and Mrs McWilliams	-	Hodgins' uncle and aunt

Gowrie opened by saying that he was pleased to have this opportunity to meet the relatives, although of course the meeting had been called at their request. He appreciated the difficulties that confronted them as the families of the hunger-strikers, and said that he was disposed to be helpful to them. He stressed that it was to be a private meeting. Mr McWilliams opened for the relatives by saying that there did not seem to be much hope of solving the problem. Relatives had put their heads on the block by coming to see the Minister, and they wished to know whether or not he had the authority to bring the problem to an end. In reply, Gowrie said that the Government had been meticulous in trying to preserve the position of the families. It had not in any way sought to bring pressure to bear on them, nor would it do so in the future. He urged the families to bring their views out into the open so that they could be discussed; he would see how things developed thereafter. Mr McWilliams then spoke to say that the families did not have power over the hunger-strikers and were critical of what they considered to be HMG's intransigence. They (the families) were unclear about HMG's responses to the five demands, and thought that the conflict had developed into a battle of wits as to who could endure for longer. It had been suggested that they ought to seek a meeting with someone in the NIO, perhaps the Secretary of State, but they had been surprised at the speed with which that day's meeting had been arranged. He asked what the Government's position was on the five demands, and complained that none of the relatives had been told directly by the NIO or by Ministers what the details were.

Lord Gowrie explained that his position was as follows. The Government would not negotiate over the five demands, either through intermediaries or directly with the hunger-strikers, nor would it be forced to act under duress. It had been the view of successive Governments that more would be lost by doing so than would be gained. Whilst he recognized the courage and conviction of these young men, nonetheless he considered them to be misguided. If, however, the hunger strike did come to an end, Gowrie promised that the following things would happen. First, the Government would not claim a large public victory and crow about success, (this was not of course to deny the press the freedom to express a resolution of the problem in such terms). Second, as Minister responsible for prisons, he had absolute authority to build on and make further improvements to the prison regime for all prisoners. Although he believed that improvements had already been offered, prison life was not a static existence; ideas moved on, and the chance of further improvements could be examined in relation to work, association, remission and clothing. As a realist he knew that if the men finished their fast they would be looking for something to save face, but he as the Minister could not say 'You come off and we will offer you X, Y and Z'. The decision to come off the hunger strike had to be taken by the strikers themselves, but thereafter Ministers would try to be helpful.

There then followed a general discussion about the nature of the various protests. The relatives seemed to be unable to agree about the reasons behind them. Mrs Hodgins said that they had nothing to do with prison conditions because the prison was a modern one. Mrs Pickering seemed to attribute them to the way that prisoners were ill-treated by prison officers, whereas the Sheehan sisters were of the firm view that it was the prisoners' status as political prisoners that was at stake; they wanted to be treated differently. Mr McWilliams said that it all went back to the political problem of the Irish versus the English. He maintained in effect that sentencing policy in the courts varied depending on an individual's political point of view. He compared his nephew's sentence of fourteen years with that of a Loyalist who had been given three years. His relative (Hodgins) had not been found in possession of anything; the Loyalist had been found in possession of 1,600 rounds of ammunition and six rifles. Thus he saw his community as cornered by the political situation, Diplock Courts, and the like. William Whitelaw had granted political status, which had then been retracted. In such a situation it was inevitable that the prisoners would see themselves as political prisoners, and they saw no alternative to a hunger strike.

In reply, Gowrie did not dismiss the hunger-strikers out of hand. He acknowledged their courage, but could not accept their motives, nor could he negotiate with them 'without calling into question the credibility of the whole of our civil system.' He rejected any suggestion that the judiciary sentenced differently along sectarian lines, and pointed out that the Diplock Courts only existed as a response to the problem of intimidation of jurors. The same problem existed in the Irish Republic. Gowrie reiterated that the decision to end the hunger strike lay in the hands of the strikers themselves, and that the Government would try to be helpful once the strike had ended, but that it would not contemplate changes under duress. As a Minister he had to tread carefully, not least because the problem not only encompassed the prisoners themselves, but also the organizations behind the prisoners. After Gowrie had restated his offer of help, and the terms under which he would be prepared to offer it, Mrs Hodgins urged him to put his commitment in writing. She thought that if the Minister did this, the strike could be ended in a matter of days. In reply to this request, Lord Gowrie said that he would try to think whether there was anything he could say, and any way in which he could say it, that would be seen as an earnest of his good faith. He believed that a good deal of work had been done on the areas of work, association, remission and clothing, and that there was scope for still further change, but not under pressure of a violent protest, since violence was violence, even if self-directed.

Mrs Hodgins, meanwhile, thought that if the hunger-strikers were given their own clothes, plus free association within each block, they would bring all forms of protest to an end. Mr McWilliams maintained that prisoners were already segregated on sectarian lines in the prisons. At this point, John Blelloch assured him that they were not; other than in the protesting blocks, prisoners were mixed within the wings and in some cases within individual cells. Mr McWilliams then also said that if the Minister were to make a statement or put something in writing to the effect that improvements would be made, the hunger strike would end. Lord Gowrie asked how it would be if he gave an undertaking to see the hunger-strikers, to hear what they had to say and explain to them what improvements would be made after they had properly come off the hunger strike. The Sheehan sisters urged him to go and see them immediately; they said that the hunger-strikers had come to the point where they needed to negotiate; there was no possibility of them ending their fast of their own accord. They thought that the gesture of the Minister meeting the strikers and listening to them might help. Gowrie reiterated that he could not act under duress, not least because in a 'life and death' atmosphere, anything said was liable to be misunderstood or distorted in a way that could lead to further unnecessary deaths. It was suggested that the Minister might instead go in to meet McFarlane, but Gowrie dismissed this on the grounds that, whilst he might be able to do something to help the hunger-strikers individually, the organizations behind them were a different matter. Mr McWilliams accepted the point entirely – that the Minister could not negotiate with the PIRA. One of the Sheehan sisters then said that she now realized that the Minister was never going to negotiate with the prisoners whilst they were still fasting. Lord Gowrie agreed that this was so, but reminded the meeting that he was willing to re-examine clothing, and matters pertaining to work and remission, once they had finally come off. He would also be prepared to meet them then. He asked the relatives to recognize the serious political ramifications for him of the latter undertaking.

As the meeting drew to a close, Mr McWilliams urged Gowrie to give them some form of statement, as Mrs Hodgins had suggested. The Sheehan sisters did not think that what was on offer would make any difference, but urged Gowrie to make a statement anyway as there was nothing to lose. Mr McWilliams took a more optimistic view. He had not come to the meeting with any hopes at all, but had found a small amount of reassurance in what the Minister had said. He too would welcome a statement. Gowrie, though, foresaw the difficulty from his point of view of putting out a statement that the relatives had now told him would have no effect, and that would in any case bring criticism to bear upon him from other quarters. Blelloch agreed regarding the difficulty of drafting an unequivocal statement; the experiences of the previous Christmas had demonstrated the immensity of such a task. Mrs Hodgins ventured to suggest that if the hunger strike were brought to an end, the blanket protest would cease too. The Sheehan sisters disagreed, and envisaged hunger-strikers going on to the blanket protest whilst waiting for any promised improvements to be made. One of the Sheehan sisters asked whether Gowrie would be prepared to talk to ex-hunger-strikers who were on the blanket protest rather than fully conforming. The Minister said that under controlled conditions he would, but that he would have to choose how he went about it. The meeting closed after nearly two hours with the relatives again urging the Minister to seriously consider making some form of statement. Gowrie contented himself with saying that he had been happy to meet them, at their request, and he advised them to say, if they were asked about what had taken place once they were outside the meeting, that they had put their points fully and that he had listened. This they agreed to do.[27]

The meeting with Gowrie left the families in no doubt that the Government would not make any concessions to the prisoners as long the hunger strike continued. Events now seemed to converge, undermining the hunger strike fatally. On 24 September, Bernard Fox, (day thirty-two) ended his fast as he seemed to be 'dying too quickly'. Two days later Liam McCloskey (day fifty-five) ended his fast after his family stated that they would call for medical intervention if he became unconscious. When it became clear, on 2 October, that the families of all the remaining hunger-strikers were prepared to intervene to prevent further deaths, leading Republicans prepared the ground for the ending of the hunger strike. Danny Morrison claimed that: 'The hunger strike ... is being actively subverted by people within the Irish establishment, by the SDLP but particularly by the Irish hierarchy who are working on the emotions and putting moral pressure on the understandably distressed relatives'. Richard McAuley stressed that if the hunger strike tactic were to succeed, more deaths were necessary, although he concluded that: 'The future of the hunger strike rests with the prisoners'.[28]

On the following day, 3 October, the hunger strike ended. A statement from inside the Maze announced:

> We, the protesting political prisoners in the H-Blocks and the men on hunger strike, have reluctantly decided in this the seventh month of the hunger strike to end our fast.
>
> We have been robbed of the hunger strike as an effective protest weapon principally because of the successful campaign waged against our distressed relatives by the Catholic hierarchy, aided and abetted by the Irish establishment (the SDLP and Free State Political Parties) which took no effective action against the British Government and did everything to encourage feelings of hopelessness among our kith and kin. The success of this campaign meant that the British Government could remain intransigent as the crucial political pressure which flows from the threat of death or actual death of hunger strikers was subsiding not increasing.[29]

Once the hunger strike had concluded, members of the NHAC were quick to deny that it had been defeated. Bernadette McAliskey announced: 'Our compassion goes out to the families who decided to intervene in the hunger strike … The British may think they have beaten one half of us and intimidated the other half. They have made a mistake. We have international support and we will not accept that our political prisoners are criminals'. Gerry Adams adopted a similar theme: 'National consciousness has been aroused; internationally, the prisoners are recognised as political and all that remains is the securing of conditions suitable to that status.' He looked forward to the Government moving towards the implementation of 'the conditions outlined by the prisoners on July 4 and August 6', which he claimed 'would permanently end the prison protest'. Although he did not comment on whether the prison protest would continue, he doubted whether there would be a third hunger strike. He announced, however, that 'we could well field candidates if the Secretary of State launches an initiative involving elections'. On the military front, Morrison claimed that the British Government privately regarded the Provisional IRA as a legitimate anti-imperialist force and that one day the British would be forced to negotiate with them. An unnamed Sinn Féin spokesman was quoted by the *Observer* (4 October) as saying: 'The position of the IRA is stronger now than it has been for years'. Nevertheless, there was no immediate military backlash to the ending of the hunger strike.

Cardinal Ó Fiaich said that the ending of the fast provided the authorities with an opportunity to show 'generosity and compassion in their attitude to prison reform', and John Hume added that it was now 'a time for the Government to show magnanimity and to make a serious and positive effort to solve the entire prison crisis'. The Taoiseach, whilst also welcoming the news, at the same time called on the IRA to end its campaign of violence. Unionists, however, were more cautious. The Reverend Robert Bradford (UUP) commented: 'It smells of a deal. I believe there are very serious concessions being granted including remission and clothing', while Jim Molyneaux (the UUP leader) said that, although he did not believe a deal had already been struck, he hoped that the Government 'would not make the mistake of rushing into concessions under the threat which has been made by certain churchmen that the hunger strike will be renewed unless concessions are granted'. A DUP spokesman said that their party was also 'gravely suspicious' and hoped that the Government would not be foolish enough to 'reward' the IRA with concessions in the jail.[30] From Canberra, Mrs Thatcher issued a short statement declaring: 'I am delighted to hear that this waste of life is at an end.'[31]

From within the NIO, the Government now turned its attention to what it could and could not do in terms of modifying the prison regime. Prison Rule 63 provided that: 'Every convicted prisoner shall be provided with clothing sufficient for warmth and health in accordance with a scale approved by the Department, and shall, except as otherwise approved by it, be required to wear such clothing.' It was noted that a decision by the Secretary of State that prisoners in Northern Ireland prisons may wear their own clothes at all times could be put into effect under this rule under the exception clause. In due course the NIO would envisage a new rule, but immediate action could be taken to put such a decision into effect by means of a circular to Governors and a guidance leaflet for prisoners and their families. On the provision of association, the NIO turned to the Irish Commission for Justice and Peace. They had been concerned to increase opportunities for association between prisoners, and suggested that, subject to satisfactory arrangements for supervision and control, provision might be made for adjacent wings in each H-Block to share association in recreation rooms and exercise yards. With certain physical and staffing changes, it was decided that limited movement between wings could be provided, broadly in line with the ICJP suggestions. The designated association periods were from 5.30 p.m. to 8.30 p.m. each weekday, and on Saturday and Sunday from 2.00 p.m. to 4.00 p.m. and from 5.30 p.m. to 8.30 p.m. The proposed new system would operate as follows:

(i)   during any designated evening association period any prisoners wishing to use the exercise yard (summer period weather permitting) would elect to do so and they would proceed to the designated exercise area – only one yard would be used in the first instance to avoid self-imposed segregation between Republican and Loyalist prisoners;

(ii) during any designated association period any prisoner wishing to proceed to the recreation room in the opposite wing in the H-Block would elect to do so.

The only restriction on movement under (i) or (ii) above would be the physical limitation of numbers in either of the two recreation rooms or the exercise yard. The proposed maximum was forty-five in any one room or yard. This figure would ensure some capacity for inter-wing movement in all H-Blocks. The new shared association provision would be termed a privilege, thus enabling any individual to be deprived of it by the Governor if it was abused. The Governor would also be able to discontinue the system, in part or totally, at any time for any specified period, in the interests of good order in the prison. While some additional supervisory staff would be required for the new system, the physical change of a new grille gate between adjacent wings (two per H-Block, and sixteen in all at the Maze) was the main limiting factor. This physical change would take some weeks to achieve, but a reasonable objective would be to have the first grille gate installed in about three weeks, when the system could begin to operate. The NIO envisaged that the new grilles, and consequent provision for inter-wing association, would be made first in the H-Blocks holding fully conforming prisoners.

Next to be decided was the position on work. There were at this point just under 400 protesting prisoners. The only work they were doing was keeping their own cells clean. The other domestic chores in the H-Blocks (serving meals, cleaning the general areas, the exercise yard and so on) were presently carried out by orderlies (about ten per Block) brought in from elsewhere. The first step, once the protesting prisoners put on their own clothes, would be for these orderlies to be returned to their own Blocks and ten orderlies selected from each of the four protesting H-Blocks to carry out those domestic cleaning duties. The second step would be for interviews by the Governor's staff, Prison Medical Officers, the Education Officer and the Industries Manager with all the ex-protesters to determine whether the ex-protestors were fit for work, and if so, to what form of work or training they were best suited and would wish to pursue. These interviews 'could prove a watershed.' The prisoners might refuse to co-operate and simply indicate that they were not available for work of any kind. If so, that was 'the end of the matter and we have a "no work" protest.' If, however, they did co-operate, it was estimated that these individual interviews would take around two weeks to complete for all protesters. In these interviews it would be made clear that there were available a number of different work alternatives – orderly duties in servicing the prison outside the Block; vocational training; industrial work; and where appropriate remedial education: 'Clearly we cannot provide all prisoners with the work of their choice immediately though it may be possible to do so over a period of time.' There was at the Maze a prison labour allocations board chaired by the Governor, which was responsible for allocating prisoners to the various forms of work and to training, and it would be for this board, after taking into account the results of the interviews, to make the appropriate allocations. Again, at this stage 'we could have a watershed either by some prisoners refusing the allocation of work which was not their choice or a refusal as a co-ordinated response by all the ex-protesters to co-operate in the area of work other than on their own terms.' The NIO decided to follow up the suggestions of the ICJP on the widening of prison work to include work for certain approved charities, and the Department of Finance Works Division was drawing up plans for the building of three small chapels at the Maze using prison labour. A provisional scheme was worked out on the following lines:

WORK ETC PLACES FOR 400 PROTESTERS

Orderly duties in Block	40
Orderly duties on Prison Services e.g. gardening	30
Available industrial work places	50
New Vocational Training courses	150*
Special education/pre-Vocational Training Course: (English, Maths, handicrafts)	120
Remedial education ?	20
	410

* Available after 8 weeks approx.[32]

Publicly, James Prior announced changes to the prison system, but not, of course, the more detailed plans being outlined within the NIO: 'The hunger strike has ended, as it began, by the voluntary action of the protestors. It is time to heal the deep wounds and fresh divisions caused by the strike both inside and outside the prisons, and help to bring to an end the violence which for so long had prevented the social, political and economic development of Northern Ireland.' The Secretary of State confirmed that now, no longer under the duress of the hunger strike, he wanted to 'play my part in seeking reconciliation and an end to violence by introducing changes along the lines set out by my predecessor on 30 June and 8 July.' But first:

I must make it quite clear what I am not prepared to do. The protestors' views on work and association are not compatible with a civil prison system, especially the modern and humane system which makes the principal jails of the Province as advanced as any in the world. There is room for development here as elsewhere. But there will be no question of a political or military system of administration or any return to special category status.

Prior confirmed that the changes he had decided to make would apply to all prisoners in all prisons in Northern Ireland.

On clothes, prisoners would in future be able to wear their own clothing at all times as of right. To avoid any misunderstandings, the practical arrangements for this change would be set out in a leaflet, which Lord Gowrie would circulate to prisoners. These arrangements covered, for example, the need to ensure that clothing worn by prisoners did not resemble that of prison officers, was not tantamount to a uniform, and was not offensive or unsuitable so as to be an abuse of the privilege. There would also be a need to specify the quantities of clothing and finalize laundry arrangements. These were 'practical matters and need cause no serious problems.' The change would take perhaps two or three weeks to complete. Families could bring clothes to the prisons when they had been informed of the details in the leaflets: 'Of course, those who prefer to continue to wear the prison-issue civilian-style clothing will be able to do so.' At present, prisoners who had lost remission as a penalty for certain protest action might have 20% of that lost remission restored after three months of full conformity with the prison rules. A number of prisoners had already gained from this. Prior announced a more generous scheme for restoration of lost remission. Lord Gowrie would make the full details known, based on the following principles:

(i) The new scheme will extend to all prisoners who have lost remission other than as a result of violent acts against prison officers or other prisoners;

(ii) The amount of lost remission which may be restored will be increased to a maximum of 50 per cent i.e. those who have already qualified for the earlier 20 per cent restoration will gain a further 30 per cent, and those who newly qualify will gain the full 50 per cent;

(iii) The new scheme, like the present one, will apply only after a period of 3 months' conformity with prison rules. However as a gesture of goodwill I am prepared exceptionally, to ensure that the first eligible prisoners can be home by Christmas.

The new scheme applied to past behaviour, and did not mean that prisoners who in the future lost remission for breaches of prison rules would have lost remission restored. On association, Prior explained, conforming prisoners already had many opportunities for mixing with one another at mealtimes, work, exercise, and during their period of association each evening and at weekends. There was little immediate scope for expansion, 'but I have accepted that there should be some provision for prisoners in adjacent wings of H-Blocks to share association in recreation rooms and exercise areas.' Before this change could be implemented, new arrangements for the control and supervision of such movement and certain additional physical changes would be required. These would take some weeks. The Government, continued Prior, had made it clear that the development of a prison system was a continual process; in particular, the possibility of widening the scope of work in the prisons could be examined within certain well-defined limits. There were obvious practical and financial limitations on what could be arranged: 'Here I should like to pay tribute to prison officials for successfully maintaining an enlightened system for conforming prisoners while coping with the great stress and strain occasioned by the protest. I am very conscious that many, indeed most of the prisoners, are young men.' Even in the context of deservedly long sentences on conviction for violent crimes, many of them would, in the normal way, be released before they were middle aged: 'I do therefore want to encourage a system where the very advanced training and educational facilities available, which have much impressed me, may be freely used by all prisoners. Lord Gowrie will continue to keep a close eye on developments in this field as the new arrangements settle down.' In order to create a breathing space and ease the changeover in the prison system, for twenty-eight days no loss of remission would be imposed as a penalty for breaches of prison rules arising out of the refusal to wear prison-issue clothes. Finally:

I hope that the end of the hunger strike, together with the measures I have described above, will help end the confrontation which has caused so much tragedy and suffering inside and outside the prisons. We must never forget that while 10 young men have died tragically in the Maze, many more people have died during the period of the strike as innocent victims of the violence outside.

Our task is to stop the men who are causing that violence, so that we can turn all our energies to creating a better future for all the people of Northern Ireland. I want to get on with this task and I have made it clear that my priority will be to tackle our economic difficulties. In the spirit of reconciliation with which I have put forward my prison reforms I look for co-operation and support in this wide purpose from all the leaders of the community.'[33]

Reactions came quickly to Prior's statement of 6 October. Cardinal Ó Fiaich praised the speed with which Prior had acted, and welcomed the measures as 'a step in the right direction'. John Hume called the reforms 'a positive response from the Government'. Unionists, however, were very angry. Ian Paisley, accompanied by his deputy, Peter Robinson, met the Secretary of State that evening and expressed outrage at the 'concessions' to the IRA. The proposals were, he said, 'a complete sell-out to those engaged in the campaign of murder against the Protestant community'. He had 'won the war but lost the peace'. Jim Molyneaux had earlier accused Prior of 'snatching defeat from the jaws of victory'. Later that same evening, at a reception for council leaders given by the Secretary of State at Hillsborough Castle, eleven DUP members walked out after telling Prior that they saw the proposals as a sell-out to the IRA.[34]

As for wider considerations, in his report to Lord Carrington on the effect of the hunger strikes in the Republic, Sir Leonard Figg described them as one of the most difficult periods in Anglo-Irish relations for many years: 'As I said at the time, the Irish Government were not too alarmed by Sands's death and the general public took it calmly. What did worry us was the prospect of further hunger strikers dying, as they had said they would, at carefully timed intervals.' The hunger strike in the Republic – as in Northern Ireland – used moral blackmail to appeal to traditional Irish Republican emotions: 'the past intimidating the present', as one journalist called it. Many Irish people could not tell how their country would react to deaths from the hunger strike, partly because they could not be sure of their own reactions: 'Logically they could not ask us to surrender but emotionally they could not accept a succession of deaths. Hence the appeal to us to show "flexibility", to make changes which would fluff the issue of political status as they had successfully done to end a hunger strike in Portlaoise in 1977. This missed the essence of the problem for us': that the strike had become a political trial of strength; that in the Republic the number of terrorist prisoners was only 15% of the prison population (while in the North it was about 70%); and that in the South the religious and cultural backgrounds of prison warders were the same as those of the prisoners and of the public at large. In the North 'we have to contend with a cultural and religious difference between warders and Republican prisoners and with a critical Protestant audience outside.' While in quieter times an Irish Government:

> ... might accept that these differences form a serious constraint on our ability to run a prison system in the way they do in the South, they ceased to accept them as the pace hotted up. When the violence flowed down to the South in June and July the Irish Government's pressure on us to end the strike grew in proportion to their fears that they might not be able to control events and that the institutions of the State might collapse. I must say I never shared their fears, but I put this down more to ignorance of the country on my part than to over-anxiety on theirs.

'How far has the hunger strike affected our relations with the Republic?' asked Figg: 'I should like to say, probably not very much. What we called the "1916

Syndrome" (increasing fury at a succession of deaths for which Her Majesty's Government was held responsible) never developed, though we came close to it in early July until the demonstration and rioting ... showed the opposition in their true colours.' For the Republican fringe, the hunger-strikers had already entered the litany of martyrs, but while the IRA might have gained individual recruits in the Republic from the strike, 'I do not believe they have extended their area of support beyond the traditional hardline Republican element which is significant in the border counties (perhaps 10 to 15 per cent) but may only approach 2 to 3 per cent elsewhere in the South.' For the majority of Irish people, the hunger strike would remain a painful memory. The IRA may attract an increasing share of the blame as emotion fades, 'but I think it is too soon to forecast how our part will be seen.'[35]

In the Foreign Office, Patrick Eyers commented, to Fergusson, on how Figg's dispatch showed that the effects of the hunger strike in the Republic were much greater and more lasting than those in Britain. The success of a recent Anglo-Irish summit, though:

> ... had probably healed any lingering sores in Anglo-Irish relations. But we must bear in mind the very different perception that the Irish Government have of events in Northern Ireland and take account of it in our dealings with them next time that there is trouble in the Catholic community in the north. If the IRA murder campaign continues and the Protestant backlash develops further, this may not be very far off.[36]

In his comments to Figg, Eyers observed that there were lessons 'for us all' to learn for the future handling of similar problems. Two points particularly struck Eyers. The first was that events in the Catholic community in Northern Ireland had a much more direct effect on the Government in Dublin than the Government in London. HMG was under no domestic pressure to settle the hunger strike. Indeed, the pressures were all in the opposite direction. On the other hand, Dr FitzGerald was subjected to strong and emotional forces, and had to suffer the frustration of having no responsibility for the source of the problem and no powers to act directly to resolve it. In the circumstances, all he could do was pass on his frustration to HMG. The other point was the tendency of Irish Governments to take an unrealistic view of the problems in Northern Ireland, despite their close contacts with 'the Province' and knowledge of it. Seen from London, their actions seemed to be guided less by reality than by wishful thinking. In the case of the hunger strike, this was exemplified by the assumption that the ICJP was going to produce a compromise. HMG did not set great store by the ICJP's chances: 'we gave them a fair wind but never expected them to work a miracle. When the ICJP failed our reaction was conditioned by our scepticism. The Irish Government's reaction was conditioned by their undue expectations and they felt that we had let them down.' Wishful thinking also seemed to be behind the view that HMG could make changes in the prison regime in Northern Ireland that would fluff the issue of political status: in Figg's words, 'this missed the essence of the problem for us'.

What this all amounted to was that there was a wide, and worrying, gap between perceptions in Dublin and London: 'We need to try to bridge this gap because it can cause serious differences of opinion between us on matters on which it is in our interests to work in harmony.' On the broader political front there was the view, held widely in Irish-America as well as among Republicans in both parts of Ireland, that HMG only had to put pressure on the Loyalists, by for instance removing the constitutional 'Guarantee', for them to accept that their future lay in a united Ireland. 'As seen from here, this is nonsense': the current unrest in the North showed only too well that any British Government had to tread a very careful path between Protestant and Catholic communities, maintaining a balance in its actions and attitudes towards both. As Eyers admitted to Figg: 'You were right in concluding that we must expect difficult times ahead.' The centre of the Northern Ireland stage, having been held by the Catholics for the previous twelve months, saw the Protestants 'now having their go. Paradoxically, this backlash may make it easier for us to persuade Republican wishful-thinkers that the facts of life in Northern Ireland are not as straightforward as they like to think.'[37] This last comment proved to be an example of British wishful thinking.

NOTES

1   TNA FCO 87/1263 Dublin to FCO Telegram Number 288 of 10 August 1981.
2   TNA FCO 87/1263 Dublin to FCO Telegram Number 290 of 12 August 1981.
3   TNA FCO 87/1263 Dublin to FCO Telegram Number 291 of 12 August 1981.
4   TNA FCO 87/1263 Dublin to FCO Telegram Number 292 of 13 August 1981.
5   TNA FCO 87/1263 Dublin to FCO Telegram Number 297 of 15 August 1981.
6   TNA FCO 87/1263 Summary Record of Meeting in Northern Ireland Office: 3.15 p.m. 11 August 1981.
7   TNA CJ4/3624 Harrington to PS/Secretary of State 12 August 1981.
8   TNA FCO 87/1263 Fergusson to Moriarty 17 August 1981.
9   TNA FCO 87/1264 Moriarty to Fergusson.
10   TNA FCO 87/1263 Harrington to Douglas.
11   TNA FCO 87/1263 Telegram Number 310 of 27 August 1981.
12   PRONI CENT/1/10/62 Blatherwick to Blelloch 17 August 1981.
13   PRONI CENT/1/10/62 Local Effects of the Hunger Strike.
14   TNA CJ4/3624 Note for the Record, 11 August 1981 (1st note).
15   TNA CJ4/3624 Note for the Record, 11 August 1981 (2nd note).
16   NAI D/T 2011/127/1057 Lillis Memo.

17   NAI D/T 2011/127/1058 M Lillis Memo, 14 August 1981.
18   NAI D/T 2011/127/1058 To Taoiseach from Lillis, 19 August 1981.
19   TNA CJ4/3624 Note for the Record, 19 August 1981.
20   NAI D/T 2011/127/1058 H-Blocks – Some Considerations Department of Foreign Affairs, 20 August 1981.
21   TNA FCO 87/1263 Protests and Second Hunger Strike – Weekly Bulletin No. 26.
22   *An Phoblacht/Republican News*, 29 August 1981.
23   PRONI CENT/1/10/62 Mr Alison's meeting with Mr Owen Carron – Friday, 28 August 1981.
24   TNA FCO 87/1264 Protests and Second Hunger Strike – Weekly Bulletin No. 28. 09.00 hours Thursday 3 September – 09.00 hours Thursday 10 September.
25   PRONI CENT/1/10/62 D. J. Wyatt to Blelloch, 21 September 1981.
26   PRONI CENT/1/10/62 J. N. Blelloch to PS/Secretary of State, 24 September 1981.
27   TNA FCO 87/1264 Note for the Record.
28   TNA FCO 87/1265 Protests and Second Hunger Strike - Final Bulletin No. 32. 09.00 hours Thursday 1 October – 09.00 hours Wednesday 7 October.
29   TNA FCO 87/1264 Cabinet Office to Melbourne Telegram No. 031534Z of 3 October.
30   TNA FCO 87/1265 Protests and Second Hunger Strike - Final Bulletin No. 32. 09.00 hours Thursday 1 October – 09.00 hours Wednesday 7 October.
31   TNA FCO 87/1264 Ukdel to FCO Telegram Number 57 of 4 Oct.
32   TNA FCO 87/1264 To Harrington to Eyers, 5 October 1981.
33   TNA FCO 87/1264 FCO to Dublin Telegram number 153 of 5 October.
34   TNA FCO 87/1265 Protests and Second Hunger Strike - Final Bulletin No. 32. 09.00 hours Thursday 1 October – 09.00 hours Wednesday 7 October.
35   TNA FCO 87/1265 The Hunger Strike: View from the Irish Republic, 19 October 1981.
36   TNA FCO 87/1265 Eyers to Fergusson, 19 November 1981.
37   TNA FCO 87/1265 Eyers to Figg.

Conclusion

Years after the hunger strikes, Mrs Thatcher reflected: 'you really had to hand it to some of these IRA boys ... poor devils ... if they didn't go on strike they'd be shot ... What a waste! What a terrible waste of human life ... I don't even remember their names.'[1] The former Prime Minister admired the courage of the hunger-strikers even if she did not admire the cause for which they died. In the short term it was clear that Mrs Thatcher 'won' the hunger strike: it, and the years of protest by Republican prisoners, did not deliver special category status. But did Mrs Thatcher lose the peace? Should the Thatcher Government have confronted the Republican prisoners in the manner in which it did? Clearly, the political advancement of Sinn Féin suggests that, from the British point of view, it would have been better to have avoided a hunger strike, but this is a retrospective position. The Government's response to the hunger strike has to be seen in the context of what it knew at the time. The electoral benefit for Sinn Féin was a consequence of the hunger strike; it was not the main issue of the confrontation. That was the deeper, fundamental issue of claims of political status by the prisoners, and this was something on which no British Government could concede after what was considered to be a serious misjudgement by William Whitelaw in 1972, which had handed the Provisionals a major coup in their propaganda campaign.

Mrs Thatcher's Government inherited the basic position on the prisons from the previous Labour Government, whose strategy was that of Ulsterization: putting local security forces, particularly the police, in the forefront of the fight against terrorism. Alongside this was criminalization: the claim that political killing was a crime, whatever its motivation. From the Government's perspective, criminalization was another part of the strategy of denying the PIRA legitimacy for its actions. In this respect it was part of a wider psychological and political battle. Defining political violence as 'crime' was a concerted attempt to disavow the claim that paramilitary combatants had any justification in resorting to armed struggle: they were 'terrorists'. This did not mean that the Labour Government failed to recognize the political origins of paramilitary violence. The aim of the Labour Government, as during the 1975 PIRA ceasefire, was to convince the Republican Movement to pursue its aim of a united Ireland through peaceful means.

The winning of 'hearts and minds' in the wider community involved both consent and coercion. Criminalization was also an important policy in terms of deterrent – while there was a continuous stream of young men and women willing to join paramilitaries, there were many more who did not. While one cannot say how many people, if indeed anybody, were deterred by criminalization, it was a key part of the Government's aim to delegitimize paramilitarism. The image of paramilitaries imprisoned behind barbed wire, in Nissen huts, gave some credibility to Republican attempts to claim that its prisoners were POWs engaged in a war against a foreign occupier. It was a PR disaster from the Government's point of view. It also entailed a significant loss of control over the prisoners who, engaged in free association within the compounds, effectively policed themselves, made mock weapons and undertook drilling. Not for nothing were the Maze compounds known as a 'university of terrorism'. Criminalization meant a less glamorous image of convicted terrorists in cellular confinement with no prospect of an amnesty following an end of hostilities (even with the release of paramilitary prisoners, following the 1998 Good Friday Agreement, it was under licence and not as part of an amnesty).

The confrontation between the Republican prisoners in the H-Blocks and successive Governments was a titanic struggle that symbolized the legitimacy, or otherwise, of the PIRA's armed struggle (and it was essentially a conflict led by the Provisionals). The protesting prisoners were prepared to go to extreme lengths to resist conforming to the Maze regime, from refusing to wear prison uniform to the 'dirty protest'. It is important to remember that the conditions the Blanketmen endured were self-imposed. The Maze was, in terms of facilities, one of the best prisons in western Europe. But the prisoners were not interested in improving the prison regime – they were interested in breaking the control of the prison authorities over them. They regarded themselves as prisoners of war, and believed that the reintroduction of special category status would give them de facto, if not de jure, POW status – in the sense that they believed this would grant them 'political status'. Of course the Thatcher Government, like the Conservative and Labour Governments before it, did not accept that special category status equated with either political status or POW status. After the introduction of criminalization, there remained the anomaly of special category status prisoners still being sentenced for offences committed before 1 March 1976. The reintroduction of special category status, however, would undermine the Government's strategy of isolating paramilitaries, as far as was possible, from the communities from which they came. Successive Governments had sought to reduce the support that the PIRA received from within the Catholic community. The PIRA also contributed to this with Nationalist war-weariness and disenchantment at the actions carried out by paramilitaries. This went hand in hand with 'normalization' and the police primacy of the RUC in security operations.

The tragedy of the confrontation was that while, in terms of principles, there was a fundamental gulf between the Government and the prisoners, when the conceptual framework was stripped away, the practicalities of work and association meant that the two sides were not that far apart in the end. On clothing, remission and visits/parcels, it was clear what was on offer, but it took a monumental struggle to reach that position, including years of struggle on the part of the Republican protesters, before the prisoners realized that the Government was not going to give in to intimidation. The prisoners wanted a deferential system for themselves to distinguish them from other, 'ordinary', prisoners, whom they regarded as criminals. The prison authorities reacted with harsh punishments to the prisoners' refusal to conform. There was violence inside the Maze, from some prison officers to prisoners, while the H-Block staff were vulnerable to paramilitary attack outside it: twenty-one staff, working in Northern Irish prisons, were murdered between 1976 and 1980, including two Governors.

The prisoners were involved in a constant struggle to undermine the prison system. This is illustrated by what happened after the end of the hunger strike when there was a more 'relaxed' atmosphere between the prisoners and staff: in 1983, thirty-eight PIRA prisoners escaped from the Maze. The official inquiry into the escape found that the escapees 'exploited human and design weaknesses'. In particular, the prisoners broke down the 'human contribution to security; they did so by adopting a deliberate policy of conditioning staff to reduce their alertness.' Many prison officers in H7, where the breakout began, 'were complacent and the Block had acquired the reputation of being "liberal".'[2] As Bobby Sands made clear in the 1980 hunger strike, any relaxation by the authorities was to be exploited.

As for HMG, the Thatcher administration was not a monolith: there were debates and tensions within it, particularly between the NIO and the FCO. The latter was concerned with how Britain was perceived overseas, with the United States as the key audience. American opinion was crucial to Britain because of HMG's wider strategic concerns: the Cold War had entered a new period of tension following the Soviet invasion of Afghanistan; medium-range nuclear weapons had been deployed in East Germany by the Russians; and there were continuing tensions in Poland, where martial law was to be imposed by the end of 1981. With regard to Northern Ireland, the Reagan Administration offered Mrs Thatcher the support she wanted after problems with the Carter Administration, which had been under Congressional pressure. The diplomatic influence and resources that the British could mobilize were in sharp contrast to those of the Irish Government. The hunger strike was more of a problem for Dublin than for London: for Charles Haughey and Garret FitzGerald it became the main political issue in their diplomatic relations because it had such an impact domestically; for Mrs Thatcher, with no real domestic pressure in Great Britain, it was one of a long series of issues, including severe economic problems. The Irish were often exasperated by what they regarded as the British mishandling of the hunger strikes, but despite

Dublin's despair over its apparent impotence in influencing HMG, there were key moments when the FCO did succeed in persuading Mrs Thatcher and the NIO to take on board Irish concerns – the intervention of the ICJP was the key one. But there were limits beyond which the British would not move. Despite the severe strains between Dublin and London, an Irish breach with the British was never seriously on the cards because of the propaganda coup this would have given the Provisonals.

In London, the Prime Minister was the ultimate arbiter of policy, although she depended on advice from Humphrey Atkins more than most. Atkins, in particular, remained hard-line on the hunger strike, as did the NIO, generally on core issues such as control of the prison and that no concessions would be made under duress. Aside from these non-negotiable points, though, the Thatcher Government was relatively flexible: from internal documents there was clearly a desire to implement a prison regime that would accommodate many of the prisoners' demands – albeit not their key demand that this would be for paramilitary prisoners alone. The Government did not rule out scenarios it did not want to concede, such as recognizing the paramilitary command structure, which it had with Sands during the first hunger strike; the Government, on the other hand, dug its heels in on this point during the second hunger strike, when the stakes were raised. After the hunger strike, paramilitary OCs were informally recognized again. Some issues that were initially non-negotiable, to both sides, during the wider prison protest and the hunger strikes, appeared, away from the glare of the public, acceptable afterwards. This may seem bizarre given the huge consequences that stemmed from the confrontation, but the very act of paramilitary prisoners demanding certain things meant that the Government was bound to resist them at that point. Demand and resistance became political acts taken in a wider political game.

A turning point in the confrontation was reached during the second hunger strike when, after struggling since 1976 for differential treatment, the prisoners surrendered this point in their 4 July 1981 statement and conceded that the five demands could be applied to *all* prisoners in Northern Ireland. One could say that, at this point, the Government had defeated the prisoners in their demand for special category status. Before this point, and from the moment Kieran Nugent refused to wear prison uniform, the key demand from Republican prisoners was for a separate regime to distinguish themselves from non-paramilitary inmates. The demand of the hunger-strikers from here on in was for the implementation of the five demands – even if this applied to all prisoners in Northern Ireland. Why then did the Thatcher Government not offer concessions to the hunger-strikers? The reason was that the Government still adhered to the core position that it would not negotiate with the prisoners under duress. The hunger strike had to end first. Although the prisoners had conceded their fundamental position, the hunger strike continued because neither side trusted the other. The prisoners wanted some guarantee about what would be introduced once the fast ended; Mrs Thatcher feared that any concessions would be pocketed before new demands were made later, with the possibility of yet another hunger strike. The issue of who controlled the prison was also key to the Government's refusal to move. This was not because the Government was unwilling to implement any of the five demands, but because it adhered to the principle that it would be for the prison authorities to decide if, when and what would be implemented, particularly in terms of work and association.

Mrs Thatcher and her Government were intransigent on the principle that the hunger strike must end first; but it is equally true that Republicans were intransigent on the implementation of the five demands. The continuing pursuit of the five demands seems to have become an end in itself when, in reality, the fundamental point of special category status had already been conceded on 4 July. There seems to have been no strategy on the part of the Provisionals outside the Maze to end the strike beyond a continuous conveyer belt of dying hunger-strikers until Mrs Thatcher gave in. When, at the end of July, the hunger-strikers Quinn and McElwee expressed concern about saving the lives of their comrades Lynch and Doherty, 'if a way could be found through a change in tactics', Brendan McFarlane, in his own words 'tore it to shreds' on the basis that the issue was the 'five demands or we capitulate. No in-between solutions.'

At face value, it seems extraordinary that the hunger strike should continue after its main demand had been surrendered. The five demands were now a totem. No one on the Republican side – including the leadership inside or outside the Maze – seems to have questioned the wisdom of carrying on the hunger strike, with more men dying for a regime that could be applied, at any time the authorities wished to do so, to all prisoners in Northern Ireland. Prior to July it is very difficult to see how any compromise could have been reached. Those who believed that a solution was available had the Government compromised on certain issues, such as the wearing of prison clothes, were wrong: they underestimated the resolve of the prisoners to secure the five demands as part of a differential regime for themselves. In July, however, the ICJP came up with a scheme that was, in the end, more or less, adopted by the Government after the collapse of the hunger strike.

This raises another important question as to why the prisoners and the Provisionals outside the Maze rejected this, and what was coming through the backchannel with the British? One of the problems in deciphering the position of the PIRA is that it was part of a movement that engaged in propaganda, all facets of which were geared to forwarding the struggle. The most obvious example of this was the Republican claim that there was a deal with the British in December 1980 that ended the first hunger strike, on which HMG reneged, leading to the second hunger strike. This was a straightforward lie, issued for propaganda purposes. There was no deal in December 1980. There was a deal in July 1981, although it was derailed for a number of reasons. There was clearly an issue of trust on the part of the hunger-strikers – they wanted guarantees about the prison regime that would be implemented after the end of the hunger strike. The hunger-strikers, in this sense, were in control of their own destiny. They were autonomous. But they also relied on the interpretations of others, from outside, of what was going on through the backchannel, and this was that there was not enough in the HMG clarifications to end the hunger strike. This was correct – in the sense that the British did not go far enough for Republicans in outlining what could be done on work and association.

One of the key objectives of the Republicans co-ordinating the hunger strike outside, and McFarlane inside the prison, was direct negotiations with the British, whether through the latter as PIRA O/C in the Maze or through the backchannel. This became a point of principle as rigid as any adopted by Mrs Thatcher. Republicans regarded this as granting belligerent status on them. The key aim was to open negotiations. This was the fundamental mistake: on two separate occasions, through the backchannel, the Provisionals sought to push the British into negotiating on work and association. The British said no on both occasions. There would be no concessions during the hunger strike and no negotiations: despite the claims of her official biographer that the Prime Minister in effect did 'negotiate with terrorists' in contrast to her protestations, the fact is that one of the reasons the hunger strike dragged on for so long was that her Government refused to negotiate with Republicans. To the outside observer, differences between 'clarification' and 'negotiation' may seem semantic, but given that it is naïve to expect that Governments should not have some line of communication open to insurgents, the devil is in the detail of these exchanges. And, fine line though it was, clarification, not negotiation, is what occurred down the Duddy backchannel.

Nevertheless, the exchanges, signed off on by the Prime Minister, raise issues on the handling of these contacts by Republicans outside the prison. Firstly, it was perfectly reasonable, from their perspective, to ask whether the British clarification could be negotiated, but it was an error to continue to push for this when it was made clear that there would be no direct negotiation. But secondly, although what Mrs Thatcher personally signed off on was quite limited, it is also apparent that what Brendan Duddy was being told at the other end of a telephone were unofficial elaborations of the sort of things that would occur, with regard to work and association, if the hunger strike were called off. This, combined with what the ICJP was also suggesting, through the speculative conversations with Alison that caused such controversy, were enough for the outside Republican co-ordinators to have recommended to the prisoners that here was a basis for calling off the hunger strike. Instead, the considered opinion sent into the Maze was that more was needed. But there was no more, and there was never going to be. The Government was clearly not going to move any further in terms of putting something into a document that could be used to embarrass it later; but, even without doing this, it was obvious what sort of options were available on work and association, for the prisoners, once the fast ended. The hunger-strikers were ill advised by their superiors inside and outside the prison on this issue; while Richard O'Rawe's claim that he and McFarlane agreed that there was an acceptable deal is unprovable, his assertion that there was a deal on the table, from the British, is supported from the documentary evidence.

By this stage, each death had less impact on the Government. It was this realization, coupled with the reality that the Government was not going to give in, that led to the families seizing control and intervening to end the hunger strike. While there is no direct evidence that the hunger strike was continued, at the expense of more lives, in the pursuit of advancing an electoral strategy for Sinn Féin, all that can be said is that the continuation of the hunger strike certainly benefited it. Whether the momentum for the continuation of the hunger strike came from Republicans inside or outside the Maze, its perpetuation made no sense, apart from saving face, because by July 1981 even the concession of the five demands for all Northern Irish prisoners would have represented the defeat of the original struggle for special category status.

This brings one to whether, in the long term, Sinn Féin 'won' the hunger strike. Sinn Féin, by the time of Baroness Thatcher's death, was the largest Nationalist party in Northern Ireland, sharing power at Stormont with Unionists. It had also become a considerable electoral force in the Republic of Ireland. Sinn Féin's Martin McGuinness, the Deputy First Minister of Northern Ireland, reflecting on the old Unionist-dominated Northern Ireland recalled, in 2013:

> I grew up in that state. So did many generations of nationalists before me. We experienced, in a very stark way, the denial of human rights. We experienced first hand institutionalised discrimination. Our cultural rights were systematically trampled upon. We were denied democratic participation. Many many nationalists ... have borne the brunt of various British government attempts to suppress their sense of Irishness and the expression of their Irish identity.[3]

In the same year, Gerry Kelly (a senior Sinn Féin member of the Northern Ireland Assembly, and a prisoner in the Maze during the hunger strike), when commemorating two young PIRA Volunteers killed by their own bomb, explained how: 'There was a war, which the Orange Apartheid State caused through its institutionalised and endemic discrimination and oppression of the Catholic population over generations.'[4]

Despite the retrospective claim that the PIRA's campaign was necessary to establish equality between Catholics and Protestants in Northern Ireland, this was *not* what the armed struggle was about. It was to end partition. Danny Morrison criticized the suggestion by former PIRA prisoner Tommy Gorman:

> ... that the current outcome of the struggle (the Belfast/Good Friday Agreement) as apparently having been the real objective: that the campaign was about reform and redressing the wrongs which the civil rights movement identified, rather than about ending partition and establishing a 32-county socialist republic. Clearly, given that Tommy did not believe this at the time he joined and was active in the IRA (or did those large numbers of republicans from the South who sacrificed their freedom and their lives), he has to come up with an explanation for the flaw in the campaign and all our eyes being wiped.

Instead, Morrison pointed out that the demand for a British withdrawal from Ireland was the 'goal which generated our passion and was what we were actually fighting and prepared to die for'.[5]

The PIRA regarded itself as a legitimate army fighting for the liberation of its country from an occupying power. This, in essence, is what the hunger strike was really about, from the prisoners' perspective. The Republican Movement has compared its struggle against British colonialism to other anti-imperialist struggles around the world, particularly in Palestine–Israel and South Africa. The African National Congress (ANC) fought against the apartheid regime that repressed political dissent and institutionalized racial economic exploitation. Strict segregation placed limits on where blacks could work and live. The ANC's political aim, set out in its 1955 'Freedom Charter', was the establishment of equal rights for blacks. It was committed to non-violence, but this became more difficult as State repression became more intense. Gerry Kelly's claim was that the PIRA's war came about through similar repression, but Northern Ireland was not South Africa.

British State violence and coercion during the Troubles included Bloody Sunday and collusion by elements of the security forces with Loyalist paramilitaries, the first of which certainly drew young Nationalist men and women into the Republican Movement. But these indefensible actions occurred as part of an emerging conflict between the State and the PIRA. They were reactive responses to the situation created by the proactive PIRA campaign of violence to drive the British out of Northern Ireland. The PIRA's decision to wage war (*jus ad bellum*) against the British State in Northern Ireland was taken in 1970. When that decision was taken, the then Labour Government was instituting a series of political reforms, through pressure on the then Unionist Government, including all the original demands of the Northern Ireland Civil Rights Association to end discrimination against Catholics. Political dissent was not repressed by the British Government: Nationalists who were not satisfied by the reforms had the right to continue protesting for further reforms, including the ending of Unionist majority rule; and the pursuit of a united Ireland by peaceful means was recognized as a legitimate goal by London.

The Provisional leadership took a unilateral decision to begin their own war, without any mandate except the claim of the right of resistance to foreign occupation of their land by an imperialist power and the belief that their Army Council was the legitimate government of Ireland, and not the Irish Government in Dublin. Republicans refused to recognize the electoral legitimacy of the independent Irish State, arguing instead that the final all-Ireland general election in 1918 was the last expression of Irish national self-determination (although this was also the last all-British Isles general election, as the whole of Ireland was in the United Kingdom at this time). Within this ideological framework, the Provisional IRA launched its war against the British when a British Government was engaged in reforming Northern Ireland. It was the wrong war against the wrong enemy. British Governments, including Mrs Thatcher's, did not stay in Northern Ireland for any imperialist colonial desire to exploit the island for selfish strategic or economic reasons. Indeed, many, in and out of Whitehall, shared a similar view to that held by Mrs Thatcher's husband, Denis, who thought: 'If the Irish want to kill each other that does seem to me to be their business.'[6] Mrs Thatcher's Government, like previous British Governments since the outbreak of the Troubles, refused to declare its intent to withdraw from Northern Ireland or to persuade its inhabitants that their future lay in a united Ireland for the simple reason that it was the will of the majority of people there to remain British and in the United Kingdom. For Nationalists of all persuasions this principle of consent was frustrating and amounted to a Unionist veto over progress – usually to a united Ireland – but only Republicans saw in it the need to take up arms to expel an imperialist British State that existed only in their own minds.

Throughout the hunger strikes, and the Troubles, Republicans claimed that they were political prisoners and, therefore, had a right to be treated differently from other prisoners. They were not criminals, they believed, because their actions were politically motivated. This raises a fundamental question about the nature of the Government–prisoner confrontation in the hunger strikes. The PIRA and INLA prisoners in the H-Blocks were there because they had engaged in acts of political violence and were convicted in special non-jury courts constituted under emergency legislation. But they were not political prisoners in the sense that they were incarcerated for their political beliefs. Republican politically motivated prisoners were not political prisoners of conscience. They were in prison because they were engaged in political violence – in both Northern Ireland and Great Britain and, sometimes, in the Republic of Ireland. They chose to try and resolve the political conflict in Northern Ireland by acts of violence. In this, they made a choice. Other Nationalists, even in the face of State violence, did not choose to kill. The H-Blocks were a battleground in which the conflict represented a reflection of the wider conflict of legitimacy between Republicans and the British State. The Provisional IRA had no legitimate right to kill people because their political views were different to theirs. Political murder was a crime in that sense.

There were alternatives to politically motivated violence. There was an alternative to achieving Republican aims: the PIRA's campaign, in any event, did not achieve a united Ireland; Northern Ireland was clearly reformable, and Catholics need no longer be second-class citizens within it – for how else can Sinn Féin now justify being involved in a Northern Ireland power-sharing Government with Unionists? In the 1970s and 1980s, Republicans were a minority of a minority – the majority of Nationalists in Northern Ireland rejected violence as the way to achieve a united Ireland. John Hume and the SDLP were, despite Republican claims to the contrary, as committed to the ultimate unification of Ireland as were the Provisionals. But the SDLP – and the Irish Government – sought to achieve this through negotiation and persuasion; they rejected the argument that the Unionist majority in the North could be bombed into a united Ireland or that the British Government could be driven out of Ireland by violence. There was an alternative to the Provisional IRA campaign. That armed campaign was not instigated as a measure of last resort – a key element of what constitutes a Just War. Whatever the historic rights and wrongs of British involvement in Ireland – and the partition of the island – the political reality was that Northern Ireland existed and the British Government remained there, not because of selfish strategic interests, but because a majority of the North's citizens wished to remain part of the UK. The whole thrust of international law, since the end of the Second World War, had been to resist the changing of borders by force. The obstacle to a united Ireland was not the British Government but the real British presence in Northern Ireland: the Protestant/Unionist majority.

This was the reality that Mrs Thatcher confronted during the 1970s and 1980s; not what historical wrongs were done in 1170, 1603, 1845 or 1920. Throughout the hunger strike – and the Troubles generally – Whitehall had to take into account the effects of policy on the majority community. This was realpolitik: during the hunger strikes, any concession to the hunger-strikers had to be measured by its impact on the Protestant community. The Republican answer to all of this was to ignore the implications of the Unionist community in their thinking: their core belief that Ireland constituted one political nation had a major problem if there were any acknowledgement of the Northern Irish Protestant consciousness of Britishness, the logical consequence of which was that there were two political nations on the island of Ireland. Then, as now, the route to a united Ireland lay in persuading a sufficient number of Northern Protestants, not a British Government, that that this was a desirable goal.

The basic position of the Thatcher Government was that of its predecessors: the principle of consent. It was enshrined in the Northern Ireland Constitution Act, passed by Westminster in 1973, which stated that a majority of the people of Northern Ireland should determine whether that entity should remain within the United Kingdom or not. It was also set out in the 1949 Ireland Act before it, which declared that the Northern Ireland Parliament should decide whether Northern Ireland remained in the UK. Arguably, consent formed part of British policy as far back as the Government of Ireland Act 1920, which partitioned the island, and affirmed that the then Northern and Southern Irish Parliaments could vote themselves out of existence and create an all-Ireland Government/Parliament in their place. The principle of consent is now Sinn Féin policy. On 14 August 2011, to mark the thirtieth anniversary of the 1981 Hunger Strike, Sinn Féin President, Gerry Adams, told a commemoration in Camlough, South Armagh, that:

> The Hunger Strike changed the political landscape in Ireland. The political gains that have been made since then owe much to the men and women political prisoners and to the sacrifice, resolve and perseverance of the Hunger Strikers and their families ... The prison struggle, like the struggle on the outside, became a battle of will about the right of the Irish people to self-determination and independence and freedom. The prisoners knew that. So did the Brits. It was about uniting Ireland ... The Sinn Féin strategy brought the British and the unionists and the Irish Government to the negotiating table. Thirty years ago, there was an Orange State. The Orange State is gone. The Government of Ireland Act is gone. The right of citizens to opt for a united Ireland is equal to that of those who wish to retain the Union ... There is now an entirely peaceful way to bring an end to British rule ... Britain's claim to the North is now reduced to a simple majority vote ... Sinn Féin is the largest nationalist party in the Assembly and on local councils. There are five Sinn Féin ministers, including Martin McGuinness, who as Deputy First Minister shares the Office of First and Deputy First Minister with [the DUP's] Peter Robinson as an equal in all matters. The DUP and UUP, who opposed power sharing, are sharing power in government. There are all-Ireland political, functioning institutions...

Thus, Gerry Adams' position has moved from, in the 1970s and 1980s, demanding a British Declaration of Intent to withdraw from Northern Ireland to the position of the British Government, as set out in the Northern Ireland Constitution Act 1973, nearly forty years before. This raises elemental questions as to how the PIRA's war against the British State can be justified retrospectively if the present Sinn Féin leadership has arrived at a position it could have adopted decades earlier. The lament of Bobby Sands' sister was that he 'didn't die for cross-border bodies' as were set up under the Good Friday Agreement. The North–South Ministerial Council established by that Agreement is a toothless talking shop – unlike the Council of Ireland, envisaged in the Sunningdale Agreement, and negotiated in 1973, which had executive powers (with the potential to act as an all-Ireland embryonic government). At that stage the Provisionals regarded Sunningdale as a sell-out. The Government of Ireland Act 1920, repealed under the auspices of the Good Friday Agreement, was trumpeted by Sinn Féin as removing the British claim to sovereignty to the North (section 75 stated that the Westminster Parliament was sovereign over all things in Northern Ireland); yet, constitutionally, its repeal meant nothing as Westminster's parliamentary sovereignty is inherent throughout the United Kingdom. It was the Act of Union 1800 that established Westminster's sovereignty over what is now Northern Ireland, and that remains the constitutional cornerstone of the United Kingdom.

The Good Friday Agreement also expressly recognizes British sovereignty in Northern Ireland, as did the Northern Ireland Constitution Act 1998, which replaced the Government of Ireland Act. The outcome of the Peace Process certainly sees Republicans sharing power with Unionists; yet this is a position that the SDLP advocated and achieved in 1973, but which was opposed, again as an 'internal solution' and sell-out, by Adams in exchanges with John Hume in the late 1980s. As all executive power in the UK stems from the Crown, Martin McGuinness, as Deputy First Minister, is, constitutionally, Her Majesty's Deputy First Minister in Northern Ireland – although that term is politically unacceptable to Republicans. It could be said that the historic and symbolic meeting between him and the Queen was, in constitutional terms, where the Deputy First Minister met his boss.

If one accepts the Clausewitzian concept of strategy – that the 'political object is the goal, war is the means of reaching it, and the means can never be considered in isolation from their purposes' – then the stark reality of the situation is that, in strategic political terms, the Republican Movement lost the 'war'; are now at a position accepted by previous Nationalists, who opposed the unification of Ireland by force decades earlier; and agreed to a worse deal in 1998, in terms of North–South structures, than were on offer in 1973. The only basis on which a united Ireland can occur is that advocated by Unionists and successive British Governments for several generations: the principle of consent. In one respect, given the opinion poll evidence that support in Northern Ireland for a united Ireland has declined sharply since the Good Friday Agreement, the principle of consent remains a 'unionist veto' over Irish unity, albeit with a small 'u' given that the Union with Britain has increased Catholic support.

The question, therefore, from a Republican perspective is whether the Provisionals' armed struggle was worth it, or indeed necessary? The irony is that Sinn Féin's contemporary position on how to achieve a united Ireland is exactly the same as Margaret Thatcher's in 1981.

NOTES

1   Moore *op.cit.* p.617.
2   *Report of an Inquiry by HM Chief Inspector of Prisons into the security arrangements at HM Prison, Maze relative to the escape on Sunday 25th September 1983, including relevant recommendations for the improvement of security at HM Prison, Maze* (HMSO 1984).
3   http://www.sinnfein.ie/contents/25293 (accessed 15 August 2013).
4   http://www.newsletter.co.uk/news/regional/in-pictures-gerry-kelly-s-speech-in-full-1-5376906 (accessed 1 October 2013).
5   *An Phoblacht,* 6 February 2012.
6   Moore *op.cit* p.587.

Select Bibliography

Primary Sources
The National Archives (TNA)
CAB Cabinet Office
PREM Prime Minister's Office
FCO Foreign and Commonwealth Office

Public Record Office of Northern Ireland (PRONI)
CAB Cabinet Records
CENT Central Secretariat
NIO Northern Ireland Office

National Archives of Ireland (NAI)
Department of the Taoiseach (D/T)

Thatcher Foundation (TF)
Manuscripts/speeches/interviews

Periodicals & Newspapers
An Phoblacht
Belfast Telegraph
Daily Ireland
Irish News
The Irish Times

Secondary Sources

Adams, Gerry, *The Politics of Irish Freedom* (Dublin: 1986).
Adams, Gerry, *Free Ireland: Towards a Lasting Peace* (Dublin: 1995).
Adams, Gerry, *Before the Dawn: An Autobiography* (Dublin: 2001).
Aughey, Arthur, *Under Siege: Ulster Unionism and the Anglo-Irish Agreement* (Belfast: 1989).
Bean, Kevin, *The New Politics of Sinn Féin* (Liverpool: 2007).
Bell, J. Bowyer, *The Secret Army: The IRA 1916–1979* (Dublin: 1979).
Bell, J. Bowyer, *The Irish Troubles: A Generation of Violence 1967–1992* (Dublin:1993).
Beresford, David, *Ten Men Dead: The Story of the 1981 Irish Hunger Strike* (London: 1987).
Bew, John, Frampton, Martyn and Gurruchaga, Inigo, *Talking to Terrorists: Making Peace in Northern Ireland and the Basque Country* (London: 2009).
Campbell, Brian (ed.), *Nor Meekly Serve My Time: H Block Struggle, 1976–81* (Belfast: 1994).
Coogan, Tim Pat, *On the Blanket: The Inside Story of the IRA Prisoners' "Dirty" Protest* (Basingstoke: 2002).
Crawford, Colin, *Inside the UDA. Volunteers and Violence* (London: 2003).
Cunningham, Michael J., *British Government Policy in Northern Ireland 1969–89: Its Nature and Execution* (Manchester: 1991).

Edwards, Aaron, *Defending the Realm: The Politics of Britain's Small Wars Since 1945* (Manchester: 2013).

Edwards, Ruth Dudley, *Patrick Pearse: The Triumph of Failure* (Dublin:1977).

English, Richard, *Armed Struggle: A History of the IRA* (London: 2003).

English, Richard and Walker, Graham, *Unionism in Modern Ireland: New Perspectives on Politics and Culture* (Dublin: 1996).

Farrell, Michael, *Northern Ireland: The Orange State* (London: 1976).

Frampton, Martyn, *The Long March: The Political Strategy of Sinn Féin, 1981–2007* (Basingstoke: 2008).

Hadfield, Brigid, 'The Belfast Agreement, Sovereignty and the State of the Union', (1998) *Public Law* (Winter) pp. 599–616.

Hamill, Desmond, *Pig in the Middle: The Army in Northern Ireland 1969–1985* (London: 1985).

Hennessy, Peter, *Whitehall* (New York: 1989).

Hennessey, Thomas, *A History of Northern Ireland 1920–1996* (Dublin: 1997).

Hennessey, Thomas, *Dividing Ireland: World War One and Partition* (London: 1998).

Hennessey, Thomas, *The Northern Ireland Peace Process. Ending the Troubles?* (Dublin: 2000).

Hennessey, Thomas, *Northern Ireland: The Origins of the Troubles* (Dublin: 2005).

Hennessey, Thomas, *The Evolution of the Troubles 1970–72* (Dublin: 2007).

Hennessey, Thomas and Thomas, Claire, *Spooks: The Unofficial History of MI5* (Gloucestershire: 2009).

Holland, Jack and McDonald, Henry, *INLA: Deadly Divisions* (Dublin: 1994).

Jackson, Alvin, *Ireland 1798–1998* (Oxford: 1999).

Mallie, Eamon and McKittrick, David, *The Fight for Peace: The Secret Story Behind the Irish Peace Process* (London: 1996).

McEvoy, Kieran, *Paramilitary Imprisonment in Northern Ireland: Resistance, Management, and Release* (Oxford: 2001).

McKittrick, David, Kelters, Seamus, Feeney, Brian, Thornton, Chris and McVea, David, *Lost Lives: The Stories of the Men, Women and Children Who Died as a Result of the Northern Ireland Troubles* (Edinburgh: 2004).

McGrattan, Cillian, *Northern Ireland 1968–2008: The Politics of Entrenchment* (Basingstoke: 2010).

Moloney, Ed, *A Secret History of the IRA* (London: 2002).

Moloney, Ed, *Voices from the Grave: Two Men's War in Ireland* (London: 2011).

Moore, Charles, *Margaret Thatcher: The Authorized Biography, Volume One: Not For Turning* (London: 2013).

Morrison, Danny (ed.) *Hunger Strike: Reflections on the 1981 Republican Hunger Strike* (Dublin: 2006).

Murray, Gerard and Tonge, Jonathan, *Sinn Féin and the SDLP: From Alienation to Participation* (London: 2005).

O'Brien, Brendan, *The Long War: The IRA and Sinn Féin 1985 to Today* (Dublin: 1993).

O'Dochartaigh, Niall, *From Civil Rights to Armalites: Derry and the Birth of the Irish Troubles* (Cork: 1997).

O'Hearn, Dennis, *Nothing But An Unfinished Song: The Life and Times of Bobby Sands* (New York: 2006).

O'Leary, Brendan and McGarry, John, *The Politics of Antagonism: Understanding Northern Ireland* (London: 1993).

O'Malley, Padraig, *The Uncivil Wars: Ireland Today* (Belfast: 1983).

O'Malley, Padraig, *Biting at the Grave: The Irish Hunger Strikes and the Politics of Despair* (Belfast: 1990).

O'Malley, Padraig, *Northern Ireland: Questions of Nuance* (Belfast: 1990).

O'Rawe, Richard, *Blanketmen: An Untold Story of the H-Block Hunger Strike* (Dublin: 2005).

O'Rawe, Richard, *Afterlives: The Hunger Strike and the Secret Offer That Changed Irish History* (Dublin: 2010).

Patterson, Henry, *The Politics of Illusion: A Political History of the IRA* (London 1997).

Patterson, Henry, *Ireland's Violent Frontier: The Border and Anglo-Irish Relations During the Troubles* (Basingstoke 2013).

Ross, Stuart, *Smashing H-Block: The Popular Campaign Against Criminalization and the Irish Hunger Strikes 1976–1982* (Liverpool: 2011).

Sands, Bobby, *Writings From Prison* (Dublin: 1993).

Shirlow, Peter, Tonge, Jon, McAuley, James W. and McGlyn, Catherine, *Abandoning Historical Conflict? Former Political Prisoners and Reconciliation in Northern Ireland* (Manchester: 2012).

Taylor, Peter, *Families at War* (London: 1989).

Taylor, Peter, *Provos: The IRA & Sinn Fein* (London: 1997).

Taylor, Peter, *Loyalists* (London: 1999).

Taylor, Peter, *Brits: The War Against the IRA* (London: 2001).

Tools, Kevin, *Rebel Hearts: Journeys within the IRA's Soul* (London: 1995).

Townshend, Charles, *Political Violence in Ireland: Government and Resistance since 1848* (Oxford: 1983).

Warner, Geoffrey, 'The Falls Road Curfew Revisited', *Irish Studies Review*, 14, 3, pp. 325–42.

Whyte, John, *Interpreting Northern Ireland* (Oxford: 1990).

Wichert, Sabine, *Northern Ireland Since 1945* (Essex: 1991).

Index